CENTRAL MEXICO HANDBOOK

MEXICO CITY, GUADALAJARA, AND OTHER COLONIAL CITIES

CENTRAL MEXICO HANDBOOK

MEXICO CITY, GUADALAJARA, AND OTHER COLONIAL CITIES

CHICKI MALLAN

PHOTOS BY

OZ MALLAN

MOON
PUBLICATIONS INC.

CENTRAL MEXICO HANDBOOK
MEXICO CITY, GUADALAJARA, AND OTHER COLONIAL CITIES

Published by
Moon Publications, Inc.
P.O. Box 3040
Chico, California 95927-3040, USA

Printed by
Colorcraft Ltd.

Please send all comments,
corrections, additions,
amendments, and critiques to:

**CENTRAL MEXICO HANDBOOK
MOON PUBLICATIONS, INC.
P.O. BOX 3040
CHICO, CA 95927-3040, USA**

Printing History
1st edition—November 1994

Library of Congress Cataloging in Publication Data
Mallan, Chicki,
    Central Mexico Handbook : Mexico City, Guadalajara, and Other
    Colonial Cities / Chicki Mallan
        p.   cm.
    Includes the Federal District and the states of Mexico, Hidalgo,
    Jalisco, Michoacan, Puebla, Queretaro, Tlaxcala, Veracruz,
    Guerrero, Morelos, and Guanajuato.
    Includes bibliographical references and index.
    ISBN 1-56691-023-4
    1. Mexico—Guidebooks.   I. Title.
F1209.M335   1994   94-9364
917.204'835—dc20   CIP

Front cover photo: adobe house, Banco de Mexico, courtesy of Photo Network
All photos by Oz Mallan unless otherwise noted.

Distributed in the United States by Publishers Group West

Printed in Hong Kong

To my special friends and

most vigorous supporters—

Barbara, Tony, Denise,

Scott, Beth, Guy, Patti, and Bryant

ACKNOWLEDGMENTS

Gratitude goes to those who helped me gather the thousands of details in this book, especially Forat Bernardo with the Mexican Government Tourism office in Mexico City, who not only provides facts and data, but has a wonderful knack for telling stories (all true, I'm sure) about life in Mexico. Thanks also to Nancy Felling, who trekked the outback of Queretaro; to Alma Flores and her brother Henry Flores for the telephone work in Mexico City; to Paul Piacentini who likewise tracked down little known facts in the heart of the country; and to Amy Bortz and Felicia White, both with Edelman PR, who understand the writer's craving for current details.

Particular kudos to the Mexican people; to all the Mexican waiters who still come chasing after me with the belongings I've left behind in their cafes. To the nameless folks willing to take the time to answer so many questions. That goes double to the kids selling Chiclets and the corn vendors in the parks and plazas who were cheerful and gracious and spent many of their valuable "business hours" in long conversations with the nosey "gringa-lady" carrying the big purse.

I would also like to mention a few people who very early in life taught me what the *mexicano* was like. My dad of course, the late Tony Pa-nariello, who instilled in me a great excitement (that never left me) as I crossed the border for the first time—before age six. My next happy impression was from the Mexican-American Saldana family, friends and neighbors who lived on Catalina Island (where I grew up). And later, while I *commuted* to Flintridge Sacred Heart Academy on the southern California mainland, I had the pleasure of getting to know classmates Eugenia Azcarraga and Ruth Gomez (also *commuting*), from Mexico City. It was through them that I first perceived, intimately, the true spirit and warmth of the people of the country. Later, thanks to my dear childhood friend Guilli Zobelein, who chose to live and work with the local Tzotzil-speaking communities in the outlying areas of San Cristobal de las Casas in the state of Chiapas, I discovered still another facet of Mexican life. Guilli worked to help the campesinos preserve their ancient culture, but at the same time, to improve their way of life. She generously included us in many experiences with these people in Chiapas that today are treasures in light of current events. Thanks to all these folks for their considerable Mexican influence on my life and my books—thank you Mexico.

CONTENTS

MAPS

MAP SYMBOLS

MEX. FEDERAL HIGHWAY

MEX. STATE HIGHWAY

WATER

ARCHAEOLOGICAL RUIN

PEMEX GAS STATION

DIVIDED HIGHWAY

MAIN ROAD

OTHER ROAD

UNPAVED ROAD

TRACK / TRAIL

BRIDGE

STATE BORDER

HOTEL / ACCOMMODATION

POINT OF INTEREST

TOWN / VILLAGE

CITY

MOUNTAIN

AIRPORT

CHARTS AND SPECIAL TOPICS

IS THIS BOOK OUT OF DATE?

If there's anything in this life that we can absolutely count on, it's change. No doubt by the time you have this book in your hands there will be changes in hotels; more have opened, some have closed or changed names. Chefs, in restaurants that we love, come and go. Prices go up, prices go down, so remember that they are listed in this volume to be used as a *general guideline only.*

We enjoy your comments, especially if you find discrepancies with the information given. If you have a phenomenally wonderful time someplace that we have not yet discovered, we'd love to hear about it. We'll do our best to keep things up to date. Address your letters to:

Central Mexico Handbook
Moon Publications, Inc.
P.O. Box 3040
Chico, CA 95927-3040, USA

K. A. ESCOVEDO SANDERS

INTRODUCTION

For years the hidden star of Mexico has been the colonial cities nestled in the rugged highlands of Central Mexico. The central plateau offers visitors a vast variety of adventure, an opportunity to discover how the past invented the present, an occasion to observe the essence of nature, and, if you stop to smell the roses, a chance to experience the warmth of the people. Here the outdoors combines soaring volcanic peaks, high meadows, placid lakes, tumultuous waterways, caves with crystalline formations, and forests that house a myriad of flora and fauna.

The architecture in Central Mexico is a combination of Spanish-European influences and native American artisans. A hotel can be a modern glass high-rise, or a 400-year-old mansion on a narrow cobblestone street. A city can be a high-tech wonder saluting eight-lane highways, and yet have a city center that embraces pedestrian-only streets bustling with people of the '90s. Many of these streets are lined with antique domed and porticoed structures, boasting ornate stone and tile facades—and they were built to last for centuries. Looking closely at these churches, palaces, and homes, you'll slowly realize the native American artisan within these creations—the intrepid fusion that has evolved into the rich Mexican culture. Nowhere is it more apparent than in the colonial cities of Central Mexico.

The Mexican states covered in this book are located in the high plateau, with a sidetrip to the tropical state of Veracruz, the original gateway to the New World. We'll lead you through Mexico City and surrounding Mexico State as well as Querétaro, Guanajuato, Jalisco, Tlaxcala, Michoacán, Puebla, Morelos, Guerrero, and Hidalgo, following in the footsteps of Cortés.

THE LAND

Size And Area
Mexico covers an area slightly less than three times the size of the state of Texas; 1,972,550 square kilometers (761,602 square miles). It shares a northern border 3,362 kilometers long with the United States. Mexico's beautiful coastlines stretch 9,330 kilometers along the Atlantic and Pacific oceans, the Caribbean Sea, and

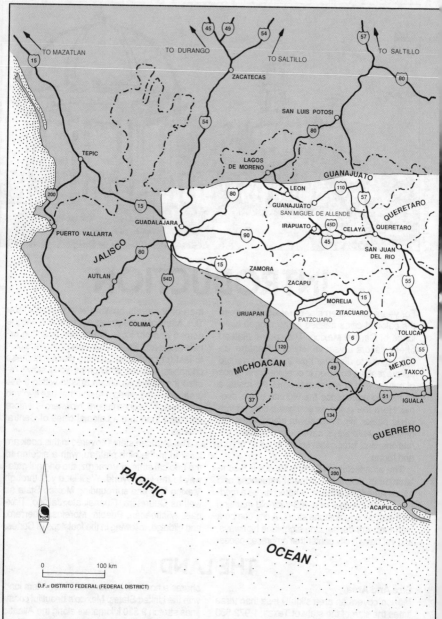

0   100 km

D.F.= DISTRITO FEDERAL (FEDERAL DISTRICT)

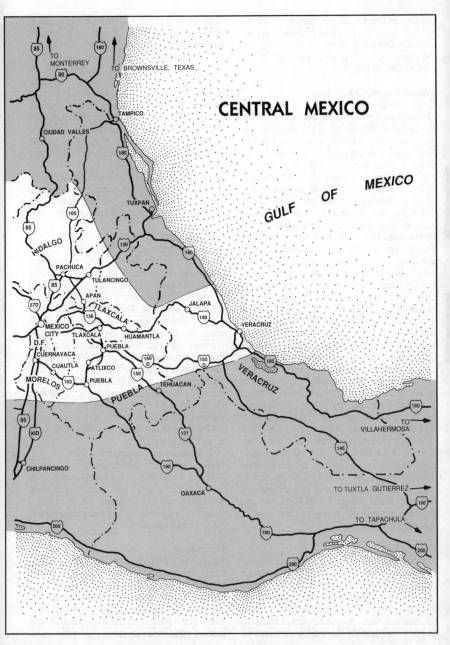

CENTRAL MEXICO

GULF OF MEXICO

TO MONTERREY

TO BROWNSVILLE, TEXAS

TAMPICO

CIUDAD VALLES

TUXPAN

HIDALGO

PACHUCA

TULANCINGO

APAN

JALAPA

TLAXCALA

VERACRUZ

MEXICO CITY

TLAXCALA

HUAMANTLA

D.F.

PUEBLA

CUERNAVACA

CUAUTLA

ATLIXCO

MORELOS

PUEBLA

PUEBLA

TEHUACAN

VERACRUZ

TO VILLAHERMOSA

CHILPANCINGO

OAXACA

TO TUXTLA GUTIERREZ

TO TAPACHULA

the Sea of Cortez. Mother Nature shows her strength every so often; earthquakes have been known to shake the central and southern part of the country once in a while, especially in and around Mexico City.

Principal Rivers And Lakes Of Central Mexico

Six principal rivers drain into the Gulf of Mexico: the Bravo Norte, Grijalva, Usumacinta, Papaloapan, Coatzalcoalcos, and the Pánuco. Major rivers draining into the Pacific are the Colorado, Balsas, and the Lerma-Santiago. The central plateau is a basin of interior drainage, and its principal rivers either evaporate, flow into various lakes, or disappear underground.

The **Lerma-Santiago** river system (927 km) is the longest waterway in Central Mexico. The headwaters of the Lerma River are located in the Toluca basin and are diverted to Mexico City. To the west, it forms Lake Chapala (the largest natural lake in Mexico). Exiting the lake is the Río Santiago, which flows northwest to the Pacific. The Río Balsas (724 km) begins in the high peaks of Puebla state as the Río Atoyac at the confluence of the San Martin and Zahuapan rivers. It flows southwestward and then westward through Guerrero state, where it becomes the principal river, known as the Mezcala. It drains into the Pacific at Mongrove Point.

The rivers of Mexico have long been used for irrigation, though half the irrigation water of the country comes from wells. Hydroelectric plants are seen often in Central Mexico, introducing electricity even to the most remote areas.

In Central Mexico, surface water has diminished over the centuries. When Cortés arrived lakes flourished on the plateau, but due to dense development, quirks of nature, dams, and diversions, only the remnants of once copious bodies of water remain. Lakes Pátzcuaro and Cuitzeo are examples, and even Lake Chapala is shrinking every year.

Mountain Ranges

The central plateau of Mexico displays impressive mountainous landforms. Mexico's highest point is 5,747 meters at Mt. Orizaba, located near Puebla in the mountain chain referred to as the **Transverse Volcanic Sierra**. This chain extends east-west across Mexico at about 19 degrees north latitude. Central Mexico's colonial cities are located in these mountain highlands, all above 1,500 meters (5,000 feet). North to south, two mountain ranges cross Mexico. To the east, the Sierra Madre Oriental rises to more than 4,000 meters. To the west, the Sierra Madre Occidental soars to 3,300 meters. The Occidental range was the "roadblock" that for centuries held back the masses, both indigenous people and even some foreign explorers, from the beautiful Pacific coast of Mexico. This territory has often been compared with mountainous European countries: France, Switzerland, Spain, and Portugal, for example.

Between the two ranges is the central plateau. At the extreme southern end of this "Plateau in the Valley" lies the ever-growing Mexico City, formerly the ancient city of Tenochtitlán.

Volcano Belt

If you draw a line across Mexico from the east coast at Tuxtla San Andres (Veracruz) to Cape Corrientes on the Pacific coast, you would be tracing the tectonic seam that was the site of an immense upheaval of the earth's crust thousands of years ago. This is part of the circum-Pacific Ring of Fire. Along this seam, which measures about 160 kilometers wide and 1,280 kilometers long, you'll find the volcanoes of Mexico: **La Malinche** (4,462 meters), **Popocatépetl** (5,452 meters), **Ixtaccíhuatl** (4,330 meters), **Nevado de Toluca** (4,558 meters), and **Paricutín** (2,774 meters) in Central Mexico; **Nevado de Colima** (4,330 meters), **Sanganguey** (2,360 meters), and **Ceboruco** (2,164 meters) toward the Pacific end; and finally the tallest of all, **Orizaba** (5,747 meters).

This upheaval created the central plateau where most of the colonial cities are located. Perhaps it was this monumental shake-up of the earth that pushed vast quantities of silver and gold closer to the surface. These precious metals were the main reason these cities grew in difficult mountainous terrain.

Geography

Mexico ranges from beautiful beaches to marshlands, low meadows, high meadows, woodlands, jungles, tall mountain ranges, and volcanoes. Natural resources include silver, copper, gold, crude oil, lead, zinc, natural gas, and timber. Twelve percent of the land is arable, one percent with permanent crops. Forest and wood-

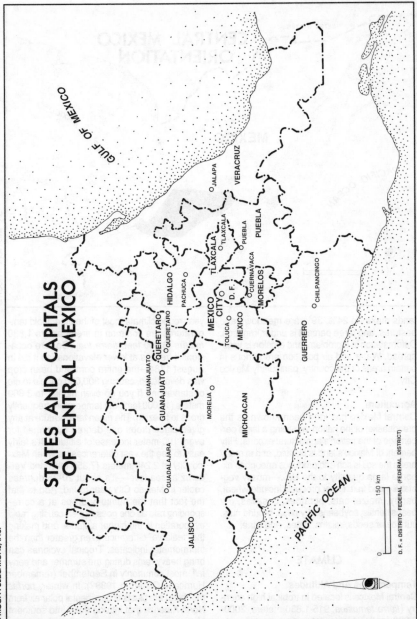

STATES AND CAPITALS
OF CENTRAL MEXICO

GULF OF MEXICO

JALAPA VERACRUZ

TLAXCALA
Tlaxcala
Puebla
PUEBLA

PACHUCA
HIDALGO

MEXICO
CITY
D. F.

CUERNAVACA
MORELOS

CHILPANCINGO

QUERETARO
Queretaro

TOLUCA
MEXICO

GUERRERO

GUANAJUATO
Guanajuato

GUANAJUATO

MORELIA

MICHOACAN

GUADALAJARA

JALISCO

PACIFIC OCEAN

0   150 km

D. F. = DISTRITO FEDERAL (FEDERAL DISTRICT)

© MOON PUBLICATIONS, INC.

CENTRAL MEXICO
ORIENTATION

UNITED STATES

MEXICO

GULF OF MEXICO

PACIFIC OCEAN

0   500 km

© MOON PUBLICATIONS, INC.

lands make up 24%, 39% are meadows and pastures, and three percent is under irrigation. Deforestation is a problem, and erosion is widespread. Water and air pollution are serious in certain areas of the country, particularly Mexico City.

Agriculture
Central Mexico has long been known as the breadbasket of the nation, providing a large percentage of the nation's agricultural exports. Fifty percent of Mexico's land is planted, and in many areas the soil is rich and produces enough to export a large quantity to the U.S.—mostly vegetables and fruit. Other products include wheat, barley, maize, oats, potatoes, casavas, dry beans, lentils, soybeans, dry peas, ground nuts, sunflower seeds, raisins, dates, and wine.

CLIMATE

Temperatures And Altitudes
Central Mexico is located in tropical high country (*tierra templada;* 915-1,830 meters, 3000-6,000 feet), which creates a very temperate year-round climate most of the time. Cold temperatures are common in areas above 1,830 meters (6,000 feet; *tierra fria*). On rare occasions it freezes at lower elevations (as it did in August 1784—the entire corn and bean crop was devastated, causing 300,000 people to die of starvation). If you go even higher, to 3,660 meters (12,000 feet), the temperature frequently drops to freezing. The mean temperature at any given place drops one degree fahrenheit for every 100-meter increase of altitude. It's fairly easy to see the vast differences between Mexico City at 2,240 meters (7,350 feet) and Veracruz at sea level—it's about 20-25 degrees cooler in Mexico City year-round. Add to that the fact that the humidity drops at a corresponding rate as one goes higher, causing rapid evaporation in the higher altitudes and making the "feelable" difference even greater than the thermometer indicates. Tropical cyclones can bring heavy rains during the summer and early fall, most commonly in September (remember Hurricane Gilbert in 1988?). In winter, *nortes* (northers) are blasts of continental polar air from North America that intrude deep into southern Mexico.

Rain

The rainy season in the central highlands usually begins in June and lasts till October. And since Mother Nature has never read the rain chart, it can be wet in May and November. Spring and fall are touted as the finest times of the year, with pleasant temperatures, very little rain, and never too much heat in the mountains. In tropical Veracruz it can get very hot year-round, and the humidity is much heavier, making the heat more noticeable.

When To Visit

Generally speaking, high season is 15 December-15 April, low season is July-August, and the shoulder seasons are May-June and September-October. When to go is an individual decision. Are you visiting coastal areas or mountain regions? The weather might determine your choice; coastal areas will be hot, humid, and rainy in the summer, slightly cooler in the winter. The mountains are very pleasant year-round, but in the winter it can get very cold at night, maybe even dipping into freezing temperatures. Do you prefer to visit when there are fewer people? The off season, then, would be preferable, although the shoulder seasons may be the best. Do you like crowds and big *típico* celebrations? Vacationing during a national or religious holiday is lots of fun; reserve in advance—you'll be competing with the Mexican population. Some people are forced to travel during school vacations. If so, remember summer is Mexican family-vacation time also and some hotels will be crowded; again, reserve in advance. You'll find many Americans and Canadians in high season escaping the cold weather north of the border.

ECOLOGY

The Mexican government is putting forth increased effort to deal with the ecological problems in Mexico thanks to the endeavors of people like Romero Arigis and his Group of One Hundred. This novelist and poet grew up near a village where the monarch butterflies returned each year, a happy part of his childhood. Today he defends the trees and the environnment; he feels that even the poorest child should have

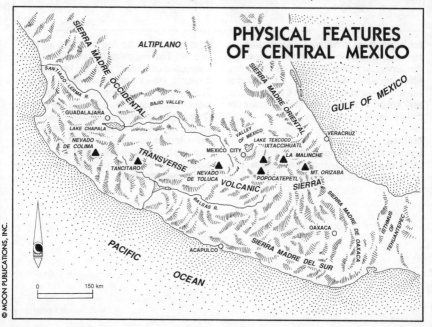

PHYSICAL FEATURES OF CENTRAL MEXICO

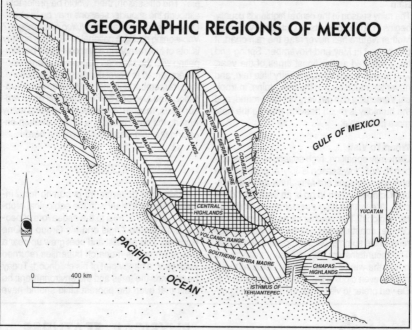

GEOGRAPHIC REGIONS OF MEXICO

BAJA CALIFORNIA

SONORA PLAINS

WESTERN SIERRA MADRE

NORTHERN HIGHLANDS

EASTERN SIERRA MADRE

GULF COASTAL PLAIN

GULF OF MEXICO

CENTRAL HIGHLANDS

VOLCANIC RANGE

SOUTHERN SIERRA MADRE

YUCATAN

CHIAPAS HIGHLANDS

ISTHMUS OF TEHUANTEPEC

PACIFIC OCEAN

0   400 km

© MOON PUBLICATIONS, INC.

rich experiences in nature. His leadership has been instrumental in the creation of new laws concerning the forests as well as the sea turtles, which have survived extinction for millions of years. He likes to point out that it is the responsibility of each person to see that the turtles live on for millions of years more.

Progress

Small victories are important in the ecological battle, and the war continues on all fronts. One recent success story concerns a six-month bat-tle to have one of the new proposed toll roads rerouted. The controversial highway would have trespassed on some of Mexico's top ecological treasures. The road connecting Mexico City and Tuxtla Gutiérrez would have cut through the **El Ocote** rainforest reserve in Chiapas and the **Chimalapas** rainforest in Oaxaca. These areas, among the few remaining rainforests on the North American continent, are vital to protecting Mexico's biological diversity. The revised route extended its length by some 80 kilometers—morality won this one.

FLORA AND FAUNA

FLORA

Central Mexico is a densely populated area, and because of human habitation, most of the endemic plants and flowers have been decimated over the centuries. Some parts of the highlands are arid, and shrub grasses and cactus still grow wild in undisturbed areas. In the higher elevations coniferous and oak-tree forests are seen in humid areas of the mild and cool climates, including the Sierra Madre Oriental, the Sierra Madre Occidental, and the Transverse Volcanic Sierra of Central Mexico. Many flowering plants were originally found in the Mexican countryside when the Spaniards arrived. However, with the exception of cactus, if you wish to see those plants now you can only enjoy them in private homes, botanical gardens, or parks.

Cactus

The variety of size, shape, and growth pattern of cactus in Central Mexico is huge—from a tiny button of brilliant color to an immense mammoth (called elephant cactus). Many think of cactus as growing only in the desert. However, they also grow in semidry, well drained soil, and they do need moisture. The elephant cactus can grow to 18 meters and weigh many tonnes. Some cactus stems and trunks are smooth; others are covered with spines and/or fine hairs. The spines of some plants point downward and act as tips to concentrate the light rain or heavy dew into droplets of water that then fall to the ground where better use is made of the precious moisture. Some root systems can preserve large amounts of water in their tubers.

Many cactus have flowers: all beautiful, some waxlike, and in vivid colors that vary from white through yellow and red to purple. Fruits frequently develop from these flowers and are popular sources of food in some parts of Mexico. The most common is from the opuntia, the prickly pear. Once the prickles are cut off, the small purple fruit makes a juicy refreshment. Luther Burbank developed a spineless variety that is used as cattle feed in some parts of Mexico.

In the open markets of Central Mexico, you'll see women removing the spines from the flat paddlelike leaves of the nopales cactus before selling them. The leaf is cut into narrow strips and cooked like other vegetables or eaten raw in salads. Drinks and folk medicines are two other common uses of these frequently seen plants.

Probably the most characteristic sight is the "living fence"; straight rows of tall cactus planted around a small ranchito—this is usually the pipe-organ cactus.

Dahlias

This lovely perennial tuberous plant is part of the Compositae group. Dahlias were first discovered in the mountains of Mexico in the 16th century by a Spanish expedition, though named later in honor of a Swedish botanist who worked to develop the plant. The blossoms can be small or large, with vivid colors in every range except blue. In really cold climes the tubers must be lifted and protected over the winter.

Poinsettias

The Christmas flower, the poinsettia, was also first seen in Mexico. This showy plant is part of the spurge family, and the most common color is vivid red, though it also comes in yellow, white, or pink. The poinsettia "flowers" are actually bracts, or modified leaves, and the flowers are the tiny blossoms in the center of the bracts. In subtropical and tropical climates it grows easily in the garden.

Nasturtiums

This crepe-papery little blossom is almost weed-like once it gets started. An herb, the nasturtium thrives in highland regions of Mexico. The flowers are red, orange, and yellow, and the blossom is shaped like an elongated funnel. In Mexico (and now trendy restaurants in southern California), the leaves and young blossoms are used raw in salads, and the seeds are sometimes pickled and used like capers.

Bougainvilleas

Enjoyed for its long-lasting beauty and brilliant colors, the bougainvillea is one of the most common flowers in all of Mexico. It seems to thrive whether in the highlands or in the jungle. In Central Mexico, the bright pink, fuchsia, red, and white blossoms tumble over old colonial walls flashing a happy greeting to all who pass. We saw a plant recently that grew both pink and white flowers. The bougainvillea is a heavy duty vine and the branches are studded with sharp thorns. It will climb to the top of a high building if helped with a little support on the way up.

Monkey Flowers

This pretty little flower is part of the snapdragon family and, like the familiar snap, resembles a monkey face. Native to Mexico (as well as other countries), it may be either a perennial or an annual, erect or creeping. It grows to two feet high, is tubular, two-lipped, and colored yellow with a red-spotted throat. It's usually found in wet places.

Roses

This is a popular flower all over the world, and Mexico is no exception. The difference between Mexico and the U.S. is the difference in price of a dozen roses. In the U.S. you're lucky if you can find them for less than US$35 a dozen; in Mexico you can buy the finest for US$15 or less (one dozen) in the market. Expect to pay a higher price in a fancy hotel florist shop, especially in Mexico City.

Squash Flowers

This wouldn't usually be placed in the floral category, but when walking through an open market, if you wonder about the colorful bunches of orange blossoms piled in with the vegetables, they are more than likely squash blossoms, highly prized in Mexico for making soup; in gourmet restaurants now they are used in crepes as well. They are usually obtained from the zucchini squash.

Juniper Trees

Seen frequently in Central Mexico, the cypress family includes about 35 species ranging from short shrubs to tall trees. The wood is fragrant, colored from red to brown, and durable. The oil distilled from the wood is used in perfume and medicines. The distinctive flavor of gin is obtained from juniper berries. The trees grow in temperate as well as cold climates.

Soapberry Trees

Another indigenous tree, this one has been used by the campesinos as a cleaning agent for years. First a small white flower blooms, and then it ripens into a brown fruit that contains the soapy cleansing substance.

FAUNA

Monarch Butterflies

Anyone who has a chance should take a walk through the woods where the monarch butterflies cluster on trees and hang on each other for a winter of semisnoozing, creating a vivid mass of fluttering orange and yellow color that is one of nature's most extravagant displays.

Hundreds of thousands of monarch butterflies migrate from the U.S. and Canada every fall and spend the winter in Mexico. This is an amazing flight of some 8,000 km from the northern part of North America to Mexico's central states of Michoacán and Mexico.

Gathering in the north, the monarchs embark on their long journey south late August and September. They can travel as many as 600 kilometers in a 24-hour period. Their flight pattern takes them above patches of milkweed (their main food supply), but they can fly 1,000 kilometers without stopping to feed. Clouds of butterflies arrive at specific tree groves. Drowsily

---

DIFFERENCES BETWEEN MOTHS AND BUTTERFLIES

1. Butterflies fly during the day; moths fly at dusk or at night.

2. Butterflies rest with their wings folded straight up over their bodies; most moths rest with their wings spread flat.

3. All butterflies have bare knobs at the end of both antennae (feelers); moths' antennae are either plumy or hairlike and end in a point.

4. Butterflies have slender bodies; moths are plump. Both insects are of the order Lepidoptera. So, lepidopterists, you are in butterfly heaven in the jungle areas of Central Mexico.

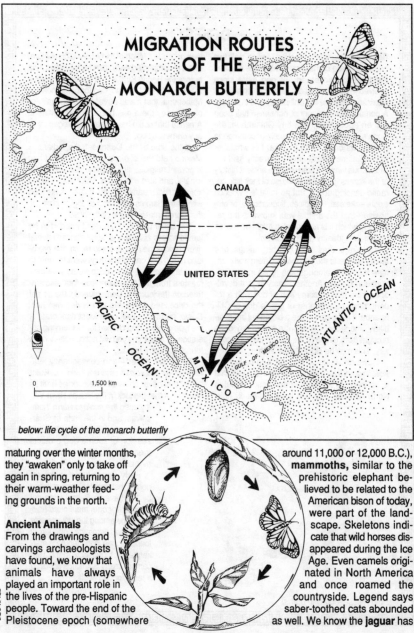

MIGRATION ROUTES OF THE MONARCH BUTTERFLY

CANADA

UNITED STATES

PACIFIC OCEAN

ATLANTIC OCEAN

GULF OF MEXICO

M E X I C O

0   1,500 km

© MOON PUBLICATIONS, INC.

BOB RACE

below: life cycle of the monarch butterfly

maturing over the winter months, they "awaken" only to take off again in spring, returning to their warm-weather feeding grounds in the north.

Ancient Animals

From the drawings and carvings archaeologists have found, we know that animals have always played an important role in the lives of the pre-Hispanic people. Toward the end of the Pleistocene epoch (somewhere around 11,000 or 12,000 B.C.), **mammoths,** similar to the prehistoric elephant believed to be related to the American bison of today, were part of the landscape. Skeletons indicate that wild horses disappeared during the Ice Age. Even camels originated in North America and once roamed the countryside. Legend says saber-toothed cats abounded as well. We know the **jaguar** has

DOGS

Before the Spaniards reached Mexico, only two creatures were domesticated here; the dog and the turkey. Two breeds of dog have since evolved in Mexico and are regarded typically as Mexican; these are the Chihuahua and the *sholo*. A considerable amount of nonsense has been written about both. The tiny Chihuahua, the world's smallest dog, is actually uncommon in Mexico. Its origin is an enigma. For whatever reason, some writers have incorrectly said the Chihuahua was involved with the ancient history of the Aztecs (probably because of their little ceramic dancing dogs). But no reliable evidence exists—skeletal, in codices, linguistically, or otherwise—that the animal was known in the regions to which it is attributed. It might be a case of mistaken identity (with the *sholo*).

If you're interested in dog beginnings, one theory suggests the dog evolved from a wild canine that lived amongst the rocks in the Chihuahuan Desert. Another theory says it developed from mating some sort of dog with a rodent, perhaps a gopher or prairie dog of Chihuahua. These claims are a biological impossibility. One story tells about a pair of tiny dogs brought from China at the end of the 18th century. This may be closer to the truth.

However, there is another dog called the *xoloitzcuintli* (usually abbreviated to *sholo*) that is believed to be the first domestic animal in North America. The dog is almost totally hairless or "nude." Much of its history is conjecture; that it accompanied early man from Eastern Asia across the Bering Straits; that its nearest relative is another form of "naked" dog formerly known in Manchuria; that it was never a wild animal. Zoologists say there has been no wild canine in America that could have been the progenitor of any domestic dog.

At the time of the Conquest, the Indians in Mexico held the *sholo* in great esteem; it had important religious significance, was used medicinally, and also was eaten. The Nahuatl name *xoloitzcuintli* means "he who snatches his food with teeth sharp as obsidian [i.e. dog], and who is the representative of the god *Xolotl*."

The belief was that the dead needed to be ferried across at least one "subterranean infernal river" before their souls could reach "the promised land," and only black dogs were thought to be able to do this. These dogs would save their masters from the "fiendish crocodiles" encountered on the journey. Consequently, the dog of the deceased was killed and buried with him. *Sholo*, normally black or at least dark gray, is the type of black dog chosen for this ferrying operation. In museums you will notice pottery dogs found in ancient burials.

Today this naked—and consequently flealess—body of a *xoloitzcuintli* is a living "hot water bottle" that never cools off. Their bodies emit so much heat that the sick in the Balsas River Valley used the *sholo* to warm themselves, and in the state of Guerrero some still believe that possession of such a dog protects them from colds and other ailments.

Early Spanish historians reported that dog flesh was relished by the Indians. Bernal Díaz del Castillo, for one, mentioned hairless dogs among the innumerable exotic food items the conquerors found for sale in the fabulous marketplace of Tlateloctl. In the 16th century, many Spaniards acquired a taste for dog flesh.

BOB RACE

sholo *(vessel-dog with horns)*

been around for centuries—the Aztecs believed that **Tezcatlipoca,** god of darkness and evildoers, assumed the disguise of a jaguar, its spotted skin representing the nighttime sky filled with stars.

Bats

BOB RACE

Bats are numerous in Mexico, as are the caves that many of them live in. The Nahuatls called a bat *tzinacan.*

bat

In some areas of Mexico they're called *ratones viejos* (old mice). The superstitious believe that a dead mouse is resurrected as a bat, although bats are not members of the Rodentia order. *Vampiro,* blood-sucking bats, are found in certain countryside areas, though they seldom attack humans. They love to go after birds, and on occasion they attack cattle. Interestingly, while the word "vampire" is of Slavic origin (remember Count Dracula), there are no blood-sucking bats in Europe. Vampire bats are confined to the American continent.

Bats were revered as gods by the ancient Maya, Aztecs, Zapotecs, and other pre-Hispanic peoples. They're very adaptable and can live in any climate, barring the frigid polar regions. Different species eat a variety of foods: from fruit, to insects, to rodents, to birds—there's even a fishing bat with sharp little clawed feet. Some bats help the ecology; those that thrive on the nectars of a flower help the pollination process of night-blooming flowers. Fruit bats that take their fruit away from the tree drop the seeds wherever they're dining and in turn are doing a little "cultivation" and reforestation.

Free-tailed bats from the north migrate yearly as far south as Mexico City and Cuernavaca. Here they gather in abandoned buildings or even tall belfries (bats in your belfries?), where they mate and then return to their "home caves" in the spring. There the young are born and nurtured. These caves are called "maternity caves"; that is, no males allowed.

Jaguars

The jaguar is found in the low-lying tropical areas of Mexico, but the only place you may ever see one is in a zoo, since it's rarely out and about in the daylight. The jaguar is heavy-chested with sturdy, muscled forelegs, small rounded ears, and a relatively short tail. Color ranges from tan on top with white on the underside to pure black. The male can weigh 65-115 kilograms, females 55-75 kilograms. The largest of the cats in Mexico and the third-largest cat in the world, the jaguar is about the same size as a leopard. It is nocturnal, spending most daylight hours snoozing in the sun. The male marks an area of about 170 square kilometers and spends its nights stalking deer, peccaries, agoutis, tapirs, monkeys, and birds. If hunting is poor and times are tough, the jaguar will go into the rivers and scoop fish with its large paws. Females begin breeding at about three years and generally produce twin cubs.

Pumas

Known as the *león* in Mexico, the puma has been seen in many parts of Mexico at almost every altitude and latitude. In the U.S. it's called a mountain lion and will adapt to conditions ranging from humid tropics to high, cold regions. In Mexico, pumas are usually shot on sight, especially by farmers who have livestock. Here again, they thrive where there are few people.

The adult male puma measures about two meters in length and can weigh up to 40 kilograms. It thrives in any environment that supports deer, porcupine, or rabbit. They will hunt day or night, but in actuality are seldom seen.

Bobcats Or Lynx

This tufted-eared, short-tailed cat can be found throughout two-thirds of Mexico. Its nickname is *gato montés* (mountain cat) or lynx. It's found only occasionally in the central highlands. The cat's numbers are diminishing radically in densely populated areas since bobcats, like coyotes, grab their prey where they find it, putting all farm animals at risk. In the northern, more isolated areas of Mexico they are thriving.

Peccaries

Other names for this piglike creature are musk hog and javelina. Some compare these nocturnal mammals to the wild pigs found in Europe, though in fact they are native to America. The feisty collared peccary stands 30 centimeters tall at the shoulder and can a meter long, weighing as much as 30 kilograms. It is black and white with a narrow semicircular collar of white hair on the shoulders. In Spanish *javelina* means "spear," descriptive of the two spearlike tusks that protrude from its mouth. This more familiar peccary is found in deserts, woodlands, and rainforests, and travels in groups of five to 15.

Birds
In Central Mexico the best places to observe birds are the rural areas, especially archaeological zones where there has been little construction for centuries. The best time to birdwatch is either early in the morning or at dusk. To listen to the birds by the thousands, visit any of the old parks surrounded by Indian Laurel trees such as in San Miguel. There are times,

especially at dusk, when it's hard to carry on a conversation because of the chirping.

Hummingbirds: The hummingbird is an amazing little creature with legs like rubber bands and wings that "hum" in flight or while hovering, but even more remarkable is that they can fly, nonstop, distances of up to 800 kilometers. They feed on nectar with a long bill that reaches deep into the heart of flowers. They are known to mark their feeding areas and will run off other hummingbirds infringing on their territory. The hummingbird was an important part of the ancient religious culture and is often seen in carvings done by the Aztecs and other indigenous groups.

Bananaquit: Bananaquits build their unusual domed nests out of banana-leaf fibers. Because they can nest wherever banana trees are located, there small singing birds enjoy a variety of landscapes—from home gardens to scrub vegetation to open woodlands.

DIANA LASICH-HARPER

HISTORY

EARLIEST MAN

During the Pleistocene epoch when the level of the sea fell (around 50,000 B.C.), people and animals from Asia were thought to have crossed the Bering land bridge into the North American continent. For nearly 50,000 years, humans continued the trek southward. It is believed that the first people reached Tierra del Fuego, at the tip of South America, in approximately 1000 B.C.

As early as 10,000 B.C., Ice Age man hunted woolly mammoth and other large animals roaming the cool, moist landscape of Central Mexico. Between 7000 and 2000 B.C., proto-agricultural society evolved from hunters and gatherers to farmers. Such crops as corn, squash, and beans were independently domesticated in widely separated areas of Mexico after about 6000 B.C. The remains of clay figurines from the pre-Classic period, presumed to be fertility symbols, marked the rise of religion in Mesoamerica, beginning around 2000 B.C.

Around 1000 B.C. the Olmec culture, believed to be the country's earliest, began to spread throughout Mesoamerica from the Gulf of Mexico coast. The large-scale ceremonial centers grew along Gulf of Mexico coastlands, and much of Mesoamerica was influenced by the Olmec religion, whose followers worshiped curious jaguarlike gods. They were also responsible for the New World's first calendar and an early system of writing.

Classic Period

The Classic period, beginning about A.D. 300, is now hailed as the peak of cultural development among the cultures throughout Mexico, aptly called the florescence of ancient Mexican civilization. Until A.D. 900, phenomenal progress was made in the development of artistic, architectural, and astronomical skills. Impressive buildings were constructed, and codices (folded bark books) were written and filled with hieroglyphic symbols that detailed complicated mathematical calculations of days, months, and years. Only the priests and the privileged held this knowledge, and they continued to learn and develop ideas until there was a sudden halt to this growth. For years there were many theories for this so called "end" including disease, invasion, etc.—but researchers now feel strongly that the collapse was caused by a combination of overpopulation and destruction of the environment.

Postclassic

After A.D. 900, the Toltec influence took hold, marking the end of the most artistic era and the birth of a new militaristic society built around a blend of ceremonialism, civic and social organization, and conquest.

CULTURE OF THE AZTECS

It was at the end of the postclassic period that we first hear about the Aztecs, and what we know about their early beginnings is fuzzy and no doubt misrepresented. It is believed that once they established themselves as rulers, they destroyed most of their earliest chronicles. It is also believed they began their long journey in the year A.D. 1111, accompanied by their bloodthirsty gods, the most important of which was Huitzilopochtli ("Hummingbird of the South"). The group called themselves Mexica (say meh-SHEE-kah), but we know them as Aztecs. From what historians can surmise, this was a ragtag group of brutal nomads who originated on an island that some believe was located off the coast of Nayarit. This island was called Aztatlán (or Aztlán); hence, the name Aztecas.

An Aztec myth tells of their long quest for a homeland. They were commanded by their gods to look for a particular sign: specifically, an eagle with a serpent in its beak. They wandered for many decades in their search. Finally in the Anáhuac basin they found what the priests had described; an eagle perched on a cactus with a serpent clutched in its beak. They continued their journey into the Valley of Mexico, disrupting the residents and earning a reputation as a barbaric, warlike bunch. To their credit they were tremendous warriors, and their combativeness would earn them an empire with its island core at Tenochtitlán.

On their journey the Aztecs came first to a snake-infested area of Chapultepec woods, where they roasted and ate the serpents they lived with. Next they fought their way to the mosquito-infested marshes of Tenochtitlán, on a small island with little fresh water. This would become their homeland. They continued their barbarian habits, often invading and conquering their neighbors. Despite their rituals, many groups in the Valley of Mexico began to rely upon the Aztecs to do their dirty work, to be their hired slayers—paid mercenaries. Little by

little they gained power by their wit and cunning. And though they started life in the most scurrilous of conditions and in the worst location, after about a hundred years they ruled a major part of the country now known as Mexico.

The Flowery Wars

The Aztecs were determined to take over the entire area around the Valley of Mexico. They very nearly did. The Aztecs and the Tlaxcalans began the Xochiyaoyotl ("Flowery Wars"). These wars were essentially expeditions to gather captives (on both sides, for both groups) to sacrifice to their gods. At first, strict rules regulated these en-

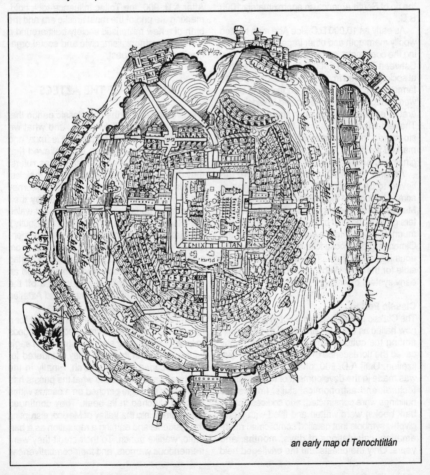

an early map of Tenochtitlán

counters, the object being to collect only *live* captives, much like the tournaments of ancient European knights. Eventually, however, the confrontations became bloodletting events resulting in many deaths.

Mexcaltitlán

Some believe the Aztec homeland is what is now called **Mexcaltitlán,** located in the swampy Río San Pedro, just off the west coast. Others have conjectured that they originated on the island of Janitzio in Lake Pátzcuaro. For now it is an unsolved mystery. But historian Wigberto Jiménez-Moreno points out many similarities between Tenochtitlán's island existence in Lake Texcoco and Mexcaltitlán. During the rainy season, Mexcaltitlán becomes a small Venice when all the streets become canals, and transport is most likely by canoe as it was in Tenochtitlán, also an island with canals.

A Culture Develops

From this astonishing beginning the Aztecs became a strong militaristic society, with surprisingly strong moral values yet bloody religious rituals. While they dearly loved their children, they would sacrifice them to their gods. Their old were treated with great respect and were

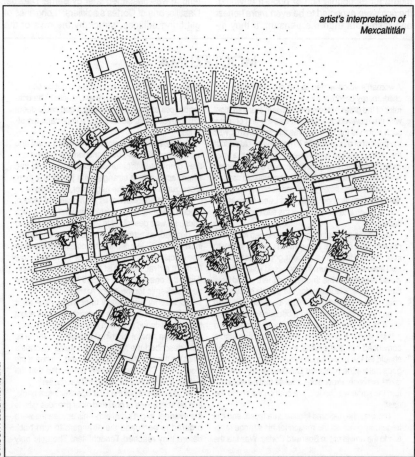

artist's interpretation of Mexcaltitlán

allowed to legally drink the sacred *octli* (pulque) whenever they wished. Ordinarily it was used for religious ceremonies only, and normally if its use was abused the penalty was death. The average man was forbidden *octli*, but it was okay to use other mind-altering drugs. Both *octli* and powerful hallucinogens were believed to be magical because of their effect on people.

To the Aztecs, fairness was paramount for all people rich or poor. If anything, the rich were expected to be even *more* honest and respectful than the peasant; if they di-

gressed, punishment was more severe for the noble. A judge was always present at the enormous Tlateloctl market to make sure that all business was conducted honestly and fairly. By 1426, the Aztec empire was flourishing, and they were the most powerful group in the midst of hundreds of different indigenous societies. From some very undesireable real estate in Lake Texcoco, they had created Tenochtitlán, a beautiful homeland. It was described later by Bernal Díaz del Castillo, one of Cortés's soldiers: "Long lines of glittering edifices, struck by the rays of the

BOB RACE

MOCTEZUMA

A woman's voice wailed in the still dark night, "my children, my children, ruin is at hand." Moctezuma, ruler of the great Aztec nation woke in fear that night with unanswered questions. It was the first of many such nights to follow. Who was this spirit? What was the portent of this message? The 52-year-old ruler of the Aztecs waited and feared. This was the year called "one-reed," and many strange events had already taken place: a volcanic upheaval had caused the waters of the lakes to roil and flood the streets of Tenochtitlán, strange lights had been seen in the northern sky, and the temple of the sun had burst into flames.

Magicians and astrologers surrounded Moctezuma and filled his ears with ominous events surely to take place. Hadn't the ancient god, Quetzalcoatl, said that he would return in a one-reed year? That he would reestablish his throne, and there would be a time of great "tribulation for the people?" Quetzalcoatl, the white-skinned, black-bearded god, had been run off centuries before because of his opposition to the bloodletting that was rampant with the priests and the populace. Moctezuma's advisors convinced him the omens were grim and that he should let the blood run in the streets to satisfy the gods before the banished Quetzalcoatl returned to take his throne. Prophecies foretold that he would return the same way he left, in a craft on the sea to the east.

This was the dilemma Moctezuma faced, and it is frequently given as the reason for his strange reaction to the arrival of the Spaniard Cortés. Was this the

returning god? The Aztec king could not be certain, but he also could not take any chances! The consequences of physically injuring a god could doom him forever in this life and, more important, the afterlife.

The Aztecs were notorious for being cruel and unforgiving soldiers. They conquered and killed and they dominated the surrounding areas, and yet, when faced with a stranger with just a few men, Moctezuma became the negotiator, the gift giver.

Before his appointment as the monarch of Mexico, Moctezuma had been a great general and a high priest; he was described in the *Codex Mendoza* as ". . . learned, an astrologer, a philosopher, and skilled in all the arts." He ruled the nation as First Speaker (the official title of the monarch) for 17 years before Cortés's arrival. Was it just fate when Cortés *did* arrive in the one-reed year of 1519? It would prove to be cataclysmic for the entire Aztec nation.

Moctezuma was clearly unnerved by the tales brought back to the palace by coastal soldiers about this white skinned man with a full black beard wearing strange "metal clothing" astride a "deer." His men described the "moving mountains" (Cortés's ships) in the sea. And most disturbing, he heard the stories that Cortés continually demanded that the Aztecs give up their ritual bloody sacrifices.

What he heard put the First Speaker into a panic, and he sent bribes of gold and other precious gifts to the stranger to get rid of him—his emissaries were ordered to persuade the strangers to turn back before they reached Tenochtitlán. The gold only

evening sun, trembled on the dark blue waters of the lake. It looked like a thing of fairy creation rather than the work of mortal hands." Though they would never dream it possible then, at the end of another hundred years, all that the Aztecs had created would be destroyed.

The 1500s

As the 16th century began, the Aztecs were entrenched in most of Central Mexico and (excluding Maya regions) much of southern Mexico as well. However, there were still a few groups of people who managed to resist Aztec control and the control of their cruel gods. Among these were the Tarascans and the Tlaxcalans. Tarascan territory encompassed what is now the state of Michoacán, where rich copper deposits were

part of the economy of the people. After one confrontation with 24,000 Aztecs, the Tarascans killed 20,000. As a result, the Aztecs left the Tarascans and their copper weapons alone.

Tlaxcala territory was on the eastern slopes of the Valley of Mexico and their beginnings were rooted in the Chichimec culture, a powerful people who managed to maintain their independence against the Aztecs.

Religion

Nature was the essence of Aztec religious beliefs. The Aztecs believed that they ventured into life from a cave—from the womb of the earth. Caves were everywhere and were an important part of the lives of the early people. The very earliest people used them for shelter as

---

intensified Cortés's lust for riches and his desire to meet Moctezuma—he pressed on.

For weeks the Aztec monarch tried bribery, then deceit, even ambush, to keep the Spaniards from getting to his kingdom. When with the help of Moctezuma's Indian enemies (anxious to team up with someone who might be able to conquer the Indian leader), Cortés prevailed, Moctezuma presumed that this was the great god Quetzalcoatl. The once dauntless leader was paralyzed with fear. Cortés and his few men conquered thousands with his Indian allies, his wily tongue, and roaring cannons that shot fire, never before seen by these people. He eventually reached the fabulous city of Tenochtitlán and the palace of Moctezuma.

Moctezuma's dilemma made him a cooperative prisoner in his own palace, surrounded by Cortés and his men. Even then, the Aztec was a gracious host. He was willing to do almost anything to placate this powerful man/god, Cortés/Quetzalcoatl. But he would never accept the Christian religion (even at his death).

However, others in Tenochtitlán were unwilling to give up to these usurpers. When they finally decided to fight (too late), Moctezuma was unable to lead his people; he was dethroned by the populace, and another, more pragmatic man (his cousin, Falling Eagle) was made First Speaker of the Aztecs.

Through six months of turmoil and imprisonment, Moctezuma never strayed from his belief that it would be unwise to use physical force on this bearded deity. As it turns out, he was right. By the time the real fight began, the Aztecs were struck down by the thousands with smallpox, the Spaniard's disease. This was just what the Spaniards needed, or they surely would have been defeated.

It was obvious from the words of Bernal Díaz del Castillo (one of Cortés's soldiers) that Moctezuma had earned the respect and admiration of the Spanish soldiers who guarded him in the palace for many months. But Moctezuma was an enigma. As kind and intelligent as he was, he was still part of the mysterious world of a savage religion, and the Spaniards could never accept his ritual inhumanity or understand his total belief that the gods craved human blood. Moctezuma and all the Aztecs truly believed that if the gods were denied they would destroy the earth.

Moctezuma maintained his dignity to the end. He had saved Cortés on several occasions, believing Cortés when he said he and his men would leave. When the Aztec finally realized his trust was misplaced, the old soldier lost heart but was forever the dignified leader. Even the last time, when Cortés begged Moctezuma to speak to his people in the midst of a battle that the Spaniards were losing, the monarch agreed. Dressed in his finest official garments, with grief and sadness he stood on the wall of the palace where rocks and arrows bolted into the courtyard. He pleaded with the crowds to quit the fight, but his people no longer trusted him—their answer was a volley of heavy rocks, one hitting him in the head. He died several days later.

With the advantage of almost 500 hundred years of hindsight, we can safely say it was inevitable. Even if the Aztecs had been able to stop the Spanish in their attack at that moment, it was just a matter of time. Their world was discovered and no circumstance could have stopped the incursion of Europeans.

they wandered, and in later years caves took on a mystical aura; they were a place to conduct secret ceremonies of the religion. It's not unusual to find evidence of indigenous life in caves across the landscape of the country.

As people changed from nomads and gatherers, settling into villages, leaders took on more responsibilities. Those in charge had to oversee the survival of the people, and growing food was the main issue. It was apparent that in order to grow food, the soil needed rain, yet these early people had no understanding of the erratic flights of nature. They believed in many gods, to whom they attributed natural wonders; if the rain didn't come, they offered "bribes" to their gods. At first small offerings were put on top of small dirt mounds. All of this was encouraged by the priests who were gaining more power because of their supposed influence on and communication with the gods. As time passed, little earth mounds became tall stone structures and became the blood of the people. Religion became the most compelling force in the life of the Aztec, nobleman or peasant.

Each day there was an agenda of ceremonies, whether it was to recognize the birth of children, mark farm plots, or pay daily homage to a specific deity at a determined time. And there were many gods to satisfy. Their religion was a powerful force that thrust bloody demands on the people; at the worst, captives' hearts were cut out and offered still beating to the god —then they were eaten. The populace feared many things and saw themselves in imminent danger of destruction by their gods. Even today, there are those who adhere to some of the old beliefs and go to special *curanderos* who have an "in" with those old gods.

To say they took their beliefs to extremes might not be strong enough. Under Lord Ahuitzotl (a savage leader), a new temple was built to honor the bloodthirsty Huitzilopochtli. Completed in 1487, a mass inauguration ceremony was held. Historians tell us that at least 20,000 hearts were wrenched from the bodies of captives. This took four days and the streets ran with blood. There were more bodies than could be eaten, so thousands were disposed of in the canals.

Note: Cannibalism was not unusual in the history of other civilizations. In the case of the Aztecs, it was practiced much later in the de-

velopment of the people, rather surprising in light of their progressive development in almost all other areas.

The Catholic Transition

With Cortés a new religion came to the continent. This religion recognized only one god. While the Catholic god was said to be a gentle one, some priests (and followers) were notably cruel.

The first priests wasted no time ordering the burning of codices filled with characters and symbols they could not understand. They believed the codices contained only superstitions and Satanic preachings. Since then, only three codices have been found and studied, though only parts of them have been successfully deciphered. The Spaniards destroyed much of the history of these ancient peoples. A few wise men, like Bishop Sahaguin, regretted that rash move and began a search into ancient traditions. He quizzed the Indians and put down in great detail the facts of their lives, including their methods of growing and preparing food, the structure of their society, the priesthood, and the sciences. In all, he filled 12 volumes that today have been thoroughly studied.

In some ways it was an easy transition from the old religion to the new. Statues of the Christian religion (namely saints) were introduced and took the place of the hundreds of statues of the ancient religion (destroyed by the Spanish). The indigenous people saw the saints as an extension of their array of deities and, in isolated areas, they still are. Over the years, the majority of Indians were indeed baptized into the Catholic faith. With a few cruel exceptions, Catholic priests were kind and did their best to educate the people, teach them to read and write, and protect them from the growing number of Spanish settlers who used them as slaves. The majority of Mexicans today practice Catholicism, but in rural areas it's a special "mix" of Catholicism and traditional indigenous beliefs. Some people still cling to many of the old, traditional beliefs.

Agriculture

Scientists believe one of the prime reasons Indian priests were so important is that they studied celestial movements. The elaborate temples were built to strict astronomical guidelines, and one of the priests' prime functions was to chart the changing seasons and decide when to begin the planting cycle, which in some areas involved the slash-and-burn method of agriculture. Those living in the lake districts had little land and needed to know when to prepare their cleverly developed *chinampas* (floating "farms"). Water was also a prime concern.

Although priests could track the seasons, they could not guarantee rain, and that's where superstitous followers were led astray. Their religious leaders/priests (in the earliest years priests were the rulers of the tribes) believed that the rain gods would produce rain as long as they were presented with blood offerings. Early recorded history tells of severe years of drought, when great numbers of people died of starvation. Frightened it would happen again and believing the priests personally knew the gods, the resistance to human sacrifice was not what would be expected. During drought periods survival was tough. People found sustenance available in other forms. Since they lived surrounded by lakes, they looked to the muddy swamps. How many people in your hometown would be desperate enough to take a net and capture mosquito larvae for dinner? (They turned out to be a good source of protein.) The larvae served double duty: In addition to being the main course, a handful of dried larvae was very portable and nutritious; it was often carried into battle by warriors.

When water was abundant, women collected the eggs of a tiny green insect attached to reeds growing in the lake. At home the tiny eggs were made into patties. Tiny algae fish called *amarillos* (about the size of aquarium fish) are still eaten by the locals. One of today's delicacies is the *huitlacoche* (corn smut/mushroom), a fungus that grows over corn kernels in the rainy season. This too, dates back to the time of the Aztecs. Today in gourmet restaurants you'll pay a pretty penny to eat them in crepes, stews, and soups (so let's not call them "smut"). Actually, they have a fine flavor, though different from any mushroom I've eaten.

When the time is propitious (before the rains begin in the spring), Indians cut the trees and weeds on a section of land, leaving stumps about half a meter above ground. Downed trees are spread evenly across the landscape in order to burn uniformly; residual ash is left to nourish

the soil. At the proper time, holes are made with a pointed stick, and four precious maize kernels are dropped into the earth, along with a thin bean and a fat bean. At each corner (the cardinal points) of the cornfield, offerings are left to encourage the gods to give forth great rains. With abundant moisture, crops are bountiful and rich enough to provide food even into the following year.

The indigenous people knew the value of allowing the land to lay fallow after two seasons of growth, and each family's cornfield was moved from place to place around the villages scattered through the bush; a lot of forest land was destroyed. Often, squash and tomatoes were planted in the shade of towering corn stalks to make double use of the land.

The Aztecs were a clever lot. Out of necessity, they devised a way of "creating" plots of land along the coastal fringes of their island in order to raise food; these were *chinampas*, basically floating farms. Pilings made of young trees were driven into the marshy shallows then laced with sapling limbs, creating criblike affairs that were filled with layers of rotten reeds alternated with rich lake-bottom sludge. Eventually, these *chinampas* became rooted. As the population increased, more *chinampas* were added. Channels were left between rows along the shoreline for ease of access. This land reclamation grew, canals became established waterways, and the populace traveled mostly by canoe. Rich floating farms grew quantities of foodstuffs to take care of the island residents, with enough left over to barter with mainland folk. The Spaniards found this successful lifestyle when they first arrived.

All of the indigenous groups of Mesoamerica share the belief that human life began with corn. It was not just their nourishment, it was a sacred entity. Corn was the heart of nutrition and was eaten at each meal. From it they made tortillas, stew, and beverages—both alcoholic and nonalcoholic. Because growing corn was such a vital part of life, it is represented in drawings and carvings along with other social and religious symbols. Corn tortillas are still a main staple of the Mexican people. Native women in small towns can be seen early in the morning carrying bowls of corn kernels on their heads to the tortilla shop. Here the kernels are ground into tortilla dough. This was done by hand for centuries (and still is in isolated places). Today with electricity and neighborhood entrepreneurs, it's much quicker to pay a peso or two and zap—tortilla dough! Others pay a few more pesos (price is controlled by the government) and buy their tortillas by the kilo hot off the griddle. It's amazing that the indigenous people came up with the combination of corn and beans without a dietitian telling them it was a complete protein.

Music

The entire Aztec culture was directed by religion. Music was composed for religious ceremonies and there was no such thing as a written note. Musicians played for high stakes. If they made an error in a note or a drumbeat, they would displease the gods (according to the priests), and the penalty was death. Musicians memorized their entire repertoire. Instruments consisted of conch shells, flutes, rattles, and drums of many different styles, shapes, and sounds.

Arts And Crafts

Most of the arts that developed over the centuries before the Spanish were connected in some way to ancient religious beliefs and ceremonies. Later, the Spanish influence would become apparent. The early priests devoted much of their time to instructing the populace, in hopes of teaching them trades. Colonialists from Spain brought artisans who passed on their skills to the indigenes. These local artists were already great masters of wood and stone carving, gold and silver masonry, paper art and painting. They were skilled in the use of colors found in nature. These existing skills, along with newly introduced European crafts, created a special flavor. This flavor has blended into the unique "touch" of Mexico. The specialties of Mexico have continued to evolve and flourish throughout the centuries, making Mexican art comparable in quality and originality to any country in the world.

Medicine

Aztec healers and European physicians during the same era demonstrated very similar techniques. Healers on both continents bled the sick, set broken bones, and treated tooth decay. Aztec practitioners even performed brain surgery. They depended on an enormous array of herbs, roots, and barks to treat their patients. Many of these same elements continue to be used by isolated groups, and several have been found to be an important basis for modern medicines. They've since been synthesized into 20th-century caplets, pills, and elixirs.

Education

Priests were probably the most educated segment of Aztec society, each having had a specialty, such as music or dancing. School was compulsory for children. Status determined which of two schools they would attend and what they would learn. Children of nobles attended a school taught by priests. Boys were taught a broad curriculum including history, philosophy, poetry, astronomy, religion, and oratory —they were trained for either a military post, the priesthood, or life as a noble. If they were being trained for the priesthood (girls as well) they learned the art of writing. All girls were taught to work in the home.

Commoners attended schools where they learned trades and other skills to prepare them for life. Though the Aztecs used the written word, only the most outstanding events were recorded on paper. Most lessons were taught orally, and history was handed down from generation to generation. All children were taught modesty, humility, and courtesy; these were important elements of their education. Society maintained strict moral codes that were publicly enforced, whether or not the offender was royalty or a commoner.

THE SPANISH CONQUEST

The early 16th century was a time of mass exploration in other parts of the globe. The world was hungry to see what was beyond the horizon, to find a shorter sea route to get to Asia and its rich trading market. The Spanish were feeling triumphant after finally ridding themselves of the Moors following decades of fighting. At last, there was a Christian world (or so the powerful Pope pronounced). And though Columbus failed to find the passage he searched for, when he returned and reported the wonders he had observed in his "accidental" New World, it was only natural that adventurers awaited ready to take a look. Kings and ad-

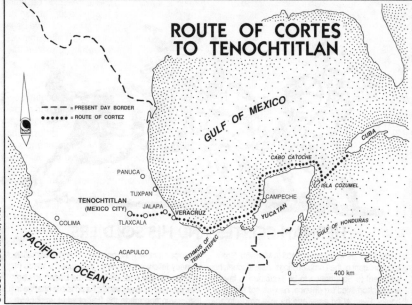

ROUTE OF CORTES TO TENOCHTITLAN

- - - = PRESENT DAY BORDER
•••••• = ROUTE OF CORTEZ

GULF OF MEXICO

PACIFIC OCEAN

CUBA

CABO CATOCHE

ISLA COZUMEL

PANUCA

TUXPAN

TENOCHTITLAN
(MEXICO CITY)

JALAPA

VERACRUZ

CAMPECHE

YUCATAN

GULF OF HONDURAS

COLIMA

TLAXCALA

ISTHMUS OF TEHUANTEPEC

ACAPULCO

0   400 km

© MOON PUBLICATIONS, INC.

venturers were greedy, and the promise of gold and great riches lured many explorers to forsake their homeland and move to Nueva España.

The free-spirited vagabonds who followed Columbus were an amazing lot—particularly courageous were the conquistadores, a handful of men led by Hernán Cortés. Cortés was a gutsy man of great vision and immense confidence, with a con artist's tongue—who else, while surrounded by six million hostile natives, would burn his ships to stop the grumbling in the ranks, precluding any possible escape from a strange land thousands of miles from home? He had tremendous motivation that some attribute to greed and a compelling desire for power. Against amazing odds, he managed to conquer the unknown land and to make the first sweeping strokes on a landscape that would become the Americas, then and now the richest piece of the earth.

In his search for new lands and riches, Cortés discovered a civilization of pagans who worshipped multiple gods and who had an appetite for human blood. Their leaders wore trinkets of gold. This society was in many ways advanced beyond that of Europe. Pope Alexander VI had already given the Spanish explorers carte blanche in any lands they discovered, *as long as they taught them the "word of the Christian God."* There it was, another saving reason (or rationalization) to conquer land and people, to save "heathen souls" and turn them all into "good Christians"—no matter what the cost. In the paths of these explorers/saviors, magnificent cities grew and a rich cultural blend of European and American tradition became Mexico.

Destruction Of A Society

As the Spaniards evangelized the New World, an entire society of indigenous people was destroyed. The Catholic Spaniards were shocked by the bloodthirsty practices they discovered as they traveled through the beautiful, well-developed cities from Veracruz to Tenochtitlán in their quest to find Moctezuma. But the Aztecs' methods did not intimidate Cortés. Right from the beginning, he began spreading the Christian doctrine—and extracting promises (under pain of death) that said they would give up their beliefs and worship the Catholic way. Bernal Díaz del Castillo, other conquistadores, and the letters

HERNAN CORTES AND HIS SOLDIERS

Hernán Cortés was born in 1485 in Medellin, Spain, a descendant of the Lombard kings. As a student, he was sent to Salamanca to be educated in law. It was a short-lived experience; he was not a man of books. Even at an early age he was prone to adventure, though then it was the amorous variety of adventure. He dreamed of Columbus's New World and the mystery that it held. At 17 he became a cavalier and eventually sailed to Hispaniola in search of gold and adventure. Instead he became a country gentleman who owned land and servants, but still he yearned for his dream. In 1511, Cortés sailed with Diego Velasquez to conquer Cuba. From that voyage it became evident that Cortés had definite talents in this direction. Velasquez was made governor of Cuba, and he brought the young explorer along. Again he was awarded land and slaves, and he ended up with gold mines that paid off handsomely. But his life was still filled with swashbuckling dreams that frequently landed him in Cuban prisons—each time he was clever enough to escape. He and Velasquez had a precarious relationship, including moments of respect and/or jealousy. Both came together when Velasquez appointed Cortés the captain general of an expedition from Cuba to the New World to find several Spaniards believed held prisoners by the Indians in Mexico. Cortés's explicit orders were to patronize the Indians and to barter with them, to learn about the races of their people and the natural resources of the country, and above all to do nothing to embarrass the crown or offend God.

As Cortés threw himself into the preparations for

this expedition, with the good spirits and cooperation of many fellow adventurers, Velasquez's seeds of jealousy on the possible outcome began to nag. The younger man got wind of a possible change in leadership and made the first of what would turn out to be many gambles.

After hearing rumors that Velasquez was about to change his mind and appoint a new captain, Cortés and his men sailed, ill prepared and in a hurry. In Cortés's defense, he had spent considerable amount of his own funds equipping the ships and the stores. More than anything he could not accept being denied the opportunity to go to the New World.

And so, on 10 February 1519, 34-year-old Hernán Cortés sailed from Cuba. With 11 ships, 120 sailors, 550 soldiers, 200 Indians, and 16 horses he set out in search of a dream, with or without the blessings of governor Velasquez. The search for the Spanish prisoners began on the Yucatán coast. But it was on the Gulf of Mexico coast, in what would become the state of Veracruz, that Cortés's destiny was put in motion. Much was to happen very quickly. And though over the next days the Indians presented Cortés with a variety of gifts, including gold trinkets (those definitely got his attention), one gift in particular would prove to be the most helpful of all, the young woman named Marina (also called Malinche and Malintze). Doña Marina would become his skilled interpreter, advisor, and eventually his lover and the mother of his son. Today she is considered by most Mexicans a traitor to her homeland for her assistance in the Conquest.

Cortés's soldiers, who lived through the amazing subjugation of Moctezuma and the Aztecs, were promised a piece of the booty. In 1522, though it was not the gold they all had hoped for each man was rewarded with a piece of land, his own little kingdom. Unlike today's soldiers who receive pay, many of the explorers who accompanied Cortés not only did not receive pay, but in fact paid for part of the expedition, at the least for their own equipment, arms, and horses. Some went into debt to go on this venture. It was obvious to the men under Cortés that there was no gold to divvy up in the end. So, their leader agreed to give each of these irate men (who had suffered so much and fought so hard) native villages and villagers. The idea was, the *encomiendero* would receive the tribute of the natives as well as their (free) labor. He would treat them kindly and teach them to be good Christians. After all was said and done, however, these Indians were slaves. They were treated poorly, and in some cases inhumanely; thousands died as a result. The Spanish crown could have stopped this, but it seemed to be the easiest way to placate the soldiers who had given so much, and who now demanded some sort of payment.

In some cases the *encomiendas* were many thousands of acres in size, and each warrior expected to strike it rich finding gold and silver. However, it was a crapshoot; few of the soldiers found the precious metal they all longed for.

Cortés was a man of many appetites. One was his love of riches, but it almost seems that his love of adventure, conquest, and fame

BOB RACE

were even more important to him. His complete defeat of the Aztec empire and Moctezuma included the destruction of millions of Indians (whether directly or indirectly). After that, in the early 16th century, the door was open for the exploration and colonization of millions of acres then called New Spain, now called Mexico. Immense amounts of silver and gold were returned to Spain and the crown, Spaniards flooded the country, and cities grew. Though it would seem to be a direct result of the courage and cleverness of Cortés, he never received the recognition he desired.

Cortés was allowed (by King Charles V) to choose 22 towns for his own personal *encomiendas,* naturally he chose the richest areas in New Spain. In the mid-1530s, thanks to his sugar mills, livestock, mines, and tribute from 23,000 Indian families on his widespread *encomiendas,* Cortés was the richest Spaniard in the world with the exception of King Charles. However, his real desire was for power, to be the governor of the lands that he had conquered, or at the least a duke in the court of Spain. He was awarded neither. He left Mexico in 1540, never to return and never to carry the titles he dreamed of. He died in Spain in 1547. At his request, his remains were returned to Mexico. Today, one seldom hears or sees reminders of Cortés in Mexico, despite his impact on the country. A small bust of Cortés lingers over his bones in the Templo y Hospital de Jesús in Mexico City. The only other public memorial is a statue in the Cuernavaca Hotel, which is the palace he built and the home he seemed to most enjoy in Mexico.

from Cortés to the King of Spain spelled out clearly the lifestyle of the people, their rulers, and especially their powerful priests who encouraged the cannibalism of their captives.

It took Cortés and the Spaniards only three years to totally subdue the Aztecs and the Valley of Mexico. Once that was accomplished the rest of the country fell into line. Important changes would take place over the next 100 years. At the heart of it all was evangelization and gold. Aztec temples and cities were systematically destroyed. New European-style structures took their places, almost always constructed over the old.

Moctezuma's promise was real—the gold and silver were there, it just took a while to get to it. With each new strike in the mines throughout the mountain highlands, the country grew; it was the Indians who labored under the worst conditions and paid with the heaviest price, their lives. Even though most of the precious metals were sent to Spain, there was enough for the creation of rich men, and cities of magnificent buildings, plus the institution of a new culture.

Cortés cannot take all the credit for bringing an entire nation under control; much of it was bad luck, the most profound of which was the smallpox carried over by a Cuban soldier. It swept across the country, killing as many as 80% of the people—precisely at the moment that the Indians began to realize what had to be done to conquer the Spaniards; fight back! Note: In 1519 the indigenous population was 25,200,000. By 1650 disease and destruction had reduced that number to less than 1,000,000. Even though by 1810 the indigenous count had more than tripled to 3,676,281, most of the world was conquered.

Trek Of Discovery

That first trek from Veracruz to Tenochtitlán (in 1519) was filled with unexpected discoveries. The Spaniards were impressed with the layout and design of Indian cities, the rich farmlands with unusual fruits and vegetables, the clever infrastructure (plumbing and roads), the use of color, and the amazing woven textiles often incorporating beautiful feathers. But especially, they were particularly wide-eyed at the gold and silver trinkets and religious ornaments they saw.

THE CHANGING FACES OF NEW SPAIN

When Cortés arrived, the indigenes were part of a well-structured society. Even then there was a caste system. After the conquest and through colonization and evangelization, many new ethnicities developed over the years.

Gachupines Peninsulares

The *gachupines,* those born in Spain and living in Mexico, had not only the richest lifestyle and ownership of vast *encomiendas* (which meant they had land *and* slaves), but they were also the most prestigious and received the most respect from the crown in Spain. If we are to believe the writings of Fanny Calderón de la Barca, wife of the first envoy from Spain to independent Mexico, life was a series of parties, grand affairs on religious feast days, and public or private celebrations.

Criollos

The criollos, pure Spaniards born in Mexico, were just as rich with all the gracious pastimes of European gentry. Their *encomienda* status also provided them with servants and vassals of the land. They mingled freely and frequently at the social affairs of the *gachupines,* or at parties of their own (a marvelous excuse for the women in both groups to dress in imported European silks and satins that arrived yearly aboard the galleons). But the respect was missing. They were treated like second-class citizens as far as the Spanish crown was concerned. There was a certain blight on them because of their birth country, even though they were the descendants of the people who left their homeland for the New World, endorsed by the crown. Without these original pioneers, merchants, and mining barons, the country would never have developed.

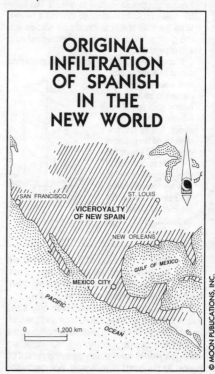

ORIGINAL INFILTRATION OF SPANISH IN THE NEW WORLD

SAN FRANCISCO   ST. LOUIS

VICEROYALTY OF NEW SPAIN

NEW ORLEANS

GULF OF MEXICO

MEXICO CITY

PACIFIC

0   1,200 km   OCEAN

© MOON PUBLICATIONS, INC.

Mestizos

The next class tier was not nearly so lucky. The mestizos, born in Mexico of mixed Spanish and Indian blood, or any other two mixed groups, found little of their *jefes'* (bosses') luxury. Their lot in life would seldom change; they were always on the bottom rung, and it remained that way until Benito Juárez (a full-blooded Zapotec) came along and tried to make life more bearable.

Indigenes

Below the bottom rung of this social ladder were the "Indians," whose ancestors ruled and developed the society that the Spaniards crushed in 1520. While the lower classes of the ancient lifestyle had been subject to sacrifice, slave labor, and a humble lifestyle, *all* of the people were treated with respect and within the moral rules of their society. The indigenous people were the wheels that cranked out progress.

Under Spanish rule, however, they were subject to inane laws that controlled their development; for example, Indians were forbidden to wear European clothes. The penalty for a transgression was 100 lashes and a month in jail.

MONEY SENT TO THE SPANISH CROWN, 1786-1789

A phenomenal amount of money was made in the New World, and much of it was the direct result of hard working early settlers from Spain and their descendants, the criollos. Spain spent it as fast as they got it, using it to conquer new lands around the globe and old governments in Europe.

FROM	PESOS
Tobacco Monopoly	16,000,000
Sales Tax	15,500,000
One-tenth of Precious Metals	9,000,000
Coinage	6,000,000
Pulque Monopoly	3,500,000
Indian Tributes	3,500,000
Customs Duties	3,000,000
TOTAL	**56,500,000**

Birth Of A Nation

The long arm of the Spanish throne continued to reach across the seas to New Spain, to make tougher laws, raise taxes, and claim an ever larger share of the silver. Spain seemed far removed, the old conquistadores and their loyalty to the throne were long gone, and Spanish rule was resented more and more. While the criollos had wealth, they had little power; *that* remained in the hands of the *peninsulares*. Mestizos and Indians were powerless and kept in a condition of eternal poverty. And though their circles never touched, the criollo, mestizo, and Indian were juxtaposed by a growing Mexican nationalism. The *peninsulares* and their Spanish royalist soldiers ruled with an iron fist until finally a revolt erupted.

THE SEEDS OF DISCONTENT

That it took 300 years for a revolt against the Spanish is amazing; that it was the criollos who instigated it is even more amazing. But it was the criollos, the descendants of the original Spaniards, who longed for the power and the stature enjoyed only by the *gachupines*.

Miguel Hidalgo

In 1810, throughout Central Mexico, groups of agitated criollos met under the guise of social events and "literary clubs." Long nights were spent debating their future, their plans, their dreams, and eventually a revolution. Among these groups, one of the most active was The Literary and Social Club of Querétaro. Although the group included many sincere individuals from all walks of society, the one whom we hear about most was an aging criollo parish priest, Miguel Hidalgo y Costilla. He was a passionate man with an ongoing concern for the poor and a resentment toward the Spanish hierarchy. It was this heirarchy that gave the "plum" jobs in the big city churches to *gachupines peninsulares*. But that was only part of the problem. At the same time in Europe, Spain was having problems with France. It was unthinkable to the populace of New Spain to imagine the reins of the country being taken over by a "foreign" government (France). Perhaps the line of thinking was that if anyone was going to take over the New World, it would be the populace. As it happens many of these people would not live through the next 10 years to (indeed) see the French try to take over the country.

War Of Independence

The world watched both the American and French revolutions and their fights for freedom; role models had been established. Spain's problems now included the invasion of Napoleon Bonaparte. Nonetheless, the "discontented" in the highlands of Mexico were still in the planning stages of a *peaceful* revolt. It was only when the plan was unexpectedly uncovered that it erupted prematurely into a violent war. Father Hidalgo shouted his **Grito de Dolores** on 16 September, 1810, a passionate cry for freedom, pitting peasants and criollos against the power and firearms of the Spanish royalist army.

Independence

It took until 1821 to achieve independence from Spain, and contrary to the belief of all who fought in the bloody war, it was only the beginning of Mexico's problems. For the next one hundred-plus years, the country would struggle through politicians who were crooks, a clampdown on the power of the Catholic church, a division of the wealth between the country and the peasants (or so it was supposed to be), and periods of great development.

Mexico also suffered great losses, especially during the **Mexican-American War** in 1833 during the regime of president/general Santa Anna (a self-made dictator who gave away half the country and who was made president 11 times!). A series of more wars left behind scars and chaos. In 1858, the civil **War Of Reform** was between the powers of Mexico City and Veracruz. The big outcome concerned the wealth of the Catholic church and the takeover of its property. Zapotec Indian and future president of Mexico Benito Juárez played an important role.

Enter The French

In 1862, the **French Invasion** enabled the French to take over the country and attempt to turn the fledgling republic into a monarchy. Napoleon III sent Ferdinand Maximilian Joseph and his wife Carlota to Mexico as emperor and empress. Their reign was a short and tragic

one. The enormous size of the country, the bickering among his counselors, the corruptness of everyone in authority, the duplicity of the Church, and the U.S. commitment to the Monroe Doctrine combined to end the experiment of "Empire" with Maximilian's death before a firing squad in Querétaro and Carlota's insanity as she pleaded in Europe for her husband's safe return. By 1867, Benito Juárez was back in control.

JUAREZ TO SALINAS DE GORTARI

From Juárez's time to the present leadership of Miguel Salinas de Gortari, the country has seen extremes in government and suffered with patience through a "reform" and the dictatorlike regime of the **Porfiriata** (Porfirio Díaz, president 1877-1911). When patience ran out there was the **Mexican Revolution** (1911-1917). A president was assassinated (Francisco Madero, 1913), and in 1917 the country put into place a new constitution to begin massive reforms, sweeping education programs, and the nationalization of many foreign industries, including U.S. oil companies. Within the next couple of decades the nation would see two more presidents assassinated (Obregón and Venustano Carranza) as well as the coming and going of such colorful folk heroes as Francisco "Pancho" Villa and Emiliano Zapata.

Mexico has seen its star rise with the oil industry and they've watched it sink with the price-cut of oil around the world. They have endured triple-digit inflation and have seen it finally relax into a more bearable single-digit figure. Salinas de Gortari has been given much of the credit for the period of stabilization between 1987 and 1993. Now, if the new regime can make NAFTA (the North American Free Trade Agreement) work between the U.S., Canada, and Mexico, the new president will have a historical feather to tuck into his cap; only time will tell if it was the best way to go for all parties concerned.

Modern-day Explorers

Today's explorers of Mexico are visitors—visitors discovering for the first time the art and beauty of a rich historical past and the joys of the Mexican people. Central Mexico, mineral laden still, is the scene of this colorful tapestry. Some visitors find similarities between the appearance of cobblestone streets of Europe to the cobblestone streets of Central Mexico. But there the similarity ends. Visitors learn that Mexico's culture is all its own and unlike any other in the world. Its gringo neighbor to the north has had a heavy influence and Mexico continues to grow, expand, improve, and maintain its historical sense of its past.

Foreign travelers are falling in love with the mosaic that has become Mexico. More and more visitors are coming from Europe, and now Japan, but the U.S. and Canada still represent the highest number of foreign visitors.

GOVERNMENT AND ECONOMY

GOVERNMENT

Theoretically, Mexico enjoys a constitutional democracy modeled after that of the United States. A president, a two-house congress, and a judiciary branch see to the business of running the country. Theoretically, Mexico's elections are free. Realistically, for 66 years the country has been controlled by one party, the PRI (Partido Revolucionario Institutional, or Institutional Revolutionary Party). Political dissent—represented primarily by PAN (Partido Acción Nacional) and PMS (Partido Mexicano Socialista)—has never had much voice. The president, who can serve only a single six-year term, hand-

Benito Juárez

picks the next PRI candidate who historically has been guaranteed the office through use of the state-controlled media and dubious election procedures.

In addition to Mexico's 32 states, the country has the **Distrito Federal,** or Federal District in Mexico City, which encompasses the government center. The states are allowed a small measure of autonomy, but the reach of the federal government is long. City mayors, called *presidentes municipales,* appoint federal *delegatos* to represent the national government at the municipal level.

Fraud and corruption have been ugly mainstays of Mexican government from its beginning. In the 1988 presidential election, PRI candidate Carlos Salinas de Gortari officially garnered 51% of the vote, a figure many critics believe was invented by the PRI after polls closed. (A suspicious "breakdown" in the election computer delayed the results for several days.)

CHRIS PARMENTER/2

Porfirio Díaz

But Salinas's term will likely be remembered as a time of historic reforms, such as expanding the number of Senate seats to allow more for the opposition, limiting campaign spending, and changing the rules of the body that oversees Mexican elections.

The only certainty in Mexico's tumultuous political arena is that, after decades of a government static in its ways, things are changing fast. The U.S. Congress's passage of NAFTA in 1993 sealed a free-trade deal between Mexico, the U.S., and Canada that will likely change Mexico's economic landscape forever—the political ramifications of which are still unclear. The March 1994 election-year shooting of PRI presidential candidate Luis Donaldo Colosio in Tijuana was Mexico's first major political assassination since 1928. Soon after, Colosio's campaign manager, technocrat Ernesto Zedillo, was nominated to fill the candidacy. Mexico's political future is anyone's guess.

ECONOMY

Central Mexico Cities
Mexico City is the heart of the colonial cities. With 20 million people, it is the largest city in the world. Each year 800,000 people enter the city's job market, yet only 400,000 jobs are available. Roughly 65% of the national population resides in cities, partly due to continuing migration from rural areas. In addition, a certain number of young Mexican adults, many accompanied by their families, continue to make their way across the U.S. border (both legally and illegally), where there's more hope of getting jobs; about six million Mexicans presently live in the United States. Because of this leave-the-land movement, the country's agriculture has suffered.

Industries, Imports, Exports
Mexico imports corn, cereals, and sugar, among other products, and exports coffee, cotton, sisal, honey, bananas, and beef cattle. Mexico's chief industries are oil, mining, and tourism. After the oil industry was nationalized in 1938, a time of transition slowed down production. Pemex, the state oil corporation, does not belong to the Organization of Petroleum Exporting Countries (OPEC), but keeps its prices in line with it. Most

of the oil produced in Mexico is shipped to the U.S. (its number-one customer), as well as Canada, Israel, France, and Japan. Rich in natural gas, the country sends the U.S. 10% of its total output. Two-thirds of Mexico's export revenue comes from fossil fuels. The slump of oil prices has forced the government to think about other alternatives for revenue, and thus many new industries are growing.

Mexico is still the world's largest producer of silver and fluorspar. It also processes large quantities of barite, antimony, bismuth, copper, and sulphur. Other minerals mined are gold, tin, manganese, zinc, coal, and iron. Although mining has always been important to Mexico's economy, growth of the industry is slow, about a two percent increase per year. Around 60% of the country's industrial plants are concentrated around Mexico City, although the government is trying to change that by establishing manufacturing areas and encouraging private industry to build in the provinces. Petrochemical processing industries along the U.S. border continue to grow.

Maquiladoras
An industry that's growing rapidly all over Mexico, the *maquiladoras* provide jobs for hundreds of Mexicans. Products from the U.S. such as clothing, small equipment, and leather goods originate in the U.S. and are then sent to Mexico to be completed by the cheaper labor force. These *maquiladora* plants are enthusiastically being developed.

NAFTA
With the 1993 ratification of NAFTA, Mexico expects many more of these developments to succeed. Mexico has pinned its hopes on NAFTA and has implemented many changes to woo U.S. and Canadian corporations.

Tourism
Tourism is developing into the number-two contributor to the economy. **FONATUR**, the government's national trust fund (established to finance the development of beautiful areas of the country to attract investors and visitors), has been very successful. Cancún is probably the most successful example thus far, but an advertising campaign to bring people into the colonial cities, Munda Maya, and other little

known but beautiful areas is coming along. Government money is used to develop the infrastructure, and then private enterprise takes over. Millions of tourists visit the country every year, and travelers from America make up the largest percentages.

THE PEOPLE OF MEXICO

The people who live in Central Mexico are an interesting mix: some are sophisticated, well-educated, modern thinkers from well-developed cities, and yet pockets still exist of almost-pure-blooded indigenous groups that continue to live a lifestyle similar to that of their ancestors. These rural villages are in isolated mountains and valleys, and the groups have varying languages and backgrounds, but times are changing. As roads are built, they are more in tune with the everyday life of the '90s, and they are more apt to mingle with their neighbors. Mostly you see these people on market days in hub-cities around the countryside. These groups are easily recognizable in their individualized village costumes.

For a historical look ath Mexico's many ethnic groups, please see "The Changing Faces of New Spain" under "History," above.

Population Facts
As of 1990 (the last census until 2000), the population of Mexico was 75,000,000; some, however, believe this is on the low side. It is estimated that 50% of the country's population lives in Mexico City alone. The urban population of the country is 66.3% of the total population. Overall, 41.5% are under the age of 15, and 3.6% are over 65 (in the U.S., the latter percentage is much higher). The life expectancy for men is 68 years, for women it's 76 years. The ethnic division is 60% mestizo (Indian/Spanish) and 30% Amerindian (divided up among a large number of different groups—the largest is the Nauhua). Nine percent of the remaining people are white, and only one percent are from other races. Roman Catholics make up 97%, and three percent are Protestant. Interestingly, Mexico has an 88% literacy rate—and it's growing.

Women
The women of Mexico have a complex position in the lifestyle. All mothers are greatly respected by their children. Women also have a very independent nature, and though they know the position they hold is to run the home and the family, it's not unusual today for women to receive a good education and hold down professional jobs. This used to hold true only for those of the upper classes, but it has filtered down to the middle class as well. **Note:** This is definitely not the case for the pockets of pure indigenes, where women have *no* rights whatsoever.

But today's woman in the middle to upper class has a better life than a century ago. The social mores of husbands may not have changed a great deal; they still have the final word in the house, and they still take pride in a *machismo* attitude (mostly to impress their male friends).

Early Women's Rights
In the colonial era, parents often chose a woman's future—either a husband or a life in the convent—and she accepted her fate. And though the terminology was unknown then, New Spain can rightfully boast the first women's rights activist, Sor (Sister) Juana Inés de la Cruz (1651-1695). Brilliant even as a child, she was considered a genius and was much admired in Spanish court circles, giving her the opportunity to enter into a good (probably rich) marriage. But this independent woman had already noticed the treatment of women in the male-dominated society. So, to the shock of her social circle, she left would-be suitors behind, entered the convent, and spent her life meditating, praying, and writing. She wrote thousands of poems deriding the treatment of women. Sor Juana is still remembered as the brightest literary personality of the colonial era.

Not until the era of the Porfiriato (1876-1911) were women allowed to enter professions formerly reserved for men only, and even then it was very limited. By the late 1890s women became involved in medicine, pharmacy, dentistry, law, and higher education, but they were still held at arm's length.

Laura Torres was also ahead of the times when in 1904 she organized the Admiradoras de

Juárez, a feminist group that was a little too militant for the likes of most Mexican men, especially those in power. Despite the gains made over the years, it wasn't until 1955 that women were given the right to vote.

Family Planning

The stereotyped image of Mexican women giving birth to a baby every year is no longer valid. Social advances have changed that tradition. The old adage that Mexican families had lots of children to help on the *ranchito* may or may not be true, but it *was* true that women had little control over the situation. Today, 45% of married women use contraceptives. Interestingly, though contraceptives have been around for years, it wasn't something most women used or even knew about.

Enter soap operas (even the poorest families have TV today if they have electricity). Anything is acceptable on soap operas, even in Mexico. These shows "taught" Mexican women that they could limit their family size. The show called **"Acompañame"** ("Come Along With Me") was first broadcast in 1977 and is credited with propelling more than half a million Mexican women to family planning clinics for the first time, fueling a 32.5% increase in contraceptive use.

Another plus in today's Mexico: the government provides child care services for little or no money for working mothers. These centers are mostly available in the larger cities where there's a growing segment of working women.

Note: Indigenous rural women are not part of this changing tide, and they continue to have many children. They may not even be aware of packaged contraceptives. Indian women for centuries knew which bark to chew on to discourage pregnancy (they just couldn't let their husbands in on it). It was this bark that sparked the first oral-contraceptive research, today known as the "Pill."

The Middle Class

Some say the growing middle class is Mexcio's hope for the future. At one time there was only a wealthy class or the poor. Today that's changing. A veritably free education is more available to children all over the countryside, and that has been instrumental in encouraging this impor-

tant part of society. More and more moderate-income families are able to buy homes. It's probably this group more than any other that is in love with U.S. goods, whether it's McDonald's hamburgers or shampoo or disposable diapers. Huge shopping malls and supermarkets are becoming U.S. clones. Rumors circulate that large public *mercados* such as those in Guadalajara have lost tenants because middle-income people have switched their loyalties away from the open market stalls to such modern markets as **Comercial Mexicanas** and **Wal-Mart**. And who knows what NAFTA is bringing?

EDUCATION

Education is high on the priority list of the Mexican government. In the cities, the majority of children go to school and have access to higher education at little cost. In most schools the children must wear uniforms, and they must pay for their own books and pencils. For some this is a problem, but there are private agencies that help out. In small villages the problem escalates; often families do not have the money to buy the uniforms *or* the pencils. (You might notice that children who surround tourists in small villages don't ask for money; they ask for pencils.) We have found that in cities such as Guadalajara and Chapala, where there are large groups of Americans and Canadians, many of these children's needs are met by organizations set up by the expats. The Huichols in Jalisco and Nayarit have greatly benefitted from these charitable organizations.

Children are required to go to school from age six to age 14. At that point many of the poorer families then must keep their children home to help the family or to go to work. **Note:** Females over 15 make up the largest percentage of illiteracy (11.7%). After primary school those that go on must choose between trade or academic education. All students can go to college for free or nearly free. Some question the quality of public education as well as the education of the teachers. Their pay, however, recently has been increased. In 1993 the starting salary for primary teachers in Mexico City was US$451.60 per month. In other parts of the country it is as low as US$362.90.

LANGUAGE

The majority of people speak Spanish, and it is the language taught in Mexican schools. In recent years, there's been an outcry by ethnic groups (or by foreign supporters) for their native languages to be preserved in writing and taught to their children. In most cases this hasn't happened. One exception is in Chiapas, where Robert M. Laughlin (who has lived and studied among the people for 30 years) produced the *First Great Tzotzil Dictionary of San Lorenzo Zinacantán* (published by Smithsonian Institution Press). In the small villages, many of these children speak only the language of their ancestors until they begin school, and then they must learn Spanish; most have never seen their traditional language written.

There are many pockets of other-language speakers scattered about the country, and if you drive through small villages in the central highlands you will undoubtedly hear these almost bygone tongues. Nahuatl is the most common in Central Mexico, since that was the language of the Aztecs, the largest group in Mexico when Cortés arrived.

Visitors And Language

In Mexico, English is not spoken except perhaps by corporate businessmen and those involved in tourism. Often a Mexican waiter or salesperson appears to know the language and is able to do his/her job in English. However, if you try to go beyond an order from a menu, or any other request pertinent to the business, you'll get no further. To improve your time in any foreign country, it helps to come armed with at least a few basic phrases such as "hello," "please," "thank you," and "where is the bathroom?" And if you are fluent in Spanish, you can be guaranteed a grand welcome from the people. In most bookstores you can find Spanish-English dictionaries as well as phrasebooks. Even if your pronunciation isn't perfect, Mexicans are usually appreciative of your effort to communicate in their language.

Language Schools

Spanish is the third most-often used language in the world behind English and Chinese. Many foreigners are attending language schools in Mexico these days. Most of these courses are immersion courses that include not only grammar and conversation, but give students a one-on-one experience with the Mexican people. Students are given a great opportunity to learn up close about traditions and daily life. Schools help students find housing with local families for US$10-15 per day, depending on the number of meals and the length of the stay. Certain Mexican cities are becoming havens for language students. Cuernavaca alone has 20 Spanish-language schools, San Miguel Allende has many favorites, and in Guadalajara the number of schools is growing. Quite a few U.S. university programs are available.

Class Information

For more information, check at your local university or college, or write to the Council on International Educational Exchange (CIEE). A few of the catalogs to ask for are: *Work, Study, Travel Abroad, Volunteer!* and *Student Travels*. This organization offers the **International Student Identity Card,** and **Go 25: International Youth Card.** Travel information designed to help the budget traveler is available through **Council Travel,** and this includes information on youth fares, rail passes, travel gear, and insurance. For more information contact CIEE at 205 E. 42nd St., New York, New York 10017, tel. (212) 661-1414, fax (212) 972-3231.

RELIGION

In the big cities, there's little difference between Catholic ceremonies in Mexico and those in other countries. In the rural areas (for the most part) it is a rarified form of the Roman religion with subtle and not-so-subtle additions of the ancient beliefs that were practiced before Cortés. These mystic yet Christian ceremonies are performed in baptism, courtship, marriage, illness, farming, housebuilding, and fiestas. The more isolated the town, the more intertwined the religion. Other religions are gaining a foothold in the country, but still, the largest percentage of Mexicans practice Catholicism in one form or another.

K. A. ESCOVEDO SANDERS

OUT AND ABOUT
THE ARTS

Mexico's Muralists

Mexico muralists have made an enormous impact on the world of art. But more than that, they have interpreted political messages that graphically point out the failings and successes of society since the time of the Aztecs. Some of the most well-known artists are from Mexico's central plateau. A few names to look for are: Diego Rivera, Pedro Coronel, Miguel Covarrubias, Jean Charlot, Juan O'Gorman, Rufino Tamayo, Pablo O'Higgins, José Clemente Orozco, and David Alfaro Siqueiros.

Regional Arts And Crafts

Central Mexico is noted for a variety of crafts, some of collectible quality. The specialties of several Central Mexico states are listed below.

Guanajuato—Varied styles of pottery and ceramics, including Talavera. Papier mâché piñatas and masks.

Guerrero—Silver jewelry. Traditional ceramics, decorated gourds, traditional jaguar masks.

Hidalgo—Birdcages.

Jalisco—Ceramics and glass, both traditional and ultramodern. Excellent quality pre-Columbian reproductions.

Michoacán—Inlaid gold lacquerware, special green-glazed pottery, copperware of every description, colorful woven textiles, exceptional carved furniture, guitars, woven fibers, wooden carvings.

Puebla—Talavera pottery and ornate tiles of every description. Beaded and embroidered clothing. Cross-stitch embroidered blouses called *quechquemetl*. Onyx, *amate* paper artwork.

Querétaro—semiprecious stones such as opals. Basketry and other woven items.

Tlaxcala—Wool serapes.

Veracruz—Palm leaf mats and other woven palm items. Huastecan Indian cactus fiber bags. Coral jewelry.

MURAL LOCATIONS OF MEXICO'S GREAT ARTISTS

IN MEXICO CITY

Ignacio Aguirre
Nuclear Power for Construction not Destruction.
1953. Building on Campo Elyseos and Temistocles.
Col. Polanco.

Ramón Alva de la Canal
Landing Of The Cross.
Fresco, 1922. Escuela Nacional Preparatoría, San
Ildefonso 43, center of city.

Arnold Belkin
Meeting of Emiliano Zapata and Francisco Villa.
1979. Hall No. 10, *The Revolution of 1910,*
Museo Nacional de Historia, Castillo de
Chapultepec. Chapultepec Park.

Ernesto Garcia Cabral
Mural in encaustic, 1922. Escuela Nacional Preparatoría, San Ildefonso 43, center of city.

Jorge González Camarena
Carranza with the Constitution of 1910.
1967. Hall No. 10, *The Revolution of 1910,*
Museo Nacional de Historia, Castillo de
Chapultepec. Chapultepec Park.

Jean Charlot
The Conquest of Tenochtitlán.
Fresco, 1922. Escuela Nacional Preparatoria, San
Ildefonso 43, center of city.

Eduardo Solares Gutierrez
Allegory of the Mexican Revolution.
Fresco, 1933. Main staircase, Museo Nacional de
Historia, Castillo de Chapultepec. Chapultepec
Park.

Pedro Coronel
The Country Its People.
Glass mosaic, 1952. Sindicato Nacional de Traba-
jadores del Seguro Social, Calz. de Tacubaya 126.

Miguel Covarrubias
Geography of the Folk Art of Mexico.
Tempera, 1947. Hotel del Prado, Av. Juárez 70,
center of city.

Fernando Leal
The Dancers of Chalma.
Encaustic, 1922. Escuela Nacional Preparatoría,
San Ildefonso 43, center of city.

Juan O'Gorman
The Metaphysics of Aviation.

Egg tempera, 1937. Puerto Aéreo Internacional.

The History of Culture.
Mosaic of natural stones and colored glass, 1949-51.
Biblioteca Central de la Ciudad Universitaría.

Allegory of Mexico.
Mosaic of natural stones and colored glass, 1951-53.
The north, east and west walls, and the vestibule
of the north entrance, Secretaría de Comunica-
ciones, Av. Universidad y Xola, Col. Narvarte.

*Madero Leaving Chapultepec Castle for the
National Palace.*
Hall No. 10, *The Revolution of 1910,* Museo Nacional de Historia, Castillo de Chapultepec. Chapultepec Park.

Pablo O'Higgins
Life and its Social Problems.
Fresco, 1933. Escuela Emiliano Zapata, Fundidora
de Monterrey 179, Col. Vallejo.

The Worker's Struggle Against The Financiers.
Fresco, 1933. Mercado Abelardo Rodríguez, Calle
de Rodríguez Puebla y Venezuela, center of city.

José Clemente Orozco
*Man's Struggle with Nature, Christ Destroys His
Cross.*
Fresco, 1922. Escuela Nacional Preparatoria, San
Ildefonso 43, center of city.

Catharsis.
Fresco, 1934. Palacio de Bellas Artes, Av. Juárez y
Lázaro Cárdenas.

*The National Wealth, The Proletarian Struggle,
Justice.*
Fresco, 1941. Suprema Corte de Justicia, Pino
Suárez 2, center of city.

Apocalypse.
Fresco, 1944. Templo y Hospital de Jesús, República de El Salvador y 20 de Noviembre, center of city.

Juárez.
Fresco, 1948. Museo Nacional de Historia, Castillo
de Chapultepec. Chapultepec Park.

Diego Rivera
The Creation.
Encaustic, 1922. Anfiteatro Bolívar de la Escuela
Nacional Preparatoría, San Ildefonso 43, center of
city.

The Life and History of the Mexican People.
Fresco, 1923-28. Secretaría de Educación Pública,
Av. Argentina y González Obregón, center of city.

(continued)

MURAL LOCATIONS OF MEXICO'S GREAT ARTISTS

(continued)

The History of Mexico.
Fresco, begun in 1929, completed in 1951. Palacio Nacional, Zócalo, center of city.

Man in the Time Machine.
Fresco, 1934. Palacio de Bellas Artes, Av. Juárez y Lázaro Cárdenas.

Manuel Rodríguez Lozano
Piety in the Desert.
Fresco, 1941. Originally in the Penitenciaría del D.F., now in the Palacio de Bellas Artes, Av. Juárez y Lázaro Cárdenas.

David Alfaro Siqueiros
The Elements, The Myths.
Encaustic, 1922. Stairway of the Colegio Chico de la Escuela Nacional Preparatoría, San Ildefonso 43, center of city.

Burial of the Martyred Worker.
Fresco, 1923. Stairway of the Colegio Chico de la Escuela Nacional Preparatoría, San Ildefonso 43, center of city.

The Call to Liberty.
Fresco, 1924. Stairway of the Colegio Chico de la Escuela Nacional Preparatoría, San Ildefonso 43, center of city.

Portrait of the Bourgeoisie.
Pyroxylin, 1939. Cube of the stairway of the building of the Sindicato Mexicano de Electricistas, Antonio Caso 45, Col. San Rafael.

Cuauhtémoc Against the Myth.
Pyroxylin, 1944. Moved from its original location at Av. Sonora 9 to its permanent home just behind the Tecpan Suites at Reforma Norte 630, Tlatelolco.

From Porfirioism to the Revolution.
Acrylic, 1957-1966. Sala de la Revolución, Museo Nacional de Historia, Castillo de Chapultepec, Chapultepec Park.

Drama and Comedy in the Social Life of Mexico.
Acrylic, 1958. Mural was banned for eight years. Lobby of Teatro Jorge Negrete, Edificio de la ANDA, Altamirano 128, Col. San Rafael.

Rufino Tamayo
Song and Music.
Fresco, 1933. Ex-Conservatorio Nacional de Música, presently offices of the Government, Moneda 16, center of city.

Revolution.
Fresco, 1938. Museo de las Culturas, Moneda 13, center of city.

Tribute to the Race.
Vinylite,1951. Palacio de Bellas Artes, Av. Juárez y Lázaro Cárdenas.

Birth of Our Nationality.
Vinylite,1953 Palacio de Bellas Artes, Av. Juárez y Lázaro Cárdenas.

Duality.
Acrylic, 1964. Museo Nacional de Antropología, Chapultepec.

Francisco Zúñiga
Obstacle Race.
Bas-relief, terra-cotta, 1949. Frieze of the Deportivo Chapultepec.

MURALS IN OTHER PARTS OF THE COUNTRY

Raul Anguiano
Revolution and Counterrevolution.
Casein, 1936. Confederación Revolucionaria Mexicana del Trabajo, Plaza de San Francisco, Morelia, Michoacán.

Luis Aragon Valladar
The Ship of Life.
Red stone, 1962. Dirección de Pensiones del Estado de México, Toluca, Estado de México.

Santos Balmori Picazo
Morelos.
Tempera, 1937. Confederación Campesina Emiliano Zapata, Puebla, Puebla.

Liberty.
Tempera, 1937. Confederacionaría Revolucionaria Michoacana, Plaza de San Francisco, Morelia, Michoacán.

David Barajas
The Teacher and the Family.
Vinylite, 1950. North corridor of the Museo del Estado, Guadalajara, Jalisco.

Alberto Beltran
Quetzalcoatl and the Man of Today.
Mosaic of stones and shells, 1968. Exterior, Museo de Antropología de la Universidad Veracruzana, Jalapa, Veracruz.

The Twelve "Tajines" and the Clouds.
Mosaic, 1969. Over central staircase, Museo de la Ciudad de Veracruz, Veracruz.

Amado de la Cueva
The Farmers and Workers Ideals of the Revolution of 1910.
Tempera, 1926. David Alfaro Siqueiros collaborated on this mural. Oficina de Telégrafos Nacionales, Colón y Pedro Moreno, Guadalajara, Jalisco.

Roberto Cueva del Río
Education and the Revolution.
Fresco, 1941. Escuela Secundaria de Jiquilpan, Michoacán.

José Chavez Morado
The Liberation Of The Slaves.
Fresco, 1955. Alhondiga de Granaditas, Guanajuato.

Morelos and the Independence of Mexico.
Tempera and oil, 1948. Casa de Morelos, Caracuaro, Michoacán.

Xavier Guerrero
Mexican Motifs.
Egg tempera, 1923. Home of ex-governor Zuno, Bosque 626, Guadalajara, Jalisco.

José Clemente Orozco
Social Revolution.
Fresco, 1926. Centro Obrero, Orizaba, Veracruz.

Man the Creator.
Fresco, 1936. Cupola, 14 meters diameter, Universidad de Guadalajara, Guadalajara, Jalisco.

The Rebellion of Man.
Fresco, 1936. Universidad de Guadalajara, Guadalajara, Jalisco.

Hidalgo, The Phantoms of Religion in Alliance with Militarism.
Fresco, 1937. Palacio de Gobierno, Guadalajara, Jalisco.

The Carnival of Indeologies.
Fresco, 1937. Palacio de Gobierno, Guadalajara, Jalisco.

The Pariahs.
Fresco, 1937. Palacio de Gobierno, Guadalajara, Jalisco.

The Spanish Conquest of Mexico.
Fresco, 1939. Hospicio Cabañas, Guadalajara, Jalisco.

Maternity, Allegory of Health.
Fresco, 1959. Lobby of the Sanatorio Guadalajara, Justo Sierra 388, Guadalajara, Jalisco.

Man in Liberty.
Acrylic, 1965. Cupola, Salón de Sesiones del Palacio de Gobierno de la Cuidad de Puebla, Puebla.

Diego Rivera
Here It is Taught to Exploit the Earth not the Human.
Fresco, 1926. Escuela Nacional de Agricultura, Chapingo, Estado de México.

David Alfaro Siqueiros
Monument to General Ignacio Allende.
Vinylite on cement, all surfaces of the room were to be painted including the floor. Begun in 1949, the mural is unfinished and in its initial stage. Ex-Convento de Santa Rosa, San Miguel de Allende, Guanajuato.

Excommunication and Execution of Hidalgo.
Pyroxylin on masonite, 1953. Universidad Michoacana de San Nicolas de Hidalgo, Morelia, Michoacán.

Ramon Sosamontes
The Passage of Villa and Obregón Through Vista Hermosa.
Two exterior walls, fresco, 1930. Escuela de Vista Hermosa, Municipio de Cortázar, Guanajuato.

Rosendo Soto
Worker's Movement.
Pyroxylin, 1938. Escuela Normal de Puebla, Puebla.

Alfredo Zalce
The Defenders of National Integrity.
Fresco and colored cement, 1951. Museo Michoacano, Morelia, Michoacán.

Hidalgo and the Independence.
Fresco and colored cement, 1957. Palacio de Gobierno, Morelia, Michoacán.

Converting the Indians to the Christian Faith.
Fresco, 1962. South corridor of the Camera de Diputados de Michoacán, Morelia, Michoacán.

José Guadalupe Zuno
Conquest of New Galicia.
Fresco, 1953. Museo del Estado, Guadalajara, Jalisco.

The Reform.
Fresco, 1953. Sala de Consejos del Palacio Municipal de Guadalajara, Jalisco.

FIESTAS, CELEBRATIONS, AND ENTERTAINMENT

Having a good time in Central Mexico is easy, and it doesn't matter whether you're in a big city or a small village—if you plan ahead. Mexico City in Mexico state is as cosmopolitan as any of the world's great cities. Here you can attend a variety of concerts from classical to rock, listen to fine opera, find big name international entertainers and film celebrities, or watch the fabulous **Mexican Folklorico Ballet.** Casual and elite dinner clubs offer intimate jazz bands and dancing. Small restaurants have strolling guitarists. Discos take on a whole new meaning in Mexico; you'll find glamorous buildings with high tech light shows, floor fog, and well-dressed "in" crowds attending. Big ticket entertainment is everywhere. However, for those on a budget there's no deprivation. Local museums can clue you in to free art and musical events, and if you check the **Calendar of Holidays** chart, you can plan your trip during those dates to see some of the best entertainment in Mexico. Holiday time means *ferias* (fairs), and that usually includes a *corrida* (bullfight). The Mexicans really know how to throw a party, and at a fiesta or fair you can expect music, dancing, fireworks, and lots of good food.

As well as the public festivities listed, a birthday, baptism, graduation, saint's day, wedding, departure, return, or good crop is a good excuse to celebrate with a fiesta. One of the simplest but most charming celebrations is Mother's Day. Children, both young and old, serenade mothers (often with a live band) with beautiful music outside their windows on the evening of the holiday. Last Mother's Day we sat in a lovely plaza in Oaxaca and watched virtually everyone pass with a bouquet of flowers. If invited to a fiesta, join in and have fun. Even the most humble family manages to scrape together money for a great party on these occasions.

RAIN CEREMONY

Today in many rural areas farmers still call on their old deities for help. Maybe this is not so much a religious act as it is a practiced routine that's been part of the planting process for generations. In Guerrero in early May, countryfolk meet at a holy spot in the country and chant throughout the night with musicians playing traditional music on traditional instruments. A number of crosses are set up, and at 4 a.m. they begin making their offerings. Cigarettes, colas, chicken, candles, flowers, tortillas, and bread are all offered at a sacred spot, maybe the mouth of a cave, or a pond or lake; if it's a big group, they have fireworks. In Nahuatl the leader all but scolds the gods, chanting something like this: "Accept what you are offered! Let those who have come here rejoice in good crops. Bless their seeds. May no one return to his home without rain. Bless us, keep misfortune from us, give us water." Throwing flower petals into the air to simulate rainfall, women sing to the bread gods in the hopes they'll appeal to the rain god on their behalf.

FIESTAS AND CELEBRATIONS

Mariachis

The music most often identified with Mexico is mariachi music. This originated in the state of Jalisco not too far from Guadalajara during the period of occupation by the French. The word mariachi is a bastardization of the French word for wedding, *mariage.* Guitarists and other musicians were recruited at that time to make music for wedding parties and soon it was the common practice to have a mariachi band for any party or celebration. A mariachi band generally consists of at least one each of a guitar, violin, and trumpet. We have seen plucked stringed instruments from smaller-than-a-ukelele to a very fat, broad

CALENDAR OF HOLIDAYS

JANUARY

1: **New Year's Day.** Legal holiday.

6: **Día de los Reyes Magos.** Day of the Three Kings. On this day Christmas gifts are exchanged.

FEBRUARY

2: **Candelaria.** Candlemas. Many villages celebrate with candlelight processions.

5: **Flag Day.** Legal holiday.

FEBRUARY/MARCH

Carnaval. The week before Ash Wednesday, the beginning of Lent. Some of the best planned festivals of the year are held this week. Veracruz is noted for one of the finest celebrations in the *world*. Easter parades with colorful floats, costume balls, and sporting events.

MARCH

21: **Birthday of Benito Juárez** (1806). Legal holiday.

MAY

1: **Labor Day.** Legal holiday.

3: **Day of the Holy Cross.**

5: **Battle of Puebla,** also known as **Cinco de Mayo.** In remembrance of the 1862 defeat of the French. Legal holiday.

12-18: Honors the Virgin of the Immaculate Conception. Music, bullfights, and religious processions in almost all cities.

JUNE

29: **Day of San Pedro.** All towns with the name of San Pedro celebrate. Fiestas often held in early July.

SEPTEMBER

15-16: **Independence Day.** Legal holiday. A big event all over the country. Mexico City and Dolores Hidalgo have especially good celebrations.

OCTOBER

4: **Feast Day of San Francisco de Asisi.** A week-long fiesta precedes this day in many cities.

12: **Columbus Day.** Legal holiday.

31: **Eve of All Souls' Day.** Celebrated all through Mexico. Flowers and candles placed on graves, the beginning of an eight-day observance.

NOVEMBER

1-2: **All Souls' Day** and **Day of the Dead.** Graveside and church ceremonies. A partylike atmosphere in all the cemeteries. Food and drink vendors do a lively business, as do candy makers with their sugar skulls and skeletons. A symbolic family meal is eaten at the gravesite. One of the most powerful holidays of the year.

8: **Conclusion of El Día de los Muertos.** Day of the Dead.

20: **Día de la Revolución.** Revolution Day of 1910. Legal holiday.

DECEMBER

8: **Feast of the Immaculate Conception.** Fiestas in many cities.

12: **Our Lady of Guadalupe.** Big religious celebration all over Mexico, especially at the shrine of Guadalupe.

25: **Christmas.** Legal holiday.

guitar. The music is happy, romantic, emotional, and lighthearted and the players are highly respected. The mariachis are usually dressed in sharp looking, traditional Mexican suits with short jackets over ruffled white shirts. All costumes are liberally decorated with silver. On their feet they wear pointed boots, and on their heads a heavy, broad-brimmed felt sombrero with embroidered designs and silver trim. Some of these men are fantastic musicians with classical training. Others are just friends who like to sing and play.

Many cities have plazas where the mariachis hang out, an outdoor "hiring-hall" where potential clients come to listen and negotiate a deal for parties and weddings. These plazas always attract visitors just to listen as well. They *do* expect a tip, especially if you request a song, and make sure it's US$3-5.

Village Festivities

Small village holidays are really fun—maybe even the most fun. The more money the fancier the fireworks, and somehow these un-rich folks always have a great firework display. Half the fun is watching preparations, which generally take all day and involve everyone. Both big and little kids get goose bumps watching the *especialista* wrapping and tying bamboo poles together with mysterious packets of paper-wrapped explosives. When finished, this often-tall *castillo* (structure holding the fireworks) is tilted up and admired by all. Well after dark, at the height of the celebration, the colorful explosives are set off with a spray of light and sound, accompanied by appreciative cheers of delight.

Village fiestas are a wonderful time of dancing, music, noise, colorful costumes, good food, and usually lots of drinking. A public fiesta is generally held in the central plaza surrounded by temporary stalls where you can get Mexican fast food: tamales (both sweet and meat), *buñuelos* (sweet rolls), tacos, *refrescos* (soft drinks), *churros* (fried dough dusted with sugar), *carne asada* (barbecued meat), and plenty of chilled beer.

Beware "The Egg"

In the smaller villages you'll find innocent-looking little old ladies selling the "dreaded eggshell," filled with confetti, ready to be smashed on an unsuspecting head. So be prepared if you're the only gringo around! Your head or any convenient body part will be pummeled with the colorful bombs by anyone tall enough. This is followed by a quick getaway by the bombardiers and lots of giggles from onlookers. The more you respond good-naturedly, the more you will continue to be the target—and what the heck, whether the headache is from too much beer or too many eggs doesn't matter. (Besides, it might be time for you to plunk out a few pesos for your own bombs!)

Independence Day

Some celebrations are really huge affairs, and the plazas are jammed with people. You can expect thousands of people in a plaza on Independence Day, especially in Mexico City. The president repeats the **Grito** just before midnight, and then a flamboyant show takes to the sky; fireworks and cannons go on for an hour. Families buy flags and wave them, and in general feel very patriotic. If you like crowds it's a moving celebration.

Religious Holidays

Many festivals in Mexico are in honor of religious feast days, which honor Catholic saints. (If someone was so inclined, he or she could travel the length and breadth of Mexico and find a fiesta going on every day of the year.) You'll see a unique combination of Catholic fervor and ancient beliefs mixed with plain old good times. In the church plaza, dances that have been passed down from family to family since before Cortés continue for hours. Dancers dress in symbolic costumes of bright colors, feathers, and bells, reminding onlookers of their Indian past. Inside the church is a constant stream of the candle-carrying devout, some traveling long distances to peregrinate (make a devout journey), sometimes even traveling several kilometers entirely on their knees to a church, repaying a promise made to a deity months before in thanks for a personal favor, a healing, a job found, or similar good fortune.

More Religious Days

Christmas and Easter are wonderful holidays. The **posada** (procession) of Christmas begins nine days before the holiday, when families and friends take part in processions that portray Mary and Joseph and their search for lodging before the birth of Christ ("posada" is the word for "inn"). The streets are alive with people, bright lights, and colorful nativity scenes. Families provide swinging piñatas (pottery or papier-mâché covered with brightly colored crepe paper in the shape of a popular animal or perky character and filled with candy and small surprises); children and adults alike enjoy watching the blindfolded swing away with a heavy board or baseball bat while an adult moves and sways the piñata with a rope, making the fun last and giving everyone a chance. Eventually, someone gets lucky, smashes the piñata with a hard blow (it takes strength to break it), and kids skitter around the floor retrieving the loot. Piñatas are common, not only for Christmas and Easter but also for birthdays and other special occasions in the Mexican home.

Fiesta Practicalities

A few practical things to remember about fiesta times. Location cities will be crowded. If you know in advance that you'll be in town, make hotel and car reservations as soon as possible. Easter and Christmas at any resort city will be jammed, and you may need to make reservations as far as six months in advance. Some of the best fiestas are in more isolated parts of the country, you just have to know about them. Respect the privacy of people; the native people have strong feelings and religious beliefs about having their pictures taken—ask first and abide by their wishes.

BOB RACE

ENTERTAINMENT

Discos And Nightclubs

Discos are very popular in Mexico, especially with Mexicans. Look around; you'll find all kinds of discos and nightclubs, from the dressiest that charges a cover and allows only couples, to the casual-dress, over-18 crowd. Most of the discos in the hotels are open six nights a week, but the smaller spots are often open only Thurs.-Sat.; most go on till 4 a.m.

Classical Entertainment

In the larger cities such as Mexico, Guadalajara, Morelia, Guanajuato, and San Miguel Allende (and many others), you will find world-class artists presenting some of the finest musical entertainments from around the globe. Check with the local newspapers, tourist publications, your hotel clerk, or the local tourism office for schedules of these events.

Traditional Entertainment

Every month you'll find traditional music and drama reenacted as it has been for centuries, in both the large and small communities of the country. Usually these are events that are pertinent to the particular town or village, often during fiestas, and the occasion can be either religious or civil.

Cultural Lectures

In almost every town of Mexico you'll find a Casa de Cultura. Often they're located in some ex-palace, or ex-church, or other extravagant structure that is well worth seeing. In most cases these lectures are in Spanish, so it helps to understand the language. These Casas are the heart of Mexican culture. Universities also welcome outsiders to attend cultural lectures.

Coffeehouses/Bookstores

Especially in university towns, you'll find lively social stimulation in bookstores where students gather to talk and drink coffee; often an evening will include a little casual music, so bring your guitar. You have to sniff these places out; they're generally found around a campus.

Plazas

The all-time favorite of many people who visit Mexico is to stroll the heart of the town, village, or city, listen to band concerts (usually twice a week), watch real life (strolling lovers, grandparents enjoying the fresh evening on the arms of loving adult children, and tiny tots splashing their hands in the fountain, running and playing on kiosk steps, or climbing the broad trees of the park under the watchful eyes of parents). It's quality entertainment and it's free.

SHOPPING

Mexico is a wonderful place to shop; the rich crafts vary from region to region, and the problem isn't *finding* something to take home, but making the choice of *which* of these wonderful gifts to pass by. And speaking of passing by, if you see something you really like and want, presuming that you'll get it later on down the road can be a big, disappointing mistake. You may *never* see it again.

Bargaining

Bargaining is a common everyday happening in Mexico, especially if you're shopping in a public market. However, don't substitute *cheating* with bargaining. This is a lighthearted art, a friendly way to arrive at a price that's fair to everyone. Don't be insulting, but be definite about the price

you think an item is worth, and then offer a little less. Be prepared to walk away if your final price is not met, but always be cool and convincing; often the vendor will call you back and make the deal. In the end, you might save 20-30%. Generally speaking, trendy shops and malls don't bargain as much, but try anyway in a polite amiable manner. If you're shopping for really expensive items like silver or gold, find out the most reputable jewelry shop in town and pay with your credit card. If you should have a problem later on, your credit card affiliate at home is usually a big help.

Shipping

Mailing and shipping from Mexico is easy within certain limitations. You can send one package per day to the U.S., provided its value is less than US$25. The package must be marked "Unsolicited Gift—Under US$25" and addressed to someone other than the traveler. If you do wish to ship your purchases to your home, major stores will handle shipping arrangements on larger items and a duty must be paid; this is in addition to the US$400 limit carried in person across the border.

Again, when you plan to ship a purchase home, pay with your credit card, and if for some reason you don't receive your merchandise in the proper condition, it's an easy matter to stop payment. We have shipped glass, silver, and pottery from Mexico for years and everything has arrived, well packed, unbroken, with no problems—so far! On the other hand, we had the Lladro company in Spain ship several porcelain pieces for us, and they all came with broken heads—yes they were insured, but it was a big disappointment. I only mention this because it can happen, even when packed by a big producer who ships all the time. It may take a while to receive your package, but it's so exciting when it comes, especially when it's all in one piece.

CLOTHING SIZES

If you want to shop for clothing but can't figure out the size equivalents, here's a quick guideline.

WOMEN'S DRESSES/SHIRTS

U.S.	Mexico
6	30
8	32
10	34
12	36
14	38
16	40

MEN'S SHIRTS

U.S.	Mexico
14	36
14 1/2	37
15	38
15 1/2	39
16	40
16 1/2	41

SPORTS AND RECREATION

SPORTS

Jai Alai

This is a popular sport in Mexico City. A vital part of the activity is the betting that goes on. This fast moving game was brought from Spain's Basque country to Cuba in the last century, and from there to Mexico. And when we say fast, we mean bulletlike action with a hard rubber ball that travels up to 290 kmh. Hard-bodied athletes look like they fly as well as scramble six to eight meters up the wooden support wall to capture the ball in the cesta and return it for a point; you get tired just watching!

In the Basque country, lumberjacks would secure a log to their forearm to hit the hard ball. This genre of the game was called fronton, and it continues to be popular in Cuba. Fronton is still played (usually by amateurs) in various parts of Mexico as well. The jai alai version is slightly different. The ball is "caught" in the basket-shaped cesta and thrown. The first fronton arena in Mexico City was open-air and constructed in 1895.

Cesta: This precisely woven wicker basket is the most important part of the game (besides the great ability of the athletes, of course). Each player buys his own cesta at about US$350 each. It lasts from two to three months (equivalent to about 30-45 hours of playing) before it must be replaced. The cesta is attached to a leather "glove," which is sewn to the outside of the basket and bound at the wrist to the wooden handle of the basket. The basket is woven of special reeds (imported from Spain) over a light frame of two wooden ribs. The balls have a hard latex core of Brazilian rubber, and are made in the Philippines. They're hand-wound with linen thread and covered by two layers of goatskin. Much like a baseball, the regulation weight is 25 grams. These little hardballs become dangerous missiles when hit 290 kmh.

Mexico City's famous **Fronton** is the second largest in the world at 62.5 meters long with a metal protective cage surrounding it (Cuba's court is the largest at 63.4 meters).

Yes, these young men are in top physical condition and continue with the constant aerobic movements for 75 nonstop minutes. Because of the high speeds accomplished, the traditional Basque beret has been exchanged for high-tech helmets; this sport can be dangerous. Besides the warmup exercises they all do before running onto the court, they have their moment of prayer as well.

Soccer

Mexicans are great soccer fans, and they have an enormous stadium in Mexico City that holds thousands of people. Games are usually played on Fridays and Saturdays during the season.

Charreada

Most big cities have stadiums where they put on really fantastic *charreadas* (rodeos). Men and women take part in these events. Dressed in handsome silver-bedecked clothes, they turn some fancy footwork on their horses. Check with local tourism offices for seasonal dates and times.

Horse Races

Mexicans love to ride horses, and most big cities have racetracks. In Mexico City you'll find the finest of all, **Hipodromo de las Americas** (see the Mexico City chapter).

Hiking And Backpacking

The best hiking in the country is around the high peaks **Popocatépetl, Ixtaccíhuatl,** and **Citlaltepetl** (Mt. Orizaba). For the most part, these are long treks rather than intense mountain climbs; in fact, the rocks on these mountains can fall apart easily. Small primitive cabins (with no utilities or amenities provided) are available for overnight treks. For information in the U.S., contact Colorado Mountain Climbing School, tel. (303) 586-5758, fax (303) 586-6677, or write to P.O. Box 2062, Estes Park, Colorado 80517, U.S.A.

Water Sports

Along the Veracruz coast, plenty of water sports

are available. Beaches stretch forever, and you'll find many hotels with pools and equipment for a day on the water. Water-skiing and parasailing are good on a few bays where resorts attract tourists. Big-game fishing is very popular, with boat rentals and guides available. Scuba diving and snorkeling are popular at a few locations. However, diving is a small but "lively" industry here. If you're used to diving along the Yucatán Peninsula, don't expect to find the same atmosphere. If you talk to oldtimers, they'll tell you that there are sunken ships scattered all about, and that many of them still hold immense treasures in gold and silver! Unless you know the area, scuba divers should go with a group that includes a master diver; check out his boat and make sure you know his reputation.

Fishing
A fishing license is required for all persons 16 years or older. Good for three days, one month, or a year, licenses are available for a small fee at most fresh- and saltwater fishing areas from the local delegate of the Fishing Secretariat. Ask

---

BULLFIGHTING

The bullfight is not for everyone. Many foreigners feel it's inhumane treatment of a helpless animal. There is bloodletting. If you can't tolerate this sort of thing, you'd probably be happier not attending a bullfight. Bullfighting is big business in Mexico, Spain, Portugal, and South America. The *corrida de toros* (running of the bulls) is made up of a troupe of (now) well-paid men all playing an important part in the drama. In the country's largest arena (in Mexico City), 50,000 people fill it for each performance on Sundays and holidays. The afternoon starts off (promptly at 4 p.m.) with music and a colorful parade of solemn pomp with matadors and picadors on horseback, banderilleros, plus drag mules and many ring attendants. The matadors ceremoniously circle the crowded arena to the roar of the crowd. The afternoon has begun!

Tradition
Traditional customs of the ring have not changed in centuries. The matador is the star of the event. This ceremony is a test of man and his courage. He's in the arena for one purpose, to kill the bull—but bravely and with classic moves. First the preliminary *quites* and then a series of graceful *veronicas* heighten the excitement; he brushes the treacherous horns with each move. The matador wills the animal to come closer with each movement of the *muleta*. He is outstanding if he performs his ballet as close to the bull's horns as possible (oh, how the crowd cheers!). He must elude the huge beast with only a subtle turn of his body (now they love him!). To add to the excitement, he does much of this on his knees.

At the hour of truth, the crowd gives its permission for the matador to dedicate the bull to a special person in the crowd. He throws his *montera* (hat) to the honored person and will now show his stuff.

At just the right moment he slips the *estoque* (sword) into the bull's neck. If he's an artist, he will sever the aorta and the huge animal immediately slumps to the ground and dies instantly. If the matador displays extraordinary grace, skill, and bravery, the crowd awards him the ears and the tail, and their respect. If he isn't and has not performed to their satisfaction, they loudly let him know.

Bullfighting has long been one of the most popular events in Mexico. Aficionados of this Spanish artform thrill to the excitement of the crowd, the stirring music, the grace and courage of a noble matador, and the bravery of a good bull. A student of Mexican culture will want to take part in the *corrida*, to learn more about this powerful art. *Art* is the key word. A bullfight is not a fight, it is an artistic scene of pageantry and ceremony, handed down from the Middle Ages, and was once celebrated all over Europe.

Records of the first primitive bullfight come to us from the island of Crete, 2,000 years before the time of Christ. At the same time savage wild bulls roamed the Iberian Peninsula. When faced with killing one of these vicious animals, young men, not to be outdone by the Cretons, would "dance" as closely as possible to the brute to show their bravery before finally killing the animal with an axe.

K. A. ESCOVEDO SANDERS

in the small cafes at the more isolated beaches. Check with the closest Mexican consulate, where you can get a permit for your sportfishing craft; you can also get current information there on fishing seasons and regulations, which vary from area to area.

Fishing gear may be brought into Mexico without customs tax; however, the customs officials at the border crossing from Brownsville, Texas, into Mexico are notorious for expecting a mordida or "bribe" before allowing the RVer or boater to cross the border. In the past we have told others (as we ourselves have always done) to go with the flow, pay the mordida, and get on with your trip without any more delays. We always suggested you start with $1 bills (have lots of them with you); there are several people who need to be soothed before you can cross. If you choose not to pay the bribe, they can keep you hanging around for hours, even days, before they will allow you to cross. Sadly, it's a no-win situation.

However, times are changing in Mexico. Not all officialdom goes along with "graft." So, if you

---

The Romans began importing Spanish wild bulls for Colosseum spectacles, and the Arabs in Spain encouraged tauromachia (bullfighting). In 1090, El Cid (Rodrigo Díaz de Vivar), the hero of Valencia and subject of romantic legend, is believed to have fought in the first organized bull festival. He lanced and killed a wild bull from the back of his horse showing great skill. In this era, only noblemen were allowed to use a lance, and the corrida soon became the sport of kings. Even Julius Caesar is said to have gotten in the ring with a wild bull. Bullfighting quickly became popular, and it was the daring event for the rich. Spain's ancient Roman coliseums were used. A feast day celebration wasn't complete without a corrida de toros. The number of noblemen killed while participating in this wild event began to grow.

To try to stop the corrida, Pope Pius V issued a papal ban threatening to excommunicate anyone who was killed while bullfighting (?). This didn't dull the enthusiasm of the Spanish; the ban was withdrawn, the danger and the fight continued. Queen Isabella and then finally King Philip ordered these encounters halted, and the fight ceased.

Since the lance was forbidden, commoners (who did not own horses) intrigued with the excitement of the event began fighting the bull on foot, using a cape (muleta) to hide the sword (estoque) and confuse the bull. This was the beginning of the corrida as we know it today.

The corrida has changed little in the past 200 years. The beautiful clothes originally designed by the famous artist Goya are still used. Richly embroidered silk capes add a gala touch draped over the railing of the arena. Even in the smallest village corrida, the costume design persists. Though made of simple cloth (rather than rich satin and gold-trimmed silk) and delicately embroidered with typical designs, the torero's costume is impressive.

Gone are the wild bulls; the animals (all of Spanish ancestry) are bred on large Mexican ranches just for the bullring. Only the finest—those showing superior strength, cunning, and bravery—are sent to the ring. El toro is trained for one shining day in the arena.

The season begins in December and lasts for three months. The rest of the year it's the novilleros (neophyte matadors) who are seen in the plazas across the country. They must prove themselves in the arena before they are acknowledged as respected (which means highly paid) matadors. Bullfighting is as dangerous now as when the pope tried to have it banned in the 16th century. Almost half of the most renowned matadors in the past 250 years have died in the ring.

Outside of special events, bullfights take place on Sunday afternoons and the best seats are on the shady side of the arena (la sombra)—and are more costly. Ask at your hotel or local travel agency for ticket information. But remember, the corrida is not for everyone.

A Kinder Gentler Corrida

Some villages offer a corrida (bullfight) as part of the festivities. Even a small town will have a simple bullring, and the country corrida has a special charm. If celebrating a religious holiday, a procession carrying the image of the honored deity might lead off the proceedings. The bull has it good here; there are no bloodletting ceremonies and the animal is allowed to live and carry on his reproductive activities in the pasture beyond the corrida. Only a very tight rope around its middle provokes sufficient anger for the fight. Local young men perform in the arena with as much heart and grace as professionals in Mexico City. And the crowd shows its admiration with shouts, cheers, and of course, música!—even if the band is composed only of a trumpet and a drum. Good fun for everyone, even those who don't understand the art of the corrida.

find yourself in this position, make a fuss, ask for their names, ask to see the officer in charge, tell them you are going straight to government authorities. Certainly you can refuse to pay the bribe. It's your choice. What the outcome will be, if and when you'll finally cross the border, is unpredictable.

For more fishing information write to: Mexican Fisheries Information, 2550 Fifth Ave., Suite 101, San Diego, California 92103-6622, tel. (619) 233-6956. In Mexico, contact General de Pesca, Av. Alvaro Obregón 269, Mexico 7, D.F. Allow plenty of time whether you are requesting a license or information.

Hunting

Some feel it's not worth the effort involved to go hunting in Mexico. There are many things you need to know: how to get a license (one for your firearm and one or more for the type of game), the seasons, where you can and can't hunt, what you can hunt for, and what's involved in bringing your game home. This information can be obtained at your nearest **Mexican consulate,** or at the **Dirección General de la Fauna Silvestre,** Aquiles Serdan 28, 7th floor, Mexico 3, D.F. Include a self-addressed envelope and they will send you information. Allow plenty of time for all of this to go back and forth. Now, the U.S. has rules about bringing your game back into the United States. Send a self-addressed, stamped envelope to the U.S. Customs Service, P.O. Box 7118, Washington, D.C. 20044; request a pamphlet called *Pets and Wildlife.* All of these things take time so plan accordingly.

RECREATION

Investigating Archaeological Zones

In Central Mexico many people wish to explore the sites of the ancients. Because **Tenochtitlán** (today's Mexico City) was the focal point of the conquistadores and their drive to conquer Moctezuma and his religion, most of the ancient structures were destroyed, and though much is buried under the sprawling city, there are still several areas of great interest nearby. If you only wish to see one site, you might choose **Teotihuacán,** one of the more spectacular sites with a rich history—and only 50 kilometers from

Mexico City. Or if you want to see something closer, you can choose to see **Templo Mayor,** which hasn't nearly so many structures but is located in downtown Mexico City and has a wonderful history. It was home of Moctezuma and is within walking distance from the heart of the city. These are just two of the choices for the archaeology buff. The following is a list of the primary zones (there are many more smaller sites) located in Central Mexico; more details are available in their respective state chapters.

Archaeological Zones
Tenochtitlán—Mexico City
Tula—Hidalgo State
Xochicalco—Morelos State
Tzintzuntzan—Michoacán State
El Tajin—Veracruz State
Teotihuacán—Mexico State
Cholula—Puebla State
Cacaxtla—Tlaxcala State
Tehuacán—Puebla State

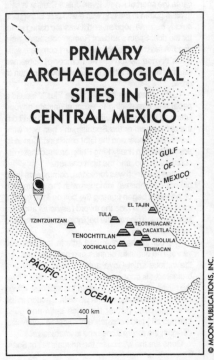

PRIMARY ARCHAEOLOGICAL SITES IN CENTRAL MEXICO

© MOON PUBLICATIONS, INC.

Mineral Baths

This is a popular pastime in the central highlands where hundreds of hot/mineral springs gurgle up from the ground. In many cases fancy hotels have been built near and around the hot water sources, but almost always you'll find a *balneario,* a public bath where the price is just a few pesos to take a hot soak. Some of these hot pools are found in caves. See individual cities for listings.

Nature Study

Birdwatching is wonderful throughout Mexico, but some areas are better than others. Where humans have moved in and roads and traffic sounds are common, you'll not find many. But take a look around the archaeological sites. If there are any trees around, more than likely you'll find abundant birdlife. From north to south the variety of birds is broad and changes with the geography and the weather. Bring binoculars, and wear boots and lightweight trousers if you plan on watching in mountainous forest or jungle areas. Studying **flora** is also a popular activity.

For this you most certainly will be in the back-country—don't forget bug repellent and be prepared for an occasional rain shower, even in the dry season. Near the Gulf of Mexico coast in the more tropical areas, look up in the trees for most orchids and bromeliads. Remember, don't take anything away with you except pictures. Bring your field-guide books for both birds and fauna.

Photography

There's a world of beauty to photograph here: the mountains, the sea, the people, and the wonderful old structures of the country, both colonial and pre-Hispanic. If you plan on **video-taping,** check with your local Mexican Tourist Office for information on what you can bring into the country. Most archaeological zones prohibit tripods and you must pay a fee to bring in your camcorder. For the photographer who wants to film *everything,* small planes are available for charter in the larger cities and resorts. (For further photography information see "Photography," under "Travel Tips," below.)

kingfisher

LOUISE FOOTE

ACCOMMODATIONS

Mexico offers a wide variety of accommodations. There's a myriad of hotels to choose from in big cities as well as options at smallish villages, lake resorts, mineral-water spas, beaches, mountains, and camping sites—in all price ranges. If you like the idea of light housekeeping and preparing your own food, condos are available in many locales. If your lifestyle is suited to outdoor living, drive your motorhome and park on the side of a mountain or in a forest.

CAMPING WITH OR WITHOUT AN RV

If you are traveling in your own vehicle, a vehicle permit must be obtained when entering the country (see "Getting There and Around," below). Traveling with a vehicle allows you to become a "luxury camper," bringing all the equipment you'll need (and more!). A van or small camper truck will fit on almost any road you'll run into. With an RV you can "street camp" in the city (some of the smaller ones). Parking lots of large hotels (check with the manager) or side streets near downtown activities are generally safe and offer easy access to entertainment. Note: In some of the more crowded cities, driving around the narrow streets filled with traffic is uncomfortable (and sometimes impossible) with a large RV.

A few reminders and some common-sense planning make a difference when traveling and camping with a vehicle. Country roads have no shoulders and near lakes and spas it's not unusual to encounter swampy areas, so check for marshy ground before pulling off the road. When beach camping, park above the high-tide line. Remember that gas stations are not as frequently found in the rural areas as in the cities. If you plan on traveling for any length of time, especially in out-of-the-way places, carry extra gas and fill up whenever you see a gas station. Along with your food supply, always carry enough water for both the car and passengers. Be practical and come prepared with a few necessities (see "Getting There and Around," below).

Sleeping Outdoors

Sleeping under a jeweled sky in a warm clime can be either a wonderful or an excruciating experience. (Two factors that will make or break it are the hot/cold extremes and the mosquito population in the immediate vicinity.) Some campers sleep in tents to get away from biting critters, which helps but is no guarantee; also, heat and cold get heavy inside an ordinary closed tent. Sleeping bags cushion the ground but tend to be much too warm at the beach. If you have a bag that zips across the bottom, it's cooling to let your feet hang out (well marinated in bug repellent or wearing a pair of socks—a dark color the mosquitos might not notice). In the high mountains make sure you have a *cold weather* bag. An air mattress softens and insulates the ground (bring along a patch kit).

In The Mountains

Although daytime temperatures usually hover in the 70s in the mountains of Central Mexico (over 1,500 meters in altitude), nighttime can get cold, especially in the winter months. Come prepared with cold weather camping gear. It has been known to freeze once in a while.

RV Parks

More and more trailer parks are popping up in Mexico. It's slowly catching on as a recreation option for Mexican families, too. Until now, this has been an activity only for the more well-to-do Mexican family, since trailers and motorhomes here are very costly to buy; perhaps that will change with NAFTA. You'll find more parks now with complete facilities and full hookups. Check out the *AAA Mexico Travel Guide;* it includes a campground supplement. Also check out *Trailer Life's Camping Index.*

HOTELS

Reservations

Traveling during the peak season (15 Dec.-15 April) requires a little planning if you wish to stay at the popular hotels. Make reservations in advance. Many hotels can be contacted through an 800 number in the U.S., Canada, and Mexico, and of course travel agencies and auto clubs as well. Many well-known U.S. chains are represented in the larger cities and their international desks can make reservations for you. Fax communication is instantaneous. If a fax or telephone number is unavailable, write directly. Many require a deposit check for one night. Ask (and allow plenty of time) for a return confirmation. If traveling May-June or Sept.-Oct., rooms are usually available.

Luxury Accommodations

Some of the familiar hotel names found all over Mexico are the Presidente Stouffer, Camino Real, Hyatt, Sheraton, Omni, Holiday Inn Crowne Plaza, and Hilton. They offer endless luxuries: hair dryers, marble fixtures, separate showers, thick, fluffy towels, in-room safes, cable television, minibars, a/c, heat, good beds, suites, junior suites, balconies, terraces, gorgeous views, green garden areas, hot mineral-water spas, pools with swim-up bars, nightclubs and fabulous restaurants, entertainment, travel agents, car rentals, giftshops, and delicatessens; almost all accept credit cards. Refunds are handled on an individual basis. The price range can start as low as US$70 and go right through the stained glass skylight. It's best to check these out in advance with reservations. In the higher priced hotels it's not unusual to get a discount if you ask (of course not during high season, or if the hotel is packed). Most hotels will give you a business discount with your business card or a AAA card. If you know the hotel you want to stay in before leaving home, call direct to the hotel (on an 800 number) and ask about package prices. It's often a pleasant surprise to find out that there are many of these available.

Moderate Hotels

In most Mexican cities it's not difficult to find moderate hotels. They aren't nearly as glitzy, might not have telephones, multiple restaurants and bars, or swimming pools, and maybe they're a little way out of town. However, the better ones are in town, and/or are near a bus stop. Generally you can find some very comfortable rooms from about US$35-55. Prices can be as much as one-third the cost of the upscale hotels. Some of these hotels take credit cards, but don't ever count on that without asking in advance.

Budget Hotels

Travelers looking to spend nights cheaply can find overnight accommodations in every city of the highlands and Veracruz. During peak seasons (Christmas and Easter) it takes a little (sometimes a lot of) nosing around (starting out early in the day helps), but inexpensive hostelries are available, and searching for one offers a good way to see the city and meet friendly locals as well.

These places are not always the cleanest, may have a shared bathroom, no hot water, no heat or air, and there might even be a curfew for guests. On the other hand, there are many fine little family-run places with only a few rooms that are really charming. And you can expect to meet lots of interesting travelers. Prices are usually in the neighborhood of US$15-30; remember it's supply and demand, so a lot depends on the city you're looking in. These cheap hostels seldom give discounts; have cash and be ready to pay, even in pesos.

In small rural villages, ask at the local cantina, cafe, or city hall for a *casa de huéspedes* (really cheap guesthouse, or boardinghouse-type accommodation). They're *usually* clean (but look!), and more than likely you'll share a toilet and (maybe) a shower. Sometimes you'll share the room itself, a large area with enough hammock hooks scattered around the walls to handle several travelers. The informed budget traveler carries his hammock (buy it in Mexico if you don't already have one) when wandering around the coastal areas. When staying in the cheaper hotels in out-of-the-way places, come prepared with toilet paper, a towel, soap, and bug repellent, and expect to buy bottled drinking water. Most of the villages have a small cantina that serves a *comida corrida* (set lunch) or ask your host; credit cards are *not* the norm. However, the price will be right and the family that runs it will offer a cultural experience you won't forget.

OTHER ACCOMMODATIONS

Condominiums

Condos, long popular in beach areas like Cancún and Puerto Vallarta, are sprouting up in other cities of Mexico. If you're vacationing with your family or a group, condo living can be a real moneysaver while still providing the fine services of a luxury hotel. Fully equipped kitchens make cooking a snap. In many cases the price includes daily maid service. Always ask, as some do not have cooking facilities but instead have a restaurant on the premises. Details are given in the appropriate travel sections.

Youth Hostels

Youth hostels, though few, are good bargains in Mexico; expect dormitory type accommodations—some offer cooking facilities. Some have lockers and provide linens if you need them (for a fee), and bathroom facilities are shared (bring your own soap, towels, and toilet paper). Price is about US$4-5 per night, and many have cheap cafeteria food (US$2-3 per meal). Expect them to be out of the downtown area, and often they're located in the center of a sports compound with playing courts nearby. Most are run by CREA (Consejo Nacional de Recursos para la Atención de la Juventud), which is affiliated with the International Youth Hostel Association. For more information about CREA youth hostels, write to **Asociación Mexicana de Albergues de la Juventud** Av. Francisco I. Madero 6, Despachos 314 y 315, Mexico 1, D.F.

CREA YOUTH HOSTEL LOCATIONS IN CENTRAL MEXICO

DISTRITO FEDERAL

Insurgentes Sur y Camino a Sta.Teresa,
Delegation Tlalpan, Mexico, D.F.

GUADALAJARA

Av. Prolongación Alcalde 1360, Barranquitas
Guadalajara, Jal., Mexico

MORELIA

Villa Deportiva Juvenil
Oaxaca y Chiapas 180
Fracc. Molino de Parras
Morelia, Mich., Mexico

QUERÉTARO

Av. Ejército Republicana, ex-Convento de la Cruz
Querétaro, Qro., Mexico

VERACRUZ

Paso Doña Juana
Municipio de Ursulo Galvan
Veracruz, Ver., Mexico

FOOD AND DRINK

Many of the crops now produced by American farmers were introduced by the indigenes of Mexico, including corn, sweet potatoes, chocolate, tomatoes, chile peppers, squash, pumpkins, and avocados. Many other products favored by Americans are native to various parts of Mexico: papaya, cotton, tobacco, rubber, vanilla, and turkey. Mexico is the largest exporter of honey in the world.

Mexican Cuisine

Mexico has given the world much in the way of gustatory delights. And if you think you're only going to see tortillas, beans, and peppers, you're in for a treat, as long as you're a little daring. Avocados, vanilla, and chocolate added much to the menus of the Europeans, even though the original colonialists considered their foods "barbarian and earthy." How times have changed! They ate food containing much of what we today consider healthful: fresh vegetables, little or no meat, no frying or fat (they had few fat sources). Much of what they ate was stewed and often wrapped in leaves (banana and maguey), then baked in the earth. As Spaniards began setting up housekeeping and using Indian servants (among them a cook for the family), the indigenous foods gradually began to creep into daily menus out of necessity—there was a lack of the ingredients that the Europeans were accustomed to. However, as the foreigners brought the familiar with them into the country, fat was

PULQUE, MEZCAL, TEQUILA

The heart of the maguey plant (known as the century plant in the U.S.) is the source of the most popular Mexican alcoholic drinks: pulque, mezcal, and tequila. Contrary to what some people believe (those who haven't tasted all three), there's a great deal of difference between these three drinks, determined by the type of maguey plant from which they come.

A Few Facts

Mezcals are distilled saps from various maguey plants. They are called "firewater" because distilled Spaniards in their search for a potent distilled alcholic beverage came up with this high proof (80 and up) usually clear and colorless intoxicant; it's not unusual to find a worm at the bottom of a mezcal bottle, not just any worm, but the one that is found on the maguey plant.

Pulque, on the other hand, is a fermented, milky, slightly foamy, and somewhat viscous beverage, mildly alcoholic (more like beer), and touted to be a good source of vitamins.

Tequila is a distilled beverage from the "blue" maguey plant. The blue maguey grows well only in two areas in Mexico, both near the city of Guadalajara, Jalisco. Probably the most well known area is that centered around the town of Tequila, and the other area is around the town of Tepatitlán.

Production

The hearts, weighing from 36 to 80 kilograms, are chopped into several pieces and roasted. The primitive system is to bury them, cover them with maguey leaves, and build a fire on top. Modern distilleries use huge steam ovens. The cooked substance is then shredded and the juice pressed out. A course and degree in Tequila Engineering are offered at a local university. Tequila producers are as much concerned about "authentic" tequila as are wine makers in France who tell the world that Burgundy wine (for example) is only grown and produced around the city of Burgundy. Contents must conform to the government regulation requiring that all liquor labeled as "tequila" contain at least 87% distilled blue maguey juice. And while the production continues to flourish each year as the demand grows, the plant itself imposes limits; its sap will not yield the characteristic tequila flavor except when grown in Tequila and Tepatitlán.

added and the creative natives began integrating New World agricultural products and traditions with the beef and pork of Spain. As a result, Mexico offers a unique cuisine. It continues to grow in originality and popularity all over the world.

Taste as many different dishes as possible during your visit; you'll be introduced to spices that add a new dimension to your diet. Naturally, you won't be wild about everything—it takes a while to become accustomed to squid served in its own black ink, for instance. Or a hamburger might not taste like one from your favorite fast-foodery back home. It should also not come as a shock to find your favorite downhome Tex-Mex enchiladas and tacos are nothing like those you order in *real* Mexican restaurants. Be prepared to come into contact with new and different tastes—you're in *México,* after all!

Seafood
You won't travel far before realizing that one of Mexico's specialties is fresh fish. All along the Gulf of Mexico coast are opportunities to indulge in piscine delicacies: lobster, shrimp, red snapper, sea bass, halibut, barracuda, and lots more. Even the tiniest cafe will prepare sweet fresh fish a la Veracruz, using ripe tomatoes, green peppers, and onions. Or if you prefer, ask for the fish *con ajo* (with garlic) sautéed in garlic and butter—scrumptious! If the menu says *al gusto* they're telling you they'll cook it any way you'd like.

Legend says that Moctezuma had runners bringing him fresh fish from the Gulf Coast (they also brought him snow from the mountaintops surrounding Mexico City). I guess it worked more or less like our old pony express; one would run as long as possible, then pass on the goods at the old coach stop or pueblo to a fresh runner, until it reached its destination.

Wild Game
Mexicans in the countryside are hunters, and if you explore much, you'll commonly see men and boys on bicycles, motorscooters, or horses with rifles slung over their shoulders and full game bags tied behind them. The game hunted varies. *Pato* (wild duck) is served during certain times of the year and is prepared several ways—try as many as possible. Though deer is

on the endangered species list, many rural citizens still hunt and eat it. Tacos and *enchiladas venado* are common, as are *birria* or *cabrito* (goat kid) tacos, and in some places tacos made from wild boar. If you're near the sea or a lake, *tacos pescados* (fish tacos) are also popular.

Coffee
Depending on where you are, if you ask for coffee in a restaurant you'll probably get a cup of hot water and a jar of instant. If you want fresh-brewed, you have a better chance of getting it if you ask for *cafe Americano*. Many restaurants have only powdered decaf. Remember that in Mexico (as in many foreign countries) you pay for each cup of coffee you order—no free fillups. And unless you specify that you want your coffee *ahora, por favor* (now, please), you will receive it at the end of your meal.

Cafe Olla
This is the traditional coffee usually served from large, colorful, clay pots sitting on a small flame at fiesta buffets. Know that it is usually quite sweet (from *pila,* raw sugar) and spiced with cinnamon. It makes a nice light dessert, but if you're used to black coffee, this might not be your style.

CAFE OLLA RECIPE

An earthen pot to fit the quantity you make.

3 tablespoons dark roasted, course ground coffee

1 cinnamon stick

3 cloves

dark brown sugar to taste

1 liter of water

Mix all ingredients together and boil until it reaches the strength you like.

Dining Customs
Although the Mexicans eat breakfast, lunch, and dinner just as Americans, the timing is slightly different. Most families, especially working

people, start the day with a small snack for breakfast (*desayuno*), often coffee and sweet roll. Later in the morning you might see businessmen having a bigger breakfast with beans, eggs, and tortillas (*almuerzo* or *lonche*), and then 1-4 p.m., many shops close, offices shut down, and most families will eat their main meal of the day (*comida*), a three or four course meal including soup, rice, entree, beans, tortillas or bread, dessert, and coffee. Workers then go back to the office or shop and work until 7-8 p.m. In the evening, *cena* is a light snack; a bowl of soup, tortillas and beans, or a sandwich.

La Cuenta Por Favor

In Mexico (as in Europe), you will not get your check without requesting it; it's considered bad manners. Simply say, "la cuenta, por favor," and that should do it. If you have a hard time getting your waiter to bring it, make a writing motion into the palm of your hand. And it sure doesn't hurt to check the check. See if the *propina* (tip) has already been added in (15% is customary), that the math is correct, and that you're paying for what you ate. In small cafes, the waiter often leaves all the dirty dishes and empty beer and pop bottles on the table in order to tabulate the bill when the time comes.

Restaurants

Most small cafes that cater to Mexican families are open all day and late into the night. The Mexican custom is to eat the heavier meal of the day 1-4 p.m. In most of these family cafes a generous *comida corrida* (set lunch) is served at this time. If you're hungry and want an economical (but filling) meal, that's what to ask for; though you don't know exactly what's coming, you get a table full of dependably fresh fare—often the pride of the kitchen. Always expect a large stack of tortillas, and five or six small bowls filled with the familiar and the unfamiliar: it could be beans, a cold plate of tomatoes and avocado, *pollo mole* (chicken cooked in a spicy sauce), fish, or whatever. Cafes in the larger upscale hotels that cater to tourists don't serve this type of a set meal. Late in the evening a light snack (*cena*) is served 9-11 p.m. Hotels with foreign tourists offer dinner earlier to cater to British, Canadian, and American tastes. Be sure to check; some restaurants add a service charge

onto the bill. If so, the check will say *incluido propina*. It's still gracious to leave a few coins for the waiter. If the tip isn't added to the bill, leaving 15% is customary.

Strolling musicians are common in Mexican cafes. If you enjoy the music, US$3-4 is a considerate gift. In certain cities, cafes and bars that cater to Mexicans will commonly serve free *antojitos* (snacks) in the afternoon with a beer or cocktail. The more you drink, the more generous the *antojitos*. These places are always packed with locals ordering the *comida corrida* or drinking, all complete with live entertainment. You get the real essence of the city and the people, and you may be the only gringo present. Remember, we said the cafes are good—not spotless!

Not too long ago, women were not allowed in these taverns. Now, such historic cantinas as **La Opera** in Mexico City have opened their doors to women. However, this is not necessarily so in small towns that seldom get tourists. Ladies will get shouted out of these.

Mexico has its own version of fast food. You'll find hole-in-the-wall stands selling *tortas* (sandwiches), tacos, tamales, or *licuados* (fruit drinks), as well as corner vendors selling mangos on a stick, slices of pineapple, peeled oranges, candies of all kinds (including tall pink fluffs of cotton candy), and barbecued meat. The public markets have foods of every description, usually very cheap. In other words, there's a huge variety to choose from, so have fun. See the "Health" section, too, before indulging in any uncooked fruits or vegetables.

Note: In the U.S., when bread is included with dinner there's no extra charge. In certain restaurants in Mexico, however, you will find a *cubierto* charge on your check; this is for the breadbasket, linen napkin, etc. This charge is generally specified on the bottom of the menu; ask if it's a concern. Tortillas are generally brought automatically with a Mexican entree.

A ploy used by many seasoned adventurers when they're tired of eating cold food from their backpacks: In an isolated village where there isn't a cafe of any kind, go to the local cantina (or grocery store, church, or city hall) and ask if there's a housewife (señora) in town who, for a fee, would be willing to include you at her dinner table. Almost always you'll find someone, usually at a fair price (determine price when you make your deal). With any luck you'll find a woman renowned not only for her *tortillas por manos* (handmade tortillas), but also for the tastiest beans this side of the border. You gain a lot more than food in this arrangement; the culture swap is priceless. The traveler should really know some Spanish in this situation.

MEXICAN COLONIAL CUISINE: THE PERFECT MARRIAGE

BY PEG RAHN

Mexican culinary art parallels history and culture through the ages. During the pre-Hispanic era, each major indigenous group had its own distinctive cuisine, eating rituals, and religious ceremonies connected with the foods that sustained them. Corn, chiles, beans, tomatoes, avocados, peanuts, sesame seeds, vanilla, turkey, potatoes, exotic fruits, herbs and roots, game, and fowl were all part of a healthful diet the natives enjoyed. Foods were eaten raw, steamed or stewed. Once the Spaniards conquered the Aztecs, they turned their thoughts to the comfort foods of home. What resulted was a second strong cuisine that evolved as nuns tried to recreate European favorites using strictly local ingredients.

During the colonial period, which began in 1524, food in Mexico changed again. The Spaniards imported barley, rice, wheat, olives, vines, eastern spices, cattle (cheese), sheep, pork, and lard from Spain. These ingredients were incorporated into the developing cuisine of Nueva España (new world Spain).

The art of frying was introduced. Lard was the natural fat; olive oil was not available. Early colonial foods and sauces were simpler than those of the indigenous groups, who preferred complex, layered flavors. Political and cultural change was reflected in the food. Two well-defined cuisines emerged—Nueva España competed with indigenous Indian.

Although the Spanish tried to impose their culture on the natives, it was they who eventually adapted and broadened their tastes. Intermarriage was a strong force behind this change. Spanish men married Indian women who brought their cuisine with them. Even in pure Spanish marriages, Indian woman cooked for the great colonial mansions. Slowly, these cooks introduced tortillas and chiles to Spanish tables. Native herbs and vegetables eaten in Indian villages were cooked with imported ingredients. Mexican colonial cooking was born.

Convents became famous for their Mexican cuisine, as nuns developed recipes from ingredients unknown to the European old world. The care and feeding of monks, priests, and the hierarchy of the church pushed Mexican cuisine to new heights.

Pastry-making flourished. Nuns invented all sorts of desserts, candies, custards and sweetmeats—*cajeta* and *buñuelos* among them. The convent kitchen at Santa Clara is credited with *rompope*, a Mexican version of the creamy alcohol-laced European *advocat*. Because the new archbishop in Puebla didn't like spicy food, María del Perpetuo Socorro tamed an Indian dish called *mulli* with peanuts, sesame seeds, cinnamon and chocolate. She called the new dish mole and served it in the churchman's honor.

Mexican colonial cuisine became a delightful blend of the culinary traditions of the two cultures. The court of Maximilian of Hapsburg (1863) added French, Austrian, and Italian influences, which were transformed into colonial cuisine by the use of native Mexican ingredients. In turn, the court's European influence refined the developing cuisine. But the most memorable thing that Maximilian is credited with is giving Mexico its beloved football-shaped, crusty French rolls called *bolillos*.

During the 19th century, food became so important that young upper-class women were sent to convents for cooking lessons. Culinary skills were part of every eligible young woman's dowry.

Today, Mexico's culinary tradition continues to evolve, positioning it as one of the most exciting in the world. Many culinary experts rank it third after that of France and China. Mexicans disagree. It's *número uno* they say!

COLONIAL RECIPES

Huachingo A La Veracruzana—Red Snapper Veracruz Style

Spanish capers and olives marry with Mexican chiles and tomatillos to present a perfect union, colonial style. This dish is a showstopper made with a whole fish and served over rice.

2 pounds red snapper fillets or whole fish about that size

salt and pepper

2 tablespoons olive oil or lard (authentic fat of choice)

1 onion, cut in half and sliced

2 pounds ripe tomatoes, finely chopped

1 cup water

10 peppercorns

2 bay leaves

3 cloves garlic, minced

2 bell peppers, sliced in strips (or a Mexican pepper such as Poblano or Anaheim)

3 tablespoons capers, drained

1/2 cup stuffed green olives sliced

Season fish and saute in oil. Add onions and peppers and saute until golden. Add the rest of the ingredients and cook, covered, until fish no longer has a shiny raw look to it. This dish can also be finished in a 350° oven. A two pound fish cooks in 20 minutes. Serve over rice. Makes six servings.

Pozole—Pork And Hominy Soup/Salad

Each diner chooses the garnishes of his choice, which he puts on top of the soup. The result is that each dish is a custom meal. ¡Muy sabroso!

1 chicken, cut up

2-3 pounds pork, cut up coarsely

1 pork foot (optional but good)

2 onions, chopped

3 cloves garlic

2 pounds hominy, drained

2 tablespoons oregano

red chile sauce:

10 guajillo chiles, seeds and membranes removed

1/2 cup water

1/4 onion

4 cloves garlic

3 tablespoons oil

salad garnish: offer sliced radishes, shredded lettuce, chopped onions, slices of lime, chopped cilantro, leaf Mexican oregano, more chile sauce.

Place chicken, pork, onions, and garlic in a large (three-quart) pot of water and cook until tender, about one hour. Remove meats to cool. Cool soup in refrigerator and remove fat layer that rises to top. Skin chicken and shred along with pork. Put back in pot along with soup, hominy, and oregano.

To make red chile sauce, soften guajillos or dried chiles of your choice in boiling water for about 20 minutes. Seed and remove membranes. Add water and chiles to blender, along with onion and garlic. Puree until smooth.

Heat oil in a skillet over high heat and fry chile puree about five minutes. Add about 1/2 cup of chile sauce to pozole and cook another 15 minutes. Serve in open soup bowls with garnishes. Makes eight servings.

(continued)

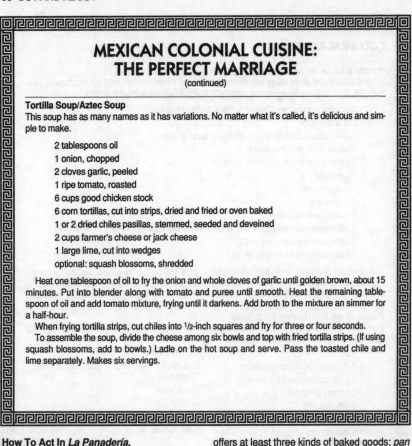

MEXICAN COLONIAL CUISINE: THE PERFECT MARRIAGE

(continued)

Tortilla Soup/Aztec Soup

This soup has as many names as it has variations. No matter what it's called, it's delicious and simple to make.

> 2 tablespoons oil
> 1 onion, chopped
> 2 cloves garlic, peeled
> 1 ripe tomato, roasted
> 6 cups good chicken stock
> 6 corn tortillas, cut into strips, dried and fried or oven baked
> 1 or 2 dried chiles pasillas, stemmed, seeded and deveined
> 2 cups farmer's cheese or jack cheese
> 1 large lime, cut into wedges
> optional: squash blossoms, shredded

Heat one tablespoon of oil to fry the onion and whole cloves of garlic until golden brown, about 15 minutes. Put into blender along with tomato and puree until smooth. Heat the remaining tablespoon of oil and add tomato mixture, frying until it darkens. Add broth to the mixture an simmer for a half-hour.

When frying tortilla strips, cut chiles into 1/2-inch squares and fry for three or four seconds.

To assemble the soup, divide the cheese among six bowls and top with fried tortilla strips. (If using squash blossoms, add to bowls.) Ladle on the hot soup and serve. Pass the toasted chile and lime separately. Makes six servings.

How To Act In *La Panadería,* A Mexican Bakery

This is *almost* better than a *dulcería* (candy shop). But if you've never been before, you'll see a stack of metal trays (probably with fresh crumbs on them) and long handled tongs. Take your tray and tongs and help yourself to the fresh goodies on the shelves and trays lining the walls. When you're done loading up, bring tray and all to the front counter—the cashier will ring you up.

Every bakery has a big fan; I often wonder whether it's to cool the place off, to shoo the flies away, or to swoosh the wonderful aromas out onto the street to lure passersby. Whatever the intention, it works on all three levels. And speaking of "three," every bakery worth its salt

offers at least three kinds of baked goods: *pan salado* (hard rolls); *bizcochos* (sweet rolls); and cookies, cakes and pastries. The hard rolls are known by everyone as *bolillos,* which are baked three times daily in huge quantities that get sold out very quickly (delicious, hot, and crispy). These marvelous rolls can be converted into *tortas* (sandwiches) or *molletes* (an open roll smeared heavily with beans or other goodies). They're great just plain, or spread with butter or salsa, or dipped in hot coffee or chocolate. A bolillo is a good all-purpose snack; it's best to eat it the first day, because by the next, it's *muy dura* (hard as a rock!).

Bizcocho dough is sweet and spongy and is blended with a number of additions, such as cinnamon, lemon or orange peel, chocolate, vanilla, rose water—we have barely scratched the surface. The cookies can be pink, or sugar, or stuffed. (Don't be shocked if when you finish you see pink in the loo; it's just the dye from Mexico's pink cookies, and we have been presuming for years that it's harmless.)

Holidays are fun in a *panadería;* around the **Day Of The Dead** you will find all kinds of "bread for the dead" with skulls (sugar imitations) and saints' faces attached. Special little cakes are made that look like graves and gravestones decorated with sugar skeletons. In January (Day of the Three Kings), bread is made with bits of dried fruit, and concealed inside is a tiny plastic infant Jesus; whoever finds it is then required by custom to host the supper of tamales and hot chocolate on Candelaria, 2 February.

When you finish with your selections, take your tray to the counter and a clerk will have the total so quickly it makes your head spin. Have pesos with you, preferably small denominations. Some of the bakeries you see in the big cities these days are really huge and very modern, and many have coffee shops attached where you can have a tasty, inexpensive breakfast of croissants and coffee or chocolate, or yogurt or *pan dulce,* or whatever you wish.

Mercado

Public markets are the places to discover many unknown, exotic new foods. If you're interested in herbs, spices, and medicinal roots and barks, this is where you'll see them. If you don't speak the language, it's best to have an interpreter along in this department to help you out. You'll see piles of marjoram, juniper berries, dried roses, cinnamon sticks, coriander, and mushrooms. Those vendors who specialize only in medicinal herbs often have them neatly packaged in cellophane bags, and it is said (whisper whisper), that you can generally buy a magic spell to go along with the potion if you know the right person at the market. But even without the spells you can buy *berro* (watercress) for headaches, *tomillo* to aid digestion, and *romero* (spirit of rosemary) to massage into sore joints, and you can order chamomile tea in any restaurant—just because you like it. About 25% of the

world's modern prescription drugs sold today were discoved as natural plant compounds (many right here in Mexico), most of which are modified versions of folk remedies.

Ladies sit on the ground and cut the thorns out of cactus pads called *nopalitos,* which they marinate or stew with chiles and tomatoes. You'll see a huge variety of chiles; light green, dark green, red, miniscule, medium, and immense, each with its own measure of *picante,* and all with *lots* of vitamin C. Pretty orange pumpkin blossoms are sold at certain times of the year, along with the *huitlacoche* fungus, both used in crepes for special occasions.

Food Safety

When preparing your own food in the backcountry, a few possible sources of bacteria are fresh fruit and vegetables, especially those with a thin skin that aren't normally peeled (e.g. lettuce or tomatoes). When washing these foods in local water (and they should definitely be washed thoroughly before consuming), add either bleach or iodine (8-10 drops per liter) to the water. Soaking vegetables all together in a container or plastic bag for about 20 minutes is easy; carrying along Ziploc bags is essential. If at the beach and short of water, substitute sea water (for everything but drinking). Remember not to rinse the bleached food with contaminated water; just pat dry, and if they have a distasteful lingering flavor, a squirt of lime juice tastes great and is very healthy. Nature has packaged some foods hygienically; a banana has its own protective seal so is considered safe (luckily, since they're so abundant). Foods that are cooked and eaten immediately are also considered safe. The general rule, according to doctors, is to avoid raw fruits and vegetables that you haven't peeled yourself. Unpeeled produce is generally fine.

Bottled Water

At a restaurant, it's probably safer to order a bottle of mineral water, either *sin gas* (without bubbles) or *con gas* (with bubbles). With the current cholera scare, take extra precautions, including careful consideration about the ice.

IMMIGRATION AND CUSTOMS

Documents

With proof of citizenship (birth certificate, passport, voter's registration, or notarized affidavit), U.S. and Canadian citizens can obtain a free tourist card good for 180 days. It can be obtained at any Mexican consulate or tourist office, at all border entry points, from airport ticket offices, and from most travel agents. Hang on to your tourist card for the entire trip; you'll need it to leave the country. If visiting Mexico for 72 hours or less, a tourist card is not necessary. Watch the date; don't let the card expire before you leave—it can be "fixed," but it becomes a bureaucratic waste of time, and you might have to pay a fine. Ask at the Mexican consulate about extensions for longer periods before it runs out. If you're a naturalized citizen, carry your naturalization papers or passport. Citizens of the U.S. or Canada are not required to obtain certificates of vaccination to enter Mexico; other nationalities should check with a local Mexican consulate.

Those under 18 without a parent or legal guardian must present a notarized letter from the parents or guardian granting permission to travel alone in Mexico. If a single parent is traveling with a minor, he or she should carry a notarized letter from the other parent granting permission. This is important going in both directions.

Bring A Passport

If you have a passport, bring it along even though it's not required (tuck your tourist card inside); it's the simplest ID when cashing traveler's checks, registering at hotels, and going through immigration. If you're visiting an area that has a current health problem and you have a health card with current information, keep that with the passport also. Keep all documents in a waterproof plastic case and in a safe place. Write to the U.S. Secretary of State for the most recent information about isolated areas that might be on the list for immunization. If traveling to such places, you'll need proof of vaccination to get back into the U.S. and perhaps other countries as well.

Driving Procedures

See **"Getting There and Around,"** below.

Pets

If traveling with a pet, you'll need two documents: a veterinarian's certificate, issued within 72 hours of crossing the border, that verifies good health; and proof of a rabies inoculation within the last six months. These certificates will be validated by any Mexican consulate for a small fee. Keep it with you for the trip back.

Purchases

When departing by land, air, or sea, you must declare at the point of reentry into your own country all items acquired in Mexico. Customs agents suggest that to facilitate this procedure, it is wise to register any foreign-made possessions with customs officials before entering Mexico and to retain the receipts for purchases made while there. In reality, we haven't done this in years and have never had a problem. With more and more imported items sold in all countries, there doesn't seem to be as much emphasis on this anymore. However, beware of the possibility. Limitations on the value of imported, duty-free goods vary from country to country and should be checked before traveling. U.S. citizens are allowed to carry through customs US$400 worth of purchases per person duty free (up to US$1000 worth of purchases for 10% tax) and one quart of alcoholic beverage. About 2,700 items are exempt from this limit, most of which are handcrafted or manufactured in Mexico. Consular offices or embassies in Mexico City can supply additional information on exempt items. Plants and certain foods are not allowed into Mexico or back into the United States. Authentic archaeological finds, colonial art, and other original artifacts cannot be exported from Mexico. And, of course, trying to bring marijuana or any other narcotic in/out of Mexico or the U.S. is foolhardy. Jail is one place in Mexico a visitor can miss. It's wise to carry a written prescription for any legal drugs you are carrying, just in case someone asks.

Studying In Mexico

In addition to fulfilling the requirements for a tourist card, students must present documents to a Mexican consulate demonstrating that they have been accepted at an educational institution and that they are financially solvent. A number of courses and workshops are offered throughout Mexico lasting two to eight weeks in addition to full-time study programs. Many adults as well as younger folks are taking part in language programs where the student lives with a family (that speaks only Spanish to them) for a period of two to four weeks and attends language classes daily. This total immersion into the language, even for a short time, is quite successful and popular as a cultural experience.

Write to the National Registration Center for Study Abroad (NRCSA), 823 N. Second St., Milwaukee, Wisconsin 53203, USA, or call (800) 558-9988. Request their *Directory of Educational Programs,* which describes programs in a number of cities in Mexico.

GETTING THERE AND AROUND

Backpackers

If you plan on hitchhiking or using public transportation, don't use a large external-frame pack; it won't fit in most small cars, buses (at your seat), or public lockers. Smaller packs with zippered compartments that accommodate mini-padlocks are most practical. A strong bike cable and lock secures the pack to a YH bed or a bus or train rack. None of the above will deter the real criminal, but it might make it difficult enough to discourage anyone else.

Experienced backpackers travel light with a pack, an additional canvas bag, a small water- and mosquito-proof tent, a hammock, and mosquito netting.

BY CAR

An international driver's license is not required to drive or rent a car in Mexico. However, if you feel safer with it, get one from an auto club. At AAA you need two passport pictures and US$10, along with a current driver's license from your home state. The international license is another good form of identification if you should have an accident or other driving problem.

Border Crossings

If while driving you should happen to reach a remote border crossing at night, you may find it unmanned. *Do not* cross the border with your car until you have obtained the proper papers; if you do, it will cause problems when you exit the country. Flash: We have just been told that AAA is now able to process many of the forms to drive into Mexico; this is supposedly going to cut border crossing time from one hour to 15 minutes. Great!

Checkpoints

Be aware that it is becoming more commonplace to run into checkpoints near the border. You are flagged down, and a uniformed man will ask where you and your car are from, and if he can look at your tourist card and/or passport. These are generally in areas where drug traffic is more frequent.

Auto Insurance

When you cross the border from the U.S. into Mexico, your car insurance is no longer valid. You can, however, buy insurance from AAA or an auto club before you leave home. Mexican vehicle insurance is available at most border towns 24 hours a day. Sanborn's is one of the largest insurance companies. (Ask Sanborn's for their excellent free road maps of the areas you plan to visit.) For more information write Sanborn's Mexican Insurance Service, P.O. Box 1210, McAllen, Texas 78501, USA; tel. (512) 682-3401. However, in every Mexican border city you'll find insurance companies selling automobile insurance. A couple more good companies to check out are **ClubMex,** P.O. Box 609, Bonita, California 91908, USA; tel. (619) 422-3028; **International Gateway Insurance,** tel. (800) 423-2646.

Auto Regulations

Following is a list of **no drive days** in Mexico City, according to your license plates.

Monday: No driving if final digit is 5 or 6

Tuesday: No driving if final digit is 7 or 8

Wednesday: No driving if final digit is 3 or 4

Thursday: No driving if final digit is 1 or 2

Friday: No driving if final digit is 9 or 0

Saturday and Sunday: all vehicles may drive

This past year has seen regulations that have caused a lot of confusion when traveling to Mexico by car. The government is trying to work with the U.S. authorities to crack down on Americans bringing in stolen cars and selling them in Mexico. The first plan did not work at all. Hopefully the new Mexican Government Regulations will eliminate some of the confusion. All vehicles traveling more than 20 kilometers (12 miles) below the U.S.-Mexican border must carry the following documents: **vehicle title** (original only), a **notarized affidavit** of consent from the **legal owner (bank)**, or **rental agreement** and a notarized affidavit of consent from the rental company. A nonrefundable US$10 car permit fee must be charged on a major credit card (Visa, MasterCard, or American Express). *No checks or cash accepted.*

Or, a surety bond issued by a Mexican company for the entire Blue Book value of the vehicle will do. The bond must be purchased at the border and is refundable only at the point of purchase when the vehicle leaves Mexico.

The US$10 fee or surety bond receipt purchases a six-month car permit. The value of the vehicle is noted by Mexican Customs officials and will be charged to the credit card if the vehicle does not return across the border. This permit must be carried at all times and must be returned upon leaving Mexico, or by the expiration date. The permit *cannot* be purchased at the ferry ports in Baja. The registered owner must accompany the vehicles. *No borrowed vehicles are allowed.*

These new regulations do not alter the need for obtaining Mexican insurance when traveling anywhere in Mexico. In addition all drivers must carry:

✔ Proof of nationality and a tourist card

✔ Driver's license

✔ Vehicle registration

✔ Mexican automobile insurance (U.S. insurance is not recognized by the Mexican Government).

These regulations went into effect on 1 April 1992 and are subject to change without notice at any time. **Note:** Before leaving on a driving trip with your car, check at both your closest **Mexican Government Tourist Office** and at a reputable auto club; AAA and Sanborn's are just two (in the event that new regulations have gone into effect). We have had lots of letters from readers with some real horror stories. Hopefully, this latest regulation will work and be simpler for the driver.

Car Parts

No matter the condition of the roads throughout the area, before taking your car into the country consider the manufacturer and the condition of the car. Will parts be available in the event of a breakdown? Volkswagen, Renault, Ford, General Motors, and Chrysler have Mexican branches and parts should be available. If you drive an expensive foreign sports car or a large luxury model, you might be better off making other arrangements. Repairs might be unavailable and you could be stranded in an unlikely place for days waiting for a part (I speak from experience when our "big car" broke down in the small town of Navajoa in 1956. We didn't get the part for a week, and ended up spending one of the finest weeks ever in Mexico, even though we were stranded). It's always wise to make sure you and the mechanic understand the cost of repairs before he begins—just like at home! **Note:** Selling your car in Mexico is illegal.

Green Angels

These very visible green trucks are government-sponsored tow trucks that cruise the main roads several times a day on the lookout for drivers in trouble. They carry gas and small parts and are prepared to fix flat tires. Each car is equipped with a CB radio and the driver is trained to give first aid, or will call a doctor. If you foolishly travel an isolated road after dark and break down, your best bet is to lock yourself in and stick it out for the night; go for help in the morning. The Mexican people are friendly, especially when they see someone in trouble; sometimes you have more help than you want.

Gas Stations And Unleaded Gas

In Central Mexico finding a gas station is fairly easy since towns are not too far apart and the

GREEN ANGEL TELEPHONE NUMBERS

Mexico City: (5) 250-8555

Guanajuato: (473) 2-0119

Taxco: (762) 2-0905

Guadalajara: (36) 35-0755

Toluca: (721) 4-4249

Morelia: (43) 5-6568

Cuernavaca: (731) 38-1420

Puebla: (22) 30-1774

Querétaro: (42) 13-8443

Tlaxcala: (246) 3-3606

Jalapa: (281) 8-4847

Veracruz: (29) 32-1613

population is large. Remember, if your car uses unleaded gas, look for the **Magna Sin** pump. For those who use regular, ask for **Nova**. More and more stations have Magna Sin these days, and usually you'll see a small sign posted along the highway that tells you the next station that sells Magna Sin. In fact, there are 2,000 Pemex stations in 74 Mexican cities selling Magna Sin, a big improvement!

When you are at the pump, always get out of the car, tell the attendant to give you N$15 or so worth of Magna Sin or Nova, show him the amount in your hand so he knows exactly what you want (make eye contact), and then make a point of checking the gas gauge (was it zeroed out?) before you unlock your own gas tank. Then watch the entire operation. Sounds far out, but you don't want any claims afterward of any misunderstanding. Whatever you do, don't ask them to *fill* the tank, some of the attendants are so fast that they zero it out before you can see how much gas you received. It doesn't happen all the time, but we get more letters of complaint about this issue than any other. If after all of this, you still have a problem and get overcharged or cheated, complain to the manager. Tell him you know how much gas your car uses and that you will report him to the police if he persists in this scam. If it was an honest mistake, he will be more than happy to refund the overcharge; if he's really a con man, you'll probably

end up paying, but do report it to the police, and then take precautions that it won't happen again. Outside of the large, new Pemex stations, don't expect to receive much service. Often there's a young boy washing your windows; he works for tips only, so a new peso (about US$.30) would be a nice gesture if he does a good job. The newer Pemex stations are really quite nice and most have clean restrooms. **Note:** Credit cards are *not* accepted at gas stations. Expect to pay in the neighborhood of 42 cents per liter (US$1.60 per gallon) of gasoline.

Out Of Gas

It's not unusual for gas stations to run out of gas, especially unleaded, so fill up whenever you pass a station. This frequently happens during long holidays. On different occasions we have found it necessary to buy gas from an accommodating villager who siphoned gas from his truck and sold it to us (for a slightly inflated price) so we could be on our way, or searched the village asking for someone who would sell us gas; and there's almost always a business that keeps a large drum of gas on the premises.

VEHICLE SUPPLIES

✔ couple of extra fan belts

✔ long towing rope or chain

✔ bottle of Windex

✔ set of spark plugs

✔ points and condenser

✔ emery boards

✔ feeler gauge (to set the points)

✔ oil filter and gas filter

✔ gas can

✔ oil

✔ fuses

✔ extra tire, patch kit

✔ air supply

✔ good-sized machete to hack your way through vines and plants

✔ shovel

✔ flares

✔ flashlight

✔ a few basic tools

✔ paper towels

Night Driving

In Mexico, it's recommended that you don't drive outside the cities at night unless it's a necessity. The highways have no streetlights—it's hard to see a black cow on a black road in the black night. Also, pedestrians have no other place to walk; shoulders are nonexistent on the roads. Public phones are few and far between, and gas stations close when the sun goes down. If you should have a problem while driving during daylight hours on a *main* road, stay with your car. The Green Angels should find you.

Toll Roads

New toll roads are popping up around the country in accordance with the federal government's plans to have a network of more than 5,000 kilometers of high-quality, four-lane toll roads finished within the next three years. Toll costs on these new roads are almost prohibitive to the average Mexican, and not cheap for the average visitor! The tolls range from 13-27 cents per kilometer (20-43 cents per mile) as compared to an average toll road cost in the U.S. of five cents per mile (three cents per kilometer). Before reaching a highway, there will be a sign that di-

CAR RENTAL TIPS

Renting a car in Mexico is usually a simple matter but is very costly, much more so than in the U.S.—and is always subject to Murphy's Law. If you know exactly when you want the car and where, it's much smarter to make reservations with a U.S. company in advance. If you wait until you get to Mexico, you'll pay the going rate, which can add up to about US$60-80 per day for a small car; most offices give little or no weekly discount. This is not to say that you can't take part in the favorite Mexican pastime, bargaining. You might get lucky. *If* it's just before closing time, and *if* someone has cancelled a reservation, and *if* it's off-season, it's possible to get a car for a good rate. However, that's a lot of "ifs" to count on when you want and need a car as soon as you arrive. Also, it's often difficult to get a car without reservations; you may have to wait around for one to be returned.

Mexican Franchises Of U.S. Companies

Representatives of Hertz, Avis, and Budget can be found in many parts of Mexico. These are separate franchises. Though not run by the mother companies, U.S. corporate offices will honor a contract price made in the U.S. before your arrival in Mexico. If you should run into a problem and you still want the car, pay the higher price and write a brief protest on the contract right then.

Avis is currently the cheapest of the big three; before leaving home do a little telephone shopping (Avis, Hertz, and Budget all list 800 numbers in the Yellow Pages; ask for the international desk). The prices they quote hold only, of course, if you make your arrangements before you leave home. Always ask for the best deal, usually a weekly arrangement.

Even if you only plan to use the car for four or five days, use your calculator; it might still be a better deal, especially with unlimited mileage. If you're planning on driving a lot, don't rent a car unless you get unlimited mileage. Look into Hertz's Affordable Mexico, which in the past was a good deal, but of late can't beat Avis's best deal. If you belong to AAA or other auto clubs, the car rental agency might give you a 10-20% discount (be sure you bring your membership card), but not in conjunction with another offer.

Read All The Fine Print

Really take the time to go over your contract carefully before signing and taking off. Make sure everyone does their math correctly, that you're getting the price promised and no unexpected extras, and that it does indeed state *unlimited mileage*. Some contracts have limitations on where you can use the car. Note the time and date written in, and if they don't have the car you were promised, don't settle for anything less; ask for an upgrade. Make sure you have an emergency number to contact in case of problems with the car. If you don't catch these things now, you are probably out of luck afterwards.

Insurance

Mexican insurance from the rental car agencies runs about US$17 per day and covers only 80% of the damages (which many travelers are unaware of). You are responsible for the deductible even with insurance—this can be expensive. However, it's dangerous to skip insurance; with most accidents in Mexico, the police take action first and ask questions later. With an insurance policy, most of the

rects you to either the *libre* (free road) or the *cuota* (toll road), so you do have a choice. For more information about the toll roads, call the **Mexican Government Tourism-Surface Travel** office in Houston, Texas, (800) 662-MEXI. In Mexico, call the 24-hour toll free number for information, 91-800-90329; you will be connected to an English-speaking operator with information.

Some of the old routes are in miserable condition, some are not, but for the most part, they have changed little and are still congested with Mexican motorists who don't think the new toll roads are worth the price. Despite a local re-

luctance to pay the heavy tolls, the federal government continues its diligent project. Many American motorists are willing to pay the price because of the safety factor—a few mountain roads were before quite dangerous.

A unique construction program commits the government to let private companies bid to build toll highways and operate them for a predetermined period of time (10 years is usual). The enterprise was begun in 1989 to transform Mexico's very poor roads into a first-rate network of highways. This network will provide five arteries crisscrossing the country from the northern bor-

---

problems are eased over. Rental agencies also offer medical insurance for US$6 per day. Your private medical insurance should cover this (check). Also, ask your credit-card provider exactly what insurance you can expect with their card when renting a car in Mexico. There might be certain coverages you already have. However, it will be your responsibility to pay for everything until the insurance kicks in. Make sure you understand all the details.

Getting The Car
Another advantage to making reservations in advance is the verification receipt you receive—be sure to ask for it when reserving the car before you leave home. Hang on to it; it's like money in the bank. When you arrive at the airport and show your verification receipt (be sure you get it back), a car will almost always be waiting for you. Once in a while you'll even get an upgrade for the same fee if your reserved car is not available. On the other side of the coin, be sure that you go over the car *carefully* before you take it far. Go over the following checklist and then drive it around the block:

✔ Gas cap.
✔ Spare tire and working jack.
✔ All doors should lock and unlock, including trunk.
✔ The seats should move forward, have no sprung backs, etc.
✔ Windshield wipers work.
✔ All windows should lock, unlock, roll up and down properly.
✔ Check for proper legal papers for the car, with addresses and phone numbers of associate car rental agencies in cities you plan to visit in case of an unexpected car problem.
✔ Horn, emergency brake, and foot brakes should work properly.

✔ Check clutch, gearshift, and all gears (don't forget reverse).
✔ Lights, head and tail.
✔ Get directions to the nearest gas station; the gas tank may be empty. If it's full, be sure to return it full, since you'll be charged top dollar per liter of gas. Ask to have any damage, even a small dent, missing doorknob, etc., noted on your contract, if it hasn't been already.
✔ Note the hour you picked up the car and try to return it before that time: a few minutes over will cost you another full day's rental fee, or at the least a costly hourly rate.

Payoff Time
When you pick up your rental car, the company makes an imprint of your credit card on a blank bill, one copy of which is attached to the papers you give the agent when you return the car. If you have had the car for several weeks, keep in mind that the car agency has a limit of how much you can charge on one credit card at one time (ask the maximum when you pick up the car). If you go over the limit be prepared to pay the balance in cash or with another credit card. If you pick up a car in one city and return it to another there's a hefty drop-off fee (per km). Most agents will figure out in advance exactly how much it will be so there aren't any surprises when you return the car.

More than likely all will go smoothly. However, if you run into a problem or are overcharged, don't panic. You might be at an office that has never heard of Affordable Mexico (for instance), even though it is specified on your verification. Go ahead and pay (with plastic), save all your paperwork, and when you return home, make copies of everything, call the company, and chances are very good that you'll get a refund.

der of Chiapas and Oaxaca in the south, and from Acapulco and Manzanillo on the west coast, to Tuxpan and Veracruz on the east coast. As we go to press, 39 toll road projects have begun, and 13 projects and about 1,200 kilometers are complete. The private companies who build and operate the new highways for a fixed period of time use toll proceeds to pay for their building costs and return a profit. After the concession period, the operation of the highway returns to the government, which aims to use the proceeds to offset the cost of building 13,000 kilometers of smaller roads around the country. In theory it's a great idea.

The program is providing an enormous boost to the construction industry and the economy, although some projects turned out to be a financial boondoggle for the concessionaires who had to refinance the project and negotiate longer concession periods in order to recover their losses. The Mexico City-Toluca toll road, the first of these projects, began operating in October 1990. Because of negative reaction on the part of Mexican motorists regarding the high toll (N$18/US$6 for 22 kilometers), traffic flow never reached projected figures and an extended concession period to the road constructor had to be implemented. Other high-cost toll roads built in the last three years include Nogales to Mazatlán and Tepic to Guadalajara. Another that should be completed is the Mexico City-Acapulco road. The highway is being engineered to eliminate dangerous curves and time-consuming obstacles; the new driving time between these two cities will be cut to three hours and fifteen minutes. Rumors claim the projected toll is high.

Another toll-artery in the works is Mexico City-Guadalajara via Morelia, a 340-kilometer stretch. This road should cut driving time between Mexico's two biggest cities from eight to four hours, and tolls will be about half as expensive as the Toluca toll road.

This writer guesses that tolls will eventually be lowered, since many complaints are flying around the heads of the federal government. As one retiree living in Guadalajara complained, anyone traveling from Guadalajara to Nogales, Arizona, better come with a thick wad of pesos. The 3,427 kilometer (2,130 mile) stretch costs US$150.38 in tolls roundtrip, and that doesn't count the cost of the unleaded Mexican gas.

He also added that some of the roads were top quality, similar to interstate highways in the U.S.; however, some were no more than upgraded two-lane blacktop roads. The airplane is looking better all the time.

City Streets

The narrow streets that were designed for horses and buggies are scenes of high-tech traffic snarls to match any you'll find in the U.S. or Canada. Add to that hilly areas with one way roads, dead ends, and narrow steep alleys; this is especially true in Guanajuato. Park your car and take the bus! While the streets in Mexico City are wider, the traffic is really thick. Big city driving is probably the most difficult.

Highways To Mexico

In California, main highways cross the Mexican border from San Diego to Tijuana and from Calexico to Mexicali. From Arizona go through Tucson to Nogales. From Texas, El Paso leads to Juárez, Eagle Pass to Piedras Negras, Laredo to Nuevo Laredo, and Brownsville to Matamoros. From each of these gateways, good highways will bring you to the capital of the country, Mexico City.

BY AIR

Today, flying to Mexico is easy with many airlines and international gateways scattered about the country. Jets arrive daily, with connections from most countries in the world. From the U.S. you can enter Central Mexico in either Guadalajara, Mexico City, or León. There are several small landing strips for private planes and small commuter airlines that fly in and out of Mexico City.

Airlines

The following airlines have offices in Mexico City as well as U.S. toll-free numbers:

Aero California, Reforma 332, tel. 207-1392; (800) 237-6225.

Aeromar, Leibnitz 34, tel. 592-1995; (800) 950-0747.

Aeromexico, Reforma 445, tel. 327-4000; (800) 237-6639.

American Airlines, Reforma 300 1st Fl., tel. 203-9444; (800) 433-7300.

Canadian Airlines International, Reforma 390, tel. 208-1654 or 208-1691; (800) 426-7000.

Continental, Reforma 325, tel. 203-1148; (800) 231-0856.

Delta Airlines, Reforma 381, tel. 202-1608; (800) 221-1212.

LACSA, Río Nilo 88, tel. 525-0025; (800) 225-2272.

Lufthansa, Av. de las Palmas 239, tel. 202-8866; (800) 645-3880.

Mexicana de Aviación, Xola 535, tel. 660-4433; (800) 531-7921.

United Airlines, Hamburgo 213, tel. 627-9476; (800) 241-6522.

Some airlines have direct flights from the U.S. to the larger cities in Central Mexico with international airports (Guadalajara, León, and Mexico City; otherwise flights are routed with a stop in other international gateways, such as Mazatlán, Puerto Vallarta, and of course Mexico City. Check with the airlines or your local travel agent, or call Mexico specialists who give outstanding service, such as **Four Seasons Travel,** 49 W. Montello St., P.O. Box 487, Montello, WI 53949; tel. (800) 552-4550, (608) 297-2332.

Charter Flights

This is a business that's booming! Many large tour groups use charter flights, and it can be considerably cheaper as long as you fit into their scheduling "slots" (some leave on Sunday and return on Saturday; it doesn't change from week to week). Often it's a package that includes hotels. Worth looking into, but remember it can be a more crowded trip since they usually put in extra seats to make it worthwhile. Your local newspaper travel section often lists the companies that operate out of your city in their Sunday edition.

Airport Tax

Before we go any further, please remember not to spend all your money in Mexico before you get to the airport to catch your plane home. You'll need about US$12 for an international departure, and if you're traveling within the country, it costs US$6 for a flight to another Mexi-

can city. Over the past few years I personally have loaned three different (panicked) U.S. travelers the airport departure tax; they had nary a peso left; each repaid immediately after returning home, thank you. Tuck the tax away before you start shopping so you don't have to worry about it.

BY TRAIN

For many years Mexico has had a fairly efficient railway service. Traveling by train is relaxing, and the scenery is outstanding. You can make the entire trip from the U.S. to Mexico City by rail. Today's passenger cars are second-hand Amtrak, 15-20 years old. They aren't "peasant" trains with wooden-bench seats, etc., but they are far from glamorous—although very acceptable. The cars are arranged with two reclining seats on either side of the car, are heated and air-conditioned, have a restroom, and you can make reservations in the U.S. and get your tickets by mail (allow 30 days). Many of the routes have eliminated Pullman overnight sleeping cars. The more popular tourist routes offer first class. A couple of the more popular day-trips are from Mexico City to Guanajuato and San Miguel Allende. There are two routes in Central Mexico that still offer Pullman service: Mexico City-Guadalajara, and Mexico City-Veracruz. As an example, the cost of the Veracruz routing is US$60 OW and includes two meals, usually a cold box lunch. It departs Veracruz at 9:30 p.m. and arrives in Mexico City at 6:30 a.m. To get information, you must ask specifically about the destination and boarding point you're interested in. For more information and reservations, write to **Mexico Rail** (8607 Wurzbach Rd., Suite V100, San Antonio, Texas, 78240; tel. 210-641-6449).

From several stateside cities along the border you can walk over the border and pick up a Mexican train; you should have reservations.

RAILWAY STATIONS ALONG THE U.S.-MEXICO BORDER

Mexicali	Nuevo Laredo
Nogales	Matamoros
Ciudad Juárez	

Some of the trains do not offer a dining car, so either carry your own snacks or depend on vendors that sell Mexican fast food, tamales, etc. at the many stops along the way (use common sense when buying). For information on other departure points along the border plus schedules, prices, etc., deal directly with the railway companies (in Mexico) or Mexico Rail if in the U.S.; schedules and prices change frequently.

BY BUS

Bus service in Mexico is very efficient. Fares will fit the most meager budget, scheduling is frequent, and even the smallest village is accessible from most hub cities in Mexico. From the U.S. it's smart to make reservations with Greyhound/Trailways to your final destination. Frequently, you can board an ongoing bus to a Mexican city at the U.S. border bus station on a scheduled bus. Or Greyhound drivers will take you to the border and then help you make the transfer (including your luggage) to a Mexican bus line. Ask about this when making reservations in the United States. This service saves you a lot of time and confusion when in a strange bus station. When making return reservations, make them straight through across the border, even if only to the first town on the U.S. side.

Class Choice

You have a choice of super-deluxe, first, second, or third class. Third-class passengers can bring their animals (and often do); buses are usually older models with no toilets or a/c, are crowded, and allow passengers to stand in the aisles. Third-class bus tickets can be as cheap as 60 cents. Most buses in Mexico have been upgraded in the last two years, especially long-distance buses. First-class and super-deluxe buses have assigned seats, are more comfortable, and are still very moderately priced.

Super Deluxe Bus Service

Some of the new super-deluxe buses have a stewardess, airline seats, plenty of room, a/c, and new equipment. They use express routes and include snacks and electronic entertainment. Drivers are given special training and

there's a device on the bus that tracks their speed, keeping it at a controlled 95 kmh (60 mph). At the end of each journey this is checked and if the driver has exceeded the speed limit, he is fined and can be suspended. One thing to note, most of the buses have heavily tinted windows and/or drapes that make it really hard to look out. And you cannot open the windows. The front seats are not necessarily the best seats, since you'll have the TV monitor directly in front of you, and you may not like the offering of the day. The **ETN** (Enlaces Terrestres Nacionales) company is our favorite. Expect ticket prices to be at least triple that of first class. They seem to have the tightest controls and so far have maintained high quality. We have found that some buses have tried to upgrade their equipment to call it a "deluxe" service, but that in reality they still are not truly deluxe.

A Few ETN Numbers In Central Mexico

Guadalajara, Jalisco: (36) 57-4353
León, Guanajuato: (47) 13-1410
Morelia, Michoacán: (45) 13-7440
Pátzcuaro, Michoacán: (454) 2-1060
Querétaro, Querétaro: (42) 14-4334
Toluca, Mexico: (72) 17-7308
Guanajuato, Guanajuato: (473) 2-3134
Mexico City, D.F.: (5) 277-0889

New companies keep popping up, so check them out; two more to consider are **Primera Plus** and **Satellite Plus** in San Miguel de Allende, tel. (465) 2-0084. Make reservations in advance with all buses if possible. Your ticket will say *asiento* (seat) with a number.

If you're traveling a long distance, buy at least first-class; the difference in comfort is worth the small, added expense. Second- and third-class buses stop for anyone who flags them, and at every small village along the way. First class operates almost exclusively between terminals. This cuts a lot of time off a long journey.

Luggage

If it fits in the overhead rack, almost anything can be carried on board. Usual allowance is 25 kilograms, but unless you're ridiculously overloaded, no one ever objects to what you bring aboard. If a driver should refuse your load, usu-

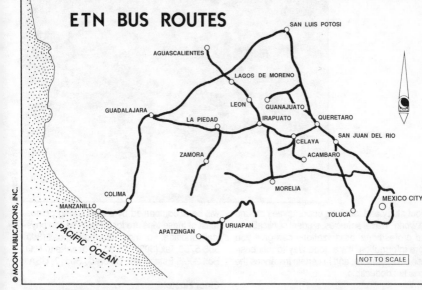

ETN BUS ROUTES

SAN LUIS POTOSI

AGUASCALIENTES

LAGOS DE MORENO

LEON

GUADALAJARA

LA PIEDAD

GUANAJUATO

IRAPUATO

QUERETARO

SAN JUAN DEL RIO

ZAMORA

CELAYA

ACAMBARO

COLIMA

MORELIA

MANZANILLO

MEXICO CITY

TOLUCA

PACIFIC OCEAN

APATZINGAN

URUAPAN

NOT TO SCALE

© MOON PUBLICATIONS, INC.

BOB RACE

ally you can come to an amicable (monetary) agreement. Larger luggage is carried in the cargo hold under the bus where breakables have a short lifespan. Purses and cameras are best kept between your feet on the floor, rather than in the overhead rack—just in case. Luggage should always be labeled, inside and out, with your name, address, and telephone number; it doesn't hurt to watch it be loaded and unloaded.

Seat Comfort

If you can, choose the shady side of the bus during the day; going south sit on the left side and going north sit on the right. At night sit on the right, which eliminates the glare of oncoming headlights. The middle of the bus is the best place to be. Steer clear of seats near the bathroom, usually the last few rows. They can be smelly and the aisle traffic and constant door activity can keep you awake. Bring a book and ignore the bus driver and his abilities; in other words, just relax.

GROUP TRAVEL

Travel agents offer many choices for escorted tours. You may pay a little extra (but not necessarily), and all arrangements and reservations are made for you to tour by plane, train, ship, or RV caravan. Also, special-interest groups with a guest expert are another attraction. For instance, archaeology buffs can usually find a group through universities or archaeologists that includes a knowledgeable professor to guide them through chosen Indian ruins. Evenings are spent together reviewing the day's investigation and discussing the next day's itinerary. Archaeology laymen will find many opportunities, including trips offered through **Earthwatch** (P.O. Box 403, Watertown, Massachusetts 02172, USA); volunteers can work on a dig under the supervision of professionals; destinations change regularly. **Transitions Abroad** (18 Hulst Rd., P.O. Box 344, Amherst, Massachusetts 01004, USA) is a magazine that offers information

snow trekkers

© MIKE DONAHUE

about study and teaching opportunities around the world. Travel agencies, student publications, and professional organizations can give you more information. It's a good way to mix business with pleasure, and in certain instances the trip is tax deductible.

TOURING COMPANIES

The next two groups promote ecological tours, so most of the people traveling will have similar interests.

Ecogrupos De Mexico
Centro Commercial de Plaza Inn, Av. Insurgentes Sur 1971, CP 01020, Mexico D.F., tel. (5) 661-9121, fax (5) 662-7354.

Balam Expediciones
Insurgentes Sur 3756, CP 14060, Tlalpan, Mexico City, tel. (5) 606-6016, fax 606-5883.

Colorado Mountain School
This group offers climbing trips to the mountains of Central Mexico, and most often to those interested in trekking into the higher altitudes. They make all the arrangements and the group will be accompanied by expert hiking guides. Most of these trips are for those in tip-top physical condition. For more information, call (303) 586-5758, fax (303) 586-6677, or write to P.O. Box 2062, Estes Park, Colorado 80517, USA.

Elder Hostel
This group is dedicated to oldsters not ready for the rocking chair. The founders combine the best traditions of education and hosteling designed exclusively for older adults who now have the time for new experiences and enrichment around the world. For more information, write to 76 Federal St., Boston, Massachusetts, 02110-1941, USA, tel. (617) 426-7788, fax (617) 426-8351.

Sightseeing Mexican Style
Some of the best bargains to see Mexico are those trips offered to Mexican travelers. While in Mexico City check out the **Paseos Culturales** located in the basement of the National Institute of Anthropology and History. They offer many one-day tours locally, plus longer ones as well. Good hotels are used on overnighters. Located on Av. Reforma corner of Ghandi Street.

TRAVEL TIPS AND PRECAUTIONS

Time Zone
Central Mexico is in the Central Standard time zone.

Electricity
Electric current has been standardized throughout Mexico, using the same 60-cycle 110-volt AC current common in the United States. Small travel appliances can be used everywhere; if you have a problem, it will be because there's no electricity at all. In some rural areas electricity is supplied by small generators and is usually turned off early in the evening. Some hotels will offer you gas lanterns after the lights go out. These areas are gradually shrinking.

Before You Leave Home
Probably the best way to save money is to make sure you don't lose anything along the way. Be practical; leave expensive jewelry at home. Take five minutes to go through your wallet before leaving and remove all credit cards you won't be using and put a good part of your money in traveler's checks. Make two copies of your passport picture page and any credit cards you carry. Leave one copy of each with someone at home you can reach in case of emergency. After you get your tourist card, also make a copy of that for your wallet. Keep these copies where you'll have them in the event your wallet and cards are stolen, e.g., in another piece of luggage. If your cards should get pinched, the copies will expedite replacement wherever you are in the world. Keep the original tourist card with your passport in a hotel safe when sightseeing, swimming, or whatever.

The Hotel Safe
Even the smallest hotels have safety deposit boxes or some other security system for their guests. Many of the more upscale hotels have in-room safes now, which is very convenient. Use it for your airline tickets and passports, along with other valuables. Don't leave anything valuable laying around your room. Why create a tempting situation? Most hotel employees are honest (honestly!); working in a hotel is a good job, and for the most part that's far more important to the employee than stealing. However (you knew a "however" was coming didn't you?), you might be the unlucky person to draw the unscrupulous thief/maid/bellhop, though they're in the minority. Some travelers feel it happens more in the large glitzy hotels than in the smaller, less upscale places. Of course, this is not a rule of thumb, but perhaps there's a higher employee turnover in the larger hotels than at the smaller, often family-run establishments.

A hotel robbery is less common than, say, a set-up on the street (a jostle, attention diverted by one person while the other grabs your purse or cuts the strap of a carry bag). It has happened (albeit rarely) while a guest was in the shower, or at night while visitors are asleep with a sliding glass door left open for fresh air. Take precautions, act sensibly, be aware of what is going on around you at all times; don't flash large wads of cash, and don't give out your room number to strangers. If you're invited to go anywhere with a stranger, suggest meeting him/her there. And let someone know where you are going, even if it's the desk clerk.

Pickpockets
Don't forget pickpockets; they love fairs and all celebrations where there are lots of people; it's really easy to jostle people in crowds (that includes buses), so make sure you've got your money where a quick hand can't get to it, e.g., a money belt or holster worn over your shoulder under your clothing. Many types are available; check out the trendy travel stores and travel catalogs. (It's a good idea to put everything in a plastic bag before you stash it in your belt/holster; sweat makes ink run.) Does this sound like paranoia? Not really. We are not trying to make Mexico a villain; if we wrote a book about New York, Chicago, Los Angeles, or Paris, we'd give the same advice (in fact we give the same advice in our *Belize Handbook*). In all honesty, in the 37-plus years we've been traveling in Mexico, we've never been the victims of a robbery or a mugging, but we keep our eyes and ears open and are aware that these things can happen.

Legal Help

If after all precautions you still have a problem, contact the 24-hour national hotline of the office of **La Procuraduría de Protección al Turista** ("Attorney General for the Protection of Tourists"). Each state has an office (the following number is located in Mexico City); tell the English-speaking operator you have an emergency and she will direct your call; tel. (5) 250-0293, 250-0151, or 250-0589.

In the event you should be arrested for whatever reason, contact the nearest American Consul's office. If nothing else, they will visit you and advise you of your rights. Whatever you do, don't get caught with illegal substances; there's little that anyone can do with the current pressure the U.S. is putting on Mexico to stop this trafficking. If it's an American offender, it's even worse (if that's possible).

Insurance

Most homeowner's policies cover loss of property while on vacation; check it out before you leave home. *Do* make a police report if you're robbed. It's a long bureaucratic chore, but sometimes your property is recovered as a result. It also helps to have the report in hand when you deal with your insurance back home.

Churches And Clubs

Mexico is predominantly a Catholic country. However, you'll find a few churches of other denominations in the larger cities, including a couple of synagogues (in Guadalajara and Mexico City). Local telephone books and hotel clerks have these listings. Many international organizations, including Lions, Rotary, Shriners, and other foreign social groups have branches in the larger cities and welcome visitors.

Women Travelers

Women traveling alone need to use good common sense, wherever they are in the world. Especially, don't wear beach clothes (short shorts, tight brief T-shirts etc.) in the cities, although walking shorts are certainly acceptable all over the country. Although you will probably see other tourists doing so, it is insensitive to wear shorts into a church. Take a look at a few commercial items for travelers going anywhere in the world where toilet facilities are iffy—or if you're in the bush where there aren't *any* facilities at all. **Le**

Funelle is a scooplike paper funnel with a wide mouth and easy-to-hold handle that enables women to stand up to urinate in comfort and safety. Made of biodegradeable paper, a pack of four is US$2.85, for 20, US$8.99.

This and some other really clever toilet articles and traveling items can be seen in a great little catalog called *Magellan's Essentials for the Traveler*. Take a look at the antibacterial wipes (pre-moistened towelettes with germ killers). A box of 20 is US$4.85. To receive your own catalog, call (800) 962-4943.

Toilet Tips

Finding a public restroom can be difficult in much of Mexico; the smaller the town, the harder it is. One can always go into a restaurant, buy a cold drink, and use the facilities. And if there are no restaurants in the village, you must either stop at the local tienda or cantina and ask, *"¿Dónde esta el baño?"* (Where is the bathroom?), or take a walk into the countryside. Not too many years ago, no facilities were available in any of the archaeological sites. However, in all of the mid- to large-size sites today, you'll find restrooms, hurrah! (See also "Women Travelers," above.)

When you see a wastebasket in the toilet stall and it has toilet paper in it, that's because you are not supposed to flush paper down the toilet: you drop the used paper into the wastebasket. Often the toilet will overflow if you put paper in it.

WHAT TO PACK

Coastal Destinations

Whatever time of year you travel to Mexico's Veracruz coast, you can expect warm weather, which means you can pack less in your suitcase. Most airlines allow you to check two suitcases, and you can bring another carry-on bag that fits either under your seat or in the overhead rack; this is great if you're planning on a one-destination trip to a self-contained resort hotel and want a change of clothes each day. But if you plan on moving around a lot, keep it light.

Clothing

A swimsuit is a must, and if you're not staying at one of the larger hotels, bring a beach towel.

In today's Mexico, *almost* any clothing is acceptable. If traveling during November, December, or January, bring along a light wrap since it can cool off in the evening. The rest of the year, you'll probably carry the wrap in your suitcase. For women, a wraparound skirt is a useful item that can quickly cover up shorts when traveling through villages and some cities (many small-village residents really gawk at women wearing shorts; whatever you do, don't enter a church wearing shorts). The wraparound skirt also makes a good shawl when it cools off. Cotton underwear is the coolest in the tropics, but nylon is less bulky and dries overnight, cutting down on the number needed. Be sure that you bring broken-in, comfortable walking shoes; blisters can wreck a vacation almost as much as a sunburn.

Mountain Destinations

High altitude vacations should be accompanied by a light jacket or sweater for evening wear since it does get chilly in the winter. And remember that most hotels do not have heat, so if you think that's a problem, bring your coziest pj's.

City Destinations

If you're staying in a bigger city for any length of time and planning on taking in some of the more upscale dining rooms or a show, you might want to bring something a little dressy. A few restaurants in town require male customers to wear a tie and jacket, and women in jeans are not welcome. Many travelers come in their most comfortable clothes and just bypass the fancy places, but you never know when you might miss the "really big show!"

Necessities

Experienced women travelers pack a small foldable purse into their compartmented carry-on, which then gives them only one thing to carry while en route. And be sure to include a few overnight necessities in your carry-on in the event your luggage doesn't arrive when you do. Valuables are safest in your carry-on stowed under the seat in front of you rather than in the overhead rack, whether you're on a plane, train, or bus.

If you wear glasses and are planning an extended trip in Mexico, it's a good idea to bring an extra pair or carry the lens prescription; the same goes for medications (make sure the prescription is written in general terms), though most Mexican pharmacies sell prescription drugs over the counter.

PHOTOGRAPHY

Bring a camera to Mexico! You will find some of the most unforgettable panoramas in Mexico, well worth taking home on film to savor again at your leisure. Many people bring simple cameras much like my 35-mm PHD (Push Here Dummy), which are easy to carry and uncomplicated. They are easier than ever to use, and are available in any price range. They can come equipped with built-in light meter, automatic exposure, self-focus, and self-advance—with little more to do than aim and click. Others prefer ultra-complicated 35-mm cameras (that's what Oz carries, in fact he carries three of them), which offer higher-quality pictures. For the really casual photographer, Kodak disposables are said to be a snap. I've seen some of the pix and they really aren't bad for memory photos! Kodak tells us that when the unit is sent in for processing, they are able to recycle parts of the disposable unit.

Film

Two reasons to bring film with you: it's cheaper and it's more readily available in the United States. Two reasons *not* to bring lots of film: space may be a problem; and heat can affect film quality, both before and after exposure. If you're traveling for more than two weeks in a car or bus a good part of the time, carry film in an insulated case. You can buy a soft-sided insulated bag in most camera shops or order one out of a professional photography magazine. For the average vacation, film kept in your room shouldn't pose a problem. Many varieties of Kodak film are found in camera shops and hotel gift shops in the larger cities in Mexico. In the smaller towns you may not be able to find slide film.

X-ray Protection

If you carry film with you when traveling by plane remember to take precautions. Each time film is passed through the security X-ray machine, a *lit-*

tle damage is done. It's cumulative, and perhaps one time won't make much difference, but most photographers won't take the chance. Request hand inspection, although with today's tight security at airports, some guards insist on passing your film and camera through the X-ray machine. If packed in your carry-on, it's wise to keep film in protective lead-lined bags, available at camera shops in two sizes; the larger size holds up to 22 rolls of 35-mm film, the smaller holds eight rolls. If you use fast film, ASA 400 or higher, buy the double lead-lined bag designed to protect more sensitive film. Carry an extra lead-lined bag for your film-loaded camera if you want to drop it into a piece of carry-on luggage. (These bags also protect medications from X-ray damage.)

If you decide to request hand examination (rarely if ever refused at a Mexican airport), make it simple for the security guard. Have the film out of boxes and canisters placed together in one clear plastic Ziploc bag that you can hand him for quick examination both coming and going. He'll also want to look at the camera; load it with film *after* crossing the border.

Film Processing

The traveler has several options. Most people take their film home and have it processed at a familiar lab. Again, if the trip is lengthy and you are shooting lots of photos, it's impractical to carry used rolls around for more than a couple of weeks. Lengthy periods in the heat can damage the film. Larger cities have one-hour photo labs, but they only handle color prints; color slides must be processed at a lab in Mexico City, which usually takes a week or two and is more expensive. If you'll be passing through the same city on another leg of your trip, the lab is a good cool place to store your slides while you travel. Just tell the lab technician when you think you'll be picking them up. Kodak mailers are another option, but most serious photographers won't let their film out of sight until they reach their own favorite lab.

Camera Protection

Take a few precautions with your camera while traveling. At the beach remember that a combi-

nation of wind and sand can really gum up the works and scratch the lens. On 35-mm cameras keep a clear skylight filter on the lens instead of a lens cap so the camera can hang around your neck or in a fanny pack, always at the ready for that spectacular shot that comes when least expected. If something is going to get scratched, better a US$45 filter than a US$300 lens. It also helps to carry as little equipment as possible. If you want more than candids and you carry a 35-mm camera, basic equipment can be simple. Padded camera cases are good and come in all sizes. A canvas bag is lighter and less conspicuous than a heavy photo bag, but it doesn't have the extra protection the padding provides.

Safety Tips

Keep your camera dry; carrying a couple of big Ziploc bags affords instant protection. Don't *store* cameras in plastic bags for any length of time because the moisture that builds up in the bag can damage a camera as much as leaving it in the rain.

It's always wise to keep cameras out of sight in a car or when camping out. Put your name and address on the camera. Chances are if it gets left behind or stolen it won't matter whether your name is there or not; however, miracles do happen. (You *can* put a rider on most homeowner's insurance policies for a nominal sum that will cover the cost if a camera is lost or stolen.) It's a nuisance to carry cameras every second when traveling for a long period. During an evening out, we recommend leaving your cameras and equipment (out of sight) in the hotel room, locked in a bag—unless it makes you crazy all evening worrying about it. Some hotel safes are large enough to accommodate your equipment.

Cameras can be a help and a hindrance when trying to get to know the people. Traveling in the backcountry you'll run into folks frightened of having their pictures taken. Keep your camera put away until the right moment. The main thing to remember is to ask permission first and then if someone doesn't want his/her picture taken, accept the refusal with a gracious smile and move on.

MONEY AND COMMUNICATIONS

MONEY

New Pesos

The current exchange rate at print time was about N$3 to US$1 (give or take a *centavo*). On 1 January 1993, Mexico's monetary system underwent a cosmetic change. Three zeroes were dropped from the current designations to make the **new peso** (N$). The value by and large remains the same, although the "change" has in most cases been rounded off to the next largest peso; Instead of 10,999 pesos, round it off to 11,000 pesos, drop the three zeros, and voila, you have a simple N$11. Most shops will mark goods with both old pesos and new pesos for the next year or so. New currency and coins have been issued. The peso, the basic medium of exchange in Mexico, has floated on the free market since 1976.

Usually your best rate of exchange is at the bank, but small shops frequently give a good rate if you're making a purchase. Hotels notoriously give the poorest exchange. Check to see what kind of a fee, if any, is charged. You can learn the current exchange rate daily in all banks and most hotels. Try not to run out of money over the weekend because the new rate often is not posted until noon on Monday; you will get the previous Friday's rate of exchange even if the weekend newspaper may be announcing an overwhelming difference in your favor. Cashing personal checks in Mexico is not easy; however, it is possible to withdraw money against your credit card in some banks. **Note:** Wearing a money belt is always a good idea while traveling—in any country.

After talking to many foreign travelers in Mexico, most find that it's easier to exchange U.S. dollars for pesos than many other currencies, perhaps with the exception of Canadian dollars. So you might want to come prepared with either U.S. dollars or traveler's checks. Also, you might try to spend all your coinage before leaving the country, since most banks or money exchangers will not buy peso coins with U.S. dollars.

Money In Rural Villages

Always go with pesos in hand to the small rural areas of Mexico. Even better, take them in small denominations. In most cases it's a real hassle to cash dollars or traveler's checks.

The Cost Of Traveling In Mexico?

If we had a crystal ball we could provide an answer to this question. However, like supply and demand, costs constantly change. However, we can give you a *rough* idea as long as you don't yell at us if we don't hit it on the head. We don't know your eating or drinking habits, or your choice of entertainment. Prices are in constant motion, but a conservative estimate would be as follows: *real* **budget** travelers can expect to spend around US$20-35 per day, per person. **Moderate** spenders who want more leeway can expect to spend US$35-50 per person, per day, and for the **luxury** seekers, you could hold it down to US$50-75. Of course when it comes to luxury, the sky's the limit in Mexico. Everyone must add more if renting a car and deduct a little if traveling in pairs. A lot depends on how you get around; taxis are lots more expensive than buses—trekkers get the best bargain of all.

Credit Cards

Major credit cards are accepted at all of the larger hotels, upscale restaurants in big cities, travel agencies, and many shops throughout the country. But don't take it for granted: ask. The smaller businesses do not accept them. In some cases you will be asked to pay a fee on top of your charged amount. In Mexico, gas stations *do not* accept credit cards.

Banks And Business Hours

Banks are open 9 a.m.-1:30 p.m., Mon.-Friday. Business offices are open from 8 or 9 a.m. to 1 or 2 p.m., then they reopen between 2:30-4 p.m. and stay open until 6 p.m. Government offices are usually open until 3 p.m. Stores in cities are generally open from 10-7 p.m. and close between 1-4 p.m. Government offices, banks, and stores are closed on national holidays.

Tipping

If not already included, 10-20% of the bill is standard. Tips for assistance with bags should be equivalent to 50-75 cents (U.S.) per bag. Chambermaids should receive about US$1 per day. It is not necessary to tip taxi drivers unless they have performed a special service. Tour guides should receive US$2-3 for a half-day trip and US$4-5 per day for longer trips, if they do a good job of course! Gas station attendants are tipped about 30 cents for pumping gas, cleaning the windshield, checking the oil and water, and providing other standard services. Often tips are the main part of the provider's income.

Moneda

The "$" sign in Mexico means pesos. Shops that accept dollars will often price items with the abbreviation "Dlls." If you see a price that says "m.n.," that indicates pesos, *moneda nacional.* Most large airports have money exchange counters, but the hours generally depend on the flight schedules. Always travel to a small village with pesos in your pocket. Few locals are able to exchange dollars—and especially not traveler's checks.

Traveler's Checks

Traveler's checks are the easiest way to carry money. However, certain moneychangers will pay more for cash and some banks charge a fee, so always ask before making a transaction. If you're in a really small town, don't expect the shops or vendors to cash a traveler's check; gas stations deal *only* in pesos—so far. Be prepared. If you need to change money after bank hours, look for a sign that says **Casa de Cambio.**

The favored credit cards in Mexico are **Bancomer** (Visa) and **Carnet** (MasterCard)—American Express is way down the list; in fact most businesses refuse American Express as well as Diners Club. Look for automated teller machines (ATMs) in the more modern banks. Before leaving home, ask your bank teller if your particular card is authorized for use in Mexico, and, if so, at which branches.

Admission Fees

Admissions to the archaeological sites have taken large leaps in the past few years. INAH (Instituto Nacional de Antropología e Historia) is the arm of the government that directs the museums and archaeological sites of the country. The increase in fees certainly goes hand in hand with the improvements made on the sites. All the larger sites now have, or will have soon, modern visitor's centers that include restrooms, gift shops, snack shops, museums, and auditoriums. The smaller sites will eventually all have restrooms. INAH also sets the fees, and as we go to press (and this could change at any moment) these attractions are rated "A" N$13, "B" N$10, "C" N$7, and that computes to (roughly), US$4.35, US$3.35, and US$2.35. We have in all sections of the handbook rounded off the fees to the nearest fifty cents (US$4.50). One or two sites are still in *way* out-of-the-way places that have not added restrooms or visitor's amenities—and they don't charge at all. Admission to all sites and museums is free on Sunday. **Remember:** Your video camera will cost more to admit to an archaeological site than you, about US$10. The current rumor around archaeological zones says a fee is impending for your camera as well. Admission fees do not include the services of a guide; having an English-speaking guide is really worthwhile but before you say "yes," be sure to negotiate the fee (for your entire group), how long he/she will be with you, and where you'll be taken. For up to six people, US$25 is a good starting point for negotiations. If he was *really* good, a tip is fair. By yourself expect to pay at least US$10 for the larger sites (much cheaper by the dozen) per half a day.

Admissions to state and national parks is free on Sunday. Fees range from US$0.75-2.75. At most museums picture taking is forbidden; however, in some cases if you are willing to pay a fee at the office you can then take photos—but without a tripod. Price can be per photo.

Taxes

A 10% IVA tax is added to room rates, restaurant and bar tabs, and gift purchases. When checking in or making reservations at a hotel, ask if tax has already been added. And once again, don't forget that when you leave the country or travel from Mexican city to Mexican city you must pay an airport departure tax: national departures, US$6; International departures, US$12.

COMMUNICATIONS

Telephone

One of the newest additions to Mexico is the Direct Dial USA telephone booths scattered about. Shiny new touch-tone phones bring you in direct contact with an American operator who will either charge the call to your telephone credit card or make it collect. It's quick and efficient and eliminates the language barrier as well as the often long waits. However, until they are universally installed, in the small towns still expect the same old rules; find a *larga distancia* office, jot down the number you want and wait while the operator makes the connection—have plenty of pesos handy. Hotels add enormous service charges to room calls—*always* ask what it will be first. Calling collect is cheaper, but even then, some hotels add a service charge. **Note:** Fax machines are becoming very common, but can also be expensive. In some smaller towns there is one fax that services the entire town, so if you are expecting a message it will not get to you very promptly, simply because the sender must compete with everyone else and could encounter a constant busy signal. In many of the large new modern hotels, sending a fax is a breeze.

Telegraph And Postal

Even the smallest village has a telegraph office. Wires can often be sent directly from the larger hotels. Almost every town in Mexico has a post office. If you're in a small town and can't find it by looking about, ask—it may be located in someone's front parlor. Airmail postage is recommended for the fastest delivery. Post offices will hold travelers' mail for one week if it is marked "a/c Lista de Correos" ("care of General Delivery"). Hotels will extend the same service for mail marked "tourist mail, hold for arrival."

Using The Mail

A few suggestions about the mail both going and coming to/from Mexico: **From the U.S.** never put the zip code at the end of the address, like "Guadalajara, Jalisco, Mexico, 11111"; instead, put it between the city and the state: Guadalajara, 11111, Jalisco, Mexico. When it is on the end, it has been known to go to a city in the U.S. with the same zip code.

When mailing **from Mexico,** don't drop your mail in a street slot; instead either take it to the post office or drop it in the hotel mail deposit. It arrives much quicker—usually. Always use airmail postage from Mexico, and mark it clearly with **por avión.** One more thing: don't put American postage stamps on letters or cards from Mexico, please. Don't laugh; for some reason many folks think it's okay and then cannot understand when their mail disappears.

New efficient services are popping up all over Mexico. If you need to get something to the U.S. in a hurry, you'll find all three worldwide courier companies with offices in most cities in Mexico: **DHL, Federal Express,** and **United Parcel Service.** You can get quick service both coming and going.

Radio And Television

AM and FM radio stations in Spanish are common in the cities; a few with a large contingent of retirees also broadcast in English. Television is already common. In the major cities hotel rooms have TV entertainment via satellite dishes. The large resort hotels have one or more cable stations from the U.S., on which you can expect to see all the major baseball and football games, news, and latest movies. In isolated mountain areas, broadcasts are made in several indigenous languages over the same station. The radios are also used as emergency communications since many of these areas are without telephone lines.

Reading Material

Avid readers in any language besides Spanish should bring a supply of books; English-language reading materials are for sale in limited quantities, mostly in big hotel gift shops and a few bookstores—and they're expensive. Both small and large hotels have book-trading shelves. If they aren't obvious, ask at the desk. Most travelers are delighted to trade books. In several cities in Mexico you'll find good English-language newspapers: *Mexico News* in Mexico City, *Colony Reporter* in Guadalajara, and *Atención* in San Miguel de Allende. The *News* is published in Mexico City and available in most larger cities and heavily visitied tourist destinations.

Newsletters

Some fine newsletters come out of Mexico for those interested in keeping up with tourist info and other south-of-the-border information. Many of these newsletters are put out by Americans who have retired in Mexico. They began by answering questions for others interested in doing the same thing. *AIM* is one of the best, it publishes six issues per year and is mailed to you in the U.S. for US$15. Write to Apdo. Postal 313-70, Guadalajara 45050, Jalisco, Mexico.

Another is the bimonthly *Mexico Now* from Mazatlán. It really gives a good overview of the political, corporate, and financial events going on in Mexico; bi-monthly, for subscription info, Apto. Postal 1192, Mazatlan, Sinaloa, Mexico.

Cuernavaca Calling is simpler, not nearly so professional, but it really gives a down-home feeling about the city. For information write to Apdo. Postal 4-587, Cuernavaca 62431, Morelos, Mexico.

MRTA: These folks put out an informative newsletter as well as a book for those interested in retiring in Mexico. The newsletter comes out six times a year and the fee is US$20; write to **Mexico Retirement And Travel Assistance,** P.O. Box 2190, Henderson, Nevada 89009, USA. Though they have a U.S. mailbox, that's just to expedite the post; they live in Guadalajara and are an endless source of information about living south of the border. Ask them about their book.

HEALTH

IMPORTANT NEW HEALTH REPORT

Isolated incidents of cholera have been reported in Mexico, although the U.S. has not issued a travel advisory regarding the disease for Mexico. The **Mexican Tourism Department** issued a recommendation to visitors in 1992 to be cautious; they recommend that you avoid Mexico's raw seafood delicacies (such as ceviche), drink only bottled water, and eat only cooked vegetables. In Guadalajara, the city health department has closed a number of street food stalls that sell seafood, and advises citizens to eat seafood only from reputable restaurants with proper refrigeration. The Mexican advisory stressed that the potentially deadly disease is "isolated" and "confined to rural areas." For information on specific areas contact the Centers for Disease Control in the U.S. at (404) 332-4559, or ask for the current travel advisory at the U.S. State Department, (202) 647-5225.

Cholera Symptoms

In the very unlikely event you're caught unaware, haven't spoken to your doctor, and are suddenly gripped with a watery diarrhea, vomiting, cramps, and extreme weakness, you may be suffering from cholera. Begin drinking purified water or boiled tea right away and get medical help. If you plan to visit an isolated area where there are probably no doctors, be wise; talk to

your doctor before you leave home about the wisdom of traveling with tetracycline.

Remember, pharmacies in Mexico sell many prescription drugs over the counter. Don't count on a cholera vaccination to protect you; most of the medical world is feeling it does little good. Early treatment is the best cure for cholera.

Traveler's Medical Insurance

Check to see if your medical or homeowner's policy provides coverage if you're out of the country—Medicare does not, and some of the supplemental policies do not. **Travel Med** is a company who will provide medical insurance while traveling in Mexico; for information contact Sanborn's Mexico Insurance Service, Box 310, McAllen, Texas 78502, USA.

TRAVELER'S DISEASE

Some travelers to foreign countries worry about getting sick the moment they leave their own country. But with a few simple precautions, you may be able to avoid sickness altogether. The most common illness to strike visitors is **traveler's disease,** known by many names (tourista, Montezuma's Revenge, Green-Apple Two Step) but, in plain Latin, it's diarrhea. It's no fun, and it can cause uncomfortable cramping, fever, dehydration, and the need to stay close to a toilet for a few days. It's caused by, among other things, various strains of bacteria managing to find your innards, so it's important to be very careful about what goes into your mouth.

Studies show that the majority of tourists who get sick do so on the third day of their visit, and that traveler's illness is common in every country. They say that in addition to bacteria, a change in diet is equally to blame. They suggest that the visitor ease slowly into the eating habits of the country, especially if the food tends to be spicy. In other words, don't blast your tummy with the *habanero* or jalapeño pepper right off the bat. Work into the fried food, drinks, local specialties, and new spices gradually; take your time changing over to foods you may never eat while at home, including the large quantities of wonderful tropical fruits that you'll want to eat. Blame is also shared by mixing alcohol with longer-than-usual periods of time in the tropical sun. The body chemistry is changed with alcohol, and it becomes very difficult to handle excessive heat.

It's The Water

While the above theories are often valid, water is probably the worst culprit. Drinking water from the faucet in most Mexican cities is not a good idea, nor in smaller villages and more isolated areas. Some of the larger hotels have their own purification plants on the premises, but a good rule of thumb is: if you're not sure about the water, ask the desk clerk at your hotel. They'll let you know the status. Hotels prefer healthy guests—this assures they'll return. If you are the slightest bit concerned, ask for bottled purified water.

In the backcountry, hikers may want to carry their own water and then, whether the source is out of the tap or a crystal-clear pond, boil it or purify it with chemicals (see below). That goes for brushing your teeth as well. If you have nothing else, a bottle of beer will make a safe (though maybe not sane) mouth rinse. If using ice, ask where it was made and if it's pure: *"¿purifica-do?"*. Think about the water you're swimming in as well. You may want to avoid small local pools.

The easiest way to purify the water is with purification tablets: **Hidroclonozone** and **Halazone** are two, but many brands are available at drugstores in all countries. Or carry a small plastic bottle of liquid bleach (use 8-10 drops

---

DISEASE AWARENESS

It's no fun to have a mosquito bite or two or a dozen. But if you're planning a trip to the tropics you say it's almost inevitable?—well not necessarily! Beware: a mosquito bite can be more than an annoyance; it can be the introduction to a particularly nasty ailment, malaria. But you can fight back against these flying, buzzing critters.

First of all, check with the Centers for Disease Control and Prevention, tel. (404) 332-4559, or with a physician who specializes in tropical diseases. They can advise you about the area you're going to visit. If it happens that you're going into a malaria-infected zone, there are precautions you can take. It used to be a simple matter of popping a quinine pill once a week and not to worry. But in *some* areas mosquitoes have developed a resistance to the common medications. Medication is still important. However, if you can avoid getting bitten in the first place that's the way to go.

Centers For Disease Control

Check on your tetanus shot before you leave home. If you anticipate backpacking in jungle regions on the Gulf, call the **International Traveler's Hotline** at the **Centers for Disease Control and Prevention,** tel. (404) 332-4559. This hotline advises callers of the conditions abroad and what areas are experiencing an outbreak of disease, and they will make suggestions for immunizations. It is updated as conditions warrant. A booklet also is available, *Health Information for International Travelers,* from the U.S. Government Printing Office. To obtain a copy, send US$5 to the Superintendent of Documents (U.S. Government Printing Office, Washington D.C.).

---

per liter of water) or iodine (use five to seven drops per liter) to purify the water. Whichever you use, let the water stand for 20 minutes to improve the flavor. Boiling the water for 20-30 minutes will purify it as well. Even though it takes a heck of a lot of fuel that you'll probably have to carry on your back, don't be lazy in this department. You can get very sick drinking contaminated water, which you can't identify by looking at—unless you travel with a microscope!

News Flash: We have been hearing about a rash of "new businesses" bottling water. These are often backyard operations, and while the water that they're putting into the five-gallon jugs is indeed purified, our source tells us it's the bottles that are not properly sterilized. Solution? Buy name brands that you're familiar with.

Giardiasis/Giardia

Giardia is a parasite that can be present in streams and ponds almost anyplace in the world. It can be destroyed by boiling the water. However, if fuel is a problem, the water can be treated with iodine. The amount and most efficient form of iodine (crystals or liquid?) to use are up for debate, so check with your doctor, or check out Moon's own *Staying Healthy in Asia, Africa, And Latin America.*

Water Filters

If you're going to be gone a reasonably short time, and you don't travel in the water danger zones that often, a compact, inexpensive water treatment kit (perfected by NASA) is the **PUR Traveler**, available from **Long Road Travel Supplies.** The mini Traveler is seven inches tall, weighs only 12 ounces, eliminates disease-causing protozoan cysts, bacteria, and viruses; it's effective to .005 microns (the size of the smallest virus). This little filter will give you peace of mind if you're concerned about Giardia. The replaceable cartridge purifies up to 400 liters (100 gallons) and includes a durable acrylic cup. We have used this little dynamo (while traveling in an isolated jungle area in Sulawesi, Indonesia, and we suffered nary a day of gastrointestinal problems. A couple of things to consider: the Traveler is tiny and only makes four ounces of water per pump-action; of course it's instant, so one person will find it comfortable to use. We travel with two, then we can each pump our water through without "waiting." It fits easily into a roomy pocket, even a roomy fanny pack. The PUR people have several other models that have specific purposes. Price of the Traveler is around US$60, and the replacement cartridge will get you another 400 liters (100 gallons) of water for US$20.

If you're a traveler who uses more water, travels into these areas more often, and is willing to pay more money up front, investigate the Swiss-made **Katadyn Mini** filter that will handle 4,000 liters (1,000 gallons) of water before needing replacement. This cuts the per-gallon cost of water considerably. For more information, contact **Long Road Travel Supplies,** tel. (800) 540-4763, fax (510) 540-0652. The company also sells fine-mesh insect net-tents, perfect to keep out potentially dangerous mosquitos.

Other Sources Of Bacteria

Money handling can be a source of germs. Wash your hands frequently, don't put your fingers in your mouth or rub your eyes, and carry individual foil packets of disinfectant cleaners, like **Wash Up** or the **Antibacterial Wipes** from the Magellan catalog. They're handy to use, and refreshing in the heat. Hepatitis is another bug that can be contracted easily if you're around it, especially in the rural areas of Central Mexico.

When in backcountry cafes, remember that fruit and vegetables, especially those with a thin edible skin (like tomatoes), are a possible source of bacteria. If you like to eat food purchased from street vendors (and some shouldn't be missed), use common sense. If you see the food being cooked (killing all the grubby little bacteria) before your eyes, have at it. If it's hanging there already cooked and is being nibbled on by small flying creatures, pass it by. It may have been there all day, and what was once a nice sterile morsel could easily have gone bad in the heat, or been contaminated by flies. Be cautious of hotel buffets; their shellfish may have been sitting out for hours—a potential bacteria source unless they are well iced. When buying food at the marketplace to cook for yourself, use the hints given in "Food Safety," under "Food and Drink," above.

Treatment

Remember, it's not just the visitor who gets sick from bacteria. Each year locals get sick from the same germs, and though great strides have been made in sanitary conditions in the rural areas, the government is still working hard to remedy all the problems. Tremendous improvements have taken place in the cities that ultimately will be accomplished all over the country, but it's a slow process involving new infrastructure in many cases. In the meantime, many careful visitors come and go each year without a touch of the trots. If after all your precautions

INSECT REPELLENT

There are many insect repellents around, some better than others. Read the labels and ask questions. Some formulas were designed to spray the outdoors, some a room, others your clothes—none of these are for the skin. Some repellents are harmful to plants and animals, some can dissolve watch crystals, and others can damage plastic eyeglass lenses. This can be a particular problem if labels are written in a foreign language that you cannot read. It's best to bring your repellent from home.

Many of the most efficient repellents contain diethyl-toluamide (DEET). Test it out before you leave home; the more concentrated solutions can cause an allergic reaction in some people, and for children a milder mix is recommended. Avoid use on skin with sores and abrasions.

Long Road Travel Supplies has come up with the **Indoor Travel Tent.** This lightweight, portable, net housing is made of ultra-fine mesh netting and fits right on top of the bed. A nylon floor and lightweight poles provide you with a roomy rectangular shape and free-standing protection from both flying and crawling insects that can make sleeping impossible. Convenient with a zipper door, folding flap for extra foot room, and an inside pocket for keeping valuables close at hand. Packed in its own carrying bag, and weighing just one kilogram (2.3 pounds, single bed), the price is US$79 (double weighs 1.3 kilograms—2.8 pounds—and the price is US$99). Ask about the budget-priced Indoor Tent II, with a drawstring door; single size is US$49 and weighs .55 kilograms (1.25 pounds). For more info call (800) 359-6040 or (510) 540-4763, P.O. Box 9497, Berkeley, California 94709, USA.

When using repellents remember:

✔ If redness and itching begin, wash off with soap and water.

✔ Apply repellent by pouring into the palms of your hands, then rubbing together and applying evenly to the skin. If you're sweating reapply every two hours. Use caution if perspiration mixed with repellent runs down your forehead and into your eyes—an absorbent headband helps.

✔ If you swim, reapply after coming out of the water.

✔ It's helpful to either dip your socks, or spray them heavily, or (as suggested by the World Health Organization) dip strips of cotton cloth two or three inches wide and wrap around your lower legs. One strip is effective for several weeks. Mosquitoes hover close to the ground in many areas.

✔ Apply liberally around the edges of your sleeves, pants cuffs, or shorts cuffs.

✔ Sleeping in an air-conditioned room with tight-fitting windows is one good way to avoid nighttime buzzing attacks; in other situations use a mosquito net over the bed. It helps if the netting has been dipped in repellent, and make sure it's large enough to tuck well under the mattress. A rectangular shape is more efficient than the usual conical, giving you more room to sit up so you'll avoid contact with the critters that might bite through the net.

you still come down with traveler's illness, many medications are available for relief. Most can be bought over the counter in Mexico, but in the U.S. you may need a prescription from your doctor. **Lomotil** and **Immodium** are common, and certainly turn off the faucet after a few hours of dosing. However, they have the side effect of constipation. These medications do not cure the problem, only the symptoms; if you quit taking it too soon your symptoms reappear, and you're back to square one. In their favor, Lomotil and Immodium work faster than **Pepto Bismol** or **Kaopectate,** and if you're about to embark on a seven-hour bus ride cross-country, you might consider either one of those "quick-

stop" drugs a lifesaver. **Note:** Immodium no longer requires a prescription; Lomotil, however, does.

If you're concerned, check with your doctor before leaving home. Also ask him about formulas called Septra and Bactrim that attack the "bug" that's causing the problem. Something else to be aware of; Pepto Bismol can turn the tongue a dark brownish color—nothing to be alarmed about.

For those who prefer natural remedies, lime juice and raw garlic are both considered good when taken as preventatives. However, they need to be taken in large quantities. Douse everything with the readily available lime juice (it's delicious on salads, fresh fruit, soups, rice, meat, and in drinks). You'll have to figure your own ways of using garlic (some believers carry garlic capsules, available in most health-food stores in the U.S.). Fresh coconut juice is said to help (don't eat the oily flesh; it makes your problem worse!). Plain, boiled, white rice soothes the tummy. While letting the ailment run its course, stay away from spicy, oily foods and fresh fruits. Drink plenty of pure water. Don't be surprised if you have chills, nausea, vomiting, stomach cramps, and run a fever. This could go on for about three days. But if the problem persists, see a doctor.

SUNBURN

Sunburn can spoil a vacation quicker than anything else, so approach the sun cautiously. Exposure to the sun should be only for short periods the first few days; wear a hat and sunglasses. Apply a good sunscreen to all exposed areas of the body (don't forget your feet, hands, nose, ears, back of knees, and top of forehead—especially if you have a receding hairline). Remember that after every time you go into the water, sunscreen lotion must be reapplied. Even after a few days of desensitizing the skin, wear a T-shirt in the water to protect your exposed back, especially if spending the day snorkeling, and thoroughly douse the back of your neck with sunscreen lotion. PABA—para-aminobenzoic acid—solutions offer good protection and condition the skin. PABA is found in many brand names and strengths, and is much cheaper in the U.S. than in Mexico. **Note:** Some people are allergic to PABA and it is said to cause cancer in isolated cases; check with your doctor before using. The higher the number on sunscreen bottles, the more protection.

If, despite precautions, you still get a painful sunburn, do not return to the sun. Cover up with clothes if it's impossible to find protective deep shade. Keep in mind that even in partial shade (such as under a beach umbrella), the reflection of the sun off the sand or water will burn your skin. Reburning the skin can result in painful blisters that might easily become infected. Soothing suntan lotions, coconut oil, vinegar, cool tea, and preparations like Solarcaine will help relieve the pain. Usually a couple of days

out of the sun will cure it. Drink plenty of liquids (especially water) and take tepid showers (see also the special topic "Simple First-Aid").

High Altitude Sunburn

Remember, all of the above goes double if you're trekking in high altitudes. The best preventative is layering clothes to keep the sun at bay.

ALTITUDE SICKNESS

It's not your imagination! You felt perfectly good when you got on the plane and all during the flight, but as soon as you landed in Mexico City at almost 2,240 meters (7,350 feet), you find yourself short of breath, feeling weak, and maybe a little shaky in the stomach; you might even have a headache. That's called altitude sickness. Your body needs to acclimate to the change in barometric pressure and lesser amounts of oxygen. It affects different people at different levels. Even the young athlete in tiptop body condition will need a few days to adjust—for the rest of us it can take as much as a week. Until you adjust, take it easy; not too much physical exertion, no running or climbing the pyramids—yet! Also, stay away from alcoholic beverages; they will intoxicate you much quicker and with much less alcohol than usual. If you have medical problems that relate to your heart and lungs, check with your doctor before leaving home.

HEALING

Most cities in Mexico have a hospital or medical clinic. More than likely someone there speaks English. In the bigger cities you can usually find a doctor who will make a house call. When staying in a hotel, get a doctor quickly by asking the hotel manager; in the larger resorts, an English-speaking doctor is on call 24 hours a day. A taxi driver can be your quickest way to get to a clinic when you're a stranger in town. In small rural villages, if you have a desperate problem and no doctor is around and you cannot get away, you can usually find a *curandero*. These healers deal with the old natural methods (and maybe just a few chants thrown in for good measure). This person could be helpful in a desperate situation away from modern technology. Locals who live in the dense, jungle areas inhabited by poisonous snakes go to the local "snake doctor." Again, this might be a possibility in a remote emergency situation where help is needed quickly, but yet, medical people say every time, *"no matter what,* don't go to a snake doctor." A **Cutter's Snake Bite Kit** can be helpful if used immediately after a bite, though its use/misuse is controversial in medical circles.

(continued on page 84)

SIMPLE FIRST AID

Acute Allergic Reaction

This, the most serious complication of insect bites, can be fatal. Common symptoms are hives, rash, pallor, nausea, tightness in the chest or throat, and trouble speaking or breathing. Be alert for symptoms. If they appear, get prompt medical help. Start CPR if needed and continue until medical help is available.

Animal Bites

Bites, especially on the face and neck, need immediate medical attention. If possible, catch and hold the animal for observation, taking care not to be bitten again. Wash the wound with soap and water (hold under running water for two to three minutes unless bleeding heavily). *Do not* use iodine or other antiseptic. Bandage. This also applies to bites by human beings. In case of human bites the danger of infection is high. (See also "Rabies" and "Snakebite.")

Bee Stings

Apply cold compresses quickly. If possible, remove the stinger by gentle scraping with a clean fingernail and continue cold applications till pain is gone. Be alert for symptoms of acute allergic reaction or infection requiring medical aid.

Bleeding

For severe bleeding apply direct pressure to the wound with a bandage or the heel of the hand. Do not remove cloths when blood-soaked; just add others on top and continue pressure until bleeding stops. Elevate bleeding part above heart level. If bleeding continues, apply a pressure bandage to arterial points. *Do not* put on tourniquet unless advised by a physician. *Do not* use iodine or other disinfectant. Get medical aid.

Blister On Heel

It is better not to open a blister if you can rest the foot. If you can't, wash the foot with soap and water; make a small hole at the base of the blister with a needle sterilized in 70% alcohol or by holding the needle in the flame of a match; drain fluid and cover with strip bandage or moleskin. If a blister breaks on its own, wash with soap and water, bandage, and be alert for signs of infection (redness, festering) that call for medical attention.

Burns

Minor burns (redness, swelling, pain): apply cold water or immerse burned part in cold water immediately. Use burn medication if necessary. **Deeper burns** (blisters develop): immerse in cold water (not ice water) or apply cold compresses for one to two hours. Blot dry and protect with a sterile bandage. *Do not* use antiseptic, ointment, or home remedies. Consult a doctor. For **deep burns** (skin layers destroyed, skin may be charred), cover with sterile cloth; be alert for breathing difficulties and treat for shock if necessary. *Do not* remove clothing stuck to burn. *Do not* apply ice. *Do not* use burn remedies. Get medical help quickly.

Cuts

Wash small cuts with clean water and soap. Hold wound under running water. Bandage. Use hydrogen peroxide or other antiseptic. For large wounds see "Bleeding." If a finger or toe has been cut off, treat severed end to control bleeding. Put severed part in a clean cloth for the doctor (it may be possible to reattach it by surgery). Treat for shock if necessary. Get medical help at once.

Diving Accident

There may be injury to the cervical spine (such as a broken neck). Call for medical help. (See also "Drowning.")

Drowning

Clear airway and start CPR even before trying to get water out of lungs. Continue CPR till medical help arrives. In case of vomiting, turn victim's head to one side to prevent the victim from inhaling vomitus.

Food Poisoning

Symptoms appear a varying number of hours after eating and are generally like those of the flu—

(continued)

SIMPLE FIRST AID
(continued)

headache, diarrhea, vomiting, abdominal cramps, fever, and a general sick feeling. See a doctor. A rare form, botulism, has a high fatality rate. Symptoms are double vision, inability to swallow, difficulty in speaking, and respiratory paralysis. Get to an emergency facility at once.

Fractures
Until medical help arrives, *do not* move the victim unless absolutely necessary. Suspected victims of back, neck, or hip injuries should not be moved. Suspected breaks of arms or legs should be splinted to avoid further damage before victim is moved, if moving is necessary.

Heat Exhaustion
Symptoms are cool, moist skin, profuse sweating, headache, fatigue, and drowsiness with essentially normal body temperature. Remove the victim to cool surroundings, raise the feet and legs, loosen clothing and apply cool cloths. Give sips of salt water—one teaspoon of salt to a glass of water—for rehydration. If the victim vomits, stop fluids and take the victim to an emergency facility as soon as possible.

Heat Stroke
Rush the victim to a hospital. Heat stroke can be fatal. The victim may be unconscious or severely confused. The skin feels hot and is red and dry with no perspiration. Body temperature is high. Pulse is rapid. Remove the victim to cool area and sponge with cool water or rubbing alcohol: use fans or a/c and wrap in wet sheets, but do not over chill. Massage arms and legs to increase circulation. *Do not* give large amounts of liquids. *Do not* give liquids if victim is unconscious.

Insect Bites
Be alert for an acute allergic reaction that requires quick medical aid. Otherwise, apply cold compresses and soothing lotions. If bites are scratched and infection starts (fever, swelling, redness), see a doctor. (See also "Spider Bites," "Bee Stings," and "Ticks.")

Jellyfish Stings
The symptom is acute pain and may include a feeling of paralysis. Immerse in ice water for 5-10 minutes or apply aromatic spirits of ammonia to remove venom from skin. Be alert for symptoms of acute allergic reaction and/or shock. If this happens, get the victim to a hospital as soon as possible.

Mosquito Bites
See "Insect Bites."

Motion Sickness
Get a prescription from your doctor if boat traveling is anticipated and this illness is a problem. Many over-the-counter remedies are sold in the United States: Bonine and Dramamine are examples. If you prefer not to take chemicals or if these make you drowsy, then something new, the Sea Band, might work for you. It's a cloth band that you place around the pressure point of the wrists. For more information write:

Sea Band
1645 Palm Beach Lake Blvd. Ste. 220
W. Palm Beach, Florida 33401

Medication is also available by prescription from your doctor that's administered in adhesive patches behind the ear.

Muscle Cramps
Usually a result of unaccustomed exertion, "working" the muscle or kneading it with the hand relieves cramp. If in water, head for shore (you can swim even with a muscle cramp), or knead the muscle with your hand. Call for help if needed. *Do not* panic.

Mushroom Poisoning
Even a small ingestion may be serious. Induce vomiting immediately if there is any question of mushroom poisoning. Symptoms—vomiting, diarrhea, difficulty breathing—may begin in one to two hours or up to 24 hours. Convulsions and delirium may develop. Go to a doctor or emergency facility at once.

Nosebleed
Press bleeding nostril closed, pinch nostrils together, or pack with sterile cotton or gauze. Apply cold cloth or ice to nose and face. The victim should sit up, leaning forward, or lie down with head and shoulders raised. If bleeding does not stop in 10 minutes, get medical help.

Obstructed Airway
Find out if the victim can talk by asking "Can you talk?" If so, encourage the victim to try to cough up

the obstruction. If the victim cannot speak, a trained person must apply the Heimlich maneuver. If you are alone and choking, try to forcefully cough object out. Or press your fist into your upper abdomen with a quick upward thrust, or lean forward and quickly press your upper abdomen over any firm object with a rounded edge (the back of a chair, the edge of a sink, or a porch railing). Keep trying until the object comes out.

Plant Poisoning

Many plants are poisonous if eaten or chewed. Induce vomiting immediately. Take the victim to emergency facility for treatment. If the leaves of the diffenbachia (common in the Yucatán jungle) are chewed, one of the first symptoms is swelling of the throat. (See also "Mushroom Poisoning.")

Poison Ivy, Poison Oak, Or Poison Sumac

After contact, wash affected area with alkali-base laundry soap, lathering well. Have a poison-ivy remedy available in case itching and blisters develop.

Puncture Wounds

Usually caused by stepping on a tack or a nail, puncture wounds often do not bleed, so try to squeeze out some blood. Wash thoroughly with soap and water and apply a sterile bandage. Check with a doctor about tetanus. If pain, heat, throbbing, or redness develops, get medical attention at once.

Rabies

Bites from bats, raccoons, rats, or other wild animals are the most common threat of rabies today. Try to capture the animal, avoiding being bitten, so it can be observed; do not kill the animal unless necessary and try not to injure the head so the brain can be examined. If the animal can't be found, see a doctor who may decide to use antirabies immunization. In any case, flush bite with water and apply a dry dressing; keep victim quiet and see a doctor as soon as possible. (See also "Animal Bites.")

Scrapes

Sponge scrapes with soap and water; dry. Apply antibiotic ointment or powder and cover with a nonstick dressing (or tape on a piece of cellophane). When healing starts, stop ointment and use antiseptic powder to help scab form. Ask a doctor about tetanus.

Shock

Shock can result from any kind of injury. Get immediate medical help. Symptoms may be pallor, a clammy feeling to the skin, shallow breathing, a fast pulse, weakness, or thirst. Loosen clothing, cover the victim with a blanket but do not apply other heat, and lay the person on the back with feet raised. If necessary, start CPR. *Do not* give water or other fluids.

Snakebite

If the snake is not poisonous, toothmarks usually appear in an even row (an exception, the poisonous gila monster, shows even tooth marks). Wash the bite with soap and water and apply a sterile bandage. See a doctor. If the snake is poisonous, puncture marks (one to six) can usually be seen. Kill the snake for identification if possible, taking care not to be bitten. Keep the victim quiet, and immobilize the bitten arm or leg, keeping it on a lower level than the heart. If possible, phone ahead to be sure antivenin is available and get medical treatment as soon as possible. *Do not* give alcohol in any form. If treatment must be delayed and a snakebite kit is available, use as directed.

Spider Bites

The black widow bite may produce only a light reaction at the place of the bite, but severe pain, a general sick feeling, sweating, abdominal cramps, and breathing and speaking difficulty may develop. The more dangerous brown recluse spider's venom produces a severe reaction at the bite, generally in two to eight hours, plus chills, fever, joint pain, nausea, and vomiting. Apply a cold compress to the bite in either case. Get medical aid quickly.

Sprain

Treat a sprain as a fracture until the injured part has been X-rayed. Raise the sprained ankle or other joint and apply cold compresses or immerse in cold water. If swelling is pronounced, try not to use the injured part till it has been X-rayed. Get prompt medical help.

Sunburn

For skin that is moderately red and slightly swollen, apply wet dressings of gauze dipped in a solution of one tablespoon baking soda and one tablespoon cornstarch to two quarts of cool water. Or take a cool bath with a cup of baking soda to a tub of water.
(continued)

SIMPLE FIRST AID
(continued)

Sunburn remedies are helpful in relieving pain. See a doctor if the burn is severe.

Sunstroke
This is a severe emergency. See "Heat Stroke." Skin is hot and dry; body temperature is high. The victim may be delirious or unconscious. Get medical help immediately.

Ticks
Cover ticks with mineral oil or kerosene to exclude air and they will usually drop off or can be lifted off with tweezers in 30 minutes. To avoid infection, take care to remove the whole tick. Wash area with soap and water. Check with a doctor or the health department to see if deadly ticks are in the area.

Wasp Stings
See "Bee Stings."

Self Help
The smart traveler carries a first-aid kit of some kind. Especially if backpacking, at least carry a minimal first-aid kit:

- ✔ adhesive tape
- ✔ insect repellent
- ✔ alcohol
- ✔ Lomotil/Immodium
- ✔ antibiotic ointment
- ✔ aspirin
- ✔ painkiller
- ✔ baking soda
- ✔ sterile, adhesive strips
- ✔ sunscreen
- ✔ cornstarch
- ✔ tweezers
- ✔ gauze
- ✔ water-purification tablets
- ✔ hydrogen peroxide
- ✔ iodine
- ✔ needle

Many first-aid products are widely available, but certain items, like aspirin and Band-Aids, are sold individually in small shops and are much cheaper if bought in your hometown. Even if not out in the wilderness you should carry at least a few sterile strips, aspirin, and an antibiotic ointment or powder or both. Travelers should be aware that in the tropics, with its heavy humidity, a simple scrape can become infected more easily than in a dry climate. Keep cuts and scratches as clean and as dry as possible.

Another great addition to your first-aid kit is David Werner's book, *Where There Is No Doctor*. It can be ordered from the Hesperian Foundation (P.O. Box 1692, Palo Alto, California 94302). David Werner drew on his experiences living in Mexico's backcountry to create this practical, informative book. Another excellent resource for preventing, diagnosing, and treating illnesses away from home is Moon Publications' *Staying Healthy in Asia, Africa, and Latin America*, by Dirk G. Schroeder, ScD, MPH. Schroeder has spent seven years researching health issues in, among others, Mexico and Central America.

K. A. ESCOVEDO SANDERS

MEXICO CITY
INTRODUCTION

> **Altitude:** 2,240 meters, 7,350 feet
> **Population:** 20,000,000
> **Area Code:** (5)

Located in the heart of the country, Mexico City—the world's second largest metropolis—is sandwiched between Mexico State and Morelos State. Originally, the city itself lay neatly within the borders of the country's federal capital, Distrito Federal (much like the District of Columbia in the U.S.). Today, however, with a population of 20 million and growing, Mexico City's "borders" are no longer clearly defined. The city has essentially consumed the 1,500 square kilometers of D.F., and is moving outward into surrounding Mexico State.

But none of this will be obvious (or even important) to the visitor. All you *really* need to know is that you're in the cultural epicenter of the country. Whether you're interested in ancient Aztec pyramids or rich colonial art, Mexico City (called simply "Mexico" as you'll soon discover) has it.

Mexico City is crammed with sights to see and sites to explore; archaeology and anthropology, architecture, great art, and a rich history. Don't come unprepared; this is a city of high fashion, big money, international trade, modern high-rise structures, and the best in *haute cuisine*. Length of stay is always the deciding factor, but all the time in the world wouldn't be enough for some people to probe Mexico City.

HISTORY

Mexico City cum Tenochtitlán has been the thriving center of commerce in the same location for 700 years. (See "Culture of the Aztecs" under "History" in the Introduction chapter for more.) Not many cities on the continent can make that claim. At one time, the **Valley of Mexico** was filled with numerous lakes and islands. When Cortés first saw Tenochtitlán in Lake Texcoco, its islands were covered with splendid palaces that reflected the sun in clear blue skies. Homes were built on interconnecting canals, the main

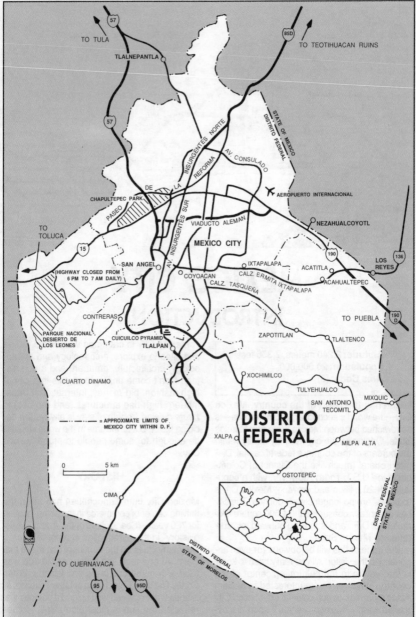

© MOON PUBLICATIONS, INC.

transport was by canoe, and efficient drawbridges kept out enemies. Marketplaces bustled with crowds of people dressed in brilliant woven and embroidered fabrics that included flamboyant feathers and gold threads. Generous varieties of fruits, vegetables, fowl, spices, and fresh fish were bartered, and rich traders from other parts of the country conducted *big* business with bird-quills filled with gold dust. It was a city of rare beauty and economic success. The Spanish would come in and change all of that, however. (See "History" in the main Introduction for more.) The next hundred years saw the destruction of Tenochtitlán, the building of the new city, the ascendancy of viceroys and bishops, the Inquisition, and plagues that would kill 70% of the native people.

Much has happened since then: Mexico City has become the second largest city in the world with about twenty million people, and the population continues to advance at a rate of 2,000 people a day.

The Indigenous People In Mexico City

The city has its ironies—colonial Mexico City was built on Indian ruins by Indian labor. Indian heritage is celebrated all around, yet the pureblooded Indian has no place here. From the days of Moctezuma, the common man may have fared better under Aztec rule than under the Spaniards. The Aztecs had their own system of class distinction. On the top of the heap were *pipiltin,* the rulers and nobles who could own land. Their children attended special schools where religion, reading and writing glyphs, and Toltecan art were taught.

The average citizens, *maceguales,* were educated in the trades learning farming and warfare; some were taught the arts, and a few became merchants. Lowest on the hierarchy chain were the *mayeques,* serfs and slaves. Though their lives were not nearly so grand as the *pipiltin,* they were not *terminally* doomed to a life of servitude (though many never made it up and out). An outstanding warrior could achieve a high rank, which held much clout in the society; a low-born woman could marry into a family of nobles. If a *maceguales* came upon hard times and was desperate he could sell himself and

his family into slavery for a given length of time (or forever), and though it surely couldn't have been pleasant, he and his family would have their most basic needs taken care of.

Today's pure indigenous groups are few. They are still independent and prefer to do things the old traditional way, and there's a new sense of pride of heritage that is no longer kept under wraps.

Visit *Now*

Sadly, the air of Mexico City is polluted with the impurities of a dense population. But it should keep no one away! The city is filled with fascinating palaces of the past. They vary from remarkable pre-Hispanic structures, to the sometimes stark stone of the 1500s, to the baroque facades and tiled domes of the 1800s. Add to that sleek steel and glass towers and together the landscape is one of the unique skylines of world capitals. But even more important, Mexico City is one of the most cosmopolitan cities of the world.

Though life on the avenues is bustling and often hectic, ambling the streets brings a new surprise at every corner. In the center of this monumental cement city, parks and plazas provide trees and flowers and bubbling fountains—small havens of tranquility. The sounds of dozens of native dialects are heard coming from people with chiseled profiles resembling those seen in ancient art. Mexico the country is a melting pot of diverse peoples with a multitude of originations. Mexico City is its nirvana, the paradise that the poorest villagers from around the vast country strive to reach. They dream of jobs and education—and not surprisingly, they often accept much less than their expectations. They stay, though, and see the possibilities of modern life all around them. Statistics prove that some of them eventually will enjoy a "piece of the pie" in this often cruel, bustling metropolis.

In Mexico City you'll find one of the most successful commerce centers in Latin America. Big corporations and foreign interests are located in the financial center of Mexico. With NAFTA now a reality, the corporate heart of the city will boom; even without it, world business is growing at a remarkable pace.

THE LAND

The city is built on an old lake bed without a rudimentary rock foundation; the result is a porous and spongy soil. As water has been pumped out of the aquifers, the city has sunk as much as nine meters over the years. Buildings are straightened and supported, but they have been structurally damaged to some extent. Newer buildings are built on floating foundations, subway tunnels float in the soil, but everything else is sinking.

Modern engineers have experimented with new ideas to eliminate the problem when building new high-rise structures. The area is a volcanic region and subject to earthquakes that have on occasion been devastating.

Weather

The city is located in a tropical latitude, but because of the high altitude (2,240 meters, 7,350 feet), the searing heat and humidity of the tropics has been "gentled" to a year-round spring. Expect summer (May-Sept.) to be warm and springlike by day, cooling down a bit in the evenings. Afternoon showers are almost a daily occurrence. A definite change of season comes Oct.-April: Dry, daytime temperatures are just slightly cooler, but evenings can be cool enough for a sweater or light jacket. Pollution is worse in the winter because of thermal inversions.

THE POPULATION OF MEXICO CITY

Yes, all roads lead to Mexico City. For over 2,000 years the central plateau has been the center of government. In 1930 the population of Mexico City was one million people, in 1970 eight million, by 1980 it had doubled again to 16 million. Today it is estimated that over 20 million people call Mexico City home—20% of the country's population lives on one percent of the land.

Air quality is bad and getting worse, potable water is scarce and diminishing quickly; still the people find those roads and come to Mexico. The government "octopus" lives here, industry lives here, and half the students in the country live here.

GEOGRAPHY OF THE CITY

MAJOR NEIGHBORHOODS OF THE CITY

Where to start? In Mexico City that's something to consider because the city runneth-over with attractions of all varieties. To see it properly, visitors should have a plan of attack; the historic center alone is a division of about 650 blocks with over a thousand buildings that hold an interest for someone, whether you enjoy the architecture, the history, the parks and plazas, the art, the people and how they meld into this city of palaces, or whether you're simply a curious traveler who's interested in seeing it *all*.

To help you implement a plan we have broken the city down into comfortable gulps of information that tell you about some of the most interesting sights in each section. Most of the areas we mention offer clusters of attractions. However, half the fun of exploring a new city is to discover it on your own.

The city is broken up into *colonias* (neighborhoods); 350 of them to be exact. Don't panic; the average visitor need only be concerned with a few. However, if you're corresponding via mail, be sure to include the full Colonia name—e.g., Rosas Moreno 71, Col. San Rafael, 06050, D.F. Mexico.

Centro

This is the heart of the city and includes the financial center of the city (perhaps even the country), with modern offices and high powered banks and financial institutions.

Zócalo

This was the focal point of the ancient Aztec city, **Tenochtitlán**. It barely skipped a beat when the Spaniards transformed it into the nerve center of Mexico. Surrounded by the most important colonial structures of its time, the Zócalo, located in the Centro, remains the hub of today's Mexico for everyday living, government buildings, and for visitors who wish a look backward to the beginnings of society on the North American continent.

La Alameda Park

Near the town center, today's Alameda Park is a broad expanse filled with trees for shade and people having fun. It gives absolutely no indication of its once barbaric past. No, not some Aztecan sacrifice, but the site of the flames of the Spanish Inquisition devouring the so-called "heretics" of the time.

Zona Rosa

Just south of Paseo de la Reforma, the Zona Rosa (the "Pink Zone") is bound by the streets Paseo de la Reforma, Insurgentes Sur, and Florencia; they form an almost triangular-shaped area. The Metro station is at Insurgentes. When you notice that all the streets are named for world cities, you're in the Pink Zone. Conveniently close to the center of the city, it is one of the trendiest areas, with smart boutiques, European-style coffee salons, lively nightlife, and upscale and moderate-price hotels.

Chapultepec

Located about five km from Centro, Chapultepec Park is the centerpiece of this area of the same name: it's filled with some of the finest museums, a castle, green grass and trees, small lakes, plenty of history, and a place for families to have a grand time. Really crowded on Sundays. The Metro stations servicing this area are **Chapultepec, Auditorio,** and **Constituyentes**. Be alert for signs that say Bosque de Chapultepec; that's Chapultepec Park.

Colonia Polanco

Located on the north end of the Reforma and north of Chapultepec Park, Colonia Polanco is fast growing into a Rodeo Drive kind of place, with modern high-rise hotels, elegant shops, art galleries, embassies, outdoor cafes, and some of the best "coat and tie" restaurants in the city. The main street running through is Presidente Mazaryk.

Xochimilco

Twenty-four km south of Centro, Xochimilco (so-she-MIL-co) is a village of canals that show just a bit of what the ancient Aztec lifestyle must

have been like on the lakes and canals surrounding Tenochtitlán. Today's visitors enjoy flower-covered Mexican gondolas drifting along the waterways; on weekends there's music and vendors floating by as well. Take Metro line 2 from downtown and get off at Tasqueña, then board a bus for Xochimilco.

San Angel

Roughly nine km south of downtown and once a tranquil little village separated from the bustle of the big city by open fields, San Angel is now an important suburb. Life still remains at an even pace, with cobblestone streets and old haciendas converted to restaurants and other businesses, but with a distinct feeling of another era. Get off at either **Viveros** or **M.A. Quevedo** Metro station and go west.

Coyoacán

About eight km south of Centro, Coyoacán is still another outlying village that the city has all but swallowed up. Today, an affluent suburb with some fine museums, plazas surrounded by outdoor cafes, and the historical fingerprint of Cortés side by side with local artists and musicians who add Bohemian color with their street displays and impromptu concerts. Take the Metro to **Viveros** station.

North Of Centro

Several important pieces of the city are near **Terminal Central del Norte,** the largest of Mexico City's four bus terminals, reached from Metro Norte del Autobuses. Or, if you're traveling by train, the lovely new **Buenavista railroad station** can be reached by the Guerrero Metro. The ancient marketplace of the Aztecs, **Tlatelocti** can be reached by Tlatelolco Metro. Nearby, the **Plaza de Tres Culturas** exhibits the cultures of the Indian, the Spaniard, and *modern* today.

MAJOR STREETS OF THE CITY

Insurgentes

Insurgentes is the longest boulevard in the city, and a major north/south route crossing Mexico City and the state of Mexico. The only name change is from "north" to "south;" Insurgentes Norte and Insurgentes Sur. Using the intersec-

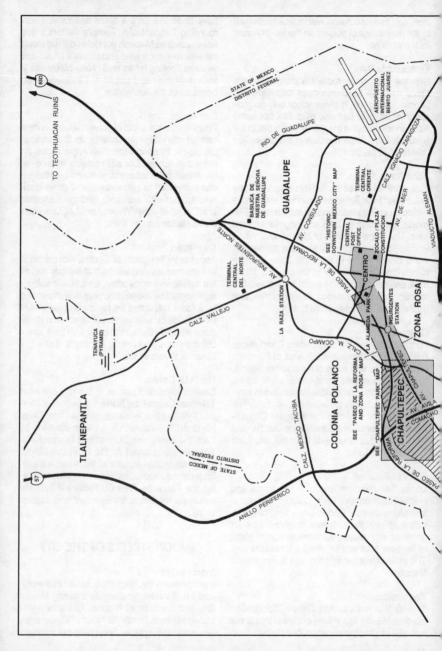

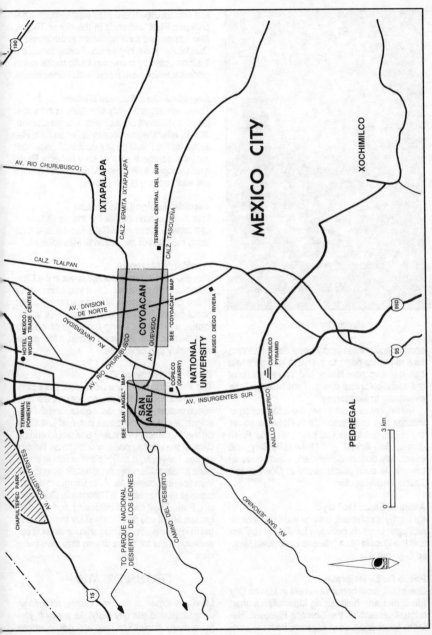

© MOON PUBLICATIONS, INC.

Mexico City avenues

OZ MALLAN

tion of Insurgentes and Paseo de la Reforma as a reference point, to the north Insurgentes is called Insurgentes Norte, and it takes you past the archaeological site of **Teotihuacán**, and eventually to **Monterrey**.

Insurgentes Sur: From the intersection of Insurgentes and Paseo de la Reforma south, the boulevard takes you past the **Zona Rosa** district, **San Angel**, and **University City**, and eventually becomes Hwy. 95, which goes all the way to such points south as Cuernavaca, Taxco, and Acapulco.

Avenida Cinco De Mayo

It's a fairly short street, but one you'll use as a direct path to travel between **La Alameda Park** and the **Zócalo** (see "Historic Downtown Mexico City" map).

Paseo De La Reforma

One of the most beautiful streets in Mexico City (designed and built during Maximilian's short reign, it resembles the Champs Elysées), Reforma takes a jog, so in essence, from the junc-

tion with Insurgentes it runs west through Chapultepec Park and ends in the city of Toluca. And it turns and runs northeast to the shrine of Guadalupe. It is a large road of many lanes, but it is interrupted by numerous traffic circles called *gloriettas*, which have monuments in the centers.

Avenida Juárez/Avenida Madero

These streets are really one fairly short street (several different blocks) with a name change. Juárez, after the intersection of Paseo de la Reforma (at the Plaza de la República) goes east past the southern side of **La Alameda Park**, then changes to Avenida Madero and continues east, ending at the Zócalo.

Avenida Hidalgo/Calle Tacuba

This avenue runs parallel to the north side of La Alameda, changes to Calle Tacuba, and runs along the back of the Catedral Metropolitan.

Presidente Mazaryke

This is becoming an important street in the Chapultepec-Polanco area. On it you'll find some of the classiest hotels and restaurants. It just about parallels (to the north) Paseo de la Reforma, which runs along the edge of what is now referred to as Polanco Colonia, a fast growing, trendy part of the city.

Periférico (Highway 57)

The Periférico is really a good idea, but again, can be confusing. Just remember that the Periférico makes a very broad loop around the city edges, and if one becomes lost, and just stays on the Periférico, eventually one would end up back at the starting point, which can be the city center. However, a major pitfall is that in some parts it has a different name; heading north, for instance, it becomes Av. Avila Camacho once it crosses the Paseo de la Reforma in Chapultepec Park. So, it can be confusing and you can get lost on it if you don't really study the map and get to know the street. This particular street is especially useful for those driving their own vehicles.

TRANSPORTATION

Mexico is expert at moving (literally) millions of people around the city daily. As a result you have many choices to help you get to where you want to go: buses, minibuses, *colectivos,* taxis, or the Metro. (Avoid the Metro during peak business hours!) Buses run frequently, and taxis are reasonable. Once at your general destination, plan on walking a lot.

Before you start out, make sure you have your most comfortable walking shoes; a fanny pack is perfect to carry necessities (put everything else in a hotel safe if available). If it's summer, and you plan to be out all day, either take cover in a cafe when the daily rains come (and they *will* come!), or attach a small folding umbrella to your fanny pack. The rain never lasts too long, and it is refreshing, cooling, and cleans the air, if only briefly. If it's winter, tie on a sweatshirt or sweater; after the sun goes down it can get a bit nippy. Now you're prepared for the weather but your hands are still free (to carry this guidebook and its maps of the areas). Enjoy!

Reminder: Mexico City is about 2,240 meters (7,350 feet) high (higher than Denver), and as such can cause problems for some people at first. If you find yourself huffing and puffing as soon as you land at the airport and begin the *long* walk to the baggage area, it's probably just the altitude. Climbing steps and running cause

the same reaction. If you're bothered (some folks aren't), for the first couple of days go easy on *really* strenuous activity. Sometimes headaches and mild stomach upset can also be part of it; doctors suggest staying away from alcoholic drinks and eating light for those first days (see the "Health" section in the Out and About chapter for more information).

Renovations

As we go to press, the downtown area is getting a facelift. Over 100 square blocks are currently being restored and renovated. Streets are being torn up and replaced with cobblestones, and old-fashioned streetlamps are replacing the less aesthetic overhead lights. Buildings are being scrubbed of age-old pollution. This may take a long time, so don't hang around and wait for it to be finished before you plan a trip. Just grin and bear it, and step around the equipment and workers. It seems that at the end of each presidential term (every six years), the money set aside for urban renewal must get spent before the next election. So, hopefully, by the time you read this, the city (and lots of other cities) should look shiny and bright and new.

HISTORIC DOWNTOWN MEXICO CITY

IN AND AROUND THE ZOCALO

The Zócalo is the second largest public plaza in the world; the largest is Red Square in Moscow. Also called **Plaza de la Constitución,** it has been a public square from the time of Moctezuma, only then it was surrounded by Azteca palaces and temples. Just south of the Zócalo was the university during the colonial era; some of the old college schools are some of the most lovely structures to visit. It continues to be the gathering place for special events in the 20th century. On particular holidays, when the plaza is crammed with locals and tourists, vendors and merchants turn out in large numbers hawking their wares. Women in black *rebozos* ask for alms at the doors of the Catedral Metropolitan next to itinerant workers sitting by their signs advertising "work for food" (getting to be a common denominator of all the big cities in the world?).

Thousands of inhabitants of Mexico gather to see the president of Mexico stand on the balcony of the National Palace and shout the Grito de Dolores just before midnight each 15 September. This is still a stirring, patriotic moment for all Mexicans, and actually for all who see it. Originally the Grito was shouted by Miguel Hidalgo in the small village of Dolores Hidalgo, and his words became the most famous in the history of Mexico: "Long live Our Lady of Guadalupe! Down with bad government! Death to all Spaniards!" It was a call to arms, a plea to end the grip of Spain from across the ocean, the beginning of what would become Mexico's independence.

And if you like churches, Mexico City has an inordinate amount of churches for a country that closed them and treated them so poorly for so many years. True, many of them are just museums today (owned by the state), but there are literally hundreds in the city.

Catedral Metropolitan

Begun in 1573, consecrated in 1667, and completed in 1813, it was the Archbishop's cathedral. Architectural style includes examples of the Gothic, baroque and churrigueresque styles. The cathedral was onceived and reconceived by the finest architects: Claudio Arciniega, Damian Ortíz de Castro, and Manuel Tolsá. The interior is buttressed by scaffolding, which detracts from the overall beauty. The main altarpiece is a stunning array of niches filled with statuary covered with gold leaf. Five naves, 14 chapels, three side altars and the sacristy are filled with colonial and European religious canvasses representing the past 450 years. The choir balcony is intricately carved and contains still more artwork and an impressive pipe organ. This cathedral is enormous and takes up one entire side of the Zócalo.

Sagrario Municipal

To the right of and adjacent to the cathedral is actually a separate church; the largest parish in the city. The richly worked facade is a monument to José Churriguera, the creator of this architectural form (churrigueresque) of expression. It is a small museum full of plans, drawings, paintings, and photos of the men responsible

for and the builders of the cathedral. The colonial ex-residence has tilting tile floors, which echo when walked on, and large windows that offer another view of the Zócalo outside.

Palacio Nacional ("National Palace")

With its *tezontle* (a type of local stone) facade this building stands on the site of Moctezuma's castle on the east end of the Zócalo. The bell above the entrance is said to be the very one that Fray Miguel Hidalgo y Costillas rang as he proclaimed his *grito*. The tradition continues each year just before midnight on 15 September, when the president of Mexico rings the bell and starts the Independence Day festivities. The overflow crowd in the Zócalo is a scene reminiscent of Times Square on New Year's Eve.

The murals depicting Diego Rivera's visions of the Great City of Tenochtitlán, the Legend of Quetzalcoatl, and the American Intervention grace the main staircase and mezzanine. The **Benito Juárez Museum** (tel. 5-522-5646) is also located here; admission is free.

Nacional Monte De Piedad ("National Pawnshop")

In case you didn't recognize the name, this is the National Pawnshop. Opened in 1777 with the dual purpose of offering low interest loans and helping the needy (literally translated the name means "Mountain of Mercy"). What a place to browse! There are all kinds of trinkets and "things" here, modern and antique, from jewelry to musical instruments (tel. 5-597-3455). Mon.-Fri. it's open 8:30 a.m.-6 p.m., Sat. hours are 8:30 a.m.-1 p.m.; closed Sunday. At 7 Calle Monte de Piedad.

Palacio Del Ayuntamiento

Occupying two buildings, which were once just one, City Hall is directly across the Zócalo from the cathedral, separated by Av. 20 de Noviembre. The facade was replaced, and a floor added to the structure by Porfirio Díaz. The original building was torched during a riot in 1692 and rebuilt in 1724. Due to the growth of bureaucracy another floor was deemed necessary and was completed in 1948.

Museo De Las Culturas

Formerly the 16th-century mint, millions of dollars worth of silver was stored here on its way to

---

WHY ZOCALO?

The word *zócalo* means "base of a pedestal." Many years back, the powers that be in Mexico City decided to construct a statue in the square and began by building the pedestal. For whatever reason, that's as far as the project got, and with their usual good humor in observing the confusion of their government, the Mexicans just laughed and began calling the square the Zócalo. This lasted long enough for the name to stick, and no matter what the formal name of many plazas, squares, and central gardens all over Mexico, they are often called *zócalos*. And by the way, the statue was never placed, and eventually the *zócalo* was removed.

HISTORIC DOWNTOWN MEXICO CITY

© MOON PUBLICATIONS, INC.

the treasury of Spain, a holding tank for the precious metal while waiting for the arrival of the yearly ships. The former mint now houses objects from around the world. The building is in an ongoing renovation mode, but it's still open for business. Calle Moneda 13 (tel. 5-512-7452). Hours are Tues.-Sat. 9:30 a.m.-5:45 p.m. and Sun. 9:30 a.m.-3:45 p.m., closed Monday.

José Luis Cuevas Museum

When you visit Mexico City see a large exhibit of the works of contemporary artist José Luis Cuevas at his own museum. The "enfant terrible" of Mexican plastic arts now has his own center for the pictorial work of Latin American artists. The José Luis Cuevas Museum, located in Mexico City's historic center, is newish and located in a 16th-century stone building, formerly Santa Ines Convent, that has been beautifully renovated. Cuevas donated about 1,000 paintings, drawings, and small sculptures to open the museum; many are his own work. You'll find a large collection (32 pieces) by Picasso and many works by Latin American artists of Cuevas's generation. One of the highlights of the museum is a striking eight-meter high bronze sculpture of a female figure that Cuevas designed especially for the center patio. Open daily except Wed., 11 a.m.-7:30 p.m., Sat.-Sun. 10 a.m.-5:30 p.m. Calle Academia 13, two blocks northeast of the National Palace and across from the San Carlos Arts Academy.

Museo De Templo Mayor

Once the holiest shrine in Tenochtitlán, the Great Temple was stumbled upon in 1978 by a utility crew working near the site. It was a magnificent discovery to find this treasure from the past. After the conquest, it was torn down by Cortés in order to build the Catedral Metropolitan. Rediscovery has yielded countless antique remnants from the earlier era. A walkway allows visitors to view the twin altars—one to the war god, Huitzilopochtli, the other to the rain god, Tlaloc—and the faded murals that surround them. The new museum alongside the temple displays many of the artifacts. A large, round stone carving shows the dismembered body of the goddess Coyolxauhqui.

The museum relates the history of the Aztecs and contains a model of Tenochtitlán. Life-sized statues of eagle warriors stand menacingly over the skulls of their victims. Located next to the cathedral; access is at Calle Seminario 8, on the corner of Seminario and Guatemala. Open Tues.-Sun. 9 a.m.-5 p.m., US$4.50 admission, free Sunday. Tours in English are available Tues.-Saturday.

Templo Mayor, The Great Temple Of Tenochtitlán

This must have been a magnificent structure. It had been rebuilt at least six times when the Spanish arrived. It is described as a truncated pyramid crowned by twin temples. Because of its location in the heart of Mexico City, the Tenochti-

Templo Mayor

OZ MALLAN

tlán site was never investigated, at least not until the accidental discovery of Templo Mayor during the subway excavations. Although there are many historical documents to relate the history of that culture, nothing tells more about a society than walking in their footsteps together with the historical data. In this case, most of those footsteps are buried under a bustling city. So, these serendipitous discoveries make archaeologists very happy. The Mexican government was very supportive at the time of this discovery; they stopped all construction on the municipal project for as long as it took to make new plans to work the modern construction *with* the temple.

Central Mercantil

Formerly the grand mercantile building, it is now the **Howard Johnson Gran Hotel de la Ciudad** (on the west side of the Zócalo). Even though it has the Howard Johnson name, which conjures visions of New York turnpikes, this is a building that everyone should stop and look at.

Built in 1899, this lovely structure makes a neck stretcher out of all comers. The art-deco interior includes a large Tiffany stained-glass dome and open-grill elevators, really quite dazzling. On Av. 16 de Septiembre 82, tel. (5) 510-4040/49, fax 512-2085. Rooms are US$99, suites are US$129.

Hotel Majestic

Next door, a 16th-century building was reclaimed some years back as the Hotel Majestic. Take a look around: on the first floor you're surrounded with stone archways and fountains; on the second floor the mix includes a glass-brick floor. Go to the seventh floor for dining while overlooking the Zócalo. If it's early enough (6 a.m.) you'll see the flag-raising ceremony, complete with uniformed guards and drums. Or, if you miss that, you may see a practically deserted plaza with only the orange-clad workers, sweeping the center of this immense plaza. The views across the Zócalo on a (rare) clear day are quite impressive. Rates US$94.50, suites US$110, at 73 Avenida F. Madero, tel. (5) 521-8600, (800) 528-1234, fax (5) 518-3466.

Along Avenida Francisco Madero

This street, from the Zócalo to La Alameda Park, contains many outstanding old buildings and established jewelry stores. **Bazar del Centro,** 30 Calle Isabel la Católica, dating to the 17th century, provides both colonial charm and modern shopping convenience in a patio setting. Shop for silver and gold jewelry and ceramics. Open Mon.-Fri. 10 a.m.-7 p.m., Sat. 10 a.m.-3 p.m.

The **Iglesia de la Profesa** ("Church of the Nun"), is on the corner of Av. F. Madero and Calle Isabel la Católica. The **American Bookstore** at Av. F. Madero 25 has a large selection of English-language books on all subjects. It's good place to stock up on reading materials if you are heading into the country (tel. 5-512-7284). Hours are 9:30 a.m.-7 p.m. Mon.-Saturday. **Palacio de Iturbide** at Av. Francisco Madero 17 is an 18th-century mansion that was restored by Banamex in 1972. This former home of Agustín de Iturbide, who was briefly Agustín I, self-proclaimed Emperor of Mexico, now houses offices of the bank and a courtyard art gallery. Open Mon.-Fri. 10 a.m.-5 p.m., Sun. 10 a.m.-7 p.m.; free.

Much of this area was residential in colonial times, and the homes all appear to be palacelike. The **Casa de Azulejos** ("House of Tiles") at Av. Francisco Madero 4 is a **Sanborn's Restaurant,** where it is always possible to see and hear Americans. There are gifts, books, and magazines as well as food and beverages; it's a great browsing place (tel. 5-518-1026, 512-9820, or 518-6676; open 7:30 a.m.-11 p.m. Mon.-Saturday. It was built in 1596 by a son to disprove his father's low opinion of him. The father's prophecy was "You will never build a house of tiles" (because the son was either shiftless or lacking in business acumen). Either way the son proved him wrong. Across the street is the **Church of San Francisco,** which was built by Cortés in 1524, using masonry stripped from Aztec temples. The painted ceiling was recently restored. The Franciscan monastery, of which it was a part, was destroyed in the 19th century.

Along Avenida Cinco De Mayo

Av. 5 de Mayo is another short street going west from the Zócalo on which many historic buildings and interesting shops can be found—plus a couple of well known eat-stops. If you have a craving for something sweet look into the **Dulcería Celaya** at Av. 5 de Mayo 39, which has a varied selection of candies and confections (tel. 5-521-1787; hours are 10:30 a.m.-7:30 p.m.).

And if you'd like a little history thrown in with lunch or dinner, or just a cold *cerveza,* stop in at the **La Opera Bar** (a long-time favorite). It's almost always crowded and you'll probably have an interminable wait for service. But it's worth it; this is a place where the walls all but shout classic history. Women weren't allowed in this male domain until the 1970s. This dark, baroque cavern of a place was built with plenty of wood and huge, mirrored booths big enough to hold a large party of revelers, or conceal a couple deep in their recesses. It is said that Pancho Villa brought his horse here for lunch, and fired his *pistolas* into the ceiling (unhappy with the service perhaps?). That's just one of many stories that could be told about La Opera. Open Mon.-Sat. noon-midnight. At Av. 5 de Mayo 10, tel. 512-8959.

South Of The Zócalo

On Av. 20 de Noviembre are shops and department stores. Calle Seminario becomes Pino Suárez, a bustling avenue due to the popularity and proximity to the Metro station, where a temple to **Ehecatl** was unearthed during the station's construction. The 21 rooms of **Museo de la Ciudad de México,** with scale models, drawings, and photos, follow the evolution of Mexico City from its founding to the present. Located in the former palace of the Count de Santiago de Calimaya, three blocks south of the Zócalo, it was built in 1558 (Av. Pino Suárez 30, tel. 5-542-0083). Open Tues.-Sun. 9:30-6:30 p.m., admission free. By the time you have this book, it (hopefully) will have reopened after repairs. The **Templo y Hospital de Jesús** was the first hospital built in Mexico City. In the chapel of this 16th-century building lie the remains of Hernán Cortés. (See also the special topic "Hernán Cortés" in the main Introduction.)

On República de Uruguay and Talavera is the **Claustro del ex-Convento de la Merced.** Moorish in style, the cloister is all that remains of the 18th-century convent that stood here. It was built in 1753 and restored in 1964.

Around Plaza De Santo Domingo

All around this plaza, which is five blocks north of the Zócalo, are buildings rife with history. The **Old School of Medicine** on the northeast corner was the center of the Court Inquisition, where trials were held and sentence passed.

The **Portales de los Evangelistas,** where letters were written for the uneducated people, now contains antique printing presses turning out handbills.

The interior of the **Ministry of Education** building is incomparable in splendor with other buildings close by, but the walls are covered with murals by Diego Rivera and his students Jean Charlot and Amado de la Cueva. Located at República de Argentina 28.

The baroque **Templo de Santo Domingo,** with neoclassical features, boasts an altarpiece executed by Manuel Tolsá and occupies the site of the first Dominican church in Mexico. It's two blocks north of the Zócalo on Calle Gonzalez Obregón, between República de Argentina and República de Brasil.

AROUND LA ALAMEDA PARK

Pushcarts and food stands, lovers arm-in-arm on benches, shoeshine stands, and the ever-present balloon sellers stand amid a moving kaleidoscope of people in La Alameda Park. The **Hemiciclo de Benito Juárez,** a marble monument built to celebrate the 100 years of Independencia, is on the south side of the park on Av. Juárez. The **Museo de la Alameda** (also known as Museo Mural Diego Rivera) houses the mural by Diego Rivera called *Dream of a Sunday Afternoon in Alameda Park.* This work once graced the lobby of the former Del Prado Hotel, a victim of old age and the 1985 earthquake. The mural portrays many of the sights seen in this lovely park, as well as the likenesses of Hernán Cortés, Porfirio Díaz, and Francisco Madero. In the forefront of the picture is a middle-aged José Guadalupe Posada (the artist who first began this unusual style) strolling with the Santísima Muerte on his arm. Santísima Muerte is a softer, less frightening descendant of the goddess Coatlicue, sort of a Mexican grim reaper often symbolized by the confectionary skulls and skeleton candies that abound on the Day of the Dead. When death comes for the macho men of Mexico, it is said to come as a woman. "Most sacred death, beloved of my heart" is a well-used phrase, I am told. Study this mural and find the artist as a young boy. Here in this beautiful park, heretics were burned during the Inquisition (alive if they refused to

Hemiciclo de Benito Juárez

OZ MALLAN

repent; renouncing their heresy brought mercy from the executioners, who would then strangle them before immolation).

In the 1800s, the memories of these dastardly acts were erased, the park was redressed with lovely fountains, a kiosk for the band, and sculptures—indeed a place for romantics, a place to see and be seen. Elegantly dressed dandies would arrive in their fancy coaches and promenade around the park. In the 19th century, La Alameda was the social "event" of the week.

The west end of the park was full of squatter shelters beginning in 1989, a protest scene for everyone who had a grievance against the government, and there were many. Now they have been relocated to the Plaza de la Solidaridad close by.

Palacio De Bellas Artes

Just a block farther you can't miss the Palacio de Bellas Artes ("Palace of Fine Arts"), located on Av. Angela Peralta. This is the showplace of Mexican culture, bordered by La Alameda, the largest park in downtown Mexico City. Construction began in 1900, during the reign of the enlightened despot, Porfirio Díaz, but then interrupted by the *revolución* and subsequent turmoil. Completed in 1934, this beautiful vision, rendered in Italian marble with neoclassic, art deco, and art nouveau motifs, was something of a white elephant from an economic point of view (total cost in depression-era dollars was US$15 million). It is so heavy that it has already set-

tled over 4.5 meters into the old lakebed. The lobby is open to the public (10 a.m.-6 p.m., tel. 5-510-1388 or 714-2111), and there's a restaurant off to the side. Several ticket windows open for advance sales to the **Ballet Folklorico** (showtimes Wednesdays at 9:30 p.m. and Sundays 9:30 a.m. and 9 p.m.) and the **Orquestra Sinfonica Nacional** ("National Philharmonic Orchestra," showtimes Sunday 12:30 p.m. and Friday 8:30 p.m.); admission is US$1.75. Murals by Rivera, Siqueiros, and Orozco cover the mezzanine walls. The only opportunity to see the Tiffany glass curtain depicting the volcanoes *Popo y Ixti* is before showtime.

Along Avenidas Juárez And Hidalgo

These two streets border La Alameda Park, and still more historical buildings abound. German-born Franz Mayer collected a vast assortment of art during his lifetime. It is now well represented at the **Museo Franz Mayer,** a 16th-century, ex-hospital building, sandwiched between colonial churches (and rebuilt after the earthquake). It contains a few canvasses by European Renaissance artists as well as *objetos de arte,* crafted in precious metals, ceramics, jade, ivory, and fabric, but mostly the exhibits are the applied arts, Mexican colonial ceramics, antique *rebozos,* furniture, weaving, silver pieces, and clocks. Av. Hidalgo 45, tel. (5) 518-2266, Tues.-Sun., 10 a.m.-5 p.m., US$1.80, Sun. is free.

Museo de la Estampa ("Engraving Museum"), just east of Museo Franz Meyer, is another reconstructed mansion of the 16th century which has a large collection of printing plates in wood and metal. So important in the past to illustrate books and periodicals, it's now a dead art because of photography; there is much of interest to see here. The etchings of José Guadalupe Posada, whose works all feature variations of the skeleton figure **La Santísima Muerte** ("Most Sacred Death"), are seen here. He is credited with inspiring the social consciousness of the great muralists, especially Rivera and Orozco, who hung around his studio as neophytes. Open Tues.-Sun. 10 a.m.-6 p.m., US$2.60. Av. Hidalgo 39.

Near the Paseo de la Reforma on Av. Hidalgo is the archaic and charming **Hotel de Cortés,** where generations of sightseers have stopped in the cool courtyard for *bebidas y antojitos* (drinks and snacks) and music. This lovely old stone building has a long history (including its use as a sanitarium) and is worth a look. Today it's also a nice central place to stay when in town (see "Mexico City Accommodations," below).

More To See Along The Avenidas
North of the Bellas Artes, between Av. 5 de Mayo and Calle Tacuba on Eje Central Lázaro Cárdenas, are the turn of the century **Bank of Mexico** and **Central Post Office** buildings (ex-palaces!). South, at the corner of Madero and Eje Central Lázaro Cárdenas, is the **Torre Latino Americana** ("Latin American Tower"), once the tallest building in Mexico. The observation deck on the 44th floor has the best view of the city and environs (when there's no smog of course!); tel. (5) 585-4200. Open daily 10 a.m.-11:30 p.m., admission charge. Check out the restaurant on the 41st floor. Built to survive the "shakes" that occasionally rattle Mexico City and its spongy foundation, the structure has withstood a couple of good ones—guess these hydro-engineers knew what they were doing!

Around the corner since 1982 is the **Museo Nacional de Arte** ("National Art Museum"). It's a lovely building, with art from all eras represented: pre-Columbian, colonial, and modern.

el Caballito

The building, once the home of the Ministry of Communication during Díaz's regime, was later used to store the National Archives. The sculpture of the mounted rider (Spain's Charles IV) in front of the museum is Manuel Tolsá's well-loved and oft-travelled *El Caballito* (only the horse is remembered fondly here in Mexico). This piece has been seen in the Zócalo, on the Reforma, and several other places since creation in the 18th century. Open Tues.-Sun. 10 a.m.-5:30 p.m. Admission is US$3.50, but Sundays are free. There's a small gift shop here. At Calle Tacuba 8.

The **School of Mining** across the street, also designed by Tolsá, has several meteorites on display in the lobby. Open 9 a.m.-8 p.m. Mon.-Fri.; at Tacuba 5.

PASEO DE LA REFORMA AND ZONA ROSA

Paseo de la Reforma starts on the west side of Chapultepec Park and runs north through the city toward the **Plaza de Los Tres Culturas** and the **Basílica de Guadalupe.** The Emperor Maximilian used the Champs Elysées as his blueprint for this wide boulevard. Along the stretch between Chapultepec Park and Av. Juárez are traffic circles, or *gloriettas,* which boast statues of historic figures or a fountain.

ZONA ROSA

Traveling northeast on Reforma from Chapultepec Park you'll enter the **Zona Rosa,** a *colonia* (neighborhood) that has been the center of charm and trend since the 1950s. The gilded statue in the first *glorietta* (at Av. Florencia) is called the *Monument to Independence,* with the *Angel of Independence* atop. It marks one end of the Zona Rosa. The angel fell off her pedestal during the earthquake of 1957, but was restored. She continues to light up the night high above the busy *glorietta* below. Note: All the *calles* within the area are named for cities of the world.

You'll find shops and restaurants, major hotels, airlines, banks, and European-style outdoor cafes. There's a **Craft Market** on Londres and Amberes, and most of the shopkeepers in the area speak English; some accept U.S. dollars. Calles Copenhagen and Génova are pedestrian-only streets full of shops, sidewalk cafes, and a pleasant respite from the peccadilloes of Mexican drivers. The **U.S. Embassy** is on the north side of Reforma, near the **Sheraton Hotel.** Nightlife is abundant in the hotels, and shopping is the activity of choice. One block southeast of **Sullivan Park** (also known as **Jardín del Artes**) there are impromptu showings by local artists each Sunday.

A statue of **Cuauhtémoc,** the leader of the Aztecs who directed the last defense of Tenochtitlán and who was executed by Cortés, stands at the Av. Insurgentes *glorietta.* This marks the eastern boundary of Zona Rosa.

The Zona Rosa started as the "in" place in the 1950s, where classy hotels dominated the skyline, and lovely homes accommodated the crème de la crème of the city. And then the zone started to age following an earthquake or two, and Colonia Polanco began competing for the *numero uno* title. Zona Rosa got the message, and has since spruced up; it's looking better all the time. Granted, a lot of the hotels have some years on them, but they also have acquired their own unique character. Look around for yourself, and stop for *un cafecita,* a cup of coffee (and remember, no free refills).

Colonia Polanco

This neighborhood is on the north edge of Chapultepec Park. No doubt about it: If you want upscale lodgings, dining, and shopping, you're looking at the right place. Some really fine hotels are located here, and more are coming. Trendy shops carry top-of-the-line designer clothes, and if you're looking for gourmet food, you will find many possibilities here. Just bring your wallet, since most of these are well above the moderate price range.

EAST OF THE ZONA ROSA

Avenida Juárez

Av. Juárez crosses Paseo de la Reforma after leaving the historic district and comes to an end at the **Monumento a la Revolución** ("Monument to the Revolution"). Here the remains of two colonial heros are interred: Venustiano Carranza and Francisco Madero. This massive memorial of marble and basalt stands amid the glass-faced buildings of modern Mexico. Porfirio Díaz planned this as the new capitol building; his successors in the 1930s turned it into a reminder of his downfall. The **Fronton** on the north side is where the speedy game of jai alai is played. A lovely branch of **Prendes Restaurant** also can be found here; tel. (5) 546-0487, Plaza de La República 17-A.

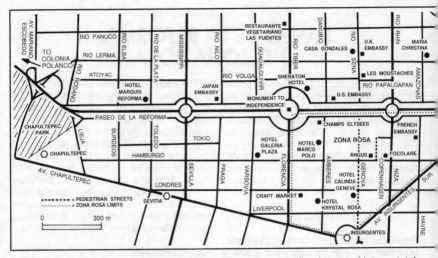

On the southeast end of the memorial is Calle La Fragua, which will join Reforma at the **Glorietta de Colón,** dedicated to the founder of the New World, Cristóbal Colón (Christopher Columbus), one block south of the monument.

The **Lotería Nacional** tickets are drawn three times a week at the headquarters building. You can't miss it; look for the art-deco building. Everyone is invited to come to the auditorium and watch the numbers pulled (begins promptly at 8 p.m.). Mexicans take their lottery very seriously. Located at Plaza de la Reforma 1, 6th Fl., Col. Tabacabra.

Avenida Hidalgo

Across Reforma, Hidalgo becomes Puente de Alvarado, a tree-lined street of large, stately residences. On the corner of Calle Ramos Arizpe is the **Museo de San Carlos,** an 18th-century mansion designed by that busy architect, Manuel Tolsá. Early on it was the home of the Marqués de Buenavista, later an art school once attended by Diego Rivera and José Clemente Orozco. Today it is filled with the work of European artisans of that early epoch, donated by King Charles IV. Titian, Rubens, El Greco, Rembrandt, Velázquez and Tintoretto are all represented. Open Wed.-Mon., 10 a.m.-5:50 p.m., tours available, admission US$2.50; Sun. admission is free (Puente de Alvarado 50). A small bookstore is on the premises and a charming little park is next door.

CHAPULTEPEC PARK

Long before the Spanish set foot in the New World, Chapultepec Park was important to the inhabitants of the Valle de México. Even then it was called **Cerro de Chapultepec** ("Grasshopper Hill"). The drinking water for all the people in the valley came from the underground springs in the Chapultepec foothills. Historians tell us that Aztec kings kept summer homes in these woods, and here they would have a gentleman's hunt. Eventually, Spanish viceroy Matias de Galvez imitated the Aztec leaders, and he too kept a summer home in the park, which ultimately became Mexico's **Military Academy.**

Today, this is very much a people's park; no signs here say Stay Off The Grass! In fact, on Sunday the grass is littered with people of all ages. Families come to have picnics and relax in the quiet strip of green in the middle of this busy city of cement. The park offers flowers and trees, sculptures and monuments, lakes with swans and boat rides, and wide paths filled with people bicycling and jogging. The large numbers and

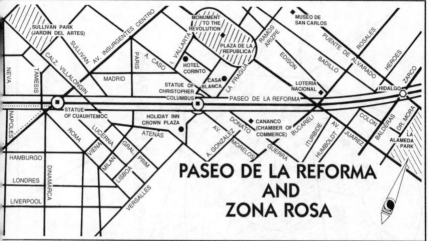

PASEO DE LA REFORMA
AND
ZONA ROSA

© MOON PUBLICATIONS, INC.

the size of the park (850 hectares) have created a logistical nightmare to keep up, and keep clean, but for the most part it's accomplished. It is usually quite inviting, especially after the summer rainy season when the grass is lush and green. The only time it looks a little messy is after a holiday weekend when thousands of people have picnicked in the park; however, you'll see all kinds of trash cans, even ones marked to separate glass, paper, etc. Within the confines of the park is an authentic castle and five other marvelous museums, including the **Museo de Antropología** ("National Museum of Anthropology"), one of the most extraordi-

nary museums in the world. The museums are world class and kept accordingly. The president's official home, **Los Pinos,** is also located in the park.

Seeing The Park

If you plan on covering the entire park thoroughly (that's eight square kilometers), it will take several days to do it properly. And like the Louvre in Paris, that's really the way to do it. Study the maps and the various installations, and allot a day or a time for each museum or site that you wish to visit. Otherwise, much of your time will be spent getting from point A to point B.

PAPALOTE CHILDREN'S MUSEUM

A wonderful thing has happened in Mexico's Chapultepec Park; a brand new children's museum. And it is attracting children from one to 100, it's that fantastic. One of the most impressive displays is the musical staircase. Remember the giant piano keyboard Tom Hanks "played" in the movie *Big?* This was designed by the same man. Come and "climb" your favorite tune. That's just one of the great presentations that all kids (young and old) will enjoy. Check out the five-story maze, a motion machine that runs for 600 feet, an immense mobile that is either a kite or a butterfly (depending on the viewer's perception), a wonderful rainforest tree, plus 250

more exhibits that give kids a hands-on, foot-stomping experience they won't soon forget. Probably the most spectacular is the fantasy maze and light show within a green tile sphere that's five stories tall.

This was the baby of Cecilia Occeli de Salinas (wife of president Carlos Salinas de Gortari. Opened on Nov. 5, 1993, it's the newest museum in the park. You can't miss it; it's a beautiful building covered in bright blue tile (the first tile building constructed in Mexico in 100 years!) Located at Chapultepec Park, on Constituyentes s/n, in the second section. Open daily except Monday 9 a.m.-6 p.m., admission US$5, tel. (5) 286-0505 or 286-0510.

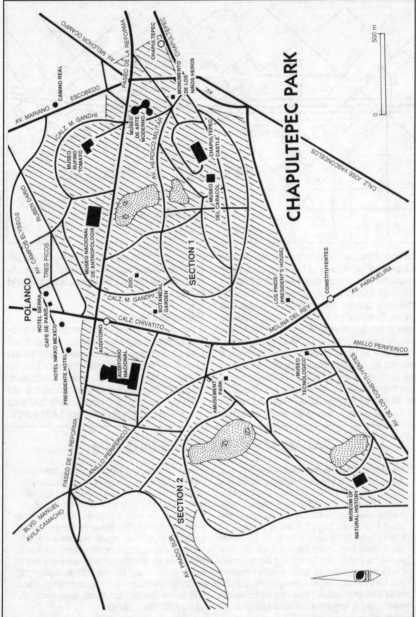

CHAPULTEPEC PARK

500 m

0

AV. MELCHOR OCAMPO

PASEO DE LA REFORMA

MONUMENTO CHAPULTEPEC

CHAPULTEPEC

AV. NINOS HEROS
DE LOS

ESCOBEDO

AV. MARIANO

CAMINO REAL

CALZ. JOSE VASCONCELOS

CALZ. M. GANDHI

Museo
DE ARTE
MODERNO

AV. HEROICO MILITAR

CHAPULTEPEC
CASTLE

MUSEO
RUFINO
TOMAYO

MUSEO
DEL CARACOL

RUBEN DARIO

AV. CAMPOS ELYSEOS

MUSEO NACIONAL
DE ANTROPOLOGIA

SECTION 1

TRES PICOS

ZOO

CALZ. M. GANDHI

POLANCO

BOTANICAL
GARDEN

CALZ. CHIVATITO

LOS PINOS
(PRESIDENT'S HOUSE)

HOTEL SIERRA

AUDITORIO

AV. PARQUELIRA

CAFE DE PARIS

MOLINA DEL REY

CONSTITUYENTES

HOTEL NIKKO MEXICO

AUDITORIO
NACIONAL

ANILLO PERIFERICO

PRESIDENTE HOTEL

AV. DE LOS CONSTITUYENTES

AMUSEMENT
PARK

MUSEO
TECNOLOGICO

ANILLO PERIFERICO

PASEO DE LA REFORMA

SECTION 2

BLVD. MANUEL
AVILA CAMACHO

AV. PRADO SUR

MUSEUM OF
NATURAL HISTORY

© MOON PUBLICATIONS, INC.

There are many vendors and several cafes at the park; the cafes in the second section are for the most part expensive and quite nice, and as is the case everywhere, vendor-food is always chancy. So if you're on a budget, you might want to bring a snack to eat in the park. If money is no object, stop in at one of the two lovely cafes on the lake. They serve a sensational champagne brunch on Sunday, and it is a little dressy (and costly).

Getting To And Around Chapultepec Park

The park is divided into **Section 1** and **Section 2.** On Paseo de la Reforma, look for any bus that's marked with Ruta 76 "Auditorio," or "Km 13." The bus goes along Reforma and will stop at the entrance of the Anthropology Museum; this bus runs frequently throughout the day. Once you have become familiar with the Metro, that's another option. Line 1 goes to the Chapultepec Station (on the east edge of the park), and Line 7 will take you to Auditorio, which is closer to the Anthropology Museum. See "Mexico City Metro" map for more information. If you take a taxi, be definite about where you wish to be dropped off; the park is quite large. It's easy to spend a whole day at the park, and for the real museum buff, it's not enough time.

Museo Nacional De Antropología

Without a doubt, this is the most important museum in Mexico. The treasures of all the civilizations that made the country great are displayed in this beautiful, understated, showcase-building designed and built in 1964 by Pedro Ramírez Vázquez. As you pass the entrance into the central patio, a sheer curtain of water drops from the top of a huge concrete column. The column is covered with reliefs that portray events in the development of the country, and it's topped with a concrete overhang referred to as an "umbrella." The effect is lovely, tranquil, and cooling—liquid art. The patio is surrounded by exhibit salons. Within the rooms visitors will see precious jade carvings, stylish gold jewelry, funerary pottery, polychrome pieces, animated whistles, obsidian carvings, reproduced murals from excavated sites deep in southern jungles, immense Olmec carvings, and maybe the most exciting of all, the Aztec Calendar Stone in the Aztec Salon.

The museum is arranged on two floors and around several courtyards. Each salon on the first floor exhibits a geographic area or culture; the second floor addresses the ethnography or characteristics of the people in today's Mexico. Each of these salons is well marked.

A real museum buff would spend a *minimum* of an entire day touring. Take in the museum's 20-minute orientation film (*Man in Mesoamerica*), study its exhibits, browse through its great Spanish and English bookstore (with a lot more than books for sale), walk its four kilometers of walkways and salons, and catch your breath under an umbrella while enjoying an alfresco lunch or snack at the lower-level cafe. Save a little time to observe a slice of everyday Mexican life; lots of schoolkids come to the museum on field trips, and they all love to play, touch, and splash in the fine waterfall that spews from its modernistic "umbrella" in the central courtyard.

At The Entrance: Buy your ticket at the entrance, and if you wish to take pictures you have to get special permission (and pay a fee). The last time out, no one (in charge that is) was too thrilled about the picture-taking; if you have a video camera, it's even less welcome, and the fee is US$10 (for your personal use only; for professional use it's much more). **Note:** No flash photography is allowed. If you don't want to pay the fee, you can check your cameras and anything else not needed. Entrance fee is US$4.50 (and has been going up each season lately), but is free on Sunday (when it's always jampacked!); open 9 a.m.-7 p.m. daily except Monday.

Chapultepec Castle

This is the castle of the gallant but ill-fated couple, Emperor Maximilian of Hapsburg and Empress Carlota of Saxe-Coburg, who sought to bring the European pomp, ceremony, culture, and court to a republican nation. On a 60-meter-high bluff overlooking the city, Maximilian commented that the views from Chapultepec, taking in the valley and the mountains, reminded him of the views from his Miramar Palace in Trieste. Carlota stood in her formal rooftop garden and could watch Maximilian in his carriage all the way along the Reforma to the palace. No doubt the air was totally free of smog and remarkably clear then.

Chapultepec was desirable real estate from

the time the Aztec kings kept a hunting residence here. The Spaniards constructed a chapel in 1554, and in the 1780s built a summer palace for the Spanish viceroys. But not until Maximilian and Carlota took over did it attain the regal flavor of an emperor's residence, a real castle. Apparently, Maximilian devoted much of his time to creating his own bit of Europe, with flowered terraces, a formal rooftop garden, and grand salons; he was criticized by his contemporaries for the time and money spent to beautify his palace and the city.

After Maximilian and Carlota were overthrown by Benito Juárez, the castle was never the same. It was used as the presidential residence until the 1930s, and in 1940 it became a museum while the surrounding area became a park.

The castle has been restored to an approximation of its grandeur at that time. Murals by Diego Rivera, José Clemente Orozco, Juan O'Gorman and David Alfaro Siqueiros have been added since Maximilian's occupancy. Visitors find a gallery of the Viceroys, also known as the Accountants of the Empire. No one should

castle guard

OZ MALLAN

miss a visit to the castle, with its arrow-straight, statuelike guards dressed in tall crowned hats. They look as though they're straight from the pages of a Grimm's Fairy Tale Storybook. Tours are available in English; the castle is open 9 a.m.-5 p.m.; admission is US$4.50. The castle is at a hill in the first section of Chapultepec Park, on Av. de Los Niños Héroes.

Museo Caracol

This museum is also called **Museo Galería de la Lucha del Pueblo Mexicano por su Libertad.** Though quite close to the castle, the entrance is a little difficult to find, so keep looking. This snail-shaped building is named for the struggle of the people on the road to liberty. The circular building contains exhibits that include dioramas, photographs, and displays explaining Mexico's fight for independence, freedom, and reform. Weapons and uniforms are also on display. At the end of the winding corridor the impressive stark, red-stone display of the Mexican flag depicts a carved eagle standing guard above a replica of Mexico's 1917 Constitution. Open Tues.-Sat. 9 a.m.-5 p.m., US$2.35; Sun. 10 a.m.-4 p.m., free. Look for this building partway down Chapultepec Hill on the south side of the castle.

Monumento De Los Niños Héroes

Nearby, this monument commemorates the six young cadets who lost their lives when Chapultepec Castle was stormed by U.S. troops during the American Intervention of 1847. On 13 September 1847, the six young men defended their academy with all the strength they could muster. Finally, when their position seemed hopeless, they wrapped themselves in their flags and jumped from the castle to their deaths.

On 13 September, the anniversary of the event, a somber memorial to their death is relived. Roll call is taken and as each boy's name is called out to the silent crowd, they answer as one, "He died for his country."

Museo De Arte Moderno

Designed by Pedro Ramírez Vázquez (of Museo Antropología fame), the Museo de Arte Moderno ("Museum of Modern Art") shines with glass and marble everywhere you look. Galleries are located in four main salons, and you can't miss the impressive stairway in the main lobby. Three galleries have changing exhibits, and a permanent collection of 20th-century Mexican art is well represented by the big names of Rivera, Siqueiros, Orozco, and Tomayo. Cross the moat and you'll find other salons and displays. Good stuff here! Open daily except Mon. 10 a.m.-6 p.m., admission US$3.

Museo Rufino Tomayo

Rufino Tomayo was first a Mexican (a Zapotec Indian from Oaxaca), and secondly an artist. The man deeply loved his people and used his talents to bring them beauty and art. On canvas he brought to life what he felt *was* Mexico. He used magnificent deep earth colors, and his imagination would fly like the wind; his works are universal and timeless. Tomayo died in 1991 at the age of 91. In 1981, he and his wife Olga gave the people of Mexico this airy museum along with a fabulous collection of modern art, consisting partly of his works, and partly of the work of others. Tomayo is highly respected by the people of Mexico. A modernistic red sculpture sits in front and the bulding is surrounded by fine gardens. World-class traveling exhibits change frequently. Check the local newspapers or the tourist office for a current list of exhibits. Open Tues.-Sun. 10 a.m.-6 p.m., admission US$3; it's located east of the Anthropology Museum, very close to Paseo de la Reforma.

Amusement Park

Not just for the kids, there's an amusement park for the adults, two for the kids, and one for very young children. Admission is about a dime, and that includes all rides except the roller coaster. It gets wild with "short" people on the weekends. Open Wed. and Thurs. 11 a.m.-5 p.m., Sat.-Sun. 10:30 a.m.-7 p.m. It's a 15-20 minute walk north from the Museum of Natural History.

Zoo

The most famous inhabitants of the Chapultepec Zoo are the pandas and their babies. They have a deluxe home behind glass and seem as happy as larks—or pandas. As we write this, the zoo is undergoing major renovations; hopefully by the time you read this, it's completed. There's a lot to this zoo, however, and if you're tired of walking take the mini-train from the station in the center of the zoo. The train will take you past the animals, from polar bears to zebras. Of course you can expect a lot of kids joining you on board; it's all part of the fun. Admission to the zoo is free, but there is a small charge for the train ride. Open Wed.-Sun; located next to the Botanical Garden.

Botanical Garden

Along with the zoo, the Botanical Garden is closed and also undergoing a facelift. We have heard rumors that the "new" garden will be brilliantly redesigned, separated into ecosystems—jungle, selva, desert, etc. From the outside it looks like there will be a giant walk-through aviary. By the time you visit, the Botanical Garden of Chapultepec Park should be in full service.

Museo Tecnológico

Just as it says, technology is the star, from the planetarium in the polyhedral dome to the masters of science who started with telephones and ended up with fax machines. You'll find mockups of a variety of high-tech exhibits, including trains and planes—and you'll see tons of students enjoying every bit of it. Downstairs is a cafeteria with snacks and cold drinks. Open Tues.-Sat. 9 a.m.-4:45 p.m., Sun. 9 a.m.-1:45 p.m., free.

Museo Nacional De Historia

This natural-history museum exhibits the evolution of the planet and how the species have developed over the years. Note the dioramas with animals placed in their natural habitats. Located in the second section of the park; open Tues.-Sun. 10 a.m.-5 p.m.

AROUND MEXICO CITY

SIGHTS NORTH OF THE CITY

Guadalupe
Basílica de Nuestra Señora de Guadalupe:
The shrine of the patroness of Mexico is the most visited in the country. The village around the new basilica (1976) contains the old basilica (1709), the Capuchin Church and ex-convent (1787), and the Capilla Pocito (1791). The religious art museum contains oils and sculptures of the vice-regency.

Every year, 12 May brings a million people to worship at the shrine from all over the country. This is where you see the holiday of Guadalupe and its emotional impact on the people. The **Basílica de Guadalupe** is eight kilometers north of the city center and can be reached by either the Basílica or La Villa Metro.

Tenayuca
On the northern edge of Mexico City, in a neighborhood called **Tlalnepantla,** is a classic Chichimec-Aztec pyramid, Tenayuca, with two parallel stairways that lead to separate temples on top. Occupied at least during the 11th century and possibly before, six known buildings were raised here, each built over the other at 52-year intervals. The last-built was destroyed and only the stairs remain. Remnants found of **Talud Tablero** (a building style of the Toltecs) indicate it was occupied by Teotihuacáns at one point in time. Note the striking architectural similarities between Tenayuca and the Templo Mayor downtown. Open daily except Mon. 9 a.m.-5 p.m.; admission US$3.35. To get to Tenayuca from the **La Raza** Metro station, look for a *pesero* that's marked "Pirámide." These small vans run frequently and are pretty cheap.

SIGHTS SOUTH OF THE CITY

At one time most of the following areas were really suburbs of Distrito Federal, but the busy city has overlapped them all. A few blocks south of Paseo de la Reforma, on the edge of the Zona Rosa, is the Insurgentes Metro station, a bustling plaza of shops, stores, eateries and street vendors. Av. Insurgentes Sur bisects the city, the main artery feeding the suburbs to the south. The neighborhoods near the city center have shops and restaurants with moderate price tags; farther out the prices rise steeply. South of the Miguel Alemán Highway the unfinished Hotel Mexico/World Trade Center monolith rises high into the air.

Pedregal Copilco
No matter how many times I do it, it's still a little shocking to think that you can just flag a taxi and ask to go to the nearest remnant of a thousand-year-old society. Such is the case in Mexico City.

Before the construction of Teotihuacán, about 100 B.C., lava from the eruption of the **Xictle Volcano** covered a 40-square-kilometer area south of Mexico City, and buried what is believed to have been the oldest settlement in the Valley of Mexico. At the quarry of nearby **Copilco,** archaeologists have found remnants of a civilization dating back to the mid-pre-Classic period (1200-400 B.C.).

If you're visiting Pedregal and you have the opportunity to look around, go through a residential area called **Gardens of the Pedregal;** you'll find contemporary modernistic homes in the lava landscape—it's a stunning setting.

Cuicuilco Ruins
We see only a few "round" structures built by the early indigenous people of Mexico. Cuicuilco was built in approximately 600 B.C. and the ceremonial center was active around 600-200 B.C. The pyramid measures 118 meters in diameter and is 18 meters tall. The site contains a rare circular platform with two ramps leading to the top. When Xictle erupted, the base of the pyramid was buried with lava, along with other structures that made up the settlement of about 20,000 inhabitants. Much of the lava has been removed, making it possible to see the construction of the pyramid.

Take a look at the small **museum** nearby for information about the people and a few artifacts found at the site, along with descriptive paintings, and note the image of the fierce fire and volcano god. Cuicuilco site and the museum are open Tues.-Sat. 10 a.m.-5 p.m., Sun. 10 a.m.-4 p.m.; admission to the museum is US$2.50, free on Sunday. It's easy to get here from the University on a bus marked "Cuicuilco" traveling south on Insurgentes.

COYOACAN

Once an affluent suburb but now part of the city, Coyoacán is a place favored by artists and academia alike. Located eight kilometers south of the Centro, Coyoacán means "The Place of Coyotes"; the only coyotes evident today are found in the central fountain of **Parque Centenario.** Coyoacán is a marvelous combination of beautifully sculptured shrubs, rainbow beds of flowers, narrow streets, and alleyways that are barely wide enough for a car. Discover good cafes under brightly colored awnings, and organ grinders playing beneath towering trees. Sample the varied menus or just have a banana split at **El Fogoncillo.** If you're into the current "I Love Frida" craze, you'll find still another museum dedicated and filled with artifacts and art that describe the life of Frida Kahlo (see below). If you're just here for the day, wear your good walking shoes and enjoy exploring the city.

Iglesia De San Juan Bautista
Built in 1589, the church graces nearby **Plaza Hidalgo,** and one of Cortés's *casas* is located behind it. The surrounding streets are chockablock with beautifully renovated colonial homes.

Museo Frida Kahlo
Coyoacán is lined with signs pointing to the Frida Kahlo Museum—it's worth the walk if it's open (sometimes it's not). Acclaimed by critics and collectors worldwide, this woman's works are selling for seven digit denominations (US$). Madonna has become one of her biggest fans and hopes to portray her in a movie. Frida Kahlo was married to artist Diego Rivera for many years (actually she married him twice), and was an artist in her own right. She suffered a crippling injury in her early years; her life was one of pain and self-loathing. She was born in this startlingly blue house; she later lived with (and without) Rivera for 25 years until her death in 1954.

BOB RACE

Frida Kahlo

Kahlo collected an eclectic assortment of art. The collections in the museum contain excellent pre-Columbian artifacts, and Mexican folk art, as well as representations of some well-known artists including José Clemente Orozco, Paul Klee, and of course Rivera. Probably the most fascinating are the works of Kahlo depicting her life-long search for serenity, which included a love affair with the Communist ideology. Stalin appears in her work as a champion. Kahlo was said to have had a close relationship with Leon Trotsky (his museum is nearby). The garden here is a nice stopping spot for reflection on the artist's life. Calle Londres 247, tel. (5) 554-5999, open Tues.-Sun. 10 a.m-1 p.m. and 3-6 p.m., US$3.35.

Museo Leon Trotsky
Leon Trotsky's house really does look like a fortress; this was done intentionally to offer him protection. His retreat has been preserved as a historical museum. His furniture and possessions are of less interest than the house itself, except for his study. Once great friends with

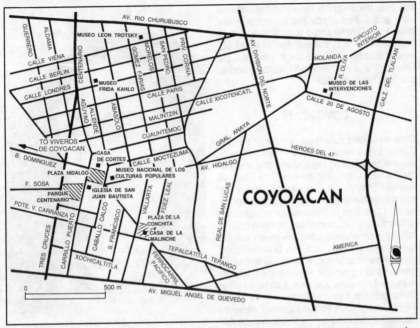

Rivera, he moved here after an affair with Frida Kahlo. There are photographs of Trotsky, his wife Natalia, Rivera, and Kahlo.

He came to Mexico in 1937 to seek asylum at the invitation of Rivera and Kahlo; because of them, then-president Lázaro Cárdenas allowed him to stay. Convinced that Joseph Stalin was trying to kill him, Trotsky hired mercenaries as protection and seldom ventured out of the house.

In 1940 his worst fear became reality. A Spaniard, Ramon Mercader, after convincing him of his friendly motives, murdered him inside the house while he worked at his desk. The room was left untouched; every paper and book remains the same. On Calle Viena 45, open Tues.-Sun. 10 a.m-5 p.m., admission US$4.

Casa De La Malinche

Another bit of Cortés's past can be found just off **Plaza de la Conchita;** it's the house of his Indian lover/interpreter, Malinche. Her house is rife with history, myths, suppositions, and maybe even a ghost. Today's Mexicans revile Malintzin (Indian name) for her part in conquering Mexico.

She was more than just an interpreter; she taught Cortés how the people thought and acted, enabling him to conquer the land.

Viveros De Coyoacán

The *viveros* (nurseries) of Coyoacán make up a cool park where you might want to rest your feet under shady trees, and just enjoy. Open to the public 6 a.m.-7 p.m.

Museo Nacional De Los Culturas Populares

The National Museum of Popular Cultures is a place where different customs and crafts from all over Mexico are performed and created. Exhibitions are changed frequently, are very informative, and are always fun to watch. On Calle Hidalgo 289, open 10 a.m.-6:00 p.m., free.

Museo De Las Intervenciones

On the grounds of the **Churubusco ex-Convento,** where General Anaya surrendered his sword, the convent has been turned into the Museum of Interventions, a Mexican term for invasions. Here you'll find dioramas of gigantic proportions depicting various battles against French and U.S. forces. Of particular interest to history buffs, all sides are treated fairly and without animosity. Note a plaque that commemorates a group of Irish-American soldiers who fought on the side of the Mexicans. Called the St. Patrick Battalion, those who survived the battle were executed in 1847. Calle 20 de Agosto at Gral. Anaya, tel. (5) 604-0699; open 9 a.m.-6 p.m. Tues.-Sun., US$3.50.

Museo Anahuacalli/Diego Rivera

Designed and built by Diego Rivera to contain his massive collection of pre-Columbian treasures, over 60,000 artifacts from the Zapotec, Toltec, Teotihuacán, Veracruz, Mixtec, and Aztec cultures are presented here, another testament to the prolific artists of ancient times. The upstairs studio has opened Rivera's life to inquisitive eyes, revealing his day to day objects and his sketches, some incomplete as though awaiting his return. Calle de Museo 150. Open Tues.-Sun. 10 a.m.-2 p.m. and 3-6 p.m., free. This museum is best reached by taxi from Coyoacán central.

Food And Entertainment

Walk north on Allende to the tile-covered facade of the busy **Fonda El Morial,** which specializes in regional foods. Have a complete breakfast (US$4.50), *antojitos* (US$3-5), or entrees of fish, fowl, and beef (US$8-15), all served in a colorful and festive environment. If you're looking for some intellectual stimulation, you might find it over a cappuccino at the **Cafe El Parnaso** (and bookstore). This is the gathering place for people who aren't afraid of expressing or listening to new ideas whether they're left or right of the political line. You'll find lots of books here, mostly in Spanish, but covering all subjects. Open daily 9 a.m.-9 p.m., off the plaza at Felipe Carrillo Puerto 2, (5) 554-2225.

For years **La Guadalupana** has been a popular refreshment stop; though a traditional cantina, they've been letting women in for quite a while. Try the tasty bean *quesadillas* people always talk about; located at the plaza.

El Hijo del Cuervo is another cantina where women are welcome. Come here to eat *botanas* (snacks), drink Cuervo, and see a show in the lit-

tle theater in the back, Open Tues.-Sun. 7-11:30 p.m., performances Thurs.-Sun. 7 p.m. On the Parque Centenario.

If you're in the mood for some off-the-wall entertainment and don't mind being shocked a little, stop in at **El Habito.** Entertainment can be about *anything* or *anyone,* politicians most certainly included (people who understand Spanish will really enjoy this). If you've always wanted to see and hear singing waiters, this is the place; Saturday night is cabaret night. For reservations call (5) 524-2481.

SAN ANGEL

Another one-time suburb that the spreading city has grown to meet (nine km from Centro), San Angel is now part of the city—it's a delightful quiet neighborhood that has retained its small town charm. You'll still find cobblestone streets with marvelous old colonial homes.

Like the entire Valley of Mexico, San Angel has a historic past filled with pre-Columbian events. Its Indian name was **Tenanitla** ("At the Foot of the Stone Wall"), referring to El Pedregal, the lava field just south. Another historic footnote puts the U.S. Army in a decisive battle, defeating General Anaya, who had disobeyed Santa Anna's order to withdraw his troops during the American Intervention. Anaya chose to fight, and it was a fatal mistake for many Mexican soldiers. This charming little city was in 1928 the site where former president General Alvaro Obregón was assasinated by a religious monomaniac. Setting aside the fanatics in the world, strolling through the cobblestone streets is a pleasant occupation.

Museo Estudio Diego Rivera

Designed by well-known artist Juan O'Gorman in 1928, the two-story Diego Rivera Museum was where Rivera lived and worked with wife Frida Kahlo for a time. Mostly this building was a studio for Kahlo and Diego, and it has been decorated as it might have looked when the artists were in residence. Rivera's life and his work are depicted on two floors here, including a few self portraits. On Av. Altavista and Cda. Las Palmas, tel. (5) 548-3032, open 10 a.m.-6 p.m., US$2.50 admission.

Museo Carrillo Gil Arte Contemporano

You may see another (more complete) name for this museum: **Museo de Arte Alvar y Carmen T. Carrillo Gil.** This slick four-tiered building is publicly owned. Exhibits include an excellent collection of works by the more talented Mexican artists such as Rivera, Siqueiros, and Orozco, along with lesser known, avant-garde artists and well-known foreign masters. But they welcome the offbeat; a recent exhibit lampooned the current "love affair" with Frida Kahlo. This is one of Mexico's finest art museums. Av. Revolución 1608. Open Tues.-Sun. 10 a.m.-6 p.m., admission US$3, less for students.

Plaza San Jacinto

Walk up the hill (on Calle Madero) to the lovely colonial plaza. It's always a brilliant splash of color on Saturday, a pleasant scene surrounded by charming colonial buildings. Still another plaque bears testimony that in 1847, U.S. soldiers who chose to fight for Mexico were executed here on the Plaza by order of Gen. Zachary Taylor. The soldiers were Irish-Catholic immigrants; Catholic priests persuaded them that the Church had been wronged and that they should fight for Mexico. Check out the 16th-century church of San Jacinto on the west side of the plaza. The church was at one time part of the Dominican monastery.

Bazar Sábado

On Saturday (*sábado*), there is a *tianguis* (bazaar), one of the finest in Mexico where you can find quality crafts. It takes place in the centerpiece of **Plaza San Jacinto**, a large, 17th-century house on the plaza's north side. Both the U.S. (in 1847) and the French (in 1863) used this old building as headquarters during their attacks on Mexico. Today talented artisans sell wonderful handcrafted items such as jewelry, pottery, leather, and clothing in the two-story plaza, which can really get crowded. Some of the finest artists have regular shops here, selling the highest quality crafts. On the outside, the usual sprawl of tarpaulin-shaded tables fans out on all sides. Surprisingly, bargaining is taboo *inside* and can cause an ugly response. With the artisans *outside,* haggle all you wish. You can get a snack at the patio.

Casa Del Risco

While on the north side of the Plaza San Jacinto, look at the house at number 15. This 18th-century house encloses two museums and two courtyards. The **Museo Colonial Casa del Risco** exhibits artifacts indicative of the European lifestyle as it was exported to Mexico in the colonial era. Also in the building is the colonial library, **Centro Cultural y Biblioteca Isidro Fabela.** Both are open Tues.-Sun. 10 a.m.-6 p.m.; free.

© MOON PUBLICATIONS, INC.

Plaza Del Carmen

Northeast of Plaza San Jacinto, at the 17th-century Carmelite ex-convent, you'll find a diverse collection of colonial art. Even more amazing is the basement crypt containing mummified remains of priests and nuns, discovered during a building project. Open Tues.-Sun. 10 a.m.-4:45 p.m.; free. There's a **Sanborn's** close by.

San Angel Inn

A hacienda built in the 17th century as a home for counts and marquéses, San Angel later served as a temporary home to the likes of Fanny Calderón de la Barca, wife of the first envoy from Spain to independent Mexico in the mid 1840s. Señora Calderón was a talented writer who chronicled Mexico's struggle with the growing pains of independence. Other temporary guests of San Angel Inn were Santa Anna and his troops, and then many years later the foot soldiers of Emiliano Zapata and Pancho Villa. Today, only tourists visit.

Ponderously heavy beams, casement windows, and stone fireplaces dominate indoors; outside, lush, green gardens are a perfect refreshment for the body and the mind. It is not cheap to eat here. Try to come at a slow time; when large groups come in on tour buses, they distract the chef. The food is normally outstanding. For a complete multicourse lunch and dinner, expect to pay from US$18-26. If the "troops" are on site, have a cold drink or a snack and just enjoy the surroundings. Open daily, 1 p.m.-1 a.m. Cda. Las Palmas 50, tel. (5) 548-6746 or 548-6840.

Getting To San Angel

Getting to San Angel from downtown is easy. You have a choice of the Metro, buses, or minibuses, depending on how much you want to walk and where your final destination is for the day—are you planning on going to Coyoacán, for instance, or University City? *Colectivos* marked "Ruta 2" go south along Insurgentes all the way to San Angel. The closest Metro station near San Angel is M.A. Quevedo—from there take a minibus well marked with "San Angel." Tell the driver you want to go to Plaza San Jacinto. These are two direct routes. If you plan on other stops, then study the bus and Metro lines for other alternatives. **Suggestion:** Go on Saturday for the bazaar and remember that the museums are closed on Mondays.

Near San Angel, take a look at **Polyforum Cultural Siqueiros.** It was designed by muralist David Alfaro Siqueiros, whose work covers immense expanses of this building. Its claim to fame (aside from its multishaped building) is the mural on the uppermost tier inside, Siqueiros's *The March of Humanity,* a three-dimensional sculpture/mural covering thousands of square meters. The multifaceted building covers an art gallery, theaters, a concert hall, a cafeteria, and a bookstore. There is also a plethora of arts and crafts for sale at fixed prices. Av. Insurgentes Sur at Filadelfia. Open daily 10 a.m.-7 p.m., free, tel. (5) 536-4522. To get here, flag down a *colectivo* marked "San Angel" going south on Insurgentes near the Zona Rosa; it also goes to San Angel, Bazar Sabado, University City, Pedregal, and Cuicuilco.

NATIONAL UNIVERSITY

Also referred to as **University City,** National University is definitely a city simply by the size and scope of its daily operation. This is the campus of the **Universidad Nacional Autonoma de Mexico** (UNAM). Not only is it a huge school, but it is also a showplace that tells a lot about Mexico. Though this campus has an ultramodern facade, the university has its roots in an ancient era; it was founded in the 1550s. With an enrollment of more than 300,000 students and a teaching staff of 25,000, this is undoubtedly the single largest campus in the Americas, if not the world. Offering an education to anyone for practically nothing (and oftentimes, it is for nothing), it is a "stew pot" of theories, philosophies, far-left ideas, and one of the highest drop-out rates in the world.

Contributions by all of Mexico's artistic population are evident; none are more exquisite than **Biblioteca Central,** the 10-story library building surrounded by a mosaic by Juan O'Gorman. The Olympic Stadium, whose mosaic murals were executed by Diego Rivera, emulates a volcanic cone. It was the site of ceremonies for the 1968 Olympics (where George Foreman waved his tiny flag, and African-American track stars raised clenched fists). The stadium holds more than 80,000 people.

Getting To University City

The most direct way to get to University City is by bus traveling on Insurgentes Sur (Insurgentes goes between the campus on the east side of the road and the stadium on the west). The bus stops close to both sides so it's an easy walk.

PARQUE NACIONAL DESIERTO DE LOS LEONES

Although its title says desert, that's a misnomer since it's really located in a lovely forest of mostly pines, *encinos*, and *oyameles* covering almost 2,000 hectares. High in the mountains at about 2,970 meters, it is a lovely national park. Picnickers and those seeking solace from the busy city stroll along paths through the trees. Some Sundays concerts are presented in the center of the park at the Carmelite ex-convent with still-lovely gardens. It was proclaimed a national park in 1917, the first official national park in Mexico. The road into the park, **Camino del Desierto,** from San Angel, is closed daily 6 p.m.-7 a.m.

THE CANALS OF XOCHIMILCO

In some ways, this centuries-old neighborhood is a living museum. People still live along the canals—as the Aztecs did before the Spaniards arrived.

Chinampas (artificial islands) were an imaginative solution that could be compared to "bringing the mountains to Mohammad." The low-lying lake water surrounding the islands of the Valley of Mexico could not be directed to the higher land of the islands, making farming almost impossible for the Aztecs on their small island. So the soil was brought to the lakes and with clever construction using reeds, tree limbs, and soil, the floating islands were built and crops were planted. The soil was extremely fertile, yielding two or three harvests a year. This method of raising crops saved the Aztecs in the earliest years of Tenochtitlán.

The older more established societies that looked down their noses at the Aztecs took them more seriously when this clever manner of farming proved successful. The method was soon a common practice on other islands as well. The Aztecs created more canals in and around the island, ultimately 80 kilometers of canals were in existence. After the Aztecs constructed an aqueduct to bring more water, their economy flourished and the centers of commerce subtly moved from the mainland foothills (with their underground springs) to the islands in the lakes. Transporting goods and supplies no longer required live porters; boats became the mode of travel and transport.

Homes lined the canals, bridges connected the islands to the mainland, and the Aztecs were becoming a powerful force on their island. Their time in the sun was all too short; the Spaniards had arrived. They tore down bridges, houses, temples, and civic buildings, and filled in the lakes with the debris.

Xochimilco was spared since it was the "breadbasket" of the city. Vegetables and flowers continued to grow. Today, you can get an idea of what life was like by visiting Xochimilco. Try to ignore the crowds of tourists, musicians, and vendors that also float around by boat trying to sell you things, from hot corn to tacos to trinkets. On the weekends, hundreds of boats move along the water. The government has set a standard fare that the boatmen can charge; a ride should average about US\$12 per hour. Agree on a price before you board, and give the boat a look; some are nicer than others. Most are decorated with imitation flowers in bright colors. This is popular Sunday fun for Mexican families, and it can be a lively good time, but if you're looking for peace and quiet, go on a weekday.

BOB RACE

Xochimilco boats

Xochimilco Park

If things go as planned, the country's largest urban ecological park will soon become the flower garden of Mexico once again. At a cost of $230 million and an investment of four years, one million trees were planted along 200 km of connected waterways that will irrigate the entire canal system. A colossal variety of flowers were planted, and it is hoped that the flowers will not only provide a beauty that harkens back to the time of the Aztecs, but will also become a thriving industry to provide the nation with flowers—and have enough left over to export.

Dolores Olmedo Museum

Dolores Olmedo was a lifelong friend and benefactor of Diego Rivera. The foundation bearing her name has opened her home, a lovingly restored ex-convent of the 16th century, as a setting for her collection of pre-Hispanic artifacts, native art, and works by Rivera and Kahlo. Av. México 5843, Col. La Noria, (5) tel. 676-1166.

Anahuacalli, Another Diego Rivera Museum

Still another new museum devoted to Diego Rivera, here more than 100 of Rivera's works are displayed in elegant salons. Another wing of the museum offers a lively collection of Mexican folk art, while still another offers a look at religious art from the country. This old estate served as the postrevolution headquarters of Emiliano Zapata. Av. México 5843.

Getting To Xochimilco

Xochimilco is 24 km southeast of the Zócalo; take Metro line 2 as far as Tasqueña, then board the Xochimilco bus. Go to the end of the line and you'll be in the center of Xochimilco. From here look for signs that say *embarcaderos*.

IXTAPALAPA

While you'll discover the world's biggest Wal-Mart here, the town is most famous for its reenactment of the passion play of Christ's crucifixion each year; a large segment of the population takes part. This is also the site of **Cerro de Estrellas,** where fires were lit to begin the new 52-year cycle once it was ascertained that the world hadn't ended.

Way Of The Cross

The passion play is often seen in Christian countries, and each performance has its unique touches. In Ixtapalapa, the play involves more than 2,000 people. There's no doubt that it takes immense planning and direction. Costumes perfectly portray the era, along with ample stage props—torches, spears, horses, and whips. Not one character of the Biblical story is left out, from Mary Magdalen to Judas to a Christ who carries a wooden cross. Later the Christ is hung on it. According to local historians the passion has been reenacted since 1853.

MEXICO CITY ACCOMMODATIONS

No one should have a problem getting just the kind of room they want in Mexico City. The quantity is immense, and the quality is diverse, from really budget to some of the most luxurious in the country. In the luxury class you can pretty well ask and receive any service you desire. In the budget class, it's suggested that you make sure you know *what* you are getting before moving in. There seems to be a direct ratio between the price and the hot-water supply. If it's important to you to have a window, look before accepting a room. Ask about the telephone; what fees can you expect? Check for security; is there a safety deposit box or something similar to leave your valuables in while touring? (Remember, this is a big city and pickpockets *love*

big cities.) Though the weather in Mexico is rather mild, it can get cold at night in the winter; check for heat or ask for plenty of blankets. In the summer it can get hot on occasion.

Rates

Even in the priciest hotels you can often get some kind of a discount, especially at certain times of the year, if it's a late-night arrival, or if the hotel isn't filled. A few more possibilities: **AAA members** generally can get 20% off. If you carry a **business card,** ask for a business discount. If you make **reservations** from the airport hotel desk, they frequently offer packages for a little less than the going rates. Or just ask for a discount after they quote a price.

Obviously it won't always happen, but occasionally discounts come to those who ask. It helps to do a little homework before you leave so you're at least acquainted with the prices of the hotels.

Where To Stay?

If you plan to move around and cover the entire city over a few days or a week, then it makes little geographical difference which "neighborhood" you're in; transportation is available from all accommodations. If you like the bustle of the city then stay in the Zona Rosa. If you prefer a touch of nature, stay at or near Chapultepec Park. And if you're just passing through by plane with an overnight stopover, then spend the extra money and stay at the airport (it's worth saving the roundtrip fare to and from the airport, and the hassle of going in and out of the city and the airport with luggage.

Choices

There are hundreds of hotels in this immense city. We won't even begin to scratch the surface of what's out there; we will include hotels that either we've stayed in, inspected, or that have been recommended by trusted travelers over the years. Please check everything in advance. If you find other good hotels in your wanderings, don't hesitate to tell us about them, and we will check them out on our next visit.

BUDGET HOTELS DOWNTOWN

Hotel Isabel

A charmingly ethnic old hotel that is favored by low-budget travelers, the Isabel's low-key atmosphere pervades the tiled, dark-wood accented lobby. Rooms have high ceilings and come with baths, color TV, and telephones. A restaurant and bar are on the premises; US$19 d, without bath is less. At Calle Isabel La Católica 63, near the Zócalo; tel. (5) 518-1213/1217.

Hotel Atlanta

This is a well-placed, quiet, inexpensive establishment that has a large lobby with a view of the street. Vibrant orange abounds on furniture and doors (which avoid the usual knuckle scraping by placing the knobs in the center), striped drapes, and multicolored carpeting. Double beds

are bracketed by lamps. Large closets and tile baths are standard. Elevator, color TV, and telephones. Rates are US$18, suites from US$28. On Calle Belasario Domingo 31, tel. (5) 518-1200 or 518-1203.

Hotel La Marina

This is worth checking out; the intimate white stucco and dark-wood lobby surrounds a fish tank. Though we were unable to see the inside of a room, the place had a good feeling about it and the price is right; US$16 s, US$18 d. On Calle Allende 30, tel. (5) 512-4842 or 518-2445.

Hotel Catedral

Half a block from Templo Mayor, near the Zócalo, the fabulous archaeology site in the middle of the city, these rooms are clean and comfy, if not glitzy. The location is good, and there's a restaurant and bar on the premises. Rates are US$33 s or d. On Donceles 95, tel. (5) 518-5232, fax 512-4344.

BUDGET HOTELS NEAR PASEO DE LA REFORMA AND ZONA ROSA

Hotel Galveston

Clean and cheap is what this hotel is all about—period: US$10 s, US$17 d. Av. Insurgentes Centro 50, tel. (5) 546-4996 or 546-4997.

Hotel Pennsylvania

A well-worn but serviceable place to stay if you're watching pennies, Hotel Pennsylvania's clean, sparsely furnished rooms on the first floor are great for leg watching since windows are at ground level. Double beds and tile bathrooms are included, and a popular restaurant is attached. US$12 s, US$16 d. Calle Ignacio Mariscal 15, tel. (5) 535-0970.

Hotel Edison

One block from the Monument to the Revolution, this modest, inexpensive hotel offers rooms of variable size and decor with stucco walls and light and dark woods. The staff is friendly and helpful, though not English speaking. Expect double beds of differing firmness, carpet, plenty of light sources, a writing desk, and chairs that have permanent depressions. The tiled bathroom has a separate shower stall. Elevator,

(previous page) Guanajuato; (this page, top) Guadalajara market; (above, left) Mexico's marvelous textiles often originate in home weaving shops, (above, right) creating lovely pictures with natural reeds (all photos by Oz Mallan)

TV, telephone, cold drinks in the lobby, and parking. Room rates: US$20 s, US$24 d. Calle Thomas A. Edison 106, tel. (5) 566-0933.

Hotel Gran Texas

This hotel is characterized by warm earth tones, and 52 smallish rooms overlook a quiet side street. Travelers looking for "reasonable" will find a friendly staff, a good location, simple clean rooms each with a double bed, a writing desk, a chair, a tile shower, TV, and a telephone. Rates are US$24 s, US$27 d. At Calle Ignacio Mariscal 129, tel. (5) 705-5782 or 566-9724.

Hotel Pisa

This large modern-style hotel has few amenities, but prices are reasonable and the desk staff is professional and efficient. Rooms offer TV and telephones, and some are air-conditioned (be sure to specify if a/c is important; you may get charged for something you don't want); US$25 s, US$27 d. At Av. Insurgentes Centro 58, tel. (5) 566-7133 or 566-7897, fax 566-7015.

Casa González

This charming Victorian inn has 22 rooms and a great third generation family/staff, with a parlor and dining room frozen in a time past. Yes, the furniture is a little worn, but in a comfortable loving way. This little *casa* hosts some very interesting travelers. It's at a great location near the Zona Rosa and is a good starting point for many museums and galleries of the city. The rates are reasonable, US$25-56 d. Meals are US$10 each and tasty. Río Sena 69, in Col. Cuauhtémoc, tel. (5) 566-9688.

Hotel Corinto

The Corinto is a 10-story, 155-room building one block south of the Monument to the Revolution. It's clean, modern, and attractively priced. The rooms are a little on the small side but quite comfortable, with a tile bath, color TV, telephone, pool, and underground parking; rates are US$34 s, US$44 d. On Calle Vallarta 24, tel. (5) 566-6555 or 566-9711, fax 546-6888.

BOB RACE

MODERATE HOTELS DOWNTOWN

Metropole Hotel

Modernized in the recent past, rooms now offer in-room safety deposit boxes; all 165 rooms are carpeted and nicely furnished, and in the bathrooms you'll find a separate faucet for purified water; color TV with U.S. channels; from US$60, on Luis Moya 39 near La Alameda, tel. (5) 510-8660, fax 512-1273.

Ritz Best Western

A mid-price suggestion is the Ritz, and there are always plenty of Americans to talk to if you get homesick. This is a comfortable hotel with 140 rooms, TV, minibars, telephones, valet parking, and a good location for walking to the great colonial sites around the Zócalo. Rates are US$61 s, US$66 d. Located on Av. Madero 30, tel. (5) 518-1340 or 518-1350, fax 518-3466, in the U.S. (800) 528-1234.

Bamer Hotel

This has been a traveler's old-reliable for years, facing the Alameda and within walking distance of many fine attractions. Spacious rooms and suites, comfy beds, a restaurant and good nightspot, the **Barnette**, also offers live music. Rates: US$64 s, US$70 d, more for suites. On Av. Juárez 52, tel. (5) 521-9060 or 521-9090, fax 510-1793.

Hotel Cortés

If you want a historical "experience," check out this fine old establishment with its grand history. The building dates back to the 16th century, originally built as a convent. The 27 rooms are old and for the most part archaic, but they're clean and the ambience is *very* pleasant and *very* Mexican. The candlelit courtyard is a lovely place to have supper, and on Saturday evening (twice) supper comes with a grand folkloric show. Two-story-high bushes fill the courtyard, a haven for hun-

Hotel Cortés

dreds of singing birds. Rates are US$93 d. It's located at Av. Hidalgo 85, tel. in the U.S. and Canada (800) 528-1234, in Mexico (5) 518-2181 or 518-2184, fax 518-3466.

MODERATE HOTELS NEAR PASEO DE LA REFORMA

Casa Blanca
This 12-story gem, Casa Blanca, has recently been remodeled and is thoroughly modern with 270 pastel-colored rooms. Wall-to-wall carpeting, ceiling-to-floor pleated drapes, subdued fluorescent lighting, and marble tiled baths, along with new mattresses, comfortable chairs and tables, piped-in music, and air-conditioning create the ambience. There's a rooftop pool and bar overlooking the city. Rates are upper end to moderate and service is formally friendly. Rooms start at US$79 s or d; La Fragua 7, tel. (5) 566-3211, fax 705-4197.

Bristol Hotel
Another fine location across Reforma Blvd. from the Zona Rosa, the Bristol is perfect for a healthy walk to many attractions. This clean modern facility is often filled with tour groups from various countries. You'll find 134 rooms, US$55 s, US$62 d, on Plaza Necaxa 17, tel. (5) 208-1717, fax 533-6060.

María Cristina
A perennial favorite in a quiet neighborhood on a nice shady green lawn, and yet the lovely old colonial hotel is only a few minutes walk from the Zona Rosa shops and cafes; it's even closer to Sullivan Park. Its colonial decor is comfortable and prices are US$55-60. On Río Lerma 31, tel. (5) 707-1787, fax 566-9194. Free parking.

EXPENSIVE AND LUXURY HOTELS NEAR THE ZOCALO

Luxury hotels in Mexico City can really be knock-outs, and though the cost is sometimes more than inexperienced visitors expect to pay, the price is amazingly cheaper than in hotels of the same caliber in large U.S. cities. Some offer special packages, which lowers the price as well. The secret for getting reduced prices in these hotels is making arrangements in advance with whatever promo they may be advertising; always ask.

Howard Johnson Gran Hotel
This is another historic structure filled with the beauty of the era. Location is great, near the Zócalo, and no one should miss the striking stained glass dome in the lobby; rates are US$99. At 16 de Septiembre 82, tel. in the U.S. and Canada (800) 654-2000, in Mexico (5) 510-4040, fax 512-2085.

Hotel Majestic
This hotel is a 16th-century building with a dab of character. The rooms, however, are small and nothing to write home about, but the wonderful location overlooking the Zócalo makes it all worthwhile. You can reserve a room with that view, or if staying in another hotel, have breakfast on one of the balconies of the seventh-floor dining room overlooking the Zócalo. It's a love-

ly way to start the day. If you're very early you'll see the flag-raising ceremony or the men in their bright orange jumpsuits cleaning the Zócalo; or if you're not a morning person, get a table at 6 p.m. and watch the presidential guards take the flag down. Anyone planning a trip to Mexico around 15 September (Independence Day) and interested in the big celebration should plan on staying here. Keep in mind that for these dates, reservations must be made a year in advance. Ask for a room facing the Zócalo. The square comes alive on that night! The president gives the Grito and he and his family watch the fireworks along with thousands of Mexicans waving flags and enjoying their special day! Rates from US$94.50. At Madero 73, tel. (5) 521-8600, fax 518-3466.

EXPENSIVE AND LUXURY HOTELS IN OR NEAR ZONA ROSA

Hotel Calinda Geneve

In its heyday (mid-1950s), the Geneve was a glorious art-deco hotel, with white-glove service and a constant hubbub of activity and tranquil music. Its high glass-domed greenhouse was filled with giant plants and tables for an afternoon cocktail or tea. In recent years the Calinda people have done a lot of work to spruce it up, but it is still just old. Hopefully the staff is as kind as when we first stayed there in 1956—after staying our reserved three nights in a lovely room for about US$20, we had fallen in love with Mexico City and wanted to extend our stay, but couldn't afford the cost of the room. So, swallowing our pride, we spoke to the manager and told him we would take any little closet if the price was right. He was very understanding, took us into the depths of the hotel and gave us a funky room so tiny that we had to climb over the bed to exit. He charged us US$2 per night; what an understanding man! Today's price is US$85; address is Londres 130, tel. (5) 211-0071, fax 208-7422.

Hotel Galería Plaza

This is one of the nicest hotels near Zona Rosa. The location is great, right in the heart of the action; it's modern and though pretty good size, has an intimate ambience. Rates are US$153; tel. (5) 211-0014, fax 207-5867, Hamburgo 195.

Hotel Marco Polo

This is a fine choice; the stylish modern hotel has had a fine reputation since it opened. Amenities include units with cooking facilities. The hotel staff knows how to pamper their guests, and there's a restaurant and piano bar on the premises. Rates are US$168; at Amberes 27, tel. (5) 207-1893, fax 533-3727.

Hotel Krystal Rosa

Another favorite in the heart of the Zona Rosa, this is becoming a frequent stopover for international businesspeople. Rooms are cozy, well furnished, and well kept. Guests will find a good selection in the restaurants and lively nightlife in the various lounges. We especially like the **Club Rooms** and their amenities, which include continental breakfast served in the Club Lounge (on the top floor with wonderful views of the city), for a little more than a standard room. Standard room is US$145 d, Club room is US$170 d. You can save money at the Krystal Rosa by asking for a Super Saver, which means you book and pay 21 days in advance. By doing that you save about US$30 on a standard room, and US$40 on a Club room. At Liverpool 155, tel. in the U.S. and Canada (800) 231-9860, in Mexico (5) 511-4620 or 511-4624.

Holiday Inn Crown Plaza

Modern, convenient, and attractive, the Holiday Inn Crown Plaza is located at Paseo de la Reforma 80, not too far from the Zona Rosa or Centro. The hotel offers three restaurants, live music in the lobby bar, and comfy rooms and suites. Rates from US$150, tel. (5) 705-1515, fax 705-1313.

LUXURY HOTELS NEAR CHAPULTEPEC PARK

The area around Chapultepec Park has long been lovely, and it's growing into the upscale section of the city for shopping, hotels, and top-notch restaurants. If you're looking for elegant, consider these hotels located near the park and in the Polanco neighborhood.

Hotel Marquis Reforma

One of the newest and most beautiful, it has already established a great reputation. The exterior is a marvelous mix of cantera rosa and glass in an art-deco style. Subdued elegance characterizes the lovely lobby, where marble and burnished inlaid woods have been used liberally. Rooms are beautifully furnished and carpeted. The hotel provides amenities to pamper each guest, with every convenience that a businessman or -woman might need. The hotel has established a floor for women only. Try **Joya,** the stylish Italian restaurant, as well as two bars, a gym, a sauna, and Jacuzzis, and note the lovely indoor fountain of four Aztecs. Rates start at US$195 s or d. At Paseo de la Reforma 465, tel. (5) 211-3600, fax 211-5561.

Camino Real

Across from Chapultepec Park, the Camino Real never changes. It's as lovely as ever, the master of understated decor with flamboyant art (such as the Rufino Tomayo mural) to light up each special corner. It's well kept, with attractive rooms, two swimming pools, four tennis courts, *six* marvelous restaurants to choose from—including the French **Fouquet's of Paris** (it is said the French food here is every bit as good as its Parisian counterpart)—and the popular **Cero-Cero** disco. Rates from US$230. At Av. Mariano Escobedo 700, tel. in the U.S. and Canada (800) 722-6466, or in Mexico City tel. (5) 203-2121.

Hotel Nikko Mexico

This sleek tower is modern and shiny with marble everywhere and a lobby bar that is the exact opposite of small and intimate; there's probably a hundred tables here. Decor is sleek almost to the point of stark, with just the slightest hint of the Orient. Rooms are large and comfortable, and the fitness enthusiast will enjoy three tennis courts, a fully equipped gym, a sauna, a jogging track, and a rooftop swimming pool. For either the Japanese visitor who'd like to feel at home, or the visitor who is intrigued with the Japanese culture, authentic suites of Japanese design, use, and decor are available. A women-only floor and club-priced rooms are on the top floors. Japanese, international, and Mexican cuisines are served in one of four restaurants and, yes, there's a disco and a nightclub. Rates from US$230. At Av. Campos Elyseos 204, tel. in the U.S. and Canada (800) 645-5687, in Mexico (5) 203-4020, fax 255-5586.

Hotel Sierra

Just down the street from the Nikko, the Sierra is the newest in the neighborhood. Near Chapultepec's Museum of Contemporary Art, it should be in full operational mode by now. On Campos Elyseos.

Presidente Hotel

Located next door to the Nikko hotel, the Presidente is one of the oldest of the park hotels. The hotel lobby is a multistory pyramid shape with a play of light from the immense skylight at the top. This is a big hotel (660 rooms), with restaurants, bars, and a popular disco. The lively lobby bar is always full and **Maxim's** serves excellent food. Rates begin at US$185. At Av. Campos Elyseos 218, tel. in the U.S. and Canada (800) 462-2427, in Mexico (5) 327-7700, fax 250-9130.

ACCOMMODATIONS NEAR TRANSPORTATION

Near The Airport

The **Fiesta Americana** is very convenient; it's actually connected to the ticket lobby. Just walk across the enclosed "bridge" and you'll be in the hotel lobby. For those with an early morning flight, it's very convenient, if a little costly. If nothing else, it serves a great buffet lunch, about US$16 for a large selection of hot and cold foods, and a beer is included. The coffee shop is open 24 hours, and even if you don't spend the night it's a much nicer place ot spend layover time than the terminal coffee shop. At the airport, the address is Fundidor Monterrey 89, Peñon de los Baños, Box 39-232, 15520, Mexico City, tel. (905) 785-0505, (800) FIESTA1, fax (905) 785-1034. Rates are US$190-210.

Near The Buenavista Railway Station

Both of these are spartan but adequate for an overnight: **Hotel Nueva Estacion,** 114 Zaragoza between Moctezuma and Meneses Colonia Guerrero, tel. (5) 546-0226, US$14; and **Hotel Central,** 248 Mosqueat, tel. 535-5724, US$13 s. **Hotel Ponte Vedra** is a newish hotel, clean and satisfactory, across from the station. Rates are US$23 s, US$36 d, tel. 541-3160.

Near Terminal Central Del Norte Bus Station
Hotel Brasilia is located within walking distance (from the terminal exit walk left for two blocks) to the **Terminal Norte Bus Station**. The hotel is more than adequate for a convenient overnight whether coming in late or going out on a very early bus in the morning. You'll find a decent restaurant and U.S. TV stations. On Av. de Los Cien Metros, tel. (5) 587-8577; US$28 s, US$32 d.

FOOD

In Mexico City you can enjoy, investigate, and explore the unique flavors from around this vast country. You'll find a multitude of kitchens in the city, from tiny *fondas* to elaborate gourmet restaurants. Not only do you have access to succulent Mexican food representing every part of Mexico, but also restaurants serving food from every country in the world. Locating all the restaurants in this city could be a lifelong occupation; there are that many. So if you find something really spectacular, please drop us a note and tell us about it.

FAST FOOD

Perhaps these are the types most strongly influenced by the country's northern neighbor. Chains of coffee shop-style restaurants, such as Sanborn's, Toks, VIPS, and Denny's abound. McDonald's and Burger King have hamburgers, Shakey's has pizza, even Woolworth and Sears have restaurants. Every street is full of the aromas of something cooking nearby. In the parks, vendors have a ready market and you'll find munchers with roasted corn, tacos, grilled pancakes with jelly, tamales, cotton candy, and ice cream. *Buen comer* (happy eating).

McDonald's: Blvd. Manuel Avila Camacho 137, Col. Polanco; tel. (5) 540-3003, 202-8679. Open Sun.-Thurs. 10 a.m.-11 p.m., Fri.-Sat. 10 a.m.-midnight. Other locations are Pabellón Polanco, corner of Ferrocarril Cuernavaca and Ejército Nacional, tel. 395-4924; Génova 56, tel. 208-9318; Insurgentes Sur 1121, tel. 575-0616; Centro Coyoacán, Av. Coyoacán between Universidad and Río Churubusco, tel. 688-6078.

Popular Coffee Shops
Sanborn's: Madero 4, historic downtown area; tel. (5) 521-6058 or 512-9820. Open daily 7:30 a.m.-1 a.m. Mexican and continental specialties, shop and drugstore. Also at: S. La Fragua (Reforma 45); S. Tiber (Reforma 333); Niza 30; Insurgentes 421; S. Polanco, (Ejército Nacional and Moliere); Av. Palmas 781.

VIPS: Madero 53, historic downtown area; tel. 521-6170 or 521-6448. Open daily 7:30 a.m.-2 a.m. Parking. Also at: Alabama 7, tel. 536-2437; Hamburgo 126, tel. 207-2680; Insurgentes Sur 493, tel. 272-1732; Av. Universidad 936, tel. 548-5602.

CASUAL DINING

Shirley's Cafeteria
This is popular any time of day with an a-la-carte menu offering an ample variety of coffee shop cuisine and excellent pastries and desserts. A good place to have breakfast (US$2-5) while waiting for the shops to open, located at Reforma 108, tel. (5) 390-5255, open 7:30 a.m.-11:30 p.m. daily.

Cafe La Blanca
La Blanca serves an assortment of sandwiches and regional dishes and is an inexpensive place to grab a bite while scurrying about the downtown sights. Service is fast and the turnover rate is high. The basket of bread is *not* complimentary; you're charged for what you take. 5 de Mayo 40, tel. (5) 510-9260. Open 6:30 a.m.-11:30 p.m. This little place has been on the scene since 1943.

El Mixteca
One block east of the National Lottery building is El Mixteca. This festive and enjoyable place has cold, freshly squeezed fruit drinks (the lemonade is wonderful). It's gaily decorated with paintings of the *corrida* and white lace over orange cloth-covered, formica tables. The food is very good and extremely inexpensive. The *comida corrida* (US$5) includes bread, drink, and

dessert. The family sits down to eat after every-one has been served; the small children of the family are entertained with a portable TV while they wait. El Mixteca is only open for lunch on weekdays, closing before 5 p.m. At Calle Thomas A. Edison on the corner of J. Teran, no phone.

Near La Alameda Park
Between Juárez and Hidalgo, on the west end of La Alameda, is Calle Colón, where there is a multitude of dining establishments; most have menus posted on the windows. **Cafe Trevi,** Colón 1, tel. (5) 512-3020), has been serving inexpensive pizza and pasta, as well as break-fast, for 60 years. There's a full bar; open 8 a.m.-11:30 p.m. Mon.-Sunday.

Restaurant Edelweiss
This restaurant, specializing in *comida alemán* (German dishes), has great rye and pumper-nickle bread peeking out of the breadbasket. A meal of *consomé de pollo,* fettuccine Alfredo, and a chicken cutlet with beets and *papas fritos* is under US$10. Breakfast with eggs, toast, juice, and coffee is US$4. Open 9 a.m.-9:30 p.m. Mon.-Saturday. Calle Arriaga 23, tel. (5) 705-2597.

Fonda Santa Anita
Reminiscent of Tijuana in the '60s, Fonda's has cartoon characters and caricatures painted across the walls. Waiters have that resigned, long-suffering look of people who deal with tourists. Fonda's is always bustling during the lunch hour: the food is good, the portions copi-ous, and the prices reasonable. A rich tortilla soup with bread and butter (US$4) is very sus-taining, and you'll find recognizable entrees from all over Mexico, many including *papas fritos* (US$5-10). One block below Av. Juárez at Calle Humboldt 48, tel. 518-4609 or 518-5723; open Mon.-Fri. noon-10 p.m., Sat.-Sun. 1-9 p.m.

Restaurant/Bar Del Pacifico
Loud *música norteño* is played here all night long, while the young crowd at the tables drinks mini-Corona beers served six at a time in buck-ets filled with ice. Belly up to the bar for a *cuba anejo* (dark rum served over ice with bottles of Coke and sparkling water); mix the sodas until

you get the exact flavor you want. There are beer drinking contests and *música viva* (live music) once a month; at these times it's impos-sible to find a seat after 11 p.m. and closing is postponed beyond 2 a.m. The food here (served 11 a.m.-11 p.m.) is Sinaloan, and the flour tortilla is king. Prices are moderate; located at Calle de Bacareli 43, tel. 592-2778. Hours: Mon.-Thurs. 1 p.m.-2 a.m., Fri.-Sat. 1 p.m.-4 a.m. An-other restaurant of the same name/owner is lo-cated at 33 Río Balsas tel. 208-2917.

FOR A LITTLE MORE MONEY

Restaurant Río Deva
The Río Deva specializes in Spanish and Mex-ican foods, and is easy on the eyes, the palate, and the pocket. Stucco walls, mirrored beams, dark wood wainscoting, pictures of Old Mexi-co, and silk plants set the ambience. The *paella Valenciana* is prepared to perfection, rich with shellfish and chicken. The service is pleasant and swift. Prices are reasonable: appetizers (US$3-5), entrees (US$7-15). Calle Ignacio Ramírez 11, tel. 566-9404. Open 1-11 p.m. Mon.-Sunday.

El Chato
Serving French cuisine in the charming ambi-ence of a colonial mansion, El Chato is slightly expensive for dinner. Floor show with admis-sion and drink minimum. At Londres 117, Zona Rosa, tel. (5) 511-1809. Open Mon.-Sat. 1 p.m.-2 a.m.

Prendes
The seafood on their international and national menu is the entree of popular choice. Moderate to expensive prices in a landmark building near the Bellas Artes, where there is always a crowd for lunch. Autographed pictures of international stars line the walls. On Av. 16 de Septiembre 10 (at Cárdenas), tel. (5) 512-7517, 518-2799, or 521-5404, fax 510-4370. Another Prendes is at the Fronton, Plaza de la República 17-A, tel. 546-5414.

Fonda Del Refugio
Still an all-time classical favorite, Fonda del Refugio serves traditional dishes in the lovely at-

mosphere of a charming old traditional house. If you have a hard time with the Spanish menu, ask for the English version. At Liverpool 166, Zona Rosa; tel. (5) 528-5823. Open Mon.-Sat. 1 p.m.-midnight.

Fouquet's De Paris

On the third floor of the Hotel Camino Real across from Chapultepec Park (Mariano Escobedo 700, Col. Verónica Anzures; tel. 5-203-2121), Fouquet's is open Mon.-Sat. 7:30-10 a.m., 2-4:30 p.m, 8 a.m.-11:30 p.m. French cuisine, jacket and tie required; about US$60 for two.

Ex-mansions Turned Restaurants

Beautifully remodeled mansions abound in their present incarnations of expensive restaurants, and major restaurateurs from around the world have addresses here (dinner for two in excess of US$100 is the norm). If money is still no object try **Sir Winston Churchill's,** a restored Tudor mansion, for the baron of beef or other meat and potato dishes. At Manuel Avila Camacho 67, tel. (5) 520-0065.

Hacienda de los Morales dates from the 1500s and is renowned for its Mexican specialties, high-powered service, and beautiful gardens, all in marvelous colonial surroundings. Along with deliciously prepared roast duck (US$15), excellent seafood soup (US$8), and cream of walnut soup (US$5), they also serve a wonderful brown bread. At Calle Vázquez de Mella 525, Col. Polanco, tel. 540-3225. Open daily 1 p.m.-midnight.

SPECIALTY DINING

Vegetarian Restaurants

Restaurante Vegetariano Las Fuentes is open daily 8 a.m.-6 p.m.; 127 Río Panuco, corner of Río Tiber, tel. (5) 525-7095. The **Vegetariano** is open Mon.-Sat. 9 a.m.-6:30 p.m., Av. Madero 56, tel. 521-6880. **Restaurante El Vegetariano** is open Mon.-Fri. 8 a.m.-8 p.m., Sat.-Sun. 8 a.m.-7 p.m., Filomeno Mata 13, 512-1186.

Sweet Stuff And Bakeries

Pastelería Madrid: 5 de Febrero 25.

Panificadora Novedades: Bolívar 78, no phone, open daily 6 a.m.-8 p.m.

La Baggette: Gante 1, 7:30 a.m.-7:30 p.m. Mon.-Sat., closed Sun., tel. (5) 521-0224, between Calle Madero and 16 de Septiembre.

Dulces Celaya: 5 de Mayo 39, between Isabel la Católica and Motolinia, historic downtown area; tel. 521-1787. Open daily 10:30 a.m.-7 p.m. Typical Mexican candies. Also at: Colima 143, Col. Roma, tel. 207-5858; Insurgentes 273, Col. Roma, tel. 574-4578.

La Dulcería: Oscar Wilde 29, Col. Polanco; tel. 280-9515. Open Mon.-Fri. 10 a.m.-6:30 p.m., Sat. 10 a.m.-2:30 p.m.

ENTERTAINMENT AND SHOPPING

ENTERTAINMENT

Palacio De Bellas Artes ("Palace Of Fine Arts")

Home of **Ballet Folklorico** as well as the National Opera and National Philharmonic; check the *Daily News,* the English-language paper, for current schedules. Av. Hidalgo 11, tel. (5) 510-1388.

Nezahualcoyotl Hall

Stages productions by the **State of Mexico Symphony.** Av. Insurgentes Sur 3000, San Angel, tel. (5) 665-1344.

Teatro De La Ciudad

Shows of classical and popular music. Calle Donceles 36, between República de Chile y Allende, tel. (5) 510-2197, 510-2942, 521-5083.

Ballet Folklórico

The **Ballet Folklorico Nacional** is a permanent event, with performances on Tues. at 8:30 p.m. and Sun. at 9:30 a.m.

Teatro Blanquita

Vaudeville shows seven days a week at 7 p.m. and 10 p.m.; Lázaro Cárdenas 16.

Plaza Garibaldi

At the moment, Plaza Garibaldi is all torn up! So the mariachis, from every small and large town in Mexico, who would gather and play in this well-known plaza, are now wandering the streets looking for an audience. The old Plaza Garibaldi, surrounded by 19th-century buildings that are seemingly held together by paint alone, really needed some TLC, so hurray for repairs! Watch out for pickpockets, although the plaza policeman keep an eye out, too. Find Garibaldi five blocks north of the Bellas Artes, east of Lázaro Cárdenas.

Folkloristas

If you should happen to see an announcement for groups called **Folkloristas,** don't miss them. These groups are devoted to reincarnating Latin-American folk music. **El Tribu** is a group devoted to pre-Hispanic music. The group includes Antonio Zepeda and Jorge Reyes. Zepeda sometimes performs at the Museum of Anthropology.

This art has been handed down from the ancestors of 500 to 1,000 years ago. If you've gone to even one museum, you've seen some of the colorful instruments. Some are flutes with small animals attached, or ceramic drums with something rattling inside. Drums are made of wood and animal skins, and occasionally are played as they float in a tub of water; this achieves a different sound. You'll see all manner of marimba-like instruments, as well as stringed instruments. Flutes and ocarinas come in many sizes and shapes. These musicians present an unusual show preserving the tones of the past.

Discos

This city is loaded with discos from upscale to casual funky. The nicer ones have really state-of-the-art light shows and sound systems. Expect to dress up a little (no shorts please) at most of these; anticipate a cover charge at the better ones, from US$15-25. You might notice that most of these clubs say they open at 9:30 or 10 p.m., but in Mexico not many people show up much before midnight, when things really get rolling. Most credit cards are accepted, with the exception of American Express and Diner's Club. Here are a few clubs to get you started:

Cero-Cero is a lively spot with a sensational light show. Dress up a little here; open Mon.-Thurs., 9 p.m.-2:30 a.m., Fri.-Sat., 9 p.m.-4 a.m. at the **Camino Real Hotel,** Mariano Escobedo 700, tel. 203-2121.

The **Coliseum,** at the Plaza de Toros has a cover charge. At Av. San Jeronimo 252; open 10 p.m.-3 a.m., tel. 395-1353.

Magic Circus admits heterosexual couples only; cover charge, open Thurs.-Saturday. At Rudolfo Gaona 3, tel. 557-2066.

Passage offers modern international music. Open Tues.-Sat. 9 p.m.-3 a.m.; Av. Revolución 333, tel. 271-7044. More of a nightclub.

Antillanos offers tropical music and dancing. Expect a cover charge, and reservations are suggested on Friday and Saturday. Francisco Pimental 78, tel. 592-0439.

Bar Gaona is at Bucareli 80, Col. Centro; tel. 512-4579. Open Mon.-Sat. 8 a.m.-11 p.m. Restaurant/bar.

Bar Jordugo, at Paseo de la Reforma 325, is inside Hotel María Isabela Sheraton, Col. Cuauhtémoc; tel. 207-3933. Open daily 6 p.m.-2 a.m. The best cocktails in a very Mexican atmosphere; cover charge.

Restaurant Tasca Maholo is at Av. de la Paz 32, between Insurgentes and Revolución, Col. San Angel; tel. 550-9191 or 550-8986. Open Mon.-Sat. 8 p.m.-2 a.m., Sun. 8 p.m.-6 a.m. Romantic Mexican music, reservations recommended, valet parking, cover charge.

Caballo Negro is at Paseo de la Reforma 80, between Versalles and Atenas, Col. Juárez; tel. 705-1515. Open Mon.-Sat. 11 a.m.-1 a.m. Floor show bar, valet parking, cover charge.

La Opera is at 5 de Mayo 10, downtown; tel. 512-8959. Open Mon.-Sat. noon-midnight. Traditional *cantina* lunch and dinner are served in addition to a large selection of drinks and appetizers.

Nueva Orleans is at Revolución 1653, Col. San Angel; tel. 680-1908. Open Tues.-Sun. 7 p.m.-1 a.m. Bar with a show starting at 8 p.m., valet parking, cover charge.

El Hijo del Cuervo is at Parque Centenario 17, Col. Coyoacán; tel. 658-5308. Open Mon.-Sat. 11 a.m.-2 a.m. Bar with outrageous comedy in Spanish, reservations recommended, cover charge.

EVENTS

Jai Alai
This game originated in Spain's Basque country. Most Mexicans love the game, and it certainly is fast! However, I think it must be an acquired taste for non-Latins, because after the first half hour I was ready to go. It's very monotonous and unless you know the players *and* are a gambler, don't go expecting love-at-first-sight. To its credit there's more to jai alai than just the game. Spectators are expected to dress up— suit and tie for men—during the week, and it's slightly more casual on the weekends. At the **Fronton de Mexico** you'll find some exquisite dining with outstanding food and tuxedo-clad waiters. In my opinion, most people go for the betting excitement. This is an ongoing action with changing odds, and fans continue to bet throughout a game. Betting stewards come to your table; you'll recognize them in their red berets. This game is for anyone who has sporting blood and some disposable income, and who likes good food, good wine, and high-style exposure. **Note:** The bars serve a full complement of cocktails, and if you win big, you can purchase a bottle of Moët Chandon champagne for US$130. Events Tues.-Fri. begin at 7 p.m., on Sat. at 6:30 p.m., and on Sun. at 5 p.m. However, the main event usually begins at 8 p.m. Located on the north side of the **Plaza a la República,** near the intersection of Juárez and Paseo de la Reforma. Admission is US$7.

Bullfights
Plaza de Toros Mexico, the largest *corrida* in the country, and one of the largest in Latin America, seats 50,000. Remember, choose a seat on the shady (*sombra*) side of the arena. The regular season is Aug.-Sept. In the Col. Nochebuena. Ticket information is available at most travel agencies and hotels.

Horseracing

Here's another popular event in Mexico. The season is Aug.-Sept., and the arena is the lovely **Hipodromo de las Americas** in Col. Lomas de Sotela, Av. Industria Militar. The races start at 5 p.m.

Soccer

At the **Estadio Azteca** the crowds go wild. The season is Aug.-Sept., Fri.-Sun., Calzada de Tlalpan 3465.

SHOPPING

Mercados

Mercado de la Merced: Traditional market, located between the streets of Santa Escuela, General Anaya, Rosario, and Cerrada del Rosario (takes in a complete block), Col. Merced Balbuena. Open daily 6 a.m.-6 p.m.

Mercado de San Juan: The best fruit, vegetable, meat, and delicatessen market, between Pugibet and Luis Moya streets. Open daily 6 a.m.-6 p.m.

OZ MALLAN

open market

Mercado de Sonora: Famous for selling medicinal and magical herbs and seeds, this market extends from Fray Servando Teresa de Mier to three blocks from Merced Metro.

Central Artesanal Buena Vista

Several blocks north of Reforma on Av. Insurgentes Norte near the Railroad Station is the sprawling Centro Artesanal Buenavista. This is one of the best places for people who hate to shop but feel guilty returning home empty-handed. Here you'll find an incredibly large selection of everything made or sold in Mexico—*under one roof*—and it's fun. The fixed prices mean that you will pay more than at some of the other shops and markets where wheeling and dealing is encouraged. You'll find a little bit of everything here, from silver to clothing to ceramics to crafts from all over the country. When it comes time to pay, it can be a little confusing. After you make your selection, you hand it to the first clerk and she takes it and gives you a bill. Then you go to the cashier and pay for it (with your first bill), and she gives you another ticket, which you take to the pick-up department. Your package will be wrapped and ready to go. At Aldama 187, east of the Buenavista railway station; tel. (5) 526-3700. Open Mon.-Sat. 9 a.m.-6 p.m., Sun. 9 a.m.-2 p.m.

Tianguis De Punk

If you happen to be around the Buenavista railway station on Saturday, check out this funky little market. Located on the side of the railway station, teens especially might enjoy looking at the collection of clothes and cassettes. Saturdays only.

FONART

There are several shops on Av. Juárez that are important to shoppers if only to get an idea of (usually) good traditional workmanship at a reasonable price. FONART is a government store showcasing crafts from every corner of the country. Locations are as follows:

Av. Juárez 89, Centro, tel. (5) 521-0171.
Londres 136, Zona Rosa, tel. 525-2026.
Insurgentes Sur 1630, tel. 534-4335
Av. de La Paz 37 San Angel, tel. 548-1167
Colegio de San Idelfonso, tel. 702-3783.
There are those who say the FONART at Av. Patriotismo 691, Mixcoac, tel. 563-4060, has

the best selection and display tactics. Hours are the same at all locations: Mon.-Sat. 10 a.m.-7 p.m.

Museo De Artes Populares

The Museo de Artes Populares is a combination art museum/store. The quality of the merchandise is (mostly) first rate and the prices are non-negotiable. Open Tues.-Sun. 10 a.m.-6 p.m. Av. Juárez 44, tel. (5) 521-6979. Major credit cards accepted. **CASART** also has silver, onyx, pottery, baskets, and textiles, but at more moderate prices than those above. 10 a.m.-7 p.m.

Colonia Polanco Shops

On Calle Presidente Masaryk check out the **Plaza Masaryk** where there are scads of boutiques featuring goods by **María Isabel, Luis Feraud, Scappino, Sisley,** and **Caviar y Mas.** They also have opened a delightful Japanese restuarant, **Itto.** If you're looking for top fashion designs, bring your plastic money and check out **Les Createurs,** Homero 908, for Italian suits; take a look at **Ermenegildo Zegna,** on Masaryk 427; and if you're planning a sailing trip on an elegant yacht, don't miss **Nautica** at Homero 908.

This is a wonderful shopping area, but it's a money-is-no-object area. Most people will enjoy an afternoon of window shopping if nothing else.

Familiar Discount Stores

Now you can really feel like you never left home (if that's what you want). Ask at your hotel where, but there's a **Price Club** going in (if you carry a card for the U.S., it's valid here). There's also a **Wal-Mart** located in **Ixtalapa,** but it's a bit of a distance from the city center.

Malls And Shopping Centers

These can be pretty spectacular, or just ordinary. **Pabellon Polanco** in Polanco has familiar shops such as Benetton, Radio Shack, and Sears, and you'll find frozen yogurt too. On Homero and Vázquez de Mella, Col. Polanco. Very nice.

Perisur: Periférico Sur 4690, Col. Jardines del Pedregal.

Centro Coyoacán Av. Universidad, corner of Av. Churubusco, Col. Del Carmen Coyoacán.

Centro Interlomas: Boulevard InterLomas

Sergio Bustamante's avant garde ceramics

OZ MALLAN

s/n. Fracc. Parques de la Herradura, Huix-quilucan, State of Mexico.

Plaza Inn: Insurgentes Sur 1971, between Río San Angel and Villalpando.

Plaza Polanco: Jaime Balmes 11, between Homero and Horacio, Col. Polanco.

Plaza Satélite: Circuito Centro Comercial 2251, Cd. Satélite.

Plaza del Angel: Londres 161, Zona Rosa. Interesting plaza with a number of shops whose windows are full of porcelain, old furniture, jewelry, and all sorts of curiosities and crafts. It has two movie theaters. On the weekends a kind of flea market appears with many antiques and charming knickknacks.

Mercado de la Ciudadela: Balderas and Plaza Morelos. A large variety of handicrafts are sold in any of the 150 stalls at this market.

Jardín del Arte or Sullivan Park: between Paseo de la Reforma and Sullivan. On Sundays, numerous artists come to exhibit their work to the visitors; this is the Montmartre of Mexico.

Art Galleries

For art lovers, Mexico not only has great artists, but some really avant-garde galleries.

Galería de Arte Contemporáneo: Medellin 65, Col. Roma; tel. (5) 533-4696 or 533-4607. Open Mon.-Fri. 10 a.m.-2:30 p.m., 4-7 p.m.; Sat. 10 a.m.-2 p.m. Contemporary art.

Galería de Arte Mexicano: Gobernador Rafael Rebollar 43, Col. San Miguel Chapultepec; tel. 515-1636 or 273-1261. Open Mon.-Fri. 10 a.m.-7 p.m., Sat. 10 a.m.-2 p.m. Contemporary Mexican art.

Galería Estela Shapiro: Victor Hugo 72; tel. (5) 525-0123 or 525-0326. Mon.-Fri. 10 a.m.-2 p.m., 4-7 p.m.; Sat. 10 a.m.-2 p.m. Contemporary art.

Galería Mexicana de Diseño: Anatole France, Col. Polanco; tel. 202-0260 or 202-0376. Open Mon.-Fri. 10 a.m.-7:30 p.m., Sat. 11:30 a.m.-5 p.m. Mexican art.

Galería Misrachi: Génova 20, Zona Rosa; tel. 533-4551. Open Mon.-Fri. 10 a.m.-2 p.m., 3-7 p.m. Also at La Fontaine and Homero, Polanco. Contemporary Mexican art.

Galería Nina Menocal: Zacatecas 93, Col. Roma; tel. 564-7209 or 564-7443. Open Mon.-Fri. 9 a.m.-7 p.m., Sat. 10 a.m.-3 p.m. Avant-garde Cuban and Latin-American art.

Galería Omr: Plaza Río de Janeiro 54, between Cordoba and Orizaba, Col. Roma; tel. 511-1179 or 525-3095. Open Mon.-Fri. 10 a.m.-3 p.m., 4-7 p.m. Contemporary Mexican art.

Galería Oscar Roman: Anatole France 26, Col. Polanco; tel. 281-4939 or 281-5214. Open Mon.-Fri. 10:30 a.m.-7:30 p.m., Sat. 11 a.m.-2 p.m. Painting and sculpture.

Salón de la Plástica Mexicana: San Francisco 1626, Col. del Valle; tel. 524-7740 or 524-3693. Open Mon.-Fri. 10 a.m.-7 p.m., Sat. 10 a.m.-2 p.m. Also at Antiguo Colegío de Cristo, Donceles 99, downtown; tel. 789-3100 or 789-1957. Contemporary Mexican art.

SERVICES, INFORMATION, AND COMMUNICATION

TOURIST OFFICES

In Mexico City you'll have a choice of several different sources of information. For a complete picture of the city and its many attractions, stop at any of the information offices you happen to pass; they'll have many brochures, maps, and magazines with upcoming cultural and sporting events, concert dates, and film events.

At **Secretaría de Turismo** (Federal Tourism), most of the material available is in Spanish. On Presidente Masaryk 172, open Mon.-Fri. 8 a.m.-8 p.m., Sat. 9 a.m.-1 p.m., tel. (5) 250-0123.

At the **Mexico City Chamber of Commerce (CANACO)** ask for maps, brochures, and pamphlets of the sites in the city and state, at Paseo de la Reforma 42, tel. 546-5645.

Mexico City Tourism has several booths about town: at Amberes 54, Zona Rosa, open Mon.-Sun., 9 a.m.-1 p.m., tel. 525-9280; at the International Airport in both the National Arrivals and International Arrivals halls; at the TAPO bus station.

COMMUNICATIONS

The area code for Mexico City is (5).

There's something new in Long Distance Telephones—AT&T is updating and upgrading telephone service to and from Mexico. **Ladatel** phones and many newer phones operate on a new system that erases all the waiting and confusion associated with long distance phone calls. Simply press "**01" (the "star" is at the lower left of the phone) and an English-speaking operator will handle your collect or credit card calls. The phones are large, black and silver, and imprinted with a telephone logo; if in doubt push "**01."

The **Main Post Office** is at Lázaro Cárdenas and Tacuba.

BOOKSTORES, NEWSPAPERS, AND MAGAZINES

Books

You can always find English-language books in any of the **Sanborn's** stores, as well as **Wool-**

worth, Sears, and the larger hotel gift shops. And if you're looking for even more, check out the following:

American Book Store: Madero 25, between Bolívar and Gante, downtown; tel. (5) 512-7279. Open Mon.-Sat. 9:30 a.m.-7 p.m. Also at: Revolución 1570, San Angel, tel. 548-8901, 550-0162; Circuito Médicoa 2, Ciudad Satélite, tel. 393-0682 or 393-0843.

Batik: Presidente Masaryk 393-13 and 15, Col. Polanco; tel. 281-0362 or 393-0843. Open Mon.-Fri. 10:30 a.m.-2 p.m., 4-8 p.m.

El Péndulo: Nuevo León 115, Col. Condesa; tel. 286-9493 or 586-9783. Open daily 11 a.m.-10 p.m. Bookstore and coffee shop.

Gandhi: Miguel Angel de Quevedo 134, Col. Chimalistac; tel. 548-1990 or 550-1884. Open Mon.-Fri. 9 a.m.-10:45 p.m., Sat.-Sun. 10 a.m.-10 p.m.

Newspapers

The *Mexico City News,* Mexico City's English-language paper, has the "funny papers" you know and love, as well as news, sports, and syndicated columns; it can be found in all large cities in most of Mexico. Look here for shows and exhibits, movies, and other entertainment.

American newspapers and magazines can be found in the lobbies of major (i.e., expensive) hotels.

Magazines

There's an English-language magazine called *Mexican Insights,* which offers articles about current events in the city and the country. A Spanish-language magazine called *Donde* has current program schedules of theaters and fairs, plus lots more information about the city (it's simple to read the names and titles and addresses). *Tiempo Libre* is yet another Spanish weekly; it lists current entertainment and events, and is available on the newsstands on Friday.

MONEY

Banks

It's no problem in Mexico City to find a bank to change your money. Between 10 a.m. and noon seems to be the times to exchange currency and traveler's checks. Look for the ATM stations that are springing up on many bank fa-

cades. Be sensible: Don't use them at night when few people are around.

Always check the exchange rate at your hotel; recently the best exchange rate was at the **Galería Plaza Hotel** (for guests only, of course).

ATMs In The City

Automatic teller machines work the same in Mexico as anywhere else. Usually they're enclosed by glass walls, and you'll need to insert your card into a slot at the door to access the area. Directions are in Spanish, though they're simple to follow if you've used an ATM at home. Some ATM locations are listed below.

Banco Serfin: Bolívar 30, historic downtown area.

Banco de Mexico: Callejon de la Condesa, historic downtown area.

Banamex: Isabel la Católica 44, historic downtown area.

Banco del Atlantico: Av. Hidalgo 128, Coyoacán.

Casas De Cambios

Casas de Cambios are a good bet when you need to exchange money in the banks' off hours.

Casa de Cambio Aeropuerto: very convenient at the International Airport, Sala B-47; open most of the day and into the night.

Americam: Presidente Mazaryk 89.

Impulsora Mexicana de Divisas: Extremadura 72.

USEFUL NUMBERS

Embassies

Argentina: Blvd. Avila Camacho 1, Comermex Building, 8th Fl., tel. (5) 520-9431 or 520-9432.

Brazil Lope de Amendáriz 130, tel. 202-7500.

Canada: Schiller 529, tel. 254-3288 or 254-3233.

Chile: Montes Urales 460, 1st Fl., tel. 520-0025 or 520-0219.

Colombia: Paseo de la Reforma 1620, tel. 202-7299 or 535-2877.

Costa Rica: Río Po 113, tel. 525-7764, 525-7765, or 525-7766.

France: Havre 15, tel. 533-1360.

Germany: Lord Byron 737, tel. 545-6655.

Great Britain: Río Lerma 71, tel. 207-2449 or 207-2569.

Israel: Luis G. Urbina 58, tel. 520-7553 or 520-7608.

Italy: Av. de las Palmas 1994, tel. 596-3655.

Japan: Paseo de la Reforma 395, tel. 211-0028.

Peru: Av. de las Palmas 2030, tel. 596-8288.

Russia: José Vasconcelos 204, tel. 573-1305 or 516-8870.

Saudi Arabia: Paseo Lomas Altas 164, tel. 570-6633, 570-6348, or 570-6892.

Spain: Edgar Allen Poe 91, tel. 280-4508 or 280-4633.

Sweden: Blvd. M. Avila Camacho 1, 6th Fl., tel. 540-7393, 540-7394, 540-7395, or 540-7396.

United States Embassy: Paseo de la Reforma 305, tel. 533-2325 or 211-0042.

Venezuela: Schiller 326, tel. 203-4435 or 203-4233.

Private Medical Services

American British Cowdray Hospital, on Sur 136, Col. Las Americas, tel. (5) 277-5000 or 515-8359: Although we have no personal experience here, we have spoken to others who have; they all say it's the best in the city. There's also the **Hospital Mocel** (Gelati 29, Col. San Miguel Chapultepec, tel. 277-3111) and the **Sanatorio Español** (Ejército Nacional 613, tel. 531-3300 to 3319).

Tourist Help And Emergencies

Infotur: City's general telephone tourist information service: restaurants, shows, hospitals, stores; tel. (5) 525-9380 to 9384.

Locatel: Information and assistance on lost persons or vehicles, medical emergencies, emotional crises, diverse public services; tel. 658-1111.

Tourist Assistance Patrol on highways: tel. 250-8221 or 250-8555, ext. 130, 297.

Red Cross: tel. 557-5757.

Federal Consumer Bureau: tel. 568-8722 or 761-3811.

Police: tel. 588-5100.

Highway Police: tel. 684-2142.

Local Police: To report robberies, assault, public disturbances, or abandoned vehicles, call 08.

To Report Lost Or Stolen Credit Cards

American Express: tel. (5) 326-2666.

Banamex, MasterCard, Visa: tel. 588-7999.

Bancomer: tel. 703-9113 or 703-9114.

Diners Club: tel. 580-0122.

Carnet: tel. 227-2777 or 227-2727.

Churches

Most of the churches in the city are Catholic, but here are a few of other faiths. For the closest Catholic church and hours of services, ask the desk clerk at your hotel.

Christ Church, Protestant, Articulo 123 134, Centro district, tel. (5) 512-7447.

Seventh Day Adventist Church: Lago Como 8, tel. 399-8413.

Monte Sinai Synagogue: Querétaro 110, Col. Roma, tel. 584-0039.

Templo Beth-El Synagogue: Horacio 1722, Polanco District, tel. 545-3967.

TRAVEL AGENCIES IN THE CITY

A good way to get the feel of a city is to take a city tour; most of the below-mentioned travel agencies will either provide or direct you to one. Also ask at your hotel.

Culturmex

This is a very helpful organization, not only for transportation in and out of the city, but also for city tours and some great cultural tours in the most interesting parts of Mexico. For more information, write or fax: Campeche 280, office 603; Col. Condesa, 06100 Mexico, D.F., tel. (5) 574-2255 or 574-2257, fax 574-2496.

Other Agencies

American Express: Hotel Nikko Mexico, tel. 207-6950; Campos Elyseos 204, tel. (5) 280-1111.

Turismo Antonio Perez: Río Volga 1, ground floor, Col. Cuauhtémoc, tel. 533-1148 to 533-1152.

Turismo Flamel: Alvaro Obregón 143, Col. Roma, tel. 207-1692, 208-4877, or 208-4817.

Viajes Bojorquez: Petalozzi 83, Col. Del Valle, tel. 523-9010.

Viajes Felgueres: Emilio Castelar 171, Col. Polanco, tel. 255-0988.

Wagon-Lits Viajes: Juárez 88, tel. 518-1180; Av. de las Palmas, ground floor, tel. 540-0579 or 540-1597.

GETTING THERE

BY PLANE

Aeropuerto Internacional Benito Juárez
Mexico's shiny new air terminal should be fully operational by the time you read this book; 135,000 square meters of space has been added with high-tech "chips" to help everything run smoothly in the business end. An additional 1,200 parking spaces have been added, which should help with the daily traffic jams at the entrances. New design and a people-mover is expected to expedite passenger flow, and there's a nice new Customs Hall with broad glass walls to separate the waiting area.

Note: As you head out of the arrival area with your luggage and go through customs you must either push a button to turn on a light (red or green) or put your hand in and reach for a ball. If the ball or light are red, you must stop and the customs people will examine your luggage. (So far we have never gotten the red light!) If your luggage is inspected, *you* must put it all back together.

BY TRAIN

The **Ferrocarriles Nacional de Mexico** is the national railway system of Mexico; the Central Station is located on Insurgentes Norte, in Col. Buenavista, tel. (5) 547-1097. Get there via Metro line 2, north of Revolución station. Information is available 6:30 a.m.-9:30 p.m. Connections can be made on the Mexican side of the border at El Paso and Laredo, Texas; Nogales, Arizona; and Calexico, California.

BY BUS

Coming and going to Mexico City by bus is probably the most efficient and economical way to get around this large country. Most tourist offices will give bus information, but for the most accurate schedules and prices, go directly to the bus station and if possible make reservations a day or so in advance. For long distance buses, go to the following stations:

Terminal Central del Norte ("North Terminal"): Av. de los Cien Metros 1907, tel. (5) 587-15-52. Metro line 5 goes to Terminal Norte station.

Terminal Central del Sur ("South Terminal"): Av. Tasqueña 1320, tel. 544-2101. Take Metro line 2 to Tasqueña station.

Terminal Poniente ("Western Terminal"): Av. Sur 122, tel. 271-0038 or 271-4519.

Terminal Central Oriente ("Eastern Terminal"): Calz. Ignacio Zaragoza 200, tel. 542-4210. Metro line 4

AIRLINES

The following airlines have offices in Mexico City:
Aero California, Reforma 332, tel. 207-1392.
Aeromar, Leibnitz 34, tel. 592-1995.
Aeromexico, Reforma 445, tel. 327-4000.
Air France, Reforma 404, tel. 627-6060.
Air Panama, Reforma 116, tel. 566-6860.
Alitalia, Reforma 390, 10th Fl., tel. 533-1240 ext. 43.
American Airlines, Reforma 300 1st Fl., tel. 203-9444.
Avianca, Reforma 195-301, tel. 566-8550.
Canadian Airlines International, Reforma 390, tel. 208-1654 or 208-1691.
Continental, Reforma 325, tel. 203-1148/280-3434.
Delta Air Lines, Reforma 381, tel. 202-1608.
Iberia, Reforma 24, tel. 705-0716.
Japan Airlines, Reforma 295, tel. 533-5515.
KLM Royal Dutch Airlines, Av. de las Palmas 735, tel. 202-4444.
LACSA, Río Nilo 88, tel. 525-0025.
Lufthansa, Av. de las Palmas 239, tel. 202-8866.
Mexicana de Aviacion, Xola 535, tel. 660-4433.
Taesa, Reforma 30, tel. 705-6164.
United Airlines, Hamburgo 213, tel. 627-9476.
Note: For international flight information, call (5) 571-3600.

at Morelos station. Line 1 at San Lázaro station.

Deluxe Bus Service
These comfortable buses are really getting to be the big thing for Mexico travel. The costs are higher but the buses and nonstop routes make up for it. Several companies have earned a good reputation:

ETN: tel. (5) 273-0251 or 567-3773.
Omnibus de Mexico: tel. 567-7698.
Tres Estrellas de Oro: tel. 587-5700.
Turistar: tel. 587-5377.

GETTING AROUND

Getting around Mexico City is cheap and efficient. Once visitors arrive at their destination neighborhood, walking is the best way to see everything; there are usually concentrations of attractions in each of the popular areas of the city. Some areas are still cobblestone, so dress your feet accordingly; flat, sturdy, preferably rubber-soled shoes are the best. Public transportation is the biggest bargain in Mexico; you can go almost anywhere for less than a quarter!

BY METRO

The Metro is a series of nine different lines, designed and built by a French company, that crisscross the city, linking airport, rail, and bus terminals. The fare is about 20 cents (US$) and millions of people a day use it to get around. The hours of operation vary slightly according to day of the week and the line, but they're roughly 6 a.m.-midnight, slightly later on Saturday nights.

The stations, located within easy walking distances of most downtown hotels, are clean and well-lit. Directions are indicated by the last stops at each end, so you must know where you want to go (Metro maps are available at ticket booths and info centers). The lines intersect, making multiple line trips as cheap as single line ones.

The bright, red trains ride on rubber wheels, making the ride quiet and providing for quick stops, many of which are unexpected. If standing, hold onto something or suffer the indignity of falling on someone. The subway crowd is intent on getting on and off the train at the earliest instant; stay well away from the doors. People will push and shove, so be prepared when the doors open. The best time to ride the Metro is during off-hours, but even then keep a grip on your belongings; pickpockets frequent the subways. At peak hours in some stations it is such a crush that the walkway is divided by ropes: one side for women and children, one side for men.

The station at **Pino Suárez** has a pyramid honoring Ehecatl inside it, and the station at **La Raza** is darkened to project slides of the universe.

To And From The Airport
If you're traveling light, take Airport Metro, line 5, at the Terminal Aerea station. If you have any luggage, your best bet is a taxi; excess luggage is not allowed on the Metro. Make your deal before you climb in the cab. If you have a choice, the VW Beetle cabs are usually cheapest.

BOB RACE

Pyramid of the Wind God, Ehecatl, in a Mexico City subway station

BY TAXI

Taxis come in all colors and sizes, with and without meters. Green and white VWs are in the majority and always can be found outside the airport. It *might* be cheaper to follow the Metro signs to the station steps and flag one down on the corner. This is letting fate guide you, but it is faster than waiting in the queue for a fleet cab. Ask the price before getting in; a ride to the Monument to the Revolution or the Zona Rosa should be around US$15 (depending on the type of cab you take).

There are many **gypsy cabs,** especially at bus terminals. Gypsy taxis are independent cabbies who are not part of any taxi company and are not allowed to park in front of the airport at the regular taxi stand. They'll usually park in the lots and then stand at the entrance of the airport and invite you to use their taxis. The problem is that you have no idea what their vehicles are like and even though the city taxi drivers can sometimes be wild drivers, the gypsies might be even wilder. In a really wild scenario, they may not even be taxi drivers, just brigands looking for a fast buck. For the most part they're just guys trying to earn some money. Under no circumstances allow anyone to take your bag. If you follow someone to a *carcacha* (jalopy) that isn't marked with a taxi sign, don't accept a ride. Usually they will overcharge you.

In the city, most larger hotels have a cab service; these are the most expensive cabs, but prices are posted. The cars are usually four-door Fords, and the drivers may speak English (or be licensed guides as well). There are also cab stands near the hotels; ask the doorman to point one out.

Horizontally striped VW vans, called *peseros,* run along most major streets and are always crowded. Ask the driver if he is going where you wish to go (e.g., *¿ Va a Teotihuacán?*—Are you going to Teotihuacán?). If he closes the door, that means no. Minibuses travel from one Metro station to another, with the destinations written on the windshield.

Note: If a driver wiggles his fingers out the window, he's telling you how many seats are available.

BY CAR

I don't recommend driving in Mexico City; it can be hazardous to both your physical and mental health. Reasons are many: The beautiful Paseo de la Reforma is a series of *gloriettas* (traffic circles), and traffic around these is horrendous. You're basically "playing chicken": I have yet to

MEXICO CITY DISTANCE TABLE

For an idea of what it takes from here to there, these distances are all from the downtown area of Mexico City.

Within The Distrito Federal
Airport: 6 km
Chapultepec Park: 5.3 km
Coyoacán: 8 km
Polanco: 6.5 km
San Angel: 9 km
Xochimilco: 24 km
Zona Rosa: 3.4 km

Elsewhere In Central Mexico
Cuernavaca: 85 km
Guadalajara: 535 km
Guanajuato: 356 km
Jalapa: 313 km
Morelia: 315
Pachuca: 90 km
Pátzcuaro: 377
Puebla: 130 km
Querétaro: 222 km
San Miguel de Allende: 275 km
Taxco: 185 km
Teotihuacán: 50 km
Tepotzlán: 82 km
Tepotzotlán: 43 km
Tlaxcala: 120
Toluca: 67 km
Tula: 93 km
Veracruz: 430 km

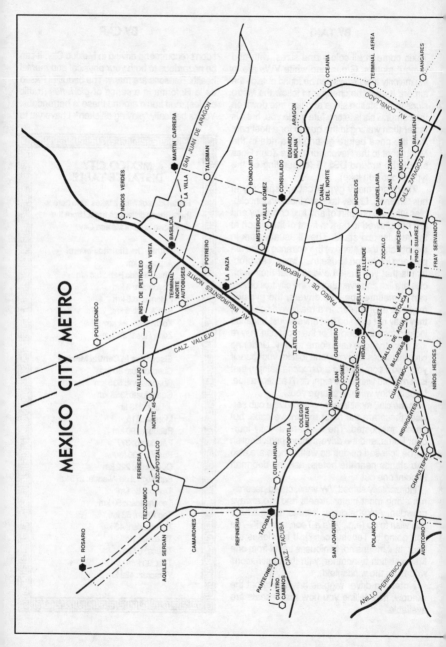

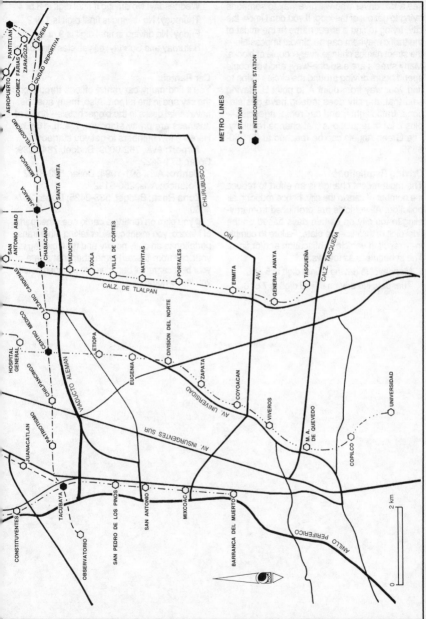

MOON PUBLICATIONS, INC.

see a taxi driver who will give way to someone trying to get out of the loop. If you don't know the city, trying to find a street name in the midst of the traffic mayhem can be almost impossible—the street names change every couple of blocks. Many streets are also one-way, and you could spend hours driving around the circles trying to find your way from point A to point B. Having said that, the city does indeed have gas stations, traffic lights, and car rental agencies—plus a lot of regulations that change regularly. The Green Angels can be reached at (5) 250-8555.

Driving Regulations

The most recent change is an effort to reduce the number of cars in the city, hence reducing air pollution. All vehicles are prohibited from traveling in the city on certain days based on the final digit of their license plate. Failure to comply may result in vehicle confiscation and/or fines. The schedule is as follows:

Monday: No driving if final digit is 5 or 6

Tuesday: No driving if final digit is 7 or 8

Wednesday: No driving if final digit is 3 or 4

Thursday: No driving is final digit is 1 or 2

Friday: No driving is final digit is 9 or 0

Saturday and Sunday: all vehicles may drive

Car Rentals

You'll find many car rental offices throughout the city and in the airport. Also, many agencies have rental desks in the bigger hotels—hours of business are pretty standard; 7 a.m.-10 p.m. Here's a few numbers to get you started:

Airport: Avis, 762-0099; Budget, 784-2289; Dollar, 571-4422

Centro: Avis, 591-1994; Dollar, 592-8312

Polanco: Avis, 250-6192

Zona Rosa: Budget, 533-0425; Dollar, 207-4060

If you plan on renting a car to see other parts of Mexico, you might consider taking other transportation to an outlying city and then picking up your car from there. Remember that some of your best car rental bargains are obtained before you leave home.

K. A. ESCOVEDO SANDERS

THE STATE OF MEXICO
INTRODUCTION

The Hub
Many visitors to Mexico State use Mexico City as their headquarters for exploring the entire state; most areas are a simple day-trip away from the capital and easily accessible either by public transport or tour group.

The Land
The geography of the state of Mexico is a wonderfully diverse landscape, from high snow-covered mountains surrounding a large valley, to towns that spread from the bottom to the top of steep hills, to flatter regions in the west. The state is overflowing with fine rivers, waterfalls, lakes, pine forests, caves, and, contrarily, almost desertlike conditions in the lower elevations. Many fine state parks are scattered about for the outdoor type. Mexico State is located in a valley on a high plateau surrounded by seven states (Hidalgo, Querétaro, Michoacán, Guerrero, Morelos, Puebla, and Tlaxcala) and the Distrito Federal (essentially Mexico City). The state itself is broken up into eight regions: Tex-

coco, Zumpango, Toluca, Coatepec, Tejupilco, Valle de Bravo, Atlacomulco, and Jilotepec.

HISTORY

The Valley Of Mexico
Known earlier as the **Valley of Anáhuac**, the Valley of Mexico has been occupied for thousands of years. Groups of warlike nomads called *chichimecas* (barbarians) migrated south from dry barren northern hills and mountains. Each new wave learned from the group it conquered, and adopted that group's farming methods and gods. As people went from being hunter/gatherers to cultivating corn and other crops, villages formed. A town of thatch houses on stilts rose at the edge of the lake at Tlatilco, 1,200 years before the birth of Christ. Stone cities such as **Cuicuilco** grew in the south and **Teotihuacán** to the north.

There are those who believe that the **Toltecs** were probably responsible for building Teoti-

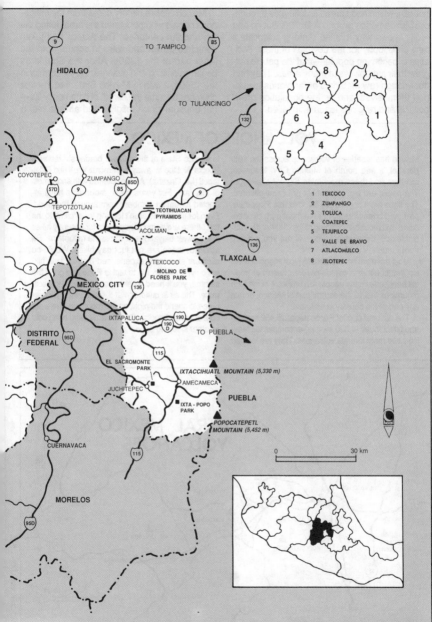

huacán, which had spread its influence throughout Mesoamerica around A.D. 700. But no one really knows why it failed. Among scientists a new philosophy for the downfall of these societies is becoming popular—that the people outgrew their capabilities in many areas. They had not enough raw materials or farmlands to support themselves, and as the population grew, political and religious leadership failed.

Mexico State's history dates from the indigenous people who populated the area during the 8th and 9th centuries. The Aztecs had taken complete power and were in control from the latter part of the 1300s. After the Spaniards began colonizing and evangelizing the country in the 1500s, it was in Mexico State that the first churches became the center of community life—not unusual since religion had always had a

VOLCANOES OF MEXICO

Mexico has a series of volcanoes across the 19th parallel, a line south of Mexico City. Mountain climbers find these mountains a great challenge. The peaks are high, and most are snow-covered. The three most popular are **Mt. Orizaba, Popocatépetl,** and **Ixtaccíhuatl.** For the most part, climbers come with mountain climbing clubs in either the U.S. or Mexico; occasionally you will run into a group from Europe or Japan.

Most travelers have a stereotypical image of Mexico that is either a cactus-covered desert or tropical beaches—many people are unaware of the high mountains that fill the central part of Mexico, or that any part of the country sees snow.

The national park of Popocatépetl (5,452 meters) and Ixtaccíhuatl (4,330 meters) encompasses Mexico's two most famous volcanoes. They are located

in Mexico State at the eastern border shared with Puebla. Not too far away in Veracruz you'll find Citlaltepetl (Mt. Orizaba). All are covered with snow most of the year. For years these mountains have attracted mountain climbers from around the world. Even for those who aren't looking for a "climb to the top," there are some lovely spots for leisurely hikes in the lower elevations of the same mountains. Be advised, these are not just day-hikes. Would-be climbers should be experienced high-altitude hikers only. If you decide to tackle Popo and go to the summit, you'll need to give yourself time to acclimate. The air is quite thin at 5,452 meters. Be prepared to spend the night on the mountain (there are huts at several spots). Dress warmly and bring cold weather sleeping bags.

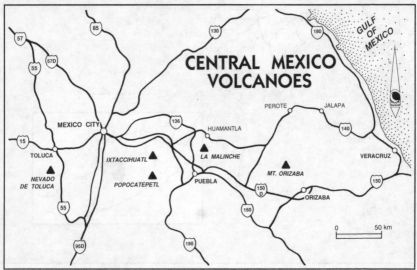

© MOON PUBLICATIONS, INC.

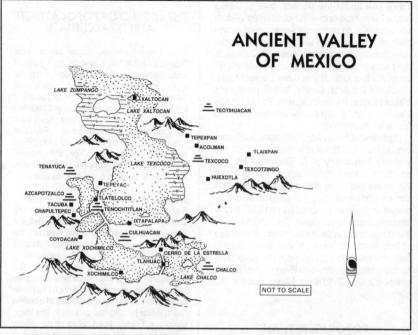

ANCIENT VALLEY OF MEXICO

LAKE ZUMPANGO

XALTOCAN

LAKE XALTOCAN

TEOTIHUACAN

TEPEXPAN

ACOLMAN

TLAIXPAN

LAKE TEXCOCO

TEXCOCO

TEXCOTZINGO

HUEXOTLA

TENAYUCA

TEPEYAC

AZCAPOTZALCO

TACUBA

TLATELOLCO

CHAPULTEPEC

TENOCHTITLAN

IXTAPALAPA

CULHUACAN

COYOACAN

LAKE XOCHIMILCO

CERRO DE LA ESTRELLA

TLAHUAC

XOCHIMILCO

CHALCO

LAKE CHALCO

NOT TO SCALE

© MOON PUBLICATIONS, INC.

strong influence on the Aztecs' daily life. The more well-known Christian centers with beautiful churches were in **Texcoco, Tepotzotlán, Tepetlaoztoc,** and **Acolmán.** The Valley of Mexico offered excellent agriculture, hunting, and fishing; **Teotenango, Toluca,** and **Calixtlahuaca,** were among the most efficient suppliers to the central cities. Mining would become the most lucrative industry of the state, and even today it's a vital part of the economy.

TEXCOCO REGION

This region is east of Mexico City, and even farther east you'll find **Ixta-Popo Park** at the foot of Popocatépetl. At the southern part of the park, please note the monument at what is called **Cortés Pass,** commemorating the route taken by Cortés and his men as they crossed the country from Veracruz to Tenochtitlán in search of Moctezuma.

AMECAMECA

Most people know Amecameca as a starting point for a trek into the high mountain peaks and volcanoes. The small city of 25,000 is at an altitude of 2,475 meters. But if you're just passing through, take a look around. In the clean brisk air of this small town, a bustling community thrives among its share of historical remnants. The **Parish Church of the Assumption** is quite lovely. Its simple red-and-white baroque facade is a welcome change to the busy exteriors of many of the churches. The church was built in the 16th century by the Dominican priests. In the cloister you'll find some very old paintings. Artisans from around the countryside bring their crafts, woolens, baskets, and ceramics (and much more) to the market that continues in the old traditions (Sat.-Sun.) at the town square.

You'll see under the portals rows of tables topped with blue-and-white checkered oilcloth covered with an immense selection of *everything,* and sprawled on the ground, a wonderful selection of *típico* pottery. **Casa de Cultura** is right next to the Parish Church downtown. Always worth a look. If you have a sweet tooth, check out the **Arts, Crafts, and Sweetmeats Market** next to the main square. The Mexicans love candy and sweet things, and don't seem to feel at all guilty about it.

Just west of town near Juchitepec, **El Sacromonte Park** is a lovely hillside area to stroll and visit the **Sanctuary of El Sacromonte.** The sanctuary is a red, domed structure located on a hill, where each year during Lent, the townsfolk carry a horizontal image of Christ that is supposed to have been created in 1521, and is decorated with sugar paste. The religious carry the image and candles to the nearby burial cave of Fray Martín de Valencia, who is said to have been the leader of the first group of missionaries to the area. If you're traveling with children, check out the **Children's Playground** in the park.

POPOCATEPETL AND IXTACCIHUATL

Most people visiting Amecameca are interested in a trek into Popocatépetl and neighboring Ixtaccíhuatl mountains. They can be approached from Puebla as well. These mountains come together as the eastern lip of the Valley of Mexico. Although both volcanoes are said to be dormant, Popo occasionally gives forth a puff of steam. But the last action of any sort was in 1921, when a new cone pushed its way from the bottom of the crater.

Scientists estimate the age of the volcanoes at 2.5 million years. Little is known about the relationship between the Indians and the volcanoes. Obviously the Indians approached these peaks on occasion, since high on the lower peak of Popo (called Ventorrillo) there's a small Toltecan enclosure dated from A.D. 900.

And in 1521, according to a remarkable story told by Bernal Díaz del Castillo, (one of Cortés's conquistadores), five of his soldiers were sent to Popo's crater on a quest for sulphur. The Spaniards were in need of gunpowder, and

THE LEGEND OF POPOCATEPETL AND IXTACCIHUATL

If you spend much time around the fire at the Vicente Guerrero lodge, and there's a group of local climbers, you'll get a barrage of stories, myths, and legends from pre-Hispanic time to the present. Some of these stories you might not want to hear, about calamities and tragedies that have occurred over the years. But at least you should know how the two peaks, Popo and Ixta, got their names. And then take a look; Popo may still be holding his torch high, and you never know when a puff of smoke will remind everyone that he's still standing guard over his love.

Smoking Mountain

A warrior, **Popocatépetl** ("Smoking Mountain"), sent off to battle by his commander, had fallen in love with **Ixtaccíhuatl** ("Sleeping Woman"), the daughter of the emperor. As much as it clutched his heart to leave her, his love empowered him to push on to a great victory far from home. But trouble was lurking, and before he arrived at his beloved's door his enemies told her he had been killed. At that news, Ixtaccíhuatl died of a broken heart. When he returned and made this tragic discovery, Popocatépetl called on his mighty powers and built the magnificent mountains just outside of Tenochtitlán. He laid Ixta's body on one range, and close by he stands guarding her for all time. The Aztecs idolized both Ixtaccíhuatl and Popocatépetl as gods, and celebrated with festivals in their honor.

Cortés, always the clever one, sent the men to get sulphur from the spitting crater. Amazingly, the men actually went into the molten crater, and after many trips lowering men on ropes, they men returned from the volcano with bags of needed sulphur.

This is a popular day-trip from Mexico City for local climbers; some even arrive, climb, and return, all in one day. They have an edge over some visitors who must become acclimated to the altitude.

If the altitude is affecting you, the sure cure is to come down to a lower elevation right away. Be sure to carry water (purified water is available in Amecameca). The town of **Tlamacas,** at 3,950 meters in the saddle between the two volcanic peaks, has become a small hiking cen-

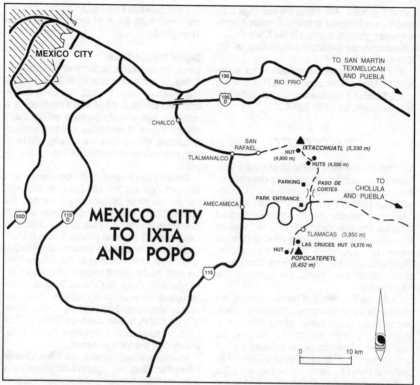

ter. You'll find two lodges, and the one recommended is **Albergue Vicente Guerrero,** set at the base of the black cone of Popo. A dorm bed and locker (bring your own padlock) goes for US$4.50 pp, and there's a restaurant, a bar, fireplaces, and lounges. Blankets and sheets are available and you can count on hot showers. It's a good idea to bring along some food and water; sometimes the restaurant is closed.

Adjusting to the altitude in steps is a good idea; spend a day or two in Mexico City (2,242 meters), then a day or two in Tlamacas (3,950 meters) before you head up to Popo (5,450 meters). Altitude sickness can hit anyone, so be alert, drink plenty of water, no liquor, and eat properly. If you're not a high climber at home, check with your family doctor for advice, and refer to the "Health" section in the Out and About chapter for symptoms and tips.

Some people don't really want to hike up to the high peaks; they're happy to wander the many trails in Tlamacas (30 km from Amecameca), after a drive brings them directly to the lodge. If you have carried anything with you, leave it locked in a locker at the lodge.

If you do decide to do a little climbing, be sure to register with the **Mountain Rescue Group** in Tlamacas before you take off, and the buddy system should be used. Ice and snow are a perennial condition on the upper slopes of Popo and Ixta. Expect freezing and below temperatures year-round, and some months are worse than others for climbing. You would be wise to check with such authorities as the **Colorado Mountain School** at P.O. Box 2062, Estes Park, Colorado 80517, USA tel. (303) 586-5758, fax 586-6677. Or the **Coordinador de Guías de Montaña** at Tlaxcala 47, Col. Roma, Mexico City, tel. (5) 584-4695 (they will provide guides). Ask about the package trips that both companies provide. Another knowledgeable group to contact is the **Club de Exploraciones de Mexico** in Mexico City, tel. (5) 578-5730.

For further detailed information about routes for all of Mexico's volcanoes, read R.G. Secor's guide *Mexico's Volcanoes,* published by The Mountaineers, tel. (206) 223-6303.

TEXCOCO CITY

Located 41 kilometers northeast of Mexico City, there's not much left of what must have been a magnificent city. Its rich history tells of its importance between the 14th and 16th century. Texcoco, a pre-Hispanic city-state, was located on Lake Texcoco (dried up now) and was an important member of the Triple Alliance (a group formed by the Aztecs to make war against the Tepanecas—the third member was Tlacolpán, a small vassal state under the thumb of the Tepanecas).

Under the leadership of Nezahualcoyotl, the city was for a time the capital of the Aztec nation. Nezahualcoyotl was known as the Indian poet-king with a love for the arts. For 40 years he reigned over Texcoco, which became the cultural center of the Valley of Mexico. This Indian poet was noted for being not only an artist, but also a keen politician, philosopher, and strong military leader. He and his people worshipped Quetzalcoatl, and did not believe in the human sacrifice demanded by the Aztec's bloodthirsty god, Huitzilopochtli. He was a clever engineer, and the records show that it was he who designed both a superior aqueduct and a giant dyke that would serve several purposes, including filtering a great deal of the salinity from the water of the lake so that it could be used to irrigate the *chinampas*. It also would control the flooding of low-lying Tenochtitlán. This was a great engineering accomplishment, and was forever referred to as Nezahualcoyotl's Dyke. Eventually, Texcoco was forced to accept the cruel gods of the powerful Aztecs. But a new threat was on the horizon; soon Cortés would arrive and end Huitzilopochtli's control. Only a few stone bits remain to tell of Nezahualcoyotl's past glory.

It was here that the defeated Cortés launched his newly built ships in order to recapture Tenochtitlán.

Sights Around Town

When the Spaniards began their colonization, America's first school was established here by Fray Pedro de Gante in 1523. The lovely **Cathedral and ex-Convent of San Francisco** is a massive, 16th-century baroque edifice that's still the scene of weddings and baptisms on Saturdays. Market days are Sunday and Monday, and the region is noted for fine woolen articles.

Constitution Square, in the town center, is a long rectangle with trees and statues, lined with the ancient stone *portales* where vendors set up their tables, selling everything from wooden furniture to sweets. The **Palacio de Gobierno** is nearby. You'll also find a large indoor market, shops, restaurants, and a bakery. Nicolás Bravo is the main street leading to the square from the east. To the west it becomes Nezahualcoyotl where the **Casa de Cultura/Casa del Constituyente Museum** is located (the State Constitution was signed here in 1827). On the corner of 2 de Marzo is **San Juan de Dios,** a 17th-century church where congress met in 1824, shortly after the Independencia.

As in most Mexican towns, you'll find **Silverio Perez Bull Ring,** two **Sports Complexes,** and a **Rodeo Ring.** Shoppers should check out both **El Crisol Glass-Blowing Factory** and **Texcoco Glass-Blowing Factory.** Nice glassware is on display, and if you're interested ask about a tour.

Los Melones Archaeological Zone, in the center of town, is also called **Cerrito de Los Melones,** on M. Abasolo, east of Juárez. Open Tues.-Sun. 10 a.m.-5 p.m. Admission US$2.50.

As you enter Texcoco from the south on Juárez, the **Agricultural University of Chapingo** is to the left. Here Diego Rivera executed some of his finest murals on the walls of the ex-chapel; open daily to the public, 9 a.m.-6 p.m.

Food And Accommodations

Hungry? **Osteoneria Catedral** is on the pedestrian street leading to Constitution Square. This is a no-frills seafood house that does a remarkable business. You have a choice of shrimp, oyster, or octopus cocktails (US$3 small, US$5

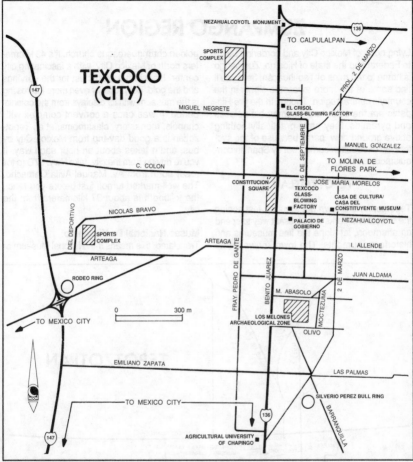

TEXCOCO (CITY)

large). *Caldo pescado* is a hearty broth with onions and tomato topped with a whole fish (US$3.25). The *camarones mojo de ajo* (shrimp and garlic) is good! (US$9).

If you're looking for a place to stay, check out **Posada y Mesón Santa Bertha,** a clean courtyard hotel with an attached restaurant.

Ex-hacienda Molino De Flores
Once an active mill for wheat and corn, the hacienda is now a very pleasant national park near Texcoco city. This 17th-century hacienda is an idyllic picnic place, or just a pleasant locale to wander among the gardens. Very picturesque, it has been used as a movie set many times. The chapel and quite a few other buildings are still standing and offer insights of the times. You can see a *tinaca* where the drink pulque was made. Every hacienda worth its salt made pulque. Take a walk through the family cemetery. The old buildings and the chapel really transport you back to colonial times. It is said that at one time this hacienda was part of the Cervantes family of Spanish Quixote fame. This is a pleasant place to explore while imagining what it was like in the 17th century.

ZUMPANGO REGION

Lying north of Mexico City and bordering Distrito Federal and the state of Hidalgo, Zumpango is home to the ruins of Teotihuacán; here you'll find some of the more awesome sights in the country's central region. Though in the pre-Hispanic era the state had innumerable palaces and pyramids, they have practically nothing above ground now, partly because of the systematic destruction carried out by Spanish conquistadores.

TEPOTZOTLAN

Tepotzotlán is a town not to miss. Just seeing the streets and parks is a pleasant way to spend an afternoon, let alone the fine museums and historic monuments. The town known for its golden churrigueresque church. It's 43 kilometers north of Mexico City, with a fascinating city center. It's worth a study just for the carvings and the gold. But probably even more interesting is the museum with its displays from the colonial period; it was once a convent complex with chapels, monastery, classrooms, et al. Tepotzotlán is a good day-trip from Mexico City by bus, and it takes about an hour each way. If you're driving from the city, take Hwy. 57D (a toll road) north from Av. Manuel Avila Camacho. The well-marked turnoff just before you reach the tollbooth is about 37 kilometers from the city.

Museo Nacional De Virreinato

Translated, this means the "National Museum of

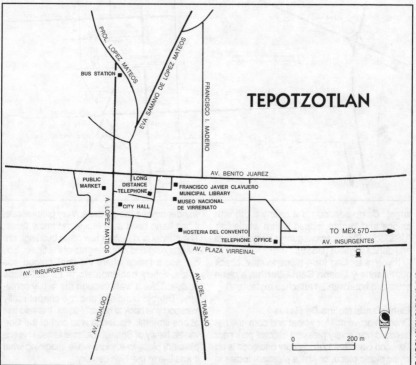

the Viceroyalty." On the plaza, this is the largest and most complete colonial history museum in the country. The 17th/18th century Jesuit ex-convent was started in the 16th century as a school to study the Indian language. Thousands of objects and artifacts pertinent to the Church's 300 years under the Viceroys are displayed here: vestments woven with precious metal, candlesticks, chalices and crucifixes of silver and gold inlaid with precious stones, an oil painting of the Virgin of Guadalupe by Miguel Cabrera. The church building is magnificent, with walls of hardwood in the Moorish style. Gold altarpieces and the carved dome of the Virgin's Chamber, a cornucopia of celestial objects and heavenly beings, are reflected in a mirror for better appreciation; this is Mexican baroque, *estilo churrigueresque* (churrigueresque style). Both the church and the ex-Convent were "made over and gilded" in the 18th century. In the 1960s the complex was renovated and cleaned up. Admission is charged. Plaza Hidalgo 99.

All around the plaza you'll find buildings and centers of interest. Stop in at the **Ex-convent** (a cultural center) and the **City Hall,** and the **Francisco Javier Clavijero Municipal Library.** A book is available in English at the site and is a recommended purchase.

Hostería del Convento is a good place to have lunch on the veranda. Located on the **Plaza Virreinal,** one of their specialties is "Crepada de Zamorra," a crepe covered with fresh berries and powdered almonds—mmm!

ACOLMAN

Either coming or going to Teotihuacán, stop on Hwy. 132 and take a look at another ex-convent, Acolmán. Built in 1560 by the early Augustinians, this monastery is in total contrast to Tepotzotlán's church. This citadel-like structure is a good example of Renaissance/plateresque style. The church contains black-and-white frescoes of the 16th century inspired by daily routines performed during the period. Note the stone cross and its carvings in the **Acolmán Convent** atrium. It is said to have been designed by the Indians. The high, curving, "flying" ceilings are quite lovely in a simple though beautifully designed way. The cloister's arched central patio looks like a peaceful place to medi-

tate. The church was filled with mud for a time due to flooding 200 years ago and was only recently restored. Said to be the locale of the original Christmas Posada in December, the celebrations here include nativity plays—and of course everyone takes part in the posada. On the road to Teotihuacán. Open 10 a.m.-6 p.m. (except Friday); admission is charged.

TEOTIHUACAN

This is one of the largest, most impressive archaeological sites in Mesoamerica. Little is known about the people who built Teotihuacán. It is known that the structures were built from about 100 B.C. and accommodated as many as 200,000 people—over 2,000 apartment compounds have been found. Where did they come from? Where did they go in A.D. 700 when the city seems to have shut down? The city was archaic when the Aztecs arrived 500 years later. The Aztecs used Teotihuacán as a pilgrimage center, and they managed to spin *their* past and present around the relics of this magnificent abandoned city, giving it a life entwined with that of their own religious beliefs. According to Aztec legend, the sun, moon, and universe itself were created here. From what has been found in important archaeological sites all over Mexico and Central America, this was the powerful social and political hub of Mesoamerica for 750 years, from about 600 B.C. to A.D.150.

The name has been translated in several ways, but all have the same basic meaning; "Place Where Men Become Gods." In most cases, the various structures were named by the Spaniards, with just a few originating from the Aztecs. Located about 50 kilometers northeast of Mexico City, Teotihuacán is considered by many to be one of the most amazing of the pre-Hispanic ruins. It's great exercise—wear good walking shoes since the **Avenue of the Dead** alone stretches about four kilometers. The majority of the popular sites are in the northern half of the ancient roadway; at one time the site covered more than 20 square kilometers. So, whether you have an avid interest or just a passing curiosity for ancient ruins, you're probably going to do a lot of walking and climbing. If you visit in the summer, it will be hot, and you can expect (like clockwork) afternoon showers.

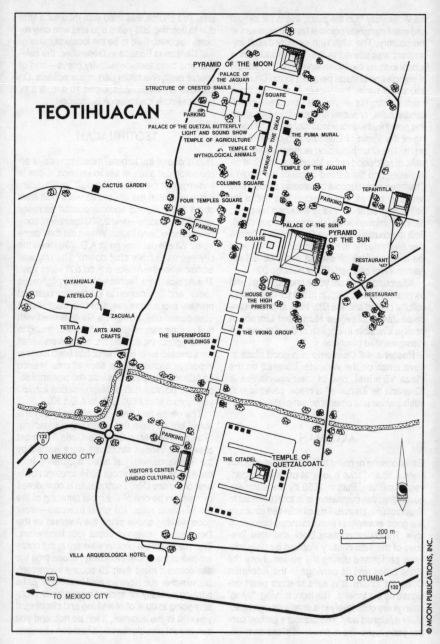

TEOTIHUACAN

PYRAMID OF THE MOON

PALACE OF THE JAGUAR

STRUCTURE OF CRESTED SNAILS

SQUARE

PARKING

PALACE OF THE QUETZAL BUTTERFLY

LIGHT AND SOUND SHOW

TEMPLE OF AGRICULTURE

TEMPLE OF MYTHOLOGICAL ANIMALS

THE PUMA MURAL

AVENUE OF THE DEAD

TEMPLE OF THE JAGUAR

COLUMNS SQUARE

CACTUS GARDEN

TEPANTITLA

PARKING

FOUR TEMPLES SQUARE

PARKING

PALACE OF THE SUN

SQUARE

PYRAMID OF THE SUN

YAYAHUALA

ATETELCO

RESTAURANT

RESTAURANT

ZACUALA

HOUSE OF THE HIGH PRIESTS

TETITLA

ARTS AND CRAFTS

THE SUPERIMPOSED BUILDINGS

THE VIKING GROUP

132 D

TO MEXICO CITY

PARKING

VISITOR'S CENTER (UNIDAD CULTURAL)

THE CITADEL

TEMPLE OF QUETZALCOATL

N

0   200 m

© MOON PUBLICATIONS, INC.

132

VILLA ARQUEOLOGICA HOTEL

TO MEXICO CITY

TO OTUMBA

132

(top left) Sergio Bustamante's galleries are found in many cities (Oz Mallan); (top right) fine pottery from Dolores Hidalgo (Oz Mallan); (above) coppersmith of Santa Clara del Cobre (Hill & Knowlton)

(top) Estudiantino serenades in Guanajuato; (above left) coconut man in Jalisco's Tlaquepaque; (above right) beautiful smiles of Mexico (all photos by Oz Mallan)

wall of masks, Teotihuacán

A hat, sunblock, and water are musts to carry with you. Remember, you are at an altitude of 2,300 meters; unless you're accustomed to this, don't try to rush around; take the steep stairs slowly. The best time of day for pictures and peace is 8 a.m., when the ticket-takers open the gate. The tour buses start arriving around 10 a.m., and the weekends are the busiest, especially on Sunday when admission is free; the rest of the week admission is US$4.50. The site is open 8 a.m.-5 p.m. daily. **Note:** The last bus leaves the main entrance at 6 p.m. Taxis cost around US$60 to get back to the city. If you're driving, there's an extra fee for parking, and you will find several different parking areas surrounding the grounds.

The Visitor's Center

This modern, efficient building is a marked contrast to what follows. Also called **Unidad Cultural,** you can't miss the replica of the water goddess, **Chalchuitlicue,** at the entrance. The original sculpture is at the National Museum of Anthropology in Chapultepec Park. This is a good place to start your visit, getting a head start on the wheres and whys of what you'll see; note the topographical map of the site layout for where you want to start and stop. Here you'll find a museum, several craft shops, a bookstore, a restaurant, and restrooms. The visitor's center is located at the south end of the site. The restaurant here is on the second floor; open Mon.-Fri. 9 a.m.-midnight, Sat. 11 a.m.-11 p.m., Sun. 10 a.m.-6 p.m. The cafe counts on a captive audience, and as result is a bit high for what you get. A sound and light show is presented daily except Sunday, in English 7-7:45 p.m., in Spanish at 8:15-9 p.m. **Note:** the show is suspended July-September).

The Citadel

Starting at the Visitor's Center across the Avenue of the Dead, you'll find the Citadel. Named by the Spanish, it was presumed to have been a military post because of its fortresslike appearance. It actually was a series of platforms that surrounded a large plaza with a stairway that led down to a sunken platform. As was the Mesoamerican custom, another pyramid covered all of this, including (at the rear of the plaza) the **Temple of Quetzalcoatl.** This striking construction contains an altar in its central plaza that is said to have been where the "new fire" ceremony was consummated each year. A hint of ancient red paint is still seen here and there. But the most impressive is the art; a series of ongoing amazing stone carvings of serpent heads surrounded by distinct feathers. The carvings and art mirror Aztec beliefs.

Avenue Of The Dead

When this was a bustling active center, this causeway was much longer than it is today, probably about twice as long. It traverses a north-south line with the Visitor's Center located at the south end and the **Pyramid of the Moon** at the north end. The roadway was named by the Aztecs, who believed that the earth-covered platforms along the way were burial chambers for a "giant" people who had all become gods. Hence the name of the site, Teotihuacán ("Place Where Men Become Gods"). As you proceed along this wide avenue, you'll pass these smaller structures, now uncovered and restored, mostly platforms with low stairways. You'll pass the the group called **superimposed buildings, Four Temples Square, Columns Square, Temple of Mythological Animals,** and **Temple of Agriculture.**

In the mind's eye, it is easy to populate the structures along this great avenue with masses of people in colorful dress going about their business, living within small apartments divided by streets and alleys, with apartment compounds designed to give each dweller a patio and privacy. Residences were densely packed in the northwest section of the city. Scientists now believe that as many as 200,000 people lived in Teotihuacán at its apogee in A.D. 600. Scraps of shiny, sharp obsidian point out the locations of workshops where craftsmen worked this material into weapons and utensils and then traded them long distances from home. These items have been found as far away as Guatemala. Archaeologists have found piles of scrap obsidian in the mines close by that were brought in and then worked by these artisans. Obsidian was also crafted into mirrors with well-rubbed, shiny surfaces.

Three quarters of the way to the **Pyramid of the Moon,** you'll find the **Pyramid of the Sun** east of the road.

Pyramid Of The Sun

This is one of the largest, most impressive pyramids in Mexico, and for that matter in the world. It sits on a base that measures 220 meters by 225 meters and rises to 70 meters in height. Be prepared for 248 steep steps to the top; the view is fantastic, especially on a clear day. Compared to many more ornate sites, the simplicity of lines in these structures adds to the drama and mystique that surround them. In 1971, a long stairway was discovered that ended in a cave 100 meters long under the Pyramid of the Sun. Ceilings had been lowered in certain areas, forcing all who entered to fall to their knees. Piles of charcoal indicate fires had been there, and stone channels imply ceremonies with water. The passage ultimately ends in an array of alcoves. Archaeologists have had a delicious time contemplating all that this could mean. One thing is for certain, caves were considered by an-

cient people to be very magical places; they were presumed to be the womb of the earth where all life began. Exploration is ongoing, with much more to be uncovered.

Palace Of The Quetzal Butterfly

Before you reach the Pyramid of the Moon, note on the west side of the road a pyramid with striking square columns covered with carvings of Quetzal butterfly symbols, stylized birds, and geometric designs. This is the Palace of the Quetzal Butterfly. If you look at the walls low to the ground you might see remnants of the red paint so frequently used in this city. The patio is called the **Plaza of the Columns,** which opens onto a stairway that leads to what was once a street. The **Palace of the Jaguar** has more open patios and rooms. If you look carefully you will see bits of the ancient murals. At one time murals covered many of these walls; within these walls were housed the elite who visited the city.

Pyramid Of The Moon

At the north end of the road you approach the Pyramid of the Moon and the large **Plaza of the Moon**. Although it looks the same height as the Pyramid of the Sun, in reality it was just built on higher ground. It is only 46 meters high; you'll notice the difference once you get to the top (not quite so steep). It's a breathtaking view down the Avenue of the Dead.

Beyond The Renovated Area

If you're not breathless, and still want more, leave the Avenue of the Dead and go to the west side of the site. The dirt roadway will bring you to several other structures that are well worth seeing. Check out the **Tetitla** and **Atetelco** palaces, plus **Zacuala** and **Yayahuala.** Again off the loop, on the opposite (east) side of the site, you'll find the **Tepantitla Palace.**

Accommodations

Villa Arqueológica is located close by at the south end of Teotihuacán. Part of the chain found at many archaeological sites in Mexico, it is a very pleasant place to spend the night if you want to do an in-depth exploration of the ancient grounds at a slower pace. The hotel offers rooms for US$70 s or d, with a/c, pool, tennis courts, a restaurant (serving both French and Mexican food), and a library filled with books about the site. From the U.S. call (800) 258-2633, in Mexico (5) 203-3086 or 203-3833.

Food

If you're hungry, you have several options outside the site. Within the site, your choices are quite limited, unless you pack your own snack. Many folks don't want to interrupt their "hike" to go all the way back to either the second floor of the visitor's center, the Villa Arqueológica dining room, or **La Gruta.** La Gruta is about a 10-minute walk east of the Pyramid of the Sun. It's a pleasant place to have lunch or a snack. Be sure to pick a table that's not out in the open, just in case a shower hits. This place is a bit costly, but they do serve light snacks and cold drinks, as well as full-course Mexican meals. Open daily 11 a.m.-7 p.m. Just outside the entrance to the site, you'll also find many small *fondas* and dining rooms serving simple Mexican food.

Getting To Teotihuacán

By Bus: At the **Terminal Central del Norte,** look for the sign **Autobuses Sahagun** at the northwest end of the terminal. Buses leave the terminal every 30 minutes 5 a.m.-6 p.m.; the trip to the Teotihuacán takes about an hour. You want the bus that says "Los Pirámides," otherwise you may end up at the nearby city of San Juan Teotihuacán. To return to the city, catch your bus at the entrance gate of the museum. Your driver can answer any questions you might have regarding times or other concerns.

By Metro: Another option is to take Metro line 3 as far as Indios Verdes. As you leave the station, note the signs directing you to the Teotihuacán buses.

By Car: You have a choice of driving toll-free on Hwy. 132D (lots of traffic and a little slower), or on the toll road (*cuota*), Hwy. 85D, just a little faster, but with less heavy traffic.

Group Tours: Many groups from Mexico City leave each day for the pyramids. Check with your hotel or travel agency.

TOLUCA REGION

The Toluca region is quite spread out and includes a couple of notable state parks, including the **Nevado de Toluca Park** where visitors enjoy climbing the (quiet) snowcapped volcano (4,558 meters). The State Tourism Office in Toluca City has good information about the parks and the peaks.

TOLUCA CITY

This is the capital of Mexico State. It's located 67 kilometers west of Mexico City. To get there, travel higher into the mountains—by the time you reach Toluca (2,680 meters), you may even be a little breathless since you're in the highest city in the country.

Toluca is a good mix—a city of modern technology yet still with an element of colonial splendor. Though it's quite large and has all the attributes of a big city (including traffic), you'll find a number of parks and plazas if you wander around. The city has a lot of churches and many have their own little plazas. The director of the State Tourism Office laughed at the idea of tourist information about his state. "There are no beaches or golf courses here," he told me. "Here is only culture." And there is a golf club now, **San Carlos Golf Club,** toward the edge of town. Evidence of the city's corporate progress is seen as you pass factory compounds such as Chrysler on the way into the city.

This city has become an industrial giant offering many jobs and a comfortable lifestyle. Early morning sees the large population on busy avenues making their way to work. Outside of the parks (mostly on holidays), you find just a few street vendors. The pace is brisk. The downtown area is clean and impressive, with manicured parks and attractive buildings. With industrial success has come modernization, a number of excellent museums, good shopping, and some fine restaurants. Add that to the remnants of prehistoric times and descendants of the Nahua and Matlatzinca people, plus the legacy of the colonial era with its often flamboyant art.

The areas of colonial interest are centrally located around the **Plaza de los Martires,** named after a group of patriots who were executed on 19 Oct. 1811 for their part in the uprising started by Father Hidalgo. The plaza faces the **Palace of the Governor, Justice Hall, City Hall Chamber of Deputies,** and the fabulous **Cosmo Vitral Jardín Botánico** just a block to the east. **Note:** Many of the buildings' facades are crafted of *tezontle* and *chiluca,* local volcanic stones.

The Portales

About a block from the Plaza, the Portales is an interesting place to spend a few hours, no matter what your interests are. It's a busy place where people meet to eat, or talk, or visit, or romance, and around Christmas you'll find lots of vendors selling the popular local candy. Stores, shops, carts, and restaurants come to life under the arches in a clean, weatherproof environment. You'll notice lots of little *fondas* selling the *típico* sweets that are unique to Toluca. A pedestrian-only walkway lies in front of the ar-

cade shops. With trees and a fountain, it's really quite nice.

Cosmo Vitral Jardín Botánico

This is one of the most original ideas of the city. The garden is located within the walls of a 19th-century building, and more recently it held the popular Toluca market (moved in 1975). The most flamboyant part is the 54 panels of stained glass, three years in the making, created by Leopoldo Flores; these panels reflect the story of mankind. It's a wonderful backdrop for the plants and flowers from the state and the country. The garden contains over 1,000 different species of flora. Open Tues.-Sun. 9 a.m.-5 p.m., admission US$1.75.

Churches

The **Chapel and Sacristy of the ex-Convent of the Assumption:** These structures were begun in 1573 and finished in 1797; you'll find the 17th-

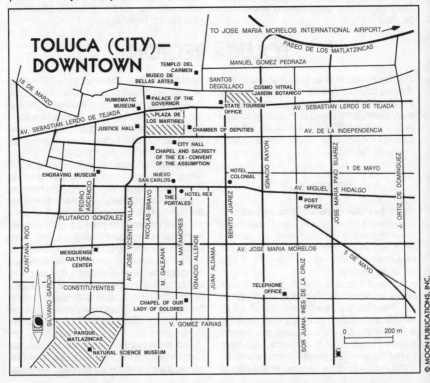

century **Chapel of Our Lady of Dolores** here.

On Calle Santos Degollado find the 16th-century Carmelite **Templo del Carmen** and the **Museo de Bellas Artes** with paintings and sculptures from the 16th to the 19th centuries. Open 9 a.m.-5 p.m. Admission US$1. At the **Cathedral,** traditional dances are performed during certain holidays of the year. This is a very colorful performance; check at one of tourist offices for dates.

Museums

Check out the **Numismatic Museum,** the **Fine Arts Museum, Natural Science Museum,** and the **Engraving Museum,** all in the downtown area.

Mexiquense Cultural Center

A bus ride out of town takes you to one of the important attractions in Toluca. The **Mexican Cultural Center** is an amazing complex with museums that contain some of the finest exhibits in the state. On the grounds visit the **Museum of Anthropology,** where you'll see several unique pieces such as the *tlapanhuéhuetl* (an intricate carved drum) from Malinalco, and the *ehecatl* from Calixtlahuaca, just two of the cultural center's fine pre-Columbian treasures. All this is contained in a beautiful, modern building designed by Pedro Ramírez Vázquez, the famous Mexican architect responsible for the National Museum of Anthropology in Mexico City. The displays and objects, discovered within the state's archaeological zones, date from the state's prehistory. A large modern **Public Library** is open for all to use.

At the other end of the compound, in the old **San Juan de la Cruz** hacienda, built by the Carmelites in the 17th century, you'll find the **Historical Archives,** plus the fine **Mexican Crafts Center,** also called the **Popular Arts Museum.** In the front hall of the building is a huge, colorful polychromed "tree of life" from Metepec, which must have been built on the spot since there is no other way to get it inside. Displays of *charreadas* clothing, saddles, stirrups, and more are located here, as well as other aspects of Mexican rural culture. See even more of those intricate colorful "trees of life" inside.

The **Museum of Modern Art** contains the canvasses of men who were accustomed to working on a larger scale; among these were Siqueiros, O'Gorman, Rivera and Orozco.

The complex also holds a bookstore and a restaurant. This is one (large) terrific compound; don't miss it. The buildings are a mix of old colonial and modern new, quite spread out with a large central area; at certain times of the year traditional dances and entertainments are held. Open Tues.-Sun., 9 a.m.-5 p.m., the restaurant is closed on Sun.; admission is free. English-speaking guides are available. Get there via bus (Linea 2 de Marzo) or taxi; it's located on the western edge of town.

Accommodations

The city has a number of good hotels that regularly accommodate business travelers. These are more expensive, but some of the less expensive are perfectly satisfactory. **Hotel Colonial** is two blocks east of the Portales. The large lobby is flanked by a restaurant on one side and a bar on the other. All are arranged around an interior patio. A well-polished wooden desk sits at the back. The marble stairs lead up to 40 rooms of varying size and decor. Some are carpeted, with white walls accenting the dark brown aged woods. The rooms are furnished with twin, a double, or two double beds, a writing desk, armoire, and a radiator for chilly nights. Tiled bath, TV, and phone; rates are US$18 s, US$22 d. Hidalgo 103 Ote., tel. (721) 15-9700/14-7066. **Nuevo San Carlos** is under the Portal Madero. The 75 rooms have recently been remodeled and upgraded with new paint and carpets. The rooms, as in all old hotels, are different sizes. The staff is friendly, and the prices are inexpensive. Tiled baths, TV and phone. Rates: US$15 s, US$23 d. Portal Madero 210, tel. 114-9419. **Hotel Rex** is across the street from the Portal Morelos. Not as nice as the San Carlos, and a little the worse from wear —wooden floor with a throw rug, yellows and brown dominant, twin beds with mismatched spreads—but it usually has room when the other's booked. Tile showers with curtain. TV in the crowded lobby. Rates are US$14 s, US$18 d. Matamoros 101, tel. 115-9300/ 115-9301. For something nicer, take a look at the **Hotel San Francisco** with 74 rooms and a split-level lobby/lounge/dining room. Rooms are comfy and you have amenities such as a mini-bar; some king beds available. Rates are US$35 s, US$47 d. Good downtown location on Rayon 104, tel. 113-3114.

Food

There are eateries of all kinds with menus for every taste and pocket under and around the Portales. The bakery on Portal 20 de Noviembre has a large selection of cakes and breads. Tamales can be bought from the couple on the corner along with a hot cup of sweet atole.

Restaurant Bar Del Rey is under the Portal 20 de Noviembre, tel. (741) 114-4863. Food, coffee and desserts, frothy drinks, and live music on weekends. Soups and *antojitos* (US$2-4), entrees like *huachinango Veracruzano* (US$5), *pollo* (US$7), and steaks (around US$10). Portal 20 de Noviembre 111.

Hostería Las Ramblas is good for low budget, regional provender. Breakfast, coffee and desserts, bar. Portal 20 de Noviembre 107-D, tel. 115-5488. **El Huipil** on the corner of Allende at Morelos, one block south of the Portales, is decorated with colorful tiles outside. Inside is spacious with a No Smoking section. The regional cuisine is tasty and inexpensive. **Casa Felipe Villanueva,** located on the corner of Morelos and Ascencia, has classical music on Friday nights. Check with the tourism office for times. Let's not forget **VIPS,** for those who might want a little American fare to go along with their Mexican food, also with a No Smoking section. On Paseo Tollocán.

If you have a sweet tooth, step into **Dulcería El Socio** and everywhere you look you'll see sugar and spice and everything—looks good! Open Mon.-Sat. 10 a.m.-9 p.m. For something to do in the evening, there is a multiplex **Cinema** on Lerdo de Tejada close to the tourism office.

Shopping

The **Mercado Juárez** takes place in the area across from the bus station (very convenient for all the villagers who bring their goods from outlying villages). Once a great place for native goods, now it's more like a giant flea market, though quality items can still be found, especially baskets. It's noisy and crowded, and the market is open all week—but Friday is the *big* day.

Casart is on Paseo Tollocán 700 Oriente, tel. 14-0742. It has two floors of goods from the state and nation at set prices. You'll see crafts-

women practicing their art; whether it be weaving cloth or baskets, it's quite amazing to watch the nimble fingers fly and create a lovely design at the same time. Of course they are there to sell their goods as well. Expect to see blown glass, ceramics of every style, lacquerware, lots of textiles in brilliant colors, wood carvings, and lots more! Open daily 10 a.m.-8 p.m. A multitude of stores and vendors sell candy and candied fruit.

Avenida Benito Juárez is another area to find many kinds of shops and stores.

Information

For good info, stop at the "?" kiosk at the bus station, as well as the **State Tourism Office** at Av. Sebastian Lerdo de Tejada 101 (3rd floor), Edificio Plaza Toluca, tel. (721) 113-3014 or 113-2142. Maps and information booklets in English are available.

Lada phones and **newsstands** are located under the Portales. The **Post Office** is at the corner of Hidalgo and Sor Juana de la Cruz.

Getting There And Getting Around

Just outside Toluca, you'll find the **José María Morelos International Airport.** However, from Mexico City, hop on a Metro to the **Observatorio** station and then go to the **Terminal Poniente** bus station. You have several choices; those marked "Toluca-Directo" are the quickest, taking about an hour. Buses to Toluca depart every few minutes throughout the day.

Once in Toluca, look for buses marked "Centro" if you're heading into the city center, and those marked "Terminal" can be caught on Morelos (near Juárez, two blocks from the Portales) when you want to return to the bus terminal.

OUT OF TOWN ATTRACTIONS

Zacango Zoo

A short distance (14 kilometers) outside of town you'll find a zoo. Located on the grounds of the old Zacango Hacienda, the zoo covers 48 hectares with treelined walkways. You'll find free-ranging animals, an African animal compound, a tropical compound, a duck pond, roller skating, pony rentals, a petting zoo, a playground, a walk-through aviary, restaurants, and, in the middle of it all, the old hacienda chapel is still in operation. This is a great place to spend a day, especially if you're traveling with children—they like the same things in any language. Open daily 9 a.m.-5 p.m. Admission charged.

Xinantecatl, Nevado De Toluca

Xinantecatl (Zee-nan-te-CAHT-el) in Nahuatl means "Naked Man." This is an (inactive) volcano. You can actually drive into the crater where you'll find two lakes: the **Lake of the Sun** and the **Lake of the Moon.** Also, there's a rather primitive lodge on the north side of the mountain. If you can catch a good day, this is a fantastic drive with an unparalleled view. The road does not go quite to the top. You must hike up the last 500 meters to the crest. The mountain has two summits; the highest is on the south, called **Pico del Fraile** ("Friar's Peak"), at 4,707 meters. **Pico de la Aguila** ("Eagle's Peak") is on the northern side of the rim at 4,620 meters. Nevada de Toluca is the fourth highest mountain in Mexico (4,558 meters, that's 15,433 feet!). For more detail about climbing the mountain, please refer to R.J. Secor's *Mexico's Volcanoes, A Climbing Guide.*

Archaeological Zone Of Calixtlahuaca

Calixtlahuaca (kah-leesh-tlah-WAH-kah—"Houses on the Plain") is small and northwest of Toluca, located on a hill overlooking the village of the same name. Exploration of this site began in 1931. Some archaeologists believe it was built as early as 1700 B.C., perhaps with a **Huastec** influence, and even nuances of the **Toltecs.** It was ultimately captured by the Aztecs in 1476. One altar with carved skull images has stone pegs along the sides indicating that real skulls were placed there. This is where the strange little round temple **Ehecatl** ("Wind God")

statue is from. (See the Ehecatl statue in the Anthropology Museum in Mexico City, and other artifacts from the site can be seen in the Anthropological Museum in Toluca.) What a fine place for a wind god to hold fort (for 3,000 years!). The breeze can be brisk whistling past the hilltop. Buses from Toluca make the trip frequently, take about 20 minutes to the village, and from there you hike up the hill, not too far. Open daily 9 a.m.-5 p.m., admission US$3.50.

Teotenango Archaeological Site

Teotenango is rather a surprise. It seems silly to say, "in the middle of nowhere," although when you're walking its broad avenues you feel that way. It's sprawled across a flat bluff, not too high, but the town of Tenango seems far away on a hazy day. This is a large site, rivaling Teotihuacán in the size of its pyramids. It was established by the **Matlazinca** people who were later conquered by the Aztecs. This was then a ceremonial center for nearby Malinalco and Calixtlahuaca. The site has been well restored (beginning in 1974) and the structures show a definite relationship to the Teotihuacán site. One of the fascinating artifacts found is a stone gargoyle eating the sun; its said to be a depiction of the solar eclipse of 1477. Stone retaining walls encircle the large broad site. There's a large ball court, and several good sized squat temples with broad staircases that probably held ceremonial structures of wood on top. As you wind up the hill you'll pass a small museum that contains some of the artifacts found during restoration. Open daily 9 a.m.-5 p.m., admission US$3.50.

Located 25 kilometers south of Toluca, and not too far outside the nearby town of **Tenango del Valle,** it's easily reached by bus and taxi combination.

COATEPEC REGION

This is another region where thermal bathing attracts many people; you'll find a series of small resorts, most with indoor and outdoor bathing facilities. But perhaps of even more interest to the explorer is the **Malinalco** archaeological site. In addition you'll find the **Grutas de Estrella** ("Star Caves"), and small towns that date back to the colonial era.

TENANCINGO

In this small town you'll find a bakery, a drugstore, and a stucco, colonial-styled hotel called **El Jardín.** And with plenty of tile, you can't miss the **Church of San Francisco.** The town is renowned for its meat products, fruit liqueurs, wooden furniture, and delightful *rebozos;* market days are Thursday and Sunday. The clean, orderly market near the bus station on Hidalgo and Ocampo is a good place to sample the products of the region. On top of the highest hill is a large religious sculpture reminiscent of Río de Janiero; from here the valley can be viewed in its entirety. Buses can be found in the plaza that will take you to Santa Anna nearby waterfall.

MALINALCO

Malinalco is a famous archaeological site on a bluff above the town of the same name. This was a religious temple Cortés could not destroy completely because it was carved from the solid stone mountainside. The climb to the site entails about 400 steep steps but is worth every panting breath, about a 30-minute walk from the parking lot. Once a school for prestigious Aztec knights, the round temple contains figures of eagle and jaguar warriors. Originally settled by relatives of the Matlazincas, the Aztecs, under Axayácatl, conquered the area in 1469. They held court here from about 1476, and apparently the construction, which began in 1501, was still underway when the Spaniards arrived and ended it all.

Malinalco

BOB RACE

Southwest of Mexico City, Malinalco is one of the four archaeological sites in the world carved from raw stone; the other three are Abu Simbel, Egypt; Petra, Jordan; and Ellora. The major monument, **Temple of the Eagles and Jaguars,** sits on a terrace of earth called Hill of the Idols, and overlooks the valley below.

Temple Of The Eagles And Jaguars

Just outside the entrance, a headless stone man greets all who come (note the giant stone reptile tongue that "swallows" all visitors). The entrance is covered with a thatch roof. For anyone who doesn't know what to expect, it's an amazement to step into this circular chamber of solid rock. It's a dark and mysterious cavern, with enigmatic sculptures of eagles and a jaguar in the floor and on the platform. It was here that the Knights of the Eagle and Jaguar learned to be tough warriors and took part in secret initiation ceremonies. The chamber is six meters in diameter, and the carved eagle in the center of the half circle is a depression where archaeologists tell us the still-beating hearts of sacrificial victims were placed.

Temple Of The Sun

Officially called **Building IV,** this is also partially carved from the stone mountain, but it was here that the beautiful little *tlapanhuéhuetl* (wooden drum) was found. This remarkable piece of art has fine carvings that include glyphs; it now resides in the museum of Anthropology in Toluca's Mexiquense Cultural Center.

There are other partial structures including some remains of frescoes. Open daily except Mon. 10 a.m.-4:30 p.m., admission US$4.50. From the city of Malinalco, the site is about one kilometer west of town, all uphill on a dirt road. Buses run approximately every two hours from the Toluca bus station.

CHALMA

This was a sacrificial site long before the Spanish arrived. About 11 kilometers from the Malinalco archaeological site, in a cave above the sanctuary there was a stone idol of Otzocteotl, god of caves, to which sacrifices and offerings were made. In 1533, shortly after the alleged appearance of the Virgin of Guadalupe, Father Nicolas Perea, an Augustinian, beseeched the natives to rid themselves of Otzocteotl and convert to Catholicism. The caciques told the Spaniards to return in three days for an answer. What the priest and his followers found when they came back was a smashed idol and the crucifix of the Señor de Chalma (Christ) standing in its place, surrounded by fragrant flowers. When the natives heard about the miracle, they came and were converted.

Pilgrims continued to come to see the **Crucifix of Chalma.** One of those pilgrims stayed, took priestly vows and through his devotion became head of the order. Fray Bartolome de Jesús María decided more room was necessary and built the sanctuary near the end of the 16th century. In 1683 the church was dedicated and the Señor de Chalma has stood there ever since.

Still an important religious sanctuary, pilgrims from villages all around the area arrive on foot carrying flowers and offerings, which they leave inside. They often approach on their knees and crawl out the door backwards, as far as the gate, so as not to turn their backs on the Señor. The ritual demanded bathing in a sacred pool in the river, scrubbing themselves and their children, and washing their clothes as well. This custom goes back to pre-Hispanic times and, like many other practices, was transferred to Catholicism after the new "miracle" took place. On the feast of the Pentecost, 3 May, thousands of people come from all over and have a big celebration. They eat and sleep here, traditional dances are performed, and a market attracts many vendors of arts and crafts.

Set among forests and gorges 12 km east of Malinalco, it is truly a place of wonder. Second-class buses leave from Mexico City's western terminal or from Cuernavaca at Flecha Roja station.

IXTAPAN DE LA SAL

If you're looking for a spa/resort of thermal springs with spa prices, you've come to the right place. Ixtapan, with about 25,000 people, is a lovely town, architecturally as well as aesthetically. There's a low-key atmosphere and a distinct flavor of the past with many colonial-style houses about. It doesn't take long to look, and there are several nice little cafes around the plaza. Around the inviting **Plaza de los Mártires,** with its shady trees, take a look at the government buildings and the facade of the **Church of the Lord's Forgiveness,** which date from the 16th century. Sunday is market day, and just a block away from plaza, the **Public Market** is open for a look. If you're interested in the crafts of the region, take a swing by **Calli Arts And Crafts** center on Benito Juárez near the corner of J. Aldama. Also scattered about

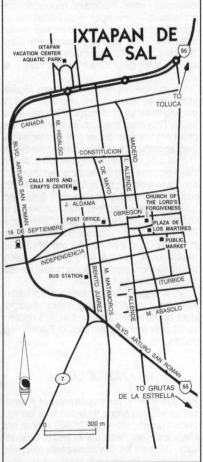

town are a number of aquatic centers if you want a hot soak or a massage, mud bath, or mud mask (anyone in town will tell you the water is radioactive and will cure anything that ails you). **Ixtapan Vacation Center Aquatic Park** is located just north of Hwy. 55 coming into town from the north (Blvd. Arturo San Roman). If you have kids with you they'll love it. Along with thermal pools, there's a small train that runs around the park, boats for rowing, an aquatic toboggan, the Crazy River, the Cheerful River, and the waterfalls—and that's just for starters. For soakers who don't want to stay overnight, check out the many **Municipal Bathing Resorts** wherever you see a sign that says *balneario publico.*

Because of its location (66 kilometers from Toluca and 120 from Mexico City) and the new **Tenango-Ixtapan de la Sal throughway,** more visitors are coming to the area. At about 1,900 meters, the weather is warm and subhumid.

Star Caves
South of town (16 kilometers) are the **Grutas de la Estrella,** electrically lit caves of interesting stalagmite and stalactite forms. As are most caves, these are quite dramatic with striking formations. Their history makes them even more intriguing—it is believed that ancient ceremonies took place in here. The tour is led by a Spanish-speaking guide; admission is charged.

Accommodations
If you decide to spend the night you'll find hotels along Arturo San Roman and around the center of town. **Hotel Casa Blanca** is located on Benito Juárez in the center of town; it's simple and pleasant with a hot pool and a restaurant that stays open all day. Rates are US$37 s, US$40 d. At Av. Benito Juárez 615, tel. (724) 3-0036.

Hotel Bungalows Lolita is a tad nicer and includes some two- and three-bedroom units, hot pool, playground, parking, dining room, and bar. Rates are US$47 s, US$69 for two-bedrooms/two people. On Blvd. San Roman 33, tel. (724) 3-0169. For something a little more upscale including meals, check out the **Hotel Ixtapan.** Rates start at US$110, and the rooms are spacious and comfortable with hot pools available, plus other services for special soaks and massage. On San Ramon, tel. (724) 3-0021.

VALLE DE BRAVO REGION

This region can boast of two lovely manmade lakes with superb views and small resorts.

VALLE DE BRAVO CITY

This beautiful city of whitewashed stucco houses is covered with red—all have red tile roofs. They're set on hills crisscrossed by serpentine streets of cobbled stone overlooking a large manmade lake. Color is everywhere, with bougainvillea dropping over white walls and terraces, and in the small park, **Plaza Independencia,** brilliant flowers attract nature on the wing, and birdsong takes on new meaning. Streets are lined with shops and galleries, restaurants and bars, their names etched on wooden signs. Restaurants offer national and international food of good quality.

Valle de Bravo, located 140 kilometers west of Mexico City, is a playground for the wealthy city dwellers who flock here for weekend getaways and more lengthy vacations. Power and sail boats can be rented for fishing (perch and bass are plentiful), relaxing, or water-skiing, and parasailing and jet skis are available. These resorts have a number of world-class golf courses and tennis courts; swimming pools are everywhere.

Lake Avandaro, which supplies hydroelectric power to the Valley of Mexico, is surrounded by miles of pine woods, rivers, and waterfalls. In the woods just outside of town, monarch butterflies come every year in April and May to reproduce in an area set aside as a wildlife refuge. If you've never seen this, it's quite a sight. Millions of butterflies cling to the trees and each other creating an atmosphere of gold.

Accommodations And Food
Hotel Mary is the bargain basement of Valle de Bravo. The majority of rooms are small, windowless, and reasonably clean (upstairs rooms in front are larger and have windows), with lots of brick and tile. Room rates depend on shower preferences: US$9 s for shared facilities; US$17 s, US$25 d for private bath. At Plaza Independencia 5, tel. 2-0609.

A much nicer, and as easily affordable (US$17 s, US$35 d) establishment is the **Posada de las Bugambillas.** Thirty cheerful, well-lit rooms with pink and white decor in a motel-like setting, freshly painted stucco, double beds, and a private bath in every room. Av. 16 de Septiembre 406, tel. 2-1966.

The **public market** occupies several blocks adjacent and to the right of the plaza. Around the plaza are the usual establishments: newsstand,

OZ MALLAN

Valle de Bravo

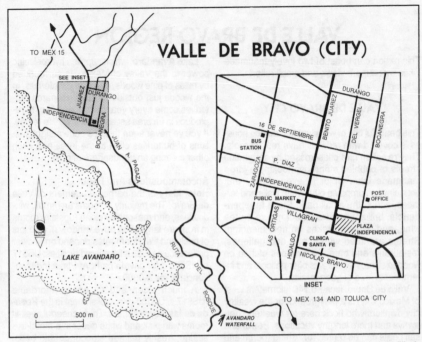

drugstore, bakery, film store, and liquor store.

Restaurant El Portal, tel. 2-0288, occupies the ex-Palacio de Gobernio. Meals are served in two tastefully decorated rooms with plenty of wood beams, brick, and tile. The menu has selections of a mostly national variety and serves all day. Breakfast runs US$2.50-4.50, soups and appetizers cost US$2-5, and entrees are US$6.50-19. Full bar. Open 9 a.m.-11 p.m. Credit cards accepted.

On Calle Juan Pagaza, going towards the lake, are **Restaurant Michoacán, El Rincón Deli,** and **La Cafetería,** to name a few. The whole town is full of delightful cafes, bistros, and restaurants. Enjoy alfresco dining under bright yellow umbrellas at **Oasis,** a second floor bar overlooking the lake (pizza costs US$17). Fine Italian food is served in a homelike setting at **D'Ciro,** as well as sushi, chicken, and seafood; the selections are vast and varied. **La Taberna de la Chef,** (reservations tel. 2-0507) offers French cuisine in a beautiful plant filled, lakefront house.

Other Practicalities

For information, tourist maps, and pamphlets stop at **Casart,** on Costera Valle de Bravo at the lake. The **Casa de Cultura** is also nearby.

Ladatel Telephones are under the portales.

Lavandería Supra Valle is open 10 a.m.-2 p.m. and 4-8 p.m. (left off Juan Pagaza a block down from the plaza).

Clínica Sante Fe offers 24-hour medical service. Calle Nicholas Bravo, a block south and west of the plaza.

To get to the Valle de Bravo from Toluca, go to the **Toluca bus station,** or taxis and *colectivos* can be found by the plaza. The "Getting Away" bus station is on Zaragoza; the first-class bus to Mexico City leaves every hour 6 a.m.-midnight.

TEJUPILCO, ATLACOMULCO, AND JILOTEPEC REGIONS

These three regions of Mexico State are seldom visited by foreign travelers, but they do offer some great wilderness parks for exploration. In most cases come prepared to camp; there are few facilities. Most of the archaeological sites have had little renovation, but there are a few more scattered about. Ask at the Toluca State Tourism Office for more detailed information about these sites and parks.

Tejupilco Region

About 103 kilometers southwest of Toluca, Tejupilco borders the states of Michoacán and Guerrero. Hikers should check out **Sierra de Nanchititla Park** (with a beautiful waterfall) and **La Goleta Park.**

Atlacomulco Region

On the west, Atlacomulco Region also borders the states of Michoacán and Querétaro. This is a productive agricultural and cattle raising center. However, mining is what really got things going here, with both gold and silver. If you should find yourself passing through the city of **El Oro,** take a look at the **El Oro Municipal Palace.** This could be a building straight out of the United Kingdom, a very lovely Victorian structure. No doubt architecturally influenced by the British during its early years when miners and consultants were brought to Mexico from Cornwall, it's just a few kilometers outside of

Atlacomulco city. Birdwatchers will find Isla de las Aves Park, where a bird sanctuary shares the neighborhood with a few humble tourist shelters. Campers will find simple camping facilities at Cruz Colorado Park. Another park to look into is Isidro Fabela near Mt. Jocotitlan, which rises to 3,900 meters. Remember, these parks vary from zero facilities to very few; primarily they're lovely open spaces dedicated to the preservation of nature.

Jilotepec

The northernmost region of Mexico State is Jilotepec. It's bordered by Querétaro and Hidalgo. **Aculco de Espinosa,** toward the western border of the region, is a charming colonial city to visit because of its slow pace and undisturbed genuine appearance left from the colonial past. It invites visitors to wander its cobblestone streets, stop in its tiny peaceful plazas, and examine stone structures with lintels, walls, and gates covered with carved medallions and images.

Acambay Aculco Park has lovely waterfalls as well as **Mt. Pelon,** a peak of 3,325 meters. Hikers will also want to check out **El Llano Park, Chapa de Mota Park** and **La Bufa Monte Alto las Cruces Park.** In Chapa de Mota Park there's a humble astronomical observatory. Another park, **El Ocatal,** is a little more upscale, with a hotel; located in the middle of woods and valleys.

K. A. ESCOVEDO SANDERS

THE STATES OF MORELOS AND GUERRERO
INTRODUCTION

THE STATE OF MORELOS

Located in southwest Mexico, in a valley beneath Mount Ajusco, Morelos was formerly the home of the Tlahuica Indians. Lying on the south side of the central plateau, Morelos, at 4,941 square km, is the second smallest state in Mexico. It's bordered to the north by Mexico City, to the west by the states of Mexico and Guerrero, and to the southeast by Puebla. The countryside presents a hilly landscape of green hills and streams with scattered waterfalls.

Morelos is an agricultural center, producing maize, wheat, and many types of fruits. It's becoming a bee center as well; honey is now one of Mexico's premier exports. you'll also find cement factories, bottling plants, and textile mills.

The state is named for José María Morelos y Pavón, a mestizo priest who joined Miguel Hidalgo's 1810 rebellion against the Spanish. After Hidalgo's 1811 execution Morelos became the leader of the government. Much of his support came from the local peasants, and he used the state as both a base and a refuge until his 1815 capture and murder by the Spanish. Cuernavaca, the capital city, and the archaeological sites Tepotzlán and Xochimilco are all within a few hours' drive from Mexico City.

History

The state has a rich history, reaching back to the Olmec, who occupied the area as far back as 1200 B.C. Recent archaeological discoveries confirm the ancient presence, though once this wasn't considered prime Olmec territory.

The indigenous peoples long considered the Morelos region, and particularly the area around Cuernavaca, as a combination refuge from political strife and holiday retreat. The Tlahuicas and Aztecs established religious sites here long before the Augustinians and Dominicans threw up their monasteries. When Cortés constructed his Cuernajala castle in 1531, he did so on the ruins of an Aztec pyramid, which he summarily destroyed.

Morelos provided many of the initial insurgents in the war of Independence; nearly a century later, the region was a hotbed of revolution, popular with Emiliano Zapata and his Zapatistas. The despotic Emperor Maximilian and his lunatic wife Carlota were also fond of the area.

THE STATE OF GUERRERO

Located in steep, rugged mountains, the State of Guerrero encompasses both sides of the Sierra Madre del Sur and lies alongside the rushing **Río Balsas.** The state is bordered to the south and west by the Pacific Ocean, to the north by the states of Mexico and Morelos, to the northwest by the state of Michoacán, and to the northeast and east by Puebla and Oaxaca. The silver center, Taxco, is about 185 kilometers southwest of Mexico City.

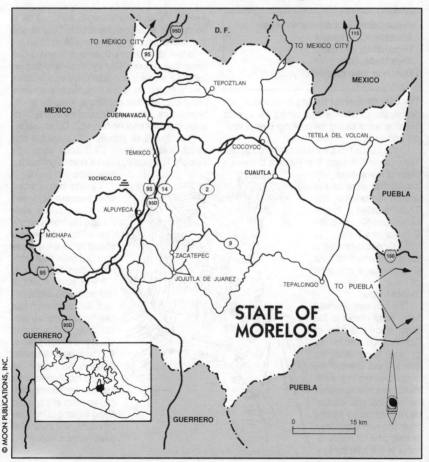

© MOON PUBLICATIONS, INC.

History

The earliest inhabitants of the region are believed to be the Olmecs, followed by the Mixtecs and the Aztecs. In the mid-15th century the Aztecs under Moctezuma I defeated the Mixtecs and brought them into the Aztec empire. Silver and gold mining were already well underway in 1522, when the Spanish in turn conquered the Aztecs.

Guerrero is believed to be the birthplace of the last Aztec emperor, Cuauhtémoc, who was defeated and executed by Cortés in 1525. Cuauhtémoc is honored in his hometown, the village of **Ixcateopan,** with an impressive monument.

Guerrero is named for the War of Independence hero General Vicente Guerrero, who later served as president of the country. He was deposed and put to death by the conservative Anastasio Bustamente in 1829.

CUERNAVACA

Pronounced: qwhere-nah-VAH-kah
Altitude: 1,538 meters
Population: 290,000
Area Code: (73)
Distance from Mexico City: 85 km

The **City Of Eternal Spring** is indeed an apt description of Cuernavaca, where the climate is gentle, encouraging the prolific growth of flowers and trees.

In the 1500s the area was controlled by the Tlahuicas and Aztecs. The Tlahuica city was a place of many trees, with leaves that were said to whistle in the wind. The Tlahuica called it Guauhnahuac, or "Place at the Edge of the Forest." In 1521 Cortés torched the city and renamed the ruins Cuernavaca, a collection of letters easier on the Iberian tongue.

The rich and powerful have been drawn to the town since the time of Cortés, who razed the city pyramid to construct his own fortress. Some of the biggest names in government have built luxury villas here, using Cuernavaca as a temporary escape from the consequences of their political machinations. In the 18th century,

Cuauhtémoc, the last Aztec emperor

BOB RACE

wealthy Taxco silver entrepreneur José de la Borda built a political mansion in Cuernavaca that was later used by Emperor Maximilian.

In the 18th century Cuernavaca was a day away from Mexico City by horse and buggy; today it's an easy one-hour drive on a modern new highway. Many are attracted to weekends in the city, whether politicians, yuppies, or entrepreneurs. Dozens of Mexico's wealthiest citizens maintain second homes in Cuernavaca.

The city is also popular with language students, featuring some 20 Spanish-language schools. The students lend a warm, lighthearted atmosphere to the city.

If you're one of those who became intrigued with Cuernavaca after reading Malcolm Lowry's *Under The Volcano,* you should know the city has changed quite a bit since his sad days there. Though still well worth a visit, it isn't what you might expect. The population has swollen to immense proportions, and includes about one million people. And with people comes pollution. So though the city has *much* cleaner air than the neighboring capital, you can still see the smog when gazing over the countryside toward the great volcano Popo.

RICARDO LINARES

LAS MAÑANITAS

G. FARIAS

LOPEZ MATEOS

TO MEXICO CITY

VICTORIA

GUERRERO

DEL PARQUE

CUERNAVACA

FLECHA ROJA TERMINAL

NO REELECCION

MATAMOROS

AV. MORELOS

ARISTA

DEGOLLADO

ARAGON Y LEON

HOTEL COLONIAL

SALINAS

MORROW

RESTAURANT VIENES

TEJADA

ARTEAGA

ZARCO

LOPEZ MATEOS

L. RAYON

JARDIN JUAREZ

JARDIN BORDA

HOTEL IBERIA

PLAZA DE ARMAS

POST OFFICE

JUAN GUTEMBERG

SALAZAR

CUAUHTEMOC

HIDALGO

CATEDRAL DE LA ASUNCION

MUSEO DE CUAUHNAHUAC / PALACIO DE CORTES

NETZAHUALCOYOTL

PALACIO MUNICIPAL

LAS CASAS

ALTACOMULCO

ABASOLO

AUTOBUSES PULLMAN DE MORELOS TERMINAL

LA POSADA DE XOCHIQUETZAL

OBREGON

GALENA

JUAREZ

LEYVA

MOTOLINIA

HUMBOLDT PALMIRA

ESTRELLA ROJA TERMINAL

CUAUHTEMOTZIN

AV. MORELOS

GONZALES

BOCANEGRA

TOURIST OFFICE

NIMNO NACIONAL

AUTOBUSES ESTRELLO DE ORO TERMINAL

0   250 m

TO TEMIXCO

© MOON PUBLICATIONS, INC.

SIGHTS

If driving to Cuernavaca from Tepoztlán (21 km), stop by the cemetery of **La Transfiguration del Señor** church and view the small monuments on the gravesites, painted in a variety of colors. The church itself is elegant and baroque.

Once in the city, you'll find roaming the streets a pleasant pastime. Try to avoid the weekends, which are usually crowded with people from Mexico City. As is often the case in these lovely old cities, the streets were not constructed for 20th century traffic, and it can get quite crowded and hectic.

A sight the tourist office doesn't mention lies near the Pullman Morelos bus station. **La Selva Park,** also known as "the woods", is a pretty park filled with trees and shrubs partially obscuring old railroad cars parked at the rear. People live in these cars. A group of expatriate women in Cuernavaca work out of nearby Guadalupita Church providing these people with at least one good meal a week. Three women began this service, paying for the food out of their own pockets. They also provide the labor. A meal might be nothing more than *bolillos,* large rolls split and spread liberally with beans and cheese and accompanied by a glass of milk.

Friday is food time. So if you're in Cuernavaca on a Friday morning about 9 a.m., you might want to help out these friends helping friends. Hopefully, contributions will allow this much-needed service to expand.

Palacio Municipal

After strolling around the lovely old 1883 building and its central courtyard, take a look at the painting on the first and second floors. You'll learn a lot about the Tlahuica, how they made cloth from maguey and wove feather mosaics. There are also representations of Aztec goldsmiths. Located on the south side of Jardín Borda, at the corner of Av. Morelos and Callejón Borda. Open Mon.-Fri. 9 a.m.-6 p.m., free.

Jardín Borda

Built in the mid-1700s, this was once the opulent holiday home of mining entrepreneur José de la Borda of Taxco silver wealth. In 1866 it served as the summer residence of Emperor Maximilian and his wife Carlota. He spent the treasury's money to renovate and beautify the home and garden, and took great pleasure in entertaining their aristocratic friends. It was here that Maximilian and his lover, the gardener's wife, conceived a son, the emperor's only known child. After his execution the house once again began to decay.

In 1987, the gardens, lakes, and kiosks were totally renovated and today it's a lovely place to wander, rent a rowboat, attend a lakeside show, feed the ducks, or have a picnic. Paintings reflect the turbulence surrounding Maximilian and his era. Note the art exhibits in the buildings at the entrance. Light snacks and drinks are available. Open Tues.-Sun. 10 a.m.-6:30 p.m., admission US$1. Located on Morelos at Hidalgo near the Palacio Municipal.

Catedral De La Asunción

One of the earliest churches built in the city, it was begun under Cortés in 1526. One comes away with two startling memories: the skull and crossbones over the main entrance, and the Japanese-style painting depicting the persecution of Christians in Japan. No one seems to know why or who the artist was; it wasn't even discovered until a renovation of the building in the 1960s. The construction typifies the early Franciscan fortress churches of Mexico; in those early days personal safety was at least as important as universal salvation. Located at the corner of Hidalgo and Morelos opposite the Jardín Borda and the Palacio. Open daily 8 a.m.-10 p.m.

Museo Casa Robert Brady

Located in the cloister of the Catedral de Cuernavaca, this museum offers a helpful service for foreign visitors. You can call in advance and make resevations for either a French- or English-speaking guide, included in the price of admission. The works of Frida Kahlo and Rufino Tamayo are represented here, as well as crafts from numerous countries. Spanish guides are available all day. Open Thursday and Friday 10 a.m.-2 p.m. and 4-6 p.m., Saturday 10 a.m.-2 p.m. If you make reservations in advance, you can make arrangements to visit the museum at other times. Admission is US$4.50. At Calle Netzahualcoyotl 4, tel. (73) 12-1136.

Museo De Cuauhnahuac/ Palacio De Cortés

Once the home of Cortés, this was built in the rugged fortresslike style of someone interested in protection as much as a comfortable home. Cortés began the structure in 1522, and lived in the palace for several years before returning to Spain in 1540. The building was held by the Cortés family for the rest of the century; later it was used as a prison, and served as the seat of the Morelos State Legislature. When the politicians moved to newer quarters it was converted to a museum. The antiquated building really shows all of its 450 years, but is still a magical place to contemplate the history of the man who built it and walked its chilly corridors.

Don't miss the **Diego Rivera** mural on the second floor, tracing the history of Cuernavaca from the Spanish onslaught to the 20th century. Theme: human barbarism in the name of profit and religion. This is one of Rivera's best, commissioned by U.S. Ambassador Dwight Morrow in the 1920s.

Wandering the salons you'll come across displays of colonial artifacts, including carriages, furniture, farm implements, and a suit of armor. You'll also find artifacts of the Tlahuica. If you look around on the ground floor you can see bits of the old Indian pyramid Cortés razed before building his own edifice.

It's located on the southeast end of the Plaza de Armas. Open Tues.-Sun. 9:30 a.m.-7 p.m.; admission is US$4.50. Check out the little stalls selling odds and ends on the bridge to the side of the castle. See especially the corn-man, who sells hot corn popular with the locals.

Plaza De Armas And Jardín Juárez

Plaza de Armas is the larger of the two plazas that make up the center of town. It comes alive in spring with flame-colored blossoms on flowering trees. And it is always alive with locals and visitors enjoying the outdoors; benches are always filled, balloons in bunches float high.

The **Jardín Juárez** is a garden next to the Plaza de Armas sporting a charming little kiosk designed by French designer Eiffel of Eiffel Tower fame. Trees and benches are shared by people and chattering birds. Find a table for a coffee or a snack.

Museo De La Herbolaría/ La Casa Del Olvido

Another name for this little house and garden is **Casa Maximiliano**. It's also known as the "House of Forgetfulness," for here Maximilian forgot for a time his unhappy marriage to Carlota, consorting with Margarita Lefuisamo Sedano, the gardener's wife. Others say the name came from the fact Maximilian "forgot" to build a room for his addled wife, though he did manage to construct a suite for his lover.

Today the house is a fine little museum devoted to Indian folk medicine. The botanical garden contains a multitude of traditional herbs and curatives used then and now by the locals. Open daily 10 a.m.-5 p.m. At Calle Matamoros 200, about 1.5 km southeast of the town center.

Teopanzolco Archaeological Site

This was first a Tlahuica pyramid, then the site of an Aztec pyramid built around the old. The stuctures were raised between 1200 and 1500 in what is now the neigborhood of Col. Vista Hermosa. The earth-covered pyramid was used during the Mexican revolution as a cannon installation. The site was first excavated in 1922, then again in 1957. Human remains have been found nearby. Open daily 10 a.m.-5 p.m., admission US$3.50.

ACCOMMODATIONS

Cuernavaca offers a wide selection of hotels and guesthouses. Budget travelers should concentrate on the streets around the Jardín Juárez, which feature several good inns at reasonable prices. If money is no object, Cuernavaca offers a couple of joints that can qualify as real knockouts.

Budget

Hotel Colonial: This hostel has a reputation as one of the nicer budget hotels. Do inspect your room: some have windows, others don't. All sixteen rooms feature a pleasant atmosphere; some include two beds; each contains a bath. At a good location three blocks from the Jardín. Rates are US$16-18. Address is Aragon y León 104, tel. (73) 12-0099.

Hotel Cadiz: This lovely old place is a comfortable family-run hostel with a small pool and a restaurant. Rates are US$17 s, US$19 d. Located close to the Hotel Las Mañanitas at Alvaro Obregón 329, tel. 12-2971.

Hotel Hortensias: Very simple, clean, featuring a tranquil garden with fountain. Rooms each have a private bath. Good location fairly close to the town center. Rates are US$26-30 s or d. At Calle Hidalgo 22, tel. 12-6152.

Hotel Iberia: Another simple but clean hotel with lovely tile, private bathrooms, and a small courtyard where you can park a small car. Rates are US$27 s, US$30 d. Located a few blocks from the plazas at Rayon 9, tel. 12-6040.

Moderate To Expensive

La Posada de Xochiquetzal: Another intimate hotel of just 14 rooms, but a little charmer with swimming pool, gardens, a real colonial feel, and an excellent restaurant. Rates are US$65-75 s or d, US$100 suite. Parking free. Located at Leyva 200, on the corner of Abasdo, tel. (73) 18-5767.

Hostería Las Quintas: This alluring spot is located about three km east of the Palacio de Cortés. It offers 43 rooms and large exotic grounds with a heated pool. Reservations suggested. Restaurant and bar, parking. Rates are US$70 s, US$80 d. Located at Av. Las Quintas 107, tel. 12-8800.

Camino Real Sumiya: A favorite in the luxury class, offering a little bit of Japan deep in the mountains of Mexico. The heart of this hotel came from Japan years ago, carried across the ocean in pieces under the direction of heiress Barbara Hutton. The original structure contains her outstanding art collection. The new section of the hotel has been built around and in the same tone as the center. The hotel offers 163 rooms and seven suites looking onto acres of oriental gardens and walking paths. The backdrop: twin snowcapped mountains. It's so like Japan here you can almost smell the cherry blossoms.

Along with the usual luxury amenities, business people will enjoy the high-tech support for computer systems. When dining in the signature restaurant you'll find an international menu highlighted by fine Japanese cuisine. The Kabuki Japanese theater offers all manner of entertainment or presentations. Located just outside of town. For reservations and information, call (800) 7-CAMINO (from the U.S. and Canada).

Las Mañanitas: This hotel is known as one of the best in Mexico. The ambience exudes luxury, with well-appointed standard rooms or suites. The surrounding grounds include verdant lawns, resident peacocks, an elegant swimming pool, intimate terraces, and all the service you can stand. There are only 22 rooms, so be sure to reserve in advance. Restaurant and bar, valet parking, no credit cards. Rates are US$85-95 d, suites up to US$300. Located at Ricardo Linares 107, tel. 14-1466/12-4646, fax 18-3672.

El Raquet Club: Each of the 33 units in this delightful renovated 16th-century hacienda offers one bedroom, a living room, and fireplaces. Swimming pool and nine tennis courts (four are lighted). Reservations suggested. Rates are US$115 s, US$140 d. On Francisco Villa 100, tel. 13-6122, fax 17-4155.

FOOD

The palate is easily pleased in Cuernavaca, and little harm need come to your wallet. The large number of students has created a market for pizza and other simple foods. The variety of ethnic cuisine includes French, Italian, Chinese, Japanese, and German.

La Estrada is located at the rear of the Palacio de Cortés downtown. The building is 300 years old, with arches and stonework around a lovely patio. Serves great lasagna.

Los Delfines offers fine fish delicacies; try the *pescado relleno*. Located near Civac on the road to Cuautla.

Log Yin is a Chinese restaurant with a good menu; delectable egg rolls. Located on Calle Morelos in Col. Acapantzingo.

La Viga is a fish house with a fresh fish market. Try the *empanisados,* a mixture of fish and shrimp wrapped in pastry. Open air, located across from Los Delfines.

Lovers of German and Viennese cooking should try **Restaurant Vienes** at Tejada 201, a block from Jardín Juárez. If you're looking for authentic German sausage and sauerkraut, try the delicatessen **Octoberfest.** They also serve Miller and Budweiser beers.

Las Mañanitas serves seriously delicious food and cocktails on a delightful terrace overlooking spacious grounds. For something really special try the fresh seafood of the day, always noted on the blackboard menu. Other continental dishes include the freshest ingredients. Expect a full multicourse meal to range US$25-45 pp. Open noon-5 p.m. and 7-11 p.m. At the hotel, tel. (73) 14-1466.

At **Hosteria Las Quintas,** Mexican food served outdoors is the specialty. Open 8-11 a.m., 1-5 p.m., and 7-10 p.m., at the Hostería Las Quintas Hotel, tel. 18-3949.

For something a little different, try a Japanese dinner at **Restaurant Sumiya.** Inside and out it looks a lot like the Japanese Imperial Palace. Great tempenyaki. Lively disco on Friday and Saturday nights. Located three km off Hwy. 160, the Cuernavaca-Cuautla Rd.; you'll see the signs. Reserve on the weekends, tel. 5-3055.

NIGHTLIFE

Sip coffee or drinks at an outside table on the Jardín Juárez at either **La Parroquia** or **Los Arcos,** or check out the concerts in the plaza on Thursday and Sunday nights. Then try drinks at **Harry's,** fun in a zany sort of way, at Gutenberg 3, open daily 1:30-11:30 p.m.

On Friday and Saturday nights the discos open around 8-9 p.m., but generally don't get rolling till about 11 p.m.; they then rage till 4 or 5 a.m.; try **Barba Azul,** at Pradera 10, and **Shadée,** toward the end of Gutenberg. Both charge a cover of US$10; drinks are US$3-4 each.

A place for great live salsa is **Vamejá Bar** in the **Las Plazas Mall.** Open Sun.-Thurs. 1 p.m.-midnight and Fri.-Sat. 1 p.m.-2 a.m. On Monday through Wednesday drinks are served two for one all day long.

INFORMATION AND SERVICES

Tourist Information
The office stocks lots of literature in English, including information on the city's language schools and archaeological sites. Open Mon.-Fri. 9 a.m.-3 p.m. and 6-8 p.m., Sat.-Sun. 9 a.m.-6 p.m. Located at Av. Morelos Sur 802, tel. (73) 14-3860/14-3920/14-3872. Another information kiosk is in the Plaza de Armas, open daily 9 a.m.-noon and 3-6 p.m.

OZ MALLAN

Palacio Cortés

Post Office
The **post office** is on the south side of the plaza, open Mon.-Fri. 8 a.m.-7 p.m. You'll find public phones in front of the post office. The postal code is 62000.

Moneychanging
All banks in Mexico observe the same hours: Mon.-Fri. 9 a.m.-1:30 p.m. Either of the banks, **Bancomer** on the Jardín Juárez, or **Banamex** on Matamoros at Arteaga just north of the Jardín Juárez, will exchange dollars or traveler's checks at the best rates.

Bookstores
Just off the Plaza de Armas, in the Centro Las Plazas shopping center, you'll find the **Librería las Plazas,** also known as the Anglo-American Bookstore. It carries a fair amount of books in English and other reading material.

Medical Services
Farmacia Blanco is at Morelos 710, tel. (73) 18-2393; **Farmacia el Sol** is at Matamoros 500,

tel. 14-1669. Both are open Mon.-Sat. 8 a.m.-9 p.m., Sun. 8 a.m.-2 p.m.

Centro Médico provides doctors on call at Juárez 507-B. The **Hospital Civil** is open 24 hours, tel. 12-5254.

Laundry Service

If you need to get the wash done you have a couple of choices. **Euro Klin** is located at Av. Morelos Sur 801, north of the tourist office. Open Mon.-Sat. 9 a.m.-7 p.m. Or try the **Lavandería Nueva Francesa**, on Juárez 2, next to the Palacio de Cortés. Same hours. Wash is washed, dried, and folded and you're charged by the kilo. It's always cheaper than laundry service at the hotels.

GETTING THERE

By Air

The Cuernavaca airport is 25 kilometers from the center of town, and the only way to get there is by taxi; there's no special airport transport. Expect to pay US$8-10 either way. Taxis only wait at the airport while flights are arriving.

By Bus

Cuernavaca is close to Mexico City and on the way to several other popular tourist destinations. Many visitors find the bus very convenient; the ride consumes one to one-and-a-half hours. Four different companies arrive from various places into Cuernavaca, each with a separate terminal; a couple are reasonably close to the center of town.

The **Estrella Roja** terminal is at Galeana and Cuauhtemotzin, about eight blocks from the city center.

Flecha Roja lets you off at the terminal at Morelos 255. Ask to be dropped off at the central plaza.

The **Autobuses Estrello de Oro** terminal requires about a 20-minute walk to town. If you don't want to flag a taxi, take a local bus going up the hill on Morelos; you can get off at the city center.

The **Autobuses Pullman de Morelos** bus terminal leaves you with a two-block walk up the hill on Netzahualcoyotl to Hidalgo; turn right and you'll see the town center. If you know what hotel you're going to, it might make more sense to just hop a cab and let the driver deliver you.

GETTING AROUND

The easiest and most economical method of travel in Cuernavaca is on foot or by local bus. For the most part, the main attractions for tourists are within walking distance of the center of town. However, if you need to go farther, check at the tourist office; they're very helpful and will give you a map of the city and make suggestions as to which bus you should take and where to get it. Buses cost about 30 cents; taxis are roughly US$2 just to get in the cab. Make your deal before you climb in the car.

TEPOTZLAN

For rugged beauty you can't beat the mountains and countryside around Tepotzlán. The town sits in a lovely valley encircled by tall craggy rock spires. If it had been built as a fortress it couldn't have been constructed better, but it's all nature's handiwork. The views are unreal, especially on a clear day, when you can spot both volcanoes, Popo and Ixta. The village is quiet except during its special fiesta days. If you haven't heard Nahuatl spoken before, you'll undoubtedly hear it here. It's the first language of many of the older residents and is taught to young people in the local schools.

This is a land of myth. Many believe the most famous myth maker of all, Quetzalcoatl, the omnipotent serpent god of the Aztecs, was born here. Mystics, artists, and adepts still trek here to try to soak up the energy that generated the mighty pagan snake.

Tepotzlán resisted colonial intrusion and is totally given over to the pre-Hispanic lifestyle. Nahautl is spoken everywhere, and the village proudly honors **Tepoztecatl**, the god of pulque. If you happen to be around on 8 September you can observe one of the town's favorite parties of the year—the pulque party. Folk dancers called Chinelos dressed in full regalia dance the traditional two-step called *el salto.*

Tepozteco Pyramid

To get to the archaeological zone around Tepozteco pyramid you must journey north to the mountains that rise above town. The site was used by the Tlahuicas as an observatory, and it also honors Tepoztecatl, the Aztec god of fertility. On 7 September each year a pilgrimage to the summit still takes place to honor the deity.

From downtown it's about three kilometers to the top; a steep climb along a narrow trail. Open Tues.-Sun. 9:30 a.m.-5 p.m., with a small admission fee to wander around the site.

Ex-Convento Dominico De La Natividad

This huge monastery was built by the Dominicans in the mid-16th century and is still the dominant structure in town. It's located behind the plaza and next to the **Capilla de Nuestra Señora de la Asunción.**

Archaeological Museum Of Tepoztlán

This museum is at the rear of the Capilla. You'll find a number of artifacts here from various groups of indigenous peoples, including Zapotec, Totonac, Aztec, and Olmec. Mostly pottery pieces. Open Tues.-Fri. 10 a.m.-2 p.m. and 4-6 p.m., small admission fee.

Accommodations And Food

Lodging is scarce in the small town, so if you plan on spending the night be sure to secure a room in advance or arrive early in the day. Don't expect to find any cheap digs here; charges start at about US$30-50. **La Posada del Tepozteco,** Paraiso 5, tel. (73) 5-0323, and **Hotel Tepoztlán,** Calle de la Industrias 6, tel. 5-0503, are pleasant little hotels, both with a pool, a garden, a restaurant and a bar.

There are many fine little cafes, and a few are outstanding. Check out **La Tapatia,** on Av. Revolución; **La Carmelita,** Av. Revolución 24; **Diana,** Plaza Principal 7; and **María Isabel,** on Mercado de los Portales. All serve quality Mexican specialties.

El Pan Nuestro is a fine spot to pause for a pastry or a coffee. For nightime entertainment with dinner, try **La Lunamextli**—live music and lots of locals. On Revolución.

Getting There

Buses are available from Mexico City and Cuernavaca. In Tepoztlán, buses arrive and depart from the zócalo.

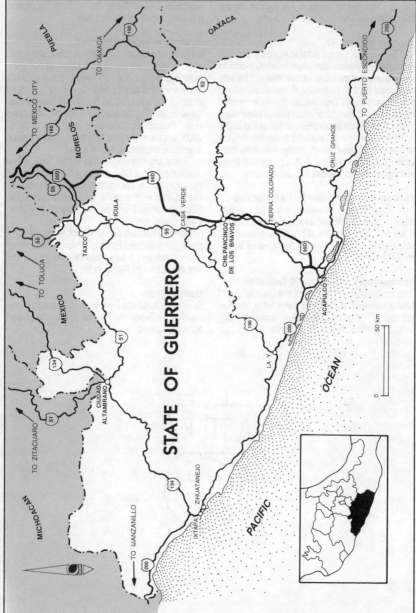

© MOON PUBLICATIONS, INC.

TAXCO

The three names most closely associated with Taxco are José de la Borda, William Spratling, and silver. For years Taxco was referred to as the "silver city," not because most of the silver of Mexico came from here, but because it served as the locus of the most skilled silversmiths in Mexico. It still does. Quantities of silver indeed came from these mountains but the veins were worked over so completely and efficiently that early on the city became a silver ghost town—until William Spratling opened a silver workshop and began creating attractive original designs.

HISTORY

Conquistadores
In 1524 Cortés was searching for tin to to make bronze cannons. He noted in the Aztec tax rolls that the Tlahuica paid tribute with, among other things, blocks of gold and silver. The greedy Cortés forgot all about tin and headed for the Tlachco area to search for gold.

Gold And Silver
The Spaniards did indeed find gold and silver, at their first mine in the New World, Socavón del Rey. The Santa Prisca Church now covers the spot. The Spanish built haciendas, smelters to process the metal, and an aqueduct to bring water into town. You can still see a section of the old aqueduct at the north end of town; the highway passes under it. One of the earliest buildings constructed here was the **Hacienda del Chorrillo,** in use today as a language school. And it was the Spaniards who first called the town Taxco, a corruption of the Nahua word Tlachco.

The 16th century was only the first gold-phase in Taxco. Though the area soon seemed played

Pronounced: TAHS-koe
Altitude: 1,784 meters
Population: 150,000
Area Code: (762)
Distance from Mexico City: 200 km

out to these 16th century miners, there was still plenty of metal in them-thar-hills.

18th-century Silver
In the 18th century came news of a new silver strike in Taxco. According to legend, it was a horse that this time discovered the stuff. The beast apparently reared, stumbled, and scraped the earth, uncovering something shiny. Voila—another rich vein of silver.

The new discovery started an 18th-century building boom, creating a fairy tale city of spires and domes, balconies and belfries, crowned by a pink baroque church called Santa Prisca. Artisans from Europe were imported to build still more beautiful estates.

The Borda Brothers
In 1708 the de la Borda brothers arrived from France and began working the mines. The eldest, Francisco, died; his brother José discovered the San Ignacio vein and became a very rich man. Soon hundreds of fortune hunters journeyed to this remote spot high in the mountains. Indian slaves brought the silver out of the earth; *patrones* gave the king his fifth and then spent the rest on ostentatious homes lining the streets of the small town.

From 1751 to 1759 the wealthy Borda supplied the funds to build Santa Prisca, supposedly the richest church in Mexico. Next door he built a lavish home for his family, part of which he shared with the local priests. His son Manuel had meanwhile found religion, and served as Taxco parish priest for 18 years.

Borda also began acquiring land not just in Taxco but elsewhere in Mexico as well. At least one of his holiday homes still stands in Cuernavaca.

Then, because his mines played out, or because he spent his silver faster than his slaves could bring it up from the earth, Borda was reduced in 1775 to begging the archbishop of Taxco to return some of the treasure he'd granted the church in wealthier times. He was eventually permitted to "borrow" several rich pieces smothered in precious stones and several gold chalices. He died two years later.

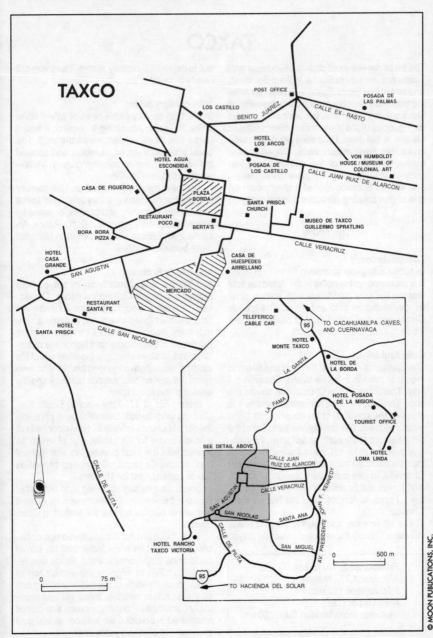

TAXCO

POST OFFICE

POSADA DE LAS PALMAS

LOS CASTILLO

BENITO JUAREZ

CALLE EX-RASTO

HOTEL LOS ARCOS

HOTEL AGUA ESCONDIDA

VON HUMBOLDT HOUSE / MUSEUM OF COLONIAL ART

POSADA DE LOS CASTILLO

CALLE JUAN RUIZ DE ALARCON

CASA DE FIGUEROA

PLAZA BORDA

SANTA PRISCA CHURCH

RESTAURANT POCO

BERTA'S

MUSEO DE TAXCO GUILLERMO SPRATLING

BORA BORA PIZZA

CALLE VERACRUZ

HOTEL CASA GRANDE

SAN AGUSTIN

CASA DE HUESPEDES ARRELLANO

MERCADO

RESTAURANT SANTA FE

HOTEL SANTA PRISCA

CALLE SAN NICOLAS

TELEFERICO/ CABLE CAR

95 TO CACAHUAMILPA CAVES, AND CUERNAVACA

HOTEL MONTE TAXCO

LA GARITA

HOTEL DE LA BORDA

LA FAMA

HOTEL POSADA DE LA MISION

TOURIST OFFICE

SEE DETAIL ABOVE

CALLE JUAN RUIZ DE ALARCON

CALLE VERACRUZ

HOTEL LOMA LINDA

SAN AGUSTIN

SAN NICOLAS

SANTA ANA

CALLE DE PILITA

AV. PRESIDENTE JOHN F. KENNEDY

SAN MIGUEL

HOTEL RANCHO TAXCO VICTORIA

0   500 m

95 TO HACIENDA DEL SOLAR

0   75 m

© MOON PUBLICATIONS, INC.

William Spratling

Eventually this boom too went bust. All those lured to Taxco for treasure packed up their silver and left for richer pastures. Taxco slipped into poverty and anonymity. The ornate city languished in a funk until 1929.

Enter American professor William Spratling from Tulane University in New Orleans. Spratling originally journeyed to Mexico to write a book, but then his publisher went out of business. American Ambassador to Mexico Dwight Morrow then encouraged Spratling to start a silver workshop. Though his early training was as an architect, Spratling possessed a certain artistic flare. While exploring Mexico on horseback, he'd accumulated a large collection of pre-Hispanic artifacts; now with just a few craftsmen, and clever designs and molds patterned after the Indian designs in his collection, Spartling began turning out beautiful silver jewelry. His business grew, continuing to create top-quality work using only the finest silver. Soon his pieces were in demand in the elite jewelry stores of the United States.

Today's Taxco silverworkers continue to improve their craft, possessing the ability to shift their designs to accommodate the latest trends. Whatever's in style at the moment, they're on top of it—perhaps they even created it. Several contemporary Taxco silver shops are owned by one-time Spratling apprentices. There are literally hundreds of quality silver shops in Taxco today.

Silver Controls

In 1940, the Mexican government imposed controls on the silver industry. It was decreed that all silver sales must be contracted through the Bank of Mexico; even silversmiths must buy their silver bars from the bank. Goods made from silver must bear the sterling seal, indicating a content of .925 pure silver. If you see that mark, you can be assured the piece is sterling.

Of course there are those who illegally apply the .925 seal. If you acquire proof of a swindle, notify the government of all details of the purchase, including the name and address of the violators. Include receipts. The government diligently works to eliminate the crooks from the industry, primarily these who substitute the cheap imitation *alpaca* for silver.

Taxco is probably one of the safest places to buy silver. Some of these craftspeople come from families who have worked in silver for generations and are proud of their heritage as fine artisans.

SIGHTS

Silver is just one of the reasons to visit Taxco. The city itself is a Spanish gingerbread lane of cobblestoned streets that climb up, down, and about, twisting in and out of the hilly landscape, occasionally opening up to reveal intimate plazas and cooling fountains. The Mexican government has designated the city a colonial monument, which encourages new construction in the colonial style and guarantees that the original old buildings will remain in good condition.

Physically handicapped folks may experience problems with the steep narrow streets. It's not unusual for pedestrians to scatter when they see a car coming; there's barely room on some of these streets for a VW bug to get by. You need to watch your step when exploring this city.

Shops, hotels, and restaurants are all clustered together here, and locals can easily direct you if you become befuddled. The main street is Hwy. 95 as you come into town from the north. It then becomes Av. Presidente John F. Kennedy winding around town to the south end before heading toward Acapulco and becoming Hwy. 95 again. Any of the many streets and alleys along Kennedy twist back up to the center of town at Santa Prisca Church. Actually it's pretty hard to get lost here. Wherever you are, just look up: you can see the church from anywhere in the city.

The weather in Taxco is considered some of the best in the country. The average high is 82°; the average low is 64°.

Santa Prisca Church

Take time to study the energetic facade of this pink baroque church, with its eclectic collection of hewn angels, saints, and shells. The baroque style, when interpreted by the Mexican artist, became the enchanting churrigueresque style of architecture so commonly found throughout the colonial cities. Here, two ornamented steeples lead the eye to a tiled dome. On the inside, you'll see recently cleaned walls and magnificent

BOB RACE

Santa Prisca church

paintings by Miguel Cabrera, a Zapotec Indian and probably the most prominent of the colonial-era artists. There's gold leaf everywhere. So many gold nooks and crannies, angels, curlicues, designs, patterns, and arrangements—it takes some time to absorb it all.

It required more than eight years to complete the structure, paid for by rich miner José de la Borda. The church faces the Plaza Borda. Open daily.

Plaza Borda

The flat center of town is shady and comfortable, a serene spot under ancient Indian Laurel trees. Along one side of the plaza sits the Santa Prisca Church. Also bordering the square are lovely old buildings containing gift shops that offer fine pottery, Guerrero masks, colorful textiles, and silver. Fine little restaurants are in the vicinity as well.

Museo De Taxco Guillermo Spratling

The two top floors of this museum contain the unique collection of William Spratling, gathered during his many years in Mexico. Here you'll find a fine display of pre-Hispanic art, from the immediate area of Guerrero and the central plateau. The bottom floor houses changing exhibits. Located at Calle Veracruz; from the Santa Prisca Church, go left, then make another left at the corner. Admission US$4.

Silver Museum

This small museum tells the history of silver in Mexico, with a special emphasis on Taxco. It's operated by a silversmith and includes a pleasant display of award-winning pieces. If you speak Spanish, this is a good place to acquire silver information. Open 9 a.m.-5 p.m., admission US$1.50. Located next to the Santa Prisca; look for a small sign.

Casa De Figueroa

Built in 1767 for the Count de la Cadena family, this home has one of the wildest histories of any building in town.

It was built by Tlahuica prisoners—men who could not pay their tributes—laboring with shackles on their legs. It quite justifiably earned the nickname Casa de las Lágrimas, or "House of Tears." Years later a Cadena descendant living there murdered his daughter to keep her from marrying a man he disapproved of. He was taken off to jail and the house remained empty for years. Eventually it was used as a barracks for independence soldiers, then as a mint, then as a residence for priests. Ultimately another arm of the Cadena family took up residence here. After some years only one member of the family remained, an elderly woman who, trusting no one, secreted her money in the walls of the house. Somehow, somebody found out about this, and burglars arrived one night to rob and kill her. The doomed edifice thereafter lay empty until 1943, when it was purchased by the Figueroa family. Stories persist that the house contains a series of tunnels leading to the church. They say several notable Americans have walked within its walls, including the late President Nixon. Located at Guadalupe 2.

Von Humboldt House/ Museum Of Colonial Art

This old house was either a one-night stopover for Baron Von Humboldt or actually served for a time as his home. Originally built in the late 1700s by the Villanueva family, it has often served as a guesthouse. Located at Calle Juan Ruíz de Alarcón 6, just a block and a half from Plaza Borda. Open 9 a.m.-1 p.m. and 3-7 p.m.

Casa Borda

Located next to the church on the square, it was built for the Borda family in 1759. Today it serves as the Casa de Cultura, a good place to see exhibits by local artists. Open daily 10 a.m.-7 p.m.

Mercado

Beside the Santa Prisca Church and behind Berta's, this market contains innumerable stalls and *fondas,* featuring stacks of fruits and vegetables, medicinal herbs, and such domestic necessities as sarapes, blankets, pots, pans, sombreros, and pottery. Lots of palm-woven items. On weekends the market is crowded with Indians from small villages in the hills around Taxco. These are the best days to look for decorative crafts.

The Teleférico/Cable Car

At the north end of town, near the highway from Mexico City, take the Swiss-built cable car 240 meters to the top of a bluff overlooking the city. The cable car runs daily 7:30 a.m.-7 p.m.; fare is US$2 one way, US$3.90 roundtrip, children are half-price. A fun trip with a spectacular view. At the top you'll find the **Hotel Monte Taxco**, with a restaurant, shops, and a golf course.

BOB RACE

Cacahuamilpa Caves

Wander through caverns two kilometers long, featuring 20 impressive "rooms" and a wondrous variety of stalactites, sta-

cable car

lagmites, and stone formations. The caves are lit with electric lights, which is a good thing, because it's *very* black when they're switched off. Guided tours leave every hour 10 a.m.-5 p.m. Not all guides speak English. Often it's very crowded, with flea-market-style *fondas* at the entrance. Buses leave daily to the caves from Taxco; inquire at the tourist office for the schedule and prices.

ACCOMMODATIONS

There are many fine little and large hostels in Taxco.

Budget And Moderate

As is customary, I suggest you look carefully at the room before checking in.

Hotel Casa Grande: this hotel is located on the Plazuela de San Juan and offers 12 clean rooms, comfortably arranged around the patio, each with private bath and softish beds. Ask for a rooftop room for plenty of light and fresh air. Only breakfast is available on the premises. Rates are US$14 s, and US$20 d; triples and quads available. Located in the same building as the Ciné Ana María, on Plazuela de San Juan 7, tel. (762) 2-0123, fax 2-1108.

Casa de Huéspedes Arrellano: Very simple but clean, with 10 rooms. Rates are US$8 s, shared bath; US$12 s, private bath; US$14 d, private bath. Facing the church; take the stairs on the right side of the Santa Prisca Church, go down two flights of stairs, then take a flight off to the left. Calle los Pajaritos 23, tel. 2-0215.

Posada de las Palmas: The rooms here are simple, with private baths; clean, with a pool on the premises. Rates are US$22 s, US$27 d. Find Restaurante Los Reyes and the post office on Calle Juárez. Ex-Rastro is a pedestrian-only street running alongside the restaurant. Follow it down to the first level and look for a sign. Once you find a door (the one on the right), you must descend some more. Ex-Rastro 4, tel. 2-3177.

Posada de los Castillo: This was one of the most beautiful mansions in Taxco during the colonial era. The charming three-story building has been refurbished and is really a pleasant place to stay, right in the center of town. All 14 small rooms have private baths, and there's greenery every place you look. Check out the nice coffee shop. Rates are US$22 s, US$27.50 d. To get there from Plaza Borda, go down the hill with the Hotel Agua Escondida on your left; at the bottom turn right. The hotel is on your right. Juan Ruíz de Alarcón 3, tel. 2-1396, fax 2-2935.

Hotel Los Arcos: The building dates back to the 16th century, when it served as a monastery. The 21 rooms are simply furnished, but with a colonial flare. Tile, fountain, rooftop terrace, pool, comfortable beds, private bathrooms, and a good location close to downtown. Rates are US$22 s, and US$31 d. On Juan Ruíz de Alarcón 12, a block down the hill from Plaza Borda, opposite Posada de los Castillo; tel. 2-1836.

Hotel Loma Linda: Motel-style living on the road from Mexico City and Cuernavaca. Rooms are large and light, quite comfortable, each with private bath. Spacious grounds with a pool and a play area for children. Ask at the desk for combi information, it passes the entrance of the hotel frequently throughout the day. Rates are US$30 s and US$36 d. At Av. Kennedy 52, tel. 2-0206, fax 2-5125. This is a popular place, so either make reservations or get there early.

Hotel Agua Escondida: The best part of this hotel is its location, right on the Plaza Borda. The rooms are spartan but bright with fresh flowers. There's a rooftop terrace, a pool, and 50 rooms, each with private bath. The place gets very crowded on the weekend. Rates are US$37 s and US$42 d. Plaza Borda 4, tel. 2-0736, fax 2-1306.

Pricey

Hacienda del Solar: If you're looking for an intimate hotel surrounded by lovely vistas, here it is. The rooms are nicely decorated in colonial style, with suites, balconies, a pool, tennis, and strolling musicians. Children under 12 are barred from the premises. Rates are US$85 s or d. Located off Hwy. 95 south of town, opposite the Tourist Information Office. Apdo. Postal 96, Col. el Solar, Taxco, 40200, Guerrero, Mexico; tel. (762) 2-0323.

Hotel Santa Prisca: This is a charming hotel with a patio, a fountain, and a library containing a good selection of English-language books. Each of the 30 smallish rooms has a private bath with a shower. A portion of the hotel is newer, with larger, lighter rooms. The dining room serves good food. Rates are US$40 s and US$46 d. On Plazuela de San Juan, one block west of Plaza Borda. Cena Obscuras 1, tel. 2-0980, fax 2-1106.

Hotel de la Borda: A little more modern and much larger than most, the hotel offers 120 clean, comfortable, and spacious rooms and suites, as well as a pool. Views from the second floor. Rates are US$50 s/d, US$60 junior suite s/d, US$130 master suite. Cerro del Pedregal 2, opposite the junction of Av. Kennedy and Calle La Garita; tel. 2-0025. Free parking.

Hotel Rancho Taxco Victoria: This one has been around for a lot of years and has a comfortable worn look to it. It's located on a hill with great views. Private bathrooms have tubs, and the furnishings are from another era. Ask for a room with a terrace. If you have luggage, take a taxi; if walking, take the winding street Carlos J. Nibbi, just off Plazuela de San Juan, to the top. Rates are US$40 s, US$62-76 d. Carlos J. Nibbi 57, tel. 2-1014, fax 2-0617.

Hotel Posada de la Misión: Another big hotel, featuring 150 rooms with private baths, suites with fireplaces, two bars, a coffee shop, a dining room, gardens and views, a swimming pool, tennis, golf, and parking. Rates are US$95-110. Located just off Av. John F. Kennedy on Cerro de la Misión 32, tel. 2-0063 or 2-0522, fax 2-2198.

Hotel Monte Taxco: One of the nicest hotels in town is perched on the top of a bluff on the north end of town near Hwy. 95. If you want a little fun getting there, take the cable car *teleférico*. The view is spectacular on the way up and down, and while you're there. The hotel offers guests (and nonguests) a golf course, tennis courts, restaurants, and other interesting ways to spend your time. If nonguests want to spend the day by the pool or playing golf they're welcome for a fee. The hotel is colonial style, comfortable with standard rooms and suites. If you're so inclined you have access to horses, a steam bath, and a fitness center. The restaurant serves good food, and a favorite attraction for visitors (wherever they're staying) is **Windows**, a great disco. You can reach the hotel by taxi.

FOOD

Taxco has some fine restaurants, and since so many visitors come to the city, they are well patronized most of the time. There are those who say the food is overpriced, and granted there are many that don't hesitate to charge plenty, especially those who serve quality fare, and you'll find several top quality restaurants in town. Order the *comida corrida* if you're looking for the most for your money. It's generally served 1-4 p.m., and is a hardy meal of three or four courses and usually quite inexpensive by comparison.

For good solid, inexpensive food check out the **Restaurant Santa Fe**, which serves *comida corrida* for US$7.50. Open daily 7:30 a.m.-11 p.m., at Hidalgo 2 down from Plazuela de San Juan. And then there's **Restaurant Ethel**, with similar prices for *comida corrida*, other main courses are US$3-10, open daily 9 a.m.-11 p.m.; at Plazuela de San Juan 14. If you want a little fun (just looking at the goofy decor is fun here) with your good food, go to **Señor Costilla's** and try the "ribs." If you can, get a table (for two) on one of the balconies overlooking the plaza; open daily 1 p.m.-midnight. On Plaza Borda 1, tel. (762) 2-3215. For a quiet intimate meal on white linen, go to **Restaurant El Adobe**, try their *enchiladas Oaxaqueños* and end with a lush mango crepe; other choices include sandwiches, and meals priced US$6-15. Open daily 8 a.m.-midnight; on Plazuela de San Juan, tel. 2-1416.

Those Old Familiar Foods

Really feeling the need for a pizza jolt? Go to **Bora Bora Pizza**. It is the best pizza in Taxco and surrounding areas. Again, if you're lucky you might get a table on one of the small balconies overlooking town, but even if not, you'll enjoy the tasty melted cheese and crispy crust amidst the purple and pink decor. Other Italian

dishes are served, along with beer and wine. Open daily 1 p.m.-midnight, on Callejon de las Delicias 4, tel. 2-1721.

If you're looking for something international, try **La Taberna Restaurant**, a favorite with Americans. Lunch in the open patio features meals from beef brochettes to chicken Kiev; US$7-20. Open daily 1 p.m.-midnight. Juárez 8, tel. 2-5226.

La Ventana De Taxco gets high marks from *Bon Appetit*. With an chef from Como, Italy, good service, and Italian specialties, it's not to be missed. The view is one of the best in town. Located at the **Hotel Hacienda Solar**, about seven minutes south of town on the highway to Acapulco. Look for the signs.

SHOPPING

Bring the bucks if you're planning on buying silver. Taxco offers some of the finest creations in

---

JUMILES

Jumiles are small beetlelike insects prized as food since the pre-Hispanic era. The locals found these bugs to be a nutricious, protein-filled addition to their diets, as well as a curative for many ailments.

Today, on the Monday after the Day of the Dead, families journey to the Cerro del Huisteco, north of Taxco, for a mass at the Huisteco Cross. Most families arrive the day of the fiesta, with all the fixings to prepare *jumiles*—including griddle, mortar, and ingredients. Cerro del Huisteco is a good place to find *jumiles*, and the whole family often helps to collect them.

The little critters are served several ways. They can be mixed in a chile sauce, grilled with lemon and onion, or consumed live wrapped in a tortilla. The *jumiles* season runs from October to December; you can buy them live in local markets. If they aren't alive, the traditional preparer won't use them.

Mexico. Don't expect any bargains here, though you'll find plenty of high-quality merchandise. This is where you come for the originals, the best. Besides silver you can purchase items with unusual mixtures of silver and ceramics, or silver, brass, copper, and ceramics.

One of the best shops is owned and operated by the Castillo family. Tony Castillo began as a Spratling apprentice and has gone on to create top-quality designs of his own. His work is sold all over Mexico. Castillo's daughter now plays an active role in the Taxco business. Los Castillo is open daily 9 a.m.-7 p.m. Located just off Plaza Borda; walk down the hill next to City Hall until you see the sign. You can watch the silversmiths at work here. If you want to take a gander at the larger operation, visit the Castillo workshop about eight km south of town on the highway to Acapulco. Open Mon.-Fri. 9 a.m.-5 p.m.

Look for **Emma's** a short distance down the street on the left of Santa Prisca. This is one of the shops where you can find lower-priced silver items, and the staff speaks English. **Elena Los Ballesteros,** between **Pineda's Taxco** and Emma's, is probably the glitziest silver shop in town.

If you're looking for more traditional gifts, stop by **Arnoldo's** at Plazuela de los Gallos 7. You'll find a fine assortment of masks used in various Indian ceremonies and dances. Check at the tourist office; folks there can direct you to a variety of shops. Or just wander around; it's impossible not to bumble into some of the town's estimated 300 silver shops.

TOURIST INFORMATION OFFICE

On Av. John F. Kennedy 28, tel. (762) 2-1525, you'll find the state tourism office.

(previous page) Lake Chapala weaver; (this page, top left) typical Querétaro architecture; (top right) The gold in many Mexican churches is dazzling; (above left) famous "Angel Monument" in Mexico City; (above right) Guadalajara Cathedral (all photos by Oz Mallan)

K. A. ESCOVEDO SANDERS

THE STATE OF MICHOACAN
INTRODUCTION

Nowhere in Mexico is the color, the texture, and the imagination of the indigenous artist more apparent than in Michoacán. The artistry has created an economic boon to artists from small villages who just 20 years ago lived a poverty-level existence by subsistence farming. Tourism has given these people a lift. Visitors spend hours browsing in stores from trendy to stall-like, in state-run workshops, public mercados, and upscale galleries. The beautiful traditions of Michoacán live on, feeding on the success of their art.

GEOGRAPHY

The Land
The state is located between the two largest cities of Mexico: Morelia, the capital, is 315 kilometers northwest of Mexico City and 367 kilometers southeast of Guadalajara, with good roads in both directions. Michoacán is bordered on the west by Jalisco and Colima, on the east by Mexico State and Querétaro, on the north by Guanajuato and Jalisco, and on the south by the Pacific Ocean and Guerrero. Michoacán's elevation ranges from sea level to 3,857 meters (10,000 feet). This geographical diversion provides a wide accumulation of flora and fauna; one of the biggest attractions each year is the arrival of the monarch butterfly—by the hundreds of thousands. Because the state occupies coastal lowlands as well as high peaks, the climate transmutes from tropical to moderate (and can get quite cool in higher elevations during the winter months). The high plateau provides beautiful rivers, waterfalls, lakes, gorges, high valleys, and the well-known volcano **Paricutín**. The high fertile valleys and a temperate climate are the basis of the state's main economy, agriculture. The tallest peak in the state is **Pico de Tancitaro** (3,857 meters).

Lakes
One of the most impressive geographical appeals of Michoacán State is Lake Pátzcuaro. The large lake is surrounded by tree-covered mountains where rivers and canyons open onto the water, with small islands scattered here and

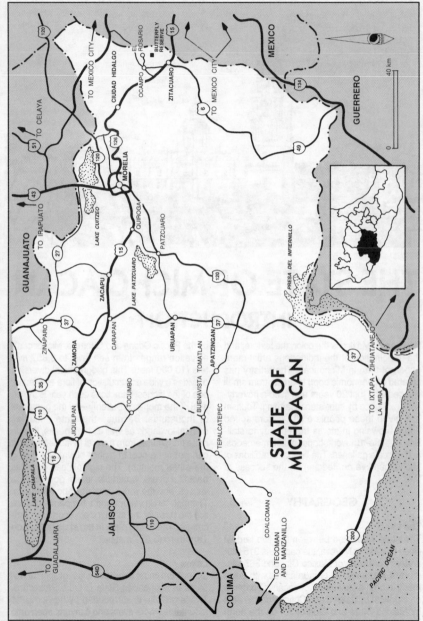

© MOON PUBLICATIONS, INC.

there. This raw natural beauty is a pleasant jolt to the senses. Of the several islands in the lake, the largest is **Isla Janitzio,** most famous for its Day of the Dead celebrations; it is jammed with tourists during this holiday.

HISTORY

Pre-Columbian

Michoacán was the pre-Columbian center of the Purépecha/Tarasca people, described by the earliest Spaniards as tall and handsome. These powerful warriors controlled most of western Mexico and managed to keep the Aztecs at bay. This was accomplished in part due to superior copper weapons made in the Michoacán area. Because of their hatred of the Aztecs, they were unwilling to join Moctezuma as an ally against Cortés, nor did they wholeheartedly resist the Spaniard's intrusion.

Although many stories circulate about the dual names of these people (Tarascan/Purépecha), we choose to repeat the most romantic one. When the Spaniards arrived and the Purépecha submitted, the Indian rulers gave the Spaniards their daughters in an effort to mollify them. After that the Indians used the term for son-in-law (*tarascue*) to address them; the Spanish misinterpreted and began calling them Tarascans.

The Tarascans

Certain artifacts and the language of the Tarascan people gave rise to speculation by a few that they were more closely related to the Incas of Peru than to any other group in Mexico. Most archaeologists don't agree. Their language is described as macro-Mixtecan. This ancient language still thrives in small pocket villages that are for all practical purposes cut off from mainstream Mexico. Their weak-kneed ruler at the time, Tangaxoan II, believed that Cortés was sent from the gods, and was unwilling to to defend his people against the Spaniard. It was a mistake.

Guzmán

One of the men who followed Cortés to western Mexico was Beltrán Nuño de Guzmán, known to make the cruelties of the Indians pale by comparison to his. He conquered and destroyed most of the Tarascans; under his control their numbers fell from 60,000 to 20,000.

Don Vasco De Quiroga

Eventually, the Spanish crown was apprised of the wicked ways of Guzmán; he was thrown out of his post and efforts were made to find better people to take charge in New Spain. They chose a gentle, fair, and intelligent man, Don Vasco de Quiroga, to look after the Indians in this part of western Mexico. He arrived in New Spain in 1531, was ordained a priest and immediately became a bishop, very late in his life. His first See was in **Tzintzuntzán,** but only for a short while. From there the Bishopric was moved to Pátzcuaro, and then to Morelia. He enhanced the work of the already talented craftsmen with easier methods and introduced new handicrafts from Spain (such as lace worked in the Andalusian style). He encouraged individual villages to excel in a single occupation. Everyone was expected to work for the community, and Quiroga taught them by example, side by side; he asked of them nothing that he did not ask of himself. He was well loved and respected, and addressed as Tata Vasco by the Indians. You'll find that the different villages in Michoacán are still noted for their particular specialties and excellent quality.

After Independence

In 1828, after independence from Spain, the capital city's Spanish name, **Valladolid,** was changed to **Morelia,** in honor of Independence hero Morelos. Despite Quiroga's efforts, when he was gone, life continued much the same way that it had before his arrival. The Purépecha people, like most of the Indians in Mexico, were still mistreated. The next break the peasants of Michoacán received was not until Lázaro Cárdenas came to power, first as governor in 1928, and then as president of the country 1934-1940. Of Purépecha descent, Cárdenas made massive land transfers, breaking up rich haciendas and giving the land to the campesinos (peasants); some 45 million acres were shuffled. The move wasn't always successful and in many cases slowed down the agricultural output due to lack of experience on the part of the Indians.

Cárdenas And Hope

The common man was for the first time given a

Wood carving is one of the specialties of Michoacán State, especially in Quiroga.

OZ MALLAN

glimmer of hope for a future. Cárdenas opened hundreds of schools for the Indians, where before there were none; he gave them a voice to air their opinions. Considered a man of the people, he lived up to his principles to the best of his ability without fear of whose toes he stepped on. During his lifetime he was instrumental in the development of the labor movement, and he nationalized the oil industry (lots of U.S. oil companies objected to that, you can bet), but then he redeemed himself with Americans when during WW II he sided with them (he was minister of defense 1941-45, and commander of forces on the Pacific coast of Mexico). This gutsy man died in 1970 at the age of 85, but he will never be forgotten, and he continues to be highly respected in Michoacán.

ECONOMY

Agriculture is still the number one industry, producing corn, avocados, sugarcane, strawberries, and melons. Timber is also a major economic factor. But a fast comer is the manufacture of steel at the newish factory called **Siderúrgica Lázaro Cárdenas,** located near the city port of Lázaro Cárdenas. If driving south along the Pacific coast, you'll cross a bridge which

crosses the **Balsas River,** the boundary between Michoacán and Guerrero. This bridge is the wall of the **José María Morelos Dam,** which irrigates certain areas of Michoacán as well as Guerrero; it also delivers water to **La Villita Hydroelectric Plant. Note:** Every year there's a fast-moving boating marathon on the Balsas River.

In Uruapan, a fascinating industry is shoes. Swiss-brand **Bally** shoes are made here, and you can really get some good buys at the factory outlet on the premises. If you're interested in seeing shoes made by hand, ask for a tour of the factory.

TODAY'S MICHOACAN

Visitors rate Michoacán as one of the more beautiful states in the country. It's modern, yet carries the stamp of the past, from its Indian roots to its colonial elegance to a high-tech city of the 1990s. Michoacán is the sixth largest state of Mexico. Prices are quite reasonable, maybe because most tourists have yet to discover the state. Don't miss traveling in Michoacán; it's another one of those secret delights of Mexico.

MORELIA

Pronounced: mo-RAYL-yah
Altitude: 1,915 meters
Population: 1,000,000
Area Code: (451)
Distance from Mexico City: 315 km

Morelia, the capital of the state of Michoacán, is a **UNESCO World Heritage Artistic Site**, and is familiarly referred to in Mexico as the "Aristocrat of Colonial Cities." The titles are well earned; the delicate pink quarrystone structures are just as majestic today as they were in the 16th century.

Founded in 1541 by the first viceroy of New Spain, Antonio de Mendoza, the city was named **Valladolid**, after Mendoza's birthplace in Spain (the name was changed after Independence, when all links with Spain were severed). It was at that time that the seat of power was moved from Pátzcuaro to Valladolid (Morelia). However, the entire area of what is today Michoacán, flourished under the fair leadership of Vasco de Quiroga. He arrived in the New World in 1531 and to Michoacán in 1533.

Probably the most Spain-like of all the colonial cities, it has a certain air of elegance. The streets are lined with countless buildings from the past, all still in use and adapted to modern-day living. It's a tribute to those who designed the city; they had an eye to the future, laying out the streets in a perfect grid and making wide boulevards. Though the traffic can be horrendous, the main streets of the ancient center are wide enough to handle automobile transport comfortably.

Michoacán has produced many free thinkers, and one of the most famous was home-grown President Lázaro Cárdenas. Morelia has been a university town for centuries and the idealistic curiosity of the students has sustained the aura of advancement in the city. Morelia is frequently the scene of high powered dissent to the government.

Industry and high-tech commerce is growing on the outskirts of the city by leaps and bounds. For balance, Morelia is also known as a musical city, with New Spain's first conservatory of music built here in 1743. The city is also home to one of the largest organs in Mexico. Still important, students continue to study here and musically perform. Morelia is a lovely city and worth several days of wandering around.

SIGHTS

The heart of Morelia is at the *zócalo*/plaza, called the **Plaza de los Mártires** ("Plaza of the Martyrs"), in memory of citizen defenders who were executed in 1830 for taking part in the War of Independence. You'll find its history ensconced in the splendid buildings surrounding this large square. It's a fine way to spend a day—or two, strolling around the Plaza, going from one historical era to the next. This is all flat ground and easy walking. A shady bench is always available if you wish to take a break—or chat with the young chiclets salesperson who will more than likely sit down beside you.

Catedral
Constructed of quarrystone, the building gives off a pink glow and has two ornate towers 200 feet high. The Catedral was begun in 1660 and completed 84 years later. One of the outstanding attractions of this church is its massive pipe organ with 4,600 pipes. Its classical tone would do justice to a New York production of *Phantom of the Opera;* the organ is a joy to see as well as to hear. Please don't take pictures during church services. Open for inspection daily 5:30 a.m.-11 p.m.; at Av. Madero Poniente, entrances on Av. Morelos Sur and Hidalgo.

Palacio Federal
This baroque masterpiece is worth visiting. It was often referred to as the foundation of the ancient city of Valladolid (now Morelia), and was used for a variety of purposes (including the storage of grains) over the centuries. Open Mon.-Sat. 8 a.m-11 p.m., Sun. 8 a.m.-2 p.m. Taking pictures is permitted in the exterior areas only. On the plaza at Portal Allende 267.

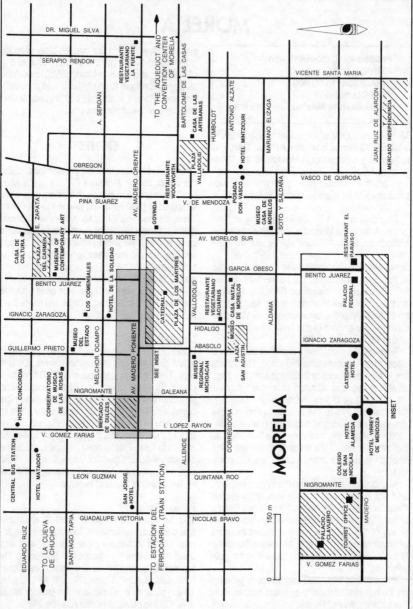

MORELIA

© MOON PUBLICATIONS, INC.

Conservatorio De Música De Las Rosas

Established in 1590 as a Dominican Convent, Convento de las Monjas, in the late 1700s it was adopted for use as a music school for boys. Today it is still a music school and the center for the **Boy's Choir of Morelia.** If you have an opportunity, go to one of their world-renowned performances. If you can, quietly slip into the conservatory and listen to a practice. Open Mon.-Sat. 8 a.m.-4 p.m. Take a look at the nearby baroque church and garden, formerly part of this Dominican Convent. On Santiago Tapia, several blocks northwest of the plaza.

Colegio De San Nicolas

Moved from Pátzcuaro in 1580, this college was originally founded in 1540 by Vasco de Quiroga. It is said to be one of the oldest institutions of learning in the Americas. It was the precursor of what is now the University of Michoacán. Several noted Mexicans attended school here from its early days: Miguel Hidalgo, José María Morelos, and Melchor Ocampo (remembered in an upstairs salon). Open Mon.-Fri. 8 a.m.-2 p.m., free.

Palacio Clavijero

Named in honor of Jesuit leader Francisco Clavijero, this building was completed in 1660 as a Jesuit college (short-lived since the Jesuits were booted out of Mexico in 1767). Today it is used as the state library. Take a look around, and don't miss the immense patio with its center fountain and graceful arches. At the southern end of Mercado de Dulces.

Mercado De Dulces

All sweets-lovers should take a stroll through this "sugar" market. One of the best times to visit is just before the **Day of the Dead,** when sugar artists go wild creating sugar skulls, skeletons, and a multitude of designs that bring a little laughter to this very important holiday. If you've never tasted *ate,* this is a good place to do it. It's a confection made of fresh fruit turned into a pastelike substance. Very tasty, and it's made in many flavors. Making candy is a tradition of the colonial era, handed down by European nuns who in turn passed on the tradition at schools for girls. Located on the west side of the **Palacio Clavijero.**

Museo Del Estado

One of the smallest museums in the city, this was formerly the home of Ana Huarte, who later married Agustín Iturbide (he called himself the Emperor of Mexico for 10 months). You can trace the timeline of the state of Morelia through the exhibits. The ground floor shows pre-Columbian history through figurines, the use of copper, gold, and silver; the second floor has a pharmacological display from the 18th century, regional clothes, and some very fine murals of the 19th century. Note the lovely wooden shelves and design that house the apothecary jars. Ask about the different events held on Wednesday evenings at 7:30 p.m.; the programs change and include art exhibits, regional dances, and other cultural events. Open Mon.-Fri. 9 a.m.-2 p.m. and 4-8 p.m., Sat.-Sun., 9 a.m.-7 p.m., free. At Guillermo Prieto 176.

Museo Casa Natal De Morelos

An eternal torch continues to burn here in memory of native son/hero José María Morelos. This is where he was born on 30 Sept. 1765. The house was built around 1650, and now is a national monument and a museum, with a public library and well-used auditorium. Many rooms display remnants from Morelos's life that somehow bring him to life. Free cultural events take place every Friday night; ask about the current schedule at the tourist office. Museum is open Mon.-Sat. 9 a.m.-2 p.m., and 4-8 p.m., free. On Corregidora 113, photos permitted.

Museo Casa De Morelos

This was the home of Morelos from the time he bought it in 1801. He added the second story. This museum provides personal history of Morelos and information about the War of Independence and his part in it. Open Mon.-Sat. 9 a.m.-7 p.m., Sun. 9 a.m.-2 p.m. Admission is US$3, free on Sunday. On Av. Morelos Sur 323. No flash photos.

Casa De La Cultura

You'll find some fine entertainment here. Each month a calendar of events is printed and distributed for free, so stop in and pick one up. It will update you on what's going on all over the city: dances, music, drama, art exhibits and lots more. While you're here, stop and look at the fascinating exhibit of traditional masks used in ceremonies from all over Mexico. Open Mon.-Fri. 10 a.m.-2 p.m., Sat.-Sun. 10 a.m.-6 p.m., free. Located at Av. Morelos Norte 485.

Museo Regional Michoacán

This structure was built for Isidro Huarte. One of its most interesting displays is the mural by Alfredo Zalce, showing the "haves and have nots" (people who have helped Mexico, and those who have not). Exhibits include pre-Columbian artifacts, ceramics, colonial arms, contemporary and colonial paintings, and one section that is a public library, including a library for children. Open Tues.-Sun. 9 a.m.-7 p.m., admission US$4; photos are allowed, but no flash please. Located on Allende 305. Check out the message board; free international films are shown in the museum auditorium on Saturdays and Sundays at noon.

Casa De Las Artesanías

This is not just a museum of state crafts, but a

Quiroga pottery can be found all over the state.

workshop and sales floor. You'll find some of the best quality crafts from all the famous little towns. There are many rooms where you can observe artisans working. The quality here is excellent and the prices are accordingly high. Located at the ex-convent of San Francisco, on **Plaza Valladolid.** Open 9 a.m.-8 p.m.; the shops upstairs are open 10 a.m.-3 p.m. and 5-8 p.m.

Bosque Park

This is the largest park in Morelia and is officially called **Bosque Cuauhtémoc Forest.** It's a pleasant place to take a walk, away from the sights and sounds of the city. It's bordered by several sites of importance; the **Aqueduct, Museum of Natural History, Museum of Contemporary Art,** and the **Tarascan Fountain.** In the small **Plaza Morelos** (on the northeast side of the Bosque), note the fine statue of Morelos on his steed.

Museum Of Contemporary Art

In another fine ex-mansion built in the early 19th century, you'll find contemporary art of local as well as international artists. Three salons exhibit artwork in a variety of media, from oils to acrylics, photography, and lithography. These displays are changed each month, so it's always a surprise. Located on Calle Acueducto 18, on the border of Bosque Cuauhtémoc. Open Tues.-Sun. 4-7 p.m., free. No flash photos.

Museo De Historia Natural

This museum was inaugurated in 1986 under the auspices of the University of Michoacán. It is devoted to the protection of the state's natural resources, and exhibits programs of investigation and history of the growth of ecology in the state. Open daily except Tues. 10 a.m.-6 p.m., free. Located on the border of the Bosque Cuauhtémoc, on Av. Ventura Puente s/n.

The Aqueduct

At one time the primary means of getting water to the city, the Aqueduct continues its path over the landscape, ending at the **Tarascan Fountain.** The graceful arches at one time stretched for eight kilometers, supplying 30 public fountains where people hand-dipped their water for home use. Today there are 253 arches, with the highest at 7.5 meters.

OZ MALLAN

MODERN MORELIA

Benito Juárez Zoo

This is a real change of pace from the intense historical walk through the the inner city of Morelia. It's a place to relax, be outdoors, and enjoy children (yours or those of others). You'll find a variety of animals, a small lake with rowboats for rent, a nocturnal display, reptiles, a mini-train that cruises around the park, restaurants, shops, a children's playground, a picnic area, and a fine ecology program. Open daily 10 a.m.-6 p.m., admission US$1.10 adult, 20 cents children under 10. Located on Av. Juárez and Av. Camelinas, about three km south of the plaza. **Note:** The combi with the maroon code going south on Nigromante can be boarded on the east side of Palacio Clavijero; this takes you right to the zoo. Tell the bus driver where you want to get off when you board.

Convention Center Of Morelia

A modern, green complex that is adaptable to many different programs in the city; the most interesting are the **planetarium,** the **orchid house** (called the orchidarium), and the **Morelos Theater.** You'll also find the **Gran Hotel Centro de Convenciones, Restaurante Cuacalli,** a **public library,** and a **travel agency.**

Planetarium

Programs are presented at the planetarium on Sunday at 6 p.m., admission US$2. There's an interesting dome where the stars and planets are brought closer to the audience.

House Of Orchids

This is a great adventure for both professional and amateur horticulturists. The variety of flora and colors are impressive, and if you're there at the right time of the blooming season, the aroma is marvelous. Open Mon.-Fri. 8 a.m.-6 p.m., Sat. and Sun. 10 a.m.-2 p.m. and 4-6 p.m. Admission is more of a donation than anything else; there's a ticket price for every pocketbook.

Teatro Morelos

This oversized modern theater is used in a grand style for large conventions as well as for cultural events. The schedule is available at the tourist office. Take the **yellow** combi going east on Calle Santiago Tapia to 20 de Noviembre. Remember to check the hour it stops running; it's a *long* walk back to the center of town. However, there are taxis around.

ACCOMMODATIONS

The hotels in the central part of the city are mostly wonderful old buildings with colonial architecture. Most have stairs to climb, some have lovely courtyards, and in many you do not find heat (bring warm sleeping clothes in the winter).

Budget

The real bargain hunters should check out the youth hostel, **Villa Deportiva Juvenil.** Everyone of any age is welcome, no card necessary. Men and women have separate dorms, with four bunks per room. The facilities are clean, and it's located about 20 minutes walking distance from downtown (take a taxi or a bus at the plaza). Rates are about US$4 pp, with a discount for those holding a membership card. Located at Chiapas St. 180 in the IMJUDE sport center at Oaxaca and Chiapas, south west of the plaza; tel. (451) 3-3177.

There are many budget hotels in Morelia, many in converted old houses. Look carefully—probably

planetarium

BOB RACE

the biggest complaint about many is that they have no exterior windows. Don't expect elevators, and some of the rooms are a little worn. Look at your room before you decide. The **Posada Don Vasco** is a popular stopover for budget travelers; it's clean, carpeted, and facing the courtyard where there are relaxing places to sit and read a book. The restaurant offers good food and cheap prices. Rates are US$15 s, US$18 d; free parking. Located at Vasco de Quiroga 232, tel. (451) 12-1484. **Hotel Mintzicuri** is hard to miss if you're walking past. Look for the bright blue tile front; three floors, 37 clean rooms, all carpeted. Rates are US$16 s, US$18.50 d, on Vasco de Quiroga 227, tel. 12-0664. Check out **Hotel Matador,** Eduardo Ruíz 531, tel. 12-4649, about US$15 s or d (a good one.) **Hotel San Jorge** is adequate at Madero Poniente 719, tel. 12-4610. **Plaza Hotel** is near the bus station, if that's important to you. Spartan, clean, small vintage rooms with a three-story walkup. Rates are US$16 s, US$20 d. Located at Valentín Farías 278, tel. 12-3095. More include **Hotel Concordia,** at Valentín Farías 328, tel. 12-3052/3054, with rates of US$16 s, US$19 d; and **Hotel Colonial,** at 15 de Noviembre 20, tel. 12-1897.

Moderate

Catedral Hotel: Earthy colors, good downtown location, and comfortable rooms make this a good choice. With 44 rooms, coffee shop, bar, restaurant, and a covered central patio filled with plants. Rates are about US$48 s, US$60 d, free parking; located at Zaragoza 1, tel. (451) 13-0783 or 13-0467, fax 13-0406.

Hotel Alameda: Here you have a choice between modern and older rooms; ask for the newer more modern rooms. The entire hotel is a mix of old and new with a little neon thrown in where least expected; charming and eclectic. Rates range US$60-80, suites are higher; 116 rooms. Bar and restaurant on premises. Located on the Plaza at Av. Madero Poniente 313, tel. 12-2023 or 12-2405, fax 13-8727.

Hotel Virrey de Mendoza: For a real step back into history, stay in the ex-mansion of Antonio de Mendoza, first viceroy of Mexico. This lovely home now offers 50 rooms that have been renovated and sumptuously furnished with antiques. The beautiful staircase, opulent public rooms with crystal chandeliers, and gold rococo mirrors give the feeling of elegance. Rates are US$70-75, suites more. Located on the northwest corner of the plaza, tel. 12-0045.

Posada Vista Bella: Located across from the luxurious Villa Montana in the hills overlooking the city, you'll find a pleasant, simple, and clean little place. The apartments make it particularly interesting; they are available for week- or month-long rentals. Rooms are about US$50 d. For other rental information, write to Apdo. Postal 135, Morelia, 58090, Michoacán, Mexico; located at Calle Galeana, Lomas de Santa María, tel./fax 14-0284.

Hotel de la Soledad: This posada is housed in an ex-mansion built about 1700. The lovely old structure has a long history of use; a convent lurks in its past. There's a beautiful courtyard, with archways and bright bougainvilleas; it's very Mexican. Rooms are spacious, and some overlook the courtyard where tables are set up for dining. The food is okay. About 60 rooms, rates are around US$75 d. Located on Calle Zaragoza 90 and Calle Ocampo, tel. 2-1888. A parking garage is across the street.

Hotel Mansión de la Calle Real: Here you'll find satellite TV, an elevator, a covered parking lot, and 66 modern and carpeted rooms, as well as a bar and restaurant. Mostly used by business travelers, rates are US$70; it's about eight blocks from the Cathedral near the Aqueduct, Av. Madero Ote. 766, tel. 3-2856.

Luxury

If you really want to stay in an upscale inn with beautiful surroundings and a great view several kilometers away from the bustle of town—if money is no object—Villa Montaña is it.

Villa Montaña: This is not only well thought of in Morelia, it is ranked as one of the finest small hotels in Mexico. Don't expect to walk to the Plaza de los Mártires from this location (in the Santa María Hills south of town); if you don't have your own car (rentals are available at the airport), expect to take a taxi. The accommodations here are all huge, flamboyant villas decorated with beautiful antiques, surrounded by well-kept, well-landscaped gardens. These gardens are filled with impressive statuary, many from the pre-Columbian period. The dining room is famed for its gourmet food. On the grounds there's a lovely pool and a tennis court. Golf is five minutes away. Reservations are suggested, and rates start at about US$120, US$150, or US$180, depending on the villa you choose; all include a full breakfast. For more information, write Apdo. Postal 233, Morelia, 58090, Michoacán, Mexico, located at Patzimba 201, Col. Vista Bella, in the U.S. tel. (800) 223-6510, in Mexico tel. (451) 14-0231, fax 15-1423.

FOOD

In Morelia you can count on most of the hotel dining rooms for good solid fare, from international to local specialties. There are several restaurants in town that offer outstanding *típico* food. The best part is the wonderful ambience of many of the restaurants set in patios of formerly magnificent homes from the colonial era. For the most part, food is reasonable in the city; look near the bus station for the cheapest. Other inexpensive choices are under the covered arches on **Plaza San Agustín**. Budget travelers all look to get the cheapest *comida corrida,* and usually prices for the other meals in these restaurants fall in line. Several of these are vegetarian, and very good:

Comida Corrida
La Cueva de Chucho, Eduardo Ruíz 620.

Govinda, vegetarian, Morelos Sur 39.

Restaurante El Paraiso, Portal Galeana 103.

Restaurante Woolworth, on Virrey de Mendoza.

Restaurante Vegetariano Acuarius, Hidalgo 75.

Restaurante Vegetariano La Fuente, Av. Madero Oriente 493-B.

El Quinto Sol, open daily 10 a.m.-6 p.m., Aquiles Serdán 72.

Los Comensales: Readers continue to recommend **Los Comensales** for breakfast and lunch especially. Meals are served in a charming interior courtyard, with colorful flowers, a fountain, and birds. Really good local food. If you haven't tried *uchepos* (fresh corn tamales) this is the place to do it. They're served with sour cream and a red chile sauce (delicious!) for about US$2; chilequiles and espresso are also good here. At Calle Zaragoza 148. Budget to moderate.

Moderate
El Gratin is a little coffee shop with good simple meals; they take pride in serving *hygienically safe* green salads. Open daily except Tues. 8 a.m.-7 p.m. On Río Mayo 610-4, in Col. Ventura Puente. Another fine little place is **Mesón San Diego,** specializing in selections from the Mexican kitchen, with nice piano bar, at Calz. Fray Antonio de San Miguel 344.

For a taste of the local traditional foods, check out **Restaurante Don Quijote** (in the Hotel Casino) serving the white fish from Pátzcuaro, as well as *charales, carnitas,* and *conejo,* and don't forget frothy traditional chocolate. Open daily 7:30 a.m.-9:30 p.m., Portal Hidalgo 229. In the mood for Italian? Go to **La Pasta Nostra.** Cocktails are served; open daily; 7 a.m.-midnight, at Lázaro Cárdenas 2276, tel. (451) 4-4946. **Mr. Muu** is known for his roasted kid goat, open daily 1:30-11 p.m., Isidro Huarte 75-A, tel. 2-4987. And if you're in the mood for prime rib, try **Rey Sol** (remember this is Mexico, and the cuts aren't always the same style), open daily 1-11 p.m., García de León 1188, tel. 5-2021.

Steak Houses
All carnivores take note of the good steaks at **El Torito** (open daily 2-11:30 p.m., at Av. Madero Poniente 867), **La Cabañita** (open daily 2-11 p.m., García de León 960), and **La Venadita,** (Ventura Puente 770, open daily 2-11 p.m., tel. 451-4-3338). Moderate to expensive.

Las Morelianas
This is an excellent restaurant with superb service in a beautiful old building. Sunday afternoon dinner is very traditional and you see many Mexican families enjoying themselves. Open daily 8 a.m.-midnight. On Calle de Retajo 90, tel. (451) 4-4594. Moderate to expensive.

Restaurante Fonda Las Mercedes
Another lovely patio restaurant; this city is filled with the most charming old courtyards, and many restaurants have set up shop within. Is the food really *so* good? Or is the atmosphere so sensational you don't notice the taste? In this case the food is excellent, and while you're eating you can admire the murals, the flowers, the plants, and the colorful birds. Try one of the unusual pasta dishes. Closed Sun., open 1 p.m.-1 a.m., at León Guzmán 47, tel. (451) 2-6113. Moderate.

Sweets

Morelia is known for its sweets. A variety of candy is made from fruit. Before Columbus introduced sugarcane into the country, the candy was sweetened with coconut, honey, and fruit. *Dulces* (sweets) are still made with those ingredients, but now, sugar has been added. *Ate* is popular all over Mexico, but especially in Morelia. It's a simple fruit paste (made from a huge variety of fruits) with sugar and water added; it's then kneaded. *Cocadas* are made with coconut, and in Michoacán, they are bite size and have a slight cinnamon flavor. Wherever you are in Mexico, as the Day of the Dead holiday approaches (31 October to 2 November), you will see sugar skulls with bright colored eyes, as well as caskets and skeletons. Take a look through the **Mercado de Dulces,** at Av. Madero Oriente, s/n. They display dozens of varieties of candy from all over the country. A few other sweets shops are: **Agustina Zamudio,** at Antonio Alzate 336; **Jorgito,** Bocanegra 1459-A; **La Estrella,** Madero Oriente 1526; and **Morelianas,** at Av. Lázaro Cárdenas 2760.

EVENTS AND NIGHTLIFE

Morelia Nightlife

Many fine cultural exhibitions are continually going on in Morelia, including regional dances, choir and organ recitals, folkloric dances (especially famous in this area is the **Danza de los Viejitos**), and many other events; check at the tourism office, and at the **Casa de Cultura.** For more lively entertainment with music that continues throughout the night, there are a few discos in town. **Bambalinas** advertises "just drinks and rock 'n' roll," at Av. Lázaro Cárdenas 2225, tel. (451) 5-5354. At **XO,** dance away the nights Mon.-Sun. 9 p.m.-2 a.m., Av. del Campestre 100, tel. 5-1035. **Bar El Mural,** at the Gran Hotel Centro de Convenciones, is open 9 p.m.-2 a.m., tel. 15-0023.

Morelia Calendar Of Events

This is a busy city, and all year-round something exciting is happening, including several great *ferias* (fairs):

1 Dec.-6 Jan.: The **Christmas Fair** both ends the year and begins the year.

May: The **Fair of Morelia** is the biggie for More-lia, a regular old-fashioned state fair with handmade items, prize animals, and produce displays; of course there's a bullfight.

May: The first two weeks in May the **International Organ Festival** attracts musicians from all over the world (you have to hear this organ!).

18 May: Morelia's "birthday"

July-Aug.: For two weeks musicians put on grand performances in various places in the city for the **International Music Festival.**

15-16 Sept.: Mexican **Independence Day** brings parades, dances, music, and speeches.

30 Sept.: The **Birthday of Don José María Morelos** inspires celebrations to remember the local Independence hero the city was named for.

31 Oct.-2 Nov.: Día de Los Muertos ("Day of the Dead").

12 Dec.: **Día de la Virgen de Guadalupe** is the day to remember the patron saint of Mexico.

SPORTS

If you're into golf, check out the **Club Campestre,** a tricky nine-hole course where nonmembers are welcome. Greens fees are around US$35 on weekdays, US$40 on weekends. Tennis is available at the club for a lot less. Ask at your hotel for more information.

Balneario Cointzio is a lovely spa about 25 kilometers west of town; good swimming here. Lots of hills for trekking. Come see the animals; there's a zoo. Open 10 a.m.-6 p.m., closed Tuesdays, small admission fee.

The Butterfly Sanctuary

Perhaps this isn't considered a "sport" per se, but it will include a trek into the countryside. It's time well spent. One hundred million monarch butterflies make a yearly migration that takes them 5,000-8,000 kilometers from Canada and the central and northern U.S. to the transvolcanic belt in Mexico. This ecosystem is located at an altitude of 2,800-3,300 meters. The climate is ideally suited for the overwintering butterflies. If you're in Michoacán during the winter months (Nov.-Feb.), take the opportunity to see the forests and the millions of butterflies clinging to the trees. Angangueo and Ocampo are the two areas in Michoacán open to the public. (In Mexico State you can see them in the Cerro Pelón Sanctuary.)

You start seeing butterflies at the small, unpretentious nearby village of El Rosario. A sanctuary guide escorts all visitors through this high forest and for about an hour you'll walk along steep mountain paths in the midst of a world that turns black and orange. Have you ever heard the flutter of butterfly wings? Here you will hear the flutter of millions. The branches of the tall green oyamel trees are shrouded by the black-and-orange striped pattern. It's an overwhelming "high" to all the senses. Near the parking area you'll find a visitor's center with toilets, cold drinks, and a video display that explains all about the doings of the monarch. Those who are unable to make the hike shouldn't stay away—the entire area is filled with butterflies before you head up the trail. This is high-altitude hiking. Admission to the sanctuary is US$3.50, and tip for the guide is generally about US$3.50; open daily 10 a.m.-5 p.m.

Getting There: This is really not a one-day trip if using public transportation. Just to get to the park in time to take the hike you must stick to a tight schedule. From Morelia's Central Camionera the 7 a.m. bus is the first of the day and the one you *must* take in order to connect to Zitacuaro (about US$3.50 and three hours). From there go to the local bus station in Zitacuaro. It's not far, but it's most expeditious to go by cab. From the station you can take a bus to Ocampo; it costs about 60 cents and takes 45 minutes. In Ocampo there's only one bus to Sierra del Companario sanctuary that leaves from the main plaza; it costs about 60 cents and leaves at 12:30 p.m. If you miss that bus you will have to pay about US$45 by taxi. This makes a very long day. However, there are several hotels along the way if you choose to go on your own.

In my book, the best way is with a tour operator, because if you miss that bus, the cost comes out the same. One of the best for this trip is **Operadora Monarcha.** The cost is US$84 for a day-trip. It sounds like a high price for nine hours, but it is the most convenient way if you don't have your own vehicle. The price includes transport, entrance fees, guide, and lunch. The trip takes you through Ocampo and Angangueo and into the beautiful mountains of the Eje Neovolcanico at 3,100 meters. They also offer two- and three-night trips to the area. For more information contact Gisela Medina (she speaks English) at (43) 13-3571, fax 12-0075, at Av. Madero Oriente 635, C.P., Morelia, 58000, Mich., Mexico.

SHOPPING

Any place you look in the historic center of Morelia has fine or funky shops. Antique collectors will delight in finding precious minutia from the past and ancient religious articles that still circulate. Other shops specialize in the local crafts.

Mercados

If you like browsing in the public market, you'll find several in Morelia: **Mercado San Juan,** at Plan de Ayala s/n; **Mercado Independencia,** at Vicente Santa María s/n; and **Mercado Vasco de Quiroga,** at Madrigal de las Torres s/n.

Arts And Crafts

Michoacán ranks high as an all-round good state to do major shopping. The variety of arts and crafts is huge, from copper *everything* to woolen garments and beautiful, brilliantly colored, modern-day woven table linens that are perfect for decorating the table of the 1990s. There's intricately wrought silver filigree, woven straw, embroidery, and lovely lacquerware with inlaid gold that rivals that of the Orient. In many of the communities you can watch the art as it's created.

The following shops are always worth looking through if you are interested in the marvelous diversity of this area's indigenous art.

Artes Michoacanas Cerda, Ignacio Zaragoza 163.

Artesanías del Centro, Portal Hidalgo 197.

Casa de las Artesanías, Fray Juan de San Miguel s/n (near the ex-convent of San Francisco).

Cerámica Morelia, Tomas Alba Edison 113.

Furniture

More and more beautiful furniture is coming from Morelia. It looks handcrafted, although I don't know that it is, but the carving is lovely and it *is* handpainted. From headboards, desks, wardrobes, and chairs, you'll find interesting art work in subtle pastel colors, designed sometimes as fruits, vegetables, or geometric designs. Many companies ship. Check out **Ex-**

portationes Guare, at Av. Heroes de Nocupitaro 421, tel. (451) 3-7946, fax 2-5763.

Bazaars And Antiques

Most of the antiques we found were of religious significance, but they were marvelous old woodcarvings or metal work regardless.

Bazar Corregidora, Corregidora 707.

El Arcano, Ignacio Zaragoza 79.

El Hallazgo, Av. Rey Tanganxhuan 549.

La Soledad, Ignacio Zaragoza 90.

Malls

These are becoming popular, and come in many sizes and styles. Check out some of the following.

Plaza Fiesta Camelinas, Av. del Campestre s/n.

Plaza Rebullones, Bosque Cuauhtémoc and the Acueducto

Servicentro, Av. del Campestre s/n.

INFORMATION AND SERVICES

Tourist Office

This office is located in a wonderful old building, a former monastery, **Palacio Clavijero.** Usually someone speaks English and they are happy to provide you with good information and maps. Ask for their free monthly schedule of events. In a glass case at the entrance look at additional booklets for sale about the city and state. Open Mon.-Fri. 9 a.m.-2 p.m. and 4-8 p.m., Sat.-Sun. 9 a.m.-8 p.m. On the corner of Madero and Nigromante, tel. (451) 3-2654. Ask about the free guided walking tours of the Morelia city center.

Communications

The **Post Office** and the **Telegraph Office** are in the **Palacio Federal** on the corner of Madero and Serapio, five blocks east of the cathedral at Av. Madero Oriente 369.

La Libreria Bookstore

You'll find very little information printed in English in Morelia. At this bookstore/coffee shop you'll find a few publications in English, but don't expect much. However, they do offer very nice cultural evenings here: International films on Fri. at 7 p.m. and Sat. at 7:30 p.m., and live music on Sun. at 7:30 p.m. There's no charge as long as you buy a snack at the cafe. This is a good place to mix and meet university students from the Cine-club. At Calz. Fray Antonio de San Miguel 284, tel. (451) 2-0287.

Newspapers

At the tourist office there are several publications filled with information and events in town. A local paper, called *La Voz de Michoacán* comes out each Monday and lists entertainment and cultural events in the city.

Money Matters

There are many banks to change currency along Madero near the main plaza, open 9 a.m.-1:30 p.m.: **Banamex, Bancomer, Banco Serfin,** and **Banco Del Atlántico.** If you need to change money in the off hours, try the *casas de cambios.* They all keep similar hours; Mon.-Fri. 9 a.m.-6 p.m., Sat. 9 a.m.-1 p.m. Check out **Casa de Cambio Majapara,** at Pino Suárez 166. They change a variety of currencies. **Trocamex** is at Melchor Ocampo 178.

Laundromats

There are several laundromats in town. One is on the corner of Nicolas Bravo, open Mon.-Fri. 8 a.m.-noon and 4-8 p.m., Sat. 8 a.m.-5 p.m. Another, **Lavandería Automática,** is on Montanez 318, in the Plaza Capuchinas. Open Mon.-Fri. 9 a.m.-2 p.m. and 4-7 p.m., Sat. 9 a.m.-2 p.m. It's really almost as cheap to let them do it as to do it yourself.

Medical Services

General Hospital Vasco Quiroga, ISSSTE is on the road to Guanajuato, Km 3, tel. 12-3013.

Centro Medico is at Bartolomé de las Casas 636, tel. 12-8031.

Farmacias El Fénix, at Allende 69, tel. 12-8492, and **Farmax Farmacias,** Av. Madero Poniente 5, tel. 12-0434, are two of the pharmacies in town.

LANGUAGE SCHOOLS

There at least three language schools in the city. **Centro Cultural de Lenguas Morelia,** on Av. Madero 560, tel. (451) 12-2743, is one. Another is **Baden-Powell Institute,** Alzate 565, tel. 12-4070. And the biggest is **Centro Mexicano Internacional,** at the Albergue de la Calzada hotel. For more information write to CMI, Apdo. Postal 56, Morelia, 58000, Michoacán, Mexico, tel. (800) 835-8863.

GETTING THERE AND AWAY

By Air
The **Aeropuerto Federal Francisco J. Mújica** is about 30 km from Morelia. It's served by **Aeromar,** Av. 20 de Noviembre 110, tel. (451) 3-8570; **Aero Sudpacífico,** Plaza Fiesta Camelinas, tel. 3-5246; and **Taesa.** All three fly to Mexico City. It's about 45 minutes by taxi from the central plaza (or hotels in the area) to the airport (about US$15). Ask for the rate if more than one person is in the taxi.

For airport service, call **Servicio Morelia Aeropuerto,** Melchor Ocampo 58-A, tel. 15-0218 or 15-6714.

By Train
On the southwest side of the city, the **Estación del Ferrocarril** ticket office is open 5:30-6:30 a.m., 10 a.m.-noon, 4-6 p.m., and 10-11 p.m., tel. (451) 16-1697. Some schedule information and tickets are available from the U.S.; contact **Mexico Air and Rail Vacation,** 8607 Wurzbach Rd., Suite V100, San Antonio, Texas 78240, tel. (210) 641-6449.

By Bus
Buses to and from Morelia are frequent and scheduled. Service to Mexico City departs every 30 minutes throughout the day. The central bus station is located near the center of town on Eduardo Ruíz near Valentín Farías. Here you will find long distance telephone and fax service, snack and coffee shops, luggage storage,

and a choice of several bus lines coming and going. One of the new luxury bus companies, **ETN,** travels to Mexico City, Guadalajara, and Guanajuato. Other companies include **Flecha Amarilla, Autobuses de Jalisco,** and **Estrellas de Oro.** Check at the bus station for the most current schedule and prices; they change regularly. A taxi from the bus station to a local downtown hotel will cost about US$1.50.

GETTING AROUND MORELIA

As in all the colonial cities, getting around the town center is easy on foot. And many of the city's historical sites are located in the center of town around the plaza. Many hotels are located downtown, but several are beyond walking distance. Taxis are quite reasonable in Morelia. There are no metered cabs, so figure about 50 cents per km, and double check your fare before you climb in. Large vans/combis provide service for reasonable rates, tickets cost 25 cents, and the color tells you where the combi is going. Check at the tourist office for more information and schedules with color codes.

Car Rentals
Dollar Rent A Car, Av. del Campestre 676 and the airport, tel. (451) 5-3050.

Quick Car Rental, Av. Las Camelinas 1454, tel. 5-4466.

Budget, at Camelinas Av. 2938, place 9, Plaza Galerías, tel. 3-6728.

Gas Stations
San Miguel, on the road to Pátzcuaro at Km 3.5.

Santa Fe, on the road to Salamanca at Km 104.

Chicácuaro, at Av. Madero Poniente 1145.

PATZCUARO

Pronounced: PAHTZ-kwah-roh
Altitude: 2,200 meters
Population: 100,000
Area Code: (434)
Distance from Mexico City: 377 km

Pátzcuaro is an enigma. It's a colonial-rich town yet it dates to a pre-Christian era, making it one of the most indigenous cities of the country, with a growing population (mostly all descendants of the Purépechas). If you can visualize the orderliness of Morelia, imagine just the opposite here. Pátzcuaro was drawn well, but no one colored within the lines. Whitewashed houses with red tile roofs climb up uneven, curvy, hilly streets; lush trees are shrouded in disorderly vines. Then it all falls into place when at the edges of this disarray the smooth green water of lovely Lake Pátzcuaro mates with the shore and drifts off dreamily to the horizon.

SIGHTS

Lay Of The Land

The center of Pátzcuaro lies about a mile from the lake, much of it on the side of the hill. But the very heart of the city is flat and easy walking, making it fun to discover colonial buildings. Lake Pátzcuaro is well known for its whitefish, and you'll find many fish-cafes near the dock on the waterfront. Commuter boats run back and forth to Isla Janitzio; the trip takes about 20 minutes.

Plaza Grande

It's officially named **Plaza de Vasco de Quiroga,** easy to figure out when you see the statue of the beloved priest in the middle of this large, peaceful center of town. On the edge of the plaza you'll find restaurants, shops, and lovely old colonial buildings.

Plaza Chica

Only a block away is the "other center of town"; its official name is **Plaza Gertrudis Bocanegra.** Gertrudis Bocanegra was a martyr for the cause of Independence and was shot in neigh-

boring Plaza Grande while tied to an ash tree. From this plaza you'll find the *mercado* going off on the west side. There's a Friday morning Indian market in the plaza where you can buy ceramics, woodcarvings, lacquerware, copper, woven goods, and even furniture. However, the market really bustles all week long. From here the walk to the lake is just a little under two kilometers. However, if that's too much for you, catch the bus leaving about every 15 minutes from Plaza Chica or any bus or combi marked **Lago;** it will get you to the docks.

Basílica De Nuestra Señora De La Salud

Vasco de Quiroga wanted only the best for the Indians, and he planned a grandiose church for Pátzcuaro. It was going to be bigger than the Cathedral of Notre Dame in Paris. Between the resistance of the powers that were in place at the time, and political and natural disasters, it didn't happen. However, this basilica (in a much smaller format) is still well worth a look. Of special interest is the statue of the Virgin encased in glass. The statue was created by Tarascan craftsmen out of corn paste and wild orchids in 1547. It's much beloved, and on the Virgin's special feast days, 8 December and 8 May, pilgrims come from miles around to salute the Virgin of Good Health. The church is located on the little hill east of the center of town.

Museo Regional De Artes Populares

Another Quiroga-built structure, the first location of the **Colegio de San Nicolas** in 1540, is now a museum that displays the wonderful crafts of the region, including those the Indians were skilled at: pre-Quiroga and the fine arts the Indians learned from Spanish artisans, such as lace-work. Here, along with the examples of the crafts, you'll see what the lifestyle was like for these early people; you'll find a full replication. Open Tues.-Sat. 9 a.m.-7 p.m., Sun. 9 a.m.-3 p.m., admission about US$4.50. At Calle Ensenaza, one block east of Plaza Grande.

Teatro Caltzontzin

In the upstairs hall, check out the murals which portray the history of Michoacán from the first

OZ MALLAN

Museo Regional de Artes Populares

meeting between Tarascan ruler Tangahxuan II and the Spanish conquistadores in 1522 until and including the reign of native son Lázaro Cárdenas in 1940. At one time this was a convent for the **Church of San Agustín** (next door), today's library. In 1936 it was converted to a theater where cultural events and movies are shown.

Biblioteca Bocanegra
Formerly the Church of San Agustín, you will find a number of English-language books in the rear of this public library. Also, there's a fine mural by artist Juan O'Gorman. Open Mon.-Fri. 10 a.m.-7 p.m., Sat. 10 a.m.-1 p.m. Located on the north side of Plaza Chica.

House Of The Giant
Also called **Casa del Gigante,** this colonial structure has a giant stone man holding up one part of the building. Located on the east side of Plaza Grande, it was built by a count in 1663 and is one of the oldest structures in Pátzcuaro.

Casa De Los Once Patios
One of the favorite stops for tourists is this centuries-old hospital-then-Dominican-Convent structure with many patios (but I sure couldn't find eleven!). Visitors spend hours in the labyrinth of small shops where craftsmen are seen creating their wares. Don't miss any of them, this is a talented bunch. Michoacán's reputation for quality crafts is well earned. You'll find a doorway that leads to weavings, woolen sweaters, table linens, silver jewelry, modern coffee sets, ceramics, and lacquerware with gold inlay (the most remarkable to me)—really incredibly beautiful work. Note that none of the men wear glasses, and with such close-up tedious work in ill-lighted rooms, that seems rather amazing—to this four-eyes. When a remark was made, the artist quietly commented that "when the work comes from the heart, the eyes follow."

SIGHTS OFFSHORE

Lake Pátzcuaro
This is one of the highest lakes in Mexico (and the world) at 2,210 meters. Small villages nestle on the shores of Lake Pátzcuaro and on the right day the view of the lake is an artist's delight with blue sky, white puffy clouds, calm green water, and the famous butterfly nets of the Pátzcuaro fishermen. Like gossamer wings, the nets give a look of grace to the bulky wooden boats as they glide across the water. Today you seldom see the butterfly nets anymore. Many fishermen have progressed to more modern means of fishing. Then they rush their catch to nearby restaurants.

Go to the dock for a ride across the way to nearby **Isla Janitzio.** The boat ride takes about 20 minutes and the most economical way is on the *colectivo* boat, which leaves as soon as it's filled; you seldom have to wait more than 15 minutes (fare is about US$3). Check the ticket office at the dock for other excursions available around the lake.

Isla Janitzio
Probably more people go to Janitzio on the Day of the Dead holiday than any other time. But on a two- to three-hour day-trip, you can see just about everything you wish on the small island. Add another hour for a fish lunch, and if you're

TO URUAPAN

TO LAKE PATZCUARO AND ISLA JANITZIO

TO MORELIA

PATZCUARO

POSADA DE DON VASCO ● ● HOTEL VILLA PATZCUARO

CALZ DE LAS AMERICAS

EFREN URICHO

CRUZ VERDE

DEL PANTEON

SAN JOSE

ALVARO OBREGON

INDUSTRIAS

LIBERTAD

HOTEL FIESTA PLAZA ■

TEATRO CALTZONTZIN AND BIBLIOTECA BOCANEGRA ●

DEGOLLADO

HOTEL CONCORDIA ●

HOTEL VALMEN ●

POSADA DE LA BASILICA ●

PLAZA CHICA

ARCIGA

BASILICA DE NUESTRA SEÑORA DE LA SALUD ●

RAMOS REGULES

GRAN HOTEL ●

LA PAZ

BENIGNO SERRATO

BENITO JUAREZ

POSADA LA TERRAZA ●

HOTEL MANSION ITURBIDE ●

ITURBE

AHUMADA

MUSEO REGIONAL DE ARTES POPULARES ■

TOURIST OFFICE ■

QUIROGA

IBARRA

ALCANTARILLAS

HOTEL LOS ESCUDOS ●

HOUSE OF THE GIANT ■

PLAZA GRANDE

ENSENANZA

EL CIPRAS DEL ESPEJO

EMILIO CARRANZA

TERAN

PONCE DE LEON

EL PATIO ■

DR. JOSE MARIA COSS

CASA DE LAS ONCES PATIOS ■

LA HUERTA

NAVARRETE

NOT TO SCALE

© MOON PUBLICATIONS, INC.

so inclined, poke around the shops that mostly sell geegaws found anywhere. Do take a walk up to the enormous statue of patriot José María Morelos. The statue is 40 meters (130 feet) tall, and a climb in the interior of the statue brings you to a mural that tells the story of Morelos's life. If you go all the way to the fist of the statue, you'll come out to a terrace where the view is breathtaking; or it would be, but you're already out of breath after the climb (US$1 admission). Often, when there are many tourists on the island, you'll get a glimpse of the butterfly boats performing for visitors.

Day Of The Dead On Isla Janitzio

Traveling to the island in the fading twilight, modern sleek boats engrave white lines on smooth dark water. The dock is filled, people jostle along small paths carrying orange flowers, blue pots filled with tasty food, and candles wrapped in a scrap of paper. This is the Day of the Dead; the church bells have already begun to "summon the departed" from the land beyond, and the bells and the hundreds of candles are to help guide the deceased back, to keep them from losing their way. The bells will continue to ring throughout the night until the sun rises. This is not a sad time; it's a happy time when families feel closer to their departed than at any other time of the year. It's almost a party, as a wake is a party.

A walk through the crowded cemetery, with the heavy smell of candle wax mixed with the earthy aroma of marigolds, evokes private memories. At each grave people are busy beautifying the site, placing flowers all over the graves, outnumbered only by candles. Each is different—photographs of the departed, a cherished toy, liquor, pots of fresh cooked favorite foods, a cigar, a preferred hat, all manner of worldly things that were special to those dear people—these worldly "things" are intended to lure them back once each year on 1 and 2 November. This is a two-day celebration; the first night is especially for the children who passed on before their time.

Today With Tourists

Years ago here on Janitzio, the Day of the Dead was such a pristine, sincere celebration that it began attracting tourists from all over the world. Today it becomes so crowded with foreigners

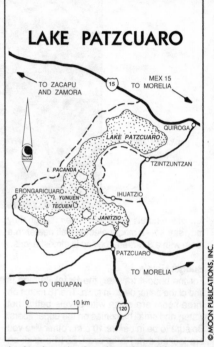

that it's almost hard to take a photo without capturing at least two or three visitors in each pic. So be forewarned. If you can look beyond the outsiders (of course we would like to think that we are not outsiders, sí?) and feel the real essence of the occasion, then on with you, across the lake to Janitzio. Some throw out the baby with the bath water complaining that the locals have made it a tawdry display, but in reality the locals are just doing what they have been doing for generations, experiencing their attachment to the dead in their own way, which dates back to pre-Christian days—it is we who have turned their private feelings into a massive photo-op. By the way, don't take photos without asking permission first, and if refused be respectful and gracious.

ACCOMMODATIONS

Hotel rooms in Pátzcuaro run to simplicity. Be sure to bring warm woollies in the winter, since

colonial Pátzcuaro

OZ MALLAN

few of the hotels have heat, even though they may say so—a single electric wall heater in a room with a 3.5-meter ceiling is almost a joke.

Budget Hotels

For the budget traveler, the **Hotel Valmen** is one of the better deals in town. The 16 rooms on three floors are clean with private baths, hot water, and small balconies on the upper floors. Be sure to be in before 10 p.m., otherwise you are locked out. Rates are US$14 s or d; on Lloreda 334, one block east of Plaza Chica. Most everyone enjoys staying at the **Posada de la Basílica** across from the basilica on a little hill with a fine view of the town. You'll find pleasant clean rooms in a colonial mansion (and loud church bells in the morning). The restaurant on the premises also has a lovely view. Eleven rooms unfold onto an open patio. Rates are US$22 s, US$26 d; at Arciga 6, tel. (434) 2-1108.

Just one of several old mansions that have been renovated to serve as hotels around the plaza areas, **Hotel Los Escudos** has 30 rooms with carpeting and TV (with a satellite dish); some have fireplaces. A TV might be something to think about in a town that closes up at 9 p.m. Rates are US$25 s, US$33 d, at Portal 73, west side of Plaza Grande, tel. 2-0138.

The newish, modernish, **Hotel Fiesta Plaza** presents a colonial flavor. This is a good bargain for the money. Three stories, all rooms have small balconies that overlook a central courtyard covered in tile and with a fountain. All 33 rooms have private baths, hot water, TV, and comfy beds. **El Pescador** restaurant is on the premises. Rates are US$36 d. Easy to find at Plaza Bocanegra 24, tel. (434) 2-2515/2-2516.

At **Posada de Don Vasco** you'll find a hotel on one side of the street and a motel opposite. More modern than most of the hostels in town, it's also the costliest. It's a large rambling affair with 103 rooms located about two km north of town. It's best if you have a car; however, the bus does stop right out front. The motel is the most modern part. There's a tennis court, a pool (don't believe them if they say it's heated), patios, a restaurant and bar, and a bowling alley. Okay, but overrated. Rates are US$75 d. On Av. Lázaro Cárdenas 450, tel. (800) 528-1234, (434) 2-0227.

A Few More Hotels To Consider

Hotel Villa Pátzcuaro is another motel, very nice with parking slots in front of 12 pleasant rooms that each have a fireplace and wood beam ceilings. There's a pool, tennis courts (for a fee), and a grassy area in the rear. Also, there are trailer sites on the property. It's beyond walking distance from town, about three km from the plazas, but the bus passes out front frequently. Rates are US$24 s, US$29.50 d, trailer fees are US$12 for two people. At Lázaro Cárdenas 506, tel. (434) 2-0767, fax 2-2571. The **Hotel Mansión Iturbe** is considered by many to be the nicest on the Plaza Grande. Guests enjoy the colonial decor, heavy wood furniture, lace curtains, and a gentle ambience of the past.

Just 15 rooms; the restaurant is open 8:30 a.m.-9 p.m. Rates are US$45 s or d; at Portal Morelos 59, tel. 2-0368, on the north side of the plaza.

More Budget Rooms

Check around Plaza Chica for some inexpensive places: **Posada La Terraza,** just four blocks west from both plazas, US$21 d; **Gran Hotel,** US$21; **Posada Imperial,** US$20; and **Posada Lagos, Hotel Concordia,** both US$10. Remember, we said cheap, not choice.

FOOD

Visitors do not come to Pátzcuaro for the food. Not even the whitefish, which this writer feels is highly overrated. Because it is becoming increasingly scarce, it is becoming increasingly expensive (commonly about US$10 for an a la carte dinner), and for the same money you can get a lot of *good* Mexican food made with masa, sauces, chiles, beans, etc. This is not to say you can't find any good food in Pátzcuaro; we found several pleasant places that served good hearty food at reasonable prices. Our favorite was **Dany's,** open all day, and equally good for breakfast, lunch, and dinner. Rather oddly shaped like a narrow rectangle, the dining room is on two floors and the kitchen is on the third floor. Prices for *tortas* (sandwiches) run US$1.50-1.75 (the ham sandwich is always good). Dinners offered include the usual indigenous specialties along with ribs, chicken, and steak ranchero for

about US$5.50. Located on the street between the two plazas.

At the **Posada de Don Vasco** the food is very acceptable, atmosphere is "colonially" charming, and this is probably the most expensive of the hotel dining rooms. Check out the adjacent gift shop and take a look at some of their "X-rated" ceramic scenes inside the pots.

The **Camino Real** (next to the Pemex gas station) serves tasty food at good prices. Try the "Tarasca Soup"—that innocent little red *bit* floating on the top is one dynamite chile, so if you don't like to blowtorch your mouth, you might want to remove it to a safe zone before it soaks in real well. The soup is great. A couple more eateries to try are **El Patio,** the nearby **Posada San Rafael,** and the dining room at the **Escudos Hotel.** For a good priced *comida corida,* check out the **Meson del Gallo.** From the railway station on down the dock you'll find a number of cafes, and they all serve lake fish.

INFORMATION

Tourism Office

For information, maps, opening hours of various buildings, help with a hotel room, boat schedules, suggestions where to find the best whitefish and almost anything else you might

BOB RACE

The remaining yácatas of the Tarascan capital at Tzintzuntzan shows a unique round design. At one time these were faced with precisely fitted pieces of volcanic stone. Only a few have been investigated and these were found to hold the rich tombs of deceased leaders.

need, go to the northwest corner of the Plaza, on Ibarra St. 2, tel. (434) 2-1214.

SHOPPING

In the town of Pátzcuaro shoppers will fall in love with the old **Casa de los Once Patios.** The market is always a pleasure, and if you have a vehicle, drive into the towns of Santa Clara del Cobre, Quiroga, and Tzintzuntzan. Lots of shops, lots of special talents, wood-carvings galore, ceramics, and straw weavings that are unique.

GETTING THERE

By Bus
Public buses from Morelia run every 15 minutes 24 hours a day on **Autotransportes Galeana,** take approximately one hour, and cost US$2.50. If traveling from Mexico City to Pátzcuaro, both **Autobuses de Occidente** and **Flecha Amarilla** leave hourly at a cost of about US$8.

By Train
You can travel to and from Pátzcuaro and Mexico City by train, as long as you don't mind sitting up all night; there are no sleeping cars or food. Going in both directions, the train leaves at about 10 p.m. and arrives at your destination, either Pátzcuaro or Mexico City, at about 7:30 a.m. Check with **Mexico Air and Rail Vacation,** tel. (210) 641-6449 in the U.S. for current schedules, prices, and reservations.

NEAR PATZCUARO

From Pátzcuaro it's convenient to take day-trips to many extraordinary small towns and villages.

Santa Clara Del Cobre
Twenty kilometers south of Pátzcuaro, Santa Clara has been a center for copper work since before the Spanish arrived. At one time, copper was mined from the surrounding hills, these mines are no longer in operation; the copper is mined out, it is said. However, the town is still the copper center of Michoacán. The copper mu-

taking the cows home in Santa Clara del Cobre

seum whets the appetite of the collector. Small shops and factories all over town produce traditional and modern sleek napkin rings, graceful flower vases, pitchers, miniatures, and whatever you might have in mind; special orders will be made. At a local factory (there are about 50 in town) you can see a fat red ingot pulled from the fire as three or four strong men beat a tattoo with 50-pound sledgehammers until the copper is cold, black, and flat. The craftsmen use every bit of scrap copper they can get their hands on. It's amazing how they manage to shape the metal in such a primitive style.

Note the lovely copper roof on the kiosk in the Santa Clara town square. Lots of small shops border the main street across from the kiosk, all with copper. The **Copper Fair** is held each August for a week. Check with your local Mexican Government Tourist Office for dates for this moveable *feria*. And if you decide it would be fun to attend, make reservations in advance. You have limited accommodations choices: **Hotel Camino Real,** US$17 d (good restaurant here), tel. (434) 3-0281; **Hotel Oasis,** US$14 d, 3-0040; **Hotel Real del Cobre,** US$12 d, no phone, just take your chances.

Lake Zirahuen

About 12 kilometers west of Santa Clara del Cobre, ask for the small dirt road to Lake Zirahuen. This is another delightful out-of-the-way spot to find peace and quiet. The Mexicans treasure this as a favorite vacation ground, so it can get busy, but a nice kind of busy. No high-rises here, just low-key wooden cabins with a few cafes. Prices for cabins run from US$30 (for a single room) to about US$95 for a three bedroom. Check out the **Cabañas del Nautico** multi-bedroomed cabins (one-three), some with kitchenettes. Call (43) 15-0624, or fax (43) 15-0491. Also check out **Cabañas del Rincón,** the **Casa Club,** or have a good meal at **La Troje de Ala,** open Sat., Sun., and holidays. Lazy days can be spent canoeing, dropping a line from the dock, or taking a boat ride. Be sure to make reservations in advance for July and August, Easter week, Christmas/New Year week, and Day of the Dead. It's about 25 minutes from Pátzcuaro.

Tzintzuntzan

At one time Tzintzuntzan was the center of Tarascan power. It's located about 15 kilometers from Pátzcuaro, on the northeast edge of the lake. The ancient people built a network of five unusual round structures called *yácatas,* believed to have been burial centers for their leaders. **Las Yácatas** site is open daily 9 a.m.-6 p.m., admission is US$4 (seniors free). Below the unusual archaeological zone, a Franciscan monastery remains from the 16th century. The aged olive trees on the monastery grounds are said to have been planted by Vasco de Quiroga (he dared to go against the Spanish Crown's restrictive ban on olive growing, which was to maintain Spain's monopoly).

The town is filled with shops selling the dark green-glazed primitive-style pottery which is well known. When you purchase the pottery you might consider what it will be used for, and whether or not its lead content is within the limits of safety (probably not). But it's lovely pottery for flowers or just to look at.

If you decide you want to stay, check out **Cabañas de Tzintzuntzan** by the lake. It's quite a lovely spot with seven cabañas that will sleep up to five people, US$85 per day. For reservations call (434) 3-1003 in Morelia.

Quiroga

This pre-Columbian town once known as **Cocupao** was another Tarascan center. After the arrival of Vasco de Quiroga, the name was changed in his honor. Today it seems to exist on its pottery business and of course its string of craft centers. It's amazing the number of shops in the small town, and the variety of crafts for sale is immense. In July, the townsfolk celebrate the **Feast of the Blood of Christ** with a fiesta and torchlight parade, featuring a statue of Christ made years ago by the Indians from corn paste.

Quiroga market

OZ MALLAN

Around Lake Pátzcuaro

If you're driving and would like to get off the beaten path, take a drive around the lake. If you don't have your own vehicle, there is a bus that stops at all of the little villages. Obviously the advantage of driving is the freedom to stop and stay where you find intrigue without a schedule to care about. Each little village has its own personality; some have nothing else.

Pollution At Lake Pátzcuaro

One thing becomes very clear as you drive from village to village; like Lake Chapala, Lake Pátzcuaro is showing signs of pollution. Trash is dumped indiscriminately along the shores of the stream, and when the rain comes, the debris is washed into the lovely lake. Along the shore plastics are becoming almost as common as wild grasses.

On the west shore of the lake, the village of **Erongarícuaro** is a pleasant, low-key little place. There's nothing spectacular to see, but the town is imbued with the feel of tranquility. Enjoy the lake from another point of view; watch the kids play soccer and basketball in the church courtyard. It's always such a pleasure to watch life in the slow lane in some of these lovely little villages.

In **Ihuatzio**, we came across a small archaeological site with another group of three *yácatas,* stepped-stone pyramids from the Tarascan era. This is a pleasant way to spend a good part of a day, almost always with the lake in view. The road, however, seems to get progressively worse once you leave Pátzcuaro, until it comes to and joins the main road between Morelia and Zamora (Hwy. 15).

K. A. ESCOVEDO SANDERS

THE STATE OF JALISCO
INTRODUCTION

Independence best describes the character of Jalisco and most especially the people. Called Tapatíos (a nickname for people who were born in Jalisco), they are proud and never forget their heritage. They consider themselves "maybe just a little bit better than those from other cities in Mexico." After all, it is the Tapatíos who can be thanked for the joy of mariachi music; they share the delicious pleasure of their "home-brewed" tequila and *charreada* (rodeo).

Most people who visit Mexico already know about the grand dame of colonial cities, capital Guadalajara—and if not, are well aware of the city's famous little sister by the sea, Puerto Vallarta. Today Guadalajara is the second largest city of the country and a leader in high-tech development. What a city of contrasts! This is one of the most beautiful historic centers in the country with exhibits of world-respected muralists including native son José Clemente Orozco, and also has become a successful community of corporate progress and development. You just

have to look at the broad skyline to see both eras vividly.

LAND

Jalisco-country is a land of differences. Volcanic mountains and pine forests dot the high country; lush jungles, rugged coastlines, and beautiful beaches in the lowlands parallel the Pacific Ocean. It's bordered on the north by the states Aguascalientes and Zacatecas, on the west by the Pacific Ocean and Nayarit, to the east by Guanajuato State, and in the south by the states of Michoacán and Colima. The highest peak is **Nevado de Colima** (4,330 meters, 14,205 feet) in the southern part of the state. Its twin, Volcán de Colima (3,937 meters, 12,916 feet) is just across the border in Colima State. The **Sierra Madre Occidental** range stretches close to the coastline from Puerto Vallarta south to **La Cumbre,** where it then clutches the shoreline all the way to Patricio de Melaque.

CLIMATE

Jaliscenses enjoy a wide range of weather; it can be cool, even cold in the higher elevations. Guadalajara, at 1,567 meters, enjoys a moderate year-round climate, but it's always good to have a sweater along during the winter months. Long-time retired Americans in Guadalajara boast that over the years they have never needed heat or air-conditioning because it never gets too hot or too cold. On the other hand, Puerto Vallarta and other towns located on the coast can be hot and humid, with lots of rain, which makes them lush and green.

Because of the springlike weather in the highlands and tropical clime near the coast, Jalisco has flowers everywhere. In the highlands, bougainvillea, hibiscus, oleander, royal poinciana, jacaranda, roses, and African tulip-trees are everywhere. Near the coast lovely orchids grow wild in the jungle attached to high trees ever-reaching for the sun.

HISTORY

Pre-Hispanic

Historians tell us the land was inhabited by simple nomadic people who occupied the area during the pre-Classic era into the Classic period. During the postclassic period, Indian states (Xalisco, Tollan, Coliman, and Zapotlan) grew in the area that is today called Nayarit, Colima, and Jalisco. These groups of people formed part of the Aztec tribes (called Confederación Chimalhuacana) and others: Purépecha (Tarascans), Chapalas, and Huicholes. They were talented artists, leaving behind highly stylized terracotta figurines (but not in large quantities), which scientists presume represent the people of the era. The high mountains of the Sierra Madre del Sur and the Sierra Madre Occidental formed a barrier to the ocean plain excluding sophisticated indigenous groups such as the Aztecs and the Maya—so most of the communities on the coast developed in a slower, less polished manner than those upscale neighborhoods on the other side of the mountain.

The Coming Of The Spanish

Unpopulated lands northeast of the Tarasco Indian realm hosted nomad tribes, hunters, and eventually the beginnings of small settlements of agriculturists. After the Aztec empire fell, a few Spanish explorers traveled through the area, still leaving the isolated areas mostly untouched. Nuño de Guzmán, a lawyer, was appointed to the Audienca, the governing body of Mexico representing the Spanish crown, in 1527. Looking back, this was the lowest point of government history. Guzmán, a long-time enemy of Cortés, jumped into action with the conqueror's absence in Spain. Guzmán's treatment of the Indians is legend; he and his soldiers managed to wipe out entire communities of indigenous people with his brutality and intense greed. He forced them to labor long and hard in the mines that produced gold and silver. This siege of brutality lasted until 1529. During that period, Franciscan bishop Juan de Zumárraga, was appointed "Protector of the Indians" and sent to Mexico. It didn't take him long to see Guzmán for what he was; a cunning man who succeeded in keeping his actions a secret from the crown in Spain. Guzmán was guilty of corruption and extreme injustice toward both Indians and Spaniards. After many attempts, the bishop was able to smuggle a letter (at great risk to his life) out of the country from Veracruz. The Spanish royalty was shocked at Guzmán's actions. Ever the wily manipulator, he was informed secretly of this exposé, so he quickly headed west in search of new lands to conquer—hoping to regain his place in the good graces of the Spanish court. Once again he dodged the bullet, and now in a much more isolated area, Guzmán continued to savage the Indians until in 1538 he was ordered to Spain. For the next 20 years he was a prisoner of the court; because of his birthright, he was treated as a "noble" prisoner.

Only when Nuño de Guzmán led his army northwest of Mexico City in 1530 did life drastically change for the indigenous people of central Mexico. Guzmán and his Spanish soldiers probed what is today Jalisco state. In Guzmán's desire for power, he called these lands **La Gran España,** his long dreamed of domain.

In the meantime, Spanish colonists continued to arrive in Mexico looking for the promised lands described to them in their Spanish homeland. They came with their horses, cattle, oxen, and other farm animals, tools, and African slaves purchased as they passed through Cuba. Ad-

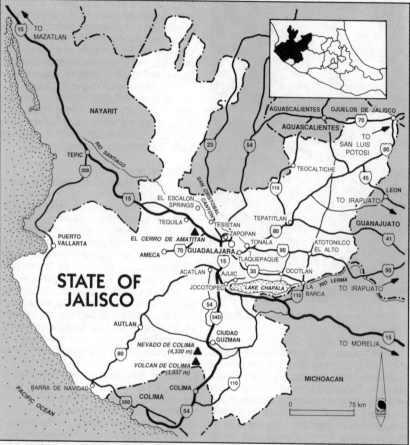

venturers had grand ideas and were looking for large plots of ground on which to establish impressive estates; many of the early groups succeeded.

The vice-regal government kept them from the Aztec empire since that was land awarded to the conquistadores and others who were in on the ground floor of the conquest. Many of the colonists headed north into territories settled (controlled) by Guzmán. He ordered the capital of *his* new "country" to be called **Guadalajara**, an Arabic word and the name of his home town in Spain. Hostile Indians and water problems made it impossible to stay at the first location, and so the search to find the perfect spot con-

tinued; it would take four locations before finally finding a permanent place to settle **Guadalajara**. Popular legend says that in the end, a brave woman, Doña Beatriz Hernandez, managed to convince the 63 colonist families to settle in the **Atemajaco Valley.** She believed in her choice of locations and also that King Charles would agree with her. And so, in 1542, with formal pomp and ceremony, with respected Spanish Army captains Oñate and Ibarra, on the spot where today stands the **Degollado Theater,** 63 families from a land thousands of miles away solemnly founded the city of Guadalajara. Four hundred and fifty years later, it remains a wise, intelligent, successful choice.

Orozco Clemente's powerful mural in the Instituto Cultural Cabañas

OZ MALLAN

When Guzmán was unceremoniously ousted, Pérez de la Torre took his place. The name of Guzmán's territory was changed to **Nueva Galicia** ("New Galicia"), and remained so until 1821 when all connections with the Spanish crown were severed after the conclusion of the War of Independence from Spain. The state was renamed Jalisco, from the indigenous capital **Xalisco,** title of one of the four pre-Hispanic kingdoms of the area.

Cradle Of The Californias

The state of Jalisco has been powerful and prosperous from the very beginning of Spanish development with a rich mineral base and fertile lands. When exploration of the territory was still being carried out by the Spanish, Guadalajara became an important link in the chain. Dozens of Spanish explorers were equipped by and departed from Guadalajara. In 1692, **Sebastían Vizcaíno** left Guadalajara on a journey that would lead to the discovery of **Monterey Bay. Gaspar de Portola** and **Father Junípero Serra** with 12 Spanish soldiers and 40 Christian Indians made the difficult journey (on horseback and by foot) that eventually led to Portola's discovery of **Drake's Bay** and **San Francisco Bay** and Father Serra's establishment of **San Diego** and all the California missions.

Independence

Jalisco and its capital, Guadalajara, managed to remain politically independent of Mexico City for decades, on its own becoming almost as rich as the capital. It has seen dramatic historical moments, such as the abolition of slavery in 1810, the Reform government of Benito Juárez briefly established in Guadalajara in 1858, and the occupation of the city by the French army from 1863 to 1866. Always a seriously religious center of the Catholic religion, another independent area on the Jalisco map, the region of Los Altos, erupted into the war of the **Cristero,** (1926-1929) in its efforts to recover the liberty and privileges that had been withdrawn from the Catholic Church by Mexico's 1917 Constitution.

With its universities, museums, modern facilities, and prosperity, the city continues to dispense an air of independence and modern sophistication. Agriculture has always been a leading moneymaker in the state. Today Jalisco is Mexico's leading producer of beans and corn, which are marketed all over the country. It's sometimes referred to as *la granadita* (the granary) of the country because of its high-tech foodstuff storage and shipping facilities. Other important products are a variety of iron and steel, textiles, and handicrafts such as glass, pottery, and leather goods.

GUADALAJARA

Pronounced: gwah-dah-lah-HAR-ah
Altitude: 1,567 meters
Population: 3,000,000
Area Code: (36)
Distance from Mexico City: 535 km

Flash: As we go to press, telephone numbers in *some parts* of Guadalajara are being changed. You will undoubtedly find incorrect numbers in the following listings, sorry!

Located in west Central Mexico, the surrounding area has rich volcanic soil, and agricultural productivity is high. Today's Guadalajara, Mexico's second largest city, is as modern as pink hair and derriere-hugging miniskirts. Yet the city is a bastion of tradition. High-tech sounds in the centuries-old **Degollado Theater** enhance musical productions, from opera to bolero to rock. Sleek new hotels mix with a skyline of aged domes and towers. Where you find young people living in the fast lane, you'll find the traditional *dons* and *doñas* with the ageless grace of old Europe. A tour of the city is indeed a shuffle between the old and the new.

Dozens of colonial plazas are scattered about the city, many with a fine old church. Actually, Tapatíos will tell you that if you try, you can find 100 plazas, all graced with a profusion of trees and flowers. I can only vouch for a few of those, and each is worth a visit. Every plaza is different; architecture includes Moorish, Tuscan, Mudejar, Gothic, Byzantine, and Corinthian. The **Plaza of the Mariachis** is noisy and fun-filled, contrasted with the **Jardín de San Francisco,** a quiet spot ideal for meditation. This spectrum adds a special depth to the texture of the city. Keep wandering and you'll find them all.

Having a cold beer on the **Plaza of the Mariachis** is a noisy, fun-filled musical experience, especially on Sundays, when dozens of mariachis give "free auditions" for which they do expect a tip of a few U.S. dollars.

BOB RACE

SIGHTS

Centro Histórico Orientation

Think of **Centro** as a giant cross-shaped area including four large plazas facing a series of colonial structures. Adjacent to the cathedral on four sides are **Plaza de los Laureles, Plaza de Armas, Plaza Tapatía,** and the **Plaza de la Liberación** with its long waterspout canal. The Centro district attracts crowds of locals as well as visitors. You really don't need a reason to visit the center; it's a grand experience to be in the pulsing center of this delightful city. Several times a year Guadalajara has large scale celebrations—crowds of people visit during the **Fiestas de Octubre.** And another colorful, busy, but low-key time to visit is during Christmas holidays. A life-size crèche is displayed in the Plaza Tapatía, entertainment is provided for the kids (and the young at heart), and sidewalk vendors offer a collection of Christmas "specials" to the holiday crowds. Ask at your hotel or the tourism office where and when a Posada for the public takes place.

The Cathedral Of Guadalajara

Construction on this monumental twin-towered cathedral was begun in 1561 and consecrated in 1618; not to say that it was really complete by then. As with most epic projects of the period, it was in process for centuries. Here, too, you will see a collection of architectural styles all lumped together: baroque, Byzantine, Greek, Moorish, churrigueresque, Gothic, neoclassical. The lovely sculpture inside the cathedral called *Our Lady of the Roses* was given to Guadalajara by King Carlos V (ruler of Spain 1520-1556). The towers of the cathedral were rebuilt after earthquake damage in 1848; the new ones are much taller than those replaced. Eleven elegant altars were presented to the archbishop of Guadalajara by King Ferdinand VII of Spain. Take a look in the sacristy (ask and an attendant will let

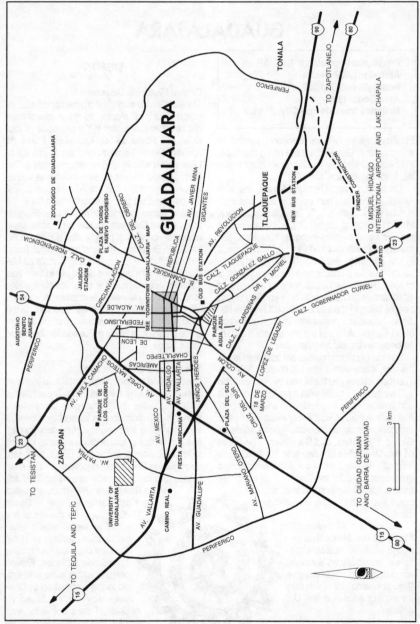

GUADALAJARA

© MOON PUBLICATIONS, INC.

you in); the painting *The Assumption of the Virgin* was painted by Bartolome Murillo in 1650.

Plaza De Los Laureles

The name gives it away. This park in front of the cathedral is filled with Indian laurel trees. Looking to the north side, note the **Presidencia Municipal,** where a mural depicts the founding of Guadalajara. This cathedral is one of the few "newish" buildings in the historical center; it was built 1949-1952.

Plaza Tapatía

Those of you who have been coming to Guadalajara for years have seen many changes. And if it's been more than 15 years since your last visit, you'll be pleasantly surprised. Probably the biggest changes have occurred in Centro. Some old buildings (not old enough to be important) were removed to make more open areas around the elegant colonial structures. By creating pedestrian-only walkways, combining plaza areas, re-stoning old walkways, and adding *more* fountains, Plaza Tapatía has become a wonderful gathering place for everyday living as well as an impressive site for visitors. In the midst of this central plaza, where clusters of historical buildings, monuments, and museums are within easy reach, you'll find lovely old hotels, shady parks, shops, and innumerable restaurants. Government money has just been set aside (1994) to work on the central district infrastructure, with many new plans to modernize and preserve the old colonial structures. In the Plaza Tapatía, at Morelos 102 behind the Teatro Degollado you'll find the tourist information office. Usually someone there speaks English. Open Mon.-Fri. 9 a.m.-9 p.m., Sat.-Sun. 9 a.m.-1 p.m.

Palacio Del Gobierno

On the pleasant Plaza de Armas, the two-story baroque/churrigueresque structure on the east side was built in the mid-1600s and was used as headquarters for the governors of Nueva Galicia. Today offices are still used by the governors of Jalisco. Stone gargoyles drain water from the roof, and stone cannons continue to protect it from attack. The entire building is worth a study of the various art forms. The front entrance is bordered by heavy Doric pillars; take a look at the sundial in the central patio.

Most visitors connect this impressive building with a comparatively modern man, artist **José Clemente Orozco.** But perhaps its greatest historical moment came in 1810 when Independence hero Hidalgo proclaimed the abolition of slavery in Mexico (fifty years before the U.S.). On the staircase of the palace, Orozco's mural of the event (painted in 1937) is powerful and invokes the heavy symbolism of an overwhelming church, the cruelties of the Spanish invasion, and a profusion of confused people lead by an angry image of Hidalgo brandishing a torch with one hand with his other fist held high. You'll find this immense work to the right of the large central patio in a deep stairwell. Open daily from 9 a.m.-9 p.m.

Plaza De Armas

After a visit to the Palacio del Gobierno and the Cathedral of Guadalajara, watch the world go by on a shady bench or have your shoes polished in Guadalajara's main square. A long-time tradition of the state band is to play music in the plaza on Thursdays and Sundays at 6:30 p.m.

Rotundo De Los Hombres Ilustres

North of the cathedral, the rotunda offers an unusual perspective of some of Jalisco's more illustrious men. While these sculptures would never be called caricatures, they certainly have brought to life each of the men's characteristics in a down-to-earth way. The men represented are buried within this handsome circular monument surrounded by graceful columns in a tree-lined park located between Hidalgo, Alcalde, Independencia, and Liceo streets. The small park was built in 1954 and contains the remains of 17 men of arts, letters, and science, and (only) two military men.

Museo Regional

An easy walk from Plaza de Armas, the **Regional Museum of Jalisco** is another old building with an impressive history. The baroque structure is two stories high with a pleasant inner courtyard. Building began in 1696, and for 163 years it served as the **Seminary of St. Joseph.** In 1810 it served temporarily as a prison for captured Spanish soldiers during the War of Independence, and in 1918 it was converted to a museum. On the first floor, displays include exhibits of pre-Hispanic artifacts, pottery figures, and jewelry said to be over 1,000 years old. Take a look at the replica of a 780 kg (1,715 pound) meteorite that fell on Zacatecas in 1792. Upstairs you'll find paintings from several eras, an ethnography area, and a peek into what life has been like in Jalisco since its colonial beginning. Open Tues.-Sun., 9 a.m.-4 p.m., admission is US$4.50, free on Sundays.

Plaza De La Liberación

Also called locally **Plaza de las Dos Copas** (from the rear of the cathedral east to Teatro Degollado) this is the commercial end of the plaza. On both sides of a long, narrow waterway fed by arching water spouts, a large number of shops and restaurants are open to the public. A statue of Miguel Hidalgo holds a broken chain to symbolize his call for the end of slavery in 1810.

Teatro Degollado

Another neoclassic-style building, the Teatro Degollado was designed by Jaliscan architect Jacobo Galvez; it was begun in 1855 and completed in 1866. The first performance, on 3 Sep-

Palace of Justice in Guadalajara

OZ MALLAN

tember 1866, was the opera *Lucia de Lammermoor,* performed by Angela Peralta, beloved Mexican soprano of the Grand Italian Opera Company. The inside was renovated a few years ago and now has a high-tech sound system for the entertainments presented, which include operas, classical concerts, rock concerts, jazz, bolero, and plays. This is the home of the **Guadalajara Philharmonic Orchestra** (several American musicians play in this marvelous orchestra). Every Sunday at 10 a.m., the **University of Guadalajara Folkloric Ballet** puts on what is considered to be the most magnificent folkloric ballet in all of Mexico. For years following this performance, the state philharmonic (Filarmónica de Jalisco) has played, but they are having major budget problems, so who knows how much longer the city will have this excellent orchestra.

Try to attend a performance of just about *anything,* but if it's impossible, take a tour of this unique old structure (open Mon.-Sat. 10 a.m.-2 p.m.). Note the classic dome and the proscenium. The multilevel interior accommodates more than 1,400 people in a plush elegance often compared to La Scala Opera House in Milan. You'll see murals everywhere inspired by Dante's *Divine Comedy,* painted by architects Galvez and Gerardo Suárez. The building is set in **Plaza Tapatía** with a high shooting fountain in front. On the triangular facade above the entrance, Apollo and the Nine Muses are portrayed in heavy relief. The back side of the building is embellished with a stunning bronze mural filled with nine-foot figures depicting the founding of the Atemajaco Valley.

Instituto Cultural Cabañas

This beautiful example of neoclassic architecture was founded to provide a home for men, women, and children who were crippled, poor, old, abandoned, or orphaned. Built in 1810, the orphanage was the pet project of Bishop Juan Cruz Ruíz de Cabañas, who financed it. Gradually the number of children grew until it was strictly an orphanage; as many as 3,000 children lived here at one time. Into the early 1970s children were cared for, educated, and given good medical and dental care by Jaliscense volunteers, mainly from Guadalajara. In 1983, children were moved to a more modern building

(top) Mexico City cathedral on the Zócalo; (above left) Teatro Degollado in Guadalajara; (above right) San Miguel de Allende (all photos by Oz Mallan)

(top) town of Tequila, Jalisco; (above left) Day of the Dead altar;
(above right) mural, San Miguel de Allende Museum (all photos by oz Mallan)

in the city, and the Cabañas was renovated to be used as a cultural center.

The Cabañas is one of the largest colonial buildings constructed in the Americas; it covers six acres and has 23 patios. Tourists come to see the collection of powerful murals by José Clemente Orozco, painted from 1938-1939. Don't miss the chapel and the dome where one of his finest works, *El Hombre de Fuego*, portrays Hidalgo as a sinister man of fire. Aside from the murals, visit the museum with its large collection of Orozco drawings and paintings. Note the *magical* bronze sculptures of artist Alejandro Colungas. Each piece depicts a magician transforming himself into a sofa or a chair, and everyone is welcome to rest awhile in these whimsical creations.

Today, young and old alike find kindred spirits interested in music, dance, painting, sculpture, and film; marvelous dance festivals are held year-round. At the entrance you'll find a small bookstore that sells a number of titles mostly concerned with the history of Guadalajara; a few are in English. Open Tues.-Sat. 10:15 a.m.-6 p.m, Sun. closing is 3 p.m.; admission is US$2, Sun. free. It's on the eastern end of Plaza Tapatía.

Museum Regional De Guadalajara

In 1992, the 450th anniversary of the founding of the city was celebrated by the inauguration of the **Museum of the City of Guadalajara.** To the east of the Rotundo de los Hombres Ilustres, it's located in a lovely old building that at one time was part of a convent built in the 17th century. The various rooms of the museum will lead you through the growth of the city from the time of the early settlers until today. Guided tours Tues.-Sat., 10 a.m.-3 p.m., Sun., 10 a.m.-5 p.m.; tel. (36) 658-3706.

University Of Guadalajara

Founded in 1791, the university offers a good education to its students for very little money and has a fine international reputation. The main administrative offices are on Av. Juárez, and the rest of the university schools are scattered about the city.

Tequila Bottling Plant

Most of the visitors to this "attraction" are fond of Mexican tequila. The main activity in this plant is seeing how the tequila is bottled, then "testing" it. Lots of people come here for the tour offered Mon.-Fri. 10 a.m.-1 p.m. The **Sauza** bottling plant in the city is on Av. Vallarta 3273. Some folks just skip the tour and come to "test." If you're interested in how tequila actually comes to fruition, from the blue-green agave plant to a taste in a paper cup, take a trip to the town of **Tequila** where there are a couple of distilleries; about 38 km east of Guadalajara.

OUTDOOR ATTRACTIONS

Parque Agua Azul

For nature lovers, this is the oldest and largest park in the city. Something is always going on; free Sunday shows, free Saturday art lessons, a flower market, an artisan's center, swimming pools, swings and slides, and a small zoo. Modern museums include the **Museo de Arqueología del Occidente de Mexico,** where you can see a small display of pre-Hispanic artifacts; it's part of the University of Guadalajara. Museums of a different type at Parque Agua Azul include an orchid house, an aviary, and a butterfly sanctuary. This year-round green complex is a must-see for a peaceful afternoon. Redesigned in 1991, the park is separated by Calz. Gonzalez Gallo but is joined by a bridge. Wandering the walkways, it's easy to see what's going on in the outdoor theater and to check out the crafts in the **Casa de las Artesanías** ("House of Crafts"). This is the site of many activities of the Fiestas de Octubres. Located on Independencia Sur, 5 de Febrero, and Dr. Michel streets.

Zoológico De Guadalajara

The Guadalajara Zoo covers 40 hectares and harbors a large selection of mammals, birds, and reptiles. This is said to be one of the top five most visited zoos in the Americas. The location is lovely, overlooking the Río Santiago Canyon. Visitors on the grounds can either walk on well-marked paths or take a train to various areas. Don't miss the huge birdcage and its fascinating residents, or the reptile building. It's easy to spend an entire day to cover it all. For the youngsters there's a children's zoo, with an amusement park, and a planetarium next door along with a performing dolphin show. Snacks

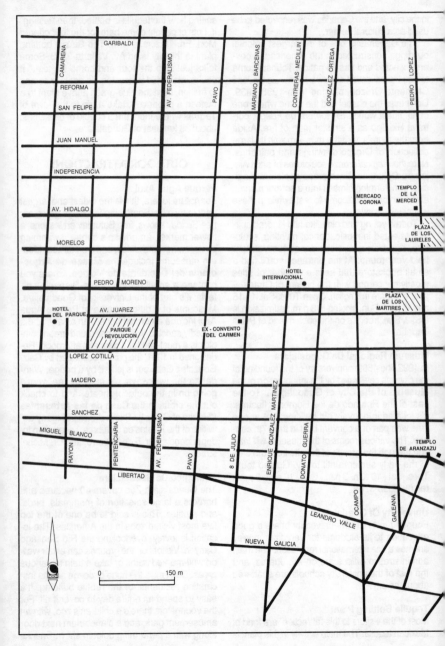

DOWNTOWN GUADALAJARA

and cold drinks are sold, restrooms are available. Admission is charged, open Tues.-Sun., 11 a.m.-6 p.m. Located at Calz. Independencia Norte and Paseo del Zoológico 600.

SPORTS AND RECREATION

Charreada (Rodeo With A Tapatío Twist)

The kissing cousin of the U.S. rodeo, the biggest difference at a *charreada* is the dress of the participants; *charros* (male riders) and *charras* (women riders) wear elaborate costumes adorned with silver. Both men and women know horses well and show off their exceptional riding skills while doing much the same thing our rodeo riders do: rope, throw, and tie calves and bulls, with more emphasis on style and less on times and competition. These events are found almost any time you visit; check with your hotel or the tourism office. A regular performance is held on Sundays at noon at the **Aceves Galindo Lienzo** (rodeo ring), located east of Parque Agua Azul, tel. (36) 19-3232.

Bullfights

On most Sundays, at the **Plaza de Toros el Nuevo Progreso,** bullfights are held at 4 p.m. Tickets range from cheap in the sunny section (*sol*) to as much as US$70 (primo location) on the shady side (*sombra*). Ask at your hotel or the tourism office for special dates and prices for bullfights; remember, you want the shady side of the arena. Tickets can be bought in advance at the Hotel Frances downtown on Thurs., or at the Plaza de Toros located at Calz. Independencia Norte.

Fútbol

Soccer is undoubtedly the national favorite of Mexico, maybe even more popular than the *corrida* (bullfight). Check with your hotel for the schedule at the **Jalisco Stadium** and join the often 70,000 shouting fans. Located across from the Plaza de Toros, on Calz. Independencia Norte.

Golf

One of the most popular sports in Guadalajara is golf. This may be due to the large numbers of Americans retired in the area. Before retiring, many of these Americans brought their clubs and took part in yearly golf tournaments at one or another of the courses in Guadalajara. Perhaps it was a natural progression that Guadalajara would be their choice for retirement. Some courses are private clubs and you need to show proof of membership in a club in the U.S. to play (with a greens fee in most cases), some are closed to nonmembers on weekends and holidays. You seldom need a tee-off time—however, it wouldn't hurt to call first. It is said that in Guadalajara, you can play golf every day of the year. Well, if not *every* day, *most* of the days; the weather is that bankable.

The oldest course is the 18-hole **Guadalajara Country Club,** considered by many to be the most beautiful—always well-trimmed and perfectly maintained. It caters to the wealthy of the city and has been well known for great tournaments for many years. Admittance to this private club is through a member or sometimes through the better hotels; presently there's an American pro who often helps American visitors get out on the greens. The Guadalajara Country Club is about five km northwest of the old city center.

Another good 18-hole course is the newer **Club de Golf Atlas** designed by American Joe Finger. This well groomed 18-hole championship course has narrow fairways lined with tall trees. It's located in the industrial area on the Chapala Hwy. between El Tapatío Hotel and the airport.

About six and a half km south of Guadalajara, the **Club de Golf Santa Anita** is on Hwy. 80 (the road to Colima). A lovely course with a prestigious country club, Santa Anita is surrounded by luxury homes on a grand scale, many occupied by Americans.

Golfers looking to retire in Guadalajara might want to check out **Bosques de San Isidro,** a newish upscale residential development and country club about 18 km north on the road to Zacatecas. This course is hilly and more of a challenge than any of the others (carts available). Besides the golf course, expect a small hotel (San Isidro Inn), a swimming pool, riding trails, tennis courts, and a bullring.

Rancho Contento is a low-key, less expensive, nine-hole course where most of the average-income retirees in Guadalajara play. The greens and fairways, comparatively, are not maintained as scrupulously as the more expensive courses, but it's still a delightful course to play; tel. (36) 621-6889.

For visitors going to the Chapala area, there are two more nine-hole courses around Lake Chapala.

Tennis

Tennis courts are found at upscale hotels around the city as well as the **Club Deportivo de Guadalajara,** located at Av. Juárez 881, tel. (36) 625-8881. Check out the courts at **Camino Real Hotel, Fiesta Americana,** and **Holiday Inn;** at **El Tapatío** you'll find 10 night-lit clay courts.

Jogging Paths

Joggers will find a path at **Parque de los Colomos** (just off Paseo Atlas Colomos 2000), a tree-lined park with good clean air. Or if you're really into the pain-gain thing, check out the 4.3 km trail down and out of **Canyon Huentitan,** a favorite path of locals. Ask for directions at your hotel or the tourism office.

ACCOMMODATIONS

Budget

When we talk about *real* budget accommodations, you must look carefully before you sign the register. Guadalajara has some of the best budget rooms in Mexico, but they still might not be as clean as you expect, or located in the best neighborhoods. Some have shared bathrooms and iffy hot water supplies, hard or lumpy beds, noisy rooms, and little air circulation with no windows. Others are charming and make you want to stay forever. As always, look carefully before you pay—and expect to pay in cash; the smaller hostels don't take credit cards. Don't forget to ask for purified water and carry your own toilet tissue and soap, just in case. If you plan on staying a week or longer ask about a discount. Some of these hotels are excellent bargains and *very* popular, so if you expect to get a room, arrive early in the day. You might meet the most interesting people of your trip at one of these budget inns.

Hotel Mexico, Javier Mina 230; tel. (36) 617-9978, is a popular spot for Mexican families. It's clean, some rooms have private bath, and all have hot water. Rates are US$12-15, s/d; near the Mercado Libertad district. **Hotel Las Americas,** Av. Hidalgo 76, tel. 613-9622, is a biggish hotel (50 rooms) opposite the **Plaza Tapatía,** in the central district. Rooms are clean, roomy, modern and the price is right, US$16-18 s/d.

Posada San Pablo, Madero 218, tel. 613-3312, is small with seven rooms, located on the second floor, opening onto a covered courtyard. This is a pleasant, family-run establishment with a European *pensión* feeling. Rates are US$11.50-13.50 s/d.

The rates at **Hotel Imperial,** Javier Mina 180, tel. 617-5042, are US$12 s, US$14. **Hotel Ana Isabel,** Javier Mina 164, tel. 617-4859 or 617-7920, costs US$15 s, US$19 d. **Motel Campo Vello,** Av. Lopez Mateos Sur 1599, tel. 621-9611, runs US$18 s, US$20 d. **Hotel Consul,** Estadio 72, tel. 619-4272, costs US$12 s, US$14 d.

Moderate

Hotel del Parque, a pretty little hotel with a convenient downtown location near the Parque Revolución, has a restaurant, a bar, a sidewalk cafe, and 81 comfortable rooms and suites. Rates are US$22-38; at Av. Juárez 845, tel. (36) 625-2800 fax 626-6648.

Hotel Frances: This hotel has been around a long time and has a special colonial charm. Originally built in 1610 as a simple inn, it has accumulated a colorful history through the years while hosting guests that include politicians, revolutionaries, tourists from around the world, and Hollywood movie stars. Many changes and renovations have taken place over the centuries going from an era when an inn provided stables for horses to the 1990s when guests expect color TV, tubs, and showers. This historic inn continues to be a favorite right down to the antiquated elevator. The hotel is centrally located and within walking distance of parks, colonial buildings, the cathedral, and the central plazas. The old inn has 60 rooms, a lovely lobby with a bubbling fountain, bar, and live music. Rates start at US$50 s, suites start at US$75 s. Hotel Francis is located on Maestranza 35, tel. 613-1190.

Hotel de Mendoza: Here's another conveniently located old downtown structure with an interesting history. At one time the hotel was a convent to the church (still in business next door), Santa María de Gracia (nearby on the other side is the Teatro Degollado). The hotel is quite nice with 104 clean modern rooms. Guests have at their disposal a swimming pool, parking, a restaurant, a bar, and a choice of room or suite. Rates are US$64 s, US$79 d; located at Venustiano Carranza 16, tel. 613-4646.

Some of the following hotels are great bargains. However, unless you're driving your own car they can be too far from the colonial center of town. In all cases it's easy to get a taxi, and bus stops are conveniently located on the main streets.

Don Quijote Plaza: Niños Héroes 61, tel. 658-1299.

Hotel Fénix: Av. Corona 160, tel. 614-5714.

Del Bosque: Av. López Mateos Sur 265, tel. 621-4020 or 621-4700.

Hotel El Parador: Carr. Guadalajara Tonalá 1500, tel. 659-0142.

Hotel Internacional: Pedro Moreno 570, tel. 613-0330 or 613-0420.

Hotel Isabel: Guadalupe Montenegro 1572, tel. 626-2630.

Hotel Metropolitan: Calz. Independencia Sur 278, tel. 612-9382 or 613-2458.

Hotel Nueva Galicia: Av. Corona 610, tel. 614-8780.

Hotel Nuevo Real Vallarta: Av. Vallarta 5549, tel. 621-9122.

Hotel Nuevo Vallarta: Av. Vallarta 3999, tel. 621-0017.

Hotel Posada Virreyes: Carr. Guadalajara-Zapotlanejo Km 1, tel. 635-0155 or 635-6622.

Spa Río Caliente: Carr. Nogales La Primavera Km 20.

Hotel Universo: López Cotilla 161, tel. 613-2815 or 613-2825.

Villa del Sol: Gante 2415, tel. 622-8022.

Hotel Azteca: Javier Mina 317-C, tel. 617-7465 or 617-7466.

Hotel Colonial: Av. López Mateos Sur 2405, tel. 621-2000 or 631-9026.

Apartment-type Accommodations

Looking for nice accommodations where you can cook your own meals? Probably because so many American retirees come to Guadalajara with the intention of settling in, there are many apartment-type accommodations available for long or short-term rental. Most of them are not in the historic central district, but usually there's a bus stop close by. Check out the want ads in the English language paper, the *Guadalajara Reporter,* which comes out each Friday.

Hotel Suites Bernini: Simple, clean, attractive, this hotel's price includes a fully-equipped kitchen and a TV. Rentals are available by the day/week/month. A one-bedroom suite is US$40 per night; two bedrooms, a living room, a dining room, and a kitchen cost US$67 per night. Av. Vallarta 1881, tel. (36) 616-6736 or 616-0858.

Luxury Hotels

Most of the luxury hotels are out of the downtown area. Again, buses are frequent, taxis are cheap, and these hotels usually have an on-site car rental agency. Many of the hotels are part of chains found all over Mexico that pamper their guests with a/c, room service, swimming pools, Jacuzzis, several dining rooms and bars, entertainment, gift shops, health spas, in-room mini bars, and beautiful decorations. For the most part they offer deluxe rooms, suites, junior suites, and king beds. If your pillow is too hard or soft, call—they'll bring a new one. For all of these amenities expect to pay more.

Camino Real: At Av. Vallarta 5005, tel. (36) 615-2507 or 621-7217 this is a lovely old hotel on spacious grounds with lots of well-kept lawn, tall shady trees, a pool, and outdoor dining. Inside a lovely lounge with beautiful antiques is the entrance to the delightful dining room. Good food! Rooms come with all the amenities you'd expect.

Fiesta Americana: On Aurelio Aceves 225, tel. 625-3434 or 625-4848; also at Av. López Mateos Sur 2500, tel. 631-5518 or 631-5566. Fiesta Americana was designed by someone whose heart was pure Mexican. You'll be dazzled by good food, a pool, lovely grounds and decor from the colonial era.

Exelaris Hyatt Regency: At Av. López Mateos Sur 5315, tel. 622-7778. This modern glass building until recently contained a very large ice-skating rink.

Other luxury hotels include **Aranzazu,** Av. Revolución Poniente 110, tel. 613-3232; **Quinta Real,** Av. Mexico 2727, tel. 652-0000, and **El Tapatío,** Carr. Chapala Km 6.5, tel. 635-6050.

Youth Hostels

The **CODE Youth Hostel** to the north of town (about 15-20 minutes by bus) has same-sex dorm rooms. Everyone is welcome, and a card is not necessary. Rates are about US$5; call ahead for reservations. Located at Alcade 1360 in the sports complex; tel. (36) 624-6515.

Camping And Trailering

On the outskirts of town you'll find two sites; both will accommodate trailers and tents, and both have electricity, water, and sewer hookups.

Hacienda Trailer Park: On four acres about 9.5 km from the town center you'll find 98 spaces in a quiet area with a heated pool, laundry facilities, a rec room, and a few shaded sites; pets are welcome. Rates are about US$14 per two persons (eighth day is free); ask about tenting fees. Located at Circunvalación Poniente 66, Ciudad Granja, five blocks southwest of Hwy. 15 (the road to Tepic). For more information and reservations write to Apdo. Postal 5-494, Guadalajara, 45000, Jalisco, Mexico; tel. (36) 627-1724.

San José del Tajo: Trailers and motorhomes have electricity, water, sewer, and cable TV hookups available, on 16 acres about 15.5 km south of the city center. Facilities include a tennis court, recreation room, swimming pool, laundry, and limited groceries. Rates are about US$15 for two. For more information write to Apdo. Postal 31-242, Guadalajara, 45050, Jalisco, Mexico; tel. 686-1738.

FOOD

Visiting businesspeople, curious tourists, and Guadalajara's 4.75 million people make for lots of eating. As a result the town is bursting with restaurants everywhere you look. No matter where you stay, walk down the street and look around. You'll find ethnic food from many countries and a price range to fit each budget. The city bustles with carry-outs, simple family neighborhood cafes, upscale restaurants with candles, crystal, and live music, typical cafes that serve only Mexican food, coffee shops, pastry shops, and lots of great delicatessens (some of these are pricey since they offer wonderful imported cheeses and delicacies). The names included are only a smattering of what's available. Remember, restaurants have a penchant for going down the tubes, and it isn't directly related to how good or bad the food is; more often it's financial. So, before making a long trip to the other side of town, call first to make sure everything is still copacetic.

Budget Food

When looking for budget meals, check around Plaza Tapatía, there are countless cheap, clean *taquerías* (taco shops); some offer seating, others are carry outs, all use the same weak-kneed paper napkins. Remember, these tacos are not fried, they are fresh floppy tortillas wrapped around almost "anything" (potatoes and veggies, chicken, pork, beef, deer meat, and sometimes fish). If you're worried about getting sick, go to the place that's jam-packed with locals; they don't want to get sick either. Remember, it's best to skip the raw fish or ceviche these days.

La Libertad Market: This dining alternative is one of the largest and most diverse public markets in Mexico, three floors and all under a roof (although current rumors say there are 2,000 shop spaces vacant because of the influx of imported goods and the NAFTA charter). If you're hungry and on a tight budget, this is a good place to shop. You'll find freshly made tortillas hot off the conveyor belt. A kilo, 2.2 pounds, goes for about 75 cents. Look for the bakery stands; you'll find huge baskets filled with French bread, and farther along you can buy chunks of cheese, fruit, pastries, candy, and Bimbo brand white sliced bread. Upstairs, a series of *fondas* (small kitchen stands, often with one or two tables) serve cheap Mexican meals that include tamales, quesadillas, sopas, and a variety of other specialties.

Mexican Food

Restaurant La Chata: This is a simple cafe, but the food is anything but, especially if you try some of the regional specials. *Pozole, pollo mole,* and their combination platter are excellent! Figure about US$4-8 for a good dinner. Breakfast is about US$3.50-4.50. Open daily 8 a.m.-11:30 p.m.; at Corona 128.

Los Itacates: For something just a little different, and very Mexican, try a few of the 19 varieties of tacos available (at 65 cents each). Or, if you want something more classical you have a choice of chicken mole, chiles rellenos, or enchiladas; every morning from 8:30 till noon they serve a breakfast buffet for US$4.50. Open daily 8 a.m.-11:30 p.m., Sun. hours are 8 a.m.-7 p.m. Located at Chapultepec Norte 110, about a 12-minute ride from downtown on the "Par Vial" bus heading west on Independencia; get off at Chapultepec.

Las Margaritas: As soon as you walk in the door your olfactory senses let you know you made the right choice. This well-known little restaurant also in the Chapultepic neighborhood, is anything but fancy. However, the food is tasty, some say the best authentic Mexican specialties in the city. Here you'll find a great *comida corrida* for about US$4.50 (more on Sunday). This is a popular place so get here by noon if you want the buffet; good fresh fruit and vegetable juices. Despite simple wood tables and chairs, the place is well patronized by businessfolk as well as tourists. Open Mon.-Sat. 9 a.m.-9 p.m., Sun. 10 a.m.-6 p.m. At López Cotilla 1477, one block west of Av. Chapultepic, tel. (36) 16-8906.

Los Otates: Though this little cafe serves great Mexican food, all worth a taste, cereal lovers will enjoy a breakfast of oatmeal with walnuts, grapes, and *piloncillo* (brown sugar). Open daily 8 a.m.-11 p.m., breakfast served all day. Av. Tepayac 57, Chapalita, tel. (36) 647-1250.

Del Monaco: This clean little neighborhood restaurant has a pleasant atmosphere with tile floors, white linens, flowers, courteous waiters, and excellent food at moderate prices. Last time I was there I had fried zucchini with a great dip (look for *calabacitas* on the menu, US$2, enough for four people as an appetizer), and a delicious combination pasta plate (US$5.10), with a selection of three different types of pasta including lasagna—delicious. Other items on the menu include fresh fish (US$8) and T-bone steak (US$9.50); salad is included with all entrees and liquor is served. Good food in a suburban neighborhood that caters to American expats. Av. Providencia 2916, tel. 642-3630. Two blocks from the supermarket Gigante P. Neruda.

Río Viejo: This lovely old mansion has been converted into a charming place to spend an evening over an international gourmet meal. Antiques decorate thick stucco walls, there are indoor and outdoor rooms, the service is excellent, and cocktails are served. Open Mon.-Sat. 1:30 p.m.-midnight, Sun. 1:30-6 p.m. On Av. de Las Americas 302, tel. 16-5321.

Expensive

If you want an evening on the town where the food is really outstanding, the wine list is to die

for, and the view is from the top of the mark, then you must make reservations one evening at the **Place de la Concorde.** The lovely decor is classical and elegant, the "white glove" service is inimitable, and it will probably be quite costly, but it continues to get rave reviews. Generally the menu is continental with a Mexican flare, and on Friday night the chef offers a butter-tender roast prime rib of beef. Located in the Fiesta Americana Hotel on the seventh floor, at Aurelio Aceves 225, for reservations call (36) 625-3434 ext. 3062 or 3116.

For another elegant evening, try **Maximino's.** Mellow background music makes for good conversation, excellent service, and a special international menu. A little pricey, but worth it; valet parking available. At Lerdo de Tejada 2043, tel. 615-3435.

International

Tirol Restaurants: You'll think you're in the European Alps when you see this colorful chalet-type restaurant. Prices are moderate and the selection ranges from enchilada suizas (US$5), to veal cutlet *Wienerschnitzel* (US$8.30), to shrimp, any way you like it (US$9.50). The atmosphere is different, the food is tasty, and the staff is friendly. Av. López Mateos and Lázaro Cárdenas, tel. (36) 621-9621.

La Trattoria: This fine Italian restaurant offers a varied menu. Salad bar is included in the price, and the pasta is made on the premises. Fettuccine Alfredo is smooth and creamy, and they have a pasta combination platter if you want a little lasagna, spaghetti Bolognese, and tortellini. Sangria is good, an ample pitcher for four is $4.75. Located on Niños Héroes 3051, tel. 622-1817.

Suehiro's Japanese Restaurant/Bar: For a change of pace, try Suehiro's for lunch or dinner. Japanese specialties such as *teppenyaki* are prepared at the table—good food. Located at Av. La Paz 1701, tel. 626-0094 or 625-1880.

Liischerly Restaurant: Feel like fondue? Liischerly Restaurant serves European cuisine in a lively family atmosphere; owned and operated by a Swiss family who speak English. Open Mon.-Sat. 1 p.m.-midnight, Sun. 1-6 p.m.; located at Duque de Rivas 5 (corner of Morelos), tel. 615-0509.

A Few More "Worldly" Restaurants: La Pagoda serves Chinese food at Av. Union 577, tel. 638-0843. For French, check out **Piaf** at Marselia 126, tel. 615-9425, and for Middle Eastern specialties go to **El Libanes** at Av. López Mateos 550, tel. 621-2702.

American Standbys

If you're getting homesick and a hamburger and fries sound good, don't fret. In Guadalajara you'll find **McDonald's, Burger King, Denny's,** and of course **KFC.** Just look around—you'll find them everywhere except in the heart of the historic center—thank heavens!

Vegetarian Food

Several stores and restaurants specialize in vegetarian food. **Megga,** on Av. de las Rosas 420, Chapalita Colonial, serves good simple food, and sells fresh-baked wheat bread. **Prasad** is a chain of health food stores that sells vitamins, Ginseng, Gerovital, yogurt, and lots more; look for them in the **Plaza Gigante Americas, Plaza Bonita,** and **Plaza Gigante Chapalita. Restaurant Acuarius** (Av. Sanchez 416) serves a great *comida corrida* (US$6); expect a crowd at lunch time. Open Mon.-Sat. 9:30 a.m.-8 p.m.

Delicatessens

La Europea: This is an upscale deli with elegant wines, liquors, cold cuts, and a large variety of imported canned meats, fish, olives, and cheeses. Need a hostess gift? Ask about fancy (though pricey) gift baskets. Located at Av. Americas 526, tel. (36) 616-4233.

Ice Cream And Bakeries

Manhattan shops are all over the place (there are 40) and they sell Blue Bell ice cream, good stuff, just like home. The **Fénix** bakery sells great pastries. Check out **Pastelería Jeffrey,** at the **Las Fuentes Shopping Plaza,** López Mateos Sur 6061. Good cookies and cakes et al. If you have a craving for good chocolate, go to **Arnoldis,** at three locations; Plaza del Sol, Plaza Mexico, and at López Mateos 1181, tel. (36) 641-4667.

ENTERTAINMENT AND EVENTS

This is a city where there's always something going on, and it's easy to find out what and where by checking with the tourist office. Remember the open air events such as an evening at the **Plaza of the Mariachis,** or the band music in the **Plaza de Armas** on Tuesday nights at 6:30 p.m. (the municipal band) and Thursday and Sunday at 7 p.m. (state band). The band has missed very few nights since the late 1800s! The concerts last an hour, and if you want to have a seat, get there a half hour early.

It's not really an entertainment, but if you happen to be downtown around sundown, note the impressive flag-lowering retreat ceremony every evening.

Teatro Degollado

The lovely theater Teatro Degollado usually has something going. Ask at your hotel, the tourist office, or look in one of the free papers or magazines found around town (hotels often have them in the lobby) for details. You can expect anything from opera to rock concerts. Open Mon.-Sat. 10 a.m.-2 p.m.

Ballet Folklórico: This excellent ballet sponsored by the **University of Guadalajara** puts on a performance every Sunday at 10 a.m. and again at 4 p.m. at the **Teatro Degollado.** This is one of the best in the country with magnificent costumes, singing, and dancing. Tickets run from US$4 in the gallery to US$17 for the better seats. On Wednesday, at the **Instituto Cultural Cabañas** a folkloric ballet is presented at 8:30 p.m.; tickets are US$5.50.

Filarmónica de Jalisco: This fine orchestra plays regularly after the ballet on Sundays. However, the organization is having financial problems so at this point in time there's no guarantee they'll still be playing in the future.

Teatro Experimental

Performances are in Spanish, and usually a little far out, but if the acting is good (and it can be great) you'll get the drift. Tues.-Sun. at 8:30 p.m., February-November. Located near Parque Agua Azul, tel. (326) 19-4121. Admission charged.

Nightclubs And Discos

Maxim's Disco in the **Hotel Frances** plays live music; there's a dance floor and a bar. While at the hotel you should stop by the lobby bar for great intimate piano music. Open 8-11 p.m. Several of the big hotels have discos; ask at the tourism office for times and addresses.

MARIACHIS

Original mariachis were home-grown groups of musicians who hired themselves out to play at weddings after the French arrived in Mexico. It soon became the custom at a traditional Mexican wedding as well as at any other celebration to have mariachi music. The word *mariachi* is a modification of the French word *mariage*.

A mariachi band can be just a few musicians or as many as they care to muster; I saw a magnificent group of 20 perform and every note of the horns and each strum of strings from the huge variety of guitars were in perfect harmony with traditional tones and classical training.

Cafe Tacuba frequently advertises good Mexican rock bands. During holidays and festivals, a good **ice show** is put on in the **Auditorio Benito Juárez.** Ask at the tourist office about rock concerts at the **Plaza de Toros El Nuevo Progreso** usually held during the Fiestas de Octubre.

Cinema

Lots of places in Guadalajara show films, including Spanish language films, art films, or foreign films. **Sala Greta Garbo** on Pino Suárez 183, and **Instituto Cultura Cabañas** often show movies. You should also check out the **Ex-Convento del Carmen** at Av. Juárez 638 for their current shows.

Yearly Events

Fiesta de Octubre: Every year thousands of people from Mexico and other countries converge on the city for a long (30 days), grand holiday. Beginning with the first Sunday in October, it's party time in Guadalajara: parades, fireworks, music—from classical to traditional pop—dances, and cultural presentations. You can expect about 340 events, including a spectacular airshow put on by Canadian Flyers. A different kind of "flyers," the **Voladores de Papantla** put on a pre-Hispanic show: men hang

The mariachis originated in Guadalajara.

attached by a rope to the top of a high pole and twirl upside down. Be sure you have advance hotel reservations in the city. For exact dates and events, call your local Mexican Government Tourist Office.

Clubs

American-Mexican Social Club: The American Mexican Social Club (Am-Ex) is a bilingual, bicultural social organization for people of all nationalities in the Guadalajara area. This club exists only for entertainment at low cost and is one of the places to meet Americans residing in Guadalajara on a semipermanent basis. Currently there are about 600 members, 55% Mexican, 40% American, and five percent other nationalities. Members enjoy dances, pool parties, and picnics, plus a bonus discount program at certain restaurants, clubs, and hotels. Headquarters are at Av. San Francisco 3376, Col. Chapalita, affectionately called **The Club.** If you want more information, write to Am-Ex Social Club, Apdo. Postal 5-742, Guadalajara, Jalisco, Mexico, tel. (36) 622-3465 or 621-4419.

Las Calas Cultural Center: This center was formed within the last decade by a group of locals interested not only in the arts, but also in social welfare. A foundation was formed to help the outlying villages of the area. A large house donated by a generous patron, private donations, and the large popular patio restaurant (profits are donated) keep the cultural center afloat. Inexpensive meatless menus (daily) and an extravagant Sunday buffet are served for US$6, including live music. The buffet is served from 10 a.m.-12:30 p.m. and 2-5 p.m. The rest of the week, the plant-filled patio offers fine dinner theater. Here you'll discover good plays, great music that varies from jazz to Latin American folk. A cover of US$5-8 is charged on Friday and Saturday. Expect simple meals of crepes, soups, salads, and beer and wine. The center has an art gallery, a craft shop, and a health shop on the premises as well as courses in art, Spanish, and music (guitar). This is a friendly place to get to know the mostly Mexican audience and contribute to a good cause. The foundation has helped a number of rural villages to install potable water, medical services, schools, and informational help in health and nutrition. The center is located at Av. Tepeyac 1156, in the Chapalito district, tel. (36) 647-0383 or 647-0279.

CHRISTMAS POSADA

About nine days before Christmas, groups of people reenact Mary and Joseph's search for an inn (*posada*). Processions of people walk through the plaza carrying candles to a variety of "inns." Frequently, museums take part in the Posada, offering the public a program of dancers and traditional drinks and refreshments served only at this time of year. Families also have their own candle-lit Posadas with relatives, going house to house and ending at a family member's home, where the traditional evening entertainment has been prepared. These are fun; if you are in Guadalajara in December, check the bulletin boards in museums, the chamber of commerce, tourist information centers, or your hotel.

SHOPPING

Mercado Libertad
This large public market, all under one roof, was built to replace the old market; entire streets were devoted to a single product. At first it's confusing getting around, but let your senses direct you; the heady aroma of leather directs you to shoes and saddles. You'll soon catch sight of artistic fruit peddlers who carve mangoes into yellow roses and display slabs of watermelon like round red tiles. Masses of traditional pottery are stacked and perched like fragile logwood. This is a hustling-bustling center for day-to-day living, bargaining, and picking up souvenirs from Jalisco.

Malls
The city has several malls, but the biggest is **Plaza del Sol** on the south side of town, on López Mateos. You'll find many stores and shops, plus cafeterias and fine restaurants. Another is **Plaza Mexico** on the west side of town. Guadalajarans must all have a "shoe fetish" judging by the number of shoe stores. Check out the **Shoe Mall** on the corner of Av. Mexico and Yaquis, near the Plaza Mexico on the west side of town. You can buy the smartest, most stylish, beautiful leather shoes for very reasonable prices.

Casas De Las Artesanías
These two arts and crafts stores are operated by the state of Jalisco and are well worth a look-around. You never know what the inventory will be for any given day, since the stock is whatever the craftsmen from around the state bring in. Frequently you find high quality with a little browsing. At two locations, both within walking distance of the town center; north, Av. Alcalde 1221, and south, Calz. Gonzalez Gallo 20 (near the Parque Agua Azul).

Department Stores
Salinas y Roche: Salinas y Roche, near Mercado Libertad and Centro, is a modern department store. Find a good selection of clothes here at reasonable to moderate prices. A reliable chain, they are located in other parts of the state as well.

Sears: In emergency situations, shoppers will find many "nuts and bolts" items that you are familiar with and you know will fit, or suit your need. You can use your Sears credit card, or pay in either U.S. or Mexican currency; don't forget that famous slogan, "satisfaction guaranteed or your money back," even after you get home! Sears is located at Av. 16 de Sept. 650, tel. (36) 614-8790 or 614-8793.

Supermarkets

You'll find supermarkets all over the city. These immense modern stores have everything from bakeries, canned goods, groceries, housewares, and clothing to disposable diapers. Look for the signs: **Gigante, Aurrera,** and **Comercial,** among others. It's customary to tip the young boys who bag and carry your groceries.

INFORMATION AND SERVICES

State Tourism Office

There's usually someone here who speaks English, and it's an excellent place for city information: calendar of events, local bus schedules, hours public buildings are open, maps of the city, maps of the state, lists of museums, and scheduled events. There's even information if you want to move to Guadalajara permanently. They offer several good (free) magazines about the city. Located on Morelos 102 on **Plaza Tapatía** (walk along the pedestrian way behind the Teatro Degollado in the building called Rincón del Diablo); open Mon.-Fri. 9 a.m.-9 p.m., Sat.-Sun. 9 a.m.-1 p.m., tel. (36) 658-2222. If you happen to be strolling on the **Plaza de Armas,** there's another (smaller) office in the **Palacio del Gobierno** open Mon.-Fri. 9 a.m.-3 p.m., 6-8 p.m., Sat. 9 a.m.-1 p.m.

American Chamber Of Commerce

This is a good place for general business information about western Mexico. Located at Marsella 570, Suite 206 at Niños Héroes, tel. (36) 615-0714 or 615-0074.

Guadalajara Visitors And Convention Bureau

This is a good place to get information about the city. They offer a few English brochures and maps; there's usually someone who speaks English. These are friendly people who go out of their way to help you. Located across the street from the Camino Real Hotel, Av. Vallarta 4095, tel. (36) 647-9281/647-9331.

Bookstores

Librería Sandi's carries a fair collection of books, as well as stationery and gift cards; at Tepeyac 718, Col. Chapalita, tel. (36) 621-0863. **Gonvil** is another place to look, on Av. 16 de Septiembre 118. **Sanborn's** can have a good selection of books in English at both the location next to the Hyatt Regency Hotel and at Av. Vallarta near Av. Chapultepic.

Benjamin Franklin Library

Visitors to Guadalajara are fortunate to have one of the largest English-language libraries in Mexico at their disposal. This library is a branch of the U.S. Information Service and offers over 11,000 volumes. Formerly located at the U.S. Consulate, it was moved in 1988. Along with book loans, you'll find a reference library, a periodical collection of over 140 titles, specialized bibliographics, an automated catalog, a video collection, and U.S. newspapers including *U.S.A. Today, New York Times,* and the *Wall Street Journal.* This library is a boon for locals and visitors alike; great place for research. The library is open Mon.-Fri. noon-4 p.m., located at Paseo Hospicio 65, directly across Plaza Tapatía from the Instituto Cultural Cabañas, tel. (36) 617-6711 or 617-6893.

Local Newspapers And Publications

Guadalajara has a number of weekly periodicals, a couple in English. The *Guadalajara Colony Reporter,* in English, comes out every Friday and gives a good overview of what's going on in the news in Guadalajara (news, activities, and cultural events) and a little less about the rest of Mexico. Resident American and Canadian expats enjoy this paper. Look for the giveaway magazines titled *Let's Enjoy, Guest Huespéd,* and *Guadalajara,* all with good info about the city as well as other popular destinations in Jalisco.

For Americans considering retirement in the area, a subscription to *MRTA,* a quarterly newsletter put out by a contemporary retired American couple, really tells it like it is. The newsletter reports current prices and availability for everyday things like milk, dish soap, gasoline, bread, and a pound of ground beef. It includes housing and utility info, popular events, where and how to meet other Americans, recommended restaurants, a short travel piece about different areas of Mexico, and other useful tips and information. The newsletter's annual subscription price is US$25; ask about their book *Guadalajara: A Great Place to Retire.* Write to Mexico Retirement And Travel Assistance, P.O. Box 2190-23, Henderson, Nevada 89009-7009.

Hospital Facilities
Medical Services are offered in English at the **Mexico-American Hospital.** The hospital offers 24-hour emergency service. On Colomos 2110, tel. (36) 641-3144 or 642-4520, fax 642-4279. **Hospital Del Carmen** also offers emergency service, and advertises that it accepts Blue Cross and Blue Shield. We have heard from expat patients of the excellent service given here. On Tarascos 3435, tel. (36) 647-4882.

Pharmacies
Guadalajara has many pharmacies. **ABC Farmacias** are familiar with U.S. prescriptions, and you'll find them at three locations: Av. Americas 404-B, tel. (36) 616-3343; Av. Chapultepic Sur 249, tel. 626-4742 or 626-4772; Plaza Del Sol, 647-4839. If you have a difficult situation and need someone who speaks English, ask for Miss Gonzalez at 626-4742.

Julio Photo Laboratorios
This chain of photo labs is scattered about the city, very easy to find. Like the U.S. they give express service, and if you don't like the results of a print, either you don't pay for it, or they will redo it for you.

Laundromats
Hotels charge a fortune for laundry service (sometimes US$1 per pair of socks)! Guadalajara has quite a few *lavanderías,* (laundries). However, most of them are not in the heart of town, or necessarily in walking distance. But, if you consider the hotel's laundry prices, it's cheaper to take a bus or call a taxi to tote you and your laundry roundtrip. Ask about pick-up and delivery service, some offer it free if they do the wash. The cost varies from laundry to laundry but averages US$2-5 for wash and dry per load, extra for soap. Most laundries are open daily except Sun. 8:30 a.m.-7 p.m. Bring your favorite crossword puzzle book; it takes a while.

Canada provides self- and full-service laundry and dry cleaning with two locations in the city: Ricardo Palma 2987, on the corner of Pablo Casals, Prados Providencia, tel. (36) 642-4473; and Av. Patria 1123-A, corner of Av. Tepeyac, Prados Tepeyac, tel. 632-6883. Another one (away from the central section) is **Splash,** offering self- and full-serve laundry service. Open Mon.-Sat., López Mateos Blvd. 5444B. **Lavandería San Antonio** is located on López Cotilla 1234.

Green Angels
The national organization whose members cruise in green trucks to give aid to drivers in distress can be reached locally at (36) 35-0755.

Language Schools
As more people travel around Mexico, more and more have discovered the advantages of Spanish-language schools. And families living in Guadalajara for any length of time have a choice for their children as well. **University of Guadalajara** offers foreign students classes in Spanish. Advanced students are offered courses in Mexican culture, literature, and art. The program includes community development, where students go into the communities to offer their services. It's a fine program, and very popular with students from all over the world.

The American School Foundation
If you and your family are planning to live in Guadalajara for a while, this is a bilingual school offering kindergarten through twelfth grade, accredited by the Southern Association of Colleges and Schools, U.S.A. and the Secretary of Education of Mexico. Located at Colomos 2100, Col. Italia Providencia, Apdo. Postal 6-1070, Guadalajara 44640, Jalisco, Mexico, tel. (36) 641-3300 or 641-2954.

Churches
Guadalajara and the Chapala areas probably have the largest selection of church-choices in all of Mexico—Episcopal (Calle San Lucas), Apostolic, Unitarian (AMSOC), Lutheran (Av. Tepeyac), Baptist (Colomos 2148), Church of Christ (Calle San Lucas), a Nondenominational,

and of course several Catholic. If you find others let me know.

CONSULATES

U.S. Consulate

This is a good place to seek help in the event of trouble. Ask for the **Citizens Consular Services.** In an emergency they can provide you with a list of English-speaking lawyers, doctors, and translators. Open Mon.-Fri. 8 a.m.-2 p.m.; after hours a duty officer is available. Located at Progreso and López Cotilla, tel. (36) 25-2700 or 25-2998.

Canadian Consulate

For the same type of support, Canadian citizens will find the Canadian Consulate at the Fiesta Americana Hotel. Open Mon.-Fri. 10 a.m.-1 p.m., Aurelio Aceves 225, tel. (36) 625-3434, ext. 3005.

GETTING THERE BY AIR

Miguel Hidalgo International Airport

This is a major hub with flights to and from Mexico from all over the U.S. and Mexico. It's located 20 km south of downtown Guadalajara on the highway to Chapala in the municipality of Zapotlanejo. If you want to go to the airport by public bus, take a local city bus to the Nueva Central Camionera (take no. 275 A or no. 275 B, going south on Av. 16 de Septiembre), and then go to module nine. The bus, one of **Autotransportes Guadalajara-Chapala,** leaves on the hour and half hour, takes 30-40 minutes, and costs less than a dollar (N$2.20). Supposedly, these buses should be available to return to the city from the airport—don't count on it. From the airport, be prepared to take the **Autotransportaciones Aeropuerto,** a combi, or a taxi: The combi can cost US$12-14, depending on where in town you wish to go. If you don't have a reservation, look for the well-marked booth by the exit where vehicles are always waiting. This company will also pick you up and deliver you to your hotel (or any location you choose) with reservations 24 hours a day. For more information and reservations, call (36) 612-4278 or 612-4308. A taxi will cost approximately US$14-

50, depending on your bargaining skills and where you wish to be taken.

Airlines Serving Jalisco

The following airlines depart from the U.S. and arrive in Guadalajara:

Aero California, López Cotilla 1423, tel. (36) 626-1962 or 626-10-64.

Aeroméxico, Av. Corona 196, corner of Madero, tel. 615-6565.

Alaska Airlines, (800) 426-0333, (322) 1-1350.

American Airlines, Vallarta 2440, tel. 616-4090.

Continental, Hyatt Hotel Plaza del Sol, tel. 647-6672 or 647-6675.

Delta, López Cotilla 1701, tel. 630-3530.

Mexicana, Mariano Otero 2353, tel. 647-2222.

Ask about commuter planes from Guadalajara to various cities in Mexico.

GETTING THERE BY BUS

Central Camionera

Well-organized, the new bus terminal in Tlaquepaque referred to as either **La Nueva Central** or **La Nueva Camionera** is located 10 km (six miles) from downtown. Each terminal holds several different bus lines, first and second class. It looks more like a modern air terminal than a bus station; passengers find seven buildings with covered walkways connecting them. An information kiosk is located at each with a well-informed staff. You'll find shuttles, Ladatel long distance telephones, cafes, accommodations information, shops, and a large new budget hotel next door.

To get to the Central Camionera bus terminal from downtown Guadalajara, go to the parking lot located on the corner of Calle Cinco de Febrero and Doctor R. Michel; a special bus leaves every five minutes 5 a.m.-11 p.m., and the trip takes about 30 minutes. To reach the new bus station from Lomas del Paraiso area, take bus no. 207; from the town of Tonalá, take bus no. 643. The buses all make the circuit of the station and passengers get off at one of the seven connected buildings. The fare is less than 50 cents until 10 p.m. when it doubles. These buses are traveler-friendly with ample space for luggage.

To save yourself a lot of running around, check with the **Servicios Coordinados** office on Independencia 254 in downtown Guadalajara for complete information about routes, departure times, reservations, and ticket purchases. **Note:** When traveling by bus, it's better to buy first class. The price distinction is small, but the difference in time and comfort is *large*.

GETTING THERE BY TRAIN

If you plan on traveling by train in Mexico, this is the easiest to get into and out of with the best facilities and second in size only to Mexico City. Several trains service Guadalajara; check at the station at Calz. Independencia for the best information (routes, schedules, and prices). From Centro take the bus marked "Estacion." By taxi figure about US$5 from the station to downtown hotels.

GETTING AROUND

Getting around the old town center is pleasantly convenient on foot. You can see all of the historical buildings this way, as well as whirl through the Mercado Libertad. Guadalajara is a large city, and getting around to the different *colonias* (neighborhoods) takes either a car, taxi, or bus. Buses are reasonable; you can travel to most points in the city for 50 cents or less. Taxis are more expensive, figure about US$7 for about 15 minutes of travel. If traveling around by car, remember to have one new peso for the new parking meters; it gives you 50 minutes parking.

GUADALAJARA SUBURBS

Several intriguing towns have become an extension of the city as Guadalajara continues to grow and sprawl outward. Art lovers should go to **Tlaquepaque** and **Tonalá.** Those with a curiosity about Old World culture should visit **Zapopan**, where each year thousands of pilgrims walk beside a 10-inch high corn-paste image of the Blessed Mother. Margarita-lovers should travel a little farther and visit the town of **Tequila.** And for those who prefer nature, an escape to many of the fine mountain areas provides hiking paths and a dip into an often nippy mountain pool or Lake Chapala, Mexico's largest lake.

For trips within Guadalajara, go to the old bus station (Niños Héroes, off Independencia Sur). For trips to Ajijic, Lake Chapala, and Jocotopec, take the **Transportes Guadalajara-Chapala,** tel. (36) 619-5675, which runs frequently throughout the day beginning at 6 a.m. Servicios Coordinador also has this information.

ZAPOPAN

This small community dates back in pre-Columbian history as an important Indian village. It's now a suburb of sprawling Guadalajara, easy to get to by bus from Centro.

The Corn-paste Virgin Of Zapopan

Zapopan is best known for a small Virgin Mary statue made of corn. Each June, the 10-inch corn paste statue is taken from Basílica de Zapopan (her home church) to visit 200 churches in Jalisco. Each year in October, pilgrims from surrounding villages and mountain communities come to the large *basílica* (built in in the 1600s) to celebrate her 12 Oct. return. People have great faith that this replica of the Virgin was responsible for saving many people from area floods. Her followers pray for special favors and in return make physical "restitution." The formal procession begins around dawn after mass at Guadalajara's downtown cathedral. It continues with about 13,000 dancers in native costumes along the eight-kilometer (five-mile) route. Even Pope John Paul II visited this well-known *basílica* in 1979.

Forty years ago, thousands walked great distances to the *basílica*. Today, many arrive jam-packed in trucks; the statue is even carried in its own brand-new car for part of the parade. A million people come to Zapopan every year for this party. The large churchyard is filled with families that have set up housekeeping for the duration of the fiesta, part of Fiestas de Octubre. Brightly colored squares of cloth make impromptu shelters in the large yard, small braziers are set up to cook the tortillas, portable *fondas* just outside the church gates sell green and orange sugar water, mariachis play music, and it wouldn't be a fiesta without fireworks. On the day the statue is returned, beginning in the wee hours of the morning, pilgrims can be seen "walking" on their knees from great distances, a kilometer or two to the *basílica* (often as a thank-you for some special favor granted during the year). Young boys and girls wearing white shirts and pants with a Red Cross band on their arm scurry around to tend to those who've fainted or have bloody knees. Other samaritans on the sidelines fold sarapes and place them in front of the pilgrims, making a pathway of soft cloth to lessen the trauma to the knees. It's a very important and moving event for Catholics from all over the country.

Museo Huichol
While at the *basílica*, go next door and take a look into this Indian museum/shop to see the intricate, colorful designs in both yarn and beads that the Huichols are known for; all for sale. This shop benefits the artisans' co-op. Open Mon.-Fri. 10 a.m.-2 p.m. and 4-7 p.m., Sun. 10 a.m. 1 p.m.

Food
On 12 October each year, a special breakfast is held at **La Gran Fonda** with a bird's-eye view of the parade. Breakfast is served from 7-11 a.m. and reservations must be made in person at Av. Avila Camacho 2012. The meal and transportation to Zapopan cost about US$15.

Getting There
Zapopan is about 10 km northeast of Guadalajara's town center; take **bus no. 275D** from Av. 16 de Septiembre to the *basílica*. **Taxis** are another option; be sure you set your rate pre-boarding. During the **Fiestas de Octubre,** expect the streets to be crowded throughout Guadalajara. Though only 10 km, figure a longer than usual ride through the city.

TLAQUEPAQUE

At one time Tlaquepaque was an out-of-town destination, but the capital city has spread out to meet the small village. It takes about 15-20 minutes to reach Tlaquepaque from the center of town, about a US$7-8 taxi ride, or a 30-cent local bus ride.

There's been a community of people on this site since before the coming of the Spaniards. It is said that these people were industrious craftsmen who created imaginative pottery using good local clay.

Over the years, Tlaquepaque village has gradually changed into a trendy little town. It took many twists and turns along the path to the 1990s; somewhere along the way quality of the art began to falter under the pressure of fame. Many more tourists with *seemingly* limitless amounts of money appeared ready to buy whatever was there. The temptation to succumb to the get-rich-quick mentality stalled artistic progress and Tlaquepaque began turning out commercial mediocrity—but only temporarily.

The true artists have now come up for air. Quality and tradition has been revived. Tlaquepaque has regained its reputation for producing stellar original art. Many well-respected artists are found in the small city, bringing new ideas, reintroducing old methods, and maintaining a deep interest in preserving the crafts of the past.

Along with the rediscovery of quality, the old mansions that line the street are gradually being renovated one by one and restored to their original beauty. They make a wonderful backdrop to display modern or folkloric art. Visitors find as much adventure in the *shop-structure* as the products being sold. It's a delight to study the antiquated buildings with two-meter-thick walls, hand-painted tile, black iron gates, great carved stone fountains sending cooling sprays of water into the air, and often a working display of antiques. Bring a lot of new pesos; today's artist recognizes his value and charges for his work accordingly.

History
During the colonial era the town became a getaway village for the rich merchants of Guadalajara. At that time people believed that Tlaquepaque was safer from earthquakes than Guadalajara.

Today's Tlaquepaque
Since the early 1970s the area in the center of town has been a pedestrian walkway, which makes it a delight to stroll and explore the small

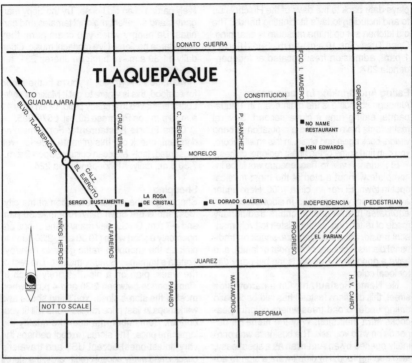

town. Visitors come in droves to wander through the countless shops that offer a huge selection of pottery, glass, textiles, wood carvings, furniture, paintings, jewelry, and metalwork; interior decorators go into feeding frenzy here. Visitors drive, taxi, or hop a bus to Tlaquepaque for the day for a real "shop-till-you-drop" sort of vacation and then stop for a fine meal. It's about a 25-minute drive from Guadalajara Centro. In a taxi expect to pay around US$8. It's a little longer by bus but the cost is about 50 cents. The town has a relaxing little plaza, El Parian, featuring music and excellent restaurants for a long late Mexican meal.

Tlaquepaque is a town of tradition as well as a visual feast of color and pattern. Some of the families date back several generations. The local museums hold some fascinating historical data.

Located in the **Presidencia Municipal**, across from El Parian, the tourism office will give you local information including maps and brochures. Open Mon.-Fri. 9 a.m.-3 p.m., Sat. 9

a.m.-1 p.m. Calle Guillermo Prieto 80, tel. (36) 635-1503 or 635-0596.

Sanctuario De Nuestra Señora De La Soledad
The centerpiece of Tlaquepaque is its plaza and wrought-metal kiosk. It's located right by the village church, a beautiful neoclassic structure built in 1878.

La Casa De Cultura
The cultural center is located in a renovated old building called El Refugio ("The Refuge") that once operated as an insane asylum for women. This is an interesting stop to look around and learn about the traditional history and customs of the city.

Regional Ceramic Museum
Look here before you start shopping in order to get a quick education about Jalisco pottery, including regional designs. Fascinating dis-

plays date back to the days of the Huichols up to and including today's fascinating trends. The old kitchen set up in the museum is charming. Open Tues.-Sat. 10 a.m.-4 p.m., Sun. 10 a.m.-1 p.m., admission free. Located at Independencia 237.

Eating And Drinking In Tlaquepaque

Although shopping is the main event in Tlaquepaque, eating runs a close second. Several restaurants have instituted a reputation to bring visitors back again and again. In this small suburb, you can find some of the finest regional dishes.

El Parian: A visit to Tlaquepaque would be incomplete without a stop at the most musical spot in town, El Parian, circa 1800. Here under a circular roof you can relax in sidewalk cafes in *equipales* (barrel-design chairs traditionally made of rattan and leather), listen to lively mariachi music, drink cold *cerveza*, snack on traditional dishes including *birria* (goat or lamb), and have a good time. Sunday is the big party day for local color.

No Name Restaurant: On a narrow side street, this old *finca* (estate) has laid-back patio dining under broad trees where colorful peacocks strut their stuff. Why the name? It depends on who you ask. The business was originally opened by an American as a speakeasy, also serving food. He didn't want a sign to advertise his illegal place, so most people referred to it as "that restaurant over there without a name." When alcohol was eventually legalized the establishment was more or less stuck with the assignation. Now the sign is barely seen because of an overgrowth of trees. The menu is delivered verbally, so listen closely and don't hesitate to ask questions—the waiters who take the orders speak English. Many sing, and there's usually a strolling troubador. The food is good Mexican/continental cuisine. Try the *queso fundido,* great guacamole, Mexican-style beefsteak, and excellent margaritas. Open daily 8:30 a.m.-9 p.m. On Madero 80, tel. (36) 635-4520.

El Patio: This is another delightful spot for good Mexican food and live music in a colonial patio/garden. Open daily 10 a.m.-7 p.m., Sun. 10 a.m.-4 p.m. On Independencia 186, tel. 635-1109.

Restaurante El Abajeno: Restaurante El Abajeno offers more dining delights in a lovely, lively garden of an old house. Try the zippy margaritas and excellent regional tamales and carnitas. Be hungry when you come here; they serve large portions. Live mariachi music. Open daily 11:30 a.m.-10 p.m., on Juárez 231, tel. 635-9015.

Mariscos Progreso: If you're in the mood for seafood, this is where to get it Mexican style. Lunch is relaxed in a shady patio. Open daily 11 a.m.-8 p.m., on Progreso 80, tel. 657-4995.

Casa Fuerte Restaurante: For something different, check out this intimate cafe for well presented, tasty Mexican cuisine. Open 9 a.m.-7:30 p.m., daily. At Independencia 224.

Shopping

Shopping is the primary attraction of the city. Most shops are open daily 10 a.m.-2:30 p.m. and 4-7 p.m. On Sunday many of the shops are open only a short while (10:30 a.m.-2:30 p.m.) to pick up the shopping traffic gone to (nearby) Tonalá's immense Sunday market. The rest of the week, plan on a nice leisurely lunch in Tlaquepaque between 2:30 and 4 p.m., when most of the stores close. You'll find shops and workshops in vast price ranges—one will fit your budget. Remember, the finer the quality the larger the price. The stores (except perhaps the very tiniest ones) accept US$ and traveler's checks, and many accept credit cards; the stores will also pack and ship products to your home. It's always a good idea to use a credit card when you have things shipped. If things don't arrive or arrive broken, the credit card company will usually replace the goods or cancel the charge. In most cases things come through beautifully (the shops no longer use straw packaging!).

Many of the shops have their workshops attached, such as **La Rosa de Cristal,** the glass factory (located across the street from the ceramic museum on Independencia 232). You are welcome to observe the craftsman. If you travel during the summer season, be sure you get to the glass factory in the morning hours; it's cooler then, and observers can't help but catch a bit of the "heat fallout" around the work space. The blowers don't work beyond 2:30 in the afternoon, and because of the excessive summer heat, they sometimes quit early. Note the lovely pitchers, plates, and figurines. If you want something special made to order, just ask the

Tlaquepaque street market

OZ MALLAN

patrón. It's fascinating to watch the craftsman and his young apprentices working with molten glass. Visitors are welcome to watch on this busy patio, just watch out for the long poles. Open Mon.-Fri. 9:30 a.m.-2:30 p.m. On Independencia 232.

El Dorado Galería: If you're looking for hand-loomed fabrics, tapestries, or bronze, take a look here. They also carry some excellent modern ceramics. Open Mon.-Sat. 10 a.m.-7 p.m., Sun. 10 a.m.-2:30 p.m., Independencia 145, tel. (36) 635-3626.

La Casa Canela: Chic and classy, it's fun to browse in this 260-year old *finca*. It's still owned by the same family. Exquisite Mexican art, furniture, and antiques can be found here. Open Mon.-Sat., at Independencia 258, tel. 635-3717.

Sergio Bustamante: By now everyone is familiar with Bustamente's fanciful ceramic work. These eclectic papier mâché pieces vary from animal to human shapes. It's located on Independencia 236, tel. 639-5519.

Getting Around

In Tlaquepaque getting around is simple; you can walk in the center of town. Most of the high-powered shops are along the pedestrian walkway (no vehicles here). The older, more popular places are within this center. However, wander out to some of the peripheral streets (where cars still drive) and you'll find more shops and factories.

TONALA

In the Nahuatl language, Tonalá means "Place of the Sun," and in the pre-Hispanic era, it was the seat of an Indian monarchy. Today, most inhabitants make their living from art. Almost next door to Tlaquepaque (15 minutes farther from Guadalajara Centro), Tonalá has become another well-known (though not as trendy) craft center. For years these factories have been manufacturing pottery to ship all over Mexico. The best days to come to Tonalá are Thursdays and Sundays; the town becomes one big street market, among other things many factory ceramic seconds are for sale, and with careful study you can get some terrific bargains.

While you're wandering around town, walk up the "Queen's Hill" where you'll find a statue of the Indian Queen **Tzihuapilli** and a great view of the entire valley. Close by you'll find the **Church of Our Lady Of Guadalupe.** The **Tourist Office** is located at Morelos 180, tel. (36) 683-0971.

Museo Nacional De La Cerámica

This museum tells the history of the popular arts in exhibits. It's located at Constitución 110; open Tues.-Sat. 10 a.m.-4 p.m., Sun. 10 a.m.-1 p.m., free.

Arts And Crafts

Tonalá's Thursday and Sunday street market shows off many artists in residence. This is becoming a primo place to find pieces worked in gesso, blown glass, ceramics, all types of metals, and hand-woven textiles. Some feel the general quality may not be as elegant as you can find in Tlaquepaque, but with careful searching you may find a really outstanding piece of craftsmanship. A few outstanding artists/potters have shops (most located in their homes) in Tonalá.

Shopping

Ken Edwards's shop/studio offers some fabulous modern creations, including lovely traditional stoneware as well as quite good "collectors items." It's well worth the time to visit while you're in town. On Morelos 184, tel. (36) 683-0313, fax 683-0716. A new shop at the **Blown-Glass Factory** is located at Av. Tonalá 161, tel. 683-2624. Ask to see the "silver" blown glass made from recycled glass one piece at a time. The shop carries fine Talavera from Puebla and the ceramic "tree of life" from Metepec (State of Mexico).

Food

You'll find several pleasant restaurants scattered around town.

Guacamayas Restaurant: The sign says, "comida and crafts," and that's just what you get at Guacamayas. Stop for breakfast or lunch in the garden dining room, and then take a peek into the **Tropiche Workshop.** Here you can watch craftsmen create whimsical papier-mâché figures. And of course, they're all for sale. Open daily 10 a.m.-8 p.m. Located at Av. Tonalá 269, tel. (36) 683-0423.

Getting There

Take the bus marked "275 Diagonal" going south on Av. 16 de Septiembre (the bus goes through Tlaquepaque). The fare is about 50 cents, and the ride takes a little over half an hour. Or take a taxi, about US$8 each way.

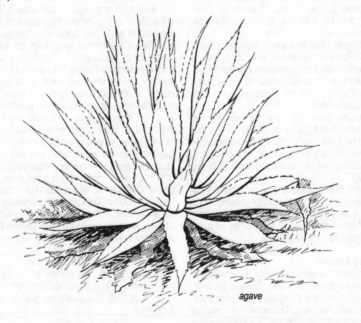

agave

BOB RACE

THE TOWN OF TEQUILA

An indigenous group of Nahuatl speakers lived in this region and discovered the beverage now called tequila. The fermented agave plant has been popular for many years and has become the favored drink of Mexicans as well as people from many parts of the world. Tequila would probably be a sleepy farm town that strangers would never know of if it weren't for the drink's popularity.

DISTILLERIES AND TEQUILA PRODUCTION

The town has been the site of distilleries since the 17th century. Acres and acres of land surrounding the town are covered with a type of blue-green colored *maguey* plant, giving the countryside a blue-green glow. This particular agave is supposedly the *best* plant for the liquor and grows only in this area. Jaliscienses are proud of their agave, and say that the liquor distilled in Tequila is the only "real stuff."

The big distilleries in town are **Sauza** and **Cuervo.** Both give tours of their factories (yes, that includes free samples).

Tequila Production

If you've never been to a distillery before it's enlightening to see the process. They strip the swordlike fronds from the plant, exposing the "heart," which looks like a giant pineapple without its crown of leaves (the heart of these plants can get very large, over a hundred pounds). Next they roast the heart and cook it in oversized copper kettles. Toward the end of the tour, you'll walk over immense tanks that hold what looks (and smells) like a witch's brew. Visitors become "experts" once they taste the standard (non-aged) clear tequila versus the well-aged tequila gold. Notice the mural at the Sauza factory—a real Bacchanalian look at life.

This small community leads the nation in tequila production, more than 15 million gallons yearly. Exports go mainly to the U.S., Germany, and England.

Sauza Family Home

This lovely old *quinta* belonging to the family that began the Sauza Distillery is now abandoned, but ask at the plant to tour the building. A stroll through the old grounds is a wonderful step into the past and what must have been a gracious lifestyle. While visiting the age-covered structure, deserted gardens, chapel, great rooms, stone carvings, and reflecting pool, it's not unusual to find an exuberant teacher with a class of young children sitting with sketching pads and pencils.

tequila vats at the Sauza Tequila factory.

OZ MALLAN

Agave cactus hearts used to make tequila. Only the blue agave, which are grown around the Jalisco area, are used for making tequila.

OZ MALLAN

GETTING THERE

It's easy to get to Tequila by bus. The town is a primary bus stop on Highway 15 from Guadalajara and buses depart Guadalajara every 20 minutes from the old bus station on Calle Los Angeles or the Nueva Camionera. The trip takes about 20 minutes.

LAKE CHAPALA

The largest lake in Mexico, Lake Chapala, is 85 km long and 29 km wide. Lake Chapala is the chief source of water for both Guadalajara and Mexico City.

The Expat Community

Some folks who have never been to Lake Chapala resist a visit due to many American and Canadian expats living here. Granted, there are many outsiders, but it has given the area a certain ambience you won't find anywhere else.

This is a beautiful area with charming small villages surrounding the lake. For the most part, the Mexicans who live here have accepted their U.S. and Canadian neighbors. Of course, along with the good things comes a downside; there's definitely a U.S. and Canadian "opinion" that pervades the town.

The weather is springlike year-round, the gardens are filled with beautiful flowers, and the surrounding forest is lush. The social life is nonstop, with all the club activity you can find in the States.

LAKE VILLAGES

The villages around the lake are very nice to explore. There's a bit of leftover grace from earlier times. (That's a long time ago, considering D.H. Lawrence wrote the *Plumed Serpent* here in 1925, and behind him came many foreign artists.) Artists are still attracted to the tranquility, the lake's beauty, and the Mexican influence on their work.

The lake villages include San Nicolas, Vista del Lago, Chula Vista, San Antonio, La Floresta, San Juan Cosala, and the three largest, Chapala, Ajijic, and Jocotepec. These villages are all over 1,500 meters in altitude. It is said that the year-long weather is better here than in Guadalajara because it is regulated by the lake, a little warmer in the winter, and a little cooler in the summer.

The Lake Itself

The lake is surrounded by mountains covered with lush forests. However, the lake is really best just to look at. It is progressively shrinking and is clogged with thick vegetation. In some areas at certain times the stench from pollution is awful. No one should swim in the lake, and in some parts of the lake, fish haven't been seen in years. Studies show that due to deforestation, millions of cubic meters of mud enter the lake from the Lerma River. The rain sweeps unprotected topsoil downriver and into the lake, causing intensive sedimentation. At the beginning of the century, the lake had an average depth of 20 meters; today, it's 10 meters. The life expectancy of Lake Chapala was originally said to be 16,000 years, but now the Jalisco Center of Engineering and Research estimates the lake to have only 500 years left. Engineers are trying to promote massive reforestation programs.

Retirees
It is estimated that about 30,000 U.S. and Canadian retirees live around the lake in three of the better-known villages: Ajijic (ah-hee-HEEK), Chapala, and Jocotepec (ho-co-teh-PEK). These people are quite content with their lifestyle, which contributes to the local economy. While few tourists come here, visitors will find a few very nice hotels, several excellent restaurants, and not much more unless you plan on staying and getting involved with the expat contingent. In that case, you'll find a raft of clubs, in-

cluding Lions, Masons, Shriners, Rotarians, DAR, AA, Spanish language clubs, bridge clubs, the Humane Society, and the Lakeside Little Theater, to name a few.

Sporting Activities
There are two lovely golf courses close by: the **Chula Vista Country Club** and the **Chapala Country Club.** Horseback riding, tennis, and limited boating are available. Thermal swimming pools are popular at spas in San Juan Cosala.

San Juan Cosala Balnearios
If passing by San Juan Cosala, ask about **Villas Buenaventura Cosala.** You'll find a choice of rooms or apartments with kitchens, Jacuzzis, thermal and hydro baths, and outdoor activities including volleyball and soccer. On the premises you have access to four pools with variable temperatures, a restaurant, and a bar. The mailing address is Apdo. Postal 181, Chapala, Jalisco, Mexico; tel. (376) 3-0302.

Motel Balneario has something for the entire family—a restaurant, a bar, and a great waterside. Relax in five therapeutic pools from mineral-laden underground hot springs. For more information contact Apdo. Postal 181, Chapala, Jalisco, Mexico; tel. (376) 3-0305, fax (376) 3-0307.

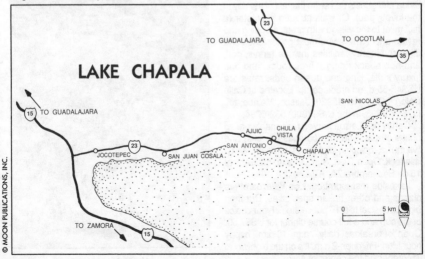

Ajijic

La Laguna Bed 'n Brunch has only four rooms, each furnished with a king-size bed and colorful locally loomed bedspreads. Brunch is served in the dining room. Special prices for two people are US$20 including brunch. Mid-day dinner, US$4. Prices vary; check to see what they are currently. The address is Zaragoza 29, Ajijic 45900, Jalisco, Mexico, tel. (376) 6-1174.

La Nueva Posada is a sophisticated inn with 17 suites and a reputation for excellent food. It's designed to relax guests with subdued pastel colors, original watercolors on the walls, and great views of the lake, a tropical garden, and a small pool. Though the Posada offers modern amenities, its heart is still colonial. The Eager family knows how to make their guests happy. The restaurant serves delicious continental cuisine indoors and out. Reservations are suggested; rates are US$67-US$85 d, including full breakfast. Write to Donato Guerra 9, Ajijic, 45900, Jalisco, Mexico; tel. (376) 6-1444 or 6-1344, in the U.S. (800) 532-0294. The "other-half" of the ownership, Judy, mails monthly menus to anyone supplying her with a mailing address.

Villa Del Gallo Cantador ("House of the Singing Rooster") is perched on a hill overlooking the lake and the village of Ajijic. Sunrises and sunsets are spectacular from up here. Continental breakfast is served on a covered veranda and guests can swim the rest of the day in the lovely pool. Or walk about a kilometer (a half mile) to the village with great shopping and restaurants (where you must go for lunch and dinner). Nearby facilities include tennis, golf, and horseback riding. Three rooms and one luxury suite, king and queen beds, rates are US$45-65 d, no credit cards. Located at Calle Colón 117, Ajijic, 45920, Jalisco, Mexico; tel. (376) 6-0308, in the U.S., (800) 532-0294.

Canto del Lagos serves reasonably priced drinks all day with free *botanas* (snacks) and live music, including jazz, blues, romantic, and a little rock. Open Tues.-Sun., 11 a.m.-midnight, at 16 de Septiembre 7A, Ajijic.

Lakeside restaurant/bar **Los Valeros** offers pizzas and other Italian specialties. But their *biggest* special is a 10 ounce steak (your choice of the cut) and a full-course dinner for US$7.50. Open for breakfast daily 8 a.m.-10 p.m., happy hour Mon.-Fri. noon-2 p.m. It's on the highway to Jocotepec, in the center of Ajijic.

Restaurant Posada Ajijic is a pleasant little restaurant with a really charming atmosphere. Good food and it's been a hangout for expats for years. The cantina comes alive with expats and fun every evening except Monday. On Wednesday enjoy live music with dancing 7-11 p.m. It's on 16 de Septiembre, tel. (376) 5-4422.

Eat pizza and pasta at **Valenciana's Pizza Ajijic** (La Montaña 1). For good creamy ice cream on the Ajijic Plaza, try **La Michoacana,** of the ice-cream chain found all over Mexico. If you're fond of Italian-style ice cream, check out **Canoli** and their sodas, malteds, banana splits, and cassatas. Cappuccino and espresso are served as well. Plaza La Montaña.

Note: If you're driving around the lake, you'll find the full service **Gasolinera Ajijic** in Ajijic, featuring Magna Sin *and* a car wash.

Chapala

Hotel Nido (budget prices, tel. 376-5-2116) has been around for a while with 30 clean rooms, a swimming pool, and a good restaurant and bar. **Quinta Quetzalcoatl**—the Inn of the Plumed Serpent or "QQ" as everyone calls it—provided

Jocotopec transport

OZ MALLAN

a bed for author D.H. Lawrence. There are a total of eight suites with fireplaces, and all are dramatically furnished. The original villa has been lovingly restored without removing the spirit of the past. Food is great, and you must book your stay in one-week intervals. The week includes daily breakfast, two gourmet dinners with wine, a midweek barbecue, and two escorted full-day tours. Rental car available, no credit cards, there is a bar, and rates are US$100-US$150 per night, seven-night minimum. Located at Zaragoza 307, Chapala, tel. (376) 5-3653, in the states call (800) 532-0294. **Note:** This hotel is part of a small group of individually owned hotels.

Mariscos La Terraza specializes in seafood. Owned and operated by the Martinez family, it's open daily 8 a.m.-10 p.m. and located on Ramon Corona 1720-A. A few specialties of the **Restaurant Cozumel** are crab legs, frog legs, and scallops. Open Tues.-Sun. 10 a.m.-9 p.m. On Paseo Ramon Corona 22-A, Chapala. **La Viuda Steak House** (Calle Hidalgo 221) specializes in good cuts of meat.

Jocotepec

Jocotepec's claim to fame is weaving. Local weavers still use old-fashioned large looms or small backstrap looms. The end results are colorful woven clothing, table linens, bedspreads, and wallhangings. These are available where made and in small shops all over town. Walk down Calle Hidalgo for a good look. It's fun to spend an afternoon browsing and watching the weavers at their tasks. I peeked into the "thread room" and was overwhelmed by the shelves filled with myriad shades of brilliant color; the room could have been a still life in itself. If you have a choice, don't go on Sunday; many weavers take the day off.

From Guadalajara city center figure about one hour. Driving is the most interesting way to go to see the sights; however, there's good bus transportation that leaves the station about every half hour, and cost is less than US$1. Many folks come here to have lunch and spend a day looking around the villages. This can be done easily with a car, or there are several travel agencies in Guadalajara that provide tours with lunch for about US$30. If you are flying into Guadalajara to go directly to Lake Chapala, you'll find taxi service available at the airport. The trip will take about half an hour.

MORE GUADALAJARA SIDETRIPS

EL ESCALON SPRINGS

If you're up for another small excursion to a pretty canyon and a swim in an unusually colored pond, take an afternoon drive to El Escalon Springs. Pack a lunch and cold drinks, bring your swimsuit, and don't forget your camera. This spot is about a half hour drive from Guadalajara and brings you to a *mirador* (lookout) where you'll see the striking **San Cristóbal Canyon.** The *barranca* (canyon) never looks the same, depending on the time of day the colors below change from tawny earthtones to dramatic grays and greens.

From the *mirador*, continue for about another five minutes until you reach a dirt sideroad on your left; travel for another five minutes and you'll come to a bridge over the river. Wade upstream just a short distance and you'll find a lovely, cool, bluish gray spring-fed pool. The stream is pristine clean, and the unusual color is due to minerals. Dark branches throw interesting shadows on the water, and unusually shaped rocks add to the intrigue. **Note:** In the dry season (the winter months), this is just an empty riverbed.

Getting There

You must have your own vehicle for this trip. Take the Periférico to the Belenes Gigante (supermarket) to the Tesistan road, drive north toward Tesistan about eight kilometers and turn right on the highway to San Cristóbal. Continue for 22.5 kilometers; you'll see a "Bienvenidos, San Cristóbal de la Barranca" sign on your right. To find Escalon Springs go north about five minutes or until you see a sign "Km 26"; take the first dirt road on your left for another 1.6 kilometers until you reach the bridge. Total driving time is about 40 minutes.

EL CERRO
DE AMATITAN

On the road to Tequila from Guadalajara, outside Amatitan, you'll find El Cerro de Amatitan. As the story goes, quite a few years ago, the townsfolk installed a large cross on the top of the *cerro* (hill). According to the same villagers, many have begun seeing the Virgin Mary's image on the hillside in the past couple of years.

All that aside, El Cerro is a low-key way to spend an afternoon. Trekkers who feel like stretching their muscles will be rewarded with beautiful views of tree groves, giant boulders perched on steep canyon edges, and jagged cliffs. As you stroll up the occasionally steep hill, you will find pilgrims enjoying picnics (especially if you go on Sunday) where the best "view of the Virgin" is available. Once you reach the cross you are at 1,846 meters. The view from the top is always spectacular. In the afternoon, the dry peaks turn golden, and the views below show acres of fields of blue-gray tequila agave. Far below, at the bottom of **Barranca Santa Rosa,** you will see the ever-moving **Río Santiago.** This is not the *most* difficult

climb, but it does get a little steep in some spots, and takes about two hours of steady walking.

Getting There

Take Highway 15 west from Guadalajara to Amatitan (about 25 minutes from the **Periférico.** When you see the sign directing you to turn right to Santa Rosa, go past it and under the footbridge that crosses the highway. Make a quick left onto Calle Juan José Flores. Go two blocks and turn left onto Hidalgo. Pass the market, turn left on Abasol, and continue on until you reach a lovely arch; turn left here and take a quick right on a dirt road. Drive just a few minutes more beyond a little arroyo creeping off to the right and watch for an opening in the stone wall big enough to drive through. This brings you to an open field. Find a cool parking place and look up; if you followed the directions you'll see a mountain with a cross on the top.

From here the directions are simple; follow the trail (on foot) south through another stone wall, bear left and head up the mountain. From the Periférico until you park it's about 45 minutes, and from the last hole-in-the-wall to the cross is about two hours, depending on how fast you hike up hill.

K. A. ESCOVEDO SANDERS

THE STATE OF GUANAJUATO
INTRODUCTION

THE LAND

Guanajuato lies near the center of Mexico, bordered to the west by Jalisco, to the east by Querétaro, to the south by Michoacán, and to the north by San Luis Potosí.

Guanajuato occupies the **Bajío,** the heartland of Mexico. Though *bajío* means lowland, Guanajuato's plains and valleys are located at a 1,675-2,135 meter (5,500-7,000 feet) altitude. When compared to the tall surrounding mountains, however, it indeed qualifies as *bajío*.

The soil is volcanic ash, mixed with rich nutrients washed down by rivers from the mountains above. Farms thrive in the fertile valleys; at certain times of the year a drive through the countryside reveals fields of brilliant green and gold. Guanajuato's beautiful orange marigold blossoms are an important ingredient in manufactured chicken feed.

Cerro Del Cubilete

In 1950, a 18-meter-high statue of Christ was erected atop a mountain said to mark the exact geographic center of Mexico. The statue, called *Cristo Rey* ("Christ the King"), lies on the outskirts of Guanajuato city; you can see it from the highway as you enter the city. Buses leave the Central Bus Terminal several times a day to visit the site.

Climate

In the mountains expect springlike daytime temperatures year-round, but winter nights are generally nippy. Bring warm clothes to sleep in since most hotels do not have heat.

HISTORY

Pre-Columbian

The **Chupicuaros** occupied this area from 500 B.C. to A.D. 1400. Chupicuaros burial sites have been excavated in southern Guanajuato state, unearthed artifacts included ceramic burial jars and ceramic dogs, along with the remains of canines. The Chupicuaros apparently consid-

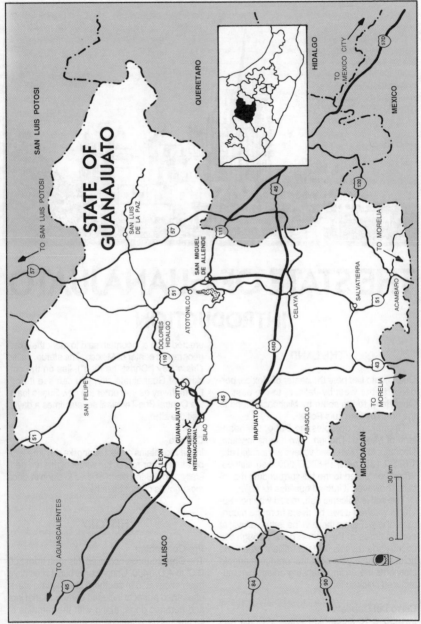

ered dogs mystical creatures; when buried with the deceased they would help lead the spirit to a proper afterlife.

Other sites reveal historic information about the **Otomi** and **Purépecha.** From the last indigenous group to occupy the area, the **Tarascans,** came the name **Quanaxuato,** which means "Place of Frogs." (There's a place overlooking Guanajuato city where the rocks take on the aspect of a pair of very large frogs.) Quanaxuato was ultimately Castilianized to **Guanajuato.**

The Spaniards Arrive

The first Spaniards arrived in Guanajuato in 1526, when the area was granted to Don Rodrigo Vázquez. He, like everyone in that era, came looking for gold and silver. It was years before anyone found sizable veins of the precious metals.

Another homelier treasure was found early on: fertile plains capable of producing bumper crops of fruits and vegetables. When ships filled with colonists embarked for the New World, Cortés convinced the powers in Spain to reserve space for seeds and plants from home. Oranges, grapevines, figs, pears, and peaches thus arrived from Spain. Farmers also grew native pumpkins, squash, cacao beans, and corn, this last probably the most important new crop among the exotic vegetables and fruits in the New World. An eager market waited for these products in nearby settlements—especially Mexico City.

The Search For Precious Metals

In 1548 the San Bernabé mine was discovered; two years later the San Juan Rayas mine opened. In 1760, a thick vein of silver was found that would change many lives, making many men rich, while bringing untold hardships to the Indians who labored deep within the earth. Mine shafts were hacked out of the mineral-laden soil, with thousands of primitive steps leading to the rich yields of minerals hidden below. Ore cars were filled with shovel and bucket, then pushed long distances to the surface. Indian laborers working under the jurisdiction of hard and cruel *encomienderos* dug the caverns and brought out the silver, slaving beyond the limits of human endurance. Many lost their lives in the tunnels, treated by money-hungry entre-

OZ MALLAN

The "gold" Church of San Cayetano at Valenciana Mine.

preneurs as expendable commodities. German naturalist Alexander von Humboldt was shocked at the conditions he witnessed at Valenciana in 1810: men carrying as much as 160 kilograms of ore on their backs for six straight hours, ascending thousands of steps at a 45-degree angle; boys under 12 and men over 60 forced to work the mines. In the beginning the ore was pulverized by hand with five-kilogram sledgehammers. Later, donkeys were used to crush the stones with their hooves. Not until the 1970s did mine operators begin to use pneumatic shovels and electrically driven cars.

Criollo Lifestyle

Sixteenth-century colonists labored hard to create cities that closely reflected what they left behind in Spain. By the 17th century Guanajuato towns featured cloistered buildings and labyrinthine rooms, flower-filled courtyards, private chapels, and opulent works of art. Universities were built, musicians and artists encouraged. Newcomers worked hard to achieve a touch of elegance from bare rock and total isolation.

Don Juan Antonio Riaño

Guanajuato was blessed with several leaders possessing great foresight. After the "year of hunger," 1784-1785, when the province endured a terrible famine, Don Juan Antonio Riaño ordered a granary (Alhóndigas de Granaditas) built in the center of Guanajuato city. Seed, grain, and other foodstuffs were stored in this stone repository against another year of bad harvests.

Riaño was a leader in other areas as well, and under his guidance Guanajuato became a center of science, letters, and the arts.

War Of Independence

The Mexican War of Independence began under an unlikely general, Father Miguel Hidalgo, a radical parish priest from the town of Dolores. A few minor skirmishes were quickly won by this reckless band; Hidalgo then hit the road to Guanajuato city with his ragtag collection of "soldiers." Fearful of attack, city leaders brought Spanish residents and their families, as well as the town's treasure, to Alhóndigas de Granaditas, a stout stone building. Folk legend tells us it was the bravery of a man named Juan José de los Reyes Martínez, known as **Pípila,** who flushed the city's defenders from the Alhóndiga, giving these inexperienced fighters their first victory.

When the insurgents entered the city they released all the prisoners in the local jail, then proceeded to fill it with apprehended *gachupines.* Three months later, when it was clear they were about to lose Guanajuato, Hidalgo's people brutally killed all their prisoners. Within a year Father Hidalgo was captured in Chihuahua, charged with treason and heresy, and executed. His head was carried to Guanajuato, where it was placed in a cage and hung outside the granary building. Three of Hidalgo's cohorts—Juan Aldama, Ignacio Allende, and Mariano Jiménez— were executed as well, their heads also placed in cages and hung on hooks in the corners of the Alhóndiga de Granaditas. Historians claim the heads hung in place for nine years and seven months.

Despite the loss of their leaders, the people continued the fight, and after 11 bloody years the new nation of Mexico forever severed its ties with Spain; independence was a reality.

The Alhóndiga serves today as an art and historical museum. There, still in place, are the hooks where the heroes' heads were hung. Guanajuato is justifiably proud of its historical part in the fight for independence. And though it's been hundreds of years since these long ago events, the city still exudes an aura of liberty, free thinking, and patriotism.

THE ECONOMY

The Broccoli Empire

The fertile Bajío produces large crops of broccoli and cauliflower; most of these vegetables are then frozen and shipped north to the U.S. market. Guanajuato's annual production of broccoli and cauliflower alone brings in more than 50 million dollars.

Mexico's first frozen-broccoli processing plant was established in Celaya 30 years ago by Birds-Eye. When in full production, the complex employs 2,000 people. This is a sizable operation; the largest of four greenhouses is bigger than a football field. Millions and millions of seedlings sprout every month. BirdsEye provides farmers with seedlings, insecticides, and fertilizer; when the plants mature, they are harvested and trucked back to the plant for processing. The broccoli is shipped from Mexico in neat frozen packages to American consumers, most of whom are totally unaware of its Mexican origins.

Water

Climatic conditions make this the breadbasket of Mexico; one farmer said that his farm produces five wheat crops a year. However, a problem is looming for Bajío farmers—water. The water table is dropping over a meter a year; if this trend continues, in 15 years half the wells in the valley will go dry.

Water pollution is another problem. Pemex refineries are probably the biggest culprits; the company now tries to recycle the water it uses in its refining process. In recent years many treatment plants have opened and more are in development.

Bull Breeding

Another Guanajuato industry is raising bulls for the *corrida* (bullfight). Several famous bull-breeding ranches are scattered about the countryside. Modern labs here store frozen sperm from the most courageous fighting bulls.

GUANAJUATO (CITY)

> **Pronounced:** wah-nah-WAH-toe
> **Altitude:** 2,020 meters
> **Population:** 75,000
> **Area Code:** (473)
> **Distance from Mexico City:** 356 km

The discovery of precious metals in the rugged Sierra Madre attracted hordes of hardy miners. Clusters of primitive shelters became the mining camps of Marfil, Tepetapa, Santa Ana, and Cerro del Cuarto. In 1554 these camps merged into Guanajuato. It was a strange little city, spread along a gorge and set very close to the river bottom located at the foot of tall mountains. The town was frequently wiped out by floods, but people kept coming. In 1741, the city had over 12,000 inhabitants, and earned from Philip IV the official designation of "city."

GUANAJUATO TODAY

As anyone who stays even a few days soon learns, Guanajuato is alive with music. **Jardín de la Unión** is the pulsing center of town, with a silvery kiosk where bands play regularly year-round. Groups of handsome young men called *estudiantinas* walk the streets strumming their stringed instruments and singing sentimental ballads of love.

The annual **Festival Internacional Cervantino** honors author Miguel Cervantes and his unique characters Don Quixote and Sancho Panza. During the festival, the intimate **Teatro Juárez** is a lively center for a variety of music, with artists from all over the world. There's dancing in the streets and every small plaza is alive with the excitement of bards, playlets, music, and dancing.

This small romantic city is best explored on foot. Museums are hidden in unlikely corners, housed in lovely old structures. The narrow, hilly streets are filled with tiny plazas, old fountains, and pastel houses with wrought-iron balconies enlivened by a host of colored flowers. Leafy vines climb old stone walls, and white lace curtains drape the windows.

The architecture is striking—you needn't know a Doric column from a Moorish proscenium to enjoy the grace of the antiquated domes, carved churrigueresque facades. Intense artistic effort went into so many of these structures. And fortunately for the rest of the world these buildings should be forever preserved: in 1989, the entire city was designated a "World Heritage Zone," preventing modernization of these old structures.

The streets are rich with the history of the past: a wonderful metal-roofed *mercado*, theaters, a university, and many old churches. And the stone form of Pípila stands guard on a high hill, visible from almost any spot in the city. Wear good walking shoes, as these streets are steep—in some areas they become staircases.

Cruise the **Carretera Panorámica,** the panoramic highway. From this circular road you'll enjoy a broad view of the city that is quite spectacular. This is also the route to noted mine sites, the **Museo de las Momias** ("Mummy Museum"), **the Pípila Monument, Valenciana Church, Presa de la Olla** and the **San Renovato Dams.**

SIGHTS

Statue Of Pípila

The statue of Pípila on the Panorámica is a true monolith, some 10 meters tall. During the siege of the city Pípila strapped a slab of stone to his back to deflect the gunfire coming his way; then, with a pile of straw, he set fire to the entrance of the Alhóndigas, enabling the insurgents to storm the fortresslike granary. In stone he continues to hold high the torch, standing above a plaque promising "there are still other Alhóndigas to burn."

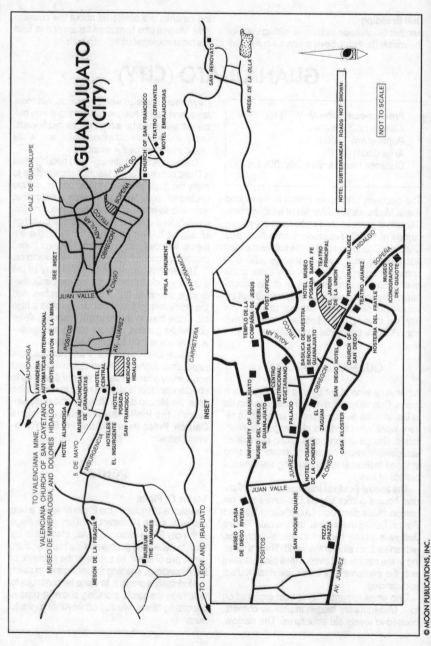

GUANAJUATO (CITY)

NOTE: SUBTERRANEAN ROADS NOT SHOWN

NOT TO SCALE

PRESA DE LA OLLA

SAN RENOVATO

CALZ. DE GUADALUPE

HIDALGO

CHURCH OF SAN FRANCISCO

HOTEL CERVANTES

TEATRO CERVANTES

HOTEL EMBAJADORAS

SOPENA

OBREGON

TRUCO

ZGY CULAR

SEE INSET

JUAN VALLE

ALONSO

PIPILA MONUMENT

ALHONDIGA

LAVANDERIA
AUTOMATICAS INTERNACIONAL

HOTEL SOCAVON DE LA MINA

TO VALENCIANA MINE,
VALENCIANA CHURCH OF SAN CAYETANO,
MUSEO DE MINERALOGIA AND DOLORES HIDALGO

HOTEL ALHONDIGA

5 DE MAYO

INSURGENCIA

MUSEUM ALHONDIGA
DE GRANADITAS

HOTEL
CENTRAL

HOTELES
EL INSURGENTE

HOTEL
POSADA
SAN FRANCISCO

POSITOS

AV. JUAREZ

MERCADO
HIDALGO

CARRETERA PANORAMICA

MESON DE LA FRAGUA

MUSEUM OF
THE MUMMIES

TO LEON AND IRAPUATO

PANORAMICA

INSET

POST OFFICE

TEMPLO DE LA
COMPAÑIA DE JESUS

TRUCO

AQUILAR

HOTEL MUSEO
POSADA SANTA FE

EL JARDIN
DE LA UNION

RESTAURANT VALADEZ

TEATRO
PRINCIPAL

HIDALGO

SOPENA

MUSEO
ICONOGRAFICO
DEL QUIJOTE

HOSTERIA DEL FRAYLE

TEATRO JUAREZ

CHURCH OF
SAN DIEGO

SAN DIEGO HOTEL

BASILICA DE NUESTRA
SEÑORA DE
GUANAJUATO

CENTRO
NUTRICIONAL
VEGETARIANO

UNIVERSITY OF GUANAJUATO

MUSEO DEL PUEBLO
DE GUANAJUATO

PALACIO

EL
ZAGUAN

OBREGON

CASA KLOSTER

HOTEL POSADA
DE LA CONDESA

ALONSO

JUAREZ

JUAN VALLE

MUSEO Y CASA
DE DIEGO RIVERA

SAN ROQUE SQUARE

PIZZA
PIAZZA

POSITOS

AV. JUAREZ

© MOON PUBLICATIONS, INC.

Visitors are welcome to climb up an inside stairway into the torch for a marvelous view of the city (there's a small charge if someone's around to collect it). Pípila is open 24 hours a day, and there's always a crowd of vendors selling snacks and souvenirs. The hardy can use a steep path to reach Pípila; start at El Jardín de la Union, then walk east on Calle Sopeña at Callejón de Calvario where the sign says "al Pípila." Uphill all the way. The bus marked "Pípila" will also take you to the monument. Once there you can spot several paths that will return you to town.

El Jardín De La Unión

In Guanajuato there are very few broad areas of flat land conducive to the construction of the typical, broad square Mexican plaza. So here the favored center/gathering place bears a rather unusual shape; El Jardín is a small flat area in the midst of myriad zigzagging up-and-down streets. This shady, smallish garden is almost entirely covered by a thick canopy of aged Indian laurel trees. A kiosk in the center is the site of music on Tuesday, Thursday, and Sunday each week. This is a pleasant place to spend an hour or two on a shady bench relaxing and reviewing the social habits of Guanajuatenses. Water spouts vigorously from the silver-colored fountain. Small children dance up and down the steps of the silver kiosk, and students and businesspeople enjoy tranquil breaks. *Mamacitas* bring small girls dressed in white veils, like miniature brides, who rush to place nosegays of flowers on the altar of the Virgin at the basilica. Elderly aristocratic women, gray hair drawn into the classic bun, dressed in black with a touch of white lace at the bodice, stroll with middle-aged sons. At this great people-watching locus the parade is nonstop.

In the evening teenage girls huddle in bunches, giggling at young boys huddled in bunches watching the girls. Vendors sell supper-in-a-cup, *vasitas de elote*—a corncob pulled from a boiling pot, the kernels scraped off, placed in a cup, sprinkled with chile powder and served with a plastic fork. The music in the park mixes swing, rock, salsa, and samba; something for everybody.

Small businesses and cafes along the perimeter of the *jardín* offer a variety of goods. One small storefront is filled with handmade baby clothes; the Michoacana ice cream shop sells fresh fruit and ice cream bars for about 50 cents. There are many dining spots around the *jardín,* including the sidewalk cafes **Cafe de Hotel Museo Santa Fe** and **Cafe El Pollo Pitagorico.** Favorite hotels are located on the *jardín* and across the street.

Teatro Juárez

Across the street from El Jardín the Teatro Juárez stands in lovely elegance. Although theater construction began in 1873, it wasn't until 1903, when Guanajuato was enjoying a period of intense wealth, that the building was finally in-

Sun, shade, and sidewalk cafes at El Jardín in Guanajuato City.

OZ MALLAN

augurated. The opening performance was Verdi's *Aida;* one of the many notable celebrities in attendance was Don Porfirio Díaz, then president of the Mexican Republic.

The top of the *teatro* is graced with life-sized statues of the nine Muses, Melpomene, Thalia, Polyhymnia, Erato, Terpsichore, Euterpe, Clio, Calliope, and Urania. The portico displays Doric-Roman columns, and the walls are constructed of stone in layers of light green and blue. Although several architects worked on the project over the years, the last to revise and complete the building was Antonio Rivas Mercado. The theater is still as handsome as ever with the same broad staircase, red wrought-iron fence, and ornate multiglobed streetlamps.

Once inside, the interior is smaller than expected. But in its day it must have been nothing less than opulent, with a European-Moorish flavor. The drop curtain was painted in France by the renowned scenographer Labasta of Paris; his subject is a panorama of the Golden Horn of Constantinople. Rich burnished woods, unique carved designs, French sculptures, foyer furniture covered with elegant damasks, and a grand chandelier from Paris all reflect the wealth of the city at the turn of the century.

The theater is open for viewing Tues.-Sun. 9 a.m.-1:45 p.m., and 5-8 p.m. Any opportunity to attend a production in the small theater offers a grand experience.

Museo Y Casa De Diego Rivera

Born in 1886 in a two-story house on a narrow Guanajuato street, artist Diego Rivera lived here until he was eight years old. Then the family moved to Mexico City, where he began painting at the age of 10. The first floor of this museum offers a pleasant display of life in the Rivera family, including furniture and antiques. The two upper floors contain about a hundred Rivera paintings and sketches.

Rivera attended art schools in Europe and became enamored of the political activists of his era. Returning to Mexico the flamboyant artist frequently became a center of controversy because of his connections and associations with communism; due to Rivera's influence, Leon Trotsky made his home in Mexico City until Stalin's henchmen sank an ice ax in his skull.

The museum is open Tues.-Sat. 9 a.m.-1:30 p.m., 4-6:30 p.m. Sun. 10 a.m.-2:30 p.m. Admission is US$2, children under 11 and those over 60 are free. Calle Pocitos 47, tel. (473) 2-1197.

Museo Iconográfico Del Quijote

Also known as the **Cervantes Museum,** this museum is located in front of the San Francisco Church. If you've ever laughed and cried at the antics of the cross-eyed conquistador and his pal Sancho Panza you'll enjoy a lighthearted visit through this amazing collection of Quixote art. Cervantes-lover Eulalio Ferrer left Spain for Mexico at the end of the Spanish Civil War, donating his immense collection of Quixotic figures to the city of Guanajuato.

Cervantes creations in 600 displays include giant wall murals, a modern depiction by Pablo Picasso, lithographs by Salvador Dali, Pedro Coronel and Raul Anguiano murals, pottery, statues, eggs, and postage stamps—all portraying the sad-eyed knight of La Mancha. The museum was officially opened by Spanish President Felipe González on 6 November 1987. Open Tues.-Sat. 10 a.m.-6:30 p.m., Sun. 10 a.m.-2:30 p.m., free. Located at Manuel Doblado 1, tel. (473) 2-6721.

Museum Alhóndiga De Granaditas

Scene of the first bloody battle of the fight for independence, this one-time city granary is today one of seven fine Guanajuato museums. Filled with historical artifacts that relate the story of the city and a pleasing art exhibit as well. From 1864 to 1964 the Alhóndiga served as a prison. In 1967 the city revamped the old building and displays today include stairway murals depicting the history of Guanajuato painted by popular artist José Chavez Morado. Open Tues.-Sat. 10 a.m.-2 p.m. and 4-6 p.m., Sun. 10 a.m.-3:30 p.m., admission is US$4.75, more with a camera, free on Sunday.

Popular Campus Museums

Three University of Guanajuato museums present changing art exhibits. Two occupy the ground floor, and one is located in the Templo de la Compañia de Jesús next door. Open Mon.-Fri. 9 a.m.-2 p.m. and 5-8 p.m., free. Naturalists might like to stop in at the **Museo de Historia Natural Alfredo Duges** on the fourth floor to see stuffed specimens of a large variety of animals, some rather unusual. Open weekdays only, 10 a.m.-6 p.m., free.

Museo Del Pueblo De Guanajuato

Formerly the home of the Marqueses de San Juan Rayas, owner of the rich Rayas silver mine, this lovely old mansion is now an art museum. Built in 1696 with its own chapel, the building's exhibits include a selection of art ranging from the early colonial period to the modern era. Check out the chapel in the courtyard; there you'll find a mural by José Chavez Morado. Open Tues.-Sat. 10 a.m.-2 p.m. and 4-7 p.m., Sun. 10 a.m.-2:30 p.m. Admission is less than US$2.

Fountain Of The Baratillo

This lovely old fountain has an interesting history. Originally commissioned by Emperor Maximilian in 1864, the fountain was constructed in Florence, Italy. Distinctly Italian in design, it was a gift to Guanajuato, placed opposite the Basílica de Nuestra Señora de Guanajuato in the Plaza de la Paz. But when Maximilian fell from power and was executed, the fountain was moved to a more inconspicuous spot about a block from the *jardín*. Today it's the centerpiece of a small plaza featuring a couple of tiny cafes and a pleasant laid-back ambience.

San Roque Square

By day this small square looks like just another bit of antiquated stone, with unusually shaped iron lanterns set in front of an old church. But during the Cervantes festival the square becomes a lavish stage straight out of old Europe, with actors dressed in the velvets and satins of the medieval period. Crowds sit on wooden bleachers to listen to the wit and wisdom of the bard. These evening playlets from Cervantes's masterful pen are productions that Hollywood could never reproduce on a sound stage. The moon, stars, and architecture present a perfect backdrop for well-performed theater.

Visitors who follow the *estudiantinas* up and down the narrow streets will also end up at this square.

Palacio

Close to the Basílica lies the Palacio, constructed in 1900 under the Porfirio Díaz regime. Seat of government for the state, it features the typical busy facade of the era. Take a look anytime 9 a.m.-10 p.m., Plaza de la Paz 77.

The Street Lacking Doors And Windows

The name refers to the subterranean labyrinth of streets that runs under and through the city. For centuries homes, churches, and businesses were flooded by the Río Guanajuato, where in the early days of the city the silver was processed. It looks as though a masterful engineer designed the throughway for the growing vehicular traffic—Mother Nature was the engineer. Perfect road beds were left when the lusty river was diverted; highways were constructed, and doors of adjacent homes were blocked off.

Churches Of The City

Guanajuato is a showcase of charming churches. The **Basílica de Nuestra Señora de Guanajuato** is a marvelous old church well worth a visit. The interior is an opulent dedication to a small wooden statue of the Virgin sent to the New World by King Philip II in 1557. It had been worshipped in Spain since 714, hidden in a cave from the Moors, and is presumed to be the oldest representation of Christian art in Mexico. It stands on a silver base and is adorned with tunics of precious inlaid stones. Each year three days are set aside to celebrate holidays dedicated to the city's protector, the Virgin of Guanajuato.

The **Templo de la Compañia de Jesús** was originally built as part of the Jesuit University in 1732. The **Church of San Diego** is located at El Jardín, and was built by the Franciscans in 1633. It has survived flood and financial difficulties and was completely reconstructed in 1786. The **Church of San Francisco** is on Sopeña, close to the *jardín*.

If you're the sort of person who collects churches, keep looking; the city features many others. They're not nearly as flamboyant as those I've mentioned, but each of the churches has its own personality and usually an intriguing history.

SIGHTS OUT OF TOWN

Local buses with frequent regular schedules can take you to most of the locales mentioned in this section; taxis are available and inexpensive.

Museum Of The Mummies

Locally known as the **Museo de las Momias.** Visiting the mummy museum is not my idea of a fun sightseeing tour! However, many people wait in long lines to see these otherworldly exhibits. This museum simply stores a collection of dried-up cadavers for viewing in glass cases. The dry mountain air and chemical mix of the soil in the tiny local cemetery combine to prevent decomposition in about two percent of bodies buried.

Here, when the deceased is buried, the family has five years to pay for the plot. If at the end of five years no payment has been received, the body is exhumed and cremated to make room for "paying" customers. Long before the museum was built, evicted bodies were propped along the fence bordering the cemetery and left there until family members returned them. One day a curious female visitor walking along the cemetery path was assaulted by a dead body that suddenly tipped over upon her. Perhaps that's when it was decided the mummies must be removed, cremated, or, if not claimed, placed in a glass case for display.

The museum is open daily 9 a.m.-6 p.m.; admission is US$1.50, more with a camera. Take the bus marked "Momias" or "Panteón," and tell the driver where you want to go; at Calz. del Panteón, tel. (473) 2-0639.

Valenciana Mine

As the Valenciana Mine continued to produce amazing quantities of silver, Guanajuato city developed into one of the major cities of New Spain, growing almost as large as Mexico City. Guanajuato prospered for two centuries, providing the world with one-half of its total silver supply. the Valenciana Mine alone produced one-third.

Only 17 Guanajuato mines remain open today. One is the Valenciana, reopened when silver prices resurged. The mine is open for inspection by the public. Statistics tell us the Valenciana mine shaft is 525 meters deep; 80 tonnes of silver are brought to the surface each month, together with 396 kilograms of gold. Although Taxco is referred to today as the silver center of the country, Valenciana actually produces more silver.

When you visit the Valenciana Mine, you might see local miners selling mineral samples around the mine shaft; check out the beautiful large quartz crystals.

To reach Valenciana by bus, take the vehicle marked "Valenciana" from Plaza Alhóndiga, Calle 5 de Mayo. Tell the driver you want to get off in Valenciana at the Church of San Cayetano; from there it's a short walk to the mine on a dirt road opposite the church.

Valenciana Church Of San Cayetano

The wealth of the Valenciana mine was unbelievable, hence this church is just what you'd expect a "gold" church to be—golden. The facade is ornate churrigueresque baroque. On the inside you'll find four enormous paintings by Luis Momay, golden altars with delicate filigree work, statues, stained glass, an alabaster holy water font, and a spectacular pulpit. The walls are one-and-a-half meters thick. If you study the walls, ceilings, altars, and pulpit you'll discover fine gold work, inlaid precious woods, ivory, and other bone. Four barrel vaults make up the ceiling, with a cupola in the transept. This is really a church that says *pesos*—lots of them.

One historian claims the church was built by Valenciana Mine owner Don Antonio de Obregón Alcocer in thanks to his maker for the vast wealth gathered from the mine. Another historian says the church was built to assuage his guilty conscience for the wealth accumulated at the cost of innumerable Indian lives. In front of the St. Cayetano Church you'll find a tiny gift shop with some interesting odds and ends, including silver and gold figurines and earrings. Worth a look around.

Mineros Club Restaurant

If you're looking for a lunch spot near the Valenciana Mine, try the "Miner's Club." The meat is a bit chewy, but the *empenadas* are tasty. Open daily just off the Valenciana Plaza, tel. (473) 2-2019.

Museo De Mineralogía

Considered one of the outstanding mineral museums of the Americas, it contains an extensive collection of rare minerals, some found only in Guanajuato. Open weekdays 8 a.m.-3 p.m., free. Take the local bus marked "Presa-San Javier" west on Juárez and tell the driver where you want to get off.

Presa De La Olla And San Renovato

Olla Dam was a gift from President Porfirio Díaz in 1903. These charming lakes provide a simple getaway for city residents. In this peaceful park you'll find a monument dedicated to Miguel Hidalgo. On Sundays, the park is always filled with picnickers, children playing, and families boating on the lake. During the week it's very quiet. Easy to reach aboard an eastbound "Presa" bus; tell the driver where you want to get off.

Ex-Hacienda San Gabriel De Barrera

Come to the ex-hacienda to stroll the beautiful grounds. Don't miss the multitude of gardens: the **Orange Garden, Arabian Garden, Pergola Garden, Rose Garden, Italian Garden, St. Francis Garden,** and **Queen's Garden.** You'll see lovely trees, beautiful statuary, unique sculpture, fountains, and reflecting pools. There's a wonderful museum with exhibits from the past, illustrating what life was like for the wealthy and the servants who slaved for them.

ACCOMMODATIONS

For some visitors, staying in a 500-year-old building is a special experience. It stimulates the imagination, conjuring a multitude of ifs, whos, and whens. Did Maximilian walk these same hallways, contemplating his future? Did the child who became muralist Diego Rivera run and skip by this old plaza? Did Carlota's skirts sweep across these worn wooden floors in dance? More so than words, these streets and structures are a physical bridge to a past that can become very real.

In Guanajuato, some of the nicest accommodations are found in renovated ex-haciendas, ex-convents, and ex-mansions. Some of these thick-walled old structures feature fabulous architecture and lovely antiques. The city also offers new modern hotels with swimming pools, tennis courts, and in-room servibars.

Reservation Considerations

Most of the hotels in Guanajuato do not have elevators. If this is a problem, be sure to ask in advance. If you plan to attend the **Cervantes Festival** or wish to visit the city in October, you must make reservations well in advance. This is true whether you desire a small unpretentious hotel or a lavish out-of-town hotel. Reconfirm a month before you go. Don't forget to bring warm sleeping clothes in winter; most rooms have no heat.

Budget

Casa Kloster: This is one of the all-time favorites for those with a small budget. A simple, clean, pleasant gathering place for European travelers, many say it reminds them of home. Though spartan, the rooms receive plenty of TLC. Only shared bathroom facilities are available. Allow time for the water to heat up before you shower; you must light the "water heater" for a truly hot shower. The patio is a relaxing place with many plants and caged birds that sing all day long. Since it has only 16 rooms, you should get there early in the day to be sure of a vacancy. Rates are about US$10.50 pp. Located across from the Telephonos de Mexico, one block west of Juárez at Calle de Alonso 32, tel. (473) 2-0088.

Hotel Posada de la Condesa: Another large, old, worn hotel with budget prices, it's located close to the Basílica. Most of the rooms are spacious, some with balconies, some with windows, some more "used" than others. Usually they're clean, with private baths and hot water. Take a look before you decide. Prices are US$14-20. Located at Plaza de la Paz 60, tel. 2-1462.

Hotel Central: This charming little hotel is cheap and clean, with nicely tiled floors, comfy beds, and a greenery-filled courtyard. No hot water, though. Rates are US$12 s, US$16 d. Located at Av. Juárez 111, tel. 2-0080.

Moderate

Hotel Socavón de la Mina: Be prepared for plenty of exercise here, as the hotel rises five stories and there's no elevator. You can choose from 37 clean carpeted rooms, each with a bathroom featuring colorful tile and a copper washbasin, all arranged around a pleasant central plaza. The restaurant/bar on the second floor is open 7:30 a.m.-10:30 p.m. Rates are US$42 s, US$47 d. Located on the road to Dolores Hidalgo, at Alhóndiga 41-A, tel. (473) 2-4885.

Hostería del Frayle: In the 17th century this old structure served as a factory for the manufacture of gold and silver coins. The ambience is very colonial, with spacious rooms, wooden floors, high dark wood beam ceilings, antiquated tall doors, and thick adobe walls. Modern touches include TV, carpet, a private bath, hot water, and lots of stairs to climb. Conveniently located in the center of town. Rates are about US$40 s, US$45 d, located just east of Teatro Juárez at Calle Sopeña 3, tel. 2-1179, fax 2-1179. Check out the small restaurant next to the lobby that features Italian food.

Suites Casas de Manrique: Eight pleasant suites downtown offer queen beds, sofa beds, minibars, color TV, telephones, large closets, safes, and private baths with tubs. Rates are US$52 s, US$69 d. Located just one block from the *mercado* at Juárez 116, tel. 2-7678, fax 2-8306.

Hoteles el Insurgente: The pleasant lobby has taken on the look of the past. The small rooms don't have much circulation and those with windows facing onto the street can be quite noisy. The quieter rooms face the glassed-in courtyard. Amenities include TVs (color, with U.S. channels), carpets, private baths, hot water, telephones, and free parking. Rates are US$40 s and US$44 d. Located six blocks north of El Jardín at Av. Juárez 226, tel. 2-3192 or 2-4090.

Hotels Within Walking Distance Of El Jardín De La Union

If you like the hustle and bustle of life on the plaza, with music floating up from the kiosk, sidewalk cafes just below your window, and restaurants, shops, and churches just a few footsteps away, then you'll want to stay downtown in the heart of the city.

Hotel Museo Posada Santa Fé: Established in 1862, this is perhaps the oldest hotel in Guanajuato. During the reign of Maximillian, historians tell us the consulate of Prussia would lodge here when on royal business to the city. On the walls, paintings by early chronicler Don Manuel Leal depict life in the early days of Guanajuato. All 50 rooms exude a feeling of the 1800s despite the addition of carpets, TV, private baths, self-serve bars, and king-size beds (suites only; in the other rooms the double beds seem quite small). Don't expect 20th-century luxury here, even though you may be paying for it. This marvelous historical landmark is filled with antiques and antiquated art. Curved stairways are lined with finely finished wood railings and spindles. A lobby bar, inside dining room, immense fireplaces, friendly, attentive staff, and a sidewalk cafe on the edge of El Jardín make this a favorite stopover. Rates are US$66 s, US$73 d. Reservations suggested. Write to El Jardín, Guanajuato, 36000, Gto., Mexico, tel. (473) 2-0084.

San Diego Hotel: Once a 17th-century convent, this hotel located on the *jardín* has historical ambience but lacks the pizzazz of some of the other historic hotels in the city. Yet the location is great, and, for some travelers, it's still one of the all-time favorite accommodations in the city. The rooms have been brought up to modern standards with private bathrooms, hot water, and shower/tubs. Some of the rooms have balconies from yesteryear; ask about the pay garage one block away. The dining room is open 7 a.m.-11 p.m.; cocktails and entertainment. Rates are US$40 s, US$50 d. Located at El Jardín de la Union 1 (Apdo. Postal 8, Guanajuato, 36000), tel. 2-1300, fax 2-5626.

Out-of-town Hotels

Some of these structures are just a couple of minutes away by taxi; others lie several miles out of Guanajuato. None are really a convenient walk from downtown.

Hotel Real de Mines: Just a short distance from the subterranean Av. Miguel Hidalgo tunnel to downtown, this large modern hotel captures a bit of the colonial spirit in its decor. With 175 rooms, the hotel often caters to large groups; it can get a bit mad. Some of the rooms have balconies, a few have fireplaces, and there's a small heated pool that crowds quickly on a hot day. Amenities include a large dining room, a cocktail lounge, a nightclub with live entertainment, and one tennis court. Rates are US$68 s and US$74 d. Located on Najayote 17, tel. (473) 2-1460, fax 2-1508.

Parador San Javier Hotel: A few blocks from the center of town, and a little pricey, this charming old structure features colonial rooms from the old hacienda days, with shiny wood floors, fireplaces and colorful tile. Other rooms are straight out of the 20th century. All are quite lovely, the suites really comfortable and located just a few steps from well manicured gardens with exquisite lawns and brilliantly colored bougainvillea tumbling over old stone walls. You'll spot some fine old antiques in the public

OZ MALLAN

Guanajuato's San Javier Hotel, once a beautiful old mansion, is now a lovely hotel.

rooms. Just wandering through the grounds is a hedonistic experience. A coffee shop and a lovely old dining room feature high ceilings, a fireplace, and colonial art, linen, and crystal as well as service from very efficient waiters. Have a drink in the El Pozo piano bar or a disco experience at La Galería. Rates are US$60-80 s, US$65-85 d; a junior suite costs US$95-125. Meals at the hotel restaurant are a set price: breakfast US$8-9, lunch US$11-12, dinner US$11-12. Remember, a Mexican lunch is generally a four-course meal. Located on Dolores Hidalgo Hwy., tel. 2-0626 or 2-0944, fax. 2-3114.

Hotel Castillo de Santa Cecilia: This unusual hotel looks like a medieval castle, sitting on a protective bluff overlooking the city. Once inside you'll find a charming, well-decorated hotel with 88 rooms, excellent service, luxurious amenities and a dining room serving excellent food. Amenities include a swimming pool, cable TV, a handicraft workshop, and parking. Dancing at the **La Cava** nightclub Fri.-Sat., a great *estudiantina* show, and live music provide entertainment. Rates are US$75-95 d. For reservations write to Camino a la Valenciana Km 1, C.P. 36000, Guanajuato, Gto., Mexico; tel. 2-0485, fax 2-0153.

Hotel Paseo de la Presa: This lovely building is located about two miles from town and offers a marvelous view of the city. The rooms are well appointed and spacious, some with king-size beds. The architectural style is a pleasant eclectic mix of modern and colonial. The **La Cascada** restaurant serves excellent international food with a fairly good wine list. **La Terraza** is an indoor/outdoor spot perfect for a casual drink. Sporting alternatives include the pool or a tennis court. This is not the sort of place for those looking for cheap lodgings, but you get what you pay for. Rates are US$82 d; during the Cervantes Festival they rise to to US$100. This Best Western hotel is located on Carretera Panorámica, tel. in the U.S. (800) 528-1234, in Mexico tel. (473) 2-3761, fax 2-2324.

Hotel San Gabriel de Barrera: This old hotel is located a couple of kilometers out of town, next to the **Ex-Hacienda San Gabriel de Barrera** museum. It's along a winding road, so you must either take a bus and then walk about 10 minutes, drive your own vehicle, or hire a taxi for about US$5. The dining room and lobby are attractive and relaxing; bedrooms and bathrooms are spacious and well appointed. The grounds are special, with flowers everywhere. Terraces, a restaurant, tennis courts, and a swimming pool complement the 137 rooms. This was formerly El Presidente Hotel. Rates are US$65-70. At Carretera Marfil Km 2.5, tel. 2-3980 or 2-3552, fax 2-7460. Take the "Noria Alta" bus and tell the driver where you're going. Don't be alarmed when he goes right past the hotel; the closest stop he can make is Calle Noria Alta. Then comes that 10-minute walk.

Casa de Espíritus Alegres ("House of Cheerful Spirits"): Located in the suburb of Marfil, this unique bed and breakfast occupies an ex-hacienda built in the mid-1700s. At one time many haciendas were located along the river about three kilometers from Guanajuato; gold and silver ore were brought here on mules for processing. In 1906, the river raged and this hacienda—along with many others—was flooded out, creating a ghost town. In the 1950s Italian sculptor Georgio Belloli took an interest in the area, restoring the old stone ghosts into charming homes.

American artists Joan and Carol Summers took over Casa de Espiritus Alegre in 1979. Plumbing and wiring were among the first improvements, then came a separate studio. Finally they worked their way through the entire house, restoring rooms, building terraces, employing playful sophistication, earthy art, and bright color.

The building now has six bedrooms, four with fireplaces, and the decor includes marvelous folk art from all over Mexico. Guests enjoy a glass-covered, tree-shaded central courtyard with tropical plants and a stone fountain. The traditional kitchen is decorated with the bright colors and style of Mexico, and includes handpainted ceramic tiles, folk art, and a dining table set in front of a large open fireplace. Each bedroom is unique: one features a collection of dolls, another the rich atmosphere of the tiger dance ritual, and a third is ready for romance with plenty of lace and flowers. All are quite charming.

The bed and breakfast is closed during the winter months, when it is then available for study groups; write for group rates. B&B rates are US$55-US$85, US$115 for a suite. No children or teenagers are allowed, and no smoking indoors. For more information and brochures write or call Joan Summers, 2817 Smith Grade, Santa Cruz, California 95060, U.S.A.; tel. (408) 423-0181. In Mexico, write to La Casa de Espiritus Alegres La Ex-Hacienda La Triñidad, 1, Marfil, Guanajuato, 36250, Gto., Mexico; tel./fax 3-1013.

Hacienda Los Cobos: This place is especially convenient for visitors arriving by car from the south; interior parking is available. The 40 rooms are comfortable but not fancy, with TV. There's a swimming pool, an average dining room, and a reading room. Rates are US$34 d, US$40 d.

Motel Guanajuato: Located on Dolores Hidalgo Highway, about 10 minutes by car from Guanajuato. The 50 rooms are clean with private bathrooms, hot water, and TV; there's also a heated pool. There's a restaurant and bar with a view of the city below. Credit cards okay. Rates are US$25-33; located on Dolores Hidalgo Hwy. at Km 2.5, Apdo. Postal 113, tel. 2-0689.

Condominiums

The **Hotel y Club Villa de la Plata** is the only time-share in Guanajuato, a great family escape located on the edge of town along a mountain road. All accommodations offer equipped kitchen, living room, TV, dining room, one or two bedrooms, and twin or double beds. Guests are guaranteed a swim in the only indoor pool in Guanajuato. The brick dome covering the pool is crowned with a sunny skylight; a small terrace overlooking the pool offers a bar and a social gathering place. The grounds are well cared for, with tree-lined walks. Parking available. Don't expect telephones, except for one public phone at the front desk. Located on Carretera a Valenciana; tel. (473) 2-5200.

Camping And Trailering

In Bario Nuevo you'll find the **Trailer Park Móvil,** a park with two levels of level camping sites. To get there you must ascend two kilometers up a steep hill north of town. Tent rates are US$5-8 for one or two people, full hookups are US$6-10. Ask for more information at the tourist office in town. On Subida de Mellado.

FOOD

Because this is a university town, those on a small budget can make out pretty well. As in all of Mexico, eating at or near the marketplace is the most economical. Dining rooms in the large hotels are usually the most expensive, though many offer excellent continental cuisine. Right on the *jardín* and up the street from the Teatro Juárez are several cafes with good food at moderate prices.

Restaurants Around El Jardín De La Union

The **Restaurant Valadez** lies directly across from the Teatro Juárez. Afternoon diners are entertained by organ music while imbibing cappuccinos, snacking on guacamole and chips, or enjoying Mexican-style steaks. There's a US$5 cover charge for the music. Food is good, but a bit pricey for what you get.

Check out **El Gallo Pitagorico Restaurant and Bar** on the *jardín* (6-C, tel. 2-1998). Here you'll enjoy good international food. During happy hours (noon-2 p.m., 6-7 p.m.) drinks are two for one and the *botanas* are free. A good-sized combination Mexican platter runs about US$8.50.

Just across from the *jardín*, the Hotel San Diego offers a nice little dining room with small open balconies where diners can enjoy breakfast, lunch, or dinner. The simple wooden tables are covered with bright red plaid linens; you'll eat good old-fashioned Mexican food at modern prices.

Budget Meals

Try **Restaurant Los Caporales** for an inexpensive, simple breakfast, less than US$2. Above the market **El Zaguan** offers decent *comida corrida* for less than US$4. **Mercado Gavira** features a series of fast-fooderies with a huge selection of such local exotic specialties as *biria* (baby goat). If you don't see the price, ask. All around the market you'll find inexpensive *comida corrida* as well as *tortas*.

Cafe Nivel 13 is a fine little coffee-and-cake spot with a "mining" atmosphere, near the *jardín*. Another place for snacks and light meals is **El Unicornio Azul,** serving *empanadas,* vegetarian sandwiches, and good yogurt. Located at Agora del Baratillo, tel. 2-0700. **Pastelaría Arnadi** serves tasty pies, fancy pastries, and yogurt at Plazuela de San Francisco, Manuel Doblado 12-B, tel. 2-6242.

Centro Nutricional Vegetariano restaurant serves vegetarian hamburgers and other sandwiches, as well as salads and soup, all prepared without meat products. Try the *molletes*, split *bolillos* (French-type rolls) spread with mashed beans and cheese. Reasonable prices. Open Mon.-Sat. 10 a.m.-9 p.m. On the north side of the basilica at Aguilar 43, tel. 2-1191.

Truco 7 serves good food at reasonable prices for breakfast, lunch, and dinner. *Comida corrida* is less than US$3. By day hear jazz or classical music, at night listen to the sounds of a live guitarist, all in a pleasant coffee-house/art-gallery atmosphere. Open weekdays 9 a.m.-midnight, weekends 11 a.m.-midnight. At Truco 7 next to the basilica.

At **Las Palomas Restaurant/Bar** clusters of artwork are everywhere and bright cloths and flowers adorn the tables. It will probably be very busy for *comida corrida* (US$5.50, served 2-5 p.m.), or come for a four-course dinner (US$5-12). Open daily 9 a.m.-11 p.m.; a few blocks north of the *jardín* at Ayuntamiento 19, tel. 2-4936.

Follow the more affluent college students to **Pizza Piazza** for humble pie. If you prefer, the place serves spaghetti as well. The large pizza will feed three or four depending on appetites (US$5-12). Sangria and beer are the popular drinks. At Plaza San Fernando 24, tel. 2-3094.

NIGHTLIFE

We would be remiss if we didn't mention **El Jardín de la Union** once again. For some visitors this is the best show in town. The state band gives free concerts in the kiosk on Tuesdays and Thursdays 7-8 p.m., and on Sundays noon-1 p.m. The rest of the week sidewalk cafes are filled with people drinking and listening to the wandering minstrels. Other nightspots generally don't open or get started until 10-11 p.m.; some charge a cover.

Rincón Del Beso

Not a disco, and not just a bar, it is instead a *peña*, an intimate Bohemian spot with dim light, tiny open rooms, plain wood tables and chairs, and a miniature stage quite colorfully done, with a backdrop representing the small winding streets of Guanajuato. If you've ever felt the urge to stand and recite a heartfelt poem you wrote over a glass or five of your favorite sangria, here's your chance: everyone here is welcome to recite, sing, or emote. Between the amateurs, plenty of professionals clamber on stage to sing the music of Mexico, Argentina, and Cuba.

It's a fun place, and you can start late and stay till early in the morning; the manager keeps the place open as long as there are customers. Wine is the drink of choice; no cover charge. At Alonso 21-A, a short walk from the *jardín*.

Disco Pequeño

The lights of the city below are just one of the attractions here. If you like students and/or loud disco music this is your place. On the road to the Pípila Monument, tel. 2-2308.

Video Bar Grill
Here you'll find young enthusiasts, lots of music, dancing, drinks, and light meals—and, of course, videos. At Insurgencia 1, tel. 2-1465; open 6 p.m.-2 a.m.

Theaters
Teatro Juárez stages elegant operas, concerts, and plays. The **Teatro Principal** and **Teatro Cervantes,** usually open Sunday, Monday, and Tuesday evenings, show international films. An announcement poster out front describes the offerings, times, and dates. All three edifices are fairly close together, near the *jardín.*

OTHER ENTERTAINMENT AND EVENTS

Cervantino Festival
Enrique Ruelas, founder and director of the university theater, introduced in 1953 the one-act street farces of Cervantes known as *entreme-ses.* The word has a double meaning, meaning both "interlude" and "farce"—very apropos, since they were originally written to entertain during the interlude between acts.

In 1972, the city broadened the affair, creating the **Festival Internacional Cervantino** and inviting dance groups and musicians from all over the world. In 1993, a group from Russia appeared; the German opera *Moctezume* was staged here recently, its Mexico debut.

For more than 20 years, the festival has enjoyed nothing but success. The streets are filled with dancers, bards, and playlets. Musicians, including Guanajuato's *estudiantinas,* stroll the streets dressed in the clothes of the Renaissance—satin knee britches, velvet puffed sleeves, and flat velvet caps with plumes up top. The Cervantino Festival is held for two weeks each year in October. For the dates, call a Mexican Government Tourism Office, ask your travel agent, or write to Desmond O'Shaughnessy at the Guanajuato Tourism Office, Plaza de la Paz 14, Guanajuato, Gto., Mexico; tel. (473) 2-0086. Advance reservations are a must if you want to secure a room during the festival.

Muses gracefully stand guard on the rooftop of Teatro Juárez.

Callejoneadas
A favorite evening pastime all year-round is following the *estudiantinas* up and down the streets of Guanajuato. These young men are well-trained classical musicians with fabulous voices working out on classical guitars, 12-string mandolins, and huge bass fiddles. In between songs they entertain the crowds with hilarious stories; translator required for full appreciation of the punchlines. The *estudiantinas* tradition began among students in Spain, who, desperate for money, hired themselves out to stroll the streets and serenade lovely señoritas at the behest of their lovers or pay tribute to mothers on their special days.

The evening promenades these days are probably more for the benefit of tourists than for those being serenaded, but it's fun. As the musicians go up and down the lanes and alleys of the city, a small donkey follows behind, wearily stumbling beneath the night's wine supply. Originally carried in skins, the vino today is transported in boxes with spigots. Anyone who wants to join in is welcome, for but a small charge for the wine and the *boron,* a spouted ceramic wine carafe.

Some local travel agents have commercialized the tradition with package tours. All tourees meet in a given spot, then wander the passageways behind the musicians, trailing behind the donkey and guzzling wine always passing through the tiny **Callejón del Beso,** or "Alley of the Kiss." The legend is told of star-crossed lovers who once pined for each other from separate houses directly across from one another, finally daring to kiss from balconies so close together the osculatory maneuver proved a remarkably easy task. The sad ending of the story finds an angry father catching them in the act, killing his daughter in an inhuman rage.

Here in the 20th century it's considered good luck to buss your lover beneath the infamous balconies, at the narrowest spot on Callejón del Beso. On tours photographers catch these kisses on color film. You're presented the photo at the end of the walk; if it pleases you, it's available for about US$6. And who wouldn't like a reminder of a kiss in such a romantic spot under a star-filled sky?

The trip around town lasts about two hours. The package price includes two wine tickets, a carafe, a poster, seats in the San Roque bleachers, and the cover at one of the local discos. Check on prices at a travel agency office; they vary considerably.

Semana Santa

Holy Week, from Palm Sunday to Easter Sunday, is a popular holiday in Guanajuato. The most moving event is the portrayal of of the Passion of Christ. Reverent processions bearing Christ on the cross and the Virgin of Dolores peregrinate to the churches. Flowers and palm crosses are everywhere; traditional altars are set up in most homes and businesses.

SHOPPING

Guanajuato is a fabulous place to shop. Besides a large selection of sleek silver jewelry, you'll find tiny shops specializing in local art, paintings, sculpture, stylish accessories for the home, trendy clothes, and local candied fruits (the strawberries are delicious). Don't expect to find things particularly cheap, however. Artists here know the market and high quality almost inevitably means high prices as well.

Mercado Hidalgo

This turn-of-the-century building features a high ceiling, broad glass "walls," and a wrought-iron stairway that leads to the wraparound balcony; one story says the building was originally designed to house a train station. The design of the building has a distinctive French flair, and you'll find dozens of small stalls offering tin pans, baskets, embroidered dresses, pottery, *rebozos,* jewelry, huaraches, vegetables, fruit, and Bimbo bread.

Estudiantinas *sing and play away the nights as they stroll the city streets.*

OZ MALLAN

If you *are* going to find a bargain it will be in the balcony, a colorful *tianguis* where you can find just about anything. Located east of Juárez.

Artesanías Vázquez
This is a good place to check out excellent quality talavera. The shop is open 10 a.m.-9 p.m. Mon.-Sat., 10 a.m.-3 p.m. on Sun. Located at Cantaranos 8, tel. 2-5231. The factory is in the town of Dolores Hidalgo (about 50 km).

The Gorky González Workshop
This well-known talavera shop has been known for years because of its master craftsman, Gorky González, and its top quality pieces. The small showroom is open weekdays 9 a.m.-2 p.m. and 4-6 p.m. Well worth a visit, it's on Calle Pastita.

INFORMATION AND SERVICES

Tourist Information Office
Located across from the basilica on Juárez, the tourist office usually has at least one friendly staff member who speaks English. The address is Plaza de la Paz 14, tel. (473) 2-1574 or 2-0086. These folks are very helpful and willing to answer all questions. Ask for a free map of the city/state. Open on weekdays 8:30 a.m.-7:30 p.m., Sat. and Sun. 10 a.m.-2 p.m. Those arriving by bus will find tourist information at the bus station on weekdays 10:30 a.m.-7 p.m., Saturday 10:30 a.m.-2 p.m.

Moneychanging
Along Plaza de la Paz, banks change foreign currency weekdays 9 a.m.-1:30 p.m. Hotels always seem to give just a little less, and often don't have the pesos available. Some shops—though not all—will accept dollars and give the top exchange rate, change returned in pesos.

Photo Supplies
If you need film, or other photo problems pop up, check out the **Macro Foto** on Alonso 44, tel. (473) 2-5566.

Post Office
Located opposite the Templo de la Compañia next to the university. Open weekdays 8 a.m.-8 p.m., Sat. 8 a.m.-1 p.m. You'll find a substation at the new bus station on weekdays 9 a.m.-1 p.m. and 3-6 p.m.

Lavandería Automaticos Internacional
With two shops, you have a laundering choice. Figure on about five hours; they usually do a good job. Three kilos of clothes for about US$7. Located at Calle Alhóndiga 35-A, tel. (473) 2-4444; also at Manuel Doblado 28 (Plazuela Ropero), tel. 2-6718.

Medical Services
The **Specialists' Surgical Clinic,** located on Juárez, features a staff of 16 specialists, including several English-speaking doctors. A relatively new **Social Security Clinic (IMSS)** opened south of town; inquire at the tourist office.

SCHOOLS

University Of Guanajuato
Established in 1724 by Jesuit priests from Spain, the university had and still contributes a great deal to the "arts and letters" ambience of the city. The university itself is huge, standing out in the town like a child taller than the rest of the class. The architecture is unusual, and the university draws students from all over Guanajuato.

Spanish Language Classes
Foreign students can attend Spanish language classes at the University of Guanajuato for very reasonable fees; about US$20 for a 10-week session. Registration takes place four times a year. The university helps students find housing with local families for US$10-15 per day, depending on the number of meals and length of stay.

For more information, write University de Guanajuato, Dept. de Servicios al Estudiante, Lascurain de Retana 5, Guanajuato, 36000, Gto., Mexico, tel. (473) 2-2770, fax 2-0278.

Instituto Falcón
This is another language school offering a flexible program. Customized classes include supervised forays into the city for exposure to customs, traditions, and typical daily life. These immersion classes are personally designed and of varied length, from one to five hours daily.

Weekly registration available. the Instituto helps secure living arrangements, including meals. Average cost: US$15 daily. Write to Callejón de la Mora 158, CP 36000 Guanajuato, Gto., Mexico; or call (473) 2-3694.

American University Programs

The following American universities offer a good summer program through the University of Guanajuato: University of Chicago; Northwestern University; Purdue University; University of Illinois; University of Indiana; University of Iowa; University of Michigan; University of Minnesota; and University of Wisconsin.

GETTING THERE

By Air

There isn't a large airport in Guanajuato city, but a number of airlines fly into the Bajío Airport in León. Flights arrive from many parts of Mexico, as well as from such U.S. cities as Chicago and Los Angeles.

From the airport you must hire a taxi. If you have reservations, some of the nicer hotels in San Miguel de Allende will send a limo to pick you up; some charge extra for this service. It's a little more than a half-hour from Guanajuato to the airport in León.

By Train

The **Constitucionalista** departs Mexico City daily at 7 a.m. with stops in Querétaro, Irapuato, and Silao, arriving in Guanajuato at 1:25 p.m. It departs Guanajuato at 2:25 p.m., arriving in Mexico City at 8:57 p.m. This is not a first-class train, and no food is served on board.

The train station is located north of town at Calle Tepetapa; usually a taxi meets the train. If not, there are several hotels close by. For some reason, the train seems to take longer and cost more than bus services.

By Bus

The bus has always been the best way to get around in Mexico, and service has only improved with the addition of new luxury-class buses traveling between most of the cities in Mexico.

Try, for instance, the **ETN.** Prices are higher than for local buses—it's US$10 to Mexico City

on the local, for example, while ETN charges US$20—but many feel the high-tech vehicles with reserved airline-type seats, air-conditioning, and attendants who bring drinks and cookies to be worth the additional expense. ETN arrives frequently from Mexico City, Guadalajara, and Morelia. Look for other deluxe bus lines as well.

Local buses are always the cheapest way to go, and in the last few years many companies have improved their services. The **Flecha Amarillo** line travels hourly from Mexico City's **Terminal del Norte.** If possible take the express and save an hour. Otherwise plan on a six hour trip, with stops at San Juan del Río, Dolores Hidalgo, Querétaro, and San Miguel de Allende. Estrella Blanca runs four daily express buses to Guanajuato from 10 a.m.-6 p.m. daily, each requiring a five-hour journey. **Omnibus de México** runs buses to/from Guadalajara, San Miguel de Allende, and Querétaro.

Guanajuato's modern bus station is located on the southwest edge of town. To get to the town center from the bus station, board the city bus marked "Centro." Traveling to the bus station look for it on the north side of the basilica. Cost is about 25 cents. The station offers a tourist information desk, a post office, shops, a cafeteria, and a communication center where you can call or fax. There's a luggage storage center as well.

GETTING AROUND

If staying in downtown Guanajuato, the best way to get around is on foot. Wear good walking shoes with thick soles to protect you from the cobblestones. Be prepared to walk up and down steep hills. Walking Guanajuato is a daily exercise in physical fitness.

By Car

Driving your own car can also be a real pain. All that up and down, zigging and zagging, trying to figure out the snaking labyrinthine subterranean tunnels—seven of them—that run under the city. The tunnels are actually a tremendous improvement over the narrow city streets, but unless you're a geographical wizard and civil engineering savant, by the time you figure out which serpentine road to take to get you where you want to go, it's time to move on to the next city. Hint: when confused in the underground tunnels, look for signs reading "Teatro Juárez" and "Jardín Union" which will lead you to the center of town.

Traffic is heavy, streets frequently become dead-ends, and when you finally find your destination, parking can be nonexistent. So, choose your poison: stay downtown and walk; stay in a hotel out of town and rely on buses or taxis; or if driving, brave the unusual traffic pattern until you get it right. It can, I hear, be done.

Handicapped folks especially should consider the topography of Guanajuato city before choosing to come. Ask lots of questions; it's not an easy place to roll a wheelchair or manipulate crutches.

By Bus
Local buses run daily 5 a.m.-10 p.m. They're helpful for reaching sites on the outskirts of town. Check with the tourist office next to the basilica for current bus schedules.

SAN MIGUEL DE ALLENDE

Pronounced: san mee-GEL day Ah-YEN-day
Altitude: 2,000 meters
Population: 61,000
Area Code: (415)
Distance from Mexico City: 275 km

A mini-pickup drove slowly along the cobblestone street. A sizable group of people followed behind. The pickup carried a small casket in the back, guarded by six men, each with a hand placed lovingly on the simple wooden box. The women trailing behind pulled their *rebozos* tight around their faces, clutching lilies to their breasts, tear-stained eyes riveted to the small box. The cadence was slow and the strangers on the street removed their hats and were silent for an instant as they shared the mourners' sorrow.

Visitors to San Miguel de Allende are often confronted with scenes such as these. No matter that many foreigners live in this quaint city, life continues here pretty much as it has for the past several centuries. Chances have been few. True, transportation now moves on wheels instead of clopping hooves, milk comes in cartons, tortillas are made by machine, and high-tech generators quickly restore electricity during bad storms. None of this, however, has anything to do with the important traditions of this small city.

HISTORY

After the Spanish conquest, and the discovery of silver and gold in the central highlands of Mexico, mule trains were needed to carry the precious metals to Mexico City. These trains had to pass through territories controlled by the independent Chichimeca Indians, and frequent frays occurred between the Indians and the muleteers, with many deaths on both sides. The Spanish viceroy decided the area must be "evangelized" and a city constructed. A Franciscan friar named Fray Juan de San Miguel was commissioned for the task, and soon the beginnings of a mission he called San Miguel sprouted in the center of Chichimeca territory.

While the missionaries forced Catholicism upon the indigenous peoples, the village grew as a natural stopover for mule trains carrying freight to Mexico City. As haciendas prospered in the surrounding area, San Miguel became the local market center. At one point it was called San Miguel de los Chichimecas, then San Miguel el Grande, to differentiate it from the innumerable other villages called San Miguel. Here *hacendados* bought and sold cattle, equipment, machetes, harnesses, knives, spurs, stirrups, woven goods, blankets, cloaks, rugs, and woolen stuffs. Whatever was needed, San Miguel would provide. The frontier town grew

BOB RACE

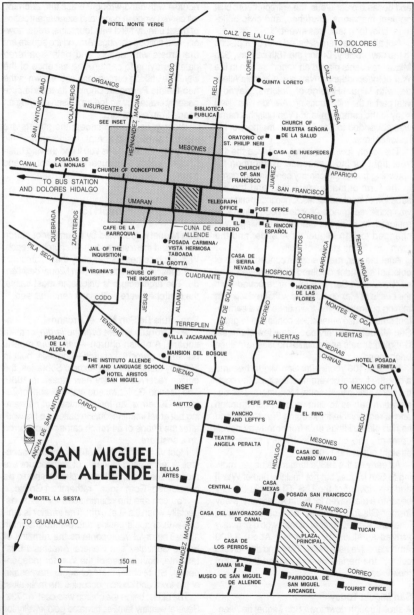

SAN MIGUEL DE ALLENDE

© MOON PUBLICATIONS, INC.

0   150 m

INSET

TO MEXICO CITY

and became prosperous; the entrepreneurs built opulent mansions, churches, and civic buildings. Life, for a few, was sweet.

Not all people were satisfied with their places in the new society. During the 18th century, San Miguel residents played an important role in the War of Independence. Native son Ignacio Allende, with Miguel Hidalgo of Dolores, played a vital part in the initial uprising. Allende was killed early in the campaign, and eventually his name was appended to San Miguel in memory of his historical role.

The lovely town just barely survived the 11-year fight for independence. Retribution for spawning one of the primary conspirators came in the form of mass executions and the destruction of local industries. Once independence was achieved Ignacio Allende's good name was restored. In 1826, the name of the village was changed to San Miguel de Allende, and the town rose to the status of a city.

After the war, many elegant concentrations of colonial splendor declined and decayed, and so it was with San Miguel. Far removed from the bustle of Mexico City, and with a reduction in mining operations, the town drifted in a somnolent state. While other cities continued to grow, San Miguel, now very poor, saw few changes. Cobbled streets and colonial houses remained unchanged.

In 1926, 100 years after San Miguel became a city, the federal government declared the community a Mexican National Monument. This declaration serves to limit modern construction and is responsible for keeping San Miguel and its rich old buildings safe from runaway development. The city still looks like something straight out of the 1700s.

As early as the 1930s foreigners began moving to San Miguel, but not until the end of WW II and the advent of the U.S. GI Bill did the city become a real haven for North Americans. Many former GIs found the schools of San Miguel ideal and a great number of men who'd originally arrived as students never left. About 3,000 Americans live here today. They find this "artist's colony" the perfect place to spend the rest of their lives.

San Miguel Today
A stroll through downtown San Miguel de Allende will take you past staid colonial buildings, houses with hand-wrought brass trim adorning tall carved wooden doors and extravagant patios of great beauty filled with fountains, trees, flowers, and antique carvings. Around the square are the artists with easels and paint-spattered palettes trying to capture the essence of the city. The striking centerpiece of the town is the neo-Gothic Parroquia Church, its facade supposedly crafted by an Indian artisan copying an image from a postcard.

Wear your walking shoes; the streets are steep, narrow, and abrupt. Inside aristocratic 300-year-old mansions you'll find thriving businesses, trendy boutiques, intimate hotels, and gourmet restaurants.

SIGHTS

San Miguel is protected by a number of patron saints, and there seems to be a church for each. With each comes a small story that contributes to the fascinating history of San Miguel de Allende. The architecture is unique; in most cases, the churches were built many centuries ago.

Parroquia De San Miguel Arcangel
The **Parroquia** towers over the *jardín,* or main square. A parish church—*parroquia* means parish, or parochial church—originally built in 1683 by architect Marco Antonio Sobrarias, the edifice received a fancy new facelift in 1880. The pseudo-Gothic facade was the work of Zeferino Gutierrez, an Indian artisan of no training but great imagination. He patterned his work after the image of a French cathedral captured on a postcard.

Most visitors find the results incredibly beautiful. A few trained students of architecture are more critical, sniping that the church should be considered "Gothesque," rather than Gothic.

You can see the church spire for miles, especially when it's lit at night. The interior is typical, with chapels beside and behind the main altar. The crypt vault contains the remains of Felipe Gonzalez and General Anastasio Bustamante, both heroes of the War for Independence. St. Michael the Archangel, namesake of the town and church, occupies the main altar.

The oldest bell in the church was cast in 1732. Several wealthy families donated gold jewelry for melting, adding other metal to enliven the sound.

hort Course

and Measurement

nce Symposium
o, California

A local once explained to me that each of the bells has a name: the largest bell is St. Michael, another is dubbed St. Peter, and the oldest and the sweetest is known as La Luz. Together they broadcast a unique melody. It's a nice sound. I hope you like it, because this town contains more than a hundred bells that start ringing early in the morning.

Chapel Of The Third Order

The Chapel of the Third Order was completed and dedicated in 1713 by the Franciscans. It's a church of great simplicity, almost primitive, with bare walls and simple doorways. Compared to nearby churches it's quite stark. Located in the small square of San Francisco, on the corner of Benito Juárez and Calle San Francisco.

Church Of San Francisco

The Church of San Francisco was contructed from 1779 to 1799, financed by local wealthy families and the proceeds from bullfights. Originally called the Church of Saint Anthony, until Anthony was deposed by Francis. The design is believed to be the work of Don Francisco Eduardo Tresguerras (1765-1833), who designed numerous churches throughout the highlands during the early 19th century. The church features the ultimate in churrigueresque design. The ceilings are notably high, and a lovely natural light filters through the high windows. The church is filled with many paintings from well known artists, interesting statues, classic Ionic and Corinthian columns, and doors and windows of carved stone.

Church Of Nuestra Señora De La Salud

The Church of Our Lady of Health, which faces the open-air market, is another bit of local history. The front door is covered with elaborate wrought-iron work; the dome is covered with yellow and blue tile; above the entrance is an enormous enveloping shell of beautiful carved stone. Just below the shell are life-size statues of the Virgin, St. Joachim, and St. Anne, each in carved niches. Flanking the entrance are St. John the Evangelist and the Sacred Heart. The dome is covered with yellow and blue tile.

This church was originally part of the **Colegio de San Francisco de Sales** next door. Here, Father Juan Benito Díaz de Gamarra taught Cartesian philosophy. This priest was well-ed-

San Miguel's Parroquia Church.

OZ MALLAN

ucated and possessed a very open mind for the era. He encouraged liberal thinking and organized public debates putting down the *scholastacism* of the period. Diaz de Gamarra instituted literary gatherings unusual for the time. His thoughts were assembled in a philosophy manual later used as a text by the University of Mexico. All the patriots of San Miguel who fought in the war of 1810 were graduates of the College of St. Francis de Sales.

Oratorio Of St. Philip Neri

The Indians of San Miguel built their own church soon after they were converted in the 17th century, calling it **Ecce Homo Chapel.** In 1712 a visiting priest, Don Juan from Pátzcuaro, fell in love with the town of San Miguel. Don Juan Antonio Pérez de Espinosa arranged a transfer to the town, and was given the authority to build a new church. He chose the site occupied by Ecce Homo, decreeing the old Indian church must come down. He managed to convince all the inhabitants of the town, except the Indians, who'd built the church with their labor and money. They didn't have a chance, of course, and through clever legal shenanigans the Indians were soon forced to give up their church. They were also ordered to build the new one. To this day the church retains a back entrance where the Indians were expected to exit and enter.

The Oratorio features many domes in myriad shapes. Some are tall and slender, others are broad, rounded, crenellated, and multilanterned. All are quite impressive. The Indian builders made use of remnants of their old church, including the pink stone of the eastern facade and the figure of Our Lady of Soledad. The Indian artisans of the highlands always managed to inject a certain mystique into their work; The feeling of the early Indians is very strong in this church.

The old leather altar screen brought over from Cordoba, Spain, features antiquated Renaissance detail embossed in gold. Thirty-three oil paintings offer vignettes of the 16th-century life of St. Philip Neri.

Chapel De La Casa De Loreto

From the Oratorio, you can enter, through a magnificent entrance with elaborate twisted columns at each side, the Chapel of the Holy House of Loreto. Manuel Canal and his wife, María de Hervas de Flores, founded and financed the construction of the chapel in 1735. Two niches contain statues in an attitude of prayer. These are said to represent the benefactors; below the niches lie their tombs. The gravestones bear the family coat-of-arms.

The chapel is supposed to be a replica of the famous Holy House in Loreto, Italy, which in turn is said to be a copy of the original home of Mary in Nazareth). The ornate chapel is covered with glazed tiles from China, Spain, and Mexico; gilded rosettes; plaster angels in relief; stars made of mirrors; and a fine golden cloth blanketing the walls. An archway inscription claims "This is the home in which the Son of God was conceived."

The chapel is usually closed, and you may have to ask to see it. In the octagonal-shaped *camarin* a reclining wax figure of St. Columbano is said to contain the saint's bones. If you study the floor tiles, you'll discern the coat of arms of the Canal family.

Church Of The Conception

Begun in 1755, this major building project was supported by funds from the Canals' daughter, as well as other wealthy villagers. The dome, however, one of the largest in Mexico, was not finished until 1891. The design is said to have been influenced by a picture of Les Invalides, and many suspect it is the work of Zeferino Gutierrez. Two stories high, it has Corinthian columns on the botton and pilasters above; there's also a marvelous gilded altarpiece. On Hernandez Macías.

Casa Del Mayorazgo De Canal

This mansion belonged to Manuel Tomas de la Canal and is often referred to as "the count's house," though Canal was never a count. It's a mansion in the true sense of the word: the original entry exhibits Corinthian columns, the family coat of arms, heraldic symbols of both husband and wife, and a niche holding an image of Our Lady of Loreto.

The grand old house is open for inspection Mon.-Fri. 9 a.m.-1:30 p.m. and 4-6 p.m., Sat.-Sun. 10 a.m.-5 p.m.; free. Check at the tourist office for information about occasional art exhibits; movies are shown here on Friday, Saturday, and Sunday. Located at Canal 4, above the arcade on the west side of the plaza.

Museo De San Miguel De Allende

This is Ignacio Allende's birthplace, another solid structure still showing neoclassic design, and now housing a historical museum. The museum displays the history of the area from the pre-Columbian era to the period of Independence. Ignacio Allende is a beloved Mexican hero and the town is proud he was born here. Local historians are quick to point out it was Allende who urged Hidalgo into the fight for Independence. One of the few trained military officers involved in the insurrection, Allende quickly became a leader and general, with only Hidalgo above him. Allende was captured and executed in 1811.

Located across from the Parroquia on Calle Cuna de Allende. Open Tues.-Sun. 10 a.m.-3:30 p.m., free.

Bellas Artes

This was originally the **Royal Convent of the Conception**; today it's operated by the government as a school. Officially called **El Centro Cultural el Nigromante,** it's the cultural heart of the city. The **Centro Cultural Ignacio Ramírez** operates from here; try to take in a dance or musical event. This big and impressive cloister at Hernández Macías 75 is a must-see, especially the lovely immense patio. Some notable paintings are inside, including work from the great muralist Siqueiros.

Jail Of The Inquisition

Located diagonally from the House of the Inquisitor, the Jail of the Inquisition is at Calle Hernández Macías and Calle Cuadrante. The corner contains a green stone cross with blue tiles around it. Now occupying the building is **El Centro de Crecimiento,** a center for handicapped children.

Casa De Los Perros

Literally translated, this means "House of the Dogs." Note the carved *perros* at the main balcony. Formerly the home of another hero of the Independence, Juan de Umarán, this lovely building is now home to the **Galería Mafuele.** At Umarán 4.

Old Home Tours

Departing from the **Biblioteca Pública** every Sunday promptly at 12:15 are home and garden tours of some of the city's lovely homes (for a fee). This is a great opportunity to see the insides of some of these ancient old buildings and observe how occupants have adapted old homes to modern lifestyles. Admission US$5.

ARTS

Those who count these things claim San Miguel has the highest ratio of art galleries per capita of any city in Mexico. No wonder it's often called the Montmartre of Mexico and compared to the art enclaves of Carmel, Key West, and Santa Fe. Art openings at galleries are one of the big attractions in the city, and occur frequently. **Galería San Miguel** is renowned for its contemporary art, and **Galería Atenea** is famed for national and international artists. The air of San Miguel is clear, attracting numerous *plein air* artists. Because art is such an important part of San Miguel, you can almost always find an art

exhibit or two; shows take place year-round. Check with **Bellas Artes** (Hernández Macías 75) and **Instituto Allende** (Ancha San Antonio 4), or obtain more information at the **Biblioteca Pública** (public library), a local hangout for American and Canadian expats. This is a great library with a large selection—14,000—of books in English. The patio is a pleasant place to sit and read; there's a bulletin board with daily info. Open Mon.-Sat. 10 a.m.-2 p.m. and 4-7 p.m.; located at Insurgentes 25, two blocks north of the Plaza Principal.

Besides the plastic arts, you'll find a concentration of musicians. Each year San Miguel sponsors a chamber music symposium. The **Ignacio Ramírez Center** offers classes in dance and music.

The Instituto Allende Art And Language School

Instituto Allende, one of the town's most popular art schools, is a beautiful old building with a rich legacy located on acres of land in the center of San Miguel. At one time it belonged to the Canal family; when purchased for the institute in 1949 much reconstruction was necessary to restore it to its original splendor. An image of the Madonna of Loreto, patroness of the Canal family, still stands in the main doorway niche. Remains of old frescoes still adhere to the walls of the chapel, while a native-style Christ occupies the altar. The campus features gardens, extensive classrooms, studios, two galleries, a theater, a library, a coffee shop, and many courtyards.

The institute offers classes ranging from three Master of Fine Arts programs to straightforward conversational Spanish courses. Art classes include multimedia sculpture, silverwork and jewelry, enameling, traditional Mexican weaving, textile design, printmaking, painting and drawing, and ceramics. The faculty is augmented by a roster of well-known visiting artists and scholars from throughout the world. It's also a campus abroad for the Rhode Island School of Design, School of the Art Institute of Chicago, Pennsylvania Academy of the Fine Arts, and Canada's Ontario College of Art.

For more information, call Mon.-Fri. 9 a.m.-noon and 3-6 p.m., tel. (415) 2-0190, or write to Instituto Allende, San Miguel de Allende, 37700, Gto., Mexico.

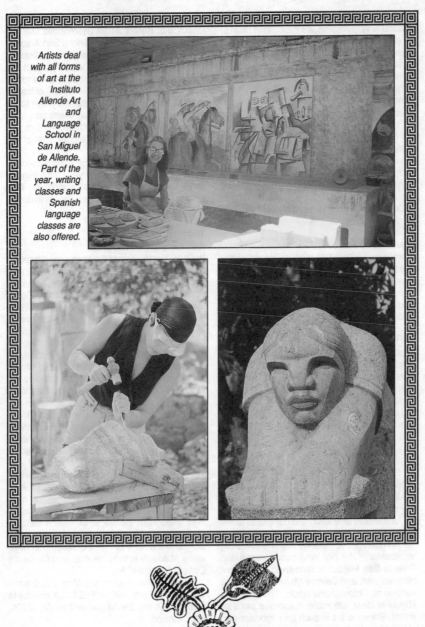

Artists deal with all forms of art at the Instituto Allende Art and Language School in San Miguel de Allende. Part of the year, writing classes and Spanish language classes are also offered.

ACCOMMODATIONS

San Miguel de Allende features a large selection of hotel rooms, though many fall in the luxury category. For the most part, they're all a better quality than other Mexico cities (as long as you're not looking for Cancún-style glitz. Old-timers complain that the prices have doubled in the last 10 years, and that the higher rates are probably due to the large concentration of American expats who live here. Whatever the reason, you'll find few dirt-cheap accommodations here.

Those coming to San Miguel should be aware that the city is hilly and steep. The more expensive hotels provide transport to and from town; when staying at the cheaper hostels you must walk or take a taxi. You'll soon learn just where the local buses go and where they don't, mostly the latter. As in most colonial cities, some of the most desirable hotels occupy antiquated buildings; hence, no elevators. Few San Miguel hotels are more than two stories tall, however. If coming during Mexico's busy seasons (e.g., Christmas, Easter, or the Cervantino Festival in nearby Guanajuato in mid-October), make reservations in advance.

Budget

Because so many people are looking for permanent lodgings, the budget hotels here have a nice feel to them. It's not unusual for people to stay for as long as six months, hence the accommodations have a more homey atmosphere and are very well cared for. Most places will give you a 10% discount if you stay a week or longer—ask. Dollars, pesos, and traveler's checks are okay; in most cases, no credit cards.

Casa de Huéspedes: This is about as cheap as it gets. With just seven units they often fill up fast, so get there early. About US$17. Mesones 7, tel. (415) 2-1378.

Other motels in a slightly higher range include **Central,** at Canal 19, tel. 2-3355; **Vista Hermosa Taboada,** at Allende 11, tel. 2-0078; and **Sautto,** at Hernández Macías 59, tel. 2-0051 or 2-0052. These hotels all charge roughly US$24-30 d.

Quinta Loreto: This is a very simple motel-type accommodation with pleasant rooms, a swimming pool, a tennis court, flowers and trees,

and a friendly efficient staff. Free parking. The restaurant offers good food at reasonable prices. Reserve well in advance, since lots of people have discovered the Quinta. Rates are US$24 s and US$29 d; add about US$10 per person for two meals daily. If you plan to stay a week or longer, ask about discounts. Located at Calle Loreto 15, tel. (415) 2-0042, fax (415) 2-3616. It's easiest to take a taxi to this hotel since it's not *really* on Calle Loreto. However, if you're on foot, walk from the *jardín* one block east on Correo and turn left on Juárez (at the post office) and continue for another two blocks until you come to Mesones, where you walk for three long curving blocks; you'll find the hotel just off Loreto.

Moderate

Posadas de la Monjas: This hotel occupies a renovated old monastery, offering 65 rooms. Rooms are comfortable and pleasant with hand-painted tiles and sunny views. The larger rooms have fireplaces. Rates are US$38-41 s; ask for small room rates. Laundry service is very reasonably priced here. Calle Canal 37, tel. (415) 2-0171.

Casa Carmen: This nice little pension has 11 rooms and is located in the heart of town. Rooms open onto a plant-filled patio and feature gas heat. The rates are reasonable for San Miguel and the food is quite good. For stays by the month the price is US$35 s and US$55 d, including breakfast and lunch. If you plan to stay less than a month, add 10%. Reserve in advance if coming during the busy seasons. On Calle Correo 31 across from the post office, tel./fax 2-0844.

Posada Carmina: At Cuna de Allende 7, tel. 2-0458, Posada Carmina offers guests a meal on the shaded patio by orange trees and umbrellas, or in the dining room which was once the old stables. Eleven rooms rent for US$40-50 s, no meals, and US$50-70 d, no meals.

Posada San Francisco: This 18th-century restored mansion is really quite lovely. Located on the *jardín,* it offers 19 rooms and 13 junior suites. Guests enjoy the pleasant courtyard, coffee shop, and convenient location on the plaza. Rates are US$40-44. At Plaza Principal 2, tel./fax 2-1466 or 2-2425.

Posada de la Aldea: This hotel across from the Instituto Allende features 66 large rooms and a pleasant atmosphere for US$40 s. On Ancha de San Antonio s/n, tel. 2-1022 or 2-1296.

El Patio: On Calle Correo 10, El Patio is pleasant, with a good location. Rates are US$83, tel. 2-1647, fax 2-3180.

Hotel Monteverde: This comfortable hotel lies about four blocks downhill from the center of town. Rooms are modern, with colonial decor, a central courtyard and a fine little restaurant. Although this hotel announces official rates of US$65, that's the charge only during Mexican holidays. The rest of the year rates run US$45 d, continental breakfast included. Long term rates are US$40 per night. Ask about senior citizen rates. The atmosphere is pleasant and sunny and the 32 rooms each feature two double beds. The fountain in the garden is said to be 400 years old. Parking available. Volanteros 2, tel. 2-1814. Credit cards accepted.

Hotel Aristos San Miguel: Next to the Instituto Allende, this hotel features large gardenlike grounds and has 65 large rooms, a swimming pool, and tennis courts. One of the nicest things about the place is its proximity to the Instituto Allende, where you can browse through the grounds, galleries, and workshops. Rates vary depending on time of year and class of room; from US$75 d to US$135 d. At Ancha de San Antonio 30, tel. 2-0392 or 2-2594, fax 2-1631.

Luxury

Casa de Sierra Nevada: This lovely hotel is a member of the prestigious **Small Grand Hotels of Mexico** and Europe's **Relais y Chateau.** The inn encompasses 18 suites in five ex-mansions, located on a cobblestone street near the cathedral and town square. Each beautifully furnished suite has its own personality and decor. Some have private terraces and many feature fireplaces. The warm atmosphere and attentive staff make this a world-class vacation. Guests will find safe deposit boxes, laundry service, room service, an in-house masseuse, a large heated pool, a spa, and one of the best restaurants in Mexico. Reservations suggested; pricey but worth it.

The hotel is owned by Swiss hotelier Peter Wirth, whose family owns the Hassler Hotel in Rome. It has been described as a perfect mix of Swiss efficiency and Mexican charm. If you like to rub shoulders with the rich and famous, this is the place to go—maybe you'll bump into such frequent guests as ex-president George Bush and his wife Barbara. Rates are currently US$120-220. For a brochure write to Hospicio 35, San Miguel Allende, 37700, Gto., Mexico; tel. (415) 2-0415, fax 2-2337, in the U.S. (800) 223-6510.

La Puertecita Boutique'otel: This is one of the newest and nicest small hotels in the city, located on the crest of a hill overlooking the town. The rooms are filled with a warm Mexican ambience, offering hand-painted sinks, woven bedspreads, and red tile floors. Services include 24-hour room service, a Jacuzzi, a spa, a heated pool, a billiard room, fireplaces, and in-house massages. No smoking. Great cuisine is available here, or a hotel van will take you down the hill to the restaurant of your choice.

The hotel also offers a unique program called Cruise Colonial Mexico. Like a cruise ship, you unpack once for the week; La Puertecita is the ship. Modern vans and English-speaking guides then take you to the most important colonial cities to shop and see the sights. Outside of one night spent in Morelia—a five-hour drive from San Miguel—each night you return to La Puertecita.

The hotel offers still another program, this for learning Spanish. Its sister guesthouse, **La Puertecita Centro,** is designed for those interested in longer stays.

Boutique'otel's prices, rooms only, run US$133-171; Centro prices start at US$70 daily or US$399 weekly. **Cruise** rates are US$998 per person, double occupancy, and include room at the Boutique'otel, breakfast, lunch, and all transportation. For more information call (800) 336-6776, or write to La Puertecita Boutique'otel, Santo Domingo 75, Col. Los Arcos, San Miguel de Allende, 37740, Gto., Mexico, tel. 2-2275, fax 2-0424.

Villa Jacaranda: This is another lovely upscale hotel, advertised as one of "Mexico's Romantic Hideaways." A few of the 15 spacious rooms and suites include private patios. The central patio contains a "Roman plunge" and solar-heated hot tub. Rates vary, from US$98 d to US$120 junior suite to US$135 suite; ask about special package rates. Credit cards are accepted. Open year-round. The hotel is known for its fabulous food and lovely dining spots, indoors and outdoors. Reservations are a must for dinner; the food is pricey but well worth the money. Address is Aldama 53, tel. (415) 2-1015 or 2-0811, fax (415) 2-0883, in the U.S. (800) 532-0294.

Hacienda de las Flores: A small and elegant hotel with a colonial personality, the Las Flores is conveniently located just two and a half blocks from the *jardín* and La Parroquia. At one time an old *quinta,* it now offers 11 rooms, a heated pool, and electric blankets. Rates are US$136, including two meals. Ask for prices without meals. Located at Calle Hospicio 16, tel. 2-1808.

Mansion del Bosque: Still a favorite with many visitors, the Bosque features gas-heated rooms, a pleasant atmosphere, and original art scattered about for US$130, including breakfast. At Aldama 65, tel. 2-0277.

Condo Hotels

Hotel Villas el Molino: Located on the old road to Querétaro above town, this hotel is quite nice with white stucco and red tile, a bubbling fountain and well-manicured grounds. Tile and wood are generously used in these nicely furnished apartments. Guests must negotiate a narrow spiral staircase to reach the rooms. No cooking facilities, but there's a restaurant on the premises and room service as well. It's a very steep walk into town, though the hotel offers free transportation. Prices range US$70-76; tel. (415) 2-1818.

Hotel Posada La Ermita: Theses condos are built into the side of a hill overlooking the city. It's named for the miniscule chapel of the same name next door. La Ermita was built by the late comedian and film star Cantinflas (Mario Moreno). A series of five terraces is connected by angled stairways. Each suite is roomy, with a sitting room, a private terrace, one bedroom, and a wonderful view of town. You'll have lots of steps to negotiate wherever you want to go. Amenities include a swimming pool, bar, and restaurant. Note the alcove off the large lobby containing Cantinflas memorabilia. Rates are about US$70 d. Rooms will handle up to five people. On Pedro Vargas 64, tel. 2-0777.

Spas

Hacienda Taboada: Central Mexico has an abundance of hot springs, resulting in many spas throughout the countryside. This is one of the nicest. The lovely white stucco and red tile rooms have balconies covered with bougainvillea blossoms or patios opening onto well-kept lawns and pools. The rooms are pleasant, though a little dark, with heavy colonial wooden furniture. Each bathroom includes a double-sized tub you can fill with natural spring water. On the grounds are colorful gardens, tennis courts, and several pools of differing temperatures—the water comes from the ground at 44° C (112° F). The water is rich in minerals and very soothing. Excellent food available as well.

The hotel will take you into San Miguel, 10 km away. For more information, write to 747 Third Ave., New York, New York, 10017-2847 USA, or call (800) 447-7462, (212) 223-2848, fax (212) 644-6840; in Mexico call (415) 2-0888, fax (415) 2-1798.

If you're really into unusual spas, contact the San Miguel tourist office and ask about **La Gruta** hot springs, located in a cave. It's rather a far out experience to soak in mineral water in the depths of the earth. Close to the village of Atotonilco. Another spa, **Parador del Cortijo,** lies nine km from San Miguel along the same road to Dolores Hidalgo. For more information call 2-1700.

Trailering

Motel La Siesta: On the Celaya Rd., about two km south of town, you'll find this trailer camp offering 62 spaces with full hookups. US$10 for two people, US$18-22 rates include breakfast; tel. 2-0207.

Lago Dorado: A pleasant trailer camp with full hookups, Lago Dorado has hot water, a swimming pool, and shady sites. Located six km from San Miguel's main plaza, near a golf course; pets welcome. Rates per night are US$10; when staying a month or more, prices drop to US$5 per night. No credit cards. Ask about long-term rates. Take the Celaya Rd. past hotel Villa de los Frailes and follow signs. For more information, contact Jacob van Dijk, Apdo. 523, San Miguel de Allende, 37700, Gto., Mexico, tel. 2-2301, fax 2-3686.

FOOD

Where you find American expats you'll find great restaurants. San Miguel's range from small coffee shops to elegant jacket-and-tie establishments. Most of the upscale restaurants specialize in international cuisine, presumably catering to the foreign community.

Budget Meals

Check out **La Princesa** at Recreo 5. For about US$6.50 you get a margarita, soup, entree with trimmings, dessert, and coffee. The surroundings are romantic, service is good, the music is live, and the food's quite tasty.

Virginia's, at Zacateros 26, is the place for breakfast. Good food at a good price—eggs, bacon, fruit or juice, and hot beverage for under US$3.

El Correo, across from the post office, is one block from the main square and serves the best soup in town. Good hearty traditional meals for US$5 and up. Open daily except Wed. 9 a.m.-9:30 p.m. at Correo 23, tel. (415) 2-0151.

Enjoy your morning coffee and paper at **Cafe de la Parroquia** at Jesús 11, open till 3 p.m. everday except Sunday, when it closes at 1 p.m. At the **Tucan,** San Francisco 2, ask for a "Cubana," a serious *torta* with lots of meats and all the fixings. Tucan serves hamburgers, too. Open daily 9 a.m.-10 p.m. **Mama Mia** fits into the budget category for breakfast only, and it's always fun to eat in the shady courtyard.

You can order a decent *comida corrida* for under $5 at: **El Mayorazgo,** Canal 19; **El Taco Tabla, H. Macías and Umarán; and** Mexicanos, Zacateros and Pila Seca.

For a great midday buffet at a good price (about US$5.75) try **La Mansión del Bosque** at Aldama 65. If it's too early for the buffet, they also serve a tasty inexpensive breakfast.

Check out the Italian menu at **Pepe Pizzas,** Hidalgo 26. They serve spaghetti, too. **La Grotta,** at Cuadrante 5, also makes a mean pizza and pasta.

Pricey Dining

Most of the really expensive restaurants are in the hotels. Dining at the **Villa Jacaranda** has been popular for years. There's a very pleasant atmosphere in all its eating areas, including a delightful glass-walled gazebo overlooking the park. Try the **Jacaranda** dining room, winner of *Travel/Holiday* Fine Dining Awards, and the newish **Salon Jacaranda,** a theater lounge offering stage shows, musicals, and dinner dancing. Most entrees are international with a few

good Mexican specialties thrown in. Service is outstanding. Reservations are a must for dinner. At Aldama 53, tel. (415) 2-1015.

Mama Mia is a casual Italian cafe set in a shady patio, serving good quality Italian specialties. They offer live music, sometimes South American, sometimes flamenco.

A typical five-course dinner at **Casa de Sierra Nevada** might consist of Atlantic shrimp with avocados and a tender vegetable salad; corn soup with fresh mintfoam; asparagus and tomato ragout in herb cream sauce; roast lamb chops with fresh herbs and homemade fettuccine; and a sinful surprise dessert. Price is US$32.50 pp. Pricey but worth it. Open for breakfast, lunch, and dinner. At Hospicio 35. For reservations call 2-0415, fax 2-2337. This is a jacket and tie establishment; the restaurant will furnish you with both.

Casa Mexas can be moderate all the way up to very expensive and caters to a lot of Americans and their favorites (hamburgers are so-so, but Tex-Mex is great!). At Canal 15. **El Campanerio,** Canal 34, offers a sedate ambience and classic menu in one of the loveliest patios in town. Green tablecloths pick up the green of the lush plants, all surrounded by old stone arches.

NIGHTLIFE

The discos in town don't really get going until 11 p.m.-midnight even though they open at 10 p.m. If the crowd is good the fun continues till about 4 a.m. Most discos charge a cover of US$5-10. Look for .**Pancho and Lefty's,** offering either American country music or disco. Then check out **El Ring** at Hidalgo 27, and **Laberintos** at Ancho de San Antonio 7, pulsing until about 4:30 a.m.

For a slower-paced evening, try **La Fragua** at Cuña de Allende, a combo dinner/music club. A nice place to eat; here in an old colonial house, Mexican music is king. At **Rincón Español,** Correo 29, dancers perform flamenco most nights.

Culturally, San Miguel has something interesting going on almost every night. Check out the **Bellas Artes** at Hernández Macías 75 for a list of activities that can include classical music concerts, poetry readings, and drama. A block away the **Teatro Angela Peralta** may be

screening to suit your mood. The tourist office can give you dates for the annual **Winter Music Festival** and the **Chamber Music Festival.** Art exhibitions are always fun here, with interesting people and often avant-garde renderings. And last but not least, the **Biblioteca Pública** has a great message board and *everything* visitors and expats are interested in will be there, plus you can pick up the English language paper *Atención* with all of its listings here at the library as well.

EVENTS AND FIESTAS

On 13 June, the Feast of San Antonio de Padua is celebrated throughout Mexico. In San Miguel, however, the festivities are a bit kinky. Saint Anthony is considered a cupid, many young petitioners demanded he deliver them spouses or sweethearts. In San Miguel these pleas take the form of men preposterously dressing as women, while the women whimsically dress themselves as their favorite characters or don duds designed to poke fun at politicians.

Another important day of celebration is 16 September, Mexican Independence Day. Shades of Pamplona, as the bulls run the streets; it's a total party time, with dancing, parades, fireworks, and flags.

The days before and after Christmas and Easter are filled with celebrations of a religious bent. Lots of fun and tradition. Make reservations well in advance.

International music festivals occur throughout the year. During the first two weeks of August the annual **Chamber Music Festival** is held at the Bellas Artes. Contact your local Mexican Government Tourism office, or the San Miguel Tourist Office, tel. (415) 2-1747.

SHOPPING

San Miguel is a shopper's paradise. Quality is high, and originality is unsurpassed. San Miguel has long been known for its metal work; look for tin, brass, bronze, copper, wrought iron, and the precious artwork of talented silversmiths. Excellent traditional art, weavings, pottery, paintings, and sculpture are available as well. And if you're looking for folk art and local crafts, you'll find terrific selections in any number of shops. Arts and crafts are not limited to Mexican art; look around and you'll see art from all over Latin America. Remember to visit the Instituto Allende for some imaginative original art for sale from the artist. As a rule of thumb, shops open around 9 a.m., close for lunch 2-4 p.m., and open again until 7 p.m., Mon.-Saturday. A few open on Sunday for a brief time. Many accept credit cards; however, not many will accept American Express. Most will take dollars and you usually get a good exchange rate with a purchase. Some shops will pack and ship to the U.S. or Canada.

A good place to start is the **Mercado de Artesanías** located in a little alleyway between Colegio and Calle Loreto not too far from the Quinta Loreto Hotel. **Joyería David,** Zacateros 53, produces extraordinary silver art. **Casa Cohen,** Reloj 18, lives up to its reputation for cast brass and bronze as well as stone carvings. **Izquinapán,** at Hidalgo 15, creates handwoven linens as soft as silk. Notice the Huichol masks. **Casa Maxwell** offers folk art from all over Mexico and Latin America. At Canal 14.

Casa Anguiano, Canal 28, has been around for some time, offering unique embroidered fabrics as well as copper and ceramic art. **Casa Armida,** next to the Instituto Allende on Ancha de San Antonio 26, is fun to browse, with goods including antiques, furniture, and local crafts.

INFORMATION AND SERVICES

Tourist Information Office

If you spot the **La Terraza** you've found the tourist office, left of the Parroquia. Usually someone in the office speaks English and will distribute literature and maps. Open Mon.-Fri. 10 a.m.-2:30 p.m. and 5-7 p.m., Sat. 10 a.m.-6 p.m., Sun. 10 a.m.-noon, tel. (415) 2-1747.

Moneychanging

For the best deal, try banks on Calle San Francisco and the Plaza Principal. These banks exchange currency 9 a.m.-1:30 p.m., Mon.-Friday. If you need an after-hours or weekend exchange, go to **Casa Cambio Mavaq,** open daily 9 a.m.-7 p.m. It closes on Sun. at 3 p.m. Located on the corner of Hidalgo and Mesones one block north of the *jardín.*

You can also take your business to **Lloyd's Casa de Cambio,** located in the lobby of the **Pośada San Francisco,** open Mon.-Fri. 9 a.m.-3 p.m.; or try the hotel restaurant, open daily 7 a.m.-10:30 p.m.

Post Office
The post office is open Mon.-Fri. 8 a.m.-7 p.m., Sat. 9 a.m.-1 p.m. Located on Correo 14 one block east of the Plaza Principal, next to the **SCT** national telegraph office. At the telegraph office you'll find a coin telephone booth and fax service. Open Mon.-Fri. 9 a.m.-1 p.m., and 3-6 p.m., Sat. 9 a.m.-noon.

Communication
There's a long-distance telephone office at the bus station, open 7 a.m.-11 p.m. You can also make long-distance calls anywhere you see the signs reading Larga Distancia.

If you plan on remaining in San Miguel for a while and expect to receive mail, faxes, or telephone messages there are several places that will accept them for you. If you wish to leave a message for a friend passing through you can use the message boards scattered about town. The **Biblioteca Pública** offers a particularly impressive message board. **La Conexión** accepts long distance telephone and fax messages, and receives mail. The place also features computer services, sells batteries and film, processes film, repairs cameras, and is a great place to have a cup of coffee. At Aldama 1, tel./fax, (415) 2-2312/2-1687. Open Mon.-Fri. 8 a.m.-8 p.m., Sat. 8 a.m.-3 p.m.

Newspapers And Books
El Colibri bookstore offers magazines and books in English, Spanish, French, and German. Open Mon.-Sat. 10 a.m.-2 p.m., and 4-7 p.m. Also check at the **Biblioteca Pública;** you'll find a used-book store with a good selection of English-language books at bargain prices. *Atención,* the English-language paper published each Friday, keeps readers informed of events.

Laundromats
It's easy to get your laundry done in San Miguel, usually in one day. Charges are about US$4-5 for a full basket, washed and folded; it's not much less if you do it yourself. **ATL Lavandería Automatica** in Pasaje Allende Mall, Mesones 5, and **Lavamagico,** at Pila Seca 5, are both open Mon.-Sat. 8 a.m.-2 p.m. and 4-7 p.m.

Consulates
You'll find the **American Consul** at Local 6, in the Plaza Colonial, on the corner of Canal and Hernández Macías. Open Mon. and Wed. 9 a.m.-1 p.m., 4-7 p.m. and Tues. and Thurs. 4-7 p.m. The emergency telephone is staffed 24 hours; call (415) 2-0068 or 2-0980. For non-emergencies call 2-2357.

Church Services
You'll find a Catholic mass in English at 11 a.m. on Sunday in a small chapel called **Church of Our Lady of Health** facing the open market. An **Episcopalian** service in English is available at Saint Paul's Church, Calz. del Cardo.

SCHOOLS

These language schools are designed for English-speaking students and offer varied approaches—from casual short conversational classes to intense immersion. For fees contact: **Instituto Allende,** Ancha S. Antonio 20, tel. (415) 2-0190; **Academia Hispano-Americana,** Mesones 4, tel. 2-0349, fax 2-2333; **Inter-Idiomas,** Mesones 15, tel. 2-2177; **Centro Mexicana de Lengua y Culture de San Miguel,** Hernández Macías 114 Altos; and **La Luna,** Cuadrante 2, tel. 2-2312.

Centro Cultural El Nigromante/Bellas Artes, also called the **Centro Cultural Ignacio Ramírez,** at Hernández Macías 75, tel. 2-0289, offers art and music classes.

San Miguel Photography Workshops occur in a zealous little school summer and winter; tel. 2-1846.

Ask around, by this time there may be more, given the way the town is attracting those interested in the arts. Not all of these schools are open year-round, some offer workshops for a comparatively short time. For more information contact the **Biblioteca Pública** at Insurgentes 325. Ask them about the **Central Internacional San Miguel** writing center.

children of San Miguel

OZ MALLAN

GETTING THERE AND AWAY

By Air
The nearest airport is in León; bus or taxi transportation is available to and from the airport.

By Bus
The other alternative is to travel by bus from Mexico City. The bus station is on Calle Canal, west of San Miguel; it's best to take a taxi to the station. **Flecha Amarilla** offers frequent trips to and from Mexico City each day. **Tres Estrellas de Oro** travels via Querétaro once daily to and from Mexico City. **Omnibus de Mexico** runs two buses daily to and from Mexico City. Buses run frequently to and from Guanajuato, Atotonilco, and Querétaro.

By Train
There is no longer a train direct from Mexico City to San Miguel de Allende. The **Constitucionalista** departs at 7 a.m. Mexico City-Querétaro; from there bus to San Miguel de Allende.

By Car
From Mexico City figure a three-to-four-hour drive whether you go via Querétaro (Hwy. 57) or Celaya (Hwy. 45).

ATOTONILCO

About 15 km north of San Miguel lies the village of Atotonilco. It's of historical interest because Father Miguel Hidalgo marched through here early in his revolt, grabbed the banner of Our Lady of Guadalupe, and carried it next to his heart as he made his famous *grito*.

So what else lures tourists to this dusty little village, where little boys and girls still tend their herds of goats? Some come for the *balnearios* (water resorts) at the bubbling hot mineral springs scattered about the highlands, some very close to Atotonilco. The small village is also known throughout Mexico as the destination for many a religious pilgrimage.

Sanctuario De Atotonilco

Many people come to Atotonilco to see this lovely church with its fine display of art by the indigenous peoples. The building was founded as a sanctuary and place of spiritual retreat by Father Luis Felipe Neri de Alfaro. Begun in 1740, the main portion was completed eight years later; additions continued over the years. You'll find chapels and courtyards; small rooms decorated with murals, canvasses, and sculptures; vaults, domes, and dome lanterns. More than in most churches, you will see good examples of authentic Mexican folk painting; the walls are alive with color and fantasy.

The church was also the site of the marriage between national hero, Ignacio Allende and María de la Luz Agustina, widow of Don Benito Manuel de Aldama.

Religious "Exercises"

The curious traveler might want to check out the activity at the sanctuary, where the beautiful architecture and sculpture almost seem lost when confronted by people milling about the church wearing crowns of thorns and and flagellating themselves with seven-tailed whips (called *disciplinas*). The Vatican outlawed this kind of thing many years ago, but it's still alive and thriving in parts of Mexico.

And it's big business. As many as 3,000 people a year stay here in small stone cells, sleeping on the floor. Businesses throughout the country operate like travel agents, organizing pilgrimages to Atotonilco, where people come to meditate, pray, and practice their "exercises," in the privacy of their cells. Vendors in front of the church sell crowns of mesquite thorns and multitailed whips of varying sizes.

On certain holidays, the dusty roads near the church are filled with penitents dressed in their best clothes, bringing arts, crafts, produce, or a hen or two to sell. The devout file into the church wearing crowns of thorns. Cannons ring out during the night to frighten the bad spirits, while women and men (during separate weeks) slip behind the walls of their private retreat. These retreats go on year-round.

Here at the Sanctuario of Atotonilco, Hidalgo stopped, prayed, and seized the Our Lady of Guadalupe banner, which became the flag of independence.

OZ MALLAN

DOLORES HIDALGO

Dolores Hidalgo is a pleasant, slow-moving little town. This sunny village, once called Dolores, is where the first cries for Mexican Independence were heard. The federal government has officially deemed Dolores Hidalgo the "Cradle of Independence." As such it's a popular destination for Mexicans interested in their country's history. There's little to attract most foreign tourists. It lies on the road between San Miguel de Allende and Guanajuato in the central part of the state, about 40 km from San Miguel, and about 50 km from Guanajuato. For most people a few hours is plenty of time to stroll through town. However, those who wish to can find fairly nice rooms. Visit the museums, the church, maybe have lunch, and investigate the ice-cream cone salesman on the plaza (you must try some of the unusual flavors that really taste quite good, such as corn, chiles, avocado,

chicharrón, cheese, and some unusual tropical fruits!).

Early Spanish History

Until 1570, the village of Dolores was just an Otomi hamlet called Cocomacán. Viceroy Enrique de Almanza then declared the town the Congregation of Our Lady of Sorrows. This no doubt became the viceroy's *encomienda,* as was the custom at the time. In 1710 a church was built and a parish priest called in.

Hidalgo Arrives

In 1804, Father Miguel Hidalgo y Costilla, punished for not conforming to the rules of the Inquisition, was shipped to the tiny village church of Dolores. He was genuinely interested in the well-being of his impoverished parishioners—in turn they held him in great esteem. Hidalgo

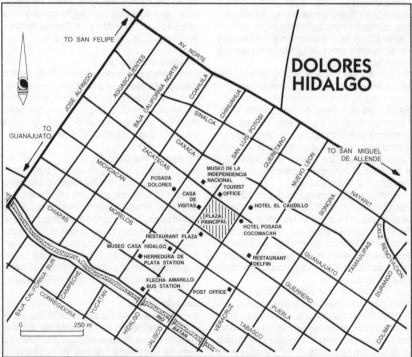

founded a pottery and tile shop in an effort to help the people economically. The pottery industry thrived, and the town today is still a popular ceramic and tile center.

Hidalgo also began other industries, including silkworm farming and the raising of grapevines. The latter was forbidden by the Spaniards, who feared it would jeopardize wine importation from Spain. He also encouraged the beginning of a band; he loved to dance, they say.

Grito De Dolores

After months of secretly plotting to peacefully take over the Spanish government, Hidalgo was awakened by a frantic accomplice who arrived on horseback in the middle of the night to announce the plot had been discovered. So in the hours before dawn on the morning of 16 September 1810, Hidalgo sounded the bells, bringing the townspeople to the church steps. The only part of his speech clearly remembered by most is his incendiary Grito de Dolores ("Cry of Dolores") a cry calling for the people to revolt against their Spanish oppressors. It's still a stirring moment when, before midnight every 15 September, in every town and city in the country, Hidalgo's cry is repeated by Mexico's president, governors, and city officials.

Criollos, mestizos, and Indians were inspired by the hometown padre and took up whatever arms were at their disposal—shovels, clubs, rocks. This was the beginning of what would become a bloody 11-year war. The agitating conditions were undeniable—the mestizos were without hope, the criollos envied the power of the *peninsulares*, and the Indians were slaves. The royalists could no longer be tolerated; the breaking point had been reached.

Hidalgo was excommunicated on 13 October 1810. But in the time he had left, he did what he thought was right. Over 50 years before the U.S. abolished slavery, Father Hidalgo demanded the Mexican government do away with this barbarous practice. The people had found a leader with a heart, one willing to sacrifice his life for their cause.

In less than a year Father Hidalgo and his three leading *compañeros* were executed, their heads hung on a Guanajuato granary as a warning to other wayward thinkers wanting freedom. But this only provoked the people to fight harder against the Spaniards. The Spaniards even-

tually gave up and returned to their Iberian homeland in 1825.

SIGHTS

Plaza Principal

The centerpiece of the shady plaza is a large statue of Miguel Hidalgo. There's also a tree which legend says is a sapling from the Tree of the Noche Triste, the tree under which Cortés wept after his army was forced out of Tenochtitlán by the Aztecs.

Shade trees provide a pleasant respite from the duties of the day. Don't forget to check out the ice-cream man, who always has a huge selection of unusual flavors in containers packed in sawdust and gunnysacks—ever had avocado ice cream? Here's your chance.

Artesanías Vázquez Factory

Here, you can watch the craftsman creating talavera art. It's fascinating to watch the procedure, from wrestling the clay to forming on a wheel to painting to firing. In Dolores Hidalgo at Puebla 56, tel./fax (418) 2-0630.

Museo Casa Hidalgo

Father Hidalgo's simple home of 1804-1810 displays his documents, furniture, eyeglasses, saddle, and the flag he used the night he urged his fellow citizens to take up arms and fight. Historical paintings that belonged to or depict the criollo priest are on display as well.

Church Of The Grito

The *parroquia* is a lovely church built 1712-1778. Its official name is **Parroquia de Nuestra Señora de Dolores.** With pink twin towers and an intricate facade, it's easily the largest building on the plaza. The bell used the night of 15 September to summon the townsfolk is kept in the National Palace of Mexico, but here in the *parroquia* a replica of the bell hangs in the belfry. The church interior contains remnants of lovely baroque art and unusual paintings. Open daily.

Casa De Visitas

It is not unusual for the president of Mexico to visit Dolores Hidalgo on 15 September to issue the *grito* where Hidalgo once stood. When he does, he stays in the Casa de Visitas, formerly

OZ MALLAN

In the plaza, barrels of ice cream are kept frozen in burlap and wood chips.

the home of Don Nicolás Fernández del Rincon and Don Ignacio Díaz de la Cortina. These two gentlemen ran the town at the time of the uprising and became the first prisoners of the fight for independence.

Museo De La Independencia Nacional

This museum chronicles the horrific events that led to the War of Independence. You'll see graphically illustrated the shocking behavior of the Spaniards, who destroyed the lives of millions of Indians. The atrocious details of their lives as Spanish slaves are really driven home. Open Mon.-Fri. 9 a.m.-2 p.m. and 4-7 p.m., Sat.-Sun. 9 a.m.-3 p.m. Small admission fee.

ACCOMMODATIONS AND FOOD

There are several simple clean accommodations and good restaurants around town. Unless you choose to visit during the Independence fiestas, you should be able to easily secure a decent meal and a fine place to stay.

Hotels

Try **Hotel El Caudillo,** US$19 d, on Querétaro 8, tel. (418) 2-0198. Restaurant on the premises, across from the church. **Hotel Posada Cocomacán,** US$18 d, on the east side of the plaza at Querétaro and Guanajuato, tel. (418) 2-0018. **Posada Dolores** is the cheapest of the three, US$9 with shared bath, US$11 with private bath. A block west of the plaza, Yucatán 8, tel. (418) 2-0642.

Food

Look around the plaza and you'll find many small snack shops, plus the **Restaurant El Delfín,** serving seafood. The **Restaurant Plaza** is good for breakfast, while **Aladino's** offers a nice steak dinner. All are within walking distance of the plaza.

INFORMATION AND SERVICES

The **Tourist Office** lies on the north side of the plaza, in the municipal building next to the church. Friendly staff will answer questions and dispense a city map. Open Mon.-Fri. 9 a.m.-3 p.m. and 5:30-8 p.m., Sat.-Sun. 9 a.m.-3 p.m.

The **Bancomer** exchanges money and traveler's checks Mon.-Fri. 9:30 a.m.-1:30 p.m.; it's located at the northwest corner of the plaza.

The **Post Office** occupies the corner of Veracruz at Puebla 22, open Mon.-Fri. 8 a.m.-7 p.m., Sat. 8 a.m.-noon.

On the south side of the plaza you'll find a **long-distance telephone** in the **Hotel Posada Las Campanas** located at Guerrero 15; open 24 hours. Other telephones are located at the bus stations.

GETTING THERE

The **Flecha Amarillo** bus station is located on Calle Hidalgo, 2.5 blocks from the plaza, and the **Herradura de Plata** station will be found on the corner of Chiapas and Chihuahua. Buses travel from both stations to many nearby towns and to Mexico City.

K. A. ESCOVEDO SANDERS

THE STATE OF QUERETARO
INTRODUCTION

The machinations of Querétaro's historic players are quite provocative. Locals love to relate the story of collusion involving a woman (Doña Josefa Ortíz) and her whispered warnings through a keyhole, patriots who secretly plotted at candlelit meetings, a militant priest and his *grito* (shout) for independence, and the movers and shakers of a small city, who in the end played a big part in the independence of Mexico.

Driving north from Mexico City for two and a half hours will bring you to Querétaro State (about 200 kilometers), near the geographical center of the country. Querétaro is bordered in the north by San Luis Potosí, in the south by Mexico State and Michoacán, in the east by Hidalgo, and in the west by Guanajuato. It is a mountainous state, with the Cerro El Gallo (3,350 meters, 10,990 feet) being the highest. This mainly agricultural area has fruitful farms and plentiful livestock, both playing an important part in the economy. The state lies in a hilly region rich in minerals, especially opals, amethysts, topaz, and silver. If you collect these fine gems, check out the local jewelry stores. The better stores can offer excellent buys on high quality gems; however, you should know your stones and *don't* be tempted by sidewalk specialists!

It's no secret that Mexico City is about to explode with its continuous influx of people. The federal government has been looking for ways to alleviate the problem and at the same time find a way to encourage the economical growth of other cities in the country. Querétaro is the doorway to a corridor that stretches for 385 kilometers across the Bajío. The population of the state currently stands close to 900,000. The state realizes the importance of developing industry and services in the countryside. One such suburb, Sanfandila, is a modern urban experiment that seems to be clicking. Several industries are in place, along with public housing, schools, and small shopping.

Other important industries in the state include manufacturing a variety of items for export, especially auto parts. This flourishing industry along with increased tourism has helped the economy to expand. The capital city gives off the aura of a comfortable living standard. As always, though, it's the Indian populations in the rural, mostly undeveloped regions that are the last to feel the benefits of increased income to the cities.

As the first stop on the new development corridor running northwest across the Bajío to León, there were only a handful of companies in Querétaro in the 1950s. Now there are 1,500 plants producing automobile parts, heavy and light machinery, and food products. Growth can be controlled if there is the willpower and interest. Otherwise Querétaro will become another Mexico City.

HISTORY

Before Independence

It is believed that about 1,000 years ago, the Otomi Indians were the first to occupy Querétaro. After them, the Purépechas came along (the name "Querétaro" is from the Purépechas

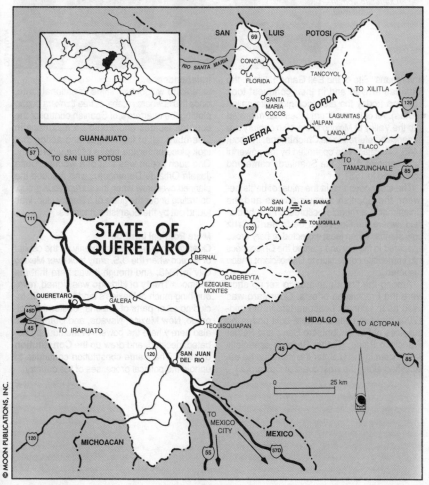

Querétaro woman
and child.

OZ MALLAN

and means "Site of the Ball Game"). Later, the **Mexicas** arrived and in their conquest took **Tlachco** (today the archaeological site called **Ranas**). All of the northern tribes that migrated into the Valley of Mexico in the 10th century are generically referred to as **Chichimecs.** In about 1445, Querétaro was controlled by the powerful Aztec empire. Next, the Spaniards came and conquered in 1531.

The story goes that in the midst of battle between the Spanish conquistadores and the Chichimecs, a miracle occured on the battlefield, where the **Convento de la Santa Cruz** now stands. When least expected, a fiery cross appeared in the sky and startled the Chichimecs into immediate conversion to Catholicism; peace resumed.

Among the first Spaniards to set up shop were the Franciscan priests. Querétaro was used as missionary headquarters in the mid-1700s and five missions were built under the auspices of Father Junípero Serra and Father Francisco Palou. (Father Serra is especially well known in the U.S. for the missions he established along the west coast of California.)

Independence

Querétaro will forever shine in national fame, since this is where a cabal of free thinkers began plotting the overthrow of Spanish control of the country. Guides and would-be historians in Querétaro tell of the intrigue and action that took place under the noses of the viceroyalty. One such action was that of a woman, Doña Josefa Ortíz de Domínguez, who rescued the planned overthrow when the surreptitious group, operating under the guise of a literary club, was found out by the Spanish authorities.

More Political Intrigue

Querétaro city served temporarily as the capital of Mexico when the U.S. army took over Mexico City in 1848. And though it was here that the infamous **Treaty of Hidalgo** was signed, relinquishing much of Mexico's land to the U.S., including all or parts of Arizona, California, Colorado, New Mexico, Nevada, and Utah, it was also here where the powers of the country debated, decided, and drew up the **Constitution of 1917.** That same constitution continues to uphold the political processes of the country.

QUERETARO (CITY)

Pronounced: keh-REH-tah-ro
Altitude: 1,500 meters
Population: 700,000
Area Code: (42)
Distance from Mexico City: 222 km

Querétaro is a city of well-ordered plazas, flower-filled gardens, ornate structures with tall carved wooden doors, uniquely etched columns, and whimsical touches of art in unexpected corners of every building. But more than that, this is a city of powerful history and fervent religious beliefs; everywhere you look you will find both historic monuments and impressive churches. If you like to hear stories, be sure to find a guide. Querétaro inspires wonderful stories. The legends told may not be accurate, but they probably have a grain of truth.

The climate is similar to Guadalajara, with the average high 27° C (81°F), and the average low at 14° C (57°F); winter nights can be chilly.

Querétaro is yet another city where people-watching is one of the best entertainments. As the shadows lengthen on the **Plaza de la Independencia** (or any one of the other fine plazas), entire families come out to enjoy the air, lovers stroll, and a light breeze carries the spray from the fountain past boys exhibiting their skateboard expertise.

One cannot help but admire the beautiful architecture and well-designed hearts of antiquated colonial cities. For more than 400 years central districts have been the gathering spots for the community. Modern technology thrives on the edge of the city. In the heart of the Querétaro (where cars are not permitted) is a place of quiet tranquility where you have a chance to get to know the people, the history, and traditions of the old city.

The Lay Of The Land

As with most colonial cities in Central Mexico, the easiest way to get around town is on foot. City fathers closed off vehicular traffic some time ago, which makes the town center an even more attractive place to explore. Most historical buildings, squares, and plazas cover a fairly close area. The *real* hub of the city is **Jardín Obregón** (also known as Plaza Principal), which is bordered by Juárez and Corregidora going north and south, and Madero and 16 de Septiembre going east and west. These streets are lined with beautiful antiquated structures, churches, museums, shops, hotels, and cafes. **Plaza de Armas,** called by most **Plaza de la Independencia,** is a small but beautiful plaza with elegant buildings, fountains, and walking-only streets that take you to other plazas and lovely old mansions. From here you can get to most any place you want. The greenest park is the **Alameda Hidalgo** with tall shade trees inviting all for a cool respite. **Jardín Corregidora** is another small park that remembers Josefa Ortíz with a statue of the celebrated woman.

SIGHTS

The Avenida Manuela Ancuna offers a taste of the past. It's a small market spread out on white sheets like dollops of paint on a palette, with vendors displaying royal limes, pomegranates, roasted peanuts, yellow guavas, black avocados, tomatillos, and already cubed bits of jicama spiked with chili and *limón.*

Aqueduct

One of the first sights you'll notice when you enter the city is the Aqueduct. In the early 1700s, this was probably the most grandiose city project. Water had become a major issue to the survival of the inhabitants until Don Juan Antonio de Urrutia, the then Marquesa de la Villa del Villar del Aguila, came up with an idea. At first it was considered "Don Juan's Folly," but the gentleman had great foresight and determination. Though encountering many delays and much scoffing, Don Urrutia continued (and paid for) the project until it was completed.

The giant manmade river (begun in 1726, finished in 1738) extends for eight kilometers. It has 74 arches, some that are 22.75 meters high, with a 15 meter span between each arch—it is

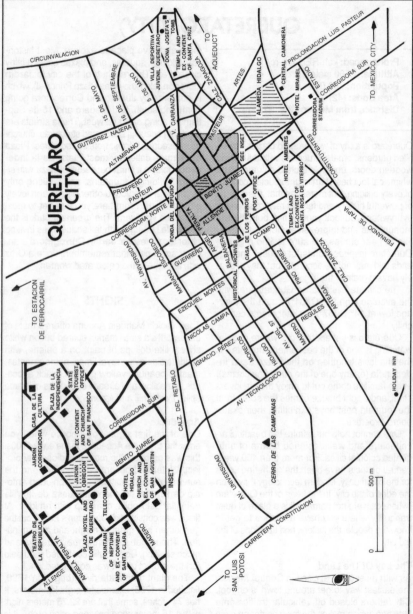

QUERETARO (CITY)

CIRCUNVALACION

TO AQUEDUCT

TO MEXICO CITY

DOÑA JOSEFA'S
VILLA DEPORTIVA JUVENIL QUERETARO
TEMPLE AND TOMB
EX-CONVENT OF SANTA CRUZ
CALZ. ZARAGOZA
ARTES
CENTRAL CAMIONERA
ESTADIO CORREGIDORA STADIUM
PROLONGACION LUIS PASTEUR
CORREGIDORA SUR
HOTEL MIRABEL

15 DE MAYO
5 DE MAYO
16 DE SEPTIEMBRE
PASTEUR
V. CARRANZA
GUTIERREZ NAJERA
ALTAMIRANO
PROSPERO C. VEGA
PASTEUR

SEE INSET
HOTEL AMBERES
CONSTITUYENTES

BENITO JUAREZ
ALLENDE
POST OFFICE
ANGELA PERALTA
FONDA DEL REFUGIO
TEMPLE AND EX-CONVENT OF SANTA ROSA DE VITERBO

CORREGIDORA NORTE
AV. UNIVERSIDAD
MARIANO ESCOBEDO
GUERRERO
EZEQUIEL MONTES
NICOLAS CAMPA
IGNACIO PEREZ
ANGELA PERALTA
BALBANERA
HISTORICAL ARCHIVES
CASA DE LOS PERROS
OCAMPO
PINO SUAREZ
CALZ. ZARAGOZA
ARTEAGA
REGULES
MADERO
MORELOS
HIDALGO
AV. DEL 57
FERNANDO DE TAPIA

TO ESTACION DE FERROCARRIL

CALZ. DEL RETABLO

AV. TECNOLOGICO

HOLIDAY INN

AV. UNIVERSIDAD
CERRO DE LAS CAMPANAS
AV. TECNOLOGICO

CARRETERA CONSTITUCION

TO SAN LUIS POTOSI

500 m
0

INSET

PLAZA DE LA INDEPENDENCIA
STATE TOURIST OFFICE
CASA DE LA CULTURA
JARDIN CORREGIDORA
EX-CONVENT AND CHURCH OF SAN FRANCISCO
CORREGIDORA SUR
JARDIN OBREGON
BENITO JUAREZ
HOTEL HIDALGO
CHURCH AND EX-CONVENT OF SAN AGUSTIN
TEATRO DE LA REPUBLICA
TELECOMM
PLAZA HOTEL AND FLOR DE QUERETARO
FOUNTAIN OF NEPTUNE AND EX-CONVENT OF SANTA CLARA
MADERO
ANGELA PERALTA
ALLENDE

© MOON PUBLICATIONS, INC.

touted as the seventh largest aqueduct of its style in the world. The tubes that carried the water were *majolica,* a quality glazed ceramic that originated in Europe. The aqueduct begins at the small village of La Cañada where the water was obtained from copious underground springs. Today it continues to stand securely and placidly—right in the center of 20th century traffic and telephone poles, a graceful reminder of the past.

There were skeptics who were so convinced that the aqueduct would never be finished that they offered to build a fountain of silver to receive the water. In the end, they were the ones to eat crow, but their "silver" fountain was talked down to copper, though it's covered to look like silver.

Jardín Obregón And The Museo Regional

The centerpiece of this park is a bronze statue of the Greek goddess Hebe. On the east side of the plaza, check out the impressive **Ex-Convent and Church of San Francisco.** You'll find the **Museo Regional** in the ex-convent. Construction (by the Franciscans) was initiated between 1540 and 1550 and continued for over a century. One of the most important convents of New Spain, it was later used for a series of historical events, and today it houses a collection of artifacts and trivia from the early years of the city. You'll find most of the artifacts on the first floor, and the upper floor displays an immense gallery of 17th and 18th century art. The building itself is worth the trip with its unique collection of archways, wrought iron fences, domes, and stone columns. Its history is as rich as its architecture, with events that turned it into a fort under Maximilian, and then a barracks for North American troops later (1867). In 1936 it became a museum. Located next to the Church of San Francisco on Jardín Obregón, corner of Corregidora and 5 de Mayo. Open Wed.-Sat. 10 a.m.-6 p.m., Tues. and Sun. 10 a.m.-3:30 p.m.; admission is US$3.50, free on Sunday.

Plaza De La Independencia

From Jardín Obregón, a lovely walking-only street (going east) takes you past many small shops and cafes to the Plaza de la Independencia. Often you'll run into Indian ladies from small villages on the fringes of town selling,

among other things, handmade embroidered cloth dolls. These (usually) low-key ladies are almost always accompanied by their beautiful children—and the dolls make fun souvenirs.

In the midst of this mini-plaza, you'll see a statue of the **Marquesa de la Villa del Villar del Aguila,** benefactor of Querétaro. Remember Don Juan and the aqueduct? On the east side of the plaza take a look at another flamboyant old house, **Casa de Ecala.** This house displays the Novo-Hispanic baroque style from the 18th century. The facade is accentuated by unusual windows and forged-iron balconies; one of the windows has a drapery carved in stone. It is occupied by offices of the DIF State's Family Integration Bureau.

Doña Josefa's House

More formally called **Casa de la Corregidora,** this is now used as the **Palacio del Gobierno.** It was originally **Casa Reales,** one of the many royal houses in the city, completed in 1770. The Corregidor Don Miguel Domínguez and his wife Doña Josefa Ortíz de Domínguez lived here. What most people are interested in seeing is the legendary room above the entrance where Doña Josefa was locked up under suspicion of being a traitor. Locked doors didn't stop Josefa—she managed to whisper vital instructions to a trusted colleague who then told Hidalgo their scheme had been discovered—the War of Independence began the next morning when Hidalgo gave his call to arms with his shout for freedom on 16 September 1810.

The house is presently the Palacio del Gobierno (seat of state government), and visitors are welcome to visit daily 7 a.m.-9 p.m. The guards are friendly and will allow you entry. Located on the north side of the Plaza de la Independencia, about a block east of Jardín Obregón.

Doña Josefa's Tomb

When this monument was built, it was planned with the idea of remembering the famous people of Querétaro. However, the one person that people really memorialize here is Doña Josefa. At the pantheon's center, a mausoleum keeps the remains of both her and her husband (the mayor of 1810), Don Miguel Domínguez. It's next to the Ex-Convent of Santa Cruz.

Temple And Ex-Convent Of Santa Cruz

Construction of the Temple and Convent of Santa Cruz began in 1654 on the hill known as Cerro del Sangremal. The ex-convent is surrounded with colorful legends (in the interior of the convent a tree with cross-shaped thorns is said to have grown from the walking stick of a saintly priest) and dramatic history. It was on this site that the Otomi Indians surrendered to the Spanish, supposedly encouraged by the appearance of a Christian saint.

The first college of **Apostles of Fide Propaganda** in America was founded here in 1683; it is still a parochial school. Several historically prominent men have walked these corridors, such as Junípero Serra (California missions) and Fray Antonio Buenaventura (who founded the mission that ultimately became the city of San Antonio). But probably the most famous resident was Emperor Maximilian. For a short time in 1867 he used the convent as a fort. But later, after his capture, he was kept in one of its cells as a prisoner before he was executed.

There are many vivid demonstrations of what everyday living (from cooking methods to water storage) was like in that era. Well worth the visit. The convent is open free to the public, and it covers a large area; the best way to see it is with a guide who will explain all of its charming aspects, legends, and history. Open Mon.-Fri. 9 a.m.-2 p.m. and 4-6 p.m., Sat.-Sun. 11 a.m.-6 p.m.; a tip is expected for the guide (usually the guide is one of the brothers and the tip is really a donation to the convent). Check at the bookstore for guide service in English and Spanish. This is about a 15-minute walk from the Plaza, once here you have a wonderful view of the city and especially the aqueduct.

Mesón De Santa Rosa

Right downtown, this hotel dates back to the 18th century. For more than a hundred years it functioned in a variety of ways, but in the end it was the Hostelry of Santa Rosa. However, the passage of time and lack of upkeep contributed to its ongoing decay. And then it was rescued from an untimely end by some talented hardworking folks who renovated and gave it new life but left its original colonial design intact. It is now one of the loveliest hotels in the city. (See also "Accommodations," below.)

Casa Don Bartolo

This is another old building to marvel at. Its unique architecture and ornamentation is from the 17th and 18th centuries and in its day was one of the city's most notable viceregal homes. The exact construction date is unknown; however, the structure today is the office of the state's Ministry of Education.

Casa De Los Cincos Patios

The "House of the Five Patios" is another architectural wonder of the city in a more graceful and simple baroque style. Moorish arches and columns separate the broad patios that are painted a delicate peach with deep sienna and white trims. Construction took place between 1742 and 1781, and it was built for Don Pedro Romero de Terreros, Count of Regia. It's now used as the **Language Center of the Mexican Culture Institute.** Take a look into the branch store of **Galerías la Estrella** located here. The last time we were here, a book fair was set up in the courtyard and along the corridors and it was filled

Casa de los Cincos Patios.

with people perusing the hundreds of volumes on display. Located two blocks west of the Plaza de la Independencia on Corregidora.

Monument To La Corregidora

This dignified statue of Doña Josefa, with its slightly Roman look, was dedicated on 13 September 1910, to commemorate the National Independence Centennial. Querétaro is indeed a town that takes its history very seriously. Doña Josefa is the only Mexican woman to have her image on a coin. Located on Av. Corregidora, one block north of Jardín Obregón.

Teatro De La República

Although it's a theater, it has always been the backdrop of important historical events. Within the decorative columns and velvet drops, the powers-in-place in 1867 pronounced Maximilian's death sentence, the present constitution of Mexico was signed in 1917, and in 1929, politicians met here to establish the principles of the PRI party—still the power force of Mexico of the 20th century.

Construction began in 1845 and was completed in 1852. In 1922, the name was changed from Teatro Iturbideto Gran Teatro de la República. For some time it was the seat of the Legislature. Today, it's used for cultural events, information about which is generally posted outside in advance. Ask at the tourism office for more information. Visitors are permitted Mon.-Fri. 10 a.m.-3 p.m. and 5-9 p.m., admission free. Located on the corner of Juárez and Angela Peralta, a block north of Jardín Obregón.

Casa De La Marquesa

This magnificent house was built during the 18th century for the Marquesa de la Villa del Villar. It has a striking design with two levels inside and a distinct mudéjar atmosphere. You can't help but notice the craftsmenship of the wooden door flanked by a stone-carved frame at the entrance. This is a house you may not be able to enter, but its worth a walk-by. On Madero, near the corner of Juárez, one block from the Plaza de la Independencia.

Fountain Of Neptune

Neptune's fountain looks just as most would expect. The stone statue portrays a well-mus-

Another reminder of Spanish architectural influence.

cled man clutching his trident, ready to protect his minions while standing tall over the denizens of the sea. The fountain was constructed in 1797, designed by Don Francisco Eduardo Tresguerras, one of the most famous architects in neoclassic design. On the corner of Madero and Allende, one block west of Jardín Obregón.

Ex-Convent Of Santa Clara

A few steps from Neptune's statue is the lovely Santa Clara church, one block west of Jardín Obregón. At one time this was part of a very large religious complex that stretched over several blocks and accommodated 8,000 Clarisa nuns. Note the door of the anteroom to the sacristy as well as the interesting forged grating that crowns the same. Tresguerras is believed to have designed the main altar of the church.

Church And Ex-Convent Of San Agustín

Construction of both began in 1731. The moderate baroque style of the facade is carved from quarry stone. The dome, on the other hand, is a lovely example of a more Mexicanized baroque style. Life-sized music-playing angels surround the dome with outstanding detail. The cloister here is quite lovely with highly decorated arches and subtle pinks and deep siennas. Located at Allende 14 Sur.

The **Museum of Art of Querétaro** is located in the cloister of San Agustín ex-convent. After the monks left in the 1800s, as happened to so many of these old buildings, it was ignored and left to decay. However, the "bones" of this antiquated structure were really sturdy, and under Porfirio Díaz's regime it was renovated and used for government offices. Almost one hundred years later it became the **Museum of Art of Querétaro.** The museum is well run and displays a fine collection of various Querétaran artists, as well as many other artists, both Latin American and European, from the 16th to the 20th century. Locals are encouraged to participate in choosing exhibits and workshops, and raising money (from auctions and concerts). The museum is open Tues.-Sun. 11 a.m.-7 p.m.; small admission. The bookstore is well worth a look, especially if you read Spanish.

Historical Archives

The building alone is worth a look. It was built at the end of the 18th century in the neoclassic style and has had many uses over the years. One of the notable uses was as the National Palace and state government building. You'll find memorabilia of the colonial era: old periodicals and newspapers, ancient birth certificates and marriage licenses, property transfers, old deeds, and all other historical records. Open Tues.-Sun. 10 a.m.-2 p.m. and 4-7 p.m. Located on Ocampo 70.

Casa De Los Perros

This charming old house was occupied by owner/architect Ignacio Mariano de las Casas until he died in 1773. Undoubtedly, it gets its name from doggy gargoyles on the baroque facade. It operates as a kindergarten now; located at Allende 16.

Cerro De Las Campanas

It was here on the "Hill of Bells" that Maximilian of Hapsburg and his generals Miramón and Mejía were executed by a cadre of sharpshooters on 19 June 1867. There's a small memorial

to Max that appears deserted. A caretaker (if you happen to be there when he is) there knows quite a bit about the details of the execution day. Farther up the hill is a large statue of Benito Juárez. Many feel this site, located on the west side of the city, is worth the half hour walk from the town center.

More Churches

Everywhere you look in Querétaro you see old churches; many are no longer religious structures and have been converted to other needs. A few still conduct masses, and you'll know this at sundown, when all the bells of the various churches ring out in a lovely symphony that harkens back to an earlier era. The facade of the **Church and Ex-Convent of San Felipe Neri** is unusual, for it's a brick facade covered with columns and ornamentation that lean more to the austere neoclassic. Built in 1786, Pope Benedict XV raised its status to cathedral in 1921. The property is known as Palacio Conín (could this be dedicated to the prominent Indian named Conín before his conversion?). It is now a state government office.

The **Church and Convent of Santo Domingo** dates back to 1692. Planned and built by architect Ignacio Mariano de las Casas, it's a large simple structure on the corner of Guerrero and Pino Suárez. Another design by architect Mariano, the **Temple and Ex-Convent of Santa Rosa de Viterbo** was built in 1752. The interior of the church is another shining example of churrigueresque as well as its own brand of baroque. Many artistic sights, large and small, will catch your eye, but in particular note the pulpit with its inlaid wood and ivory design.

MODERN QUERETARO

Querétaro 2000

On the north end of the city, a modern recreation park was opened in 1991. It has facilities for sports and recreation including an open theater and library. On the outside there's a fascinating sculpture of life-sized pre-Columbians playing an ancient ball game, stone ring and all.

Corregidora Stadium

This large arena will comfortably hold 41,673 people, and offers parking for 6,700 cars. The structure was designed so that it could be emptied of all people in 10 minutes. All soccer fans welcome! Ask at the tourism office for changing schedules and prices. Located south of the city.

Alameda Hidalgo Park

Thanks to a generous gift, this property was donated to the state in 1790. Since then, walkways have been built, trees and gardens planted, and some lovely sculptures scattered here and there. The large grassy area makes a wonderful place to spend time relaxing, picnicking, or just watching the world go by. Located in the southern part of the city, it's just across the street from the bus station.

ACCOMMODATIONS

Budget And Moderate Hotels

Fortunately it's easy to find budget accommodations in downtown Querétaro near the Jardín Obregón, a few more are farther out. As always, some are nicer than others, and to insure a budget room in the convenient central area, try to arrive in the morning; weekdays are best. As we always suggest, see your room before you decide, to eliminate any surprises. Ask about the hot water supply, which is sometimes a problem. Usually you pay extra for TV and a/c, so make sure you get what you want and that you want what you get.

Villa Deportiva Juvenil Querétaro: As expected, the youth hostel in town is the cheapest place to stay. Everyone is welcome here, even those who are no longer "youths"; card not necessary. There's a total of 72 beds with four people to a room (bunks) in separate sex dorms; rates are about US$4 per night. Check-in time is 7 a.m.-11 p.m., it's located on Ejercito Republicana next to Doña Josefa's tomb.

Plaza Hotel: By all accounts the Plaza is one of the best budget hotels in the neighborhood. Clean pleasant rooms have comfy beds and pillows, carpet, and wildflowers on the walls, and it's conveniently located on the Jardín Obregón. Ask for a room with a terrace that overlooks the plaza, or a window that overlooks the central patio. Rates are US$18 s, US$25 d. Located at Juárez Norte 23, tel. (42) 12-1138.

Hotel del Marquez: These rooms and baths are large and clean, and very red (just the carpet). Location is something to consider if you have a lot of luggage—the hotel is three city blocks north of the Jardín Obregón. **Note:** These rooms can be noisy with drifting street sounds. Rates are US$10-15 s, US$12-17 d. Located at Juárez Norte. 104.

Hotel Hidalgo: This is a pleasant little inn that's now under new ownership. They recently spiffed up the hotel (even new mattresses). Nice to look at, clean, and if you like to look out, ask for one of the rooms with a balcony. Most of the rooms are small, and the patio could be filled with cars, but the location is good, and the price is right; a budget restaurant on the premises is open 8 a.m.-9:30 p.m. Rates are US$14 s, US$18 d; it's located one block west of the Jardín Obregón.

Hotel Amberes: It's just a facade in the crowd of ordinary hotels. Modernish, clean, a restaurant, bars, and parking make it an option if you wish to be near the bus station. It has 142 rooms, and rates are about US$26 s, US$36 d. Located across from the Alameda park at Av. Corregidora Sur 188, tel. 12-8604, fax 12-8832.

Hotel Casablanca: A modern hotel that hosts more businesspeople than tourists, it's an alternative that's clean. For a brochure and current prices write to Apdo. Postal 194, Querétaro, 76030, Qro., Mexico, tel. 16-0100, fax 16-0102.

Hotel Mirabel: Not far from the bus station, this hotel is pleasant and squeaky clean. It's good-sized with 171 rooms, including five junior suites. Rooms are comfortable, if not spectacular, with everything you need on site: bar, restaurant, cable TV, elevators, a/c, swimming pool, and a convenient location. Rates are about US$36 s, and US$41 d. Located at Av. Constituentes 2 Poninte, tel. 14-3590, fax 14-3585. The hotel restaurant offers a US$8 buffet breakfast and a US$8 *comida corrida*.

More Expensive Hotels

Mesón de Santa Rosa: This delightful old colonial structure has been made into a charming 21-suite hotel. The rooms are comfortable and still have the aura of the colonial era, including arches and stone walls. The inner courtyard has an old fountain. There's a swimming pool, restaurant, and bar. Rates range US$80-95. Located at Pasteur Sur 17, Plaza de la Independencia, tel. (42) 14-5781, fax 12-5522.

Holiday Inn: A low-rise hotel with 110 rooms is not typical of the Holiday Inn chain. Decor is very colonial with a lovely entrance framed by large arches. Rooms are pleasant, clean, comfortable and well decorated with the amenities of an upscale hotel, including a minibar. There's a swimming pool, two restaurants, putting green, playground, tennis court, and access to the golf club. Price begins at US$118 d. Located on the highway to San Luis Potosí, Av. 5 de Febrero 110; tel. (800) HOLIDAY, (42) 16-0202, fax (421) 16-8902. This is far enough out of town that you may want to take a taxi.

Real de Minas Hotel: This hotel is rated five stars by the Mexican Government Tourism Office, and while it's really quite nice, I would give it more like a 3.5. It's large with 200 rooms, a/c, a swimming pool, a coffee shop, heat, a tennis court, a bar, a restaurant, and a jogging track. Rates are about US$45. Located at Av. Constituyentes 124, tel. 16-0444, fax 16-0662.

Out-of-town Hotels

The following two hotels are located out of town, but both are well worth incorporating into your journey to or from Querétaro if possible. Driving your own vehicle is the best way to get there.

Hotel Hacienda Jurica: Just 16 km from Querétaro, this former 17th-century hacienda is a delightful place to stay covering 10 hectares including a pool, tennis and squash courts, lovely gardens with inviting walkways, two restaurants, a disco, and horses; golf games can be arranged at the closest course, about five km away. The structures are beautiful with three-meter-thick stone arches and stucco walls. Rooms are spacious, and some have tiled patios. Note the old horse and buggy on the grounds. Rates are about US$140 s or d. At Km 9 on the road from Querétaro to San Luis Potosí (Hwy. 57) take the cutoff, Calle Paseo de Jurica to the hotel. Write for more information to Apdo. Postal 338, Querétaro, 76100, Qto., Mexico, tel. (42) 18-0022 or 18-0001, fax 18-0136. **Note:** It's about a 15 minute taxi ride from Querétaro.

Hotel La Mansión Galindo: If you're driving from Mexico City to Querétaro, Galindo is a one-and-a-half- to two-hour drive, right on the way. It's actually quite close to the town of **San Juan del Río.** This lovely old mansion is on spacious grounds with a pool, six clay tennis courts, and all the modern conveniences. Wander around and you'll find beautiful old halls, a multitude of arches, wood-carved balustrades, stone fountains, tile walkways, lots of shade trees, grass, flowers, and blossom-covered stone walls. Guest rooms are spacious and furnished in an elegant conservative way fitting an antique building that flourished hundreds of years ago. The dining rooms are beautiful with oil paintings, linen and crystal table settings, and excellent service. Want to throw a party? The ballroom holds 800 people. Golf can be arranged at the 18-hole **San Gil Golf Club,** five minutes away. This is not where you go for a cheap vacation; this is where you go to enjoy the finer things in Mexico. Rates start at US$85; write for more information, Carretera a Amealco Km 5, San Juan del Río, 76800, Qto., Mexico.

FOOD

In the center of town around the plazas you'll find many small cafes serving tacos and other regional dishes. On the west side of the plaza, try **Manolo's** comida corrida, US$5, and they advertise paella to go. But there's quite a choice in the city. Most restaurants offer regional menus, but several serve continental cuisine as well.

Restaurant/Bar Casa Real

In the old district, with live music, try dinner in this lovely old colonial building that serves all the foods typical of Central Mexico: pipian verde y roja, chile en nogada, and of course authentic mole poblana. Open for dinner Sat.-Sun. 7-11 p.m., located at 4 Oriente 208. Moderate.

Vegetariano

Vegetariano Comedor is for those who prefer to do without animal flesh. You can buy the usual packaged health food store items, vitamins, food supplements, etc., as well as great fresh juices, salads, and Mexican and International entrees—good whole wheat bread. Comida corrida is served 1-4 p.m., US$4.50. In two locations: at Vergara 7, and off the Jardín Obregón at Juárez 47. There's no shortage of vegetarian restaurants in town; check out **Restaurante Ibis Natura** on Juárez Norte 47, open 8:30 a.m.- 9:30 p.m., closed Sunday. Budget. **Restaurante Primavera** is on Corregidora Sur 130. Moderate.

Flor De Querétaro

This is just a simple little restaurant, but it serves a good *comida corrida* and other Mexican specialties. Downtown off Jardín Obregón, at Juárez 9. Open 7 a.m.-10 p.m. Budget.

Fonda Del Refugio

If you stroll along the pedestrian-only walkway in the historical district near Corregidora, you'll find several charming sidewalk cafes. This is our favorite. Open 7:30 a.m.-10:30 p.m. Moderate-expensive.

Coffee Shops And Fast Food

You'll find lots of coffee shops and fast-fooderies around town; **VIPS, Sanborn's, California, Burger King, KFC, and Shakey's Pizza.** If you'd like a change of pace, ask at the tourist office. They can direct you to Japanese, German, Argentinian, Chinese, French, Italian, and Lebanese cuisine.

Markets

Of course you'll find the usual *mercados,* but also look for the modern supermarket: just east of the bus station, check out the **Aurrerá supermarket** in a two-tiered shopping mall with lots of modern shops. Rumor has it more shopping is coming. The city appears to be thriving with lots of multinational firms already in place, and NAFTA has barely achieved breath. Notice firms like **Ralston-Purina, Singer, Uni-Royal,** and companies coming out of Europe and Japan.

ENTERTAINMENT AND EVENTS

Plaza Music

The magic night for Mexican plazas is Sunday evening when there's music for anyone who wants to listen—free of course. The state band plays at **Jardín Obregón** beginning at 6 p.m. On Saturday evenings at 6 p.m., the **Plaza de la Independencia** comes alive with magic, music, and mimes. Check at the tourist office for events and schedules at other plazas in town.

Discos And Nightclubs

Most of the discos in town open around 10 p.m. but really don't get rolling until later. **JBJ Disco,** at Zona Dorada 109, and **L'Opera,** at Circuito Jardín Sur 1, both offer live music.

Books for sale under the arches of a colonial building in Querétaro

University Entertainments

With two universities, **Autonoma** and **Tecnologico,** the town is loaded with students—and there's almost always something going on at night. Check at the **Universidad Autonoma de Querétaro** for evening cultural entertainments sponsored by various classes of fine arts. For the most part these entertainments will be in Spanish, but if you're having fun, you're speaking the universal language. For those into classical music, Querétaro offers some fine programs. The **Escuela de Bellas Artes** music department offers classical concerts every Friday evening at the corner of Independencia and Juárez Sur beginning at 8 p.m.; admission is under US$4. At the same place on Sundays at 6 p.m. there's a popular get-together with singalongs and a variety of popular music; it's free. **Casa de la Cultura** sponsors frequent entertainment such as dance, drama, art, or other cultural performances, at 5 de Mayo 40. Ask about the two-hour tour of the city. Another inexpensive entertainment to look into is the university theater department's presentations. Ask about "wine, cheese, bread, and theater" at **El Mesón de los Comicos de la Legua** at Guillermo Prieto 7, about US$5.50 admission. Another along those same lines is a dinner playhouse called **Corral de Comedias** at Carranza 39, reservations suggested; both begin at about 8 p.m.

Plaza De Toros Santa María
Aficionados of the *corrida* (bullfight) will find one of the finest bullrings in Mexico here in Querétaro. Built in 1963, it holds 10,000 people. The season begins each year in November and continues until February. Querétaro attracts some of the most courageous matadors and bulls. Occasional *corridas* are held out of season for special holiday events. Located southeast of the city. Check with the tourist office for schedules and other information.

SERVICES AND INFORMATION

State Tourist Office
English-speaking staff is almost always available, as well as brochures and maps. They also offer a free escorted walking tour of the most important sights of the city with a historical overview thrown in. This is a great opportunity and the price is perfect; daily (except Sunday) beginning at 10:30 a.m. The office is open Mon.-Fri. 9 a.m.-3 p.m. and 6-8 p.m., Sat. and Sun. 9 a.m.-2 p.m. Located at 5 de Mayo 61, on the Plaza de la Independencia, tel. (42) 14-5623 or 14-0179.

Money
Banks in the city are open Mon.-Fri. 9 a.m.-1 p.m., and you'll find several banks along the Jardín Obregón, on Corregidora Norte. Casa de Cambio de Querétaro will exchange cash and traveler's checks; located on Jardín Obregón at Madero 6, open Mon.-Thurs. 9 a.m.-3 p.m., Fri. 9 a.m.-1:30 p.m. Some shops accept dollars and give top exchange rates with a purchase, but most hotels give a deflated exchange.

Medical Services
Hospital Civil is a government hospital located at Reforma 21. There's a **Red Cross** office at Hidalgo Poniente 93. **Farmacia Central** is open

Mon.-Sat. 9 a.m.-9 p.m., located on the south side of the Jardín Obregón at Madero 10. **Farmacia El Feniz** is a short walk north of the Jardín at Juárez Norte 73, open daily 8 a.m.-10 p.m.

Post Office
The post office is two blocks south of the Jardín Obregón on Arteaga Poniente 7, open Mon.-Fri. 8 a.m.-7 p.m., Sat. 9 a.m.-1 p.m.

Telephone And Fax
The **Telecomm** office is located at Allende Norte 4. From here you can telegraph and fax messages. Open Mon.-Fri. 9 a.m.-8 p.m., Sat. 9 a.m.-1 p.m. For long distance telephone calls go to the *caseta de larga distancia* at 5 de Mayo 33 (the walking street to the left of San Francisco Church on the Jardín Obregón), open Mon.-Sat. 9:30 a.m.-2 p.m. and 5-9 p.m. At the bus station you can make long distance calls all day and night.

GETTING THERE

By Train
Estación del Ferrocarril ("Train Station") is located about one kilometer north of centro Querétaro at Av. Héroes de Nacozari. You can either take a local bus (look for one that says "Ruta 13") or taxi to and from the station; taxis generally meet incoming trains. Remember, in most cases you get what you pay for, and the extra you pay for a first class train ticket is well worth it for comfort (make reservations a day in advance). On the other hand, if you really are traveling light in the pocketbook, second class fares are about a third of first class (no reservations are taken; remember, bus fares are usually even cheaper).

By Plane
So far no commercial planes fly into Querétaro, which has only a small airstrip.

By Bus
The large busy bus station, **Central Camionera,** is a regional center for buses coming and going to many destinations in Mexico. From here you can efficiently and inexpensively travel to nearby colonial cities: Dolores Hidalgo (one and a

half to two hours), Guadalajara (five to six hours), Guanajuato (two and a half hours), Irapuato (one and a half hours), Mexico City (three hours), Morelia (three to four hours), San Juan del Río (45 minutes), San Miguel de Allende (one hour), Tequisquiapan (one and a half hours), and Toluca (three and a half hours).

The bus station is a nerve center for travelers. Baggage can be stored here (look for the sign that says "Guarda Equipaje"), and long distance telephone, snack shops, and other services are available. There are a couple of hotels within walking distance, but local bus service travels to and from downtown for about 25 cents.

GETTING AROUND

This is mostly a walking-around town—the local bus (Urbanos) has only a few stops in town. Much of the center of the old historic district is closed off to cars. Add that to the pleasant little parks and plazas, shops, and sidewalk cafes, and it's really a delight to walk. Taxis are reasonable if you wish to go further afield.

OUTLYING AREAS

The eastern sierra of the Sierra Madre Oriental is in the heart of the mountains northeast of the city of Querétaro. The Sierra Gorda was the arena for confrontation and evangelization over a couple of centuries. Missionaries found the Indians and pursued their "lost souls," and of course the Indians resisted, defending their ancient culture and beliefs. It becomes a more exciting trip when you put yourself in the place of the courageous missionaries who headed into uncharted territories and toward an unknown reception by people who weren't too anxious to give up their beliefs and accept a foreign god. As one descendant of those long lost souls stated, the "process has been settled, it is history." However, you don't have to look far to find remnants of the old civilization that have survived: holiday foods, designs embedded in weavings, and ceremonies that have become intertwined with the Christianity they adopted long ago.

SIGHTS NORTHEAST OF QUERETARO CITY

Cava Antonelli Winery

Just outside the town of **Ezequiel Montes**, which is on Hwy. 20, you can go through a winery. This winery has been open since 1968 and produces about one million liters yearly. It's an interesting tour since so much of the work is hand done. For instance, the bottles are turned by hand daily, the wires and corks on the champagne (called *spumoso*) are placed by hand, and 12 workers wash and fill the bottles (some-

what like we used to see in the *haut savoire* region in France 25 years ago).

Harvesting is done in October (if weather conditions allow), and Antonelli produces Chenin Blanc and traminer whites, and cabernet, merlot, and burgundy reds. They also make a small amount of sherry and champagne. Recently the winery has begun making vodka from grain alcohol and apple cider vinegar. The wine business is suffering because of the lowering of imported wine tariffs into the country.

Cava Antonelli's best customer is Mexico's Club Med. In the country, six states are wine producers. Querétaro had six wineries a while back, but since the tariffs were lowered, three have closed. No, they don't have winetasting rooms as in the United States. However, if someone wants to have a party, they buy wine (at a good price) and bring their friends. Manager Alberto Rodríguez gave us the recipe for a liquid Mexican breakfast; orange juice, two eggs, and Antonelli sherry (that might or might not get me going). If you wish to tour the winery you must make reservations in advance. (467) 7-0049.

Bernal

This is another small town off Highway 120. This is really a charming little town with mostly very friendly locals. Bernal has a popular festival to celebrate the feast of the Holy Cross, 3-4 May. Artisans come from around the surrounding areas bringing woven goods and semiprecious stones: opals (common in this area), quartz, amethysts, and some carved stones. Just outside of town you find the **Rock**, a shockingly immense monolith, second in size in the world only to Ayers Rock in Australia. It's a popular rock for climbers. And if you come on Sunday you will be surrounded by other visiting climbers, lots of them. The rock looks like sandstone with a lot of lichen, but apparently is basalt. There's a chapel about halfway up. However, the local priest is too old to say mass there anymore. The chapel is about as far as most amateur hikers get. Beyond that, special skill and equipment, or at the very least good boots and gloves to protect your hands, are needed to go to the top. It appears that some pitons have been driven into the upper rock to assist the climber. Figure about an hour to get to the chapel.

At the base of the rock there's a small free campground (rather dirty) with tables and benches. In the fall (at least in October) the lower half of the rock is dabbed with blue and red wildflowers, and it's really quite lovely. The town is 2,100 meters high, and the rock is 2,500 meters high. If you should get to the cross at the top, I'm told the view is spectacular on a clear day.

If you plan to stop over and climb, try one of two hotels. The newest is **Villa San Carlos,** clean, simple, nice, and with only six rooms right now (more rooms and a pool coming along). Rates at the Villa San Carlos are US$33 s or d. There's a pleasant restaurant upstairs with a great view of the Rock. Meals are reasonable: *carne asada* is US$5, and breakfast hotcakes are US$2. The manager speaks a little English. The only telephone in town is the central exchange, (467) 2-1903, and if you can speak Spanish, you can leave a message and it will be delivered to the hotel; or write to Villa San Carlos, Ezequiel Montes, Barrio La Capilla, Bernal, Querétaro, Mexico. Weekends are generally filled by reservation. Another small posada **Posada Pena,** is located on the town plaza, very simple but clean and adequate. Rates are US$17 s or d.

On the plaza you'll find two small restaurants, but just off the plaza on Calle Guadalupe Victoria look for **La Escondido,** a small eatery with a lovely little patio and happy doves that coo throughout breakfast. Choices are fresh fruit, sweet rolls, Mexican-style eggs, and Nescafe or Cafe Olla (sweet Mexican coffee), for less than US$3.

Cadereyta

Approaching the missions you will go through the small town of **Cadereyta.** The small municipality (population about 6,000) is located in the central area of the state. Not too many people come this way, but it does have two lovely churches in the main square, **St. Peter's** and **St. Paul's,** both ornate yet with a clean trim look in cream and sienna colors. Another reason to stop is to take a look around at the **Fernando-Schmoll Greenhouse** seed nursery. Also, those interested in the archaeology of the country should take a detour to the archaeological zones close by.

Fernando-Schmoll Greenhouse: This botanical garden in Cadereyta is rather unusual in that it specializes in cactus, with 2.5 million plants displayed on eight hectares representing 4,200 species. It's not surprising that this is the largest garden of its kind in Latin America. Actually, this is a commercial venture and seeds and plantlets are available for shipping all over the world. The public is invited to look at the cactus and other plants that cover this large area.

ARCHAEOLOGICAL SITES

About 30 km north of Cadereyta, you'll find a winding road that leads to San Joaquin, from where you can walk the rest of the way to the archaeological sites of **Toluquilla** and **Las Ranas.**

Toluquilla

If you want to see this site, you must go to the small village of **La Esperanza** and proceed about four kilometers to the lower skirt of the hill and then on foot up the long path to the site. Toluquilla hasn't really been developed for tourists yet, but the remains of a ballcourt, pyramid foundations, and part of a wall can be seen. From the late-classic period and with a distinct Huasteca influence, it is believed that this site was formerly a military fortification.

Las Ranas

Three kilometers from San Joaquin town, Las Ranas is believed to be another fortress city. Artifacts indicate the presence of Gulf coast cultures. There's more to explore here with the main structure fronted by broad flights of steps. Like so many pre-Columbian cultures, Ranas was abandoned between the years of A.D. 900

and 1000. But starting in the 16th century, the Chichimecas occupied the city and were there until the Spaniards arrived. The site is located on the upper area of two hills.

THE SIERRA GORDA MISSIONS

You really should have a vehicle to take this little detour, but it's worth the time and effort. Before Father Junípero Serra embarked on his famed mission trips north to California, he and Father Francisco Palou made their way into often rugged regions of the Sierra Gorda. Here, five missions, founded in 1744 by Don José de Escandon, were constructed and organized by these two priests. Amazingly, the state has restored many of the buildings and even operates two small hotels in the area, conveniently located near archaeological zones as well. Don't rush this trip; the roads are not freeways. You should really plan on three full days.

All five of these churches are architectural masterpieces, each with the same floorplan. As you face the front, the bell tower is to the left of the main door, with the attached convent and priest's quarters farther to the left. All are Romanesque, containing a dome with a cupola to cover the top. The combination of baroque with the cultural design of the people who built them gives each a special personality, yet with a certain commonality. As we go to press, the church facades are being restored. This is a Querétaro state government project (Environment And

SERRA

Father Junípero Serra was born in Mallorca and came to Mexico with the Franciscans to teach and evangelize the New World. Serra spent seven years in the central plateau of Mexico. His California missions are known worldwide, but those in Mexico are just now gaining fame. The last mission Serra supervised was the Mission Dolores in San Francisco. Junípero Serra is buried in Carmel, California.

Urban Development Ministry), and US$130,000 has been set aside for restoration. It's common to see a workman tied by a rope to a metal scaffolding. With a tiny brush he gently scrapes off the yellow paint in search of the original polychrome colors of terra-cotta red and black. And while the facades of these missions are so ornate, the inside of each is quite simple. Most of the churches are believed to have been built within the years of 1750-1768, although exact dates are still debated by historians.

Misión De Santiago At Jalpan

This lovely church is located 210 kilometers northeast of the city of Querétaro. Hopefully, the new facade will be complete by the time you arrive, but even if not, you can see the ornate sculptures in their individual niches. Where today the clock resides there was formerly a statue of Santa Santiago. Jalpan is the largest of all the mission towns.

Museo Historica de La Sierra Gorda: Be sure to check out the new museum recently opened across from the plaza (on Calle Fray Junípero Serra 1). It details Serra's life as well as the history of the area. All exhibits of course are explained in Spanish. Open 10 a.m.-3 p.m. Mon.-Sat., and 9 a.m.-1 p.m. on Sun., admission US$1.

Practicalities: You'll find a post office here, as well as taxis, a bus station, marketplace, telegraph office, and a small hotel (as well as one or two in progress). It's best to come with pesos, since cashing dollars is almost impossible, and cashing traveler's checks at the bank was a long, drawn out process completed only with the help of the bank manager—a very helpful gentlemen, but he might not be available next time.

Accommodations and Food: The **Hotel Posada Fray Junípero Serra** has 37 rooms and two suites, and guests will find a restaurant (the food is only so-so), bar, swimming pool, and laundry; rates are about US$35 s or d. This is part of a government-owned chain, and there's no telephone on the premises. **Posada Trejo** is a small, humble but clean hotel, rooms look out onto the courtyard, and each has a private bathroom. Rates are US$9 d, a good bargain for the money.

A good restaurant in Jalpan is the **Restaurant Jacarandas.** The food is tasty, though portions might be a bit small for a young healthy hiker. "Enchiladas Huasteca" is kind of a make-your-own taco served with tortillas, cheese, sauce, marinated beef, avocados and sliced tomatoes—roll it all up in the tortilla; US$5. Breakfast *chilequiles* were good; US$3.50.

Misión De Santa María De La Purísima Concepción Del Agua At Landa

This mission is about 231 kilometers northeast of Querétaro and 21 kilometers beyond Jalpan on the same road. The facade of this church is probably the most ornate of the five with multiple statues of saints (mostly all life size), angels, curlicues, carved curtains, stone columns, and topped with Michael the Archangel beating the dragon. This church was the last to be built. Its dome was destroyed by an earthquake 100 years ago and 50 years passed before it was replaced. The building of this mission was directed by a Mexican priest, and the Indians participated more in this construction than the other missions. Though there is some work being done on the facade here, the major restoration project is replacing the adjacent convent roof.

Misión De San Miguel Arcángel At Conca

Located 48 kilometers from Jalpan, this church facade has a different look; it's covered with bunches of grapes, is a different color, and is the smallest of the five. You really get the feeling of the Indians in these designs, since many themes come from nature rather than of saints and angels. Take time to study the front of this building; you will discover many interesting forms.

The elevation is lower here, and you can tell the difference in the climate, which is very tropical and a little warmer. Although you see cactus, much of it is entangled with vines and there's a great variety of butterfies fluttering about the plants. On the way from Jalpan you pass the Río Santa María where it converges with the Río Ayutla. Downhill from the mission is the Río Santa María; note the banks, where sugarcane, oranges, peanuts, and corn are growing. The rural area appears more like it must have been in Serra's time. Locals say there are puma, jaguar, and white-tailed deer in the area, but no one has really seen any of them for some time.

Practicalities: Next to the church you'll find a small **Tourist Office** (no sign): the woman who works here, Mary Navarro, speaks English. Open six days a week (closed Sat.). If you're interested in wildflowers, she says they are beautiful in May and June.

Misión San Miguel Arcangel

BOB RACE

In part of an old hacienda you'll find a charming 43-room hotel called **Mesón de San Nicolas** or **Ex-Hacienda de San Nicolas.** There's a restaurant, bar, and laundry. Be sure to check out the thermal pool fed by a nearby hot stream. Rates are about US$35-40 s or d. The open restaurant and bar face beautiful grounds and serve great *flautas* and *sopes* (about US$3.50). Breakfast is sweet tamales filled with a mixture including whole kernels of corn, with coffee. The price is US$2.75 for two people. Another hotel is under construction close by.

Misión De San Francisco De Asisi At Tilaco

Located 16.5 km off Hwy. 120 at Lagunitas to Tilaco, this new road recently provides access to this mission town, which used to be inaccessible by car. Apparently cars (or visitors) are still a novelty, because the vehicle I was in received plenty of attention. This is called a migrant town (as is Landa). Because there's so little work in the area, many of the men migrate to the U.S. for seasonal farm jobs and return in December—it's a 12-hour drive to the Texas border. There's not much of a commercial nature here, only a small *tienda* (store).

Although again the facade of the mission is ornate, the overall look of the church is not nearly so lovely as the first two. There are traces of the original paint if you look carefully. Wander about the grounds and inside the church for a real feeling of the era.

Misión De Nuestra Señora De La Luz At Tancoyol

This mission town is 262 kilometers from Querétaro. Just north of the turnoff to Tilaco is the turnoff to Tancoyal. The drive meanders along a canyon whose walls are covered with tall straight cactus, which looks like a forest of telephone poles (pretty green ones).

The Church: Despite the busy baroque design, the first thing you notice is an empty niche above the front entrance. At the rear of the church is a beautiful dome. Note the extravagant carved wooden doors. The interior, like the others, is simple terra-cotta and white, with a large courtyard in front.

Practicalities: Built on a hillside, this town is second in size to Jalpan. While there's no hotel, you'll find several small restaurants and stores. An elderly local man told of an old spring-fed aqueduct that was built at the same time as the mission; he led the way to the edge of town, and sure enough there it was. Today they use the water from a well closer in to town.

For more information about the Sierra Gorda region write to **Probaditur,** the state promotional office: Prospero C. Vega 31, Querétaro, 76000, Qro., Mexico, tel. (42) 12-1241, fax 14-0997.

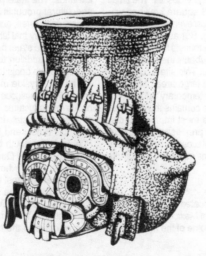

K. A. ESCOVEDO SANDERS

THE STATE OF HIDALGO
INTRODUCTION

The state of modern Hidalgo was a part of Mexico State until 1869. It was then established as its own entity and named to honor Independence hero Miguel Hidalgo y Costilla. The small province (about 20,813 square km) has witnessed significant historical events from a distant pre-Hispanic beginning. But as a destination there's very little to bring tourists for much more than a day-long visit. Probably the most visited spot in the state is **Tula.** This site at one time held the leadership of a large area of Mexico. For those more into "contemporary" attractions, this archaeological zone contains the **Atlantes** sculptures, some of the most impressive displays of strength from pre-Hispanic Mexico. Along with Tula, other places worth seeing are the collection of museums located in capital city of Pachuca.

The Land And Climate
The state of Hidalgo is located on the plateau of the eastern central part of Mexico. Northern and eastern Hidalgo are in some of the most moun-

tainous areas of the country. Peaks rise to 3,000 meters. The land in the south and west becomes flat and semiarid, eventually angling into tropical lowlands. The state produces a wide array of agricultural products including wheat, maize, barley, rice, coffee, and pulque maguey. But by far, the industry that largely affects the economy of not only the state, but also the entire country, is silver, in addition to gold, mercury, copper, and some fine opals found alongside it.

The countryside meanders along high valleys, with mountainous vistas, cactus, and dry igneous rock structures, and in many areas that's all there is. The state is bordered in the north by San Luis Potosí and Veracruz, in the east by Puebla, in the south by Mexico and Tlaxcala, and in the west by Querétaro.

It depends on where you are to determine the weather patterns. In the higher elevations it can be cool, and the state gets ample rainfall throughout the year. Daytime temperatures can be counted on to be moderate year-round (unless you take to the highest hills). And in the

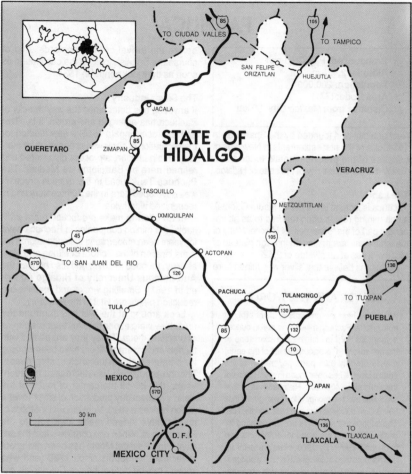

tropical lowlands temperatures are usually warm. However, the most-traveled destinations are located on the plateau, and generally the climate is quite moderate and comfortable; do bring a light wrap just in case.

Today's Economy

While silver is still a big moneymaker for the state, other forms of industry are afoot. Factories that deal in transport equipment, metalworking, textiles, cement, and more are setting roots in the little state.

Today's People

A state of contrasts, though highly urbanized and modern around the industrial centers, there are still many indigenous groups scattered about. Most of them are Otomi, and they tend their small, subsistence farms.

PACHUCA

Pronounced: Pah-CHU-cah
Altitude: 2,426 meters
Population: 200,000
Area Code: (771)
Distance from Mexico City: 90 km

Pachuca city was founded by the Spaniards in 1534, one of the first settlements in New Spain, because of the precious metals found here. Today it is the capital city of the state of Hidalgo.

The Land

Pachuca is located in the Sierra Madre Oriental, a rich mining region often referred to as an important part of the "silver belt" of Mexico. Many of the inhabitants are miners. In the high plateau of Mexico, it lies at an altitude of 2,426 meters.

Historians believe that silver was mined here

SILVER AND THE WORLD

When you hear the amounts of silver brought from just the Pachuca mines (one million ounces a year), it's hard to imagine that silver (one of the five so-called "precious metals" of the earth) makes up only 0.05 parts per million of the earth's crust. It has been found in royal tombs of the world since 4000 B.C. Historians tell us that silver was used as money (along with gold) since 800 B.C. in countries between India and the Nile. The bright white metal has been in demand for centuries around the world for ornaments and household decor. By 1960, silver's use for industrial purposes outweighed its total world production. Just a few of its uses include photography, cloud seeding for artificial rainmaking, antiseptics, cauterizing wounds, and treating diseases of the skin and eyes. Since you are probably more interested in its uses in Mexico for jewelry and decorative art, you are in the right place. Some of the most modern, beautiful silver work is done in Mexico. Strictly controlled by the government, if it is sterling it contains 92.5% silver and 7.5% of another metal, usually copper. True sterling pieces will be stamped with "925" somewhere on the item.

before the arrival of the Spaniards. And of course the Spanish took up the occupation as soon as they took control in 1534.

The Silver Industry

If anything has determined the way the city of Pachuca has emerged and grown, it is silver and its processing. In 1555, a new method for the separation of silver was speeded up by mercury amalgamation, a process discovered and refined here by Bartolome de Medina. The **Pachuca Tank** (used in the cyanide process) was developed here in the 20th century and is recognized worldwide.

In an effort to make production more profitable, the mining companies in Pachuca have for years been modernizing their operation. This is the location of the **School of Mines and Metallurgy,** founded in 1877, and also houses the **Autonomous University of Hidalgo** (founded in 1961). Smelting works and metallic-ore reduction plants are vital to the economy.

Look around at the hills that surround the area, they were at one time full treasure chests of precious metal. Today they are riddled with tunnels and caverns. Miners have been working for centuries alongside ancient slag heaps. Though production has decreased in recent years, this is still the center of much of the world's present day production of silver (over a million ounces a year). More efficient methods of mining have indeed made their way to the Pachuca hills. When one considers that the ancient mine Real del Monte has been giving out silver from its depths since 1739 (and who knows, maybe during the pre-Columbian era as well), this is one rich mountainside of unimaginable wealth.

Obsidian

While silver and gold were found in quantity by the Spaniards, obsidian, an important part of the economy of pre-Hispanic Teotihuacán and later Tula, was also mined in the area. The powerful indigenous groups mined obsidian and exported it all over pre-Hispanic Mexico. Obsidian from the Valley of Mexico continues to turn up in archaeological digs all over Mesoamerica.

SIGHTS

The Hidalgo state capital is a town of twisting hillside alleyways, with small houses that climb the steep hillsides. Though the ordinary houses are just that, the city does have a few examples of interesting early architecture and history.

This is a town of massive statues in parks and plazas commemorating the heroes of Mexican history. Take a few minutes to view **Pachuca Centro**. Wander around the **Plaza de la Independencia** and note the 40-meter high **Reloj Clock Tower,** complete with four carved statues and a carillon imported from Austria. The **Casas Colorado,** built in the 18th century, is now the city's law court. Built in the 17th century, **Las Casas** was formerly the

storage hall of the *quinta real,* the king's duty. A fifth of every bit of silver, gold, and other minerals brought from the earth was sent to the king in Spain. His fifth totaled up to a *huge* amount from this part of Mexico.

Teatro de la Ciudad is a neoclassic replica built by the clever silversmith Bartolome de Medina (he of the amalgamation process). A **Statue of Benito Juárez** by Juan Leonardo Cordero stands in front of the modern **Palacio de Gobierno,** in the civic center with murals by nativeson Jesús Becerril a few blocks from the Plaza de la Independencia. Becerril is a much-loved and honored artist here in the city, and if you look, you'll see many of his works all over the place.

Located south of the plaza and west of the civic center, **Parque Hidalgo** is a good Sunday stop. Vendors sell all manner of food and mariachis take over the day; music is everywhere. If you want quiet, this isn't the place on Sundays.

Centro Cultural De Hidalgo

A fine group of of museums is located in this former monastery of San Francisco. The **National Institute of Anthropology and History** runs this old ex-convent, which over its 400-year span has run the gamut of uses: monks were housed here, horses stabled, cattle butchered, and criminals incarcerated. In the adjoining church, the immensely wealthy Count of Regla was buried. Though there are no figures on paper, it is believed that his mines produced more than even the Valenciana mine of Guanajuato. The history and photography museums are part of this complex.

Regional History Museum

An ex-mining school, the museum displays archaeological and ethnological artifacts representing the Huastecas, Aztecs, Toltecs, Otomis, and Chichimecs. Displays of folk art, crafts, everyday utensils, and indigenous garb describe the lifestyle of early Hidalgo State.

National Museum Of Photography

Here you see some really enlightening 19th-20th century pictures of Mexico dating back to 1873. Old photos give a look at the archaeological sites before renovations, and of course, the most photographed rogue of the century, Pancho Villa, is well represented.

Casa De Las Artesanías

This is another good browsing place. Prices seemed a bit high for goods, but there were quite a number of original specimens. Check out the woven wool goods, mouth-blown glass, and some interesting ceramic pieces. Open 10 a.m.-8 p.m., closed Monday.

PRACTICALITIES

This is a big city and you'll find just about anything you need including banks and medical services.

Accommodations

Most folks come to see the sights in one day. However, if you want to wander through the countryside, there are several acceptable hotels at which to spend the night. The **Hotel Emily** is one of the nicest, located on Calle Hidalgo, Plaza de la Independencia, tel. (771) 2-6617 or 2-6618. It has reasonable prices and is tidy and friendly. **Hotel Noriega,** at Calle Matamoros 305, tel. 5-1591, has been a popular stopover for years. Rooms are large and clean, and yes, they have bottled water. Another place to check out, at Matamoros 207, is the **Hotel de los Baños,** tel. 3-0700, just off the plaza; note the fine tile. There are several others, all easy to find. Some really are cheap, and as you step into the lobbies you'll see why.

If you're driving a car and you have a fat budget, enjoy the historical drama of an old hacienda. Stop over at the **Hacienda San Miguel Regla, Hotel and Villas.** If you've been reading about the history of the mines you'll feel as though you know the gentleman who built this rambling structure. This 18th century ex-hacienda has been turned into a resort hotel in a pine forest setting and has an interesting history about a man who really struck it rich in this area.

The Count of Regla, Pedro Romero de Terreros, had good fortune with rich relatives who left him large amounts of money at their deaths. But he was also a wise man; he took his money and invested it into an engineering project that would eventually bring back to life one of the richest mines of the area, **Real del Monte.** Rejuvenating the mine, he became the wealthiest man in the country (after Cortés), so rich that he loaned King Charles III one million dollars. Even more impressive was the man-of-war ship that he had built to his specifications; when Charles III needed it, the Count graciously gave to him. It was a beautiful three-decker ship built in Cuba of cedar and mahogany.

Today, this luxurious hacienda has all the amenities needed for a comfortable vacation. Villas, suites, and rooms border walking trails through the trees, and there are bridle paths so you can enjoy horseback riding. There's also a pool and tennis courts. It's located in the town of Huasca, 16 km north of Pachuca, tel. (771) 0-0053.

Food

The food of Pachuca is tasty. One of the specialties is *mixiotes,* tamale-type ingredients wrapped in maguey leaves. Another is *barbacoa;* here in Pachuca the meat of choice is lamb wrapped in maguey leaves and baked underground. Though we have not sampled it ourselves, we've been told about another local favorite, *escamoles,* fried ant eggs.

You'll find a number of small cafes around the town center. Here are a couple of names to help you out. **Restaurante Acapulco** is at Matamoros 202, very near the Plaza de la Independencia. Seafood is the specialty here. Open all day. For an intimate taco bar, try **Mesón de Los Angeles Gomez** at Guerrero 723; watch the family in production here. Hotel Noriega has a good dining room, and there are others worth checking into. If you're really desparate for a taste and look of home, check out **Shakey's Pizza.**

Tourist Office

The tourist office is open 9 a.m.-8 p.m. There's very little in printed information in English, but the staff is very willing to try to help you. At Av. Allende 406.

Money

You'll have no trouble finding a bank to exchange money; there are several located around the Plaza de la Independencia.

Other Services

Telephone service is available at Av. Valle 106. The **post office** is at Juárez and Iglesias. The **hospital** is on the highway towards Tulancingo. **Farmacia del Pueblo** is at Matamoros 205, and check out the **Lavandería** at Centro Comercial Constitución L-14 if you need to have your clothes washed.

Trivia Note

The silver mines of Pachuca were responsible for soccer entering the country—by way of miners from Cornwall who came during the 19th century. These miners also brought a touch of Cornish cuisine in the form of pasties, which, when brought from the UK, were pastry crusts filled with meat, potatoes, carrots, and onions. Check out the menus in the neighborhood fondas, you'll find *pastes,* which are a slight variation, filled with chiles, meats, moles, and other Mexican-style adaptions. Rather a nice change of pace.

GETTING THERE AND AROUND

By Car

One of the best ways to see Hidalgo and the countryside is by driving. There are so many small communities that have reference to the past. With your own vehicle you can stop at your leisure and investigate. Be warned, many of these villages have no facilities available for tourists, so try to plan your day to end before dark at one of the cities that cater to tourists. From Mexico City, Highway 85D (toll road) is a good way to get to Pachuca and on to Actopan and Ixmiquilpan. From there follow the signs to various areas. **Note:** As in most of Mexico, it's wise to reach your destination before nightfall. In these mountainous regions, once you stray off the main highways roads can be narrow and very curvy with little or no shoulder. And though we don't hear a lot about robbers, it's always a possibility in the isolated regions.

By Bus
To get to the central bus station, hop the bus that leaves from in front of the Tourist Office on Allende. You can make connections with **ADO, Estrella Blanca,** and **Autotransportes Valle del Mexquital.**

TULA

Tula, the town, is a slow-going town with a population of 42,000 people. The altitude is 2,060 meters. The terrain of the area is semidesert. Mostly it's just the "town near the Atlantes" about three kilometers away. Buses come and go from town and from there you can either walk or take a taxi to the site.

TULA/TOLLAN ARCHAEOLOGICAL SITE

There are many unanswered questions and theories about Tula, believed to have been the ancient city of **Tollan.** The Toltec civilization, who some believe built Tula in A.D. 900, wielded a lot of power. However, like many powerful groups, something weakened their position—many authorities believe it was internal problems—and Tula fell around A.D. 1200. For 200 years the city-states of the Valley of Mexico grew, prospered, made war, and sacrificed captives.

Founded near the beginning of the 10th century, **Tollan** (today referred to as Tula) achieved its glory after Teotihuacán was crushed and before Tenochtitlán was conceived. In fact, evidence indicates that it was the many refugees from Teotihuacán that caused a rapid increase in Tula's population. It is possible that the city was the capital of the Toltec-Chichimeca Empire. And though this was a powerful nation, it never grew as large as Teotihuacán. The

Aztecs, in hindsight, declared that the Toltecs were their ancestors. In A.D. 968, new leadership of the area was taken over by **Topiltzin Quetzalcoatl,** described as fair-skinned and bearded. He was a priest-king of the feathered serpent cult who disdained human sacrifice. Apparently this was not a popular notion and history is filled with myths and legends surrounding the unusual Topiltzin.

Poems in Nahuatl tell how **Tezcatlipoca** ("Smoking Mirror"), tricked and tortured Quetzalcoatl. After being humiliated by the magic and "cheap tricks" of the evil Tezcatlipoca—a war god and giver and taker of life who craved warm, human hearts—Topiltzin was run out of town. When the bearded leader left, he vowed that one day he would return. This prophecy is what no doubt spawned the belief in 1519 that the bearded, white-skinned Cortés might be a returning god from the past. In the meantime, Tollan was taken over by Tezcatlipoca's followers until for some still unknown reason the entire region collapsed.

Still other legends propose that Topiltzin was really **Kukulcan.** Maya accounts tell of a Mexican king called Kukulcan ("Feathered Serpent"), who invaded the Yucatán in the late 10th century. Many believe they were one and the same. The architectural similarity between some of the structures at Chichén Itzá (in the state of Yucatán), especially the Temple of the Warriors, and those here at Tula are remarkable.

Archaeologists do know that the Toltecs were a tough group. Included in their military machine were the **Eagle Knights** and **Jaguar Knights,** the mightiest warriors of the Toltecs. Once they had control of the empire, it grew more warlike, and it is believed that it was they who began the excessive human sacrifice and bloodletting. They fought south to Chapultepec, east to Cholula, and as far south as Guatemala, conquering all who had the misfortune of getting in their way.

It is believed the city of Tula was engulfed in a great fire. Much was destroyed, and by A.D. 1125, Tollan began to lose its control. Sacked and looted by factions from outside the border,

Tula was abandoned before A.D. 1200. The site is small compared to Teotihuacán and not known or visited by as many people; archaeologists now believe, however, that at its peak, Tollan covered an area of 13 square km and ruled a population of 60,000 people.

Exploring Tula Site

The tales told of this ancient site of Tollan paint magnificent pictures of nirvana. The society here was rich, jewels were used as part of the mythic carvings, and walls and panels were painted with brilliant colors; no one wanted for anything. Today what you see is quite different—stripped and deserted. The Aztecs, among

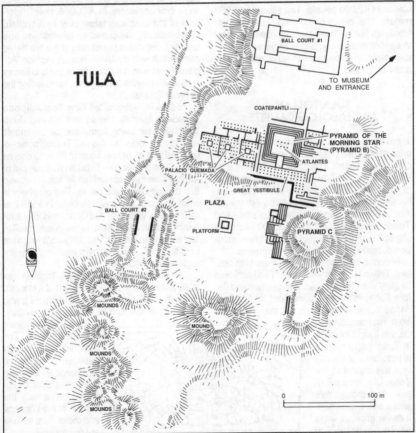

others, looted Tollan during and after its decline. Little is left of the once great city. There's a pervasive feeling of desolation here at the dusty site, more than I personally have felt at any of the other archaeological sites. Locals claim there's a magic force lurking around these ageless structures.

Pyramid B: Most everyone who visits comes to see the **Pyramid of the Morning Star** or **Templo de Tlahuizcalpantecuhtli.** This pyramid consists of five landings, the topmost holding the **Atlanteans.** These four massive stone warriors, 4.6 meters tall (15 feet) bear butterfly-shaped breastplates on their chests. Each holds an *atlatl* (spear thrower) in one hand and an incense pouch in the other, wearing a round headdress with feathers standing straight up. Stoic and austere, they present an attitude of ferocious power and their gargantuan size undoubtedly was meant to impart a warning to all who looked upon them. Around the sides of the pyramid are bas-reliefs of eagles eating human hearts, as well as coyotes, jaguars, and imaginary (and imaginative) creatures. A steep stairway on the south side takes you to the top, and it's worth the climb for the view of Tula and the arid countryside.

Palacio Quemada: Located just west of Pyramid B, the Burnt Palace is a series of plazas, benches, and walls with carvings showing a sequence of richly dressed nobles. Many of Tula's works were plundered over the years, some even finding their way to Tenochtitlán.

Coatepantli: On the north side of Pyramid B, Coatepantli ("Serpent Wall"), rises 2.25 meters high and stretches 40 meters long. This wall is covered with carvings of snakes and skeletons, and if you look closely, you can see remnants of the paint that once covered this intriguing wall.

Ball Court #1: This ball court is identical in size to one at the archaeological site of Xochicalco. This court is in excellent condition. Some

conjecture that this is where the first ball court was built, the inception of the "game" or "tournament." Another one of those unanswered questions. Was the ball game for fun or for blood?

At The Entrance: Admission is US$4 (includes parking and the museum), and the site is open daily 9:30 a.m.-4:30 p.m. You'll find a small museum, soft drinks, and the perennial souvenir salesmen.

Practicalities

If you get hungry, there are several places, either in town or on the way to the highway. **Restaurante Tollan Campestre** is located on the road returning to the toll road; look for a building with a covered wagon on its top. Back in town, check out **Cafetería el Cisne** on the main street near the *zócalo*. Another, **Restaurant Casa Blanca**, is at Zaragoza and Hidalgo.

Getting There

Buses depart Mexico City's **Terminal Central de Autobuses del Norte** about every 15 minutes 5 a.m.-11 p.m. going to Tula; fare is about US$3. Look for the ticket counter marked "Autotransportes Valle del Mezquital," (turn left as you enter the building and walk to the end). The bus will drop you off in town, and you either walk to the site (about 15-20 minutes), flag a cab, or take the minibus marked **Tlahuelilpan;** it's about three kilometers from town. You might want to make arrangements with your cab or the minibus to be picked up for the return to town. The last bus to Mexico City leaves Tula at 7 p.m. There are other buses from Mexico City available; ask at the tourist office or your hotel for more information.

By Car

Take Highway 57 from Mexico City. At Tepotzotlán it becomes a toll road, Hwy. 57D. Continue on till you see signs on the right directing you to Tula; this road is Hwy. 126, which takes you right through town. Look for the signs directing you to "Las Ruinas"; from town the sign says "Parque Nacional Tula."

Gigantes of Tula

BOB RACE

VICINITY OF PACHUCA

TULANCINGO

In the southeastern portion of the state of Hidalgo, this smallish city has remnants of history from the times of both the Toltecs and the Spanish. Situated on the **Río Grande de Tulancingo,** it lies at 2,222 meters above sea level. The Spanish took it from the Toltecs in the early 1520s. There are still several colonial churches remaining from the time (1862) when it was the seat of the Catholic Bishop. Today the city is mostly an agricultural center where barley and alfalfa are grown. This is also a textile center that is becoming more modernized each year. It's located east of Pachuca, and you can get here on the train, as well as by bus or other vehicle.

NORTHWEST OF PACHUCA

In the opposite direction, west of Pachuca, it's an interesting drive through several cities that were active during the early mining era, and since this was the heart of the indigenous world, each of these towns has its own version of pre-Hispanic history and people.

Actopan

This is another ex-convent of the Augustinians. Since they arrived in Mexico later than the Franciscans and Jesuits, they had to go farther from the cities to find their flocks. Having fewer sheep meant they could not build as prolifically as their brethren, but what they did build was worthwhile functionally and aesthetically. The thick walls and doors and windows cut at angles admit light and air yet block direct sunlight to keep the interior cool. Built between 1539 and 1560, the vaults are a stunning blend of Gothic and Plateresque style. The span of the open chapel vault is longer than that of Notre Dame Cathedral in Paris.

Ixmiquilpan

At 1,700 meters, you'll run into **Ixmiquilpan** (eesh-mee-KEEL-pawn), a pleasant little town with about 30,000 residents, most of whom are

descendants of the Otomi people. The town has a huge fortesslike ex-monastary called **St. Michael the Archangel,** built by the priests of St. Augustine in 1550. Check out the Indian frescoes inside.

This whole area is noted for its pulque production, and you'll see the maguey plant growing all over the countryside. If you happen to be around on Monday (market day) you'll find many maguey products, including popular beverages, pulque, aguamiel, and mezcal. Of course the market is filled with fruits and vegetables, but most especially some fine crafts including guitars.

Tasquillo

If you're in the mood for a swim, travel about 30 kilometers northwest of Pachuca on Hwy. 85 and stop at the town of Tasquillo, where you'll find several natural warm mineral pools.

HUEJUTLA

If you happen to be in the neighborhood, or at least close by, this small town is another interesting place to spend the **Día de los Muertos** ("Day of the Dead"), which is actually celebrated over a couple of days. In fact, here in this small village the children have a week's vacation for the celebration, called **Shantolo** in Nahuatl. During this holiday families all come from surrounding villages to be together. They spend much of the time at the cemetery cleaning and beautifying the graves of their departed. An altar is set at each grave, with a photo to identify the family member. All the favorite foods are prepared and in the home another altar is set up. Petals from marigolds are scattered in a neat path that leads to the house and through the door to help the departed find their way in the night. Fireworks go on for a week, and special Day of the Dead foods are prepared.

Pan Huasteca

In the nearby town of San Felipe Orizatlan, a popular bakery makes the "bread of the dead." Baker Josefa Rivera is well known and uses a large clay *hornito* (oven) and baking sheets made of flattened tin cut from oil drums. The oven is first warmed by building a wood fire inside and then kept warm with charcoal burning in a side-oven. She makes three kinds of bread for these holidays; cheese, butter, and egg bread—very tasty!

Other Foods For The Day

Other typical Huasteca food includes *bocoles,* which are small cakes of maize dough stuffed with beans, chiles, and chopped fresh cilantro,

all fried in pork lard. Despite the suggestion of lard, this is quite good. *Atole* is another traditional dish prepared at this time of year. This is basically a soup made of maize, beans, salt, chile, and cilantro. It can be sweetened or unsweetened—called *atole agrio.*

Practicalities

Come prepared to camp out or sleep in your car, since you won't find a hotel close by, and you really don't want to be driving these roads at night.

THE WORD HIDALGO

This is a frequently heard word in Mexico, mostly because of Miguel Hidalgo who precipitated the **War Of Independence,** freeing Mexico from Spain. But the word itself has meanings that go back much farther to the early days of Spain. That helps to explain the class system that most of us seldom think about; it is a contraction of the words *hijo de algo,* which means "son of something," in other words a hereditary title. It was bestowed upon the lesser nobility, distinct from those with more clout, such as the *ricos hombres* (rich men), and distinct from those nobles who traveled in an even less-honored path, *caballeros villanos* (commoner knights). Actually, the *hidalgos* had a good position, but they were not rich men. They were generally presented with land that paid them some rents and bestowed other prestigious privileges. From the 15th century on, they were all Christian (after the long siege of Muslim rule in Spain). For a really good look into the life of an *hidalgo,* read *Don Quixote,* by Miguel de Cervantes, and *Lazarillo de Tormes,* by Hurtado de Mendoza.

K. A. ESCOVEDO SANDERS

THE STATE OF VERACRUZ
INTRODUCTION

This is it. The place where the European world slipped into a land of magic, at once both wonderful and frightening. Veracruz was the gateway to what would be called the New World, beginning with the arrival of Hernán Cortés on Good Friday in 1519, with a small fleet, 15 horsemen, and 300 foot soldiers. Veracruz continues to be an important Mexican port for ships from around the globe.

All along the coast of Veracruz, the people are a mix of European, Indian, and African descendants. The people here are the most diverse of anywhere in Mexico.

Veracruz is where the lively *la bamba* originated, and it takes very little searching to find the music and its aficionados dancing up a storm all over the state. In every seaside port along the coast you'll find vendors selling fresh grilled shrimp and crab, with cold *cerveza* of course. Life is lively on the streets of the cities, especially in the sidewalk cafes along the historical plazas of Veracruz city, where it's "party time" most of the time, and it's a favorite vacation spot for families from all over Mexico.

The Land

Located in an undulating 1,000-km strip on the Gulf of Mexico, Veracruz touches the states of Tamaulipas, San Luis Potosí, Hidalgo, Puebla, Oaxaca, Chiapas, and Tabasco. This balmy, tropical state produces rice, coffee, sugar, tobacco, a large assortment of fruits, oil, and cattle.

Prehistory

The multicultured people of the ancient past shared various similarities and left numerous artifacts behind to tell the tale. At the archaeological sites of **San Lorenzo, La Venta,** and **Tres Zapotes** the massive basalt sculptures of the Olmec continue to stand guard through the ages. At **Cempoala** and **El Tajín,** the Totanacs, who may have been the architects of Teotihuacán, left a large footprint—the **Huastec** culture, which still thrives in the north.

The Olmecs are believed to be the oldest civilization in Mexico. Most of what is known about these people is from the trail of sculptures they left behind including the monolithic stone heads

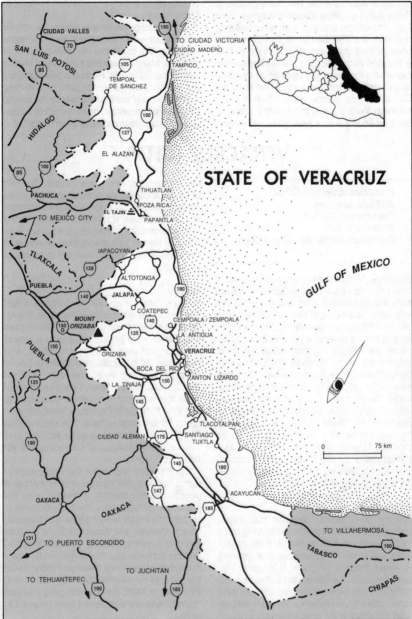

STATE OF VERACRUZ

GULF OF MEXICO

CIUDAD VALLES

SAN LUIS POTOSI

TO CIUDAD VICTORIA
CIUDAD MADERO
TAMPICO

HIDALGO

TEMPOAL
DE SANCHEZ

EL ALAZAN

TIHUATLAN
POZA RICA
EL TAJIN
PAPANTLA

PACHUCA

TO MEXICO CITY

TLAXCALA

IAPACOYAN

ALTOTONGA

PUEBLA

JALAPA

COATEPEC

CEMPOALA / ZEMPOALA
LA ANTIGUA

MOUNT
ORIZABA

ORIZABA

VERACRUZ

BOCA DEL RIO

ANTON LIZARDO

PUEBLA

LA TINAJA

CIUDAD ALEMAN

SANTIAGO
TUXTLA

TLACOTALPAN

0   75 km

OAXACA

OAXACA

TO VILLAHERMOSA

ACAYUCAN

TABASCO

TO PUERTO ESCONDIDO

TO TEHUANTEPEC

TO JUCHITAN

CHIAPAS

© MOON PUBLICATIONS, INC.

and small jade carvings. The characteristics of these carvings were always the same: thick lips—sometimes snarling—jaguarlike features, and often chubby infant faces. One of the most unusual finds is a bearded figure in the pose of a wrestler. Archaeologists are still hesistant to say where these people were from, though a large number of artifacts were found along the Gulf of Mexico coastal plain, which is today southern Veracruz and neighboring Tabasco. But new finds are now turning up in Guerrero, and it seems there's a connection in Yucatán Maya country as well.

The capital of the state is Jalapa, the Athens of Veracruz—so called because of the state university and the liberal inquisitive attitude of students. Many believe that the future of Mexico lies on the Gulf coast. Railroads and highways are well kept, and rumors of plans for damming rivers to provide water and power for the central plateau are circulating. The oil centers of Tampico and Coatzalcoalcos have been upgraded.

VERACRUZ (CITY)

Pronounced: Ver-ah-CRUZ
Altitude: sea level
Population: 375,000
Area Code: (29)
Distance from Mexico City: 430 km

Somehow, Veracruz has a different personality from the Acapulcos and the Cancúns. It's not quite the glitzy resort town and you won't see long white beaches and streamlined high-tech discos. Rather, it's a steamy seaport-city with a magnanimous history, a pride in its independence, and a flourishing international port where industry is thriving. However, it is a city whose people thoroughly enjoy themselves. **Carnaval** here ranks with the finest celebrations in the world. The town also fills up on *all* the main holidays. Today's Veracruzanos (known locally as Jarochos, the "Rude Ones") are a funloving, hardworking lot. The city is well known for its seafood. At least once try fish with the famous Veracruzano sauce made with tomatoes, onions, chile peppers, garlic, and zinger spices. Try a fish tamale, different and tasty.

Economy

The city counts 88,000 industries, businesses, and service entities, together employing half a million workers; 63% work in shops, restaurants, and hotels. The tourist sector is growing. However, industry continues to locate in Veracruz because of ample supplies of water, electricity, and gas plus quality labor and industrial zones offering convenience for plant installations. Proximity to the power-producing Temazcal Dam is another important factor. The port at Veracruz continually receives container ships carrying tons of raw materials, especially from the United States. It's located minutes from a major international airport, and the railroad links it to all of Mexico, plus there's a broad network of highways spreading from Veracruz to the rest of the country.

History

Today's Veracruz was the first community settled by Cortés and his men. However, the location is the third one for the city. The first two settlements were poor choices for a variety of reasons: bad water, swampy locations, and mosquitos (all considerations stated in Bernal Díaz del Castillo's book, *The True History of the Conquest of New Spain*. Cortés and his stalwarts first landed at San Juan de Ulúa, and the first **Villa Rica de la Cruz** (now Veracruz) was about 70 km north of here. The second Villa Rica was then moved close to Antiqua, and then finally, in 1598, today's Veracruz was established.

It is the oldest and largest port in Mexico. Veracruz has seen the historical entry of *millions* of people into the country. However, with the growth of tourism, more continue to arrive in Mexico via much newer gateways: Cancún, Puerto Vallarta, and Acapulco. Tons of silver and gold were shipped from Veracruz to Spain, and the port was also the entry point for every subsequent invasion in Mexico's history; it was the last safe haven of the Spanish, 1821-1824. However, in 1825, the Spanish gave their last "hurrah" and were banished from Nueva España.

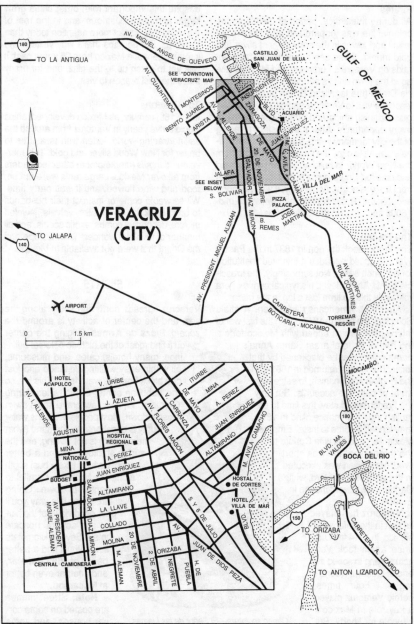

TO LA ANTIGUA

180

AV. MIGUEL ANGEL DE QUEVEDO

AV. CUAUHTEMOC

MONTESINOS

BENITO JUAREZ

M. ARISTA

AV. ALLENDE

1 DE MAYO

20 DE NOVIEMBRE

SALVADOR DIAZ MIRON

S. BOLIVAR

INSURGENTES

BLVD

ZARAGOZA

SEE "DOWNTOWN
VERACRUZ" MAP

CASTILLO
SAN JUAN DE ULUA

GULF OF MEXICO

ACUARIO

JUAN ENRIQUEZ

C. AVILA CAMACHO

VILLA DEL MAR

PIZZA
PALACE

JOSE
MARTINI

B. REMES

JALAPA

SEE INSET
BELOW

VERACRUZ
(CITY)

TO JALAPA

140

AV. PRESIDENT MIGUEL ALEMAN

AV. ADOLFO
RUIZ CORTINES

CARRETERA
BOTICARIA - MOCAMBO

TORREMAR
RESORT

AIRPORT

1.5 km

MOCAMBO

180

BLVD MA.
VALDES

BOCA DEL RIO

© MOON PUBLICATIONS, INC.

HOTEL
ACAPULCO

AV. I. ALLENDE

V. URIBE

J. AZUETA

AGUSTIN

MINA

NATIONAL

BUDGET

ITURBE

MINA

1 DE MAYO

V. CARRANZA

AV. FLORES MAGON

A. PEREZ

JUAN ENRIQUEZ

ALTAMIRANO

HOSPITAL
REGIONAL

A. PEREZ

JUAN ENRIQUEZ

SALVADOR DIAZ MIRON

ALTAMIRANO

LA LLAVE

COLLADO

AV. PRESIDENT
MIGUEL ALEMAN

MOLINA

20 DE NOVIEMBRE

CENTRAL CAMIONERA

M. ALEMAN

2 DE ABRIL

ORIZABA

NEGRETE

H. DE
PUEBLA

5 Y 6 DE JULIO

AV.

JUAN DE DIOS PEZA

HOSTAL
DE CORTES

HOTEL
VILLA DE MAR

OLID

150

TO ORIZABA

CARRETERA A. LIZARDO

TO ANTON LIZARDO

Pirates

All during this critical period of development, colonial life was jeopardized by pirates. Like many port towns in the early days of silver and gold mania, these sea rovers made frequent raids on Veracruz. Lorencillo and his men ravaged the town and its people in 1683. Sir Francis Drake (the legalized British pirate) paid at least one visit to Veracruz and continued to harrass Spanish ships and purloin their booty at every opportunity. After the constant pillaging of the city for many years, the Spanish crown finally saw fit to okay the funds (which came from the New World) to build an immense bulkhead and nine forts in Veracruz to protect themselves from the onslaught. Apparently, it was not good enough; the pirates sacked the town in the mid-1600s and again in the early 1700s.

The French

The French took the port in 1837 in the **Pastry War,** so-called because it involved restitution for a French baker. Not surprisingly, the irrascible Santa Anna played his typical comic-opera role, only this he time lost a leg in the fracas.

After that, Americans under Gen. Winfield Scott took the town in 1847 during the first war of intervention, which ended with Mexico forfeiting half of its total area; Santa Anna's name will forever be blackened by that affair. The French returned in 1861 with the English and Spanish, to settle payment of past due accounts. But only the French would stay, this time to establish their dominance. And in 1862 they landed in force to install Emperor Maximilian and his wife Carlota to the throne; that too was short-lived. Maximilian was executed in the state of Querétaro, while Carlota slowly went insane in Europe.

Veracruz has played its part in the defense of Mexico. In 1914 the U.S. once again took Veracruz, trying to speed the end of General Huerta's regime. Four times, heroic Veracruz played a key role in Mexico's struggle for liberty. But

despite this important role, other cities grew larger and more illustrious, and in the rest of the world may attract more attention today than Veracruz. But perhaps that's why visitors find it reminiscent of a Mexico from 25 years past; it has yet to catch up to the glitz, and for many that's the best reason to visit.

The Galleons

In the 16th century, as Mexico developed, ships would arrive yearly in Veracruz from around the sailing/trading world, laden with treasures to barter for New World silver and gold. This marvelous *tianguis* (marketplace) attracted traders from all over Mexico. Large tents were put up, food and wine flowed, and it was party time. Wives would come or instruct their husbands to bring back the lovely silks, velvets, jeweled mirrors, decorative combs, exotic scents, and all manner of frivolous wonders from Europe and the Orient that were not available in Mexico.

SIGHTS

Veracruz spreads north and south along the sea, and the center of activity is around the *zócalo,* **Plaza de Armas.** Edging the center you'll find most of the historic colonial buildings, many hotels, cafes, and museums, all within easy walking distance and just one block from the waterfront. This is also the bubbling center of festivities during Carnaval. While a few brave souls swim close to town, most people don't; the water purity is questionable, the sand (what there is of it) is not inviting, and the surf is shallow. To find a better beach, walk (or take a bus) south along the Malecón, parallel to the center of town. Going south, along this way you'll pass good views of the harbor and several upscale hotels. Several kilometers south you'll find a better beach at **Villa del Mar,** and another even better at **Mocambo.**

Note: Street names are posted on some corner houses, and some

Olmec sculpture—El Señor de las Llamas

K. A. ESCOVEDO SANDERS

signs relate the name that street was called in the past—there can be several numbers visible on each building. If confused, ask—or just wander; it's very hard to get lost in the old part of the city.

Plaza De Armas

The *zócalo* is known officially as Plaza de Armas; either name will get you there. This is the beating heart of Veracruz. Musicians are everywhere; marimba bands, guitarists, and mariachis, serenading couples on benches near the fountain, diners under the *portales,* and everyone nearby. Natives and visitors alike sit in large hotel restaurants drinking *café con leche* (coffee with milk) in the morning, *cerveza o coctels* (beer or cocktails) in the afternoon, and dining on a wide array of seafoods, day and night.

Catedral De Nuestra Señora De La Asunción

Built in 1721 and elevated to cathedral status in 1963, this is little more than a village church when compared to the massive cathedrals of other cities. If this is your first look inside a Mexican church, note the glass-enclosed statues, some dressed in clothing, and the people who kiss their fingers before touching the glass. Old women sitting behind tables or on the cathedral steps sell religious medals and holy cards.

Palacio Municipal

The building was constructed in 1627, greatly inspired by the Moorish architecture of Spain. The Italian-style tower, whose bell rang (in the past) to announce each ship arrival, was added a century later. The bandstand nearby holds the military band on Monday and Saturday evenings.

Coffee Customs At La Parroquia

Although this is a restaurant, it's a famous sight as well; no one visits the city without stopping at La Parroquia for a little *gnash* or a coffee. Here you find the real movement of the city. The sounds are a cacophony of music, conversation in a multitude of languages, and a steady stream of vendors selling anything from lottery tickets to live parrots. It's traditional to sit and be seen banging a glass mug with a spoon to summon the bustling waiters. The ritual begins by ordering *café con leche;* your waiter pours black coffee and disappears. Pick up the spoon and

clay vessel with effigy

NATIONAL MUSEUM OF ANTHROPOLOGY, MEXICO CITY

clink it, as if a toast were in order; another waiter, with a pot in each hand, will eventually appear. If there is too much coffee in your cup you pour the excess into one pot and he pours the milk from the other. You will learn quickly—just watch. The day starts early here, maybe 6 a.m., and goes on till well into the night. It's one block south of Plaza de Armas, at Av. Independencia 105, tel. (29) 32-2584.

Portales De Miranda

The *portales* (arches), near the cathedral, are named for Miranda, who was the merchant who did big business here. Browse through the many shops where once the scribes wrote letters.

All around the colorful facades of balconied houses bring reminders of islands touched by tradewinds, and shades of blue, green, yellow, and pink abound. Many old houses around the plaza post plaques announcing the residence or birthplace of Mexican leaders and scholars, including native son Miguel Alemán, once president of Mexico.

Malecón

From the boulevard (the Malecón) that runs along the harbor and seafront, watch the freighters and tankers come and go or take a

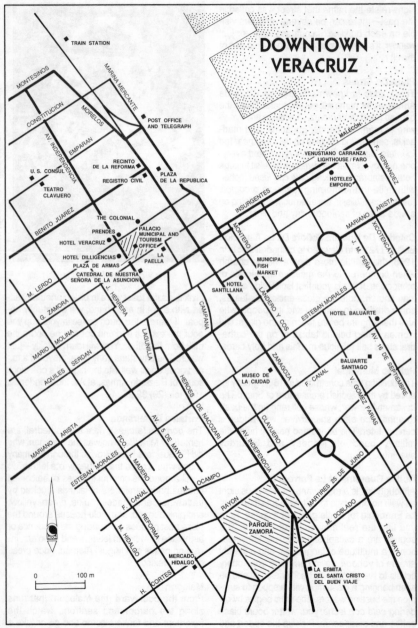

DOWNTOWN VERACRUZ

TRAIN STATION

MONTESINOS

CONSTITUCION

MORELOS

MARINA MERCANTE

AV. INDEPENDENCIA

EMPARAN

POST OFFICE AND TELEGRAPH

RECINTO DE LA REFORMA

U.S. CONSULATE

MALECON

F. HERNANDEZ

VENUSTIANO CARRANZA LIGHTHOUSE / FARO

REGISTRO CIVIL

PLAZA DE LA REPUBLICA

HOTELES EMPORIO

TEATRO CLAVIJERO

BENITO JUAREZ

INSURGENTES

MARIANO ARISTA

J. XICOTENCATL

THE COLONIAL

PRENDES

HOTEL VERACRUZ

PALACIO MUNICIPAL AND TOURISM OFFICE

MONTERO

J. M. PEÑA

HOTEL DILLIGENCIAS

LA PAELLA

PLAZA DE ARMAS

CATEDRAL DE NUESTRA SEÑORA DE LA ASUNCION

MUNICIPAL FISH MARKET

M. LERDO

G. ZAMORA

J. HERRERA

CAMPANA

LANDERO Y COS

HOTEL SANTILLANA

ESTEBAN MORALES

HOTEL BALUARTE

MARIO MOLINA

AQUILES SERDAN

LAGUNILLA

ZARAGOZA

AV. 16 DE SEPTIEMBRE

BALUARTE SANTIAGO

HEROES DE NACOZARI

F. CANAL

V. GOMEZ FARIAS

MUSEO DE LA CIUDAD

MARIANO ARISTA

AV. 5 DE MAYO

CLAVIJERO

AV. INDEPENDCIA

ESTEBAN MORALES

FCO. I. MADERO

M. OCAMPO

MARTIRES 25 DE JUNIO

M. DOBLADO

1 DE MAYO

F. CANAL

REFORMA

RAYON

PARQUE ZAMORA

M. HIDALGO

MERCADO HIDALGO

H. CORTES

LA ERMITA DEL SANTA CRISTO DEL BUEN VIAJE

0   100 m

© MOON PUBLICATIONS, INC.

tour on one of the ships tied up close by. Harbor tours are available on one of several launches (7 a.m.-7 p.m.). Prices vary, and they are often negotiable. Guides usually speak only Spanish (ask at your hotel about foreign language tours).

Castillo San Juan De Ulúa

The squat, menacing shape visible across the bay was built to defend the city in the 16th and 17th centuries, and later used as a prison. **Benito Juárez** was a one-time guest (1858-1861). Now it's a museum, where you can imagine the massive cannon that stood ready and the soldiers who watched for unfriendly sails on the horizon, and you will surely cringe at the thought of occupying a cold, dank dungeon. This prison was notorious for cruelty. The **Rampart of the Shackles** was begun in the 16th century. From here the last royalist force in Mexico was ousted in 1825. Venustiano Carranza called this building home in 1915 when he briefly made Veracruz the seat of government. It's accessible by bus (marked "San Juan de Ulúa") or taxi from the Malecón at Landero y Coss. Open Tues.-Sun. 10 a.m.-4:30 p.m.; small admission fee, free on Sunday.

Avenida De La República

Behind the *zócalo,* across Zaragoza, stroll along on the Plaza de la República, where you'll see the beautiful pastel yellow buildings of the **post** and **telegraph** offices, with stone lions guarding the columned entrance (designed by Salvador Echagaray); also notice the **Custom House,** with its frets and battlements, and the **railroad station.** At night spotlight beams bathe them in an eerie glow. The old-fashioned, clustered streetlamps add a touch of what it might have been like when they were new.

Recinto De La Reforma

On Av. Zaragoza find the ex-church of San Francisco (1715), where Benito Juárez pronounced the laws of reform here in 1859. Today it displays bold bronze statues of the courageous *Heroes of the Reformation;* open 9 a.m.-6 p.m.

Registro Civil

On the corner of Juárez, the first birth certificate of the city was officially registered, framed, and displayed near the entrance. Don't be surprised that it's the birth record of Jeronima Francisca, the daughter of priest and liberator Benito Juárez. Note the beautiful stained glass window created by Alberto Beltran.

Plaza De La República

This plaza is an island in the swift current of vehicles during the day. Close by, near the train station, look for the sculpture of Juárez, created by Italian artist Francisco Durini, which is surrounded by metallic plaques bearing the laws of reform. This well-kept park is a cool refuge when the fountains are on. You'll find buses and taxis parked here.

Venustiano Carranza Lighthouse ("Faro")

At the corner of Aquiles Serdán and Xicoten-

Veracruz port is one of the most important in the country.

OZ MALLAN

catl, a large statue of Venustiano Carranza graces the small park in front of the old *faro* (lighthouse). It's a museum filled with the memorabilia of the famous general and one-time president. Peek into a one-room version of his life as he lived in it 1914-1915, when he (and other leaders of the era) composed the **Mexican Constitution**. Open Tues.-Sat. 9 a.m.-1 p.m. and 4-6 p.m.; free.

Baluarte De Santiago

On Canal, between 16 de Septiembre and Gómez Farías, you'll find the only one of nine forts still standing (from 1635). It once marked the outer limits of the city. The cannon on its massive walls created a link to the defenses of the city and menaced attacking vessels. Now it's a museum, open daily, 9 a.m.-5 p.m., free. About a seven-block walk from the *zócalo*.

Museo De La Ciudad

Once an orphanage, the Museo de la Ciudad is an old two-story building nicely arranged around a central courtyard and housing a small collection of pre-Columbian artifacts. Other displays exhibit local traditions, arts, crafts, and regional costumes. Located three blocks from the *zócalo* on Av. Zaragoza. Open Tues.-Sat. 9 a.m.-5 p.m., Sun. 10 a.m.-2 p.m., small admission charged.

Parque Zamora

At the corner of Rayón and Av. Independencia, is a lovely green realm in which to retreat from traffic. On Sunday evenings, it's a place of stringed instruments, as well as *huapangos* and *danzons* (traditional dances).

La Ermita Del Santa Cristo Del Buen Viaje

South of Parque Zamora on Independencia stands one of the oldest churches in the Americas, La Ermita del Santa Cristo del Buen Viaje ("Hermitage of the Holy Christ of Good Journey"). Originally, the structure was built outside the walls of the city, but the old stones were torn down in 1880, so the church has been gathered into the community. The bells hanging in their niches are reminiscent of the California missions.

Acuario

Simply called the aquarium, this compound is lo-
cated in the midst of a modern shopping center. The complex is enormous—10,000 square meters of floor space. In the aquarium itself, the main tank holds 1,250,000 liters of water and contains a vigorous collection of pelagic creatures in a lovely setting that includes a reef. Large sharks, sea turtles, barracuda, and other impressive fish glide through the clear water looking at you nose to nose. Viewing is through 13 eight-tonne acrylic windows that reach from the floor to a height of 4.5 meters; each window has a screen that can be closed. A colorful light and water show entertains visitors as they wait for tickets. The entrance curves through a natural setting of lush greenery parallel to a winding stream with small water creatures. Close by, a wall is covered with a fine waterfall and hanging green vines. Other galleries offer smaller water tanks in modern shapes and settings, all with a huge variety of fish. The Acuario was designed by Hiroshi Kamio, and it's a favorite for children; the touching table includes shark teeth, blowfish, coral, turtle shells, and much more. Another table for hands-on experience offers live tidal flats with fascinating creepies and crawlies.

This is a learning institution, and at any time you will find at least 60 interns helping in all capacities, along with visiting authorities from many parts of the world. It is south of downtown on Av. Avila Camacho. Open daily 10 a.m.-7 p.m.; admission is US$5 adults, US$1.50 children, and US$3 seniors.

Just out the door of the aquarium, visitors find great shopping with lots of modern stores and a VIPS with good snacks and cold drinks.

Teatro Clavijero

The old structure was built of wood in 1700, then destroyed by fire and rebuilt in 1834. For years it was ignored and neglected and ravaged by the elements, but the city took it over and restored it to its present incarnation. The theater is a showcase for good music and theater. It's on Emparán west of Av. Independencia.

La Prueba Cigar Factory

Throughout Mexico, Veracruz has many claims to fame, one of which is its fine cigars. Tobacco is an important crop in the south of the state, and while there have been many factories, for over 100 years this small factory has been turning out cigars. Follow the aroma of fresh tobacco and you'll find workers rolling leaf at Miguel Lerdo 500. The factory is open to the public, and tours are available Mon.-Fri. 9-11 a.m.; tel. (29) 39-2061. From the *zócalo*, walk one block north on Independencia and turn left on Lerdo; keep going for another few blocks and watch on the left—you can't miss it.

The *Marigalante/Santa María*

At the waterfront, take a look at the 15th-century-style galleon built in the state of Veracruz 1981-1987. This is a true replica of Cristóbal Colón's flagship, the *Santa Maria,* originally named *Marigalante.* It was built with blueprints obtained from the Marine Museum of Spain. Not only does the fine wooden ship look like the Santa María, but it has proven its seaworthiness by duplicating the journeys of the original ship. Built to celebrate the "500 Years of America" project, it set out from Veracruz to Tampico, then went on to Brownsville, Texas, and then across the Atlantic Ocean, reaching Spain with a crew consisting of natives of each of the countries of the American continent. Finally, it returned to the United States.

This is a floating museum with typical nautical paraphernalia as well as arts and crafts from each of the countries it has visited. When you're in Veracruz, check with your hotel or tourism office to see if the ship is in town. Admission is US$1.50; it's open all day when in port.

a crewman of the Santa María replica

ACCOMMODATIONS

Veracruz has many hotels and inns, and the prices are reasonable. Right on the Plaza de Armas, you'll find a multitude of hotels popular for their old world charm and convenience. Visitors will find accommodations to fit into every pocketbook, although prices fluctuate depending on the season or the holiday (during Carnaval especially). For all your questions and information on lodging, contact the **Mexican Association of Hotels and Motels of Veracruz and Boca Del Río,** tel. (29) 31-6448, fax 31-6845, or check with the tourism office on the *zócalo*. It's a lot easier if you can speak Spanish, otherwise, ask for the person who speaks English and keep your fingers crossed. The busiest times of the year are during **Carnaval,** from the

Sun. before till Ash Wednesday; mid-Nov. to mid-Jan.; July-Sept.; and Easter week, from Palm Sunday to Easter.

Budget Accommodations

Look for **Hotel Santillana** a couple of blocks from the *zócalo*. This older hotel offers rooms situated around a central, well-lighted atrium. The scents of ammonia and bleach attest to the sanitary proclivities of the staff. The rooms are small and simple with tile baths, double beds, and a fan. Rates are US$13 s, US$16 d, and US$21 d with two beds. At Landero y Coss 209, tel. (29) 32-3116.

About halfway between the *zócalo* and the bus terminal, a half block off Díaz Mirón, you'll find **Hotel Acapulco,** with rooms large enough for two double beds and furnishings that include chairs and a writing table. A fan provides circulation and each room has a tiled bathroom. Clean, well kept, and very inexpensive with a laundry on the premises (US$12 s, US$15 d, US$3 for extra person). Parking available. At Uribe 1327, tel. 32-9287.

Prendes, next to the Plaza de Armas at Lerdo and Independencia, has comfortable, a/c rooms for US$28 d, tel. 31-0241. The **Colonial**, with an indoor pool, has rooms with fans or a/c, and some have balconies overlooking the *zócalo*. Prices range US$13-30, depending on what you choose. At Lerdo 117, tel. 32-0193. Remember that the music and celebrating in the streets do have a tendency to cut into one's sleep if in a room overlooking the plaza—unless of course you're one of the revelers.

A Few More Budget Hotels:

Hotel Domingo, Serdán 451, tel (29) 32-8285.

Hotel Amparo, Serdán 482, tel. 32-2738.

Hotel Villa Rica, Blvd. Avila Camacho 7, tel. 32-4854.

Hotel Mar y Tierra, Avila Camacho and Figueroa, tel. 32-0260.

Hotel Royalty, Avila Camacho and Abasolo, tel. 36-1041.

Budget Hotels Near the Bus Stations:

Hotel Central, Díaz Mirón 1612, tel. (29) 37-2222, one block north of first-class bus station.

Hotel Rosa Mar, Lafragua 1100, tel. 37-0747, opposite second-class bus station.

Hotel Cheto, 22 de Marzo 218, tel. 37-4241, one block east of the second-class bus station.

Moderate Hotels

Located across the street from the old fort find the **Hotel Baluarte,** with clean, cozy air-conditioned rooms, most with balconies, all with baths; there's also a restaurant and bar. Budget rooms are US$21 s, US$24 d; the more upscale rooms are US$35 s, US$45 d. Located at Canal 265 on the corner of 16 de Septiembre, tel. (29) 36-0844; parking available.

Hotel Dilligencias is in an historical old building dating from 1780. If only the walls could tell us the stories they have witnessed. In its early days it was just as important to house and protect the stagecoaches and horses as the people who arrived on them. The antique elevator always seems to rest either just above or just below floor level, and the youthful elevator operators seem to enjoy the dilemma they create. The lobby is busy, and the desk help only speak Spanish. Expect large, modernish rooms, the corner ones having balconies on two sides, with clean, painted white walls and dark wood. Each has a tile bath, air-conditioning and TV; there's

also a restaurant and bar. Rates are US$36 s, US$45 d; at Av. Independencia 1115, tel. 31-2241, fax 31-3157.

Hotel Villa Del Mar is south of the public beach at Del Mar. This hotel feels almost new (even though it isn't). Located about 2.5 km from the *zócalo* it glows in pastel shades of (mostly) red. Accommodations are roomy and comfortable, and it's considerably cooler and quieter than the *zócalo*, unless you get a room overlooking the road. You have a choice of the main building or cottages in the garden; amenities include a/c, a pool, a seafood restaurant and bar, and a large TV in the lounge. Rates are US$45 s, US$60 d. At Avila Camacho 2707, tel. 86-0224.

Expensive Hotels

One of the larger hotels in the heart of town, **Hoteles Emporio** is on the Malecón. With 200 rooms, the Emporio offers such luxurious amenities as rooms with Jacuzzi bathtubs, satellite TV, panoramic elevators, three pools, a roof garden, **Morucho's** (a great disco), a coffee shop, a boutique, a car rental desk, and a travel agency. It can get busy when a convention is here. Rates are US$85 d for a standard to US$155 for a suite. Paseo del Malecón 244, tel. (29) 32-2222 or 32-0020, fax 31-2261.

A **Howard Johnson Hotel** lies just a few blocks from the Plaza de Armas. Also near the harbor, this chain hotel has clean, modern rooms, and they really cater to businesspeople, but of course many tourists enjoy the hotel as well. **El Vitral** restaurant serves gourmet food and the **Del Paseo** coffee shop is open around the clock. Rates are US$75 s or d; located on Blvd. Avila Camacho 1263, tel. 31-0011, fax 31-0867.

Most of the rooms of the **Torremar Resort** have views of the sea. A favorite with Mexican visitors for years, you'll find a swimming pool, a tennis court, a/c, comfy beds, a palapa snack bar, and good entertainment at **Caprichos Show Bar.** Rates start at US$120 s, US$133 d, and go up. Located at Blvd. Adolfo Ruíz Cortines, tel. 21-3466, fax 21-0291.

The **Hotel Veracruz** is in the heart of the city. With 104 rooms, it has the feeling of today's Mexico. Rooms are nicely furnished, some with king beds, very modern, marble and tile, and on the seventh-floor roof you'll find a swimming pool and solarium with a spectacular view of the city. It offers good restaurants and good nighttime entertainment. Rates are from US$90 s or d, junior and master suites available. Av. Lerdo, tel. 31-2233 or 31-1124, fax 31-5134.

At the **Hostal de Cortés** you'll find a tour desk and scuba shop on the premises, as well as an exercise room, pools, a sauna—the works. The **Disco** is one of the primo party spots for the rapaciously hip. Verandas open onto a view of the Gulf, little minibars are filled with diverse choices in every room, with nicely tiled bathrooms and satellite TV, plus a restaurant, a bar, a coffee shop, room service, and parking. Rooms start at about US$115 s and d. At Avila Camacho, on the corner of De las Casas; tel. 32-0065, fax 31-5744.

FOOD

There's a lot to be said for fresh seafood, and it doesn't get any more varied or delicious anywhere else in Mexico. *Pulpos en su tinta* (squid in its ink), *caldos* (broths) of many varieties, *jaiba* (crab), and the famous *snapper Veracruzano* are just a few of the specialties. Shrimp comes any way you can imagine and then some; don't forget *ostiones* (oysters).

The **Municipal Fish Market** contains a long line of identical stands (*ostionerías*), where *coctels* of shrimp, oysters, and octopus can be sampled. The prices are low, good for a snack or a meal with an icy *cerveza* or bubbling *refresca;* don't forget to check out the upstairs. Landero y Coss, between Arista and Serdán.

La Parroquia

A visit to Veracruz would not be complete without a visit to the spirited restaurant called La Parroquia (no doubt named for its location near to the parish church *parroquia*. Whether it's just for a cup of coffee or a platter of *anything*, it's a pleasant experience; waiters are quick, no-frill meals are served for breakfast, lunch, and dinner, and prices are reasonable. This place is always crowded, and the pitch is feverish; with spoons clinking glasses, businesspeople conversing in Spanish, or visitors sending up a variety of languages, it's loud and noisy—and fun. For breakfast try the *huevos* (eggs) cooked in sundry ways; try eggs in beans, eggs with enchiladas, eggs in Veracruzano sauce, eggs with asparagus, eggs with chiles, or *algusto*—any way you want them. With coffee it probably won't cost you more than US$3-5. Open daily, 6 a.m.-1 a.m., it's just off the Plaza de Armas on Independencia 105. How *do* they serve coffee at Parroquia? See "Coffee Customs at La Parroquia" under "Sights," above.

Try the other newer, larger version of the cafe facing the harbor, **La Gran Café Parroquia,** on Insurgentes 340, tel. (29) 32-1855.

Vegetarian Food

Vegetarians can usually find no-meat dishes fairly easily in Mexico. Tortillas and cheese and beans are usually meat-free—ask, however; some folks use animal fat in the preparation of the beans. Check out **Cafe El Profeta,** which specializes in vegetarian lunches for about US$3 Mon.-Sat.; Sunday buffet runs about US$3.75. On Juárez and Madero.

Moderately Priced Food Choices

Prendes Cafe is located at the hotel of the same name; fresh seafood as well as meat dishes are recommended. An added bonus here is watching the comings-and-goings on the plaza. A good dinner for two is about US$30. At Independencia 1064, corner of Miguel Lerdo.

La Paella offers a touch of Spain. Yes, of course, try the paella (US$6) in this nice little restaurant decorated with reminders of famous bullfights. They also serve a good *comida corrida* for about US$5.50. There are many good choices on a good menu (remember, in Spain, a *tortilla* is an omelet). Located near the tourism office in a colonial building on the south side of the *zócalo*, at Zamora 138, tel. (29) 32-0322.

Brisas Del Mar has a wonderful seafood selection. Paintings of old Mexico line the walls, and potted plants are strategically placed around the room. The service is friendly and prompt from the breadbasket to the dessert. Soups include *caldo largo* (a whole fish simmered in stock with onions and tomato), or *chilpachole de jaiba*, a spicy preparation of crab (US$3-$4.50). Entrees include such dishes as *paella, huachinango Veracruzano, ostiones a diablo*, or *camarones en mojo de ajo* (US$6-9.50). All are served with yellow rice. With beverage, tax, and tip, it's about US$40 for two.

If you need a taste of home, this is the place. **California Burgers and Shakes** serves burgers, sandwiches, shakes, and fresh fruit drinks. Low prices (US$2.50-5); at Independencia 1452. **Cafe Colonial** is a relaxing change from La Parroquia, if not as much fun. Service is good and the prices are reasonable, though a tad higher than the Independencia cafes. For a breakfast of eggs, juice, toast, and coffee have a US$5 bill handy. For lunch, soups and *antojitos* cost US$2-3.50, and entrees are US$4-8. At Calle Miguel Lerdo 109, tel. 32-3840.

Avenida Independencia

Walk along here and you'll find a multitude of choices for a snack or cold drink of any variety. There are lots of places in this city to buy "walking shrimp."

Looking For Italian

Have you had enough seafood? Tired of beans and tortillas? Well, have a little taste of Italy at the **Pizza Palace.** Remember, you're in Mexico and here you get a Mexican variation of this American favorite from Italy. They also have a hot and cold buffet for a reasonable price (US$5-6.50) noon-5 p.m. Beer is served in a glass "horn" of varying sizes supported in a wooden cradle. One of many in a chain, this one's at Molino 284, tel. (29) 36-1276.

Pira, Pira, Da Liuseppe has more than a dozen choices of pizza, and their spaghetti is fixed in a variety of ways. This is a favorite hangout of the college students, and the prices are moderate. Nice Italian atmosphere. At Arista 692, tel. 31-6144. Go south three blocks on Independencia, and turn left on Arista.

Bakeries

For the sweet tooth, try one of the bakeries that tempt from a block away—if the wind is right. Sweet rolls, pastries and excellent bread rolls and croissants can be had for *centavos.* Pick up a tray, tongs, and wax paper and serve yourself. Try **Panaficadora Paris** on Av. 5 de Mayo and Calle Mario Molina (32-1213) or **Panadería Independencia** at Av. Independencia 1400, corner of Ocampo.

Tortillas And The Market

On Av. Zaragoza a block or two from the *portales* is a tortilla store; get them while they're hot! The **Mercado Hidalgo** is located at the corner of Cortés and Hidalgo, about a block off 5 de Mayo. For cheap eats, check out the fruit and vegetable stands, cheese stalls, tortilla maker, and bakers, plus myriad choices of typical snacks.

ENTERTAINMENT AND EVENTS

Nightlife

At night the discos at Hotel Prendes (**La Capilla**) and the Hotel Emporio (**Moruchos**) are popular. So are **Garlics** and the **Hostal de Cortés,** on Avila Camacho. The local *danzon* is danced on Tuesday and Thursday at the *zócalo,* and on Sunday at Parque Zamora. The band plays in front of the Palacio on Thursday and Sunday, 7-10 p.m.

While in Veracruz, take a look, or better, *take part* in the *danzon.* This is the folkloric dance of Veracruz, with its roots in Andalusia, Spain, a bit of Florence, an added African twist, and it's further spiced up with a Cuban influence. It's a dance of rapid rhythms, solemn faces, and the straight backs of the flamenco. You'll see a lot of this during the Carnaval celebration.

Carnaval

Carnaval is a time of joyous debauchery before the fasting of Lent begins. A parade of extravagant colorful floats is the highlight of **Fat Tuesday,** flamboyant dance groups perform *danzones* down the boulevard, grand balls and masquerade parties are held all over town, and wherever more than two people gather it becomes a party whether in the park, the plaza, the Malecón, cantinas, restaurants, or a front porch; there's music everywhere! For a list of Carnaval events, check with the tourism office on Plaza de Armas. In the past, men dressed as women would perform and dance at the *bomberos* (firehouse). Ask around town if this is still the custom, and if outsiders are welcome. If you plan on visiting Veracruz during this busy time, be sure you make reservations well in advance; hotels are filled to capacity. Don't miss the fun; the Veracruz Carnaval is rated as one of the best in the country. **Note:** Pickpockets flourish during this festival with the crush of people along the parade route; take precautions.

SPORTS AND RECREATION

Fishing

Boats and tackle can be arranged through the larger hotels, definitely through the **Hostal de Cortés** or the **Club de Yates Veracruz A.C.,** tel. (29) 32-0917.

Regatta Amigos

Every two years since 1966, a fleet of sailing ships leaves Galveston, Texas, for the 690-nautical-mile trip to Veracruz. Sponsored by the yacht clubs of Galveston and Corpus Cristi, the race takes four to five days, depending on weather conditions. The crews and the families who join them here are then hosted about town by city officials and parties are the theme of the week by the **Veracruz Yachtclub.**

Beaches

The water near the town center isn't recommended for swimming—the water at Villa del Mar isn't much better, but if you must swim in the ocean in the area, go south travelers, go south.

If you feel like some exercise, **Villa Del Mar** is within (*a long*) walking distance of the *zócalo* along the Malecón, but it's much quicker on a bus, about a 10-minute ride (take bus marked "Playa V. del Mar"). Entrance fee is about US$1.25. You'll find a large pool and, if you wish, chairs and umbrellas are available for a small fee. The **Restaurante Bullshot,** on the corner of A. Camacho and Zaragoza Boulevard, is a recommended pit stop for those walking and is well patronized by the locals dining on *antojitos* and cold beer.

Even better (and a little farther) is **Mocambo,** the largest, least crowded, and best beach in the city. Entrance fee is about US$1.75, and besides a swimming pool, you can rent water toys such as snorkels, water-skis and boats. The water is shallow, and there are no strong currents, but safety is up to you, as there are no lifeguards at the beaches.

Swimming

If you want to swim in a pool and your hotel doesn't have one, check out those open to the public at the **Hotel Mocambo** and **Villa del Mar.** Both charge a small fee. Suggestion: Don't swim in the polluted waters near Veracruz Harbor; go south or go north instead.

Scuba Diving

Although diving in Veracruz doesn't even come close to Mexican Caribbean diving, it has its own special attraction. The history of Veracruz has added adventure to diving by its accumulation of sunken vessels. Every diver has heard the stories of colonial ships going down and has eyes open for the possibility of discovering a chest of gold or silver; many treasure ships fell prey to pirates and in some cases they sank before the thieves could whisk away the treasures known to be on board.

Offshore Reefs: Veracruz was the site of Mexico's first underwater national park (see below), authorized in 1972. The best diving reefs are located outside of the breakwater.

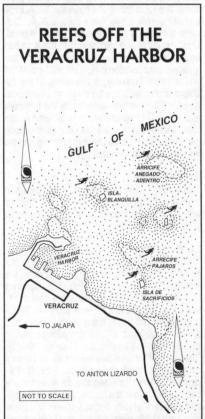

REEFS OFF THE VERACRUZ HARBOR

Miscellaneous

Tennis courts can be found at most of the more upscale hotels as well as at the **Las Palmas Racquet Club,** at Urano in Mocambo, tel. (29) 21-1970. Bicycles can be rented at **Bicicentro Lezama,** at Canal 1200, tel. 32-4965.

THE UNDERWATER PARK

A few miles outside of the harbor you'll find the underwater national park, which takes in several diving areas and reefs skirting both Isla Verde and nearby Isla Blanquilla. Diving depths average 9-30 meters. It's a good place for snorkelers. The shallow areas of the reef that face the mainland are alive with sponges, staghorn, and brain coral. The reefs facing the open sea flaunt large elkhorn corals some three meters high. Currents are usually minimal and visibility is good. Don't expect to see too many fish; this area has been overfished for centuries. Hopefully the fairly recent conservation programs will help. What you will see, however, is the wreck of the *Hidalgo,* a popular place for divers to investigate. It lies in 27 meters of water inside the bay near Isla Verde. No spearfishing is allowed in the park. These islands are a few kilometers outside the harbor, and in a fast boat expect to get to the reefs in about 35 minutes.

Isla Blanquilla

This is rather a desolate coral reef, but it is often the subject of photographers who are intrigued with large multicolored coral polyps found at fairly shallow depths.

Isla De Sacrificios

This little island has rather a gruesome history. When it was discovered by the Spaniards, the indigenous people were found performing human sacrifices. Sandy areas are said to still turn up an archaic artifact now and then. Regularly scheduled boats bring visitors interested in walking around the island and taking a look at its 35-meter-tall lighthouse. Nearby, **Hidden Reef** is another dive site known for its colorful coral polyps. North of Sacrificios, **Arrecife Pajaros** and **Arrecife Anegado de Adentro** are both rather close to the harbor, and there are limited numbers of fish, but still, divers find them both easy destinations (close), and fairly shallow depths offer interesting coral formations and a sandy bottom.

Dive Shops

Dive shops are located at **La Casa Del Mar,** A. Camacho at Zapata, tel. (29) 31-5051, or **Tridente,** Avila Camacho 165-A, tel. 32-7924; make arrangements directly with a dive group or through your hotel. Whitewater rafting can be arranged at Gómez Farías 592, tel. 36-1278.

SHOPPING

Av. Independencia is loaded with shops as well as food stores. The **Mercado Hidalgo** is located at the corner of Cortés and Hidalgo, about a block from 5 de Mayo, here vendors hawk everything imaginable. Traditional and modern clothing, fabrics, needles, crafts, Bimbo white sliced bread, chunk cheese, pots, pans, fresh fruit and veggies, and live animals; if you can name it you can probably find it. For a more familiar super-type market go to **Suprasturlos Molinos,** at Av. Gral Prim 676.

At the lower end of Av. de la República where it becomes Landero y Coss, stroll on the Malecón side where in curio and souvenir shops you can find hats, shells, baskets, yawning fish jaws with razorlike teeth, and T-shirts. On the other side of Insurgentes is the **Casa de Artesanías,** containing stalls where painters paint and carvers carve; it's pleasurable to watch them create their specialties—the crafts are for sale, of course.

SERVICES AND INFORMATION

Tourist Information Office

The **Tourism Office** is located on the south side of the Plaza de Armas in the **Palacio Municipal.** Here you can pick up a map and pamphlets describing the main points of interest. Little English is spoken but the nodding heads and smiling faces are all friendly. Open daily 9 a.m.-9 p.m., tel. (29) 32-1999.

Communication

The **Post Office** and **Telegraph** are located on the Plaza de República. **Lada Phones** are found at the bus station, train station, and *zócalo.*

Consul Offices
U.S. Consul, Edwin L. Culp, is located at Victimas del 25 de Junio 388, tel. (29) 31-0142.

Laundromats
You can find a laundromat at Gómez Faría 704, open 10 a.m.-1:30 p.m. and 4-8 p.m. Mon.-Friday. Another is **Lavamatic,** at 20 de Noviembre 133, open 8:30 a.m.-1 p.m. and 4-8 p.m. Mon.-Friday.

Medical Services
Centro Pediatrico is at M. Escobeda 289, tel. (29) 32-6902. **Hospital Regional** is at 20 de Noviembre 284, tel. 32-3690. The old stand-by pharmacies that we see in so many Mexican cities can be depended on: **El Fenix** has two branches, one at the corner of Independencia and E. Morales, tel. 32-0491, and another at Hidalgo 907, tel. 38-0110.

Money
Banamex is at the corner of Independencia and Juárez, tel. (29) 36-0964. **Bancomer** is located at Independencia 993, tel. 32-0719.
    Casas de Cambio: Monex is at 23 de Noviembre 550-12, tel. 35-1072. **La Amistad** is at Juárez 112, tel. 31-2450.

GETTING THERE

By Plane
Heriberto Jara Airport is 3.5 km from town with services provided by **Aerocaribe, Aeromexico** and **Litoral Airlines.** Flights are available to and from Mexico City, Guadalajara, and Mérida.

By Bus
First class bus line ADO, tel. (29) 35-0783, and second class bus line AU, tel. (29) 32-2376, serve most of the country from **Central Camion-**

era, located about 18-20 blocks from the town center. You can either bus to the station (look for buses marked "Díaz Mirón," for about 35 cents or take a taxi for about US$1.25. Rental lockers are available at the bus terminal.

By Train
The train station is on Plaza de la República, near the harbor. You can expect good service between Mexico City and Veracruz. As we go to press for example, the cost of the Veracruz routing is US$60 OW, and includes a sleeping room with a loo as well as two meals (generally box lunches). It departs Veracruz at 9:30 p.m. and arrives in Mexico City at 6:30 a.m. To get information, you must ask specifically about the destination and boarding point you're interested in. For more information and reservations before you go to Mexico, write to **Mexico Rail,** 8607 Wurzbach Rd. Suite V100, San Antonio, Texas, 78240, USA; tel. (210) 641-6449.

GETTING AROUND

Buses And Taxis
Buses to the beaches (marked "Mocambo-Boca del Río") can be found across from the trolley car on Victimas 25 de Junio.
    Taxis are unmetered and inexpensive; ask the price before you get in the car. **Taxi de Veracruz,** tel. (29) 34-6299 and **Radio Taxi,** tel. 38-2232 are two companies in town. **Bus tours** leave daily from the Malecón to all the popular attractions in the area; ask at your hotel or the the tourism office.

Car Rentals
Dollar is at 22 de Marzo 546, tel. (29) 31-4535, as well as at the Hostal de Cortés, tel. 32-0065. **Budget** is on Díaz Mirón 1123, tel. 31-2139. **National** is a block away from Budget at Díaz Mirón 1036, tel. 31-1756.

OUTLYING TOWNS TO VISIT

BOCA DEL RIO AND MANDINGA

Once a quaint fishing town on the banks of the lazy **Jamapa River,** Boca del Río is now a suburb of Veracruz. The small town boasts a very fine beach, good restaurants where you can sit for hours drinking beer and eating shrimp, and a few good hotels. **Pardinos Central** at Gutierrez Zamora 40 (tel. 86-0135) is one of the inexpensive eating possibilities; they specialize in crab dishes.

About eight kilometers south of Boca del Río is Mandinga, a haphazard group of wooden

huts perched between two lagoons, where you can rent a boat or gorge on the local shellfish.

ANTON LIZARDO

Just south of Boca del Río, the small mainland fishing village of Antón Lizardo offers more offshore diving. Close-by **Arrecife Blanca,** a coral islet, is said to be a good shallow snorkeling spot. If it's been raining, don't even think about going, since it's close to the mouth of a river that ruins visibility when it pours out disturbed mud. Other offshore spots to investigate are **Isla Salmedina,** a low-lying coral island. **Isla de en Medio** is a popular place for scuba divers who find maximum depths of 25 meters, with canyons and coral trenches; snorkeling is good all around the island. Camping is permitted on this island; you'll find a lighthouse and a house for the keeper. Another island south of En Medio is **Arrecife Rizo.** More reefs lie 13-24 kilometers offshore but are only a good bet during calm weather. Five outer coral banks probably offer the best selection of sea life, with tarpon, black sea bass, sharks, lobsters, and several shipwrecks.

If you're interested in shipwrecks, mention this to whichever dive shop you approach. Ask about the *Valientes* and the *Ana Elena.*

TLACOTALPAN

A town of colonial charm that sits on the **Río Papaloapan** ("River of Butterflies"), Tlacotalpan is a two hour ride by bus south of Veracruz. It's famous for its fiesta and the quality of the musicians. Beautiful stucco homes of soothing shades, some dating to the 18th century, are lovingly maintained. The *zócalo* supports two churches, a museum and house of culture, and a Moorish-style kiosk where fandango music often wafts on warm breezes.

There's a pretty park by the river where the sun rises into an azure sky and sets amid pastel hues and lovers steal kisses.

Take a leisurely boat ride on the river. Tlacotalpan claims Agustín Lara, a composer, as a

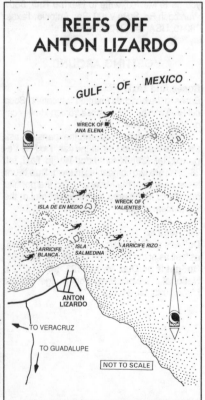

REEFS OFF ANTON LIZARDO

GULF OF MEXICO

WRECK OF ANA ELENA

ISLA DE EN MEDIO

WRECK OF VALIENTES

ARRICIFE BLANCA

ISLA SALMEDINA

ARRICIFE RIZO

ANTON LIZARDO

TO VERACRUZ

TO GUADALUPE

NOT TO SCALE

© MOON PUBLICATIONS, INC.

native son and keeps his favorite tavern as a museum. The **Salvador Ferrando Museum,** corner of Beltran and Allegre, displays clothing, furniture, and paintings of the area's past. The **Festival of Candles** takes place the last week in January and culminates on 2 February. A statue of the Virgin is carried to a waiting ship piled high with flowers and taken for a tradition-filled cruise on the river. Hundreds of young men and women on horseback parade in 19th-century finery, and bulls raised in the region run through the streets.

Food And Accommodations

The remodeled **Hotel Posada Doña Lala** is near the plaza, has a cool, dark-wood dining room and is the best the town has to offer. The variety of rooms is large and the prices vary according to the amenities of each; US$25-40. Located at Av. Carranza 11, tel. (29) 4-2580.

Small restaurants overlook the river on Av. Agustín Lara, and a bar at the north end is a place of basketball worship with posters of all the stars of the '80s plastered on the walls. The market displays the food (try any one of the almond confections) and crafts of the area, including hats and leather goods.

January-March is the best time here. When the rains start, the river rises and the streets are hard to navigate without a boat (sometimes).

Getting There From Veracruz

By **car** take Rte. 180 south. By **bus** ADO has a first-class depot in town (cost is about US$1 from Veracruz). There is also a second-class terminal close by, in case you want to go to some of the smaller towns in the area or visit the archaeological zone at **Tres Zapotes,** located outside the town of Santiago Tuxtla.

SANTIAGO TUXTLA

Magic Magnetic Black

If you're wandering around south of Veracruz and are at all close to the smallish city of Santiago Tuxtla (151 km south of Veracruz city), stop and take a wander through the **Regional Anthropology Museum.** The most well-known exhibit is called *Magnetic Black,* a sculpture found during the 1950s at **Tres Zapotes,** where two of the 15 colossal Olmec heads were found.

For many years the odd-shaped sculpture remained in the public park of the city.

LA ANTIGUA

La Antigua is a sleepy town on a sluggish river where songbirds, livestock, and falling fruit are the only afternoon sounds. In this quiet backwater, Cortés first founded his "rich city of the true cross."

Casa Cortés

It's almost a religious experience to wander the crumbling ruins that were once the home of Cortés, now held together by roots and branches of the dense jungle, aflutter with birds. The only recognizable artifacts are the oven and the cannon in front. The arches and doorways lead out to a tiny plaza where the original, oldest church of all, **Capilla de Santo Cristo del Buen Viaje,** still stands.

Discovery

From here, take a walk toward the river; your reverie may be interrupted by a soccer game played by barefoot children using coconuts to mark the goal mouth—exit the 16th century.

A ruined hotel sits on one side of the street, a gathering place for the local youth. Along this shore and under the sacred ceiba tree, it is believed that Cortés tied his vessels. Somewhere nearby is the place where he destroyed them, guaranteeing that his crew would not mutiny and sail away while he slept. A niche in the stone wall contains models of the caravels. A few steps farther is a wooden suspension bridge held up by steel cables. The sign warns to count the number of folks already on the span. Each footstep causes the bridge to sway, and multiple footsteps create more motion. The local kids love it when the gringos are thrown to and fro like leaves in a hurricane. The river below holds a small fleet of dugout canoes and a legion of exuberant kids enjoying the simple life. On the far side of the bridge is a store that sells refreshments and snacks.

The **Hotel Ceiba** sits across from the old ceiba tree, a two-story courtyard motel with clean, tile-floored rooms with twin or full-size beds, each decorated in the minimalist tradition. Rates are US$13 s, US$19 d.

Along the river, a host of patio restaurants beckon where the bountiful harvest of the sea is served. Each slightly different, all amazingly the same. **Restaurants Carmona, Tericitas,** and **Bertha** all promise ¡Música viva! ¡Pase usted! (But the signs don't say when the music starts.) Another simple cafe, **Las Delicias,** specializes in seafood and offers soups and seafood cocktails (US$2-3.50), entrees (US$5-11), a breakfast of juice, toast, and coffee (US$2), as well as beer, soda, and cocktails (US$0.75-3.50). Listen: There's always music playing beyond the trees. This road is Calle Emiliano Zapata, the first left as you enter town.

Getting There

By Car: From Veracruz go north on Hwy. 180. Take the first left turn after the tollbooth and go about 1.5 kilometers.

By Bus from Veracruz: Catch the bus to **Cardel** from either the first or second class bus station in Veracruz. Don't ask the driver if the bus goes to Antigua; he'll tell you it doesn't. Pay the fare to Cardel, and when the bus goes through the tollbooth, get off. There may or may not be a cab that will take you to town; otherwise, the walk is about 1.5 kilometers along a quiet country road. Returning to Veracruz, walk through the toll and flag down the first bus you see, or catch it where you got off and continue on from Cardel to Veracruz.

CEMPOALA/ZEMPOALA

This ancient Totonac site is located about 42 km north of Veracruz on Hwy. 180, outside of Cardel; if you're going to Jalapa, it's on the way. Another option for a day-trip from Veracruz is to take a taxi or colectivo to the ruins. Ask at the tourism office on the zócalo, often they will offer day-trips to close by attractions, or might be able to put you together with other travelers looking for the same trip—check to see if they have a bulletin board.

Totonac Archaeology

Cortés and his band of treasure seekers found their first allies here, the "Totanac people of the Fat Cacique" (this according to Bernal Díaz del Castillo). Cempoala was destined to be the last capital of that ancient culture. The well-tended ruins, which were inhabited around the 10th century and whose civilization peaked in the 14th century, contain the **Throne of the Cacique,** the **Temple of the Faces,** and the **Great Temple of Quetzalcoatl.**

This hardy group of 30,000 people was led by their fat cacique, **Chicomacatl.** The Zempoalans helped Cortés out of several tight spots, including the defeat of Narvaez, sent by Velásquez, governor of Cuba, who wanted him dead or brought back in chains. The Zempoalans were also the escort and show of force that Cortés needed as he stalked across the Mexican landscape, stopping in many small villages on his march to find Moctezuma and Tenochtitlán. Eventually, the Zempoalans fell victim to the same fate as so many of the Indians who had contact with the Spaniards; they were wiped out by Old World diseases and were gone by the 17th century.

At The Ruins

Zempoala's archaeological zone occupies a rectangular area of eight square kilometers between the Actopan and the Chachalacas rivers. Because of the changing course of the Chachalacas River, over the years sections of the ancient city have been isolated and city streets have intruded on the ceremonial center. Originally the Totonac city was divided into 10 enclosures, each with its own religious structures. Thick walls covered with smooth limestone stucco separated each zone. Surrounding the religious center, dwellings were built on platforms and embankments. Zempoala built protective walls and had a well-developed water system by 1200. Water was supplied by subterranean pipes, and adjacent farmlands were irrigated by well-developed canals.

The zone of the **Templo Mayor** is occupied by the **Great Temple** on the north and the **Pyramid of the Sun** on the east. The latter is also known as **Chimeneas** because of the series of semicircular pillars suggesting a row of chimneys on a rooftop. Its foundation measures 24 meters at the front and 22 meters at the sides. Originally the pyramid was composed of seven slightly inclined forms, the lower one covered in order to build the lateral platforms. The stairway is nine meters wide and has nearly vertical balustrades. The columns were formerly adorned by bas-relief stucco designs depicting a lizard.

In the adjoining zone is a building called **Las Caritas** because of the many small clay heads adorning its walls. Its stairway is flanked with broad balustrades and, like the Great Temple, it faces east. The first of its two superimposed platforms measures 20 meters across, 15 meters at the sides, and nearly three meters in height. A niche opens at the rear of the structure. In another section is an edifice known as **The Temple of the Wind God**, a circular temple, often associated with the cult of Ectepactl.

There's a large unexcavated area called **Las Anonas** with vestiges of numerous walls, platforms, and pyramids. The first archaeological research here was carried out in 1891-1892 after identification of the site by comparing a description of the route taken by the conquistadores on their march to Tenochtitlán. Quotations by Bernal Díaz del Castillo and Cortés, later synopsized by Torquemada, paint the following picture:

> *When the Spaniards entered Zempoala and saw the splendid city—so new and attractive, with houses made of adobe and others of lime and cantera (a local stone)—the streets filled with people who came out to look back at them. The Spaniards corroborated Grijalva's choice name, Nueva España. . . . Zempoala at that time had a very large pop-*

ulation with great buildings, finished with fine wood construction, and each house had its own orchard and irrigation system. Altogether, this garden place seemed like a delightful paradise, not only because it was so verdant and cool, but also because it was laden with fruits as well. A market was held every day of all the salable products, to which the many persons present did justice . . . the Spaniards saw that the Zempoalans lived under a well-organized political order and that all held their Lord Ruler in high veneration. Our men admired them because of these things and because unlike other Indians of the islands (the Caribbean), the Zempoalans did not go around nude.

Open every day except Monday 10 a.m.-5 p.m. Admission is US$3.50. The *voladores* (flyers) usually perform their dare-devil flying act on Sat. and Sun. around noon.

A Few Beaches

If you're driving, continue a short distance farther north (near Ursala Galvan), until you come to **Playa de Chachalacas.** The jungle opens onto some of the nicest sandy stretches of beach and sea where a swim and another helping of fresh fish are hard to pass up.

BOB RACE

Totonac site

JALAPA

Pronounced: hah-LAP-ah
Altitude: 1,372 meters
Population: 400,000
Area Code: (281)
Distance from Mexico City: 313 km

The capital of Veracruz (also spelled Xalapa), is the "City of Flowers," and offers a modern, open attitude most likely because of its large student population from the **University of Veracruz.** Most travelers come with the intention of seeing the renowned **Museo de Antropología de la Universidad Veracruzana** and the nearby ruins. But once here, they almost always want to stay longer—the city is a pleasant surprise.

HISTORY

Pre-Columbian legend tells us that it was near Jalapa that the original Totonacs emerged from the sea. As they increased in numbers they founded thirteen settlements "within a range of six leagues." The legend referred to a first settlement "four leagues beyond Zacatlan." Ten generations of chieftains ruled for 80 years. During the reign of the second leader, the Chichimecs arrived in the land, hungry and poor. They were fed and treated with great kindness by the Totonacs, and amicable relations between the two peoples were maintained for many decades. But upon the death of the eighth chieftain, his two sons ruled jointly and strife developed. The Chichimecs, taking advantage of internal dissension, seized control and occupied a dominant position until the arrival of the ambassadors of Moctezuma I. Various warring campaigns by the Aztecs continued until the northern section yielded to Moctezuma II. Like Veracruz, Jalapa is juxtaposed on the historical road used by history's famous: Cortés and his conquistadores, Spanish colonists, American invaders, the French (including Maximilian), and its favorite and/or most notorious native son, **Antonio López de Santa Anna.** The "often-ex-president" of the country was made president 11 different times between 1833 and 1855.

He built and lived at a wonderful hacienda outside of Jalapa, now a museum called **Ex-Hacienda El Lencero.**

The road to the city rises from humid jungle plains to alpine heights offering a varied and verdant climate. Winding streets are fronted by colorful houses with plenty of wrought iron. Jalapa can even brag about its own tree-capped volcano. Coffee is grown here as well as varied other crops, and it's known all over Mexico as the **jalapeño capital** of the world. Many visitors find room in their suitcase to take home some samples of both.

SIGHTS

Parque Juárez, across from the **Cathedral** on Zamora, is in a hilly part of the city. It's a lovely park with flowers in bloom year-round. Facing the park is the **Palacio de Gobierno** and the **Municipal Palace.** Wandering up and down and around there's a lot to see. Don't leave it until you have explored all of its levels. You'll find students poring over texts, lovers looking deeply into each other's eyes, old men playing chess or checkers, children competing in decibels with the birds, and the ever-present vendors of tamales and cold, colorful sugar water.

Cathedral

This lovely church was built in 1773 and improved in 1896. Semi-Gothic, with one tower high and imposing, the other squat and square, it has a lopsided appeal. Inside, the three naves are supported by columns forming pointed arches. The chapel contains the tomb of Bishop Rafael Guizar Valencia, who was beatified by the Vatican. A painting by Miguel Cabrera hangs in a place of honor.

Palacio De Gobierno

This was built in 1855 on the site of the old **Hospital of San Juan de Dios.** The murals of José Chavez Morado, depicting the coats of arms given by Charles IV to Xalapa, Cordoba, Orizaba, and Veracruz grace the walls inside the side entrance.

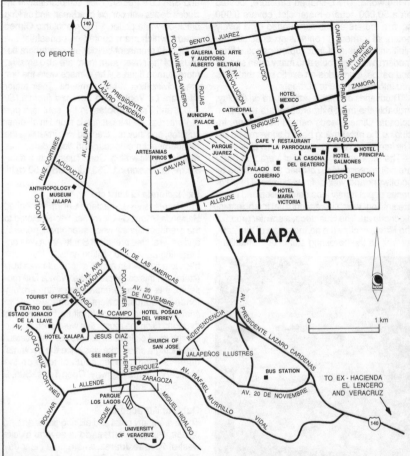

JALAPA

Markets

To the right of the cathedral the streets climb up to a street market. On Calle Zaragoza there are several alleys where the wares of the merchants are spread on tables. An **indoor bazaar** runs between Zaragoza and Zamora. Take a look at **Artesanías Piros** on the far side of the Parque Juárez on Ursala Galvan, and check the coffee houses and the better shops for quality merchandise. The **Agora de la Ciudad** on the south side of the park is frequented by students and contains bookstores and still more *things* to buy.

Church Of San José

This church on Calle Cuauhtémoc is the city's oldest, built in 1770 in the colonial style. Sebastian Lerdo de Tejada and General Santa Anna were baptized here.

Anthropology Museum Jalapa

Designed by the firm of Edward Durell Stone (of New York), this is a truly imposing museum and folk culture center at the same time. A must see, this fairly new (1986) museum took the place of one that had been on the same spot since 1959. It is ranked the fifth finest of its kind in the world. The L-shaped structure, located on a 50,000-square-meter plot, covers 9,000 square meters and is surrounded by a lovely botanical garden. It contains six spacious exhibition salons and four roofed patios. Ultramodern, with high roofs and many open spaces and patios, it provides an exotic light that fools you into feeling you're outdoors.

Thousands of notable artifacts are on display; probably the most extraordinary are the seven colossal Olmec heads carved from stone, including the only smiling head discovered so far. The largest of these monoliths weighs 27 tonnes.

The three major cultures of Veracruz State are well represented. **Totonac** art is marked by scrollwork and well-defined curves. Their figurines depict frontal lobe deformation and some are smiling, which is very unusual in ancient indigenous art. The **Huastecs,** a splinter group of the Maya, occupy the northern part of the state, as well as the bordering states of Tamaulipas

OZ MALLAN

One of the monolithic Olmec heads found in the Gulf of Mexico region. These immense stone heads all weigh over a ton and depict features and headgear still not understood by archaeologists.

and San Luis Potosí. Their sculptural style includes deities with conical headwear, and striking black-on-white pottery. The monolithic **Olmec** heads, which are mounted on pedestals, are thought to represent ballplayers or warriors because of their headgear; there are also smaller, more human figures. The Olmecs were the first great civilization of Mesoamerica. Their major sites are **La Venta, San Lorenzo** (from 1150 B.C.), and **Tres Zapotes,** in the southern part of Veracruz. Their influence is found in all other cultures, and they are credited with inventing the Mesoamerican calendar and "long dates," as well as glyphic writing. Open Tues.-Sun. 9 a.m.-5 p.m.; admission is US$3 adult, US$1.50 child.

Ex-Hacienda El Lencero

This impressive ex-hacienda (formerly called Hacienda Manga de Clavo) has been restored to the grandeur it knew when strongman, general, and several-time president Santa Anna was entertaining artists and visiting nobility. It's a look back to a time when a man's hacienda was truly (literally in this case) his castle. Now a fine museum, it is still quite impressive with carefully tended grounds, flowers and shade trees in courtyards, and elegant furniture from around the world filling the rooms that were often the site of high level diplomatic powwows. The restaurant facing a small lake was once the servants' quarters. Find it 10 km south of town on the Mexico/Veracruz highway. Open Tues.-Sun. 9 a.m.-5 p.m., free.

Outdoor Attractions

There are many quiet and alluring parks around Jalapa, **Parque Centenario** is several blocks west of **Parque Juárez,** where on a clear day **Mt. Orizaba** is visible. **Parque Los Lagos** near the college has lakes, a playground for children, and a cooling breeze. **Parque Berrios,** south of the city center (Centro), provides a large, circular space of cobbled walks among cooling swaying trees, statues, and colorful flowers, surrounded by houses of colonial charm.

ACCOMMODATIONS

Hotel Principal

The Hotel Principal is one block below Zamora (downhill) on Calle Ignacio Zaragoza at the corner of Primo Verdad. This is a well-kept older hotel. Rooms have bare wooden floors with throw rugs and some really elegant pieces of now-old furniture. Most rooms have narrow verandas with floor to ceiling doors, enough space to move around, a tile bathroom, and a big closet. A restaurant is attached, and there's a TV in the lobby. Rates are US$12 s, US$15 d. There's no phone.

Hotel Salmones

A block closer to the Parque Juárez on Ignacio Zaragoza, Hotel Salmones is also a well-preserved reminder of colonial times. It's built around a gorgeous courtyard of flowering shrubs. White walls and rich, dark wood are the norm in the rooms, which are light and spacious. Most rooms have verandas, private baths, and a few of the amenities of the more upscale hotels; TV, telephones, a restaurant/bar, and parking. The 70 rooms run US$20 s, US$25 d; at Zaragoza 24, tel. (281) 7-5431 or 7-5435.

BOB RACE

Other Hotels

Hotel María Victoria, on Zaragoza 6, has a good location near the town center with a pool, restaurant, and bar; rates are about US$45-55; tel. (281) 8-6011. **Hotel Posada del Virrey** is located at Dr. Lucio 142 and is an uphill climb, but it's still close to the center of town. Modern and comfortable, rates are about US$25-32; tel. 8-6100. And for something fancier and worth the extra expense, take a look at the **Hotel Xalapa,** located on Victoria, also a short climb uphill. This is touted as the best hotel in town. Rooms are attractively decorated with upscale amenities like minibars—plus heat, a/c, and a place to dine and wine overlooking the pool. Rates are about US$82-88, tel. 8-2222, fax 8-9424.

FOOD

The restaurant at the **Salmones** serves a nice selection of regional cuisine, is well recommended, and is moderately priced.

Have lunch at the **Hotel Mexico** at Calle Lucio 4, tel. 8-8000, not for the atmosphere but for the food, which is tasty, bountiful and inexpensive. The generous *comida corrida* will carry most people through the daylight hours (about US$6.50).

Cafe y Restaurant La Parroquia at Zaragoza 18 is a friendly crowded cafe frequented by students, businesspeople, and visitors because the food is good and the service attentive. Breakfast prices start at about US$2.50 and go up to about US$9.50 for a good dinner. Open 7:30 a.m.-10:30 p.m. Or go next door, where dinner can be taken at the beautiful **La Casona Del Beaterio.** Here, beneath high ceilings crossed by large open beams hung with plants, students congregate to discuss anarchy over *hamburguesas* and society women come to gossip over coffee and rich desserts. Casement windows frame a view of the populace on the busy streets and allow a rain-tinged breeze to come inside. Excellent picante sauce. Soups, sandwiches, and *antojitos* cost around US$3, and meat or fish entrees are US$10-15. At Calle Zaragoza 20, tel. (281) 8-2129.

There's a variety of good cafes along the streets of Jalapa, especially around Plaza Juárez and the walking-only street of **Callejón del Diamante.** Prices range from very reasonable to moderate, so look around. Don't forget to look into the bakeries around the city for great breakfast material.

INFORMATION AND SERVICES

Tourist Office

You really have to look to find tourist information in Jalapa. However, there are two locations equidistant from downtown (about two km). One is at Avila Camacho 191, tel. (281) 8-7186, hours Mon.-Fri. 9 a.m.-3 p.m. and 6-9 p.m., Sat. 9 a.m.-1 p.m. The other is at the bus station at 20 de Noviembre where someone usually speaks English, tel. (281) 8-7224 or 8-7424, fax 8-7313. **Note:** We're told there's a tourist office near the plaza next door to the Hotel Salmones, tel. (281) 7-3030; I haven't seen it myself, but I'll check it out on the next visit.

Money And Other Services

Change money at **Casa de Cambio** at Calle Zamora 36, tel. 8-6860. **Telegraph** and **Post Office** are found in the **Palacio Federal** at the corner of Diego Leno and Gutierrez Zamora.

GETTING THERE

Jalapa has a splendid bus station located on 20 de Noviembre, called **Central de Autobuses de Xalapa,** or CAXA for short. From here you can come and go by various bus companies, including one of the new luxury buses, **Uno,** which departs daily for Mexico City for about US$24, or by ADO first-class bus to Mexico City (with frequent departures) for about US$8. To Papantla on ADO, it's about US$7; Puebla on ADO is US$4.50 (or by direct second-class AU for about US$3.75). To Veracruz, by ADO, it's US$2.50; buses depart 5 a.m.-10 p.m., very frequently. Ask for prices and schedules to Campeche, Coatepec, Mérida, Orizaba, and Tlaxcala.

GETTING AROUND

Jalapa is built in the hills, and even downtown you have hilly climbs to deal with. For the most part it is still easier to walk around the central area. However, in some cases, such as going and coming to the bus station or outlying areas, you might prefer to take a bus or taxi. A local bus runs from the Plaza Juárez to the service road in front of the bus station; look for buses, minivans, or *colectivos* that are marked with "Centro" and you will get to and from downtown; fare is 35 cents at this printing. **Buses** run on the main roads around the Centro district. Walking is by far the most rewarding way to see the city, but taxis are unmetered and inexpensive. A ride from the bus station to Centro is about US$1.50.

K. A. ESCOVEDO SANDERS

AROUND JALAPA

COATEPEC

Known as the "City of Gardenias," Coatepec is 14 km south of Jalapa on the road to Xico. It's renowned for wonderful mountain coffee and greenhouse orchids that are grown here, as well as fruits and sugarcane. Crafts include textiles and ingenious pottery sugar bowls. This was once considered the wealthiest town per capita in Mexico, and there are many large and beautiful colonial-style houses.

Sightseeing

At the Parque Principal you'll see the 19th century municipal palace undergoing renovation. The **Parroquia of San Jeronimo** was built in 1702, and its unorthodox tower is a curiosity of architecture. Even more curious is the image of San Isidro Labrador inside, which is clothed in the peasant style of Russia circa 1700. On 30 September the **Fiesta of San Jeronimo,** a major celebration, is held here. The town becomes a noisy, raucous, fun-filled place to be.

Cafes

Close to the park, you'll find several cafes. **Los Arcos,** on the south side of the park, has inexpensive, regional food. **El Cafetal,** on the corner of Ocampo and Delgollado, has excellent coffee.

POZA RICA

This oil town is booming; even the cemetery exhibits vaults with windows and curtains. If you plan on going to El Tajín, more than likely you'll go through Poza Rica. This part of Veracruz is profusely green with jungle all around the town. The area grows tons of vanilla beans—and just outside of town is a waterfall famous as one of the sites where the movie *Romancing the Stone* was filmed. It's a beautiful waterfall and you can get closer on a swing bridge that crosses over a mighty deep river gorge if you're looking for a good photo.

If passing through, check out the large open-air restaurant in the center of town called Lla-marada. A river runs through the middle of town, and during the rainy season it rises almost up to the top of the banks along the streets and buildings.

Much of the population is still made up of Huastec Indians. They're said to have run 30- to 40-kilometer relays carrying fresh fish wrapped in banana leaves for Moctezuma's breakfast.

EL TAJIN

El Tajín, at its apogee toward the end of the late Classic (A.D. 600-900), is considered the most important of the Classic Veracruz sites. Though the area is now mostly inhabited by the Totonac descendants, scientists are hard pressed to say that it was the Totonac who built these structures. The name Tajín comes from the legend that the structures are occupied by 12 old men who are the lords of thunderstorms, akin to the rain god, and therefore very important and respected. The site is surrounded by rich farmlands where tobacco, vanilla, cacao, and corn grew in the ancient era and continue to be important crops for today's citizens.

At The Site

A good-size parking lot accommodates quite a few cars, even though this archaeological zone is off the beaten track and many folks don't find it. A spacious visitor's center includes very clean restrooms (be sure to have N$1 to give the ticket lady across from the door), a fine museum with many artifacts of the area, a gift shop, a snack bar, and an excellent cafe.

It's a bit of a walk on a dirt road to get to where the structures are clustered together. It's not a huge site, but the pyramids have a unique look, and they're surrounded by hills and jungle. The entire area covers 25 square kilometers, and archaeologists have located (according to the guides on the site) more than 200 temples and 17 ball courts. Michael Coe, in his most recent book on Mexican archaeology, states there are only nine ball courts—in one you will see six broad carved panels of stone that tell stories of bloody sacrifice and death.

Pyramid of the Niches

OZ MALLAN

The most exotic of the temples is the **Temple of the Niches.** It dates back to the late Classic period and is 18 meters high. If you walk around to the northeast wall you'll find a carved panel that shows a scene depicting the sacrifice of a ball player. The structure has six levels with one wide staircase to the top. At each level there are many small square niches (365—no, it's not just chance, it deliberately coincides with the number of days in a year), and hundreds of years ago, the keepers of the temple set flames burning in each. El Tajín was considered an elite ceremonial center. In typical ancient prearrangement, another structure was found within the structure, but without the niches. In its prime, the temple's facade had a stucco veneer and glowed brightly with red paint.

Most of the structures are similarly designed; another that offers architectural differences is the **Building of the Columns.** It is the largest of the palace complexes, and if you look closely at the pillars you'll see carvings that again depict ball players, captives, and sacrifice—these folks were quite serious about their ball game. Some of these structures were painted bright blue. Note the repetition of the step-and-fret motif on many of the buildings—this symbolized lightning in the pre-Hispanic era.

Look around the grounds and you'll find a *temescal,* a steam bath where herbs and roots are placed in the water that is passed over hot rocks. Many pregnant indigenous people still do this and claim that it helps ease the birth.

Papantla Flyers

One of the highlights of a visit to the archaeological zone is to watch the *voladores* or flyers (local Totonac Indians) who perform in the front of the visitor's center. No matter how many times you see it, it's still a remarkable feat. These men climb a 30-meter pole (this one is metal with steel rods protruding to help them get to the top) till they reach a small rotating platform. One man (the captain) sits in the middle and plays a flute while tapping a tiny drum hanging from the flute. The other men rotate the platform and carefully wrap their ropes around the pole. All the while they do this, the captain plays his flute, taps his rhythms and even does a little rain dance on this platform that appears no bigger than half a square meter. The men are colorfully dressed in red pants, handsome boots, a beaded apron, and a brightly colored hat adorned with mirrors and plumes. This is a dance to beseech the rain gods to send moisture to the earth. While they're at it, the flyers ask all the other gods in nature to go to bat for them, and then they pay tribute to the gods representing the four cardinal points. Thus, the four men fall over backwards and fly upside down, around and around, arms outstretched, each attached to a rope by the ankle, while they make 13 broad circles in the sky (there are 13 months in the Aztec calendar). They look like colorful birds enjoying the air currents, all the time getting lower to the ground with each revolution, till at last they gracefully step to the ground without

OZ MALLAN

Flying voladores fall backward from the small platform atop a 30-meter pole once they have secured ropes to their ankles.

omelette. Small handmade tortillas are fresh and delicious. The menu is in English and Spanish, and please note; if you order from the Spanish side of the menu, prices are a few pesos cheaper than on the English side of the menu(?). A good lunch with a cold beer or two goes for US$6-10, or for a bargain meal, order a platter of tacos, US$3-4.

Getting There

El Tajín is 225 km northwest of Veracruz. If you're traveling by bus, go to Poza Rica and from there take the Papantla bus marked "Chote/Tajin," which leaves from the side of the Juárez Market, across from the church. This bus goes right to El Tajín. However, their hourly schedule can be undependable. Another choice is to take the bus marked "Chote;" tell the driver you want to go to El Tajín and you will be dropped off at the intersection; from there you can take a taxi for about US$4. Some folks stay at the nearby town of Papantla, though there's a dearth of hotels. The **Premier Hotel** is clean, fairly nice, with a/c, TV, baths, tile floors, and balconies. The lobby is on the second floor where there's a bar that's open 9 a.m.-10 p.m. Rates are about US$45 s, US$50 d. Located at Enriquez 103, tel. (784) 2-1645.

missing a beat. Quite a performance. The flyers circle the crowd and ask for donations; US$3-4 is customary. If you wish to take photos, ask—they seem perfectly willing. The flyers generally perform Mon.-Sat. at midmorning, the noon hour, and about 3 p.m., on Sundays noon-4 p.m. Admission to El Tajín is US$3.50, free on Sunday; open daily 8 a.m.-5 p.m.

Restaurant Enrique

Around the back of the visitor's center on the left side of the walkway, you'll find a dandy outdoor restaurant that serves really good food. Most of the cafes at the sites are pretty simple, but the menu here gives some good unusual choices. Of course there are all kinds of fish dishes, tamales, and homemade fish soups. The cassoulets are a little out of the ordinary, and when you see something called a shrimp torta, it's not a sandwich but a wonderful

MOUNT ORIZABA

This is the highest mountain in Mexico, at 5,747 meters. This is probably the mountain you've seen from many spots in your meanderings in and around Veracruz State. The Aztecs' beliefs were rooted in nature. Undoubtedly, the smoke and fire that would occasionally erupt from these immense mountains must have given them cause for fear. The peaks that surround the Valley of Mexico were given names by the Aztecs, and each has at least one legend. **Citlaltepetl** in Nahuatl means "Star Mountain," more commonly known as **Pico de Orizaba.** Legend tells us that Quetzalcoatl, revered as the Plumed Serpent, was devoured by sacred flames in the heart of the volcano, but then miraculously took human form and sailed off across the seas, promising to one day return to his people.

K. A. ESCOVEDO SANDERS

THE STATE OF TLAXCALA
INTRODUCTION

This smallest and poorest of Mexico's states has rich traditions, colorful history, and a wealth of colonial architecture. One of the main attractions is an important archaeological site, **Cacaxtla.** Discovered in the mid-1970s, it continues to attract those interested in archaeology, including scientists and laymen. Along with Cacaxtla, archaeology buffs should go to **Tizatlán**, and/or check out the cave paintings at **Atlihuetzia,** all vivid reminders of early civilizations. This highland state's elevation is over 2,000 meters, the air is clear, and the sunlight sparkles. The people of Tlaxcala are mostly descendants of the Otomi. In every town and village there is an ancient church, thanks to the evangelical zeal of the early Franciscans. In August, **Huamantla** becomes a hub of excitement when the sun sets and the locals begin creating the celebrated carpet of colorful flower petals and sawdust for the 15 August procession, working straight through the night. At daybreak the faithful follow the religious caravan, walking on the magnificent colored carpet in celebration of the Virgin of the Divine Assumption.

The state is surrounded by Puebla on three sides, bordered on the north by Hidalgo, and on the west by Mexico. The population is small, 615,000, though when considering the state is made up of only 4,000 square km (less than 1,600 square miles) it is quite densely populated. Agriculture is important here; wheat and maguey leaves are important products, as is cattle. Within the state's borders visitors have the opportunity to visit the fifth highest mountain (4,462 meters, 14,637 feet) in Mexico, **La Malinche** (also called Malantzin).

HISTORY

Pre-Columbian History
Cacaxtla is believed to have been built at the zenith of the Olmec Xicalanca culture around A.D. 700, lasting until A.D. 1200. Tlaxcala was part of a unique civilization that was pretty close to being a democracy, with voting conducted in a senatorial atmosphere. The Tlaxcaltecas, as they were called, were comprised of four im-

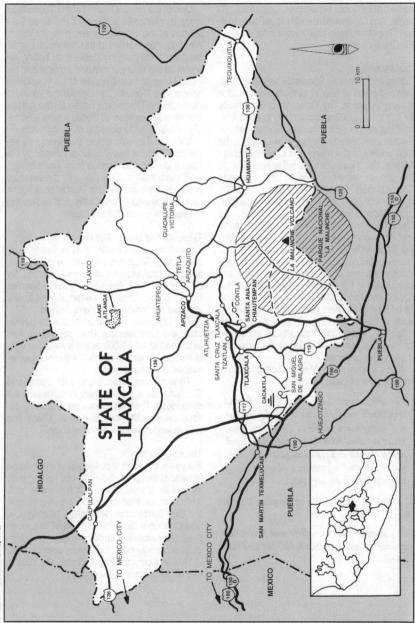

STATE OF TLAXCALA

© MOON PUBLICATIONS, INC.

portant dominions: Tepeticpac, Ocotelulco, Tizatlán, and Quiahuixtlán, each with its own chieftain. Together these chiefs were referred to as the Cuatro Señores.

Cortés Arrives

Cortés and his fellow Spaniards arrived at Tlaxcala at the end of August 1519, two weeks after leaving Veracruz. The Tlaxcaltecas were ready for him with 60,000 warriors ready to fight. After hearing of the rich gifts that Cortés sent to Moctezuma, they firmly believed Cortés to be their enemy and a friend and supporter of the Aztecs, the Tlaxcaltecas's bitter enemies. At the proper moment, the Indians charged Cortés's men, flinging stones from slings and javelins with tips "hardened to pierce any armor" (according to conquistador Bernal Díaz del Castillo's description). The Tlaxcalta army was no match, however, for the firepower that the Spaniards brought into the battle. Cortés, however, did not want to kill these men; he was more interested in aligning with the army and using them to fight and eventually conquer the Aztecs and Tenochtitlán. Cortés ended the battle by forcing captives to deliver his "message" back to the Tlaxcaltecas. Their options being alliance or death, the Tlaxcaltecas chose the former, and remained allies of the crown for many years to come.

In his *Letters From Mexico,* Cortés wrote of his first view of Tlaxcala:

The city is much larger than Granada and very much stronger, with as good buildings and many more people . . . and very much better supplied with the produce of the land, namely bread and fowl and game and freshwater fish and vegetables and other things they eat, which are very good.

After seeing more of the countryside he went on:

. . . many beautiful valleys and plains, all cultivated and harvested, leaving no place untilled.

One of the military leaders of the Tlaxcalteca army, Xicoténcatl the Younger, remained suspicious of the Spaniards and their intrusion. When Cortés learned of this, he manipulated the people into hanging Xicoténcatl. Today, Xicoténcatl the Younger remains a martyr and famous Mexican hero because of his suspicions concerning Cortés. Throughout the years, it would be the Tlaxcalteca hatred for the Aztecs that would keep them at Cortés's side, eventually resulting in the downfall of Tenochtitlán.

It was in Tlaxcala where the Spaniards recovered from the heavy wounds inflicted by the Aztecs during their escape from Tenochtitlán. And it was here that the plans for the eventual conquest were drawn. The Tlaxcaltecas built a fleet of ships under Cortés's direction and carried the vessels across the mountains.

Tlaxcaltecas Under The Crown

Tlaxcaltecas were participants in Spanish expeditions to South America and the Philippines, and in the colonization of northern Mexico. By order of Charles I, they were given the Spanish honorific title, Don, were exempt from taxes, and had the "privilege" of riding horses.

The diseases brought from Europe devastated the Tlaxcaltecas. Their population was estimated at 4,000,000 at the time of the conquest; as few as one quarter of that number remained a century later.

Their descendants, along with Otomi and Chichimecas, are the primary inhabitants of the state today. The people are very religiously devout, even by Mexican standards. Otomi and Nahua languages are widely spoken.

Tlaxcala Today

For years the state was the site of many large haciendas that produced cattle and fighting bulls as well as pulque. Some of the more famous ex-haciendas that thrived on growing pulque are **San Bartolome del Monte, Ixtafiayuca, San Cristóbal Zacacalo,** and **San Blas.** However, the revolution ended the days of ruling-class prosperity here, as in many colonial cities in Mexico's central plateau. Today the state is one of the poorest in the country.

TLAXCALA (CITY)

Pronounced: Tlahsh-KAH-lah
Altitude: 2,225 meters
Population: 41,000
Area Code: (246)
Distance from Mexico City: 120 km

The capital of the state, Tlaxcala, is located in the highlands of the **Sierra Madre Oriental.** More formally named **New City of Our Lady of the Assumption,** it was jointly founded by Hernán Cortés and the Order of San Francisco (the Franciscans) 1520-1525. The first bishopric of the country was established in 1527; in those years the bishopric was very important—it meant the difference between development and no development. Officially, the creation of the city is listed in 1537 with the construction of chapels of the San Francisco convent; take your choice of dates. The town was built on land donated by the Indian dominions of **Ocotelulco** and **Tizatlán.** Just as in Puebla, the city was planned and built on virgin territory, not the leftover grounds of an ancient Indian homeland.

Tlaxcala is a beautiful colonial city, yet the traffic on the roads and around the ancient plazas is a constant reminder of the present. University students are seen at sidewalk cafes near architecturally delightful buildings that remind all of a rich ancient past. Although located only about 120 km east of Mexico City, it still boasts a population of only 41,000 people.

SIGHTS

The downtown area is a labyrinth of interesting buildings and historical sites. Most are easy walking.

Plaza De La Constitución

The Plaza de la Constitución, in the center of the city, is near the Parroquia de San José and the offices of government. A 19th-century bandstand, surrounded by beautifully blooming flowers, next to an octagonal fountain topped by a stone cross engraved with angelic faces, a gift from Philip IV in 1646. On Monday morning, at 8:30 a.m., the army band plays, and chosen citizens raise the flag amid a fanfare of brass and drums.

Palacio De Gobierno

The 16th-century Palacio de Gobierno, on the north side of the plaza, is actually three buildings. The Royal Houses are on the right, where traveling nobles were billeted when they came to town. Burned during an Indian uprising in 1692, and partially leveled by an earthquake in 1711, only the lower part of the facade and the interior arches remain. Repaired again in 1761, it received its present French rococo plaster-and-brick work in 1928.

On the walls above and between the arches on the first floor are the murals of Desiderio Hernandez Xochitiotzin, artist and historian of Tlaxcala. They concern the coming of man to Tlaxcala, the legend of Quetzalcoatl, the *tianguis* of the four dominions, the alliance with Spain, the departure of the 400 families and the seals of the cities that they founded, and Mexican Independence. The work, which began in 1957, was interrupted for years due to philosophical differences between artists and politicians and is still in progress.

The central building, which now houses the state government, was the seat of the indigenous (elected) governor of the four dominions. The original arches, some with carved stone lacework, are intact. An upstairs room, used for state functions, is beautifully appointed, including a French crystal chandelier. Known as the Red Room, it is not usually open for viewing. Ask someone who looks important if you really want to get inside.

The third building was the corn exchange, where the grain was bought and stored. The flower-decorated facade is well preserved. The address is Plaza de la Constitución 2, tel. 2-5306, tours are available; flashless photography only. The lobby is open weekdays 8 a.m.-6 p.m., Sat.-Sun. 10 a.m.-2 p.m.

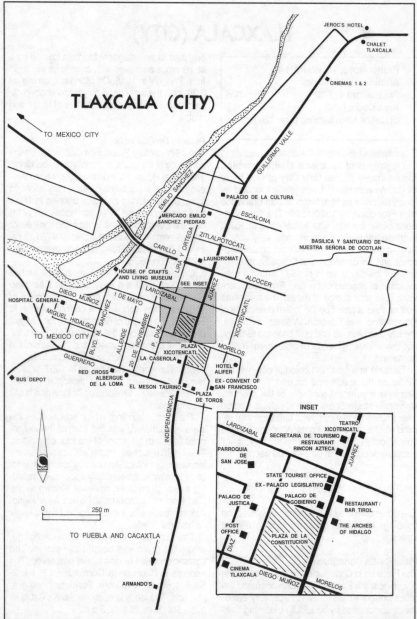

TLAXCALA (CITY)

TO MEXICO CITY

JEROC'S HOTEL

CHALET TLAXCALA

CINEMAS 1 & 2

GUILLERMO VALLE

EMILIO SANCHEZ

PALACIO DE LA CULTURA

MERCADO EMILIO SANCHEZ PIEDRAS

ESCALONA

CARILLO

LIRA Y ORTEGA

ZITLALPOTOCATL

LAUNDROMAT

BASILICA Y SANTUARIO DE NUESTRA SEÑORA DE OCOTLAN

HOUSE OF CRAFTS AND LIVING MUSEUM

SEE INSET

ALCOCER

DIEGO MUÑOZ

LARDIZABAL

1 DE MAYO

JUAREZ

XICOTENCATL

HOSPITAL GENERAL

MIGUEL HIDALGO

BLVD. M. SANCHEZ

ALLENDE

P. DIAZ

TO MEXICO CITY

GUERRERO

20 DE NOVIEMBRE

MORELOS

PLAZA XICOTENCATL

LA CASEROLA

BUS DEPOT

RED CROSS

ALBERGUE DE LA LOMA

HOTEL ALIFER

EL MESON TAURINO

EX-CONVENT OF SAN FRANCISCO

INDEPENDENCIA

PLAZA DE TOROS

INSET

0   250 m

MOON

TO PUEBLA AND CACAXTLA

ARMANDO'S

INSET

LARDIZABAL

TEATRO XICOTENCATL

SECRETARIA DE TOURISMO

RESTAURANT RINCON AZTECA

PARROQUIA DE SAN JOSE

JUAREZ

STATE TOURIST OFFICE

EX-PALACIO LEGISLATIVO

PALACIO DE JUSTICA

PALACIO DE GOBIERNO

RESTAURANT / BAR TIROL

THE ARCHES OF HIDALGO

POST OFFICE

DIAZ

PLAZA DE LA CONSTITUCION

CINEMA TLAXCALA

DIEGO MUÑOZ

MORELOS

© MOON PUBLICATIONS, INC.

Ex-Palacio Legislativo

This antiquated building was completed in 1651 to house visiting dignitaries. It has had many incarnations including a slaughterhouse, bakery, and hotel. Renovated in 1982 to house the state legislature, only the arches remain of the original ediface. It's one block north of the plaza on Juárez; open 8 a.m.-6 p.m.

Palacio De Justicia

This building was begun in 1528 by Fray Andres de Córdoba. Dedicated to Spain's Charles I and paid for by the Cuatro Señores, it was redecorated in the 17th century. There are stone bas-reliefs representing the coats of arms of Castile and León. A fire in 1796, an earthquake in 1800, and almost two centuries of neglect followed until the state rebuilt it in 1984.

The Arches Of Hidalgo

Across the street from Plaza de la Constitución note the fine old *portales* that cover what was once the market. Started in 1550 to protect the merchants and their customers from sun and rain, the arches and openings are of differing sizes because construction was done in stages. Under the arches stores sell a variety of items; look for a pharmacy, a sandwich shop, shoes, newspapers, and more.

Secretaría De Turismo

The art nouveau building at the corner of Juárez was erected at the turn of the century and housed the State Legislature until 1982. Now it is the home of the state tourism office. You can pick up maps and brochures, look at photos and displays of Tlaxcala, or hire a guide. The staff is pleasant and professional and eager to practice their English; Rene López Balderas is especially helpful! The address is Secretaría de Turismo, Av. Juárez 18, tel. (246) 2-5307 or 2-0027, fax 2-5309; hours are Mon.-Fri. 9 a.m-3 p.m. and 5-7 p.m., Sat. 9 a.m.-1 p.m.

Parroquia De San José

Parroquia de San José ("Parish Church of St. Joseph") was constructed early in the 17th century, with mortar images and the tiled facade mandated by then Bishop of Puebla, Juan de Palafox y Mendoza. The dome was tiled later to cover damage caused by an earthquake in 1864. The lone tower has a neoclassical style.

At one time the Cathedral of Tlaxcala, the interior of the church is richly appointed. The main altar, installed early this century, is silver. Two stone holy water fonts are engraved, one with the Indian deity of war, Camaxtli, the other with the Spanish Imperial seal. Large, religious oils dominate the walls between plaster saints and angels. On the right hand side of the church is a 17th-century likeness of the Virgin of Guadalupe worked in shells. The left-hand chapel has a baroque altarpiece dedicated to the Virgins of Guadalupe and the Rosary. Located on the Plaza Constitución, open Mon.-Sat. 6 a.m.-8 p.m., Sun. 7 a.m.-8 p.m., and masses go on much of Sunday morning. For permission for photos, tel. (246) 2-1106.

Around The Plaza Xicoténcatl

A slightly smaller plaza, it's located across from the Arches of Hidalgo. There are restaurants and shops here as well as a statue of the plaza's namesake on Morelos and Av. Independencia.

Ex-Convent Of San Francisco

The official name of this large compound is **Convent of Our Lady of the Assumption.** Erected between 1537 and 1540, it is one of the first four convents built in America. After the Reform it was used as a barracks as well as a jail and now houses the **Regional Museum of Tlaxcala.** The north entrance, from the Plaza Xicoténcatl, passes between fluted columns that support the arches connecting the cloister and bell tower. There is a small corner chapel, like the ones at Huejotzingo. The three arches of the open chapel are the oldest of their type in Mexico. Inside the vault, which was constructed in 1539, paintings done by the Indians can be seen. The first plays, with religious themes, were enacted here on Calz. San Francisco just off Plaza Xicoténcatl.

Catedral De Nuestra Señora De La Asunción

Still part of the Franciscan complex, this cathedral features architecture and artifacts of interest. Note the heavy cedar crossbeams that glitter with stars, the wrought iron gate of the Virgin's Chapel, a 19th-century organ, the first pulpit, and in the Chapel of the Third Order, the stone baptismal font in which the Cuatro Señores were converted to Catholicism in 1520. There is a painting behind the main altar depicting this event. Open for viewing Mon.- Fri. 6 a.m.-2 p.m. and 4-8 p.m., Sat. 6 a.m.-7:30 p.m., Sun. 6 a.m.-8:30 p.m. Photos are allowed only with permission; tel. (246) 2-1511.

Museo Regional De Tlaxcala

Next to the cathedral, located in the old cloisters of the ex-convent, the museum was installed here in 1978 and contains exhibits from pre-Hispanic to modern times. Pieces of importance include a *chac mool* (ancient Maya god) and the original State Constitution; take a look at the sun clock. There's a US$1.50 admission charge; tel. (246) 2-2913. Open Tues.-Sun. 10 a.m.-5 p.m. There is a bookstore and library, and tours are available.

Basílica Y Santuario De Nuestra Señora De Ocotlán

On a hill above the city can be seen what has been called "the high point of Tlaxcaltecan baroque." The construction, which began in 1670, presents an exterior that is often described as a "wedding cake with all of the guests represented, along with the bride and groom." Plaster columns frame the four doctors of theology, the 12 apostles, the seven archangels, and saints Joseph and Francis of Assisi. The star-shaped, stained-glass window above the choir depicts the Immaculate Conception.

The old building features twin domed towers over 30 meters high, their columns decorated with twining vines and clusters of grapes. In-side, the dome is supported by four arches, every inch decorated with ornate plaster designs. The main altarpiece contains another host of life-sized images. The niche, sanctuary, and the two hanging lamps are made of silver; the shinier one has toured the world.

The ante-vestry, vestry, and the Virgin's dressing room, located behind the main altar, are not open to the public. The dressing room, called the "Virgins Well," was conceived by Father Manuel de Loayzaga. An Indian artist, Francisco Miguel Tlayoltehuanitzin, spent 25 years completing it. Their masterpiece can only be seen in photos. Traditional processions, when the Virgin is carried through the city, take place on the first and third Mondays in May. Located on Calz. de los Misterios, tel. (246) 2-1073 at the corner of Independencia. Open daily 7 a.m.-7 p.m., no pictures are allowed without permission.

Close by is the **Chapel of the Little Well,** which is built around the spring containing curative miracle water produced by the Virgin Mary (legend says). The octagonal chapel has murals by Desiderio Hernandez Xochitiotzin. In the atrium traditional red clay ducks can be purchased to transport the water. Open daily 10 a.m.-4 p.m., tel. (246) 2-1073; photos permitted.

Plaza De Toros

Below the convent and viewable through the fence is the bullring. Built early in the 19th century, of adobe, *tepetate* stone, and limestone, it is named for Tlaxcala's most famous bullfighter, Jorge "Ranchero" Aguilar. Used only during the

The streets of Tlaxcala are lined with colonial buildings and churches.

PAUL PIACENTINI

state fair, which takes place late in October and early November, this may be Mexico's oldest surviving bullring. Open for touring seven days 10 a.m.-10 p.m., Av. Independencia 10, corner of Calle Capilla Abierta.

Teatro Xicoténcatl

The facade of the theater is embossed with cut stone, and the theater has been "doing business" since 1873. Historically, it was the site of cockfights, opera, and the city's first movie theater. Inside there is an inexpensive place for breakfast, lunch, or dinner (music on Fri. night). High ceiling, tall French windows, dark woods, and yards of red curtains and red cloth create an elegant atmosphere. Located at Av. Juárez 21, tel. (246) 2-4073.

Palacio De La Cultura

Built as a school in 1939, restored in 1991, it now houses an art gallery and exhibition rooms. The programs change monthly and a newsletter is available which lists all cultural events in the state. Lots of things go on here for the locals: art and music workshops, musical events, open air shows, and art shows in the gallery. Everyone is welcome; ask at the tourist office for the bi-monthly publication listing events. Open seven days 10 a.m.-6 p.m. At Av. Juárez 62, corner of Miguel Lira, tel. (246) 2-3969.

House Of Crafts And Living Museum

Also called **Museo de Artes y Tradiciones Populares,** this is a charming, living museum where the artist creating his crafts is on display. Everything concerning native life is found here: an Otomi kitchen, complete with three stone *tlecuil* (stoves) and large cooking vessels for preparing mole prieto (perhaps?), as well as a *típico* bedroom set-up. Designs for *huipils* (blouses) and *titixtle* (woolen dresses) can be seen. There is a *cuexcomate* (for storing corn) on display, and a working *temazcal* (sauna).

Everyone is working on something and will take the time to explain what it is, in Spanish or Otomi, usually without stopping their busy talented hands. Upstairs you can watch wool being spun into yarn on the *redina,* wound and washed on the *telecador,* then rewound on the *devanadera* into neat little balls. The balls of wool are then taken to the looms, and the weavers proceed, smiling at your interest. You'll find waist looms for making woolen sweaters (each one takes four days to make), horizontal looms for blankets, serapes and jackets, and vertical looms for rugs (over 300 knots on every row).

On the way out notice the costumes, Carnaval masks, and artifacts. Gilding and polychrome are also explained. Take a peek into the pulque culture as a wizened *viejo* (old man) stirs the pot. Check out the bookstore; there's a great little new book in English all about Tlaxcala. There is also a *fonda típico* (food stand) where you can try the local specialties. At Av. Emilio S. Piedras, tel. (246) 2-2337. Open Tues.-Sun. 10 a.m.-6 p.m. Admission is US$3. Photos are permitted with prior approval. No one should miss this museum.

Aqueducto De Atempa

On the Blvd. Revolución on the way to Santa Ana Chiautempan is a 19th-century viaduct used to run a hydroelectric plant, which operated early in the 20th century. The viaduct shows skilled stonework. The graceful arches and greenery present a picturesque design by Desiderio Hernandez Xochitiotzin.

Antiguos Iglesia Y Convento De San Juan Totolac

If you happen to be on the Tlaxcala-San Martín highway a short distance from the Totolac town limit, make a small detour to look around the ruins of this very old church. Founded in the mid- to late 16th century, it is historically fascinating. On 6 July 1591, 400 colonists and their families gathered their belongings, piled into wagons, and departed for the unsettled north (now Saltillo). King Phillip II and Pope Gregory XIV knew that settling the land was of utmost importance; in order to defend themselves from the Indians, the settlers' groups had to be large.

If you happen to be in the neighborhood on 6 July, check with the tourism office in Tlaxcala; every year on that date a play is performed on the grounds depicting this event. Large numbers of people climb the surrounding hills with lanterns. On stage, a series of vignettes include performers dressed as Indian warriors reenacting the scene of the *Battle Mural* seen at Cacaxtla, the coming of the Spanish, and a candle-lit dance of maidens in white dresses. While the crowd cheers, lanterns on the hill are lit to symbolize the colonization of Saltillo. A great fireworks display follows. Vendors sell snacks, cold drinks, and traditional sweets; most of the town turns out for this event.

ACCOMMODATIONS

Budget And Moderate

While you shouldn't expect a huge selection of hotels, there are enough for you to find one in your price range. There are several inexpensive and comfortable hotels close to the Tlaxcala city center. If you're in financial-crash stage, the cheapest hotel in town is the **Mansión de Xicoténcatl**, but look at the rooms carefully; they aren't always clean. Rates are US$14-17; it's on Juárez 15, tel. (246) 2-1900. The **Albergue de la Loma** is small and pleasant, and the 18 rooms are comfortable and well-lit, some with a view overlooking the city. The walls are white stucco, with cheery pictures of birds and flowers and a full-length mirror. The private baths have enclosed shower stalls. The restaurant/bar serves regional food at inexpensive prices while sharing a view of the town and the Ocotlán basilica. Rates are US$20 s, $24 d, extra bed $7. At Av. Guerrero 58, tel. 2-0424. Parking. Up the cobblestoned hill on Morelos, off Independencia, is the **Hotel Alifer**. Small, reasonably priced, and cozy, the rooms are of varying size and floorplan. Furnished with double beds and a writing desk, pictures of snowy mountains decorate the walls. There's a marble-tiled bath and black-and-white TV in every room; rates are US$20-23 s, $27 d; $35 for four people. At Av. Morelos 11, tel. 2-5678. Restaurant/bar, parking.

Moderately priced, and with more amenities, **Jeroc's** proffers modern clean rooms with more electrical outlets, double beds, TV, and stereo music; common areas include a pool, tennis courts, conference room, restaurant, and disco (US$45 s or d). At Blvd. Revolución 4-Bis., tel. 2-1577 or 2-0300. Another one in this same area, which is an extension of Blvd. Revolución, is the **Chalet Tlaxcala**, where the rooms are pleasant, with a pool, bungalows, restaurant, bar, live music, and parking. Rates are about US$40-50, on Blvd. Revolución 3, tel. 2-0330 or 2-0310.

Expensive

The **Misión Tlaxcala** is a drafty building of differing ages; the old section offers touches such as iron-railed balconies and high ceilings. The new section is the usual; together they offer modern amenities such as tennis courts, a pool, a drugstore, a tobacconist, dry cleaning, and room service. Rates are US$79 s or d, $10 for an extra person. Suites with Jacuzzis are available (US$105), and the presidential suite goes for US$125, plus tax.

Even if you don't stay at the Misión, the restaurant serves an excellent international Sunday brunch (US$8 per person): a beautiful selection of hot and cold foods, fruits, danishes and breads, juices and hot beverages. The lovely views around this property of verdant forest and volcanic hills include a waterfall. This is a convenient hotel if you have a car; it's located 10 km outside of town on the highway to Apizaco, tel. (246) 2-4000 or 2-4005; fax 2-0178.

FOOD

Restaurant Cafe de Teatro, at the Teatro Xicoténcatl, serves a breakfast of juice, coffee, eggs and toast for about US$4. Soups, sandwiches, and antojitos (US$2.50-5) are available for lunch. Dinner entrees cost US$5-9. The restaurant at Hotel Albergue de Loma is a nice spot for lunch or an afternoon espresso. The regional cuisine is reasonable and tasty (US$3-7). **Restaurant Rincón Azteca** on Av. Juárez, a couple of doors from the plaza, offers regional and national foods. Two large rooms (usually) insure there will be an empty table. The soups and antojitos (US$2.50-5) make a tasty lunch. **Tiende Naturalista** serves healthy food, fresh-squeezed juices and homemade yogurts. Porfirio Díaz 17.

Las Cazuelas is a moderately priced restaurant offering indoor and outdoor dining. Everardo Reyes Mendoza, the genial host/owner caters to your every need. The open kitchen, which fills the dining room with mouthwatering aromas, is his wife's domain. Perfect pictures of Tlaxcalan landmarks and prints of Cacaxtla hang on the walls; large windows overlook the patio. Gourmet adventurers should taste a few of the specialties: queso asado con nopales (melted cheese with tender cactus leaves), chorizo *santanero* (grilled sausage), or *chiles rellenos con queso o pollo mole poblano.* Figure about US$15 per person for dinner and drink. Steaks go for US$10-12; desserts cost US$2-3. Open 1-10 p.m., it's at the 20 Km mark of the San Martín-Tlaxcala Highway, one km from the Plaza, tel. (246) 2-7467.

Another restaurant to try for regional food is **El Mesón Taurino;** try the Tlaxcala steak. Also good is the international food here. Located on Independencia 12, tel. 2-4366. **La Cacerola** offers national and international cuisine; taste the Tlaxcaltecan soup; on Independencia 9, open Mon.-Sun. 2 p.m.-midnight, tel. 2-7467. And for a good, reasonable *comida corrida,* check out **Restaurant-Bar Tirol** on Av. Juárez next to the **Mansión de Xicoténcatl** hotel.

ENTERTAINMENT

Nightlife

Cinema Tlaxcala is at Plaza de la Constitución 18. **Cinemas 1 and 2** is on Blvd. Guillermo Valle 113, tel. (246) 2-3544. For a little music check out **Armando's** at Blvd. Independencia 60, tel. 2-4988. **Budweiser Restaurant and Bar** is a lively place on Saturday nights. At Blvd. Mariano Sanchez 44, tel. 2-6207.

Balnearios

Scattered about the countryside, *balnearios* (spas) are generally very simple recreational areas developed for the Mexican family, but everyone is welcome. Most have water activity of some sort, whether a pool, a lake, or a dam, plus picnic areas and children's playgrounds. The weekends are very busy especially in the summer and during school vacations. All are open for daytime use only; daily 10 a.m.-6 p.m. Only a few have prepared foods, so bring a picnic and water.

Balneario Las Cumbres is a family-oriented gathering place with three swimming pools and a children's playground. Located at 20 de Noviembre 16, Santa Cruz Tlaxcala. tel. (246) 2-3280 ext. 88. Open on weekends and holidays only, 9 a.m.-5 p.m. Small admission fee.

A few others are **Zacatelco,** 18 kilometers out of Tlaxcala by way of highways 150 and 119; **Palo Huerfano,** 16 kilometers from Tlaxcala via 150 and 119; **El Montecito,** 19 kilometers from Tlaxcala via 150 and 119; **San Benito,** two kilometers from Apizaco via Hwy. 119; **Los Pinos,** 6 kilometers from Tlaxcala via 150 and 119; and **Santa Lucia,** 16 km from Tlaxcala via 150 and 119. For more information about these *balnearios,* ask at the tourist office.

Hiking And Camping

One of the most well known hiking areas in Tlaxcala is **La Malinche Mountain Camp,** in a national park 3,000 meters high on **Malinche Volcano,** the sixth highest mountain in Mexico at 4,462 meters. From here the summit of the volcano is a fairly easy three-hour hike. The gates

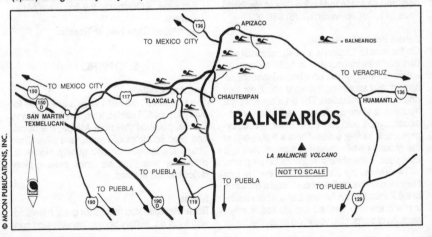

open at 9 a.m.; day-time visitors can stay until 5 p.m. The park has simple camping facilities available as well as cabins with kitchens for six to nine people; spartan but adequate. You'll find firepits, volleyball and basketball courts or just a wonderful spot to drink in nature's wonders. For more information call (246) 2-3822 or 2-3900. Daily admission is US$5 adult, US$3 for children. From Apizaco, travel east on Hwy. 136 about 13 km to a junction that will have a sign directing you to "Campamento IMSS La Malintzin." The road is paved till just past the resort, and for 4.7 km you're on a narrow dirt road. A small car like a VW bug fits. From here the trail heads south and is well marked with IMSS signs. You'll come to a ridge that connects with the summit. Roundtrip should take about six hours.

La Trinidad Vacation Center was a 19th-century textile factory that has been renovated and turned into a resort; it's a Dickensian monolith of stone, brick and tile, smokestacks, and ironwork. The traveler has a choice of large rooms (US$50 s or d, US$70 quad), campsites (US$5 each adult), or a small trailer park (US$12). The day-tripper's options (8 a.m.-5 p.m.) include picnics, swimming, court games, hiking, and horseback riding. Located 16 km east of Apizaco on the highway to Santa Cruz Tlaxcala. For info and reservations, call 2-3900 or 2-3822. Both resorts are run by IMSS (Mexican Social Security) to provide good, inexpensive fun for Mexican families; visitors are always welcome. Reservations, including transport, can be made in Mexico City at Heriberto Frias 241, Col. Narvarte, tel. (5) 639-0071.

Jardín Botánico Tizatlán

On the road to Tizatlán is a lovely botanical garden that was inaugurated in 1989 for conservation of endangered species, education, research, and spreading the word about ecology and resource utilization. The area covers eight hectares, and the dominating vegetation is subaquatic; you'll also see lots of alder, willow, cypress, and juniper pines. There's a nursery on the grounds where seedlings are grown and later used in the state's reforestation program.

Two rivers, the Zahuapan and the De Los Negros, run through the property and a deviation of the Zahuapan has formed a lake where aquatic plants are also nurtured and studied. In other sections of the garden you'll find medicinal herbs

(sage, dill, aloe, and arnica). Fruit-bearing trees include apple, pear, peach, and orange, as well as grapevines. A high-tech greenhouse imitates the humidity and shady conditions of tropical areas with a waterfall and an artificial lake, encouraging the growth of typical tropical plants such as regional, ferns, orchids, and palms. The remarkable exhibit includes an on-site auditorium, herbarium, and lecture hall, and ample parking. This is a favorite place for students to visit and learn about the ecosystems of the entire country. The guide at the Jardín Botánico tells us that botanical gardens were popular in pre-Columbian Mexico. During the Aztec era, plant specimens were collected from various parts of the country in order to study ancient medicines and cures. It's located three kilometers out of the city on the road to San Esteban Tizatlán, at Blvd. Revolución and Antigua Camino Real, tel. (246) 2-6546. Open Mon.-Sat. 7 a.m.-10 p.m., Sun. 6 a.m.-9 p.m.

REGIONAL FIESTAS

19 March: Fiesta of St. Joseph.

May: Fiestas of the Virgin of Ocotlán, first and third Mondays in May.

6 July: Fiesta of the 400 Families.

15 August: Fiesta of the Virgin of the Assumption. This is one of the biggest events in the state.

October/November: National Fair of Tlaxcala, last week of October to the first week of November.

3 December: Cane Fair, at Tizatlán.

SHOPPING

Arts And Crafts

The traditional crafts of Tlaxcala are made for everyday use. Textiles from **Santa Ana** and **Contla,** polished clay from **Atlapa,** the *huipils* and seed paintings of Atlapa, and silver from Tlaxco are famous for their quality. However, production quantities are small, making them difficult to find at times.

Shops

Bazar del Claustro makes for great browsing, with local art, history books, jewelry, and candies. The prices can be a tad high here. At Plaza Xicoténcatl 8, tel. (246) 2-2258. **Museo de Culturas** sells the work of its artisans and the quality is very good, but the wise shopper checks out **Chiautempan** town first. **Mercado Emilio Sanchez Piedras** is on the corner of Lira y Ortega, a *típico* marketplace with the usual adventure of goods.

INFORMATION AND SERVICES

Tourist Information

The state tourist office is located just off the *zócalo* at the corner of Juárez and Lardizabal. A friendly and very helpful staff will give you information and maps. If you don't speak Spanish, ask for Rene Lopez, a very helpful fellow! For complaints about hotels or restaurants contact **Sectur,** Calle Del Vecino 6, Tlaxcala, Tlax., Mexico, tel. (246) 2-5573.

Money

Thera are no *casas de cambio* (moneychangers) in the entire state. If you have to change money or cash traveler's checks you must go to a bank and stand in (usually) long lines. Banks are open 9:30 a.m.-noon. **Banamex** is in the Plaza Xicoténcatl at number 8, tel. 2-3144. **Bancomer** is on Av. Juárez 54, tel. 2-0282. Or check your hotel for the rate as well as local stores, which often accept dollars for the best exchange (for you).

Communications

The **post office** is on the Plaza de la Constitución, tel. (246) 2-0004. The **telegraph** is at Porfirio Díaz 6, tel. 2-0047. **Long distance phones** are available at Av. Juárez 56-C; hours are 8:30 a.m.-8 p.m. **Lada** phones are found under the *portales* at the plaza.

Other Services

A **laundromat** is about two blocks north of the Plaza de la Constitución at 30 Alcocer; open Mon.-Fri. 8 a.m.-4 p.m. and 5-7 p.m., Sat. 8 a.m.-3 p.m. The **Red Cross** is on Allende between Guerrero and Hidalgo, and they offer a 24-hour ambulance service, tel. (246) 2-0920. **Central Pharmacy** is in the bus depot Central

Camionera, tel. 2-5091. **Iris Pharmacy** is on Juárez 47, tel. 2-1151. Find **Hospital General,** on Av. de La Corregidora, tel. 2-0357. If you need a mechanic, try **Servicio Ocotlán,** Km 1 Tlaxcala-Puebla Highway, tel. 2-1745; or **Automotriz Pineda,** Av. Tlahuicole 78, tel. 2-0607.

GETTING THERE

By Bus And Train

Buses from Mexico City leave frequently from the **TAPO** (eastern terminal) at Calz. de Zaragoza 200; tel. (5) 762-5977. **ADO** and **AU** offer first-class buses for the two-hour ride. Buses from Puebla leave **CAPU** throughout the day for the one-hour ride to Tlaxcala. Trains leave from the **Buenavista Station,** tel. (5) 547-1084 in Mexico City. Plan three and a half hours.

The **Central Bus Station** is a half-mile from the Plaza de la Constitución. Buses to Mexico City, Puebla, and Jalapa-Veracruz leave often during the day. Buses to Apizaco and Huamantla can be found on Allende, between Guerrero and Hidalgo, tel. (246) 2-0217.

By Car

From Mexico City take Hwy 136 east out of Texcoco; travel time is about 90 minutes. From Puebla take the **Puebla-Tlaxcala Highway** north, or Hwy. 190 by way of Cholula, Huejotzingo, and San Martín Texmelucan.

GETTING AROUND

The best way to get around downtown is on foot, and the streets are laid out around the **Plaza de la Constitución** (the squarish plaza) and **Plaza Xicoténcatl** (oblong and erratic shape), in a pretty straightforward grid. However, the names of the streets change frequently, so get your bearings quickly. The streets are hilly in some areas, so wear comfy shoes.

Taxis are unmetered and inexpensive and, along with *colectivos,* can be found at Independencia and Morelos; and also at 1 de Mayo and 20 de Noviembre. Or call **Taxi Sitio Principal,** tel. (246) 2-3924.

VICINITY OF TLAXCALA

TIZATLAN

This was one of the four feudal states that together kept the Aztecs at bay. About five kilometers northeast of Tlaxcala on the road going to Apizaco, visitors will find a few remnants of what was once a major stronghold of Xicoténcatl. Even though Cortés needed and befriended the people, he never faltered in his demand that they give up their "false images" and become Catholics. In the conquistadores' impressive manner, an open chapel was built on the site of Xicoténcatl the Elder's palace (probably after Xicoténcatl the Younger was hanged by his own people, who were under the influence of Cortés and his men). One of the other four chiefs, Maxixcatzin, with Hernán Cortés, placed a cross here on the site. Remnants of old artwork can still be seen at this **Archaeological Zone** where, it is said, the Cuatro Señores allied themselves with Cortés. There are Mixtec-style columns and altars decorated with frescoes depicting legendary figures such as the god of the underworld, god of war, god of the morningstar, and Xochiquetzal, goddess of Tlaxcala. This location is believed to have been the birthplace of Xicoténcatl the Elder, as well as a training site for the fierce warriors called the Telpochcalli.

SANTA ANA CHIAUTEMPAN

Sights

Six km east of Tlaxcala and easily reached by taxi or *colectivo,* this small town is famous for its woolen textiles. A visit to the markets and shops for a round of bargaining is a must. But that's not all—Santa Ana also boasts a pair of colonial churches as well.

The center of town is bounded in the north by Allende, in the south by Morelos, in the east by Centenario, and in the west by Union. Most of the sights and markets are within this area. The **Church and Ex-Convent of Our Lady of Santa Ana Chiautempan** was built in 1588 on what was once the center of town. Occupied by a congregation of monks, it boasts many interesting architectural features, as well as a corner chapel. Located on Agustín de Iturbide 6.

The **Parish of Saint Ann** was finished at the end of the 17th century. Visitors will enjoy yet another look at the neoclassical and baroque styles. In the sanctuary, six anonymous canvasses show scenes from the life of Christ. Open Mon.-Sun. 7-1:30 p.m. and 4-8 p.m.; located on Parque Hidalgo 18. Photos may be taken with permission.

Food

El Bodegon is a moderately expensive restaurant serving national and international food. Stylish decor includes several paintings of various artists; often these paintings are of bountifully set tables. Waiters are very proper, and service is prompt *if* there isn't a large local party being catered to. Note the view of the street market from the wide window. Soup with bread, or coffee and dessert are a good call here. Upstairs at Av. Díaz Varela 8-A, tel. (246) 4-0799.

There are several inexpensive places serving regional dishes. At **Los Farolitos**, bone marrow soup may not sound too appetizing, but is one of those local (tasty) dishes worth a try. At Ignacio Pagazo 13, tel. 4-3713.

Shopping

This is the place to check out woven woolens. The town is known for good quality, and since so many of the townsfolk are employed at the same industry, you might find some good deals. Although all vendors seem to sell similar goods, you'll see many wonderful articles woven not just of wool but other materials as well, including synthetics. Some are really first rate, but others are mass produced, so browse and hunt first, compare prices, and then be ready to bargain.

Plaza Malintzin is an arcade of shops at Díaz Varela 9 (no phone). **Casa Ahuatzin,** at Antonio Varela 17, tel. (246) 2-6428; has a good selection of colorful local pottery, warm blankets, and bright-colored clothing. The **Casa del Artesano** offers a wide selection of this and that; on Ignacio Picazo Norte 16 (no phone). **El Sarape Tlaxcalteca** is a good place to pick up just what it says, sarapes. Located at Ignacio Pagazo Norte 22, tel. 4-2312.

APIZACO

Tlaxcala State's biggest, youngest, and most modern city, Apizaco, was founded in 1866 as a railroad town. It has developed into a major service center and transportation hub, and has only a few sights worth looking at. However, from here all the cities, towns and hamlets of Tlaxcala can be reached. If you are en route to almost *anywhere* you might find yourself spending a night in Apizaco; if so, take a look around.

What To See

Parque Cuauhtémoc is the center of town at 16 de Septiembre and Av. Cuauhtémoc; the **Basílica de la Misericordia** stands close by. Also, be sure to take a look at the steam engine monument located five blocks west of the Parque Cuauhtémoc.

Accommodations

One inexpensive accommodations source is **La Posada Hotel,** about five blocks west of Parque Cuauhtémoc, across from the steam engine monument. Wall-mounted bulls stare down at you, eyes bent on red. A modern hotel with 40 rooms, it's located in two buildings. The decor is white stucco, brown tile, and blonde wood. The double beds, with faux brick headboards, are comfortable, and the bathroom boasts a tile bath with enclosed shower. Rates are US$20 s, US$24 d, US$40 for the nicest rooms. Expect cable TV, a bar and restaurant, and parking. Rooms in the back get less street noise. At Av. 16 de Septiembre 911, tel. (241) 7-0815 or 7-5499. **Hotel Upton** is located one block east of the park and four blocks south, on Av. Juárez. Every room offers a different color scheme, none exactly alike, with plenty of brick and tile. A suite with hideaway Jacuzzi is one option, a small room at the top of the stairs and out of the way is another. The manager, Laura Upton, speaks English and is extremely personable. Amenities include a private bath, cable TV, FM radio, a phone, and parking. The piano bar should soon have a restaurant. Prices are as variable as the rooms (US$22 s, US$32 d; US$55 suite without Jacuzzi, US$80 with Jacuzzi). At Av. Juárez 606, tel. 7-5855 or 7-0891.

Food And Entertainment

Maruca is open for breakfast (US$2-4), lunch and dinner (US$4-12) everyday 10 a.m.-10 p.m. It specializes in inexpensive regional cuisine. At Av. 16 de Septiembre 509, tel. (241) 7-1142. **Cafe Paris** serves national and international fare. Decor is dark wood, wide windows and red-on-white cloths. Prices are moderate and up. The specialties are U.S. cuts of beef, which cost slightly more. At Av. Hidalgo 404, tel. 7-0611.

For a cup of espresso and a little people-watching try the newish **Antonio's** on the southeast corner of the park, on Av. Cuauhtémoc. The look is brown-and-white with gold-on-white tablecloths. The menu is Arabic and offers a tasty change of pace. Prices are moderate: appetizers US$3-7, entrees US$6-15. The **Mercado Cuauhtémoc** is between Madero and Serdán, one and a half blocks past Antonio's. It's a large typical market filled with foods, herbs, and crafts.

With one taxi ride to **Restaurant La Cabana de Pecos** you get two bars (side by side), a restaurant, and a dance floor too. Depending on the crowd, it's either juke box music or house tapes. **Coors Lite** boasts little American flags on the lamps over the tables, like a border bar in Texas. **La Ceiba** has a beach motif and stools to perch on. The owners often sit down and and chat with the guests. If you feel like a movie (in Spanish), go to Av. 5 de Febrero 101-H-1, tel. 7-5729. **Cinemas Apizaco** is at Av. Hidalgo 601, tel. 7-5090. **Cinema Diana** is at Av. Juárez 404, tel. 7-1540. Lively music can go on most of the night at a few discos; **Krystal Disco** is at 16 de Septiembre 305, tel. 7-0626.

INFORMATION AND SERVICES

Money

In smaller towns not really geared for tourists, money exchanging can be difficult. Come prepared with pesos, at least enough to get you through the small towns and on to the bigger cities; a night's hotel stay, bus fare, miscellaneous, and dinner. Some of the smaller hotels have a hard time exchanging dollars or traveler's checks. The banks are open Mon.-Fri. 10 a.m.-noon. **Banco de Oriente** is at Av. 16 de Septiembre 103, tel. (241) 7-0075. **Bancomer** is at Av. 16 de Septiembre 204, tel. 7-3199.

Communication

The **post office** is at Av. Francisco Madero 302, and the **telegraph office** is at Av. Hidalgo 606-Bis. **Long distance phones** can be found at Av. 16 de Septiembre, on the corner of Zaragoza; hours are 9 a.m.-2 p.m. and 4-8 p.m. **Lada** phones are near Parque Cuauhtémoc.

Medical Services

Clínica de Urgencias Medicas is at Aquiles Serdán 403, tel. (241) 7-2875. The **Hospital Central** is at Centenario 403-A, tel. 7-5077. Find **DYM** pharmacy at Francisco Madero 104, tel. 7-0299, and **IRIS** pharmacy at Cuauhtémoc 313, tel. 7-0035.

GETTING THERE AND AROUND

Everything is pretty close together downtown, and if you need one, taxis (which are reasonable) can be found at the park. The central bus station is on Jesús Carranza 108, between

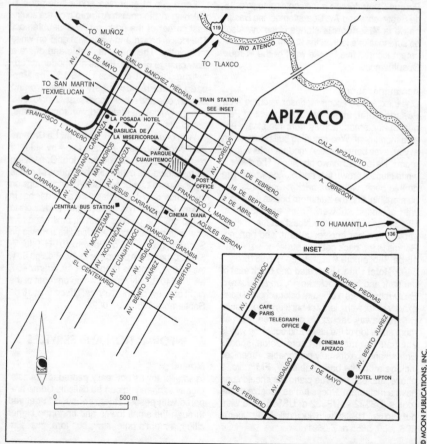

© MOON PUBLICATIONS, INC.

Cuauhtémoc and Xicoténcatl. The **Espresso Pullman** bus to Tlaxcala stops in front of the park on Av.16 de Septiembre. The **Espresso Pullman** bus to Huamantla stops across from the basilica, on the other side of the street. The phone number for **ADO** Autobuses de Oriente is (241) 7-0316. Other companies are: **EPT** (Autobuses Espresso Pullman de Tlaxcala), tel. 7-1243. **ATAH** (Autobuses Tlaxcala Apizaco Huamantla), tel. 7-1388.

The train station is located on Blvd. Emilio Sanchez, tel. 7-0985. Your best information is obtained at the train station; the tourism people seem to know little about the train schedules or the prices.

Auto Rentals

You can rent a car from **Auto Rent Apizaco,** at Libertad 701, top floor, tel. (241) 7-1933. Hours are Mon.-Fri. 9 a.m.-3 p.m. and 5-7:30 p.m., Sat. 9 a.m.-2 p.m. **Rente de Autos López Vazquez,** is at Xicoténcatl 201, tel. 7-3154, Hours are Mon.-Sat. 9 a.m.-3 p.m. and 5-7 p.m., Volkswagons and Ford Magnums are available.

VICINITY OF APIZACO

ATLIHUETZIA

Located seven km east of Tlaxcala on the Apizaco highway, Atlihuetzia can be reached by taxi or colectivo from either city.

Convent And Church Of The Immaculate Conception

The church and convent in the main square were built during that time of missionary zeal when Tlaxcaltecas and Spaniards were allies and the memory of their victory over the Aztecs was still fresh in their minds. This monastery had a relatively brief life; it was abandoned in 1770. The construction materials suggest that building took place over many years. The lower portion is composed of ashlar, the pre-Hispanic building blocks used by the Indians to build their temples. The second layer is of stone, the third of red brick. Look for the arches and vault of the open chapel on the north side. The cloister is now a cemetery. Open daily, 7 a.m.-6 p.m., on the main plaza.

Templo De La Purísma De Concepción

The 16th-century gateway once belonged to the convent across the street; the church dates from the 17th century. The bell in the tower is believed to be the first one cast in America. The original wooden pulpit and floor of the church are shiny and worn from use; the remains of ancient parishioners lie below the old floor.

On the back wall of the church, on the left, are two 19th-century paintings, which depict the murder of the Tlaxcalan *mártires los niños* (child martyrs) and are explained in Nahuatl script. One of these children, Cristóbal, the son of the chieftain of the town, was beatified in 1990 by Pope John Paul II.

The carvings and paintings are considered important for historical and religious reasons; the carving of the cross, the Virgin Mary (from the Philippines), and the Archangel Michael (with real hair) are only a part of a collection that's worth seeing.

The church is only open for mass (8:30 a.m.) on Sunday, but the caretakers can always be persuaded to unlock the door (especially if you offer to help pay the electric bill with a donation). Take no photos without permission.

Cave Paintings Of Atlihuetzia

Cave paintings dating back 10,000 years were discovered in a cave on the cliff of the **Barranca del Toro,** across from the waterfall at the Hotel Misión. The people who created these petroglyphs may have been nomads or perhaps the first settlers of the area—many questions remain unanswered. Nonetheless, they are fascinating to see and ponder over; celestial bodies, people, animals, and the ever-present red handprint (found in other early Mesoamerican sites) are some of the subjects. The trail may be slippery after a rain, so wear sensible shoes. The site is always open and free.

APIZAQUITO

Five km northeast of the city of Apizaco, Luis Garcia and Luis Becerra in 1543 founded Apizaquito. Today, its sole claim to fame is its 18th-century **Church of St. Louis King of France.** A nave of the church contains a sculpted image of Christ on the cross. This image was once located in a 16th-century hermitage on the highway and was brought to town by a muleteer under suspicious circumstances. Legend has it that his mule got as far as the church and then refused to move until the bundle was taken off its back. When discovered, the image was placed in the church. This is one of the area's most important and oft-visited images. Open daily, 6 a.m.-6 p.m., mass is on Sunday at 7 a.m.

TLAXCO

The word Tlaxco is from the Nahuatl word *tlachtli,* meaning place of the ball court. This is a quiet town of predominantly Indians, who speak only their native language. If you happen to be passing through, stop and take a look. In itself it's not usually a destination, but it's a silver center, and it's the location of an interesting silver crafts school. Several colonial structures are well worth a tour.

Parroquia De San Agustín

An 18th-century edifice, it is notable because the builder, Vincenzo Barroso de la Escaloya, was responsible for the cathedral of Morelia. The pink stone is marked by empty niches and the depiction of St. Augustine atop a two-headed eagle. Recently renovated, the main altar built in 1760, the octagonal dome, and the lovely stained-glass window inside the outer doors are of particular interest. Antique lovers, check out the 19th-century organ in the choir loft. The church is located on the main plaza.

Taller Escuela De Platería
"Silversmith School"

Strolling from the plaza along Calle Domingo Arenas will bring you to the silver school operated by Señora Eva Martinez, a local artist. Here she takes children at the ages of 13 or 14 and teaches them the art of Mixtec and Aztec jewelry making. The students stay for six years to learn, at their own pace, the 17-step process called *cire perdu* (lost wax). Wax molds are made and placed inside a larger mold of metal or clay and heated; the wax melts and is replaced by molten silver. Each wax design must be perfect, or the piece will be flawed. The students learn by their mistakes. The finished products are symbolic, as well as beautiful: birds represent purity, hands—friendship, grapes—religion. The items made are for sale; earrings are in great demand but everything is made in very small quantities. A very friendly, talented woman, Señora Martinez speaks only Spanish; call first to see if she's willing to receive visitors. Located at Domingo Arenas 26, tel. (246) 6-0307.

Vicinity Of Tlaxco

Nearby **Lake Atlanga,** on the Atlangapec-Tlaxco highway, is the largest lake in the state and has areas for barbecue picnics, as well as boat and horse rentals and a restaurant that serves trout, a fish you're probably familiar with, and mojarra, which perhaps you're not. Another fascinating spot, the **Atlanga Cattle Ranch,** is also located near here; it's a breeding ranch for bulls. Some of the old hacienda buildings can be seen and photographed, including the chapel.

If you decide to stay, we hear there is an inexpensive, recently renovated hotel on Av. Madero, close to 16 de Septiembre and 5 de Mayo; look carefully or ask at the tourism office in Tlaxcala before you head out. **Lada** telephones are near the plaza. **Osiris Drug Store** is on the main square at number 7, tel. (246) 6-0005.

Getting There

The bus to Tlaxco can be found at the **ATAH** bus station in Apizaco. There are buses of all classes available. Direct, the ride takes about 40 minutes and passes through rolling land formerly occupied by large haciendas, now called *ganaderías* (ranches). **Piedras Negro** is one, and if you're driving your own car, it's worth a stop.

CACAXTLA ARCHAEOLOGICAL SITE

A small hill, much like any other dirt- and brush-covered hill across the countryside, rises 25 meters into the blue and was ignored for 1,000 years. In 1975, as one story goes, looters took note. They began a tunnel that would bring Cacaxtla (kah-KAHSH-tlah) to the attention of the world, but hardly with the outcome they anticipated.

The looters' tunnel opened onto a blood-red wall, the background of an immense mural showing a man painted black and dressed as a bird, in a polychrome panorama filled with details that would tell a rich, though gory, story of the ancient inhabitants of Cacaxtla.

Another version of discovery tells us the site was discovered when a farmer came across one of the colorful murals while working his fields. In either case, the discovery had resounding results. Before long the site was overrun by representatives of the National Institute of Anthropology and History. And so it began, and renovation has continued ever since. Archaeologists, art historians, architects, iconographers, and archaeoastronomists are having a field day. Using clues from the ancient culture (1,100 years old) they are piecing together what life was like many lifetimes ago, aided by the continuous discovery of altars, doorways, chambers, and plazas, each with a fantastic mural.

The People Of Cacaxtla

The archaeological site is located in a corridor referred to by historians as the "trade corridor" 130 km east of Mexico City. In the ancient Aztec language, Cacaxtla means "The Merchant's Backpack." In the era of Cacaxtla's apogee, these warrior merchants were a powerful class of people that never were conquered by the Aztecs in Tenochtitlán. The earliest inhabitants are believed to have their origins in the Chontal Maya region of the Gulf coast, hence the strong Maya influences. They dominated the Puebla Valley between A.D. 100 and 1000. Still a proudly independent people when Cortés arrived, they were a mixture of Nahua, Mixtec, and Chocho-Popoloca peoples. But the capital of the Olmeca Xicalanca was all but abandoned around A.D. 1400.

Colors Of The Past

This amazing acropolis must have been a stunning sight on a sunny day during its heyday—finished in bright white stucco, with the hills and Ixtaccíhuatl volcano in the background. Probably the first thing that strikes every visitor when they walk inside Cacaxtla is the amazing color. Scientists are astonished by the brilliance after so many years. So far, five basic colors have been uncovered: white, red, yellow, blue, and black. The pigments were of ground yellow ocher, ground charcoal, and red hematite, all mixed with nopal cactus juice.

MURALS OF CACAXTLA

The murals are unbelievable, and not just because of the brilliance of the colors. As more

The amazing color of the murals at Cacaxtla remain after hundreds of years.

OZ MALLAN

study is done, they continue to relate important facts about the culture of these ancient people. One unexpected find was the discovery of the Maya presence. Scientists have pondered the identity of the painters of these murals in this area of the Mexican highlands. But even a layman recognizes the artistic style to be Maya (a group that lived 800 kilometers away in the Yucatán). Add that little mystery to the mélange of hieroglyghs and symbols most commonly found in the Mexican highlands *or* in Maya country, but never together, and indeed the origin of the murals is a wonderment.

Battle Mural

Dated A.D. 650-700, the large work displays 48 warriors. The fallen are dressed in feathered outfits (birdmen), and what seem to be the victors are dressed in jaguar skins fighting with knives and spears. The detailing of each warrior is painstaking, down to their wounds dripping blood.

The great Battle Mural contains Venus symbols from Oaxaca, Teotihuacán, and Maya territory. John Carlson, expert in Mexican and Maya Venus lore from the Center for Archaeoastronomy in College Park, Maryland, tells of wars determined by the appearance of Venus. Mesoamerican "star wars," he calls them.

At first glance these murals appear to be "stories" of horrendous battles between soldiers dressed like birds and those dressed like jaguars. The birdmen are shown fatally wounded, lances piercing their bodies, blood everywhere—these are gory scenes with the jaguar warrior the apparent victor. Scientists who study pre-Columbian culture say that this may be the scene of a huge post-sacrifice to the gods after a war was won. Others declare that the *battle* was just another gathering of blood, which seems to be the focus of the Mesoamerican belief that blood held the soul and was fundamental to the sustenance of the earth.

All clues found so far indicate that Cacaxtla was the capital of the Olmecan Xicalancas between A.D. 650 and 900, abandoned around the year 1000. These people are believed to be from the state of Campeche and consist of three ethnic groups: Nahua, Mixtec, and Chocho-Popoloca. They dominated the southwest area of the state and much of the Puebla Valley. They located on a rise of land that with the ad-

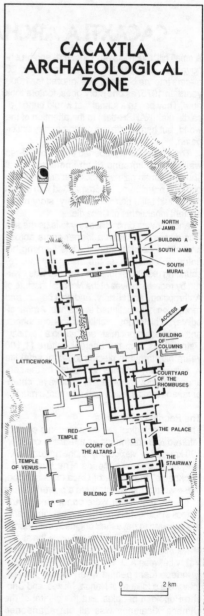

CACAXTLA ARCHAEOLOGICAL ZONE

NORTH JAMB
BUILDING A
SOUTH JAMB
SOUTH MURAL

ACCESS

BUILDING OF COLUMNS

LATTICEWORK

COURTYARD OF THE RHOMBUSES

RED TEMPLE

THE PALACE

COURT OF THE ALTARS

THE STAIRWAY

TEMPLE OF VENUS

BUILDING F

0   2 km

© MOON PUBLICATIONS, INC.

dition of walls and moats provided defensive advantage in the troubled times of the 14th century.

Uncovering The Layers

Scientists have carefully proceeded through eight layers of construction, including stairs leading to a lower chamber now called the **Red Temple** because of its brilliant red entry murals. It appears that the **North Plaza,** in front of the **El Gran Basemento,** was the scene of mob sacrifice. Also called the Palace, it was built over earlier structures, in the custom of the Mesoamericans.

Archaeologists are certain that the murals were deliberately and carefully protected. A layer of fine sand was used to cover the existing structure and its precious murals, and then a rougher fill material was added before each new edifice was built; reasons for this are still unknown.

CACAXTLA TODAY

It's just a short distance from the city of Tlaxcala, and very close to San Miguel del Milagro. It covers a space the size of four football fields and is fast becoming an important name on the "must see" list of sites for archaeology buffs visiting Mexico's central plateau. The modern look of the 20th century includes a massive metal dome to cover and protect the entire site, to keep as much weather as possible away from the flamboyant murals. The cable-supported cover was built by the state to protect the fragile adobe structure and its irreplaceable art, one of only two such covers in the world. The shape is rectangular rather than square, situated north to south. It covers 10,000 square meters, but only a small portion of this site has been explored.

TOURING THE SITE

The Entrance

Walk about 200 meters from the parking lot to the ticket office, snack shop, restrooms, and museum. From there it's about a half a kilometer more to the site, which is marked by a 3.5 tonne stone worked with attributes of a jaguar, monkey, and snake. Sometimes a van is avail-

able to take you the rest of the way. The site is open seven days a week, 10 a.m.-5 p.m. Admission is US$4.50, free on Sunday and holidays, tel. (241) 6-0000. If you're hot, hungry, and thirsty after a long afternoon of discovery, stop under the awning near the gate for an authentic blue corn taco filled with meat, squash flowers, or nopales and set up a cold beverage.

Building Of Columns

This is the oldest structure on the site and features two large columns with round bases, the only ones of that style so far discovered.

The Palace

Considered the most recent of the buildings, this was primarily used for housing the ruling class. The floor yielded the remains of 218 children sacrificed at its inauguration. The tears of the young were supposedly pleasing to the gods and it was not uncommon for children to be offered to Tlaloc (storm god) and returned as rain.

Featured here are two patios reminiscent of Teotihuacán. The expansive **Courtyard of the Rhombuses** (named after the reliefs in that shape that adorn the walls) and **Court of the Altars;** several burial chambers were found here. Facing south three pyramids can be seen.

The Stairway

The stairway is decorated on both sides by the oldest remaining murals discovered so far. In the murals you'll see the legs of four people. For some mysterious reason the artist worked in very small dimensions.

Building F is a room with two porticoes, built A.D. 600-650. Note the beautiful paneling.

Temple Of Venus (Tlahuizcalpantecutli)

Here you'll find shell designs that represent the stellar eye, relating to Venus. Two figures painted in, a priest and priestess, are viewed on the east side of the pillar. The scorpion tail denotes the male.

Red Temple

Two more murals here display a natural motif of crops (corn with human heads) and water creatures (a blue frog with turtles and snakes). A jaguar-dressed priest named **Four Dog** is almost an afterthought.

Latticework

Rather unusual, this is part of a structure built much earlier than the others excavated so far. A style never seen before in Mesoamerica, it was built with a nucleus of twigs packed firmly with mud and then coated with limestone mortar.

Building A

Aligned with the two small pyramids on the east and west sides, the murals contained here are dated 700-800. The North Mural depicts a person standing on a cat-like animal while clutching a number of water-spouting spears. Water creatures (turtles, fish, and lizards) form a border around this person, who is clad in a jaguar pelt. Due to the presence of the number "nine reptile eye," seen in flames, this is believed to be related to Quetzalcoatl in his incarnation of Ehecatl, the wind god.

The **North Jamb** supports a mural of another jaguar-clad person, this one with clawed appendages holding a snake and the water-spouting face of Tlaloc. He sports a nose pendant and a plant growing from his abdomen. Both of these murals represent Tlaloc's domain, life and fertility.

The **South Mural** is also framed with water creatures, but the person is outfitted in feathers and headdress and has taloned feet. He is standing on a feathered serpent and in his arms he holds a Maya-like snake rod. The **South Jamb** holds a richly dressed and beribboned person whose hair is elaborately made up, and who is holding a seashell with an emerging human figure.

The sunken courtyard dates from the final days of occupation. The four stairways are located at the cardinal points (north is positive, south negative, east and west neutral and equal). Of the two altars, one yielded human remains, the other, offerings. Outside, along the east wall is a well-preserved round *cuexcomate,* used then and today to store corn and grain.

Getting There

The archaeological site of Cacaxtla is 19 km from Tlaxcala near the town of San Miguel de Milagro. From there take the "Nativitas" bus from the central bus station. You will find taxis and *colectivos* that will take you to the site; expect to walk for the rest of the day (wear your favorite, well broken-in walking shoes!).

By Car: If traveling by car, once you pass Nativitas look for a sign about two kilometers out of town; the road will go to the right and is quite bumpy. Though the distance isn't great, many *topes* (speed bumps) slow you down (at least they should—these traffic bumps can wreck a fast-moving car).

VICINITY OF CACAXTLA

San Miguel De Milagro

This town is probably most known for its proximity to the archaeological site of Cacaxtla. Take a stroll around the town square, where you'll find the lovely church of St. Michael.

Sanctury Of Saint Michael

This 17th-century sanctuary was built under the sponsorship of the Bishop of Puebla, Juan de Palafox y Mendoza. The small corner chapel was built in 1712 to replace the original 16th-century one. The legend that has persisted for hundreds of years says that Archangel Michael appeared to a local Indian boy, Diego Lázaro, telling him to spread the news of a curative spring. When it wasn't done, Diego was stricken by illness for not following the wishes of the angel. It was the water of St. Michael that cured him. When the priests were made aware of the miracle they weren't receptive, they needed proof. Once again Diego was laid low; this time (it is written) he was cured by drinking from the fountain as they watched.

Inside the sanctuary is a statue of an angel sculpted from Mexican alabaster (*tecali*), bearing the date 1708. Eight paintings by Ysauro Cervantes, dated 1899, adorn the walls. Some of the 17th-century works that tell the story of the miracle are also quite beautiful. Behind the altar is the burial place of Diego Lázaro and an 18th-century baroque carving of St. Michael. It's located on the main square, visitors are welcome daily, 7 a.m.-7 p.m.

HUAMANTLA

This small city is one of the ancient boundaries of the Tlaxcalan republic, inhabited then and now by the Otomi people. Founded in 1534, Huamantla is famous for the annual fair that starts on 1 August and concludes on 15 August with a solemn procession through the streets to the church; it's the feast of the Assumption of the Virgin Mary. Highlights include the running of the fighting bulls through the village streets. On the night of 14 August, *la noche en que nadie duerme* (the night when no one sleeps), the two-km-long procession route is decorated by local artists who create a flower and sawdust "carpet," which usually takes from sundown to sunup to craft. This is a fun-filled religious event and it's almost as much fun to watch the "colorful carpet" come to life during the night as it is to follow along with the procession on the short-lived masterpiece.

History

During the War of Intervention with the U.S. a battle was fought here after the surrender of Mexico City. During the siege of Puebla, Santa Anna's army was waiting in ambush for a relief force under General Lane. When Lane heard of Santa Anna's position he sent the cavalry, of Major Samuel Walker ahead. After chasing off the Mexican cavalry Walker's men returned to Huamantla, where they were counterattacked by troops and civilians. Walker was shot and killed in the action. According to local tradition, a woman named Josefa Castelar fired the shot that killed him.

When the U.S. infantry arrived to aid the

BOB RACE

cavalry they retook the town. In reprisal for Walker's death, Lane turned his troops loose to loot, sack, rape, and pillage the town. This was the only known incident of large-scale atrocities perpetrated by U.S. troops in that war.

SIGHTS

As in most small towns in Mexico, you can often see the most interesting sights close around the town center. **Parque Juárez** is the *zócalo* of Huamantla, and is surrounded by most of the important buildings. Huamantla has two musuems of interest; museums dedicated to what some call the two national "love affairs"—toreadors, and marionettes.

The Church And Convent Of San Luis Obispo

The cloister, which is still occupied, is a 16th-century construction of the Franciscans. The main courtyard floor is covered with marble and obsidian, forming graceful geometric designs. As we go to press, the building is undergoing restoration, but the columns and portals can still be appreciated, and who knows, it might be complete and in its glory by the time you arrive.

The church foundation was laid in the 16th century, but it wasn't finished until much later, in the early 18th century. Architecturally, the building exhibits elements of baroque (the entrance), Romanesque (the floor plan), and churrigueresque (the altarpiece) features. To the side is the chapel containing the image of *The Lord* of the Convent, which is carried in the procession.

The National Puppet Museum

This is for the child in all of us. Housed in the 19th-century residence of, and donated by, the Barrientos-Carvajal family, the museum was opened in 1991. The tradition of puppet-making and shows, in Huamantla, was started by Julian Aranda and his brothers in 1850. A later collaboration with Antonio Rosete was a success and the Rosete-Aranda troupe gained widespread fame, in Mexico and abroad.

A pleasant change of pace from the usual museum, it is nonetheless an important facet of Mexican culture. The puppets, only a fraction of the Aranda's work, are complemented by puppet creations from around the world; even the U.S.A. is represented. Creative displays include a wall map that pinpoints, with lights, the countries of origin, as well as a line of puppets that moves at the touch of a button. Adult admission is $1.50, children and students get in free. Located at Parque Juárez 15, tel. (247) 2-1033, fax 2-0602. Open Tues.-Sun. 10 a.m.-2 p.m. and 5-8 p.m. Tours in English and Spanish are available by appointment.

Museo Taurino ("Bullfight Museum")

This museum has four rooms of bullfighting paraphernalia and memorabilia for the aficionado and novice alike. Huamantla has a large appetite for the sport; two native sons have made a name for themselves in the ring: Antonio "El Marinero" Ortega and Fernando "El Callao" de los Reyes Pichardo. On display you'll find posters, photos of famous matadors, costumes, capes, swords, and models of modern bullrings in Mexico. A bright mural decorates one wall. Located next to the bullring of the same name on Calle Allende 203, no phone. Open Mon.-Fri. 9 a.m.-2 p.m. Free.

PRACTICALITIES

Food

Don't expect gourmet chefs in this small city, but do expect tasty down-home specialties. El Tejado is a good place for breakfast or lunch; the prices are reasonable and the menu offers specialty dishes from all over the country. For a more international menu at moderate prices, try La Mansión at Juárez Norte 103, tel. (247) 2-1576. Lunch and dinner are served from 1-11 p.m.

Three kilometers outside of town, on the highway to Puebla, you'll find the ex-hacienda of San Francisco Soltepec. In the main house of the old hacienda, the restaurant serves good food with sterling and crystal service at less than expected rates. Try to have dinner here, or if you've already eaten, eat something again, just so you can look around this ex-hacienda dating back to the 17th century. It underwent many changes after the revolution, as did all large landholdings; for half of this century it was a teacher's college. Many aspects of hacienda life can still be seen, including the tinacle, the vat for making pulque; all haciendas made pulque in one form or another! The restaurant is located in the main house of the ex-hacienda, on Juárez Sur 216, tel. (247) 2-0498 or 2-0046. Hours are 9 a.m.-7 p.m.

Shopping And Other Services

At Centro Comercial las Doce Puertas you'll find a collection of shops selling clothing and other locally made items; Av. Juárez 102, tel. (247) 2-0235. Hospital General is at Prolongación Hidalgo 603, tel. 2-1011. Montiel Farmacia is at Parque Juárez 5, tel. 2-0302. If you need some attention for your car, try Servicio Mecanico San Luis, Hidalgo Poniente 518, tel. 2-0986. Servicio Huamantla gas station is at Hidalgo Poniente 513, tel. 2-0064. For financial transactions Banco de Oriente is at Av. Juárez Norte 8, tel. 2-0059, and Bancomer is at Av. Juárez 208, tel. 2-2189.

Getting Around

It's pretty easy to see the city on foot; however, if you need them, find taxis at Parque Juárez and ATAH buses at Zaragoza Oriente 208, tel. (247) 2-0217.

K. A. ESCOVEDO SANDERS

THE STATE OF PUEBLA
INTRODUCTION

Puebla is a state with serene pine forests, rivers, waterfalls, and magnificent high mountains. The countryside surprises first-time visitors with breathtaking views of the snow-covered volcanoes Popocatépetl and Ixtaccíhuatl in neighboring Mexico State. Some mountain climbers come to Mexico *solely* to investigate these rugged mountain peaks. These climbers are called "peak baggers" because they "collect" mountain peaks, adding each climb to their lists of conquests. However, large numbers of visitors come to investigate the capital city of Puebla, an ornate colonial center often referred to as "Talavera tile country." Taking a stroll through the city is overwhelming; you can't help but notice the tiles in nooks and crannies, ledges and domes, churches and hotels, ceilings, bathrooms, kitchens, and fountains; many of the tiles are hundreds of years old. A constant reminder of an era dedicated to color and artistic grace, Puebla is indeed filled with the glow and elaborate facade of the past.

Those with an eye for architecture enjoy the baroque churches, the churrigueresque facades, and the magnificent stonework that appears on most of the colonial structures. In Puebla there are about 70 churches and a larger number of ornate colonial buildings, all within the historic center of town. Within many of these old structures, you'll find marvelous hotels, trendy shops, and outstanding restaurants.

THE LAND

The state of Puebla is located in the region of Central Mexico near the mountain chain called the **Transverse Volcanic Sierra.** For centuries rich soil has washed down the slopes of these mountains, enriching the valleys of the highlands of Puebla. Besides fertile meadows, rampaging rivers, and tranquil streams, the nature lover will find a variety of trees from semitropical in the lower elevations to tall pines higher up. The tallest peaks, some volcanoes that have been quiet for decades, are covered with glaciers and snow most of the year.

Hidden in protected pockets and productive

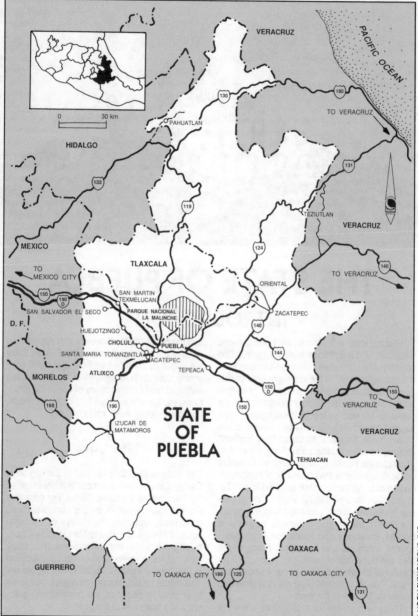

© MOON PUBLICATIONS, INC.

valleys, small villages of indigenous people are scattered throughout the beautiful Sierra Norte de Puebla and the Western Sierra Norte de Puebla. They support themselves on *ranchitos*. They grow coffee, wheat, potatoes, sugarcane, fruits, flowers, maguey agaves, eggs, beef, and pork.

Puebla shares its border with seven states; moving clockwise around it from the north, these are Veracruz, Oaxaca, Guerrero, Morelos, Mexico, Tlaxcala, and Hidalgo.

Climate

In the south, the weather is predominantly warm, but it can be quite cold in the high mountains; though uncommon, we've seen hailstorms in June in the higher elevations.

HISTORY

Historically, Puebla was a boundary between the kingdoms of **Cholula, Tlaxcala, Cuautinchan, Totimehuacan** and **Tepeaca.** These small archaic city-states were in a perpetual state of war, and though Puebla had maintained its independence for centuries, it was eventually at the mercy of Moctezuma and the Aztecs. With their increased power and daring, the Aztecs from Tenochtitlán were becoming more frenzied in their raids on the smaller city-states. They regularly kidnapped or demanded the wives and children from the people of Puebla, using them for sacrifices to their onerous gods. It's no wonder then that the indigenous people of Puebla didn't hesitate to join Cortés against Moctezuma and the Aztecs. It was their only chance to be part of the Aztec fall.

In 1519, at the port of Veracruz, Cortés and his small company of men began the first expedition to find Moctezuma and the Aztec stronghold, Tenochtitlán. It took them many weeks over unknown lands, freezing high mountain passes rising more than 3,000 meters above sea level, and countless encounters with often hostile indigenes. Puebla, almost halfway between Veracruz and Mexico, became a crucial location in the ensuing history of Mexico.

Trade Center

Puebla was a popular stopover for pre-Hispanic traders on their way to the major *tianguis* (market) in Tlaxcoco. After the arrival of Cortés it continued to be a commercial center, and because of the friendliness of the Poblanos, it became a "safehouse" for the Spaniards on the road between Mexico City (then called Tenochtitlán) and Veracruz, the main port of entry for ships to and from Spain. The route remains one of the main arteries of the country.

ECONOMY

The region is heavily populated (4.5 million people). State industries run on well-developed hydroelectric power. A few of the most vigorous industries are automaking (the Volkswagen Beetle is maunufactured here—currently a Mexican can buy a Beetle for US$7500, and the factory can't keep up with the local demand) agriculture, and the production of Talavera tiles and ceramics (which range from run-of-the-mill commercially made utility types, to beautifully crafted pieces of colorful design made in small, often family-run shops).

Poblano craftspeople create lovely Talavera pottery sold in the city.

OZ MALLAN

Tourism

Tourism adds to the economy of the state with the popularity of Puebla and nearby Cholula. Tourists flock to the state capital, also named Puebla, to explore the well-maintained colonial architecture of churches and public buildings. At Cholula, tourists with cameras and sketch pads record the graceful towers of the mountain-top church.

Mexican hikers and tourists come from around the continent to trek the famous mountains of Popo, Ixta, and Orizaba. (Although many hikers begin their treks in Puebla, Popo and Ixta are actually in Mexico State, and Mt. Orizaba is in Veracruz State; see those chapters for more details. Visitors enjoy hearty food with unique flavors and exotic ingredients that are widely proclaimed in several cookbooks that are enjoying enormous popularity in the United States. Look for Patricia Quintana's *Mexico's Feasts of Life.*

PEOPLE

Puebla is rich with indigenous cultures and people, a mix of about 400,000 Nahua and about 100,000 people from various other groups. Most of the villagers raise beans and corn, a few chickens, a pig or two, and maybe a few head of cattle on their ranchitos. Each village makes unique crafts that are endemic to its past and its village life. These traditional crafts at one time had a religious significance (some still do), but today are important as a way to supplement incomes.

The dress of the Nahua village women dates back for centuries and consists of the *quechquemetl* (an embroidered cross-stitch shoulder cape) over a white embroidered blouse, white sash, and black wool skirt. The embroidered clothing is sold in tourist shops in Puebla and Mexico City.

PUEBLA (CITY)

> **Pronounced:** PWEB-la
> **Altitude:** 4,343 meters
> **Population:** 1.5 million
> **Area Code:** (22)
> **Distance from Mexico City:** 130 km

Founded in 1531, a planned city designed from scratch by Hernando de Saavedra, Puebla city was laid out in the neat grid pattern typically employed by the Spanish, which includes a central plaza surrounded by a grand church and government buildings. The city has endured many name changes over the centuries. Before the Spaniards arrived the city-site was called Cuetlaxcoapan, "The Place Where the Snakes Change their Skin." The Spaniards first called it "City of the Angels," Puebla de los Angeles. In 1987, UNESCO, honoring the historical nature of the city, gave it the honorific title "Cultural Patrimony of Humanity." Often you will hear tour guides or those who promote the city call it "City of Monuments," or "City of Tiles." However, on 5 May 1862, after the battle of Cinco de Mayo, when the Juariztas defeated Maximilian and the French, the name of the city was changed by decree of Benito Juárez to **Puebla de Zaragoza** in honor of the Mexican general Ignacio Zaragoza Seguin. Most people, however, know it and love it as plain old Puebla.

Cinco De Mayo

For Mexicans, 5 May 1862 was a day of great triumph. More, it was a good excuse for the Napoleon government in Europe to oppose the French populace and to send more troops to Maximilian in his on-going struggle in Mexico. An additional expeditionary force of 30,000 troops was sent by Napoleon when he heard the news. It took almost a year after the Mexican victory, but the French proceeded to rout the Mexican army. So, though the Mexican victory was short lived, Cinco de Mayo remains one of the most enthusiastic holidays celebrated in Puebla today.

Architecture And Tile

Puebla is the fourth largest city of Mexico, with a population of about 1.5 million people. Only 130 kilometers from Mexico City, Puebla is a city of culture and colonial splendor as well as a modern tourist center. Gold leaf is seen everywhere, but Puebla's distinct signature is Talavera tile—it mantles rooftops, church domes, walls, fountains, kitchens, almost everything! The buildings that it covers range from hundreds of years old to brand new.

Like most colonial cities of Mexico, the historical central section is a lively conglomeration of striking buildings with more than 400 years of experience serving as a backdrop for bustling commerce, thick traffic, dozens of cafes, bars, shops, shoppers, museums, students, and scores of tourists savoring the architecture of a past era. The architecture here is almost too overwhelming, and after just a few minutes of walking around you'll suffer from sensory overload. The baroque design is combined with rich carved woods, ornate stucco abstractions, curlicues, flowers, and cherubs, which are applied in combination with colorful tiles—it creates a very distinct look.

THE CITY LAYOUT

The layout of Puebla, which was the first Mexican town built from a master plan, rather than in the midst of an existing Indian city, takes only a little study. Streets running north-south are called Calles, and those running east-west are Avenidas. Avenida Reforma/Avila Camacho (east-

west), and 16 de Septiembre/5 de Mayo (north-south) split the city.

The historic section of town is bounded by Blvd. Héroes del 5 de Mayo on the east, 11 Sur on the west, 18 Oriente to the north and 11 Oriente to the south. Avenida 16 de Septiembre becomes 5 de Mayo at Av. Reforma, which later becomes Av. Avila Camacho.

DOWNTOWN SIGHTS

The capital city of Puebla is a popular nearby destination for visitors from Mexico City, or a stopover for those traveling to Veracruz. Some make it a day-trip; others prefer to spend a night or two and haunt the Talavera shops and enjoy the excellent food. And the most popular part is meandering around the historic city center where it all began.

Around The Plaza

Plaza de Armas is the center of the city, and is surrounded by the colonial buildings of church and state. As in all Mexican cities this is where the Sunday action takes place when families come from outlying villages.

With the cathedral behind you, the **Ayuntamiento** ("City Hall") is in front of you. It was rebuilt by Carlos Hall in 1901 in the art nouveau style. The main council room is where the ancient *Royal Decree* of the city is kept.

The city center (call it the *zócalo*, the plaza, the Plaza de la Constitución or the Plaza de Armas) is situated in front of the cathedral and is bordered on three sides by the original broad stone *portales* (arches). The buildings display architectural styles including baroque, churrigueresque, neoclassic, herreresque, and renaissance. Sidewalk cafes and shops sell shoes, clothes, jewelry, and tacos. Almost anything you need can be found under the 16th-century arches, including Spanish and English newspapers (the *Mexico News*). The spacious *zócalo* is an island of tranquility with abundant shade trees, benches, and a bandstand within the crowded noisy ocean of cars, honking horns, and scurrying people. Locals escape their routine to enjoy the fresh air together with their families. Before 1854's renovation, however, the center of town was more popular for public hangings, the *tianguis* (marketplace), bullfights,

fiestas, and as a forum for *politicos*. For a flavor of the city today, get there early on a Sunday when families in their best clothes (little girls in white or colored dresses, with their hair in big red bows, or little boys dressed as clones of their papas) meander around the plaza after mass. Faded umbrellas shade the shoe-shiners and their customers, and on holidays the walkways are crowded with vendors carrying clusters of bright balloons, pink cotton candy, and a variety of food specialties.

Casa De Cultura

Formerly the archbishop's palace, the Casa de Cultura is located across from the cathedral at Av. 5 Oriente 5, next door to the Tourism Office. This long building, built in 1597 by Lic. Juan Larios, housed the Colleges of San Pablo, San Pedro, and San Juan in the 17th and 18th centuries. In 1891 it became the Governor's Palace, and it was reconstructed in 1973 due to its historical significance. Inside you'll find a movie room, exhibition space, workshops, a cafeteria, a coffee shop, and restrooms.

Up a flight of marble stairs to the second floor find the **Biblioteca Palafoxiana** ("Palafoxian Library"), believed to be the oldest library in the Americas. In 1646, Bishop Juan Palafox y Mendoza donated the first 5,000 volumes, including works of philosophy, theology, and history. The books cover a wide variety of scholars, many in Greek and Latin, others in Hebrew and Sanskrit, some printed as long ago as the 15th century.

In 1773 Bishop Francisco Fabian y Fuero constructed the library, a parallelogram 43 meters long and 12 meters wide, covered by five domes on six Doric arches. Stands of white cedar, divided into 2,472 sections, hold 50,000 volumes. Note the water flasks hung on the shelves in the event of fire! Tables inlaid with onyx stand on a red tiled floor. Faded maps of the ancient world adorn the hand hewn walls. In one corner is a beautiful chapel dedicated to the Virgin Mary.

Cathedral Of The Immaculate Conception

On the south side of the *zócalo* you cannot miss seeing the cathedral, which is considered by many visitors, as well as Catholic-church buffs, as the most beautiful church in all of Mexico. That's a huge compliment considering how many

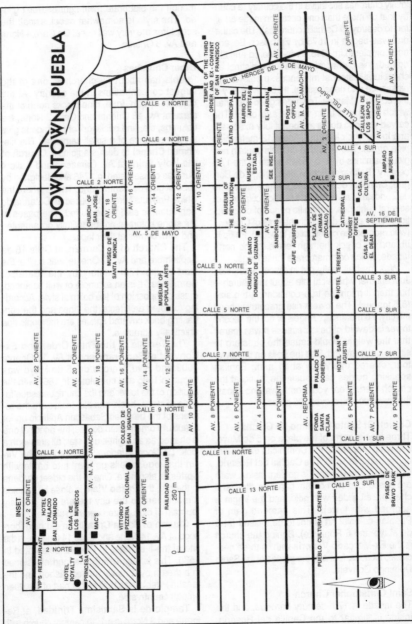

DOWNTOWN PUEBLA

AV. 2 ORIENTE
AV. 5 ORIENTE
AV. 9 ORIENTE
AV. 7 ORIENTE

Temple of the Third Order and Ex-Convent of San Francisco
BLVD. HEROES DEL 5 DE MAYO
CALLE 6 NORTE
CALLE 4 NORTE
Teatro Principal
Barrio del Artistas
El Parian
Post Office
AV. M. A. Camacho
AV. 3 ORIENTE
CALLE DEL SAPO
Callejon de los Sapos
CALLE 4 SUR
AV. 8 ORIENTE
Museo de Estada
SEE INSET
CALLE 2 SUR
Amparo Museum
Church of San Jose
AV. 18 ORIENTE
AV. 16 ORIENTE
AV. 14 ORIENTE
AV. 12 ORIENTE
AV. 10 ORIENTE
Museum of the Revolution
AV. 6 ORIENTE
AV. 4 ORIENTE
Sanborns
Plaza de Armas (Zocalo)
Cathedral
Casa de Cultura
AV. 16 DE SEPTIEMBRE
CALLE 2 NORTE
Museo de Santa Monica
AV. 5 DE MAYO
Museum of Popular Arts
Church of Santo Domingo de Guzman
Cafe Aguirre
Tourist Office
Casa de El Dean
CALLE 3 NORTE
Hotel Teresita
CALLE 3 SUR
CALLE 5 NORTE
CALLE 5 SUR
AV. 22 PONIENTE
AV. 20 PONIENTE
AV. 18 PONIENTE
AV. 16 PONIENTE
AV. 14 PONIENTE
AV. 12 PONIENTE
CALLE 7 NORTE
AV. 10 PONIENTE
AV. 8 PONIENTE
AV. 6 PONIENTE
AV. 4 PONIENTE
AV. 2 PONIENTE
AV. REFORMA
Palacio de Gobierno
Hotel San Agustin
CALLE 7 SUR
AV. 5 PONIENTE
AV. 7 PONIENTE
AV. 9 PONIENTE
CALLE 9 NORTE
Plaza de
Fonda Santa Clara
CALLE 11 NORTE
CALLE 11 SUR
Railroad Museum
250 m
CALLE 13 NORTE
Pueblo Cultural Center
CALLE 13 SUR
Paseo de Bravo Park
0

INSET
AV. 2 ORIENTE
Hotel Palacio San Leonardo
Casa de los Munecos
Colegio de San Ignacio
CALLE 4 NORTE
AV. M. A. Camacho
MAC'S
Vittorio's Pizzeria Colonial
AV. 3 ORIENTE
VIP'S Restaurant
Hotel Royalty
2 NORTE
LA PRINCESA

© MOON PUBLICATIONS, INC.

lovely churches still thrive in the country (a country that on more than one occasion made an effort to destroy all Catholic churches). The cathedral was begun in 1575 by Francisco Becerra and completed in 1648. Twin-towered and tile-domed, this cathedral shows three distinct architectural/historical influences: medieval, renaissance and neoclassical. It truly rivals any in the country. Manuel Tolsá designed the altar, which is carved from marble and onyx. The carved wooden doors are beautifully executed, and in the choir loft you'll find a 12-meter-high pipe organ. The 14 gilded chapels contain religious paintings by well-known artists of the 17th century (Balthazar Echeverioja, Diego de Borgraf, Cristóbal de Villalpando, Miguel Jeronimo de Zendejas), as well as relics and sculptures of several centuries. During its period of construction, Spain passed through the eras of Charles I (who ordered the construction to begin), Phillip II, III, and IV; check the high reliefs on the north facade, which commemorate those kings.

Was the bell really put in place by angels? Just another whimsical tale about the church—but then it might be true considering the size (8.5 tonnes). The towers rise gracefully above the city, 70 meters up. Angels or no, the second tower is devoid of bells because it was feared that the weight would cause the structure to sink into the ground. See the bells on the tower tour, offered every day at 11 a.m.; English speaking guides can usually be found at the church then. Wear your comfy walking shoes; the tower contains over 200 steps.

Church Of Santo Domingo De Guzmán

Three blocks north of the plaza on 5 de Mayo, see what remains of the Dominican monastery consecrated in 1690. The **Capilla del Rosario,** ("Chapel of the Rosary") is golden. Inside, walls are ensconced with ornate carvings, tiles, and cherubs, all gilded with gold, and the Virgin is adorned with jewels. This baroque gem of Pueblan colonial art is not to be missed (at 5 de Mayo and 6 Poniente). Behind the church is the **Ex-Mercado Victoria** with its three neoclassic facades, formerly the garden of the Santo Domingo Convent.

Saint Christopher Church

The facade is 17th-century baroque, and the inside is similar to the Capilla del Rosario, though the elaborate relief figures aren't gilded. The style is somewhat neoclassical; the sculptures are very well done. On Calle 4 Norte and Av. 6 Oriente.

Other Churches

Puebla has about 58 churches, one of the largest concentrations in the country. At the **Church of San José,** nine blocks north of the plaza at Av. 18 Oriente and Calle 2 Norte, the columns, tile, and brickwork of the facade give the appearance of a small cathedral. The tile-domed **Chapel to Jesús** adjoins it. **Church of the Holy Spirit** at Av. Camacho and Calle 4 Sur was consecrated in 1746 and designed by José Miguel de Santa María. This is where the China Poblana Mirrha, baptized as Catarina de San Juan, is said to be buried. The bases of the stone columns are beautifully ornamented and form domes at their tops.

The **Church of El Carmen,** at Calle 16 de Septiembre and Av. 17 Oriente, was built at the start of the 17th century by the "Barefoot Carmelites." It is an example of well balanced, mass composition of the colonial style. According to noted architects, the "lines and the contrasting brick covered spaces are harmonic and artistically attractive."

The **Temple of the Third Order and Ex-Convent of San Francisco** at Av. 14 Oriente 1009 and Blvd. Héroes del 5 de Mayo was begun in 1535 and completed in 1667 with the addition of the tower and the churrigueresque facade of stone, brick, and tile. Inside are the remains of the beatified Sebastian Aparicio under beautifully ornamented domes; the principal one is shaped as an eight-sided star; all are worth a look. *La Conquistadora,* the statue of the Virgin that legend tells us went into battle with Cortés, is also here. One of the oldest gardens in the city, the **Paseo Viejo** is close by; it holds a monument to the city fathers and a lovely fountain of blue glazed ceramic tiles.

Church of Santa Cruz, in an old neighborhood at Av. 14 Norte and Calle 14 Oriente, is the site of the first mass in Puebla, celebrated in 1530. This is supposedly the land envisioned in a dream by a newly arrived Bishop and the reason Puebla was built in this part of the (then empty) countryside.

Templo de la Santísima Trinidad, at Reforma and 3 Norte is a 17th century church with a glazed tile depiction of the founding of the city. Farther up 3 Norte, at 4 Poniente, **Santa Catalina** church looms with its Talavera-tiled tower and cupola sparkling in the sunshine.

Museo De Santa Monica

This religious museum tells a mysterious story of the city during the anticlerical era. There are Poblanos who disagree with these stories, but take a look and decide for yourself. After Catholic nuns and priests were banned from the country in 1857, many went "underground"—literally. This convent was discovered in 1935 after surviving secretly (along with two others) since 1857. After the discovery, the convent was left untouched and turned into a musuem. The convent was founded in 1610—originally, as one story goes, to harbor the (pregnant) daughters of prestigious citizens. After that era it is said to have been a hiding place for prostitutes (the other option was jail). Some years later it became a cloister for young novitiates. It's characterized by dim narrow halls, winding stairways that step down into the bowels of the earth (where supposedly a crypt holds the bones of babies), a secret window that looks into the church next door (where the nuns could observe mass and other ceremonies), and hidden passageways. Not everyone will be thrilled to tour this former scene of self-flagellation and total silence, for almost a hundred years a secret hiding place for a large number of women. It is also said that many influential families of Puebla helped in the religious conspiracy and saw to it that they had food and medicine.

Adding to the mystique, entrance to the convent was through the home of sympathizers through a cupboard in the dining room. Today entrance to Museo de Santa Monica is still through a private home. Apparently, this was just one of three hidden nunneries, and at Santa Monica artifacts are shown from all three. Admission is US$2; open 10 a.m.-4 p.m., closed on Monday; located at 18 Poniente 103.

Next door, the **Church of Santa Monica,** contains the glass enclosed sculpture of *El Señor de las Maravillas* ("Jesus of Wonders"), admired by both Poblanos and visitors.

Amparo Museum

The newest and brightest museum in Puebla was opened in 1991. Three blocks from the *zócalo* (follow the signs), this beautifully restored colonial mansion heralds a new policy in museumdom. Manuel Espinoza Yglesias, a banker and philanthropist, has showcased his extensive collection of pre-Columbian and colonial art here. The displays are labeled in Spanish and English; there are also pushbutton recordings in every room. Rent headphones (US$2) at the door, plug them into the audiovisual unit, and choose your language (Spanish, English, French, or Japanese). Follow instructions and learn the history and interesting details about each piece. The high-tech system has a few glitches now and then, but overall is a fine system. Open 10 a.m.-5 p.m. daily. Admission is US$3.50, free on Monday; located at Calle 2 Sur 708, tel. (22) 46-4646.

Museo Bello Y Gonzalez

Guided tours are given in Spanish (English guides are available by appointment) through this seemingly endless collection of elegant furnishings from throughout the country, as well as Europe and Asia: fine art, gold, silver, ivory, jade porcelain, glass, Talavera, wrought iron, pianos, organs, original sheet music by Beethoven, religious vestments, clothing, locks, and countless other curiosities from all over the globe. All of this was collected by José Luis Bello, a businessman who amassed a fortune during his life and, alas, was only an armchair traveler. He vicariously acquired elegant treasures for his home through the efforts of *real* travelers. Admission is US$1, free on Tues., open 10 a.m.-5 p.m. Tues.-Sun., (guide is mandatory); on Calle 3 Poniente 302, tel. (22) 32-9475.

Museum Of Popular Arts

The biggest attraction here is the Talavera-tiled kitchen (if you only have time to see one Talavera-tiled kitchen, this is the one to see) with huge caldrons and other earthenware utensils. If we are to believe the legends, this is where much of the regional cuisine was created by the now-famous Dominican nun, Sor Andrea de la Asunción. Everyone has heard the story— "Look who's coming to dinner, Sor Andrea,— uh oh, it's the bishop." In a flash she cleaned out her kitchen tubs and crocks and created the first *mole poblano,* made of more than 25 ingredients including a large variety of chiles, spices, chocolate, and turkey. It has been famous ever since, just one of the dishes that Puebla is known for. Mexican art is displayed on two floors, and a gift shop offers a selection of local handicrafts. Open 10 a.m.-5 p.m. Tues.-Sun.; admission is US$1. Located on Calle 5 Norte 1201, in the ex-convent of Santa Rosa; tel. (22) 46-2471.

Museo De Estada (Casa De Alfenique)

The word *alfenique* translates to sugar paste, and the intricate baroque facade of this colonial building could indeed be a cake maker's delight with its lacy curlicues and designs, all in white. Built in 1790 by Ignacio Morales, it is now the state museum. The first floor houses carriages and old manuscripts, the second floor will delight the history buff, and on the third floor you'll find a display of ethnography. The original *china poblana* dress is here as well as other clothing of the colonial era. Open 10 a.m.-5 p.m. Tues.-Sun., closed Mon.; admission is US$2. At Av. 4 Oriente 416, tel. (22) 41-4296.

Museum Of The Revolution

Also called the **Regional War Museum,** this was the 18th century home of Aquiles and Maximo Serdán Alatriste, who were members of the revolutionary "Light and Progress Club." This anti re-election party would eventually help to topple the dictatorship of Porfirio Díaz in the revolution that began on 18 November 1910. Sadly, Aquiles was unable to take part in the revolution thanks to an informer who tipped off Díaz. Díaz sent his men, and a barrage of bullets killed almost everyone there. Aquiles was shot and died shortly afterward. Maximo survived the attack, but along with anyone else who survived he was captured and killed—take a look at the hiding place under the floor that *almost* kept him from being discovered. The bullet holes are displayed on the building as a badge of courage. Weaponry and photos are exhibited. Admission is 75 cents; located at Av. 6 Oriente 206, tel. (22) 42-1076.

Casa De El Dean

A renaissance-style house built in the year 1580 houses antique frescoes. Visiting hours are sporadic; ask at the tourist office. Located on 16 de Septiembre and 7 Poniente.

Casa De Los Muñecos ("House Of Dolls")

The top floor of the Casa de los Muñecos is decorated with caricatures (some quite gruesome) of the town fathers who refused to let the owner, Don Agustín de Ovando y Villavincencio, add the third floor. Their complaint was that it would be taller than the old City Hall. Don Agustín went to Mexico City where, with proper politicking, he got his way. With this nose-thumbing gesture he immortalized his foes in stone parody. Today it houses the **University Museum.** Located at 2 Norte and Avila Camacho.

Teatro Principal

One of the oldest theaters on the continent, this theater was built in 1756 and opened in 1760. A tragic fire all but destroyed it in 1902, but the Mary Street Jenkins Foundation lovingly rebuilt it. The intricate stone facade may be all you get to see unless you visit on Sunday or attend a performance. On the ceilings in the lobby and on the second floor are portrait galleries honoring the **Patrones of the Comedy Corral.** These patrons of the theater provided their own homes to stage shows before the theater was built. On Av. 6 Oriente and Calle 6 Norte.

Barrio Del Artistas

Across the alley from the theater, check out the Barrio del Artistas, once called the *parian de tornos,* where spinning wheels turned out thread vital to the Poblano clothing industry. Formally named the **José Luís Rodríguez Alconado Exhibition Hall,** it is now occupied by artists. This hall provides small spaces for painters to work portraits and still lifes in pastels, watercolors, and oil. Oh, yes, the artists love to capture the roving tourist on canvas given the opportunity; make sure you clarify price before you pose. Open daily all day. Located at Calle 6 Norte and Av. 6 Oriente.

A little farther, on 6 Norte and Calle Segundo Central, is the only raised park in the city—a quiet green space with flowers, especially bougainvillea, and the ever-present courting couples. The neighborhood is well kept and the houses reflect an interesting mix of architectural styles.

VIPS Restaurant

This art nouveau building was once the home of the wealthy American William O. Jenkins. It was built at the beginning of this century, and continues as **VIPS**, a quick stop cafe for light meals. Located on the corner of 2 Oriente and 2 Norte.

House Of The China Poblana

This is said to be the house where China Poblana lived and died; on the corner of Av. 2 Oriente and Calle 2 Norte. Look at the outside; it is not open to the public.

NEAR CENTRO CIVICO CINCO DE MAYO

Take a taxi or a city bus (from Av. 6 Oriente and Calle 2 Sur) marked "Maravillas" or "Fuerte" to a complex less than two miles northeast of the zócalo at Blvd. Héroes del 5 de Mayo. Here, parks, forts, and museums commemorate the scene of Mexico's great (successful) battle with the French. It's worth the bus or cab ride to wander around and imagine the tall-hatted and overly confident French soldiers. These soldiers never counted on the motivation and determination of the barefoot peasants who came to fight. These campesinos fought with everything they had—sticks, clubs, and machetes, but mostly their hearts. After the smoke cleared and the shouting and commotion relented, the French soldiers were gone and the outnumbered Mexicans were victorious. The stone horseman you see is General Zaragoza, who led the troops—and received most of the glory.

There were "monarchists" and many Catholic clergy who aided and abetted the limping French army. It was then that President Juárez issued a presidential decree threatening to fine and imprison "priests of any cult" who further aided the French enemy. And he also made it illegal for priests of "any cult" to wear "vestments or any distinguishing garment" outside of the churches. Sadly, a year later, the French returned with thousands more troops and finished what they started on that fateful Cinco de Mayo in 1862.

Fuerte De Loreto

The primitive name of the site of this fortress is **Acuayematepec** ("Frogs in the Water of the Hill"). The church of **Our Lady of Loreto** was built here to the exact measurements of the "Saint House" in Loreto, Italy. Ciriaco del Llano

CHINA POBLANA

The *china poblana* is the national feminine folk costume and is worn on occasion by city girls and women of all classes. It is the dress of those who dance the **Jarabe Tapatio** and the *charras* in the *charreada*. The traditional costume consists of a full red flannel skirt falling to the ankles, heavily trimmed with sequined designs (the top 25 centimeters are green); a white, short-sleeved, embroidered shirt; a *rebozo* folded over the shoulders and crossed in front; multiple strings of brightly colored beads; a red or green bow atop the head; and high-heeled dancing shoes. While the costume follows a conventional pattern, there are differences in materials and adornments. *Charras* and folk singers wear sombreros.

Legend Of The *China Poblana*

There are several variations on the same theme when discussing the *china poblana*. All begin with a Chinese slave girl purchased by Captain Miguel Sosa of Puebla. Whether the girl was a Mongol princess named Mina, or a Hindu princess named Mirrha, she was noble at birth and a servant girl at death. She is said to have married a Chinese slave named Domingo Suárez, thus earning her nickname, but she refused to consummate her marriage with someone of common blood. Some say her piety was so great that she spoke with saints and had curative powers. Her funeral was attended by nobility of church and state, who carried her coffin on their own shoulders.

All agree that she did good deeds among the poor, was a devout Catholic who took the name of Catarina de San Juan, and inspired all who met her. The female servants at the time (early 17th century), called *chinas,* were enamored of Catarina and emulated her outfit, which today is called the *china poblana*.

ordered the fort built in 1821, keeping the chapel in the center. Here, on that fateful day in May, 6,000 French Zouaves under General Lorencez attacked the forts of Loreto and Guadalupe which were defended by about 2,000 Mexican troops under the command of General Ignacio Zaragoza. The defeat of the French earned Puebla the honorific title *heroica*.

Wandering through the museum you'll find dioramas of the battle, photos, drawings, and paintings. There is a picture of Maximilian in Querétaro (moments before his execution) comforting the priest who had come to ease the ex-emperor's last moments. Shortly thereafter he died in front of a firing squad, but not before his final words rang out: "Viva Mexico!" Open 10 a.m.-5 p.m., Tues.-Sun.; admission is US$2.25. Cinco de Mayo is celebrated each year here with a re-enactment of this battle and a major fiesta.

Planetarium And Natural History Museum
Puebla's planetarium (tel. 22-35-2099) boasts facilities comparable to those in the U.S., including a 360-degree screen depicting the night sky. Nearby, the entrance of the **Natural History Museum** (tel. 35-3419) displays the murals of Poblano artists Salvador Ortega and Fernando Ramirez Osorio. This is a great place to bring the kids to see animals of the various regions of the countryside. Open 10 a.m.-4:30 p.m. Tues.-Sun.; admission is US$2.50. At the **Anthropology Museum** nearby, three rooms of exhibits display pre-Hispanic, colonial, and revolutionary artifacts. Open 10 a.m.-4:30 p.m. Tues.-Sun., admission free.

ALONG THE REFORMA

In Puebla Centro, walk west on Reforma between 7 and 9 Norte and you'll see two 17th century buildings of interest. On the left side of the street is the **Palacio de Gobierno, Colegio de San Ignacio,** and on the right side is the **Hospicio,** once a house for the poor that was reconstructed in 1832 and served as a barracks in the revolution. On the corner of Reforma and Calle 9 Norte is the **Parroquia de San Marcos,** built in 1578 with typical brick and tile facade.

At the north end of the Paseo de Bravo on Reforma and 11 Norte is **Iglesia de Guadalupe,** a 17th-century baroque church with a scene of the Apparition of the Virgin captured in another tiled masterpiece. Walk through the **Paseo de Bravo Park** with its tall swaying trees and spewing fountains dedicated to the brave men and women of Mexico. Sprays of flowers and water beckon. A tiled monument depicts the planting of the cross by Cortés's expedition on their landfall.

Across from the park on Reforma and Calle 13 Sur, look for the **Pueblo Cultural Center.** This ex-penitentiary was built in the 1840s, a replica of those that stood in Philadelphia and Cincinnati. The high brick walls, towers, and turrets once held those deemed unfit to remain at large, socially or politically. Today it is a fine library and cultural center.

ACCOMMODATIONS

Budget Accommodations
There are hotels in Puebla with charm, and those with charming amenities, but there are *none* that have both at budget prices. The hotels in the budget category just aren't that much of a deal here. There are budget hotels up and down 5 de Mayo/16 de Septiembre, signified by a blue [H] sign. These old and not always clean hotels are certainly for the adventurous. If that's you, then it's worth a look. The "amenities" vary. Some might not have hot water or windows, can be noisy, and could have lumpy beds. However, they often attract interesting guests, have a friendly helpful staff who may or may not speak English, and in many cases are centrally located—this could turn out to be your most memorable stop. Ask all the right questions and look closely before you pay. Another good source of information about budget hotels is the tourism office.

Take a look at the **Casa de Huéspedes** behind the cathedral, almost adjoining the palace of the Archbishop. The courtyard is surrounded by iron-railed balconies and catwalks, behind solid noise-dampening walls. Ventilation is from open doors in these small, clean rooms, without much room for more than a bed and suitcase; a good place to meet fellow travelers. Rooms without bath are US$9 s, US$13 d; with private bath rates are US$12 s, US$16 d. A small store sells necessities in travel sizes. Once you're inside the windowless room, the street noise fades. At 5 Poniente 111, tel. (22) 46-3175.

Hotel Teresita is not very large or dramatic; some rooms have baths, and the rooms are clean, but the hot water is iffy. Most of the rooms are without windows and can be noisy. This is a popular stopover for Mexican workmen. Located one and a half blocks west of the *zócalo*. Prices without bath are US$14 s, US$17 d; with bath US$18 s, US$19 d. On Av. 3 Poniente 309, tel. 41-7072.

Moderate

The **Hotel San Agustín** offers 74 newly painted rooms. The courtyard is crowded with plants and statuary, and water spurts from a lion's head into a small pool. There's also a step-up restaurant and bar under brightly colored glass panels. The clerk is always occupied, and the lobby is always bustling. Rooms are small. There's plenty of tile, and you'll also find built-in wooden furniture, a small bathroom with curtain, satellite TV, fluorescent lights, and a double bed. Very clean, with a phone and a/c. **Note:** Look for the sign that gives you the hours when you can get a hot shower. Rates are US$23 s, US$37 d; 3 Poniente 531, tel. (22) 41-5089.

Almost every town in Mexico has an older hotel near the *zócalo* called the **Colonial.** Puebla is no different. Location only a block from the plaza and in the heart of the historic district makes it convenient to most everything (half a block north of A. Camacho). Tile floors, arched doorways, well-used wooden furniture, and paintings grace the lobby. The rooms are fairly large, and some have balconies, wood floors, and furniture that evokes a certain timelessness. Tile baths, good restaurant on the premises, parking. Rates are US$35 s, US$45 d; on Calle 4 Sur 105, tel. 46-4199.

The Hotel Gilfer, with 92 rooms, has a restaurant and a cafeteria, the **London Bar,** a beauty shop, a tobacco shop, and parking; 2 Oriente 11, tel. 46-0611 or 46-0039. **Hotel Royalty,** with 44 rooms, is located at Portal Hidalgo 8, tel. 42-4740; check out the outdoor cafe under the portals. Both of these hotels have the benefit of being on the *zócalo* and prices are fairly moderate, about US$45 d. The **Hotel Palacio San Leonardo,** with 75 rooms in a lovely old French-colonial building dating back to the early 1900s, was renovated to accommodate a hotel. There's a restaurant and bar on the premises; rates are about US$44 s, US$48d. Located at 2 Oriente 211, tel. 46-0555, fax 42-1176.

Expensive Hotels

The **Misión Park Plaza** and its modern yellow tower is on the west side of the city. Definitely at the high end of the budget, amenities include pool, spa, workout room (you can schedule time with a personal trainer), dining room, cocktail lounge, coffee shop, and a disco almost always filled with people. Tours can be arranged and tickets purchased. The rooms are tan-colored with minibars, satellite TV, twin double beds, plush carpets, and beautifully appointed tile bathrooms. Ask for a west-facing view to see the volcanoes/mountains Popocatépetl and Ixtaccíhuatl, or to the east to see Orizaba and Malinche. You have to be an early riser to catch a glimpse though, because the smog covers them quickly. Rates start at US$100 s or d, suites available. At Calle 5 Poniente, tel. (22) 48-9600 or 48-9602, fax 48-9733.

Other more expensive hotels that have merit include **Hotel Lastra,** at Calz. de los Fuertes 2633, tel. 35-9755 or 35-4111; **Hotel Granada,** at Blvd. de la Pedrera 2303, tel. 32-0966, fax 32-0424. **Hotel El Mesón del Angel** is a pleasant stopover for "down time" in a tropical green garden with two pools and a health center. Lots of businesspeople come here; rates are US$79 s, US$80 d. Located on Av. Hermanos Serdán 807, tel. 48-2100, fax 48-7935.

RV Parks In Puebla

Trailer Park Las Americas: If you're pulling a trailer, check out the **Trailer Park Las Américas;** neat and tidy, 130 spaces, fenced, laundry/rec room, pool, and ice. Located 16 km south on Hwy. 190, tel. (22) 47-0134, Apdo. Postal 49, Cholula, Puebla, Mexico. It's US$12 for two people.

Hotel Cuatro Camino: Eight spaces have full hookups, clean area, restaurant, laundry, and convenient city buses. On Av. Serdán near the highway to Mexico City.

Hotel Spa Agua Azul: Next to Agua Azul Park; you'll find a pool, mineral baths, a restaurant, and city buses.

FOOD

Puebla is noted for its wonderful cuisine, often copied but seldom matched. Bakeries are prevalent and always a good way to save pesos on breakfast. Local delis offer sandwich meats and cheeses, and *pollo* shops are easy to find, with chubby chickens slowly rotating in front of electric coils, sending out delicious aromas. A fresh whole rotisseried chicken (US$3-4) with a loaf of good fresh bread can be a great meal eaten in the park.

Food Specialties

We've already mentioned mole, which was first made at the Santa Rosa convent, but here are a few more specialties you might like to try: *Mixiotes* are made by wrapping barbequed meat (beef, pork, lamb, or goat) and spices in a maguey leaf (not edible) and steaming. *Tingas* is a meat and vegetable stew. *Chiles en nogada* is another dish credited to the imaginative cooks of Puebla. It consists of stuffed green chile poblano peppers in a white sauce of crushed walnuts, cream cheese, and pomegranate seeds. It's *¡sabroso!* (tasty!). The patriotic colors of the dish (red, green, and white) make it popular around Independence Day, 16 September. Candy, confections, and crystallized fruits are also very popular in the city. Check out the candy center north of the *zócalo* on 2 Oriente.

Besides many fine restaurants, there is a multitude of choices for meals: bakeries, *taquerias, loncherias,* and cafeterias—the food here is *muy bueno.* Restaurants usually open around 8-10 a.m. and close when there are no more customers, 9-10 p.m. The dinner houses stay open till midnight and later. Restaurants around the plaza offer good food at reasonable prices, as well as providing a great platform for people-watching.

Restaurants Indoors And Out

For an outdoor seat and a good strong cup of coffee, the **Cafe Aguirre** (Calle 5 de Mayo 4) is a good choice anytime of day. But for a solid meal, **La Princessa,** at Portal Juárez 101, tel. (22) 32-1195, is a good choice. Enjoy a reasonable breakfast (US$1.75-4), Appetizers make a great economical lunch (US$1.50-5), entrees are varied (US$6-10), and you can expect a substantial *comida corrida* (US$6.50) served 1-5 p.m. The tables in front of the **Hotel Royalty,** provide a relaxed sidewalk cafe (prices are slightly high) located on Portal Hidalgo 8, tel. 42-0202. This is a favorite American hangout.

For live music in the heart of town, come to **Restaurant Bar Casa Real** on weekends (and some weeknights). The restaurant opens for breakfast, lunch, and dinner—shows start at 9 p.m. This lovely establishment in the historical district (two blocks from the *zócalo*) serves wonderful local specialties: mole, *chalupas, chiles en nogada,* and a large selection of meats. Prices are moderate to slightly expensive; at 4 Oriente 208, tel. 46-9654.

Mac's is a modern restaurant with high wooden tables and booths. Fixed-price lunches and dinners really fill the place up. Appetizers range US$2.50-5, *comida corrida* is US$6-8, and dinner costs US$7-15. It's located on A. Camacho and Portal Morelos, tel. 46-0211.

At **Vittorio's Pizzeria,** enjoy a cappuccino or espresso alfresco, or stay indoors if it's cold. If you haven't had a Mexican-style pizza yet, here's your chance. You'll find pasta and salad on the menu as well as *típico* fare. Prices for pizza range US$5-18, depending on how many are eating; at Portal Morelos 106, tel. 32-7900.

Fonda Santa Clara is a popular and sometimes noisy restaurant serving traditional regional food. Try the *mixiotes* (*al vapor*—steamed), the *tingas,* or Poblano mole. The *antojitos* (snacks) are tasty. Paper decorations hang from the ceiling, and rave reviews are scrawled on the walls. The menu is in English and the bow-tied waiters are efficient and polite. Prices range US$3-15; at Av. 3 Poniente 307, tel. 42-2659; there's another at Av. 3 Poniente 920, tel. 46-1952.

The entrance to **Restaurante Típico la China Poblana's** is a small store-front room with three tables next to the kitchen. Decorated with local plates, masks, clothing, and a life-sized China Poblana, there's a larger dining room in the rear. The food is good here, but there's no written menu and everything is a la carte. If you don't speak Spanish, ask twice to be certain you know what you're getting and at what price. On Sunday prices tend to go up a bit; bread and tortillas cost extra here. One block south of El Parian at Calle 6 Norte 1.

La Cava Restaurant and Bar provides an ambience of soft yellow light from hanging baskets illuminating this quiet, French-service eatery on the west side of town. Soft music plays, sterno flames, and frying pans sizzle as the waiter prepares your linguine with clams—tableside. Prices range from moderate to expensive; pasta dishes and salads are US$5-9, steaks and seafood cost US$10-20. Expect dinner for two with wine or cocktails to cash out at US$25-50. No, you don't pay extra for your breadbasket here! Located across the street from the movie theater at Av. Juárez 2302.

Prime rib is the password at **London House,** which serves international food and offers unusually good upscale entertainment; it's a little dressier here than average. It's at Av. Juárez 1312, tel. 32-4538.

Bodegas del Molino is located at the edge of town on the highway to Mexico City. This old hacienda has a history of once being a flour mill that turned the land white, giving it the name of Lady of the Snows. Beautifully restored and lovingly decorated this is one of the best restaurants in town. It's a favorite choice for Poblanos for special occasions, and prices reflect just *how* special. Located at San José del Puente, tel. 49-0399 or 49-0651.

ENTERTAINMENT

Discos
La Boom Disco is at Juárez 1906, tel. (22) 42-4675. Have fun at **Cheek to Cheek Disco,** Blvd. Atlixco 47-B, tel. 48-1648. You'll find **Taboo Disco** at Diagonal Díaz Ordaz 3972.

Theaters
For a list of current performances (mostly concerts), dates, and hours, check at the tourist office. These theaters have changing events, and some are worthwhile:

Teatro Principal, 6 Norte and 8 Oriente, tel. (22) 32-6085.

Hermanos Soler, Av. 5 Poniente 318, tel. 46-9815.

Teatro U.A.P., 4 Sur 104, no phone.

Downtown Cinemas
Times and listings are easily available from the tourist office for the following cinemas:

Continental, Av. 4 Oriente, tel. (22) 32-1955.

Guerrero, Ayuntamiento 14, tel. 32-2552.

Puebla, Av. 7 Poniente 104, tel. 32-6263.

Mariachis
If you go to hear the mariachis, expect to pay. They are playing to earn a living and will circulate, expecting donations—they let you know if it's not enough! At the **Plaza de los Trabajos,** across from the Railroad Museum, mariachis play every evening; Calle 11 Norte and Av. 10 Poniente. They also play at **Plaza de Santa Inez,** Calle 3 Sur and Av. 11 Poniente.

Sporting Events
At **Estadio Cuauhtémoc,** soccer packs in the locals during the season; at Calz. Ignacio Zaragoza 666, tel. (22) 36-3746. **Estadio Zaragoza,** tel. 41-5524, is where the baseball fans go. For bullfights, go to **Plaza de Toros El Relicario,** tel. 36-8818. **Lienzo Charro,** a *charreada* (Mexican rodeo) stadium holding 4,000 people, is on the Carretera Tehuacan Poniente 1032, tel. 35-2288. *Charreada* is held most weekends and on big holidays.

Kid Stuff
Big and little kids love to come to the **Railroad Museum** to study the collection of spiffed up trains that have been put out to pasture. The antique steam engines and rail cars are open for kids (and adults) to touch, examine, and explore. This is a real hands-on experience. In some of the cars visitors find pictures and displays illustrating the history of Mexican trains since 1837; designing the routes, laying the track—there are even references to the *bandidos*. Like North American bandits, they rode their horses after trains; upon catching the train they extracted passengers' valuables. Pictures of their days of service are located in the stationlike building. Sunday is family day; lots of picnics are held in the grassy area close by. Open daily 10 a.m.-6 p.m., free; located on Calle 11 Norte between Av. 2 and Av. 6 Poniente, tel. 41-4988. **Note:** The long line behind the building is for the public telephone.

Agua Azul, tel. 43-1330, is a *balneario* (water park), where for a small fee whole families splash and play. Weekdays are less crowded; buses run regularly. **Africam,** tel. 35-8713, is a safari ride through 6,075 hectares inhabited by wild animals. Buses for Africam leave the Central Camionera (CAPU) three times every day. It's located about eight km from town.

SHOPPING

Puebla is an outstanding shopping city. Local arts and crafts are exceptional, including fine Talavera tile and pottery. The city attracts many travelers who are knowledgeable about the culture, art, and architecture that has survived over five centuries. Excellent onyx is available (along with the not-so-excellent—know your product), much of which is found in Mexico State and sent to Puebla to be carved. Modern shopping malls are springing up around the city with U.S.-style stores, but there are still many fine shops along the streets where you can browse, bargain, and find souvenir-type gifts. The indigenous people from the surrounding villages bring folk crafts to market. Sunday is market day in Puebla and the best day to find these craftsmen.

Crafts
Almost every craft that visitors admire began as something useful, often with a religious meaning for a special village. Next time you're browsing in a ceramic shop in the **Barrio de la Luz** in Puebla, ask to see the vessels made expressly for holding mole or those made expressly for tamales. Mexican-style coffee is made in a pottery pot that also has a particular shape.

In **Izucar de Matamoros** the artists create the "tree of life," which can be small or immense and tells the story of a family or a village. Onyx and marble carvings done in **Tehuacán** and **Puebla** are especially admired. As for textiles, several villages are particularly respected for

This craftsman has been making pottery for 50 years.

the quality of wool and cotton they produce: **Cholula, San Martín Texmelucan,** and **Tepeaca.** Amate paper has long been an important part of religious events in the village of **Pahuatlan.** Today they are sold for framing.

Market Days
Puebla is a small state to scurry around, especially if you have a car, otherwise bus transport is simple to these outlying areas. Market days at a few of the surrounding cities can be an expedition of discovery:

San Martín Texmelucan—Tuesday and Friday

Huejotzingo—Saturday
Cholula—Wednesday and Sunday
Zaragoza—Sunday
Tepeaca—Friday
Tehuacán—Saturday
Puebla—Sunday

El Parian
Originally built for clothing merchants at the end of the 18th century (then known as San Roque, later called Cuauhtémoc), shoppers today find rows of brick shops selling clothing, wood, leather, ceramics, silver, and onyx—practice your bargaining techniques here. Located on Calle 8 Norte between Av. 2 and Av. 6 Oriente. Check out **Centro de Talavera La Colonial,** a nifty retail outlet for the factory, at Av. 6 Oriente 11, tel. (22) 42-2340. These are renowned makers and merchants of Talavera Poblano.

Callejón De Los Sapos ("Frog Alley")
During the week this is a quiet place to meander and discover quality antique shops. On Sunday the alley comes to life with bric-a-brac laden tables and blankets, and a flea market where the common man dusts off and displays relics of inheritance and indifference; Av. 7 Oriente and Calle 4 Sur (three blocks south and one block east of the *zócalo*).

Mercado Municipal
You'll find *everything* in this sprawling indoor space. It's chockablock with all the ingredients necessary to make the mouth watering cuisine of Puebla: meats, fruits, spices, vegetables, innumerable varieties of chiles, flowers, tortillas, and breads (cooked and uncooked). There are also stands selling household goods, pots, pans,

OZ MALLAN

candles, clothing, and crafts. But maybe the most fascinating is the opportunity to witness the everyday, no nonsense life of the ordinary Poblano. At 11 Norte between Av. 2 and Av. 6 Poniente.

Indoor Malls

There are several modern indoor malls in Puebla —easy to get to. Minivans and *colectivos,* with their destinations written on the windshield, ply the streets. **Plaza Loreto** is just north of the Civic Center on Ignacio Zaragoza—restaurants and shops. **Plaza Dorado** is on Héroes del 5 de Mayo at Av. 31 Oriente near Parque Juárez— restaurants and shops. **Zona Esmerelda** is on Av. Juárez, west of Paseo de Bravo—a good selection of restaurants, discos, movies, banks and stores.

SERVICES AND INFORMATION

Laundry

Lavandería La Burbuja is at Av. 8 Poniente 2513; open 10 a.m.-1 p.m. and 4-6 p.m. There's also **Lavandería Princess,** Av. 9 Poniente 118, tel. (22) 42-2230.

Communications

Long distance telephones (Lada) are located under the *portales* at the *zócalo.* Ladatel telephones are found at the terminal, under the *portales* at El Parian on Reforma between 7 and 8 Poniente, on Juárez and Calle 23 Sur, and in front of Dikxys Coffee Shop. If you need to send a fax, go to the **Palacio Federal,** 16 de Septeimbre 504. The **post office** is in the Archbishop's Palace at the corner of Av. 5 Oriente and 16 de Septiembre, but it isn't marked very well. If you don't spot it, ask at the tourist office around the corner.

BOB RACE

Money

Several banks scattered about the center of town exchange both dollars and traveler's checks. There's also an ATM machine at **Multiban-**

co **Comermex** at the corner of Juárez and 13 Sur for MasterCard holders who wish a cash advance. **Banca Serfin** is at Av. Reforma 319, tel. (22) 46-5888 and at Av. 3 Poniente 148, tel. 46-6945; open 9 a.m.-12:30 p.m. It's best to get to the bank as soon as it opens; expect lines otherwise.

Medical

There's a **hospital** located at Av. 5 Poniente 715, tel. (22) 32-9151 or 41-3671. **Farmacia La Santísima** is on 16 de Septiembre 101, tel. 41-5869; open 9 a.m.-9:30 p.m., daily. Farmacia Juan Carlos, at 25 Poniente, 502, tel. 37-4263, is open 8 a.m.-9:30 p.m. daily.

Tourist Office

The State Tourism Office at Av. 5 Oriente 3, tel. (22) 46-1285, has one of the friendliest and most helpful staffs this writer has had the pleasure to meet. Many have a good command of English, and their love of the beauty and culture around them is evident. Manuel Salazar Riveroll and the rest of the professional staff will provide maps and direction to aid your discovery of Puebla. The office is open 10 a.m.-8 p.m. daily. There is also a kiosk at the CAPU bus terminal. As well as giving you the usual printed literature, they also sponsor tours of the city beginning at 10 a.m., a good way to get your first bearings. At 3 p.m. the microbus travels to Cholula (if enough people sign up). The tours are in English and Spanish and cost about US$17, which includes entrance fees to museums. Check tour schedules; they tend to change. SECTUR is in the Finance building, at 24 Sur and 11 Oriente, third floor; tel. 34-1239, fax 34-1224.

Books And Magazines

These can be found at **VIPS** and **Sanborns.** VIPS on the corner of Av. 2 Oriente and Calle 2 Norte is worth visiting just to see the building. Constructed at the turn of this century by the American businessman and philanthropist William O. Jenkins, it's a beautiful example of French nouveau architecture. The *Mex-*

ican News (English) published in Mexico City is usually available where you find a lot of tourists. Look for other bookstores along the Reforma.

GETTING THERE

By Air

The biggest airport is **Hermanos Serdán Airport**, about 25 minutes (or more) by taxi to the plaza. However, if you're staying in Cholula or Huejotzingo, it's even closer. A small airport is located at Huejotzingo just outside of Cholula, but as far as we know only flights from Guadalajara land here. Check at the tourist office for more information.

By Car

Driving to Puebla from Mexico City is a great trip once you leave the big city. The modern toll road (150D) goes clear to Veracruz and avoids going through the cities. To Puebla it is 130 km and takes about one and a half hours.

By Bus

First- and second-class buses depart Mexico City about every 15 minutes. The trip takes two hours. Check with ADO for first-class service. And for second class, try Autobuses Estrella Roja and Autobuses Unidos. The Puebla bus station (CAPU) is quite large, and it's located

outside of town. You have a choice of getting to the city center on the *colectivo* for US$3, or on the local bus marked "Estación Nueva" for about 45 cents.

GETTING AROUND

Most of the sights in Puebla are close to the *zócalo* and an easy walk. Anything farther can be reached by frequent bus service from CAPU, Puebla's modern bus station with cafes, shops, long distance telephone, and a place to store your luggage. It's located north of the city at 11 Norte and Blvd. Atlixco.

Taxis

Taxis and *colectivos* are cheap and go everywhere. If you board an unmetered taxi, you know the routine; don't board till you know the cost.

Car Rental

Rente Ford Budget is at Av. Juárez 2927, tel. (22) 30-3976; **Budget Calzado Ignacio** is at Zaragoza 53, tel. 35-3530.

By Minivan

A minivan marked "Centro" will take you downtown for about US$3. Get off at 10 Poniente and 2 Norte; that's as far as the vans can go.

CHOLULA

When traveling to Cholula, you'll no doubt hear tales of the churches; Cortés vowed to tear down every indigenous temple and build a Christian church instead. While traveling to Cholula, take a look at **Tonantzintla** and **Acatepec**. Both fascinating churches with a strong Indian influence, they make a worthwhile stopover. It's especially easy if you're driving, but even if you travel by bus, you can hop off and on with little interruption to your schedule. The buses run frequently and make stops at Tonantzintla and Acatepec. Check at the tourism office.

In pre-Hispanic times, Cholula was one of the most powerful provinces in the country. It had, and still has, the largest ancient structure in the Americas, the **Great Pyramid of Tepanampa**. It covers 18 hectares, is 60 meters (195 feet) high, a has a volume of three million cubic meters.

Santuario San Francisco Acatepec

On the old highway to Atlixco, five km south of Cholula, this Indian baroque church's facade is a masterpiece. They created a unique look with tile and wood carvings, combining Christian and indigenous ideals.

Santa María Tonanzintla

A town famous for its pottery, Santa María Tonanzintla is four km south of Cholula, between Acatepec and Cholula. It's the site of another important Indian style church of the 18th century. When the missionaries introduced the hierarchy of angels and saints to the new world, the natives incorporated many of their old beliefs into the new religion. Stucco, tiles, and quetzal feathers were used to adorn the walls and statues. But you will always remember the gold after you've gone home.

THE GREAT PYRAMID OF TEPANAMPA

If it weren't for the towers of the church sitting above the pyramid marking the spot, you might never know what a valuable piece of historical real estate was hidden underground and around the now overgrown pyramid. As you approach Cholula from Puebla, about 10 km to the east, you will see the church as you get closer; it's quite a spectacular view. What you *won't* see is evidence of Indian occupation. For that you must go underground.

The Great Pyramid of Tepanampa of Cholula has had many names: **Quetzalcoatl Hill**, **Tlachihualteptl** ("Artificial Hill"), **Tlalolochihuac** ("Made with Balls of Earth"), and **Machihualtepec** ("Hill Made by Hand"). Older than Teotihuacán, it was inhabited before the birth of Christ. It's still larger than anything yet discovered on this continent.

Tlahuizcalpentecutli

As was the custom in the ancient Mesoamerican civilizations, seven structures have been superimposed over the original pyramid, built over a period of 800 years. And according to historians the pyramid was in constant use until 1200. When Cortés arrived in 1519, it was still an important ceremonial center of the Indians, with a population of over 100,000 people.

Formerly called Tlahuizcalpentecutli, ("Sacred City of the Evening Star"), Cholula in Nahuatl means "Place to Escape." The Cholulans, friends of Moctezuma, secretly plotted against Cortés and devised a trap to capture the Spaniards. But Cortés's Tlaxcalteca allies discovered the ruse and the Cholulans paid with their lives. The tranquil scene today belies the dramatic blood-bath of the indigenous people that took place at this enormous ceremonial center. Six thousand warriors were slaughtered that day.

Cortés was so incensed by the Cholulans and Moctezuma's almost successful ploy that he vowed to build a Catholic church in Cholula for each day in the year. Well, he didn't quite make it, but there are at least 39.

Baron Von Humboldt's Visit

Humboldt, who visited in 1804, describes the pyramid as truncated, with three terraces. He nicknamed it "a mountain of unbaked bricks." He told of an Indian legend that describes a torrential downpour. This fierce storm destroyed all but seven giants of the primordial world. One of the giants built the pyramid in order to reach heaven, but the gods didn't approve and destroyed the pyramid with fire and confused the language of the builders; rather Babel-like.

Baron Von Humboldt relates entering through a small opening on the east side of the structure and finding a labyrinth of tunnels with walls decorated in yellow and black frescoes with butterflies and insects. In his day only people of importance were allowed into the inner sanctum of the pyramid. Today, anyone (with a paid admission) can wander through the myriad underground tunnels.

Exploring The Pyramid

Hiring one of the guides (who will undoubtedly find you as soon as you get to the entrance on the north side) is a good idea. You'll see more and have a good explanation of what you see than if you go it alone in this subterranean, though lighted, maze. These guides have no posted fees, but they do expect a tip (which is their only pay); US$4-5 is fair, and give more if there are several people in your group. After passing through the hill at the entrance, you will find yourself among the excavations that began in 1931 and are still continuing. Archaeologists have tunneled through about eight km of this amazing den.

Great Plaza

On the south side of the pyramid you'll find the Great Plaza, also called Patio de los Altares, which was the primary entrance to the pyramid. Large carved slabs are on the east, north, and west sides. You'll see platforms and unique diagonal stairways. Human bones were discovered in a pit at the south end, the scene of brutal human sacrifices. A large building, not generally opened to the public, is located west of the plaza. Check it out just in case it might be open, or ask an attendant; you might be able to get in with a tip. Within, a 50-meter-long mural depicts a pulque-drinking debacle from the third century. Slowly the marvels of the pyramid are being uncovered; there are so many in Mexico that it will probably take a couple of lifetimes (or more) to discover them all, if ever.

Follow the signs to beyond the tracks where a small museum contains pieces of pre-Hispanic art, obsidian, and ceramics. Entrance to the museum is included in the US$5 admission charge; show your ticket to get in.

Capilla De La Virgen De Los Remedios

To get to the church on the hill, turn back the way you came and follow the steep, winding path to the top of the hill—expect to sweat a little here. Built in 1666, the Capilla de la Virgen de los Remedios is so beautifully gilded it will take away any breath you may have remaining in your lungs after the climb. Drinks are available on the left hand side of the front of the church. The sodas are usually warm.

SIGHTS IN TOWN

Returning down the hill toward the *zócalo*, across the railroad tracks there's a small cafe where colder sodas, local cider (slightly alcoholic), and snacks can be purchased. Here you may come face to face with some of the local color. There's a sanitarium in Cholula, and the "inmates" are "outmates" most of the week. They are friendly and appear harmless, and some speak English; all seem to enjoy visiting with gringos. But if you meet someone who claims to be an archaeologist or a tour guide, be sure you're getting what you pay for. Nearby, along the railroad tracks, you'll find tables and blankets tended by Indian women, girls, and old men, covered with replicas of artifacts and other souvenirs for sale. The quality is what you would expect sold from a blanket. Market days in Cholula are Wednesday and Sunday.

On the east side of the zócalo you can't miss the fortresslike San Gabriel Monastery with its Moorish look, and 49 domes! The **Ex-Convent and Church of San Gabriel,** started in 1549 by Toribio de Alcarez, was consecrated by the third bishop of Puebla, Martín Sarmiento de Hojacastro. The Franciscan ex-convent is one of the original 12 built after the conquest. Construction began in 1529 and was completed in 1571. It is undergoing a massive renovation as we go to print. Tour the kitchen, dining rooms, and cloisters and peer into the sleeping quarters upstairs. Period furnishings, religious paintings on canvas, and the black-and-white frescoes of Fray Antonio de Rola adorn the walls. Wander the paths around the compound, noting the small chapels capped with triangular roofs in

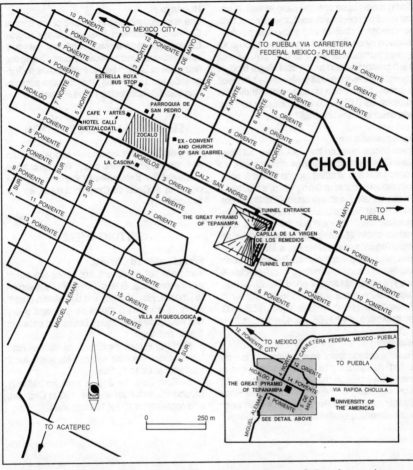

each corner. Check out the entrance door with 122 Roman nails, each a different design. Wandering around the *zócalo*, you'll find **Parroquia de San Pedro** on the north side. This old church dates back to 1641.

PRACTICALITIES

Food

A trip to Cholula is usually a day-trip from nearby Puebla. If you make a day of it, check out several small inexpensive eateries around the plaza including the **Cafe y Artes,** where you can enjoy good food and an art show at the same time. Great four-course *comida corrida* is about US$5. Pleasantly located under the arches at the north end of the plaza.

For something a little more elaborate, try **La Casona,** a lovely restaurant one block off the main street at 3 Oriente 9, tel. 47-2776, painted a cool white with plenty of trees and flowers. While you decide what to order, the waiter brings a veggie plate and breadbasket. The outdoor patio tables are usually filled with Mexican families (especially on Sunday), and the two indoor dining rooms open onto the patio as well. A typical meal can begin with *consomé de pollo,* thick with pieces of chicken, and *sopa de arroz* (rice), followed by an entree of *pipian verde con pollo* (green pumpkin seeds with chicken), all with fresh bread; that and an ice-cold Negra Modelo *cerveza* is less than US$8. Mexican-style steak is about US$9. For a cheaper lunch, they offer *quesadillas* (US$2.25) and *chulupas* (US$4), and soup and rice are US$2 each.

Accommodations

If you decide to spend the night, check out **Hotel Calli Quetzalcoatl** downtown on the plaza. It's comfortable and situated around a central patio, with modern rooms, a dining room, a bar, and a pleasant staff. Rates are about US$43 d, located at Portal Guerrero, tel. 47-1555. **Villa Arqeológica,** one of the resorts in the the Club Med-owned chain of hotels built near various archaeological zones in Mexico, is about 15 minutes from the Great Pyramid. This resort offers a/c, tennis courts, swimming, a well-stocked library, and a reasonably good French restaurant. Room rates are US$85-95. At Av. 2 Poniente 601, tel. in the U.S. is (800) 258-2633, tel. in Mexico is 47-1966; fax 47-1508.

Nightlife

This is a college town, so entertainment is easy to find. Ask your waiter to direct you to one of many busy discos that get going around 11 p.m., especially on the weekends. **Faces Rock Center** and **Disco Porthos** have both been recommended; expect to pay a cover charge.

Holidays

The enormous *zócalo* is the site of the annual **Carnaval** celebration. Festivals always include fabulous fireworks displays, and at some you'll see flamboyant indigenous dancers. During the first week of September, at the **Festival de Virgen de los Remedios,** the dancers perform traditional dances at the Great Pyramid.

SERVICES AND INFORMATION

The **post office** is located on Miguel Alemán 314, two blocks from the plaza. You can change money at the **Bancomer** or **Banamex** on the plaza, or at **Casa de Cambio Azteca,** on Av. Sur close by.

GETTING THERE

From Puebla To Cholula

Taxis are not exorbitant, but buses are much more economical. Buses from CAPU bus station to Cholula, Huejotzingo, and San Martín depart every 15 minutes (Estrella de Oro) and every half hour (Estrellas Rojas). Buses run between 5 a.m. and 9 p.m.

North of Paseo de Bravo, minibuses also leave across from the Railroad Museum, Av. 2 Poniente at Calle 13 Sur.

By Car: Take Av. Juárez west, go half-way around the traffic circle (Hwy. 190 to Cholula), and continue for about 10 kilometers.

BOOKLIST

The following titles provide insight into Mexico, its history, its drama, and its people. A few of these books are easier to obtain in Mexico, but all of them will cost less in the United States. Most are nonfiction, though several are fiction and great to pop into your carry-on for a good read on the plane, or for any time you want to get into the Mexican mood. Happy reading.

Coe, Michael D. *Mexico, from the Olmecs to the Aztecs.* London, Thames and Hudson, 4th edition, 1994. One of the most readable volumes about Mexico's ancient civilization.

Cortés, Hernán. *Five Letters.* Gordon Press, 1977. Cortés wrote long letters to the king of Spain telling of his accomplishments and trying to justify his actions in the New World.

Davies, Nigel. *The Ancient Kingdoms of Mexico.* New York: Penguin Books. Excellent study of preconquest (1519) indigenous people of Mexico.

Díaz del Castillo, Bernal. *The Conquest of New Spain.* Shoestring, 1988. History straight from the adventurer's reminiscences, translated by J.M. Cohen.

Fehrenbach, T.R. *Fire and Blood: A History of Mexico.* New York: Collier Books, 1973. 3,500 years of Mexico's history told in a way to keep you reading.

Franz, Carl. *The People's Guide to Mexico.* New York: John Muir Publications, 1988. A humorous guide filled with anecdotes and helpful general

information for visitors to Mexico. Don't expect any specific city information, just nuts-and-bolts hints for traveling south of the border.

Esquivel, Laura. *Like Water For Chocolate.* New York: Doubleday, 1992. This is just for fun, take it to read on your way to Mexico: you'll be wowed by Mexican tradition, pathos, and whimsy—and ready to go directly to a restaurant when you arrive after reading the descriptions and recipes of succulent Mexican cuisine. No, this isn't a cookbook.

Greene, Graham. *The Power and the Glory.* New York: Penguin Books, 1977. A novel that takes place in the '20s, about a priest and the antichurch movement that gripped the country.

Heffern, Richard. *Secrets of the Mind-Altering Plants of Mexico.* New York: Pyramid Books. A fascinating study of many substances, from ritual hallucinogens used by the ancients to today's medicines.

Kandall, Jonathan. *La Capital.* New York: Random House. An easy-to-read biography of Mexico City with some of the more juicy tidbits of gossip about its important historic figures.

Meyer, Michael, and William Sherman. *The Course of Mexican History.* New York: Oxford University Press, 1987. A concise one-volume history of Mexico.

Prescott, William H. *The Conquest of Mexico.* New York: Bantam Books. Another point of view of the Cortés saga in Mexico.

SPANISH PHRASEBOOK

While in Mexico, you'll find many people in the larger cities who speak English. However, once you're in rural villages, speaking Spanish becomes a necessity. Most Mexican people appreciate the effort you make, even if it's not perfect. In many villages, don't be suprised to find some people who speak no English or Spanish, only an ancient native dialect; however this group grows smaller every year.

The ideal way to prepare for your trip is to begin practicing Spanish before you leave. Most bookstores in the States sell simple Spanish-language tapes accompanied by a book. These tapes are great to listen to in the car on the way to work, or while shaving, gardening, doing the dishes, etc. Repetition succeeds.

Berlitz's *Spanish for Travelers* is a great help used along with a pocket dictionary. It is quite common in Mexico's hotel gift shops, but small English-Spanish dictionaries are not. Buy them before you leave home.

Spanish is not difficult to speak if you learn a few simple grammatical rules.

Vowels:

a: pronounced as in father

e: as in ray

i: as in gasoline

o: as in stole

u: as in crude

Consonants are similar to those in English. A few exceptions are:

g: before a, o, or u pronounced hard as in go; before e or i pronounced like an *h*.

h: silent

j: pronounced like an English *h* (with air)

ll: like y in you

ñ pronounced ny as in Spanish señor

q: pronounced as *k*

rr: rolled with the tongue (takes a little practice)

x: between vowels it's pronounced like a guttural *h*, as in Spanish Oaxaca

y: pronounced ee

GREETINGS

Hello, Hi—*Hola* or *Bueno*

Good day.—*Buenos días.* (in the morning), *Buenas tardes.* (in the afternoon)

Good night.—*Buenas noches.*

How are you?—*¿Cómo está usted?*

Very well.—*Muy bien.*

How goes it?—*¿Qué tal?*

Goodbye.—*Adiós* or *Hasta la vista.*

So long.—*Hasta luego.*

Please.—*Por favor.*

Thank you.—*Muchas gracias.*

You're welcome.—*De nada.*

COMMON EXPRESSIONS

Just a moment, please.—*Un momento, por favor. Momentito.*

Excuse me.—*Perdóneme. Discúlpeme.*

I am sorry.—*Lo siento.*

Do you speak English?—*¿Habla inglés?*

Do you understand?—*¿Me comprende? ¿Me entiende?*

I don't understand.—*No entiendo.*

I don't know.—*No sé.*

How do you say . . . in Spanish?—*¿Cómo se dice . . . en español?*

What?—*¿Cómo?*

Please repeat.—*Mande.*

Show me.—*Enséñeme.*

This is good.—*Está bueno.*

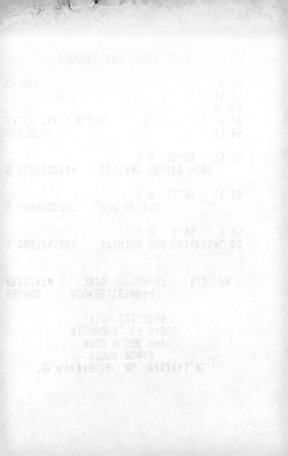

BARNES & NOBLE
STORE #2813
4000 KLOSE WAY
RICHMOND, CA 94806
(510) 222-3266

REG#02   BOOKSELLER#044
RECEIPT#   3879 07/06/97   5:31 PM

S 088729166X   SPANISH ENG UNIVERSAL DI
                1 @   5.95   5.95

S 3444000707   MAP MEXICO
                1 @   11.95   11.95

S 1566910234   CENTRAL MEXICO HDBK
                1 @   15.95   15.95

SUBTOTAL	33.85
SALES TAX - 8.25%	2.79
TOTAL	36.64
CASH PAYMENT	41.64
CHANGE	5.00

BOOKSELLERS SINCE 1873

This is bad.—*Está malo.*

Yes.—*Sí.*

No.—*No.*

What time is it?—*¿Qué hora es?*

What's going on?—*¿Qué pasa?*

How much is it?—*¿Cuánto cuesta?*

GETTING AROUND

Take me to . . . —*Lléveme a . . .*

Where is . . . ?—*¿Dónde está . . . ?*

the road to . . . —*el camino a . . .*

Follow this street.—*Siga esta calle.*

Which way?—*¿Por dónde?*

near—*cerca*

far—*lejos*

to the right/left—*a la derecha/izquierda*

straight ahead—*derecho*

open, closed—*abierto, cerrado*

How far?—*¿Hasta dónde?*

entrance, exit—*la entrada, la salida*

airplane—*avión*

airport—*el aeropuerto*

airline office—*la oficina de aviones*

train station—*la estación de tren* or *la estación del ferrocarril*

taxi stand—*el sitio*

taxi—*el taxi*

bus—*autobús* or *camión la parada*

bus stop—*la parada*

I'm going to . . . —*Me voy a . . .*

reserved seat—*asiento reservado*

reservation—*reservación*

first class—*primera clase*

second class—*segunda clase*

I want a ticket to . . . —*Quiero un boleto a . . .*

Please call me a taxi.—*Pídame un taxi, por favor.*

How long does it take to go there?—*¿Cuánto se tarda en llegar?*

What will you charge me to take me to . . . ?—*¿Cuánto me covra para llevarme a . . . ?*

How much is a ticket to . . . ?—*¿Cuánto cuesta un boleto a . . . ?*

When are there buses to . . . ?—*¿A qué hora hay camiones a . . . ?*

Is there a toilet on the bus?—*¿Hay baño en el camión?*

Where does this bus go?—*¿Dónde va este autobus?*

When does one (it) leave?—*¿Cuándo sale? (. . . llega)*

Down! (to tell the bus driver you want to get off the bus)—*¡Bajan!*

CAR AND MAINTENANCE

gas station—*una gasolinera*

gas—*gasolina*

regular (gas)—*nova*

Fill it up, please.—*Lleno, por favor.*

Please check the oil.—*Vea elaceite, por favor.*

brakes—*los frenos*

map—*el mapa*

air—*aire*

radiator—*el radiador*

battery—*la batería*

repair garage—*un taller mecánico*

mechanic—*un mecánico*

jack—*un gato*

tow truck—*una grúa*

tire—*una llanta*

hole—*bache*

speed—*velocidad*

stop—*alto*

traffic bumps—*topes*

SERVICES

telegraph office—*la oficina de telégrafos*

public telephone—*el teléfono público*

post office—*el correo*

How much is it?—*¿Cuánto cuesta?*

postage stamp—*estampilla*

postcard—*tarjeta postal*

bank—*el banco*

Where is the ladies' room? the men's room?—*¿Dónde esta el baño de damas? de señores?*

ACCOMMODATIONS

hotel—*un hotel*

a room—*un cuarto*

single—*sencillo*

double—*doble*

triple—*para tres*

with a ceiling fan—*con ventilador*

with air-conditioning—*con aire acondicionado*

without air-conditioning—*sin aire acondicionado*

bed—*la cama*

hammock—*la hamaca*

pillow—*la almohada*

blanket—*la cobija*

towel—*la toalla*

bathroom—*el baño*

shower—*la regadera*

soap—*jabón*

toilet paper—*papel sanitario*

hot water—*agua caliente*

cold water—*agua fría*

quiet—*tranquilo*

bigger—*más grande*

smaller—*más pequeno*

with a view—*con vista*

DINING

restaurant—*un restaurante*

breakfast—*desayuno*

lunch—*almuerzo*

lunch special—*la comida corrida*

supper—*cena*

dinner—*comida*

menu—*la carta*

house specialty—*especialidad de la casa*

knife—*un cuchillo*

fork—*un tenedor*

spoon—*una cuchara*

napkin—*una servilleta*

plate—*platillo*

salt—*sal*

pepper—*pimienta*

butter—*mantequilla*

bread—*pan*

French-style bread—*pan blanco*

sweet roll—*pan dulce*

pastries—*postres*

roll—*bolillo*

sandwich on a roll—*torta*

toast—*tostada*

coffee—*café*

cold water—*agua helada*

hot water—*agua caliente*

purified—*purificada*

soft drink—*un refresco*

beverages—*las bebidas*

liquefied fruit drink—*licuado*

ice—*hielo*

the bill—*la cuenta*

tax—*impuesto*

tip—*propina*

waiter—*el mesero,* or, more commonly, *joven*

to get a waiter's attention—*¡Oiga!*

Bring me . . . —*Traígame . . .*

beer—*cerveza*

a table—*una mesa*

calabash—small tree native to the Caribbean whose fruit, a gourd, is dried and used as a container.

chilaquiles—corn chips and bits of chicken

cochinita or *pollo pibil*—chicken baked with spices in banana leaves

conch—large edible mollusk common to the Caribbean; often eaten as ceviche or pounded and fried

escabeche—spicy Spanish style of cooking meat and game

naranja— sour orange used extensively in cooking

panuchos—small fried tortillas topped with black beans, lettuce, meat or poultry, and spices

pok chuc—broiled meat, tomato, onion, and sour orange

sopa de lima—chicken broth, lime juice, tomato, onion

INDEX

Page numbers in **boldface** indicate the primary reference. *Italicized* page numbers
indicate information in captions, charts, illustrations, maps, or special topics.

ABOUT THE AUTHOR

As a child Chicki Mallan discovered the joy of traveling with her parents. The family would leave their Catalina Island home yearly, hit the road, and explore the small towns and big cities of the United States. Traveling was still an important part of Chicki's life after having a bunch of kids to tote around. At various times Chicki and kids have lived in the Orient and Europe. When not traveling, lecturing, or giving slide presentations, Chicki and photographer husband Oz live in Paradise, California, a small community in the foothills of the Sierra Nevada. She does what she enjoys most, writing newspaper and magazine articles in between travel books. She has been associated with Moon Publications since 1983, and is the author of *Yucatán Peninsula Handbook, Catalina Island Handbook, Belize Handbook,* and *Cancún Handbook.* She is currently working on a new book, *Mexico Handbook,* with Moon author Joe Cummings. In 1987, Chicki was presented the Pluma de Plata writing award from the Mexican Government Ministry of Tourism for an article she wrote about the Mexican Caribbean that was published in the *Los Angeles Times.* Chicki is a member of the SATW, Society of American Travel Writers.

ABOUT THE PHOTOGRAPHER

Oz Mallan has been a professional photographer for the past 40 years. Much of that time was spent as chief cameraman for the *Chico Enterprise-Record.* Oz graduated from the Brooks Institute of Photography, Santa Barbara, in 1950. His work has often appeared in newspapers across the country via UPI and AP. He travels the world with his wife, Chicki, handling the photo end of their literary projects, which include travel books and newspaper and magazine articles, as well as lectures and slide presentations. The photos in *Central Mexico Handbook* were taken during many visits and years of travel in Mexico. Other Moon books that feature Oz's photos are *Yucatán Peninsula Handbook, Catalina Island Handbook, Cancún Handbook,* and *Belize Handbook.* He is currently traveling around Mexico once again taking photos for a new book, *Mexico Handbook.*

ABOUT THE ILLUSTRATOR

The banner art at the start of each chapter was done by Kathy Escovedo Sanders. She is an expert both in watercolor and this stipple style, which lends itself to excellent black-and-white reproduction. Kathy is a 1982 California State University Long Beach graduate with a B.A. in Art History. She exhibits drawings, etched intaglio prints, and woodcut prints, as well as her outstanding watercolor paintings. In the April 1982 issue of *Orange Coast* magazine, a complete photo essay illustrates Kathy's unique craft of dyeing, designing, and etching eggs. Her stipple art can also be seen in Chicki Mallan's *Yucatán Peninsula Handbook, Catalina Island Handbook, Cancún Handbook,* and *Belize Handbook.*

MOON HANDBOOKS—THE IDEAL TRAVELING COMPANIONS

Moon Handbooks provide travelers with all the background and practical information he or she will need on the road. Every Handbook begins with in-depth essays on the land, the people, their history, arts, politics, and social concerns—an entire bookshelf of introductory information squeezed into a one-volume encyclopedia. The Handbooks provide accurate, up-to-date coverage of all the practicalities: language, currency, transportation, accommodations, food and entertainment, and services, to name a few. Moon Handbooks are ideal traveling companions: informative, entertaining, and highly practical.

To locate the bookstore nearest you that carries Moon Travel Handbooks or to order directly from Moon Publications, call: (800) 345-5473, Monday-Friday, 9 a.m.-5 p.m. PST.

THE PACIFIC/ASIA SERIES

BALI HANDBOOK by Bill Dalton
Detailed travel information on the most famous island in the world. 428 pages. **$12.95**

BANGKOK HANDBOOK by Michael Buckley
Your tour guide through this exotic and dynamic city reveals the affordable and accessible possibilities. Thai phrasebook. 214 pages. **$10.95**

BLUEPRINT FOR PARADISE: How to Live on a Tropic Island by Ross Norgrove
This one-of-a-kind guide has everything you need to know about moving to and living comfortably on a tropical island. 212 pages. **$14.95**

FIJI ISLANDS HANDBOOK by David Stanley
The first and still the best source of information on travel around this 322-island archipelago. Fijian glossary. 198 pages. **$11.95**

INDONESIA HANDBOOK by Bill Dalton
This one-volume encyclopedia explores island by island the many facets of this sprawling, kaleidoscopic island nation. Extensive Indonesian vocabulary. 1,000 pages. **$19.95**

JAPAN HANDBOOK by J.D. Bisignani
In this comprehensive new edition, award-winning travel writer J.D. Bisignani offers to inveterate travelers, newcomers, and businesspeople alike a thoroughgoing presentation of Japan's many facets. 950 pages. **$22.50**

MICRONESIA HANDBOOK: Guide to the Caroline, Gilbert, Mariana, and Marshall Islands
by David Stanley
Micronesia Handbook guides you on a real Pacific adventure all your own. 345 pages. **$11.95**

NEW ZEALAND HANDBOOK by Jane King
Introduces you to the people, places, history, and culture of this extraordinary land. 571 pages. **$18.95**

OUTBACK AUSTRALIA HANDBOOK by Marael Johnson
Australia is an endlessly fascinating, vast land, and *Outback Australia Handbook* explores the cities and towns, sheep stations, and wilderness areas of the Northern Territory, Western Australia, and South Australia. Full of travel tips and cultural information for adventuring, relaxing, or just getting away from it all. 355 pages. **$15.95**

PHILIPPINES HANDBOOK by Peter Harper and Evelyn Peplow
Crammed with detailed information, *Philippines Handbook* equips the escapist, hedonist, or business traveler with thorough coverage of the Philippines's colorful history, landscapes, and culture. 600 pages. **$17.95**

SOUTHEAST ASIA HANDBOOK by Carl Parkes
Helps the enlightened traveler discover the real Southeast Asia. 873 pages. **$21.95**

SOUTH KOREA HANDBOOK by Robert Nilsen
Whether you're visiting on business or searching for adventure, *South Korea Handbook* is an invaluable companion. Korean glossary with useful notes on speaking and reading the language. 548 pages. **$14.95**

SOUTH PACIFIC HANDBOOK by David Stanley
The original comprehensive guide to the 16 territories in the South Pacific. 740 pages. **$19.95**

TAHITI-POLYNESIA HANDBOOK by David Stanley
All five French-Polynesian archipelagoes are covered in this comprehensive guide by Oceania's best-known travel writer. 235 pages. **$11.95**

THAILAND HANDBOOK by Carl Parkes
Presents the richest source of information on travel in Thailand. 568 pages. **$16.95**

THE HAWAIIAN SERIES

BIG ISLAND OF HAWAII HANDBOOK by J.D. Bisignani
An entertaining yet informative text packed with insider tips on accommodations, dining, sports and outdoor activities, natural attractions, and must-see sights. 350 pages. **$13.95**

HAWAII HANDBOOK by J.D. Bisignani
Winner of the 1989 Hawaii Visitors Bureau's Best Guide Award and the Grand Award for Excellence in Travel Journalism, this guide takes you beyond the glitz and high-priced hype and leads you to a genuine Hawaiian experience. Covers all 8 Hawaiian Islands. 879 pages. **$15.95**

KAUAI HANDBOOK by J.D. Bisignani
Kauai Handbook is the perfect antidote to the workaday world. Hawaiian and pidgin glossaries. 236 pages. **$9.95**

MAUI HANDBOOK by J.D. Bisignani
"No fool-'round" advice on accommodations, eateries, and recreation, plus a comprehensive introduction to island ways, geography, and history. Hawaiian and pidgin glossaries. 393 pages. **$14.95**

OAHU HANDBOOK by J.D. Bisignani
A handy guide to Honolulu, renowned surfing beaches, and Oahu's countless other diversions. Hawaiian and pidgin glossaries. 354 pages. **$11.95**

THE AMERICAS SERIES

ALASKA-YUKON HANDBOOK   by Deke Castleman and Don Pitcher
Get the inside story, with plenty of well-seasoned advice to help you cover more miles on less money. 460 pages.   **$14.95**

ARIZONA TRAVELER'S HANDBOOK   by Bill Weir
This meticulously researched guide contains everything necessary to make Arizona accessible and enjoyable. 505 pages.   **$16.95**

BAJA HANDBOOK: Mexico's Western Peninsula
including Cabo San Lucas   by Joe Cummings
A comprehensive guide with all the travel information and background on the land, history, and culture of this untamed thousand-mile-long peninsula. 362 pages.   **$15.95**

BELIZE HANDBOOK   by Chicki Mallan
Complete with detailed maps, practical information, and an overview of the area's flamboyant history, culture, and geographical features, *Belize Handbook* is the only comprehensive guide of its kind to this spectacular region. 263 pages.   **$14.95**

BRITISH COLUMBIA HANDBOOK   by Jane King
With an emphasis on outdoor adventures, this guide covers mainland British Columbia, Vancouver Island, the Queen Charlotte Islands, and the Canadian Rockies. 381 pages.
$15.95

CANCUN HANDBOOK   by Chicki Mallan
Covers the city's luxury scene as well as more modest attractions, plus many side trips to unspoiled beaches and Mayan ruins. Spanish glossary. 257 pages.   **$13.95**

CENTRAL MEXICO HANDBOOK: Mexico City, Guadalajara,
and Other Colonial Cities   by Chicki Mallan
Retrace the footsteps of Cortés from the coast of Veracruz to the heart of Mexico City to discover archaeological and cultural wonders. 391 pages.   **$15.95**

CATALINA ISLAND HANDBOOK: A Guide to California's Channel Islands
by Chicki Mallan
A complete guide to these remarkable islands, from the windy solitude of the Channel Islands National Marine Sanctuary to bustling Avalon. 245 pages.   **$10.95**

COLORADO HANDBOOK   by Stephen Metzger
Essential details to the all-season possibilities in Colorado fill this guide. Practical travel tips combine with recreation—skiing, nightlife, and wilderness exploration—plus entertaining essays. 416 pages.   **$17.95**

COSTA RICA HANDBOOK   by Christopher P. Baker
Experience the many wonders of the natural world as you explore this remarkable land. Spanish-English glossary. 574 pages.   **$17.95**

IDAHO HANDBOOK   by Bill Loftus
A year-round guide to everything in this outdoor wonderland, from whitewater adventures to rural hideaways. 275 pages.   **$12.95**

JAMAICA HANDBOOK by Karl Luntta
From the sun and surf of Montego Bay and Ocho Rios to the cool slopes of the Blue Mountains, author Karl Luntta offers island-seekers a perceptive, personal view of Jamaica. 230 pages. **$14.95**

MONTANA HANDBOOK by W.C. McRae and Judy Jewell
The wild West is yours with this extensive guide to the Treasure State, complete with travel practicalities, history, and lively essays on Montana life. 427 pages. **$15.95**

NEVADA HANDBOOK by Deke Castleman
Nevada Handbook puts the Silver State into perspective and makes it manageable and affordable. 400 pages. **$14.95**

NEW MEXICO HANDBOOK by Stephen Metzger
A close-up and complete look at every aspect of this wondrous state. 375 pages. **$14.95**

NORTHERN CALIFORNIA HANDBOOK by Kim Weir
An outstanding companion for imaginative travel in the territory north of the Tehachapis. 765 pages. **$19.95**

NORTHERN MEXICO HANDBOOK: The Sea of Cortez to the Gulf of Mexico
by Joe Cummings
Directs travelers from the barrier islands of Sonora to the majestic cloud forests of the Sierra Madre Oriental to traditional villages and hidden waterfalls in San Luis Potosí. 500 pages. **$16.95**

OREGON HANDBOOK by Stuart Warren and Ted Long Ishikawa
Brimming with travel practicalities and insiders' views on Oregon's history, culture, arts, and activities. 461 pages. **$15.95**

PACIFIC MEXICO HANDBOOK by Bruce Whipperman
Explore 2,000 miles of gorgeous beaches, quiet resort towns, and famous archaeological sites along Mexico's Pacific coast. Spanish-English glossary. 428 pages. **$15.95**

TEXAS HANDBOOK by Joe Cummings
Seasoned travel writer Joe Cummings brings an insider's perspective to his home state. 483 pages. **$13.95**

UTAH HANDBOOK by Bill Weir
Weir gives you all the carefully researched facts and background to make your visit a success. 445 pages. **$14.95**

WASHINGTON HANDBOOK by Archie Satterfield and Dianne J. Boulerice Lyons
Covers sights, shopping, services, transportation, and outdoor recreation, with complete listings for restaurants and accommodations. 419 pages. **$15.95**

WYOMING HANDBOOK by Don Pitcher
All you need to know to open the doors to this wide and wild state. 495 pages. **$14.95**

YUCATAN HANDBOOK by Chicki Mallan
All the information you'll need to guide you into every corner of this exotic land. Mayan and Spanish glossaries. 391 pages. **$15.95**

THE INTERNATIONAL SERIES

EGYPT HANDBOOK   by Kathy Hansen
An invaluable resource for intelligent travel in Egypt. Arabic glossary. 522 pages.   **$18.95**

MOSCOW-ST. PETERSBURG HANDBOOK   by Masha Nordbye
Provides the visitor with an extensive introduction to the history, culture, and people of these two great cities, as well as practical information on where to stay, eat, and shop. 260 pages. **$13.95**

NEPAL HANDBOOK   by Kerry Moran
Whether you're planning a week in Kathmandu or months out on the trail, *Nepal Handbook* will take you into the heart of this Himalayan jewel. 378 pages.   **$12.95**

NEPALI AAMA   by Broughton Coburn
A delightful photo-journey into the life of a Gurung tribeswoman of Central Nepal. Having lived with Aama (translated, "mother") for two years, first as an outsider and later as an adopted member of the family, Coburn presents an intimate glimpse into a culture alive with humor, folklore, religion, and ancient rituals. 165 pages.   **$13.95**

PAKISTAN HANDBOOK   by Isobel Shaw
For armchair travelers and trekkers alike, the most detailed and authoritative guide to Pakistan ever published. Urdu glossary. 478 pages.   **$15.95**

STAYING HEALTHY IN ASIA, AFRICA, AND LATIN AMERICA
by Dirk G. Schroeder, Sc D, MPH
Don't leave home without it! Besides providing a complete overview of the health problems that exist in these areas, this book will help you determine which immunizations you'll need beforehand, what medications to take with you, and how to recognize and treat infections and diseases. Includes extensively illustrated first-aid information and precautions for heat, cold, and high altitude. 200 pages.   **$10.95**

TIBET HANDBOOK: A PILGRIMAGE GUIDE
by Victor Chan
This remarkable book is both a comprehensive trekking guide to mountain paths and plateau trails, and a pilgrimage guide that draws on Tibetan literature and religious history. 1104 pages. **$30.00**

MOONBELTS

Made of heavy-duty Cordura nylon, the Moonbelt offers maximum protection for your money and important papers. This all-weather pouch slips under your shirt or waistband, rendering it virtually undetectable and inaccessible to pickpockets. One-inch-wide nylon webbing, heavy-duty zipper, one-inch quick-release buckle. Accommodates traveler's checks, passport, cash, photos. Size 5 x 9 inches. Black.   **$8.95**

**New travel handbooks may be available that are not on this list.
To find out more about current or upcoming titles,
call us toll-free at (800) 345-5473.**

IMPORTANT ORDERING INFORMATION

FOR FASTER SERVICE: Call to locate the bookstore nearest you that carries Moon Travel Handbooks or order directly from Moon Publications:

(800) 345-5473 • **Monday-Friday** • **9 a.m.-5 p.m. PST** • **fax (916) 345-6751**

PRICES: All prices are subject to change. We always ship the most current edition. We will let you know if there is a price increase on the book you ordered.

SHIPPING & HANDLING OPTIONS: 1) Domestic UPS or USPS first class (allow 10 working days for delivery): $3.50 for the first item, 50 cents for each additional item.

Exceptions:
- **Moonbelt** shipping is $1.50 for one, 50 cents for each additional belt.
- Add $2.00 for same-day handling.
- UPS 2nd Day Air or Printed Airmail requires a special quote.
- International Surface Bookrate (8-12 weeks delivery):
  $3.00 for the first item, $1.00 for each additional item. Note: Moon Publications cannot guarantee international surface bookrate shipping.

FOREIGN ORDERS: All orders that originate outside the U.S.A. must be paid for with either an International Money Order or a check in U.S. currency drawn on a major U.S. bank based in the U.S.A.

TELEPHONE ORDERS: We accept Visa or MasterCard payments. Minimum order is US$15.00. Call in your order: (800) 345-5473, 9 a.m.-5 p.m. Pacific Standard Time.

ORDER FORM

Be sure to call (800) 345-5473 for current prices and editions or for the name of the bookstore
nearest you that carries Moon Travel Handbooks • 9 a.m.–5 p.m. PST
(See important ordering information on preceding page)

Name: _____ Date: _____

Street: _____

City: _____ Daytime Phone: _____

State or Country: _____ Zip Code: _____

QUANTITY	TITLE	PRICE
	Taxable Total	
	Sales Tax (7.25%) for California Residents	
	Shipping & Handling	
	TOTAL	

Ship: ☐ UPS (no PO Boxes)   ☐ 1st class   ☐ International surface mail

Ship to: ☐ address above   ☐ other _____

_____

Make checks payable to: **MOON PUBLICATIONS, INC.** P.O. Box 3040, Chico, CA 95927-3040
U.S.A. We accept Visa and MasterCard. **To Order:** Call in your Visa or MasterCard number, or send
a written order with your Visa or MasterCard number and expiration date clearly written.

Card Number: ☐ **Visa**   ☐ **MasterCard**

☐☐☐☐ ☐☐☐☐ ☐☐☐☐ ☐☐☐☐

Exact Name on Card: _____

expiration date: _____

signature_____

F/94

THE METRIC SYSTEM

1 inch = 2.54 centimeters (cm)
1 foot = .304 meters (m)
1 mile = 1.6093 kilometers (km)
1 km = .6124 miles
1 fathom = 1.8288 m
1 chain = 20.1168 m
1 furlong = 201.168 m
1 acre = .4047 hectares
1 sq km = 100 hectares
1 sq mile = 2.59 square km
1 ounce = 28.35 grams
1 pound = .4536 kilograms
1 short ton = .90718 metric ton
1 short ton = 2000 pounds
1 long ton = 1.016 metric tons
1 long ton = 2240 pounds
1 metric ton = 1000 kilograms
1 quart = .94635 liters
1 US gallon = 3.7854 liters
1 Imperial gallon = 4.5459 liters
1 nautical mile = 1.852 km

To compute centigrade temperatures, subtract 32 from Fahrenheit and divide by 1.8. To go the other way, multiply centigrade by 1.8 and add 32.

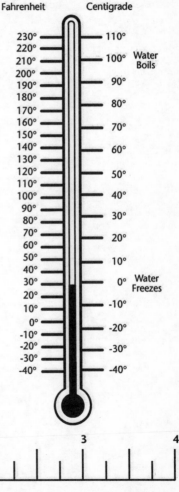

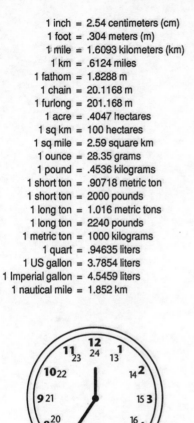